4th edition

Reading
Instruction
Diagnostic Teaching
in the Classroom

Larry A. Harris
Virginia Polytechnic Institute
and State University

Carl B. Smith
Indiana University

Macmillan Publishing Company
New York

Collier Macmillan Publishers
London

Photographs were provided by James Silliman, Alice Lloyd College, Pippa Passes, Kentucky, with the cooperation of LBJ Elementary School, Jackson, Kentucky, and the Alice Lloyd College Child Development Center.

Macmillan Publishing Company
866 Third Avenue, New York, New York 10022

Collier Macmillan Canada, Inc.

Library of Congress Cataloging in Publication Data

Harris, Larry Allen.
  Reading instruction.

  Bibliography: p.
  Includes index.
  1. Reading. I. Smith, Carl Bernard. II. Title.
LB1050.H34 1986   372.4'1   85–7124
ISBN 0–02–350580–X

Printing: 3 4 5 6 7 8   Year: 7 8 9 0 1 2 3 4 5

ISBN   0-02-350580-X

Preface

The decade of the 1980s seems destined to become one of those periods when public education and teaching practice are subjected to intense scrutiny. Because of their importance to all learning, the reading curriculum and reading instruction have occupied center stage in this scrutiny along with science, mathematics, and technology. Though sometimes awkward for educators, this special attention is not all bad. Improvements in an undertaking as vast and complex as promoting universal literacy, for example, are possible only when national concern is focused on a need.

The first edition of this textbook addressed the goal of helping classroom teachers individualize their reading instruction by providing the knowledge and tools required to diagnose each learner's needs. That theme has been carried forward through three revisions and continues as a strong message in this edition. We believe that the teacher's willingness and ability to differentiate instruction according to each child's unique pattern of strengths and weaknesses are the only sure ways to achieve the excellence in our schools sought by the educational reform movement of the 1980s.

Although the main theme of our text is unchanged, careful examination of this edition will reveal that the means for addressing the theme of individualization through classroom diagnosis have been expanded and updated. Continued research and development in the broad area of comprehension are reflected in the two revised chapters devoted to that topic, for example. The special needs of exceptional learners, who are being mainstreamed into regular classrooms at an increasing rate as a result of Public Law 94-142, are addressed in an entirely new chapter entitled "Adapting Reading Instruction for Exceptional

Children." Another new chapter written for this edition describes issues and trends in education that have special impact on reading instruction. Technology, especially in the form of computers, and competency testing of teachers and students are two of the topics discussed in the new chapter entitled "Current Issues in Reading." A major revision has also been made in the chapter on instructional systems so that the nature of basal reading programs and how they can be used effectively to individualize instruction are explored in detail. Throughout the text there has been a continuing reminder about the complex interactions readers engage in, thus reflecting recent research on the reading process. References have been added and updated where appropriate throughout the text in this new edition. More specific suggestions for improving classroom practices have been added, and suggested readings for pursuing a topic beyond the covers of this book have been listed and described at the end of each chapter.

The first two chapters of this edition provide an introduction to reading in a typical classroom and a cognitive map for the teacher. Subsequent chapters discuss the language base for reading and then the logical steps involved in guiding children through academic readiness, teaching techniques for identifying and decoding words, developing strategies for comprehending, understanding how to interact critically with the printed text (including expository writing), discussing classroom organization, diagnosing reading problems, and finally working with exceptional learners, and understanding current issues in reading instruction.

We have written this text primarily for the introductory elementary reading methods course. Given the book's emphasis on a diagnostic approach to classroom instruction, it is also appropriate to include some in-service courses and introductory graduate level courses intended to promote greater individualization of instruction. Our primary goal is to help teachers conceptualize the teaching of reading and to design activities that speak directly to the learning needs of all children in the classroom. That attitude reflects our belief that effective teaching requires regular teaching decisions in favor of the many children in the classroom. The diagnostic decision making of the classroom teacher, in our judgment, separates the professional teacher from a teacher technician. It takes an analytic teacher to identify the strengths and needs of each child and to plan instruction based on that analysis. The teacher who assumes a diagnostic role assures that the children in the classroom are receiving personalized instruction whether that instruction takes place in a large group, in a small group, or on a one-to-one basis.

This text, then, is more than a synthesis of ideas about the teaching of reading in school. It is a commitment to a point of view. We believe that children need to succeed in reading every day. They need to find joy in books as an evident part of that success. Their attitudes, interest, and feelings must be considered as well as their knowledge and their skill. Constant observation of and planning for the individual must take place in order to accomplish those ends.

Plan of the Book

The chapters for the fourth edition follow this general plan:

Part I. Decisions for Classroom Reading

The first chapter discusses reading in the classroom and gives a description of how one teacher operates reading within a language-arts framework. The second chapter provides an intellectual frame of reference from which the teacher can make decisions about reading instruction. Those decisions are explained throughout the book and involve questions about the strengths and weaknesses of children as well as organizational questions for the entire classroom.

Part II. Basic Components of the Reading Process

In Part II the language base and the psychomotor base for the child's approach to reading are discussed in chapters on language, readiness, and motivation. There follow chapters on developing word-analysis and vocabulary development. One focuses on the strategies and activities that are characteristic for the beginning reader, and the second chapter focuses on vocabulary and the strategies and activities characteristic of the more advanced reader, that is, the one who has already developed a minimal fluency in understanding and in responding to words because of early practice. Two chapters on comprehension explain the language and experience factors that are necessary to understand and to teach comprehension.

Part III. Approaches to Teaching Reading

The third part discusses means for teaching critical reading and reading in subject-matter texts. Organizational and social questions that surround the teaching of reading are included in chapters on instructional systems and materials and on organizing the classroom for instruction.

Part IV. Beyond the Fundamentals

Part IV presents techniques and tests for diagnosing children's reading performance and interests. Also included are chapters with suggestions for working with special children, parents, and volunteers in the classroom and a chapter on current issues in reading instruction.

Aids to Reading

Each chapter in this text begins with an introductory idea and a set of questions that may guide the reader in previewing the important concepts. Problem-solving activities that pose problems to be solved as a part of group discussions are also included in each chapter. Descriptions of classroom activities appropriate for use with children follow most major topics in the book. These are boxed for easy identification. At the end of each chapter are a summary and a list of discussion questions that attempt to trigger group discussions and to provide a sense of conclusion about the ideas in the chapter. A list of recommended readings along with a brief annotation for each item is provided at the end of each chapter to encourage and guide further exploration of key topics.

An index and appendixes are provided to help the reader locate terms and concepts that may be of interest. The appendixes include book-selection aids, newspapers and magazines for children, and sources of books for children that may be of continuing value to the classroom teacher. New appendixes give sources of information about reading and computer software that may be useful in the reading program.

Acknowledgment

Over the years many colleagues, students, and critics have helped us form the ideas that appear in this text. We thank them for their contributions in what we think is a much improved text on the teaching of reading. For this edition we would especially like to acknowledge the detailed readings and criticisms provided by Mary Andis, Jeanette Bartley, Laura Driggs, Dianne Monson, Eugene Reade, and Barbara Tymitz-Wolf. These colleagues have helped us in significant ways to improve the message and the accuracy of this edition.

LAH, Virginia Polytechnic
Institute and State University

CBS, Indiana University

Contents

4. Creating Interest in Reading   77

5. Readiness for Reading   109

8. Reading Comprehension: Experiential and Language Factors   225

9. Reading Comprehension: Cognitive, Affective, and Text Factors   255

Part **III**
Approaches to Teaching Reading

10. Critical and Creative Reading   301

16. Current Issues in Reading   520

Appendixes

Part I

Decisions for Classroom Reading

1

Reading in the Classroom

Each generation of teachers faces issues that define, constrain, and challenge it. Teaching does not take place in a sterile laboratory. Both national issues and local interests create a setting, an environment, in which reading is taught. At the present time, competency testing of teachers and students, the use of computers, integrating reading and writing instruction, content controlled by state legislation, and merit pay for teachers are some of the issues that affect the instructional environment. Teaching reading, therefore, cannot be relegated to learning one method or one philosophy of language. A teacher needs to learn how to thrive amid current political and academic demands and how to use a variety of teaching strategies to accommodate an inevitable diversity among children.

Reading Instruction: Content and Methodologies

The history of reading instruction in U. S. schools reveals a constant change in the content of books used for reading, changes that reflect attitudes and contemporary social values. In the early 1800s the content was religious, often taken from the Bible, because the primary purpose for literacy then was thought to be enabling children to read the Bible and learn Christian morality. In the latter 1800s the purpose of literacy had shifted to making readers into upright citizens; and so the content of readers, for example, the McGuffey readers, combined a kind of religious morality with nationalism and patriotism (N. B. Smith, 1965). Most recently, the content of readers has changed to reflect the diversity of American culture. Considerable attention is given to eliminating stereotypes about female or male roles and minority groups.

Reading instruction, then, encompasses a complex set of content requirements as well as the use of teaching methodologies. When reading methodology was viewed as learning the letters of the alphabet and attaching sounds to those letters, the instructional approach seemed fairly straightforward. In today's high-tech society, reading is seen as a tool that must be integrated into every subject in the curriculum, as a tool for learning in school and on the job. Such a view defies using a simplistic methodology, requiring instead numerous strategies for application in narratives (English), historical analysis (social studies), scientific description (science), opinions and arguments (personal development), and so on. Those reasons indicate why teachers do spend time examining various philosophies and methods for teaching reading and why reading is taught throughout grades K to eight, and sometimes into grades nine to twelve.

Definition of Reading

Reading is a subject in every elementary school curriculum in the country. In fact, it receives more time in the schedule than any other subject. More tests are given to measure it, and more effort is spent in diagnosing and tutoring children in reading than in any other subject. More public pressure and more parental pressure are applied to reading performance than to any other subject. That kind of attention should convince all those in education that reading instruction needs a special effort on their parts.

The importance of reading is an idea children should meet early and often in their school.

Decisions for Classroom Reading

What is this highly publicized phenomenon called reading? Apparently everyone does it—or at least all parents want their children to read—and everyone wants high scores on reading tests. A quick and easy way to define reading would be to say it is whatever is measured on reading tests. But reading tests are designed to measure only a narrow band of reading behavior (see Chapter 6 on the subject of assessment). Teachers are understandably concerned about what is on those reading tests because these tests are a public record of the students' performance. But teachers also want to be guided by a concept of reading that encompasses the wide range of interests, attitudes, and skills that they try to develop among the members of their classes. A working definition, then, should be broad enough to include that wide range and at the same time simple enough to act as a guide in every activity.

A good working definition is this: *Reading is the intellectual and emotional perception of a printed message.* That definition gives teachers a grasp of what has to be done to keep students on track and reminds the teachers of ways to prompt appropriate reactions and activities. Let's consider each of the important terms in the definition to see what they all mean and how they provide practical guidance.

Message implies communication, intentionality, and organization.

Printed means the use of an alphabetic code—that is, the use of sound-spelling patterns and the conventions of punctuation to approximate spoken language.

Perception indicates the role of a personal construction of the message. Perceptions may vary from reader to reader.

The word *emotional* shows a recognition of the fact that feelings and connotations prompted by the topic and by the author's formulation of the message will color the reader's perception.

The term *intellectual* identifies the activity as cognitive, rational, and meaning-driven.

Effective Teaching

One of the primary purposes of this book is to search out the guidelines and practices that enable a teacher to be effective. Rosenshine and Furst (1971) claim that the single most important characteristic of effective teachers is that they have a clear definition of goals and how to achieve them. Others might call that a philosophy, a philosophy of reading, for example. But as beneficial as it may be to have a general philosophy toward language learning or toward learning in general, those principles and attitudes become effective only when they are worked out in daily classroom practices. After years of analyzing the behavior of highly successful teachers, Kounin (1983) identified several of their characteristics:

1. They give students consistent signals by establishing clear objectives and definitions for academic and social behavior.
2. They help students see patterns in their learning and transfer

those patterns from one area to another—from reading to writing, for example.

3. They make the routine tasks of school seem real by demonstrating that these tasks have a reasonable function in the lives of their students.

After reading this text, you might find it beneficial to reread those characteristics and make some decisions on how to direct your own instructional behavior. At least that is a start. Adjustments in your thinking and in your actions will occur over time because teaching requires numerous decisions every day. The pragmatic world of classroom instruction brings up different situations hour after hour. Your initial philosophy and resultant teaching strategies will gradually modify as you make practical decisions. In that way, the rather hollow mental scheme you have for reading instruction in the early stages of teaching begins to fill out and become richer through daily decisions. Along the way, you should not overlook the rich source of ideas from other teachers. Their combined experiences can offer you techniques, activities, and guidelines that will make your own teaching decisions more beneficial for your students and give you a more useful philosophy of education.

Methods for Teaching

Learning in school poses many conceptual difficulties for teachers and for theorists. Studies of how children learn are often conducted in a laboratory environment, where the learner and the observer are isolated. Pronouncements from those studies, then, seem to give directions for classroom teachers, but they have not been demonstrated as successful in a classroom where there are twenty-five to thirty-five students. The classroom teacher makes decisions within that group-oriented framework. That doesn't exclude the needs of the individual. Those needs must be attended to. But the focus of instruction is on the commonalities of students in that class. There we have stated one of the major dilemmas of teaching: How does one direct teaching to the commonalities of the group while at the same time recognizing individual differences? Any discussion of methodology must speak to that dilemma.

Throughout this text, we will try to construct a system for teaching groups and for working with individuals at the same time. But a system for teaching reading has to be based on the teacher's perception of language learning and on ways to work with the children in a classroom environment. Because this is not a propaganda piece but an academic textbook, we will present as clear a picture of current theories and methods as we can. It is then up to each individual to construct a system for teaching reading. That system will be based on some of the following considerations:

1. How reading is defined.
2. How children in a specific age group are perceived to learn most effectively.

3. How one teacher can manage learning among twenty-five to thirty-five children.
4. How best to incorporate the content demands that school and society place on reading.
5. How to make reading an effective tool for learning and for enjoyment.

In other words, there is a challenging conceptual task that each teacher must resolve—how to work out a philosophy and a methodology among the many demands incumbent on those who teach children to learn in school.

There is no one methodology that guarantees success for all children. Yet each teacher needs to have a basic system to rely on. From that system, the teacher can branch out as needed to meet the needs of all the children in the class.

The purpose of a text like this is to identify some of the options that exist for a teacher and deliver sufficient information about the research, the characteristics, and the content of reading to help teachers have enough information to begin to make personal decisions about what reading is and how to teach reading to children.

Propaganda. If we simply delivered one point of view or described one methodology, the text and the course in which it is used would serve a propagandistic purpose. In a college course we believe that the purpose is primarily intellectual, that is, to explore various issues and means, not simply to argue for a single point of view.

The Classroom

Most teaching as we know it takes place in a classroom with from twenty to thirty-five children. That gives our discussion a focus. We are not trying to determine how to tutor a child one-on-one. We are analyzing the research and the activities that are effective in a typical classroom. Throughout this text we seek to answer one central question: What are the most likely strategies and activities that a teacher can use in a group environment?

Let's look at a classroom as a way of calling up some images of what the teacher has to work with and some of the things that a typical teacher can do in a typical classroom.

A Reading Class

What constitutes a reading class? Wiggling bodies—some that smell like a deodorant soap and some that do not—smiling faces, accepting or suspicious eyes, tousled hair. All these are superficial differences as every teacher knows. The students' faces mask an expansive range of abilities, interests, attitudes toward learning, and socioeconomic conditions. It all adds up to what is called "background," and the back-

Attractive displays and inviting activities give reading special emphasis in this classroom.

ground that each child brings to school constitutes a hidden curriculum of the child's person, personal experiences, and spirit.

Teachers clear paths for such individuals in order to help them develop competency in reading. Teachers also arrange opportunities to satisfy the range of competencies, interests, attitudes, and socioeconomic circumstances. What does that mean for the reading class?

Look at any classroom. Many tools of the profession are right there. Books, desks, tables, bookshelves, the library, the audiovisual supply—the teacher utilizes all those things to accommodate the children. But each room and each library are different. No standardized description fits every classroom. Each teacher mixes and matches tools and children to cultivate learning. And the question persists: How does one teach a class to read and adjust constantly to the varying performances of each child? Decisions must be made constantly.

The Rule Book

In the teachers' lounge many myths arise from the bustle and offhand chatter. Sometimes these myths begin with the words "You can't" or "It's against the rules." *You can't* use different books; *you can't* be yourself; *you can't.* But teachers do and are. If they want to try something different, they usually can. They find that most schools have support personnel to help them and their students. Reading consultants, remedial teachers, and administrators can help with forming new approaches to reading. It is our experience that teachers can do most of the things they want to do for their pupils if they are willing to try. Teachers cannot afford to be hampered by teacher-lounge myths.

Decisions for Classroom Reading

Additional help and resources can often be found in the community. When a teacher needs another pair of hands or a resource or when the children need another lap to sit on, parents, college students, retired people, and business and professional people in the community will frequently help out. To get this kind of assistance, though, the teacher has to reach out, has to think beyond the four walls of the classroom and the school.

The Need to Demonstrate Progress

Each pupil in a school must become successful in reading. The climate of the time—if a professional conscience were not enough—alerts teachers to the need for personalizing pupil instruction. Many states now have legislation that requires teachers to demonstrate pupil progress in the basic subjects of reading, math, and English. Clear learning objectives and a performance record for each child are obvious components of that kind of accountability. More and more parents are asking for personal performance information instead of a single quality grade from *A* to *F*. Federal and state project moneys are frequently earmarked for schools in order to increase individual competency. Accountability and competency testing are discussed in Chapter 16, "Current Issues in Reading," and procedures for diagnosing individual needs are discussed in Chapter 14.

After decades of discussion about meeting individual needs in the classroom, political and social currents are pushing educators to show tangible evidence. Reading instruction, more than any other area in the curriculum, is expected to produce results.

Those same political and social pressures work in favor of the reading teacher. Reading *is* important. Parents and children know that success in reading is the most necessary and basic part of education. They may even have in mind careers or day-to-day circumstances where fluent reading ability helps them to gain information, relaxation, or enjoyment. Basically, therefore, teachers and children have a powerful motive working for their success in the teaching and learning of reading. They are both constantly learning to read and to think for future development. Teachers, when using texts other than basal reading books, can serve as models of effective reading behavior (Manzo, 1980).

Contrary to a belief commonly accepted a few years ago, our technological, information-centered society has *increased,* not decreased, the need for reading skill. Computers have expanded the use of complex directions and the amount of time spent on the job in reading (Sticht & Mickulecky, 1984, p. 4). Even entry-level jobs now require reading, mixing formulas, checking gauges, and keeping logs of tasks and performance levels. As a result, the general level of literacy needed in the world of work has risen considerably over that required twenty-five years ago when a previous generation entered the work force. Current technology, especially the use of computers in elementary schools, serves the language-arts teacher in two ways: by acting as a tutor through computer-assisted instruction and by providing a clear example of the continuing relationship between reading and writing. (The use of computers in reading instruction is discussed in Chapters 12 and 16.)

The teacher's job is to help each child realize that he or she is making daily progress in becoming a competent reader. Exactly how is that accomplished? The beginning of this chapter is concerned with formulating means to that end. These suggest attitudes as a powerful force to change; each teacher needs to identify instructional strategies and find ways of achieving clear signs of success. As an example of an environment in which success can occur, the authors would like to describe a classroom they have visited. The description that follows should cause questions to come to mind—questions that we hope will be answered in this book and in related discussions.

One Classroom Environment

What is a reading and language-arts classroom like? No one description is adequate for the diversity that exists. Here is a description of an operating class, one that we think is within the capability of most teachers. We do not advocate that all classes should look and function alike, but we do want to present an example that stimulates thinking about how to work with children in the classroom. Depending on personal style and the atmosphere of the school, each teacher must construct his or her own "best environment" for success in reading.

Geneva—first-grade teacher, warm, smiling, and alert—moves with confidence and purpose around her classroom. She makes sure each group of children knows what to do and asks her two adult volunteer helpers if they have suggestions about the children's tasks. Then she returns to a group of six children so that she can work with them.

The classroom is clean and bright in appearance, with children's papers and seasonal decorations on two walls. There are several adult-constructed charts and wall hangings, which suggest that Geneva has an artistic flair and uses it to decorate vocabulary charts, success charts, and timely poems. There are several centers of reading activity around the room, as well as centers used for other purposes. (Figure 1.1 gives a diagram of the room, showing the reading circle, library, a place for games, oral language area, listening center, microcomputer, and general work area.)

1. *Reading Circle.* Geneva uses a rocking chair, and a small group sits in a circle on the floor on corduroy-covered cushions. With her teacher's guide on her lap and some work cards for a chart beside her, Geneva introduces a story that is in the children's readers. These books are on the floor in front of the children, who discuss concepts and purposes. Then Geneva asks them to read a couple of pages silently so they can discuss what is happening in the story. When the silent readings have been completed by everyone, they talk about the ideas they have encountered.

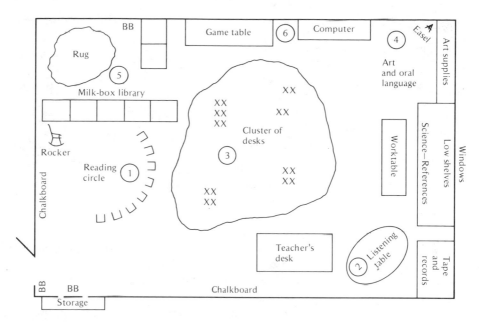

FIGURE 1.1 Sample Classroom.

2. *Listening Table.* In the tape corner, four children sit around the listening table, place headsets over their ears, open library books, and wait while one of the volunteers selects a tape and starts the tape recorder. The children read along with the taped voice, occasionally responding by smiling or nodding their heads. Then, using a work sheet, they write or draw according to directions given on the tape.

3. *Cluster of Desks.* In the center of the room where desks have been clustered, some children take out a workbook and begin to read and answer the questions. They refer to their readers in order to complete the workbook exercises. The volunteer who had helped in the listening corner circulates among this group, giving each child help as needed. When each individual finishes, he or she goes either to the library corner (Area 5) to lie on the floor and read or to the game table or microcomputer (Area 6) to practice some skill that a volunteer helps to identify from a personal folder. The folders for each child are kept in a box near the kits and games. A checklist in the folders lists the kinds or practice materials the child has used. Those skills the child has mastered have stars pasted in front of them.

   As the children at the listening table finish their tasks, they, too, go to the library corner or to Area 6. In the library corner they share books and help one another read the stories.

4. *Art and Language.* The group in the art corner works with the second adult volunteer. At first this volunteer reads a brief story, and the children assume the roles of the characters and panto-mime their actions. Then the volunteer takes picture cards,

FIGURE 1.2   Picture Card.

which the children identify and discuss; they also match word cards to the pictures. (*See* Fig. 1.2.)

Each child then takes a picture card and a piece of paper and draws a scene. The children describe one of the pictures as the volunteer writes on a piece of chart paper those sentences that the child artist agrees have meaning for the picture. The children then read their stories to each other.

The attitude pervading this classroom is one of "Let's explore a world of ideas." From that attitude follows expression of self, of enjoyment of stories, of verification of information, and of sense of autonomy. The children seem to feel accepted, for they are willing to express their ideas. Books are evidently valuable resources. This is an excellent atmosphere for learning to read.

Geneva's classroom reflects her teaching philosophy and the kind of person she is. This philosophy is valuable because it works well for her and for the children. Another classroom may not look the same because it will reflect a different teacher and different children. *Your reading class reflects you!* That's a rule for creative thought, not for intellectual apathy.

This description of a reading class raises two major questions: Why were those activities included? How does Geneva adjust class activities from day to day to meet the changing needs of the children?

Each center of activity seems to represent an aspect of Geneva's definition of teaching. Some activities are group-oriented and teacher-directed. Some are highly controlled, and some are creative. Some appeal to children's interests and independence. Directed reading, practice reading, creativity, independence—all these are options. Geneva feels that frequent contacts with adults promote children's language growth, so she trains adult volunteers to assist her. But those other adults are there because they are part of Geneva's philosophy of learning to read. A beginning teacher, for example, might find it overwhelming to organize volunteers in addition to organizing himself or herself. Each teacher must evolve his or her own philosophy.

This particular first-grade class shows a range in reading performance from some who cannot recite the alphabet to those who can

Decisions for Classroom Reading

read third-grade books with relative ease. How does the teacher adjust? Her attitude, classroom organization, and materials should aid her decisions. As indicated earlier, each child has a folder—a work and progress folder. Geneva and her two volunteers keep a record of basal units, books read, and special needs: skills, interests, and so on. Geneva reviews these folders each week to make new assignments for the following week. The work plan starts with the child's assignment to a reading group. Other assignments and personal selections follow from that basic assignment.

A teacher in a typical fourth-grade class would find some children who stumble over first-grade selections and others who breeze through seventh- and eighth-grade selections. To benefit all those children, the fourth-grade teacher must learn to prescribe reading and language activities for the typical range in the class. Other grades would have corresponding differences.

Language Arts Integration

Although this text focuses on the act of reading, the other modes of language communication are discussed throughout the book as integral parts of the reading process. In a literate society such as the one in which we live, reading cannot be isolated from writing or from listening and speaking. Television, for example, represents the regular integration of communication modes in our daily lives. We listen to a commercial message and see the same words appear on the screen. We then talk about those message, perhaps even write ourselves a reminder to try the product that has been advertised. Because all modes of language use mutual concepts, vocabulary, and sentence structures, learners naturally make use of their knowledge of one language expression in working with another. That mutuality is an assumption underlying all discussion in this text.

But for purposes of academic discussion and of clarifying one aspect of language in its relationship to another, we can analyze *reading* strictly in its own terms in order to understand the process more clearly and as a way of improving instruction. Even while targeting reading for analysis, we can incorporate listening, speaking, and writing as well. Because reading and writing both use print, it seems particularly useful to work with them together in order to show students similar patterns, conventions, and conceptual forms. Perhaps the best way for most children to learn how to read a description is to write one of their own and to learn how to read argumentative prose is to write an argument of their own.

Demonstrating Competence

All teachers need to remember that they do not operate their own classroom islands. One of the occupational beauties of teaching is its flexibility, which allows freedom for helping individuals and for exercising creative decisions, but all of that must be carried out in conjunction with other teacher-colleagues and with the guidelines developed by the community. Most communities, either through the state legislature or through local policy, require teachers to demonstrate that children have achieved identified competencies in the basic skills subjects of reading, writing, and mathematics. In a positive manner, most teachers will use this opportunity to display the progress their children are making. Competency objectives restate the need that parents and the community have for seeing progress. Like children in school or, for that matter, like any intelligent person, community members want to see that their efforts and their money are having an effect on the education of their children. See Chapter 16 for a discussion of the advantages and disadvantages of competency testing.

Teachers, of course, must bridge the gap between the classroom and the world instead of trying to isolate themselves. That may mean they must report how their students perform on selected examinations, sometimes called criterion tests because they test specific elements. Some competency tests, for example, examine decoding skills and the recognition of a specific word list, and they ask questions to reveal children's ability to follow directions or determine a cause-effect relationship, and so on. Where those kinds of examinations exist, teachers work to prepare children to be successful on those criteria as well as to prepare them in the broader aspects of reading. Those broader goals aim at cultivating the ability to think actively and at developing a sense of the lifelong values that accrue from reading efficiently.

From the community's need to see progress, *teachers can remind themselves that children, too, need to see progress.* They need to see that they are being successful, not only in tests but also in the daily hurdles that they find in the classroom. Thus their needs are not limited to skills that may appear on comparative examinations. They need to share language and books with their classmates, to become independent in finding and using information across a wide variety of subjects, to learn to manipulate ideas found in books—whether storybooks or content books. Teachers find ways of helping children achieve for tests and for life and of giving them an opportunity to display what they can do. In their concern for success on standardized tests, teachers must not forget to show the child his or her regular progress in language growth, in reading effectively.

Success and Records

Displaying success has an even broader implication for teachers and schools than has been discussed thus far. The children in a class are not the property of a single teacher. They are learners who make a constructive stop in one teacher's room before going on to other teachers and to other experiences. In order to provide continuing personal growth for each child, teachers rely on the work and the information that other teachers provide while continuing their own analyses, of course. This continuity of growth indicates the need for schools and teachers to decide what is important and to keep reasonable records of where the child is in his or her march toward independence. Some school systems develop or purchase record-keeping systems or management systems. Others ask teachers to devise their own. Either way, teachers provide colleagues and parents with a thorough and regular picture of the child's progress in reading. In the light of this discussion, it should be apparent that reading competency tests should not be seen as plateaus to rest on. Rather they are public marks of progress that are communicated to children and parents along with other signs that the children are becoming competent, efficient, and independent learners.

Summary

The active and creative life that goes on within a classroom includes the school, the professional relationship among teachers, and the important relationship that must exist among school, parents, children, and society.

This book intends to offer you opportunities to formulate a philosophy and an image of your own classroom. Each of you works from images, beliefs, principles, and personal policies that you use to create a sense of what your classroom should look like and how you will work within it. Each of you starts with a sense of how to teach reading, a sense drawn from your own experiences and studies. That early perception will change somewhat with added experience and study. Please use the chapters that follow as a means for clarifying and expanding your present concepts of teaching and learning reading.

Discussion Questions

1. Why is it helpful for a teacher to have a definition of reading?
2. Can you formulate a definition of reading that gives you practical guidance for teaching?
3. How could a teacher get a sense of the community expectations to which a reading class must respond?

Recommended Readings

Cunningham, Patricia M., et al. (1983). *Reading in elementary classrooms: Strategies and observations.* New York: Longman.
   This book presents month-by-month case studies of reading instructional programs in six different elementary classrooms from kindergarten to fifth grade.
Harris, Larry A., & Smith, Carl B. (1972). *Individualizing reading instruction: A reader.* New York: Holt, Rinehart & Winston.
   This valuable collection of articles gives help in explaining the reading process and provides a resource and frame of reference for conceptualizing reading instruction.
Kounin, Jacob S. (1983, November). *Classrooms: Individuals or behavior settings?* In *Monographs in Teaching and Learning* (General Series, Number 1). Bloomington, IN: School of Education, Indiana University.

Kounin summarizes years of observations and lists the characteristics of highly effective teachers.

Quandt, Ivan (1972). *Self-concept and reading.* Newark, DE: International Reading Association.

Quandt presents an overview of research on the relationship between reading and self-concept, and provides some practical suggestions on how the classroom teacher can improve self-concepts as well as reading abilities.

Stoodt, Barbara D. (1981). *Reading instruction.* Boston: Houghton Mifflin.

This text gives a general overview and introduction to reading instruction. Chapters 2 and 3 summarize various perspectives in reading as well as teaching and learning principles applied to reading instruction.

Van Allen, Roach (1976). *Language experience in communication.* Boston: Houghton Mifflin.

This is a useful resource emphasizing reading, writing, speaking, and listening as communication. It has valuable chapters on discussion skills, evaluation, and organization that promotes communication.

Decisions for Classroom Reading

2

An Intellectual
Map for Teaching

Children want to learn. Teachers want to teach them how to learn. These basic assumptions support most of the decisions we make in school. If you, as a teacher, are going to teach a group of children to read, you need a kind of "intellectual map" that will guide your decisions for the group and for individual children. An example will put this idea into perspective.

> Marla, a child we know, went to kindergarten filled with *Sesame Street* and stories that her daddy had read to her. She wanted to learn to read and told her kindergarten teacher of her desire.
>
> "You learn to read in the first grade," said the teacher. "Sorry, but I'm not allowed to teach you."
>
> Wait! A signal is being flashed to this child.
>
> At the start of the first grade, Marla expected to begin reading immediately. Instead, the first-grade teacher put her through a series of kindergarten readiness activities, things Marla had done when she was three years old.
>
> At a most impressionable time, Marla was told, in effect, "Schooling is only a set of rules. Watch what the group is doing and follow along."

Those two teachers were not concentrating on learning. They were concerned with something else: Their grade levels, some artificial rule, perhaps a set of books, or some plan or map guided their statements. Without intending to, they conveyed to the child a working attitude about school: "Don't push out; don't explore. Squelch your curiosity."

If Marla's learning had been the center of her teachers' attention, both teachers would have encouraged her and tried to find out what she could do and what she might try next in her quest to learn to read.

Motivation? What higher point of interest is there than when a learner says, "Oh, teach me that!"

Observing the Child

To focus on learning means to focus on the individual child. To know what to observe, the teacher must know what to look for. Otherwise, observation is random, perhaps even erratic and unproductive. What is it, then, that the teacher should observe?

TABLE 2.1 Oral Language Objectives and Activities

1. Can the child retell the story in his or her own words?
   a. Use an individual filmstrip and tell the story to the group.
   b. Read a short story and retell it to a small group.
   c. Prepare individual or small-group "book talks" or "commercials."
2. Can the child create a story, given a stimulus?
   a. Have a puppet show.
   b. "Story starters"—objects or pictures—can be used to prepare a story.
3. Can the child participate in a discussion?
   a. "Discussion starters" can be written on slips of paper. Children work in small groups to reach a conclusion.
   b. Trips around the school are helpful. The teacher talks about the five senses, about things the children feel, see, and so on. Limit the subject to keep discussion relevant.
4. Can the child organize ideas orally in a sequence of events?
   a. Explain a hobby or craft.
   b. With pictures (storyboard) or slides, explain why objects have been placed in a particular order.
5. Can the child make introductions?
   a. Have each child play the role of a person in the news or of an important historical figure.
   b. Have each child arrange for resource persons as guest speakers and introduce them.
6. Can the child interpret and restate the main idea of a spoken dialogue?
   a. Use a "magic circle"—each child repeats the gist of remarks made by preceding speakers before making additional contributions.
   b. Have the child describe the characteristics of a sport.
7. Can the child give verbal descriptions?
   a. Have pairs of children sit back to back. One must describe an object while the other draws a picture of it.
   b. Ask each child prepare and teach a lesson to the other children in the class (how to tie a shoelace, draw a picture of a cat, and so on).
8. Can the child formulate relevant questions?
   a. Hold a "press conference"—some children act as people in the news; others ask questions. This activity can also be used with questions on historical periods.
   b. Try the "gambit" game—children make up questions to be used in the game. Provide a grab-bag for prizes at the end of the game (first team to score twenty-one points).
9. Can the child adjust to different oral situations?
   a. Have each child make a tape of a nursery rhyme or fable in his or her own version, complete with sound effects.
   b. Use a large carton (such as a refrigerator box) to simulate a TV set for presenting book reports, commercials, newscasts, weather reports, and so on.

Before a doctor operates on you, you hope that he or she has passed the anatomy course. Before a teacher confronts a child, shouldn't that teacher have identified some objectives and decided what goals to aim for? The teacher is not a physician prescribing for a patient, but it is necessary to adjust to the needs of individual learners and proceed analytically in prescribing learning activities for each student.

The classroom teacher looks for alertness, family environment, language development, attitudes, and some very specific types of behavior relating to the printed page; for academic learning is related to intelligence, environment, and language development. However, the teacher cannot simply discharge the obligation to observe a child's reading performance by *"generally* observing the *general* characteristics." Such broad aspects of learning only form a backdrop and give perspective to the more specific activities of a subject such as reading.

Questions to Guide Observation

- *What language abilities does the child have?*
- *What speech and writing skills can be expected in a child of a given age?*
- *Are these skills related to vocabulary, articulation, and message-oriented utterances?*
- *Does the child surpass the expected skill level? (For reference, a sample of oral-language objectives is given in Table 2.1.)*
- *When reading or working with written symbols, does the child have an orderly sense of how to proceed?*
- *Does the child have a system for figuring out unknown words?*
- *Does the child know how to read for various purposes?*
- *Can the child think systematically about what is read?*
- *Are personal interests reflected in what is read?*

These questions should form a permanent part of any teacher's thinking because they provide guidance in making instructional decisions and in helping children make progress. They also indicate the need for goal setting.

Making Decisions About Reading

Questions about each child's language, word strategies, and comprehension skills can be answered when the teacher knows specifically what to look for. Indeed, every teacher needs a map of reading—a cognitive map that provides directions and checkpoints. (*Cognition* is the act or process of knowing or perceiving.) Cognitive clarity—knowing what is to be accomplished and how to accomplish it—is the teacher characteristic most highly correlated with learner success (Rosenshine & Furst, 1971). It has also been found that consistent application of clear, systematic procedures is one of the distinguishing features of the successful teacher (Kounin, 1983). Doesn't it seem reasonable, then, that the teacher with a sense of direction is more likely to help students than one who says, "I don't know much about teaching reading." It logically follows that each teacher should develop a definition of reading and of language growth, a definition that will work in the classroom and make it possible to solve the major problems involved in teaching reading. The teacher must determine the following:

1. The level of the child's reading-language performance.
2. The word and comprehension skills of the child.
3. The way the child extracts information.
4. The attitudes and interests that the child brings to the task of reading.

Level of Reading

The child's level of reading performance is closely tied to a reading vocabulary—the printed words that the child can identify. General comprehension is also a factor in the level of reading performance. Deciding about the level of performance is similar to determining which book in the school's reading program matches the point at which the child can begin to make progress consistently. That's the book with which to begin instruction.

Word Skills

A fluent reader can use a variety of techniques to figure out unfamiliar words. Suppose the child did not know the word *grizzly* in this sentence: "The grizzly man scratched his beard." What techniques or skills can be used to figure out what the unknown word means? Is the child able to employ context clues (the meaning of words other than the unknown word), sound-symbol correspondences (phonics), word-structure clues (structural analysis), and visual memory (configuration)? Those word skills that the child seems to need are the ones that should be taught.

Comprehension Skills

What kinds of comprehension-thinking operations can the child perform? Given content reasonable for age and background, the child should be able to do the following:

Identify the content. ("Yeah, I know bushmen live in Australia.")
Recall major details.
Analyze the information and rearrange it to suit individual purposes.
Apply some criterion to judge the content.
Use the content or extend it.

Those thinking operations that the child does not know should be taught.

Extracting Information

Learning to read includes the ability to use print from a wide variety of sources. Locating and extracting information in encyclopedias and other reference books, for example, and understanding and using charts, maps, and other forms of information are covered by the reading curriculum. Does the child know how to find information in these sources and extract what is needed? Having an efficient search-and-select strategy provides the learner with a valuable learning skill.

Interests and Motivation

People like to read material that they find appealing, but interests are far from uniform. How does one grab the child's attention and hold it throughout the process of learning to read? Built into each person are a set of reactions to reading in general and a set of reactions to the particular content of a given selection. Sometimes subtle and sometimes violent, these reactions stem from the previous experience of the learner and the personal framework that has developed. "Nobody reads at my house," says one child. This attitude then colors all that the child reads. Often labeled the *affective domain* of learning, attitudes and feelings can work *for* or *against* learning. By locating major interests and sources of positive feelings, the teacher can develop and maintain a positive attitude and a healthy interest in reading. Attractive books and interesting reading activities will gain the child's attention. Working through individual interests and showing that success is possible will help to keep each student on target throughout the school years. Helping the pupil see real-life ways to use reading will promote positive lifelong attitudes toward reading.

Toward a Definition of Reading

The teacher's major areas of decision in reading are (1) level of performance, (2) word-solving strategies, (3) comprehension strategies, and (4) interests and attitudes. Through decisions made in these areas, the teacher guides the child toward competency in reading. Armed with a definition of reading, a definition stated in operational, "real-life" terms, the teacher knows what is important and what has to be emphasized.

This is not the time to ask you to analyze various theoretical definitions. You will better serve your own learning by asking yourself what you now believe that *reading* means. What do you *do*, for example, when you read? How does your mind work? Is your process similar to that of your friends? How does your reading process differ from that of the age-group you want to teach? If you were a typical second-grader, for instance, would you read a book or a newspaper the same way that a college senior does?

Definitions of reading range from "establishing a sound-to-symbol relationship" to "giving personal meaning to printed signs." That range

Defining Reading

Before you read further, take a minute to examine your views about reading. We teach what we believe about reading and about how children learn. How would you define reading? What differentiates the best reader you know from the worst? What components or skills or processes would you include in a definition? How would you state that definition so that it could be put into practice? Use the three teaching decisions (level, skills, interests) to guide the formulation of your definition of reading in order to make it as practicable as possible. Jot down your current ideas about reading, and then reexamine what you've written after you have finished this book.

My definition:

includes theories that view reading as a very narrow, mechanistic, learned behavior and theories that define reading as an intuitive type of learning that is hindered by deliberate instruction. As you try to define your present understanding of *reading,* ask yourself if any of the following metaphors apply:

> Reading is photographing a page for safekeeping in the memory.
> Reading is pronouncing words. All else is thinking.
> Reading is a conversation with the author.
> Reading is a creative expression.

Is reading primarily passive, or is it active? Do readers simply soak up the words and ideas of the author, or do they build their own ideas, using the text as a starting point? Trying to resolve these and similar issues enables a teacher to establish a working definition that will guide instructional activity. In this textbook, the authors define reading as an active, constructive process. To us, *reading is the intellectual and emotional perception of a printed message.* With a definition like that as a starting point, we can establish guidelines for classroom instruction because the definition is simple enough to remember, yet it identifies important aspects over which teachers have influence. What are these aspects?

1. A *printed message* indicates purpose, organization, and sound-spelling relationships.
2. A *perception* means that the reader formulates a personal image or concept as a result of the printed message.
3. *Emotional perception* recognizes the personal feelings that often color the words and ideas associated with a message.
4. *Intellectual perception* identifies the cognitive work that is inherent in building an understanding of the printed message.

Our definition reminds the teacher that reading is not passive, that there is intellectual energy to be expended. Greater direction can

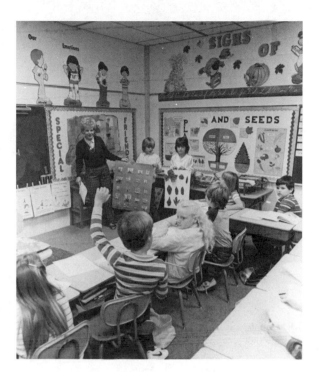

When children are helped to see reading as a functional skill, they are more likely to develop an accurate understanding of how the process works.

be achieved by enlarging that definition. Reading is the reader's interaction with a printed message across a range of thinking operations as guided by a purpose for reading. This definition can be turned into teaching directions and performance goals for students and parents, and a sense of order begins to evolve within the activity called *reading.* Interaction requires both (1) the extraction of information and (2) an active response to ideas. Extracting information is the activity most often associated with reading and involves the phonology, semantics, and syntax of written language: the sound-symbol correspondences, word meanings, and mutually understandable ordering of words in phrases and sentences. While working through those operations, the reader seeks both to make sense of the message and to make decisions about it. That is the beginning of interaction with the message. Kenneth Goodman gives this definition: "Reading is a complex process by which a reader reconstructs, to some degree, a message encoded by a writer in graphic language" (Goodman & Niles, 1970, p. 5).

For the teacher, interaction with the printed message means that the child's background and attitudes actively mix with the surface meaning of the printed words. Take the word *beard,* for example: "My nice, smiling daddy has a beard." Or, "The smelly man down the street has a beard." The word *beard* is not a sterile term for the child.

Interactions across a range of thinking operations indicate that the child's intelligence deals with the message through a variety of crucial skills, including analysis and evaluation, as guided by the child's purpose for reading: to find information, to compare, to enjoy, and so on.

Skilled or competent reading is more than simple memory activity. Skilled reading assumes analytic and judgmental operations on the text as well as assimilation or use of the information gathered from the text.

The purposes that direct a reader's activity are significant for the act of reading. Purpose arranges the perception, association, and organization of the reader's mind, thus playing a central role in determining the specific meaning extracted and the kinds of associations, analyses, and judgments made—not to mention the beneficial effect that purpose has on short- and long-range memory.

The child's career as a learner suggests a definition that helps both children and parents understand what the teacher is helping students to do. For the benefit of each child, then, reading can be defined in terms of his or her observable performance.

Reading Performance

In order to organize reading instruction and to make numerous decisions about teaching individual children, teachers need to clarify their definitions of reading and make these as concrete and directive as possible. The discussions and activities in this book should help to accomplish that end.

The child should be able to gain information and pleasure from schoolbooks and from reading done at home. Furthermore, the child should be able to figure out unfamiliar words and perform typical comprehension tasks such as recalling, analyzing, and evaluating content (according to the individual's level of development).

For discussion with parents, a teacher may want to stress the various elements included within the definition of reading. This might be accomplished in a letter such as the following:

Dear Parent,

Here is a brief list of those things we will help your child accomplish as he or she learns to read. If you want to discuss any of these goals, please call.

In the months ahead, we want your child to

1. Become increasingly aware that reading leads to knowledge and to enjoyment.
2. Have content reading skills that make it possible to read schoolbooks, magazines, newspapers, and other material outside of school.
3. Use various skills to figure out unfamiliar words.
4. Develop comprehension—thinking skills and creative reading.
5. Build vocabulary steadily from its present level.

Sincerely

Getting the attention and holding the interest of students are of necessity major concerns for teachers. As diverse as interests are and as slippery as motivation is, the teacher needs an approach that does not rely exclusively on a "thunderbolt." The thunderbolt approach employs dramatic devices akin to a flash of lightning and a crash of thunder to attract the child's attention. It may startle for a moment but soon becomes ineffective.

The organized teacher acts as a catalyst for learning by bringing together the child, the setting, the content, and the material in a way that engages both the mind *and* the emotions of each student. The word *engage* stands in deliberate contrast to the so-called thunderbolt approach. *Engagement* implies involvement, relevance, challenge, and continuity; it is like a mystery story you can't put down rather than a highway billboard that flashes by in seconds.

Teachers can design the classroom, the materials, and the exercises to appeal to the values and interests of children. They clarify the purposes of classroom activities and provide regular feedback concerning each child's growth and accomplishments. After all, what better motivation is there than knowing that you are succeeding in something that has recognized value—recognized by parents, teachers, classmates—and by the child as well. Reading stands high on almost everyone's list as a skill to be mastered. Kindergarten children, for example, stand in awe of one of their classmates who can read. For that reason, if no other, the teacher sets up systematic procedures for letting children know about their successes. Whether star charts, notes to parents, lists of skills to be checked off, or other methods are used, children should be told regularly what progress they are making. That kind of feedback often ignites enthusiasm because children want to hear again and again that they are doing something that is viewed as important and worthy of praise. To this point, however, the teacher must link *perseverance*, for each child's fuse burns at its own pace, and the ignition is not always a brilliant flash.

Promoting Interaction

Motivation to learn comes both from within (intrinsic) and from without (extrinsic). Children want to learn to read because it satisfies their desires to conquer their world and because reading feeds their interests. But they are also motivated by the pressures and pleasures that adults and classmates apply. One of the fascinating challenges for the teacher is to combine the intrinsic and extrinsic forces that keep a child moving toward fluency and competence in reading. The word *interaction* can be used by the teacher as a guide to activities: "Let's read this story and see which of you has the best solution to the problem of the missing jewels."

There should be interaction between internal and external forces. The child who delights in reading about the mysterious events on a

An Intellectual Map for Teaching

Interaction among students and with the teacher concerning something that has been read encourages a probing, reflective disposition toward reading.

haunted island should experience increased satisfaction when describing to classmates those parts of the mystery that were most intriguing. Book-sharing time as a regular classroom activity will emphasize the community value of reading and will give the child a stage on which to perform. In this way, the child interacts not only with printed material but also with people, adults as well as children. Some teachers prompt children to think about what they have read by saying, "See if you can outguess the author. Maybe you know what the author will say before you read it." This kind of predicting motivates and establishes a mental stance that leads the child to act upon the content instead of merely trying to absorb it.

Discussing stories in groups not only brings the selections alive for children but gives each of them a chance to be important. They can tell others what they found significant in the story. Discussions are also valuable for building language skills. Reading builds on the oral language of a child; speaking and listening activities are consequently very important in enhancing the reading process.

The value of the kind of personal reaction to reading just described extends beyond the immediate emotional responses. By asking themselves what is important or what makes a selection "come alive," children begin to examine their own feelings and thinking strategies for reading different kinds of exposition. Such activity may very well provide the spark for refining all kinds of reading-thinking skills. For children in their own way ask questions similar to those that the teacher asks: "What am I interested in reading? Should my interests be expanding? What must I do in order to read well? What are my reasons for

Decisions for Classroom Reading

Sharing Independent Reading
(Classroom Activity)

A combination of independence and sharing can be promoted by having two periods a week during which everyone in the class (including the teacher) reads anything that is found appealing. Each could read a story, a magazine, a selection from the science text, or whatever else is of interest. There would be only one requirement: At the end of the free-reading time, each person has to be willing to tell a small group what was interesting or important about the piece just read. The reporting can be done on a random basis by drawing names from a hat or by some other procedure that will guarantee the involvement of every child over the course of a couple of weeks. Given a two- or three-minute time limit for telling what is important to them, most children will thrive on the opportunity. Through sharing, they are alerted to many kinds of selections that otherwise might not have been called to their attention.*

* Free time for personal reading is sometimes identified as USSR: uninterrupted, sustained, silent reading.

reading one selection, and how do those reasons differ when reading another selection? How do I improve?"

Internalizing a Map

Reading comes full circle. A definition leads to improvement, which leads to a better definition. A simple outline or schema in the mind changes with experience (Spiro, 1977). Teaching reading includes many aspects of learning and needs an operational definition that incorporates skills, interests, and attitudes. These various elements should turn into a definition, into a set of terms that a busy classroom teacher can recall and use to guide instruction. When a new student arrives or when children show spurts of growth (as they always do), the teacher needs some framework as a guide for starting instruction and for keeping the children moving forward. After all, it isn't following lesson-plan directions that creates a problem for the teacher; a set of instructions for group activities can be carried out simply by following the teacher's plan book for the basal reader. But teacher expertise equates with teacher adjustment to individual differences in progress—to variation in pupil growth. In order to identify the kinds of differences that may be encountered and in order to have a sense of direction for adjusting instruction, the teacher needs an *intellectual* (cognitive) map. Just as the surgeon must have knowledge of anatomy and of operating procedures, the teacher must have knowledge of important components in reading competency and must know procedures for helping children achieve mastery of the skills required for competent reading.

A cognitive map for reading does not assure success in reading.

Teaching and learning are fraught with uncharted twists and turns, based on environment and genetics, that require ingenuity on the part of the teacher. Nonetheless, a cognitive map lays out a direction and a series of paths to follow; if one path does not lead to success, another may be tried. Such a map gives teachers and children a clear focus on objectives.

Here we will outline a concept or model for understanding the teaching of reading. In succeeding chapters, this outline will help guide the discussion of specific aspects of reading and related teaching-learning activities.

The model should help teachers reach the following goals:

1. Set objectives for learning.
2. Evaluate progress.
3. Prescribe instructional activities.
4. Observe interests and attitudes.

All of us, teachers as well as students, are searching for ways of putting order into our academic lives. As an intellectual map, the outline should help teachers put reading instruction into some sensible pattern. Thus, the authors offer a model for reading instruction.

Harris-Smith Outline of Reading

Reading never takes place in an isolated, sterile environment. Stored within every reader are knowledge, feelings, attitudes, premonitions—some in neat array, some in a clutter—filling the memory with subjective reactions and viewing each new idea within the framework available to the reader at that time (Piaget, 1952). Corresponding to Piaget's ideas on general intellectual development, Chall (1983) indicates that there are different characteristics and behaviors at each stage of reading development. If these assumptions are valid, the teacher has more reason than ever to observe the child's performance and to provide help and experience that will encourage the child to grow. Reading, like any other type of learning, is subject to the intellectual and emotional overlays that each individual brings to the task. The teacher watches and listens to the child in order to search out the language, experiences, and operations that a child can apply. For example, has the child developed mental structures that make it possible to read history with a perspective of time?

Given a general learning perspective, the teacher then asks, "What is involved in learning to read?" Teachers need a model that illustrates the major components of reading activity and indicates the direction that analysis of the reading process should take. Figure 2.1 presents a diagram that has been helpful to many teachers. It is the first in a series of diagrams designed to help in conceptualizing the reading process and should be viewed (even in this simplistic form) as a number of mental operations that are governed by the intention and the background of the reader.

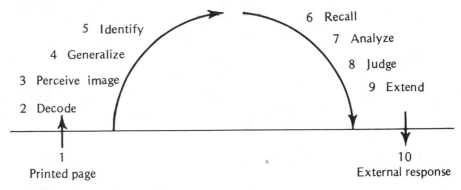

FIGURE 2.1   Operations in Learning to Read.

The major operations that a reader can perform on a printed message are shown in Figure 2.1. It therefore indicates questions a teacher can ask—classroom diagnosis, if you wish. But it also categorizes major teaching-learning activities designed to help children learn to read. A cursory look at the labels shows that reading includes a wide range of operations, both visual-perceptual responses and analytic-evaluative thinking acts. Teaching children to read involves more than a decoding phase or a simple stimulus-response bond. Reading involves an active pursuit of and interaction with the printed message.

Items 1 (the printed page) and 10 (the external response) in Figure 2.1 are those things that can be observed in a direct physical sense. We can see the eye making contact with the book page and we can see or hear the reader's responses: an explanation, a written summary, a shrug of disdain, a dance, an illustration. There are internal responses, too—for example, placing the received information into a framework of knowledge, a feat we cannot observe directly. In logical order, the reader can proceed through each category in the model.

Decode

The printed page is translated and related to spoken language. In the early stages of reading, this involves a decoding operation. The letters and patterns of letters are related to the sounds they stand for. A correct translation of symbol into sound provides the reader with a basic recognition of the word if we assume that the word is part of the reader's listening vocabulary.

Perceive Image

The recognition of a word on the sensory level evokes what is sometimes called a *perception* or a *perceptual image.* This is an image at the threshold of abstraction. It is the learner's first step toward forming a *concept,* an idea of something constructed by mentally combining all of its characteristic features into a general notion of the thing as a whole. The young reader's perception of the word *dog* is a rather specific

An Intellectual Map for Teaching

image of a particular four-legged creature that barks and answers to a specific name—for example, "Ralph."

Generalize

The image of a *specific* dog is then subsumed under the broader idea of *pet, animal,* or various *kinds* of dogs. In that way, the word *dog* becomes a generalized concept of "dogness."

Identify and Recall

As readers feel that the passage holds some meaning for them, that they can identify and recall ideas in it, they have a number of options or operations to choose from. For example, a reader can search the message for specific ideas, analyze it, and evaluate it. Given the whole message, the reader can then go back into it to recall details or parts that are important, either for personal reasons or because some specific purpose for reading was assigned. This is often referred to as *literal comprehension.*

Analyze

To analyze means to manipulate the events or ideas of a message in order to accomplish a specific end. Analysis includes activities such as categorizing elements, identifying organizational principles, differentiating between fact and opinion, and so on.

Judge

Evaluation is an operation in which selected criteria are applied to a passage to decide its worth. The reader must develop criteria based on logic, empirical studies, or the subjective feeling he or she has about an issue. These criteria can be used to judge the value of what the reader sees in the passage. This operation is often called *critical reading.* Critical and creative reading are examined later on in Chapter 10.

Extend

Readers may decide to do something with the knowledge they have gained (application). Depending on their evaluation, they may reject the selection and the author who wrote it, or they may look for a similar work in order to build additional knowledge. A reader's decision may result in an observable response expressed orally, in writing, or through a gesture; it may also result in an unobservable decision or response to synthesize or reject what has been learned. This may be called *creative reading.*

The model in Figure 2.1 is a logical interpretation of part of the reading process. Because this process is described in a step-by-step fashion, it may appear that these operations are linear. That is not

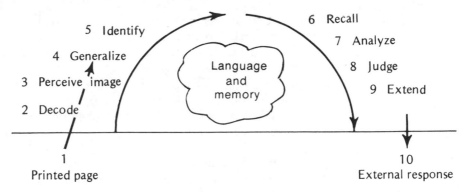

FIGURE 2.2 Mature reading in the Harris-Smith model. The mature reader may often leap automatically from the *printed page* (Step 1) to a higher level such as *generalizing* (Step 4).

necessarily true. All sorts of crisscrossing within Figure 2.1 may occur in actual reading as all the different processes interact and influence one another. In fact, it seems that in mature readers some of the processes become automatic. A mature reader very often goes automatically from Step 1 (the printed page) to Step 4 (generalize) or Step 5 (identify), as shown in Figure 2.2. For the sake of diagnosis and instructional planning, however, the teacher may find it most beneficial to classify the operations, as in Figure 2.1, from the simplest (decode) to the most complex (extend) and use that logic in analyzing children's performances and in organizing records to keep track of their progress.

Figure 2.1 is a skeleton that will be fleshed out in succeeding chapters of this text, but a word of caution is needed here with a reminder of the perspective mentioned earlier. "Teaching reading" and

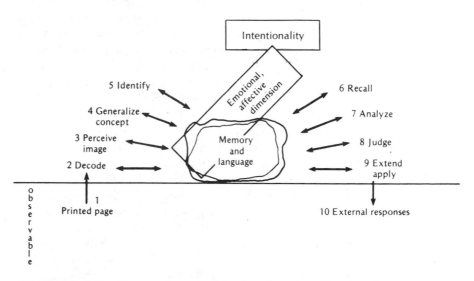

FIGURE 2.3 The reading model, showing the affective dimension and the interaction of the operations.

"learning to read" are not simply a sum of eight operations or skills such as those shown in Figure 2.1. Whether the list contains eight items or eight hundred, reading is somehow greater than the sum of its parts. Each learner brings a unique set of experiences, attitudes, and interests when beginning to read. These stored memories interact in a multitude of ways with the mental operations listed in the model. Even a single word such as *shop* calls up various images and feelings, depending on that unique storehouse of memories. *Shop* may mean a place where Mother works or something you do when you go to the grocery. It may evoke pleasant feelings or those of irritation. Aware of these nuances, the teacher remains flexible in observing and guiding the child's reactions.

Figure 2.3 expands the outline of reading. It not only shows an emotional, "affective" dimension (interests, feelings, beliefs) cutting across the entire range of reading operations or skills but also points to the constant interaction between the message, any of the various operations, and the memory bank of the reader.

The Model and the Book

Now that the model has been introduced briefly, it is necessary to consider how and where it applies in the classroom. Some perspective is needed to relate the model to teaching and to the rest of this book, for a cursory view of the chapter headings reveals no one-to-one match with the categories in the model.

The Harris-Smith model is an attempt to describe the reading process in a logical sequence from its simplest to its most complex elements. The model provides a reasonable outline of how the reader works on the printed message—at his or her own level of ability and sophistication. But activities in the classroom—and thus books and materials for teaching reading—traditionally have been organized around topics such as readiness, word skills, comprehension skills, study skills, and creative reading. These topics clearly provide convenient categories for listing activities in reading instruction. In teachers' guides, for example, the objectives and exercises are labeled in this way. These categories, therefore, constitute one important area of the teacher's knowledge. At the same that a word skill or comprehension activity is being taught, it is necessary for the teacher to know how that activity is used by the reader in the act of reading, how it fits into the total reading process. That is why we call the Harris-Smith model a *map* and why we will refer to it throughout this book to show where the activities of a given chapter touch on the model.

Over the past forty years, several terms without precise definition have been used to describe reading comprehension. Writers and teachers have talked about "literal reading," "interpretive reading," "critical reading," and sometimes "creative reading"; but it was never very clear what each writer meant when using one or another of these terms.

TABLE 2.2 Matching terms to the Harris-Smith model

Harris-Smith Terms	Other Terms
Perceive image	
Generalize	
Identify	
Recall	Literal comprehension
Analyze	Interpretive and inferential comprehension
Judge	Critical comprehension
Extend	Creative comprehension

In some instances, they referred to a type of information; and in others, to a kind of activity the reader engaged in. The Harris-Smith model focuses on operations used by the reader in constructing meaning, but because the terms *literal, interpretive,* and *critical* will appear in other writings, we want to show approximately where they match the terms used in the Harris-Smith model. Depending on an author's use of these terms, there may be a slight variation from our presentation in Table 2.2.

Following is a list of the categories in the model and the chapters that contain material related to each term. Because of the complex nature of reading, some of the reading activities described in these chapters are listed in more than one category of the model.

Decode: Chapters 4, 5, and 6 discuss listening, sound-spelling patterns, and word-structure activities.

Perceive Image: Chapters 6, 7, and 8 include basic comprehension and word-recognition activities.

Generalize: Chapters 3, 4, 7, and 8 on language growth and comprehension deal with the development of concepts and purposeful identification of a message.

Recall: Chapters 8 and 9 on comprehension and word memory provide activities on this subject.

Analyze: Chapters 7, 8, 10, and 11 on critical comprehension and content reading show how analysis is applied in reading.

Evaluate: Chapter 10 on critical reading is especially applicable to this stage of the model, as is Chapter 11 on content reading.

Extend: Chapters 10 and 13 discuss creative and utilitarian applications in reading.

Other chapters in this text describe testing, organizing, and selecting materials—concerns that extend beyond any single skill or phase of the reading process. Throughout the book, by means of frequent references to this model, the reader will be reminded that it is important to relate the various components of the model to the discussion of individual classroom practices.

Assessing and Observing

Teaching and evaluating go hand in hand. Every teacher needs to assess what children are doing and determine whether to adjust instruction to help them make progress. This text tries to show that the evaluation of learning is a continual activity. In each of the succeeding chapters, you will find evaluation activities related to the chapter topic. In addition, a separate chapter on the testing and diagnosing of reading appears later in the book (Chapter 14).

The concept of *assessment as diagnosis* is so important that it merits a separate discussion to provide an overview that will apply throughout the remainder of this text. If teaching is an intentional behavior—if it is diagnostic and prescriptive (and we think it is)—then it is important for teachers to have in mind how they are going to observe children in order to help them make progress in reading.

Formal Assessment

Ordinarily, the terms *assessment* and *evaluation* bring to mind the image of a paper-and-pencil test. Although standardized tests are sometimes useful, educators should not be seduced by the apparent sophistication of such examinations. The authors of this text view assessment in classroom teaching as a means of gaining information about children, information that will help in making instructional decisions. Teachers and administrators must ask themselves whether or not the commercially printed standardized reading tests do, in fact, promote intelligent decision making in the classroom (Farr, 1969). Many standardized reading tests are designed to rank students from low to high and do not give the teacher useful decision-making information. Such tests may be useful for administrators to report school averages, but they have little practical value for the classroom teacher. Teachers should use only the overall reading score rather than the subtest scores—and then only to determine range of classroom abilities.

On the other hand, a growing number of commercial tests have been aimed at measuring specific performance objectives in reading. Such a test is often called a "criterion-referenced test," meaning that it is designed to measure specifically described reading behaviors. By using criterion-referenced tests (discussed in Chapter 14), the teacher can tell which skills the children already have and which ones will require more work. Once again, simply because a test is commercially available does not automatically make it valuable. The teacher must determine whether or not the test *measures what has been taught.* It is fine to have a test that measure twenty different *decoding* skills, but if the teacher wants to know whether or not the child has mastered six *comprehension* skills, then the test on decoding skills is obviously inappropriate.

"Informal assessment procedures were [established as] a reaction to standardized test instruments because those instruments did not always fit the needs of particular schools and school districts," wrote Moore in 1983 (p. 961). Experienced and well-read teachers will usually observe children's performance through informal techniques. Such techniques include listening to children read aloud, examining their daily

---

When a student needs help, place a zero (0) in the box. When unsupervised practice is needed, place a check (√). When the student demonstrates strength, place a plus sign (+) in the box.

READING AREAS	STUDENTS					
I. WORD-SOLVING STRATEGIES						
Decoding:						
sound-symbol						
spelling patterns						
structural analysis						
Perceive image:						
association						
II. COMPREHENSION STRATEGIES (A)						
Generalize:						
categorizing						
labeling						
Identify:						
general experiences						
content-specific						
III. COMPREHENSION STRATEGIES (B)						
Recall:						
details						
sequence						
directions						
Analyze:						
inferences						
cause-effect						
organization						
Judge:						
personal						
external						
Extend:						
emotional						
logical						
IV. INTERESTS						

FIGURE 2.4 Reading Checklist.

An Intellectual Map for Teaching

work and noting patterns of strength or weakness, watching children solve problems through reading, and sometimes asking children or their parents to describe how they read or what problems they are having. These techniques sound deceptively simple, but it is most important for teachers to use such informal observations as indicators of performance, not as highly reliable or valid test scores (McKenna, 1983). For informal observations to be worthwhile, the teacher must have a clear picture in mind of what kinds of behavior to observe and must keep careful records of observations.

One of the primary reasons for constructing the Harris-Smith model of reading was to give teachers a mental framework that could be used to categorize children's behavior. That model could be turned into a checklist, especially where reading comprehension was concerned. The model deals primarily with processing information. The major task of the reader is to perform those operations that will enable him or her to understand the meaning of what is read. Thus, those aspects related to the development of comprehension should play a major role in a teacher's conceptualization of reading. In the very earliest stages of reading, of course, a wide variety of word skills is needed. Therefore, the teacher of beginning reading is more concerned with the alphabet code, vocabulary, and concepts: the decoding, perceptual, and conceptual elements of the Harris-Smith model.

A clear definition and a coherent instructional outline enable a teacher to collect useful information about helping children learn to read. Without a clear outline, the observations a teacher makes are likely to be random and unorganized and are not likely to be put into any useful pattern for making constructive decisions.

With an outline such as that provided by the Harris-Smith model, a teacher can either hold information in mind or construct a checklist that can be used for making simple notations during class. In this way, a record can be kept of those who need help and those who are proceeding without difficulty. A checklist or two attached to a clipboard can be used as an efficient data-collection tool and should improve significantly the decisions made about reading progress. See Figure 2.4 for a sample reading checklist.

What to Observe

Teachers learn to observe those things that help in making major decisions about reading. Consequently, several questions need to be asked continually about student performance:

1. *Can the child read the material in the book without undue frustration?*
   This is a matter of determining an appropriate instructional level. It is a fairly simple matter to check the child's reading level by providing several sample paragraphs from the textbook used in class to see if the child can read aloud and comprehend and can answer several typical questions about the material just read. If many word and comprehension errors are made, the passages are apparently

too difficult, and, for instructional purposes, the child should be given books that are easier to read. Additional details regarding the determination of reading level are found in the discussion of assessment in Chapter 14, pages 472–479.

2. *Does the child have an adequate supply of word-solving strategies?*
   No matter what their age or grade level, children are constantly meeting new words in their reading. The ability to decode those words should not rely simply on guesses but on a number of orderly and intelligent strategies. Do the children give evidence of having a system for using the context of the story? Do they have a variety of decoding and other word-recognition strategies? After deciding which strategies the children do or do not have, the teacher is able to offer instructional guidance.

3. *Does the child have satisfactory comprehension strategies?*
   Before it is possible to answer questions or determine how to use information gathered from reading, a reader needs a sense of order. Do the children know how to get the main idea and supporting details and how to use the organization of the passage to guide their thinking? Questions such as these guide the teacher's observation and instructional planning (Spiegel, 1980).

4. *Does the child use his or her interests to help with reading?*
   By helping a child identify interests and by keeping tabs on them through a checklist or some other record, the teacher encourages the child to use both background and interests in learning to read and to comprehend what has been read. Most children will need guidance in identifying and using their interests. Once again the teacher observes and collects information to provide that guidance. Then related books and materials can be provided to assist the child with reading practice and with learning in areas of interest.

Assessment Plan

It should be clear from what has been said that diagnostic-prescriptive teaching demands some kind of plan for observing children and assessing their progress. The teacher must gather adequate information about students and then make intelligent decisions after weighing the various alternatives. Assessment, then, is the information-gathering process that provides the basis for making intelligent decisions. Every teacher wants to promote learning and to develop strong, independent children. Therefore, it only makes sense that some plan to collect data about children's reading goes along with good teaching. The basic steps in decision making, then, are these:

1. Outlining the area to be observed.
2. Identifying the specific objectives to be attained.
3. Developing checklists or other procedures for collecting data.

These processes will be fully described in the remaining chapters of this book.

Communicating a Definition

If reading is defined as a type of communication, then this definition also implies an attitude toward reading. Children begin to realize that they are to interact with the printed page, that they not only work on a word but they act on the entire message. They are constructing meaning when they read. Thus, the writer and the reader both contribute to the meaning and significance of a reading selection.

The teacher defines reading in the child's terms, using material that is appropriate to the child's stage of development and environment—usually schoolbooks and the magazines that are read at home. Reading is further defined in terms of word-recognition and thinking operations. In observing these, the teacher can judge the skills of the child and can plan activities that promote continuing progress toward competent reading. That definition is made flexible by the teacher's attempts to utilize the child's unique experiences and interests in teaching him or her to read.

As Figure 2.3 indicates, each aspect of the model is affected by the background, language, attitudes, and interests of the child. There is a constant interplay among those stored and ever-changing features of human learning. Thus, no single skill or mental operation stands in isolation from all the others. That fact makes careful and intuitive observation a central feature in teaching a child to read.

Refine

All that needs to be added to our map of reading is a principle of development. From the outset, children construct meaning in the manner that their intellectual development allows. As a child's intellectual structure changes and as experience expands, he or she is more and more able to construct meaning from a message in the manner of an adult—like a fluent and competent reader. The work of the teacher, then, is to promote a continuing refinement of the operations listed in Figure 2.3.

That refinement, that progress in reading will continue—sometimes rapidly, sometimes slowly, sometimes erratically, sometimes purposefully. The teacher observes and adjusts week by week and year by year. With a cognitive map such as the one in Figure 2.3, the teacher can help the child to progress in a steady spiral. To accomplish this, the teacher

1. Determines the level of development and what operations of skills the learner has already mastered.
2. Observes the learner's strategy for solving various word and comprehension problems.
3. Uses interests and background to obtain healthy interaction with written messages.
4. Keeps providing opportunities for progress and the refinement of skills by the child.

After the teacher has determined the child's background and level of skills, the Harris-Smith model can be used to guide the child toward efficient, fluent, enjoyable reading. The reading-communication model gives the teacher a schema with which to diagnose a reader's progress at specific stages in the learning process. The teacher can ask about the reader's skill in decoding, perceiving, conceptualizing, recalling, analyzing, evaluating, and applying. Simply being aware that a reader may experience difficulty at any one of these stages serves as a reminder that the teacher must analyze each student's needs and provide assistance whenever problems arise. Means for testing and teaching arise from an awareness of these aspects of reading.

Teaching Reading and the Other Language Arts*

For the past fifty years, educators have called for a greater integration of language arts teaching than they typically found in the elementary school classroom. Integrating language arts instruction means that listening, speaking, reading, and writing are deliberately used together to show their commonalities and mutual features. For example, when a story is presented, its topic and the students' experiences are discussed and written just as adults would raise questions and share ideas if they found someone else who was reading the same novel or the same professional book. Through the interactions found in those language encounters, teachers and students have an opportunity to ask for definitions and clarification—a natural way to call attention to possibilities for language growth. Some theorists refer to a language exchange as a transaction, a giving and taking of personal language in order to make sense of the encounter (Rosenblatt, 1978). Because language encounters are based on thought and are coded in sounds or graphic symbols, it is easy to speak glibly about interrelationships. It is not so easy, however, to maneuver that simple-sounding relationship across the many demands of the language arts curriculum.

Language arts instruction in public schools is organized around achievement in vocabulary, comprehension, word skills, study skills, literary content, grammar, punctuation, spelling, and writing different forms of exposition. Teachers and children are asked to demonstrate competence in most of those areas. Attention to each, therefore, is usually required.

One of the characteristics of good teaching, according to Kounin (1983), is the ability to make those routine school tasks seem real.

* The ideas in this discussion were first presented to the Indianapolis Public Schools in a position paper entitled "Using Target Tasks in Language Arts Instruction" by Carl B. Smith (1981). Extended strategies and activities based on these ideas can be found in *The Language Arts Resource Book: Grades One Through Six* by Evelyn J. Mason, Supervisor of Language Arts (Grades 1–6), Indianapolis Public Schools (n.d.).

Teachers can accomplish that goal and can also integrate language arts instruction by focusing on whole messages, such as, the communication of a personal feeling. When children see that they are reading and writing messages that have personal significance, they may then be able to put the smaller details of language arts instruction into perspective. They are actually leading to a desirable result: A communication that makes sense in the real world. Thus, students can see some value in the structured curriculum and they are also learning to think about reading, writing, speaking, and listening as mutually beneficial language activities.

Linking Reading and Writing

Unless specific attempts are made to show the connection between reading and writing in the curriculum, most of what has been said in the preceding paragraphs will remain fairly general notions that teachers may apply in a random fashion. The following paragraphs outline a framework that an individual teacher or school system might use to link reading and writing (and, in fact, all communication modes).

By agreeing that language arts instruction is concerned primarily with communication, teachers and students could direct their attention to such things as reading and writing short stories and essays as demonstrations of their competence, just as the swimmer uses the race as a demonstration. A swimmer will endure grueling practice sessions because they lead to a race. The same is true in communication. Students will endure grammar, spelling, and decoding activities when they see that those exercises enable them to communicate more effectively—to tell stories, listen and outline, write letters, and read books more effectively. By changing the performance target and the kind of language samples that are measured, schools not only make the curriculum more real but also offer the teacher more flexibility in using practice activities to achieve a real communication goal. The practice activities—grammar, spelling, phonics—are means to the end; they are not ends in themselves.

In a communications-oriented plan, teachers and students still engage in many of the traditional activities. The major difference lies in a rather clear separation between means and ends, between practice activities and the performances that demonstrate communication. The performance of an entire message is a clear indication of an ability to communicate, providing evidence of a growing vocabulary, the use of sentences, and the understanding and use of narration or explanatory prose in school and in daily life. Students can show that they understand a short story, for example, when they can tell or write a short story themselves. It is understood, of course, that the language arts curriculum includes much more than is tested, and more than is stated here. The major performances listed here are merely sample achievements or demonstrations of a student's progress toward becoming a literate, articulate human being.

For example, in the lower primary grades the goal of speaking clearly and effectively can be demonstrated in the telling of a personal

Decisions for Classroom Reading

short story that has defined characteristics (for example, one in which characters work out a particular problem). The teacher can evaluate the performance with any personal notation system that seems appropriate, such as (1) high competence, (2) minimal competence, or (3) needs additional work.

Any selection of developmental tasks such as the one just described requires choices, and those choices obviously include some and exclude other competence indicators that the teacher could measure. As teachers, we accept that situation and do the best we can to make our choices workable and acceptable. For example, in the early stages of language arts development, a simple short story could be a benchmark: *The child will be able to tell or write a simple short story.* Implied in that target task is the child's prior ability to listen to and read a short story, as well as to identify the characters and the process by which they work out a solution to their problems. The teacher then builds toward that short-story task by providing the examples, motivation, and skills the child needs to produce the message (the short story). Whether those activities include speaking in clear utterances, writing sentences, or spelling words so that others can understand them, the teacher uses all the language arts resources available to help students improve and develop.

Using Developmental Tasks

Suppose you want to teach primary-grade children to comprehend and to write a short story but you aren't sure what they know and what they don't. How can you outline the various levels on which you may approach the task? Table 2.3 outlines the teaching of a short story by showing various entry points: vocabulary development, personal experience statements, sequence of events, complete story. Related activities may range from vocabulary development as a preparation for reading or writing a short story all the way to using an entire story as a complete communication. By moving horizontally at Level 1, a teacher could read a story or certain sentences for it, directing children to listen for certain kinds of words or to listen for the ways in which particular words are used. Then the teacher could ask children to dictate stories using special words that seem to fit the subject of their story. The teacher or an aide transcribes the statements, after which each child shares it with another student or with a small group. That gives the student a chance to see if the selected vocabulary communicates as intended. The final activity in Level 1 should enable the child to write the words that have been practiced in listening, talking, and reading activities.

At Level 4 in Table 2.3, all the listening, speaking, reading, and writing activities use complete stories. Between Level 1 (vocabulary) and Level 4 (complete sentences) there are intermediate stages: using sentences associated with a personal experience and writing descriptions of people and places to gain a sense of order and sequence in narrative writing.

Table 2.3 is not intended to serve as a lesson plan; rather, it is a broad outline showing related language arts tasks that move toward

TABLE 2.3 Sample Practices Leading to Writing a Short Story. (Lower Primary Grades)

Processing Levels	Listening	Speaking	Reading	Writing
1. Concept Vocabulary	Listen for certain words.	Dictate experience story.	Read back experience story.	Write (spell) common words.
2. Use vocabulary in a statement about personal experience.	Attend to enjoyable stories.	Use special vocabulary in classwork.	Build word recognition vocabulary.	Write stentence with capital and final period or quesiton mark.
3. Provide several details in an organized set.	Listen for specific information.	Describe places and people who live there.	Read for character and place details.	Write descriptions of people and places.
4. Final Target: A Basic Communication.	Listen to and analyze stories that have characters and action.	Tell a story with characters and action.	Read and analyze a story with characters and action.	Write a short story with characters and action.

the goal of understanding and producing a short story with character and action. As outlined, it would be appropriate for primary-grade children as well as for those in intermediate grades.

A framework for interrelating the language arts can be extracted from Table 2.3. Because the target is to listen to, tell, read, and write a short story, the teacher and the child can see their progress (moving vertically) and can also see relationships (moving through listening, speaking, reading, and writing).

Major Communication Functions

Besides a short story, what are the major messages or communication functions that people use in their daily lives? The following list contains those communication functions that seem most appropriate for an elementary school student:

1. Tell a story.
2. Give a personal message.
3. Present someone's life story.
4. Convince someone of a point of view.
5. Explain a personal discovery or a discovery made by someone else.
6. Describe a scene or an event.
7. Apply for a position or license.
8. Express personal feelings.
9. Give a formal message.
10. Explain an idea or process.
11. Explore ideas in an organized way.

A curriculum that focuses on communication of complete messages would evaluate its success in terms of evidence that a student can read and write in each message type or is at least making progress toward effective communication of those messages.

Sample Communications for Primary and Intermediate Grades

The following list indicates sample products that students may use to communicate. The entries are divided into those that are more likely to be associated with the primary grades and those more likely to be associated with the intermediate grades. These divisions are somewhat arbitrary but they do illustrate the form the above-listed messages may take.

Primary	*Intermediate*
Personal letters	Formal letters
Simple stories and puppet-show dramas	Complicated stories and TV dramas
Autobiographies	Historical biographies
Simple poetry	Various poetic forms
Description of events (personal journal)	Explanation of how to play a game
Expressing opinions	Building arguments and propaganda
Reporting information	Research report
Filling out forms and appplications	Newspaper ads and forms
Nonverbal communication (picture books)	Nonverbal communication (symbols and body language)

Each of these examples could be organized into an instructional outline similar to the one presented in Table 2.3. For any of these target communications, the teacher should start each student at a task or level of development that can be handled successfully and from which progress can be made. The older the students, the more likely they will be working on several communication targets within the same period of time—a grading period, for example. When reading, students perform each target task and mark it on a personal checklist. As they work to achieve the target communications, students practice the mechanics and skills that enable them to demonstrate competence. Those skills may be tested at the discretion of the teacher. For some children, a test in itself constitutes effective motivation. But the actual test lies in the challenge to write a message that another person will read and respond to.

The following sample outlines of several elementary school communication tasks are arranged to display instructional development (vertically) and to show mutually reinforcing tasks (horizontally). The title of a targeted communication or message is given at the top and

TABLE 2.4 Expressing an Opinion.

Listen	Speak	Read	Write
1. Identify differences between fact and opinion.	State a feeling about an issue or a book. State facts on an issue or book.	Read a belief statement and identify it as an opinion.	List feelings on a given topic. List facts on a given topic.
2. Separate facts and feelings in an opinion statement	Present feelings and facts in an order that expresses your opinion.	Read a factual selection and discuss its actuality.	On an issue (or book) write a summary of your opinion.
3. Identify the main idea of an opinion statement.	Practice making opinion statements in class.	Read a brief opinion statement such as a letter to the editor.	In an organized way write an opinion on some issue or book.
4. Tell the facts and feelings used to support an opinion.	In an organized way present opinion using feelings and facts.	Read a book review or other opinion essay and separate fact and opinion.	In an organized way write an opinion on some issue or book.

the final exercise at the bottom of the chart is the fulfillment of the title (the targeted message).

Table 2.4 suggests four developmental levels that lead students to an understanding of how to express their opinions in a public forum such as a schoolroom. In the table these four levels are organized as follows:

Level 1 - Definition.
Level 2 - Categorization.
Level 3 - Theme.
Level 4 - Organization.

The teacher selects an entry point (a processing level) that matches the current level of understanding of the student.

This arrangement provides two helpful views of a child who tries to "express an opinion." A horizontal view (listen, speak, read, write) indicates performance at a given level or in a particular type of activity. A vertical view suggests the developmental progress that is expected of a child over a longer period of time. The total figure reminds the teacher that listening, speaking, reading, and writing are interrelated, even though the activity of the moment may seem to have a more limited focus.

In Table 2.5 the major communication to be achieved is a description that uses figurative language and mood-setting vocabulary—a communication more appropriate for upper elementary students than

TABLE 2.5 Description of People, Things, Events.

Listen	Speak	Read	Write
1. Attend to the reading of appropriate prose and poetry, and discuss the reading of descriptive sentences by peers.	Give one-sentence descriptions of a sensory action or general emotional feeling or experience using one or more descriptive words.	Read sentences or brief poems describing a sensory action or emotional feeling or experience using one or more descriptive words.	Write one sentence or a brief poem describing a sensory action or emotional feeling or experience using one or more descriptive words.
2. Attend to the reading or speaking of jingles, poetry, and prose from student's writings, children's classics, and appropriate adult literature and discuss personal reactions to descriptive words and phrases.	Organize and present a description of an event, object, or place using action, emotion, and sensory-experience words.	Read jingles, poetry, and prose descriptions, including those by peers. Locate descriptive words, phrases, and sentences.	Write three or more sentences describing a scene, place, object, or event using action, emotion, and sensory words.
3. Attend to the reading or oral presentation of appropriate descriptive prose and poetry from students' writings, children's classics, and adult literature and identify the kind of description appearing in each.	Use a reporter's guide (5 W's) to present an organized description using specific and expressive verbs, adjectives, and adverbs.	Read descriptive prose and poetry from students' writing, children's classics, and appropriate adult literature and identify the kind of description appearing in each.	Write one or more descriptive paragraphs or poetic verses, using a reporter's guide (5 W's), for an event. Use specific and expressive verbs, adjectives, and adverbs.
4. Attend to the reading or oral presentation of prose and poetry. Identify the figurative language and the mood created by descriptive words.	Organize and present a description of an object, place, person, or event using figurative language and other descriptive words to create moods.	Read increasingly complex descriptive prose and poetry from students' writings, children's classics, and appropriate adult literature and identify figurative language and descriptive words that create mood.	Organize and write more than one paragraph or poetic verse describing an object, person or event using figurative language and certain descriptive words to create a mood.

for those in the lower grades. Level 1 operates within the framework of single sentences. Level 2 expects more than one sentence. Level 3 suggests using the five W's of news reporting as a guide to description (Who, Where, What, When, Why). Level 4 develops a longer description with the use of figurative language and mood words that have been introduced earlier.

Table 2.6 displays an outline that asks for an organized report based on collected data, that is, a research report. Level 1 focuses on selecting a workable topic; level 2, on collecting and organizing data; level 3, on outlining a report; level 4, on producing an organized report based on a variety of sources.

TABLE 2.6   Research and Reporting.

Listen	Speak	Read	Write
1. Listen to a report and identify bits of information the researcher had to gather for the report.	Identify a topic on which to gather information and list ways of finding information.	Read about researchers or reporters collecting information on topics of interest.	Select a topic for doing research.
2. Listen to and identify important details heard in a report.	Discuss ways of collecting data on a specific topic.	Read a report and determine where the researcher got the information.	Collect and keep data in an organized way.
3. Listen to and identify conclusions heard in a factual presentation.	Discuss how to categorize and outline data collected.	Read a report and outline its major categories and conclusions.	Outline the paper and categorize information collected in an outline.
4. Listen to and summarize (retell) the steps the speaker took in presenting a factual report.	Give a presentation of data that provides meaningful information to listeners.	Read a report and tell how to verify its information.	Submit an organized report based on a number of identified sources.

Processing Information for a Purpose

Reading and writing concern themselves with processing information. Whether acting as a reader or writer, the child has to ask, "How do I take this information and make it meaningful?" Central to that question is the guiding role of purpose or intention: "Why am I reading this?" or "Why do I want to communicate these ideas in writing?" It would be helpful if all children had those two questions emblazoned on a card in front of them throughout their school careers!

The intention of the reader or writer serves as the primary mechanism for selecting information and for organizing what is selected. After that, the ability and skill of the individual determine the outcome, that is, the synthesis that occurs in reading or the composition in writing. If children know that school assignments require a retelling of information or events in their stated sequence, that knowledge becomes their guide for selecting and organizing what they will try to retain. In like manner, their writing will tend to list details of events in chronological order with little other thought given to a composition, if that is the kind of processing children associate with school tasks.

Quantity and Type of Processing

There are two ways for a teacher to teach children how to process a message. One way looks at the message quantitatively; the other looks at the kind of thinking required to process the message. By treating the message as a quantity, the teacher can ask if the children can process

1. The entire selection.
2. A section or a paragraph.
3. A sentence.
4. The key vocabulary or a word.

If satisfactory responses are given for the entire selection, there is no need to check smaller units. But for some children, even at the upper elementary grades, processing sentences or even vocabulary poses a problem.

As an aid to reading or writing a message, teachers often find it helpful to start by listing words that represent important concepts. When a group of children is writing on the same subject, listing words on the board gives each of them a set of concepts and a vocabulary that they can start with. In the same light, children can write single statements that represent some of the major thoughts they have on a subject. Those statements could be shared or tried on a partner as a way of seeing where gaps occur and where help is needed before attempting to organize a coherent message.

Another way to approach a message is to examine the kind of thinking needed to process the information. Certainly there are many types of thinking, but we will restrict our discussion to three types that can guide instruction in reading and writing:

1. Linear thinking that retells a message in its original order.
2. Interpretive thinking that builds on a theme or a moral.
3. Evaluative thinking that measures the story against a standard or benchmark.

A teacher could demonstrate these levels of information processing by asking children to respond to one of Aesop's fables, for example, the story of the shepherd boy who cried "Wolf!" The three levels of thinking could be observed in an elementary school class by asking these questions:

Who can retell the story?
What is the moral of the story?
Why did the boy and the townspeople act as they did?

In a similar fashion, a teacher could get children to write and process on any of these levels by directing them to do the following:

1. Write a story that has a clear sequence of events.
2. Write a story that exemplifies a theme or moral.
3. Write a story that shows characters making mistakes or making judgments about something important.

Common Instructional Steps

In reading instruction, it has been common for teachers to direct reading in three steps: prereading activity, reading for a purpose, and discussion and review. Writing benefits from a similar staging: prewriting, writing with intention, and revising. In each of these steps similar thinking and classroom interaction can occur.

Step 1: Prereading/Prewriting. This preparatory step calls for making associations, drawing on background experiences, calling up vocabulary, and bringing the topic into focus. It may require motivational or interest-raising activities, depending on the children's perception of the topic. The primary objective of this step is to call forth or to develop ideas about a topic and to select those that appear useful for step two. It involves getting the mind ready. It is a preview. Some psychologists refer to these activities as ways of activating mental schemata (Anderson, Spiro, & Montague, 1977).

Step 2: Reading/Writing with Intention. Step 2 calls for reading or writing for personally established purposes. Decisions have to be made about reasons for doing the activity, the intended outcome, and what will guide the mind. The objective of step two is to keep the mind focused while reading or writing. The vocabulary, background information, and schemata from step one are called into play during the active message development of step two.

Step 3: Summarizing and Revising. This step calls for the mind to confirm its work. This may be as simple as summarizing what has been read in order to tie ideas together, or it may require rereading what has been written to make sure major points have been made. Step three may also involve adjusting earlier perceptions into a modified scheme or revising a written composition in order to have it communicate more effectively with the intended audience.

Although more will be said in Chapter 12 about a directed teaching plan, the summary given here confirms the concept that not only can reading and writing be taught in conjunction with each other but also that the same kind of directed teaching works for any communication, no matter the mode—listening, speaking, reading, or writing.

Summary

This chapter has described the need teachers have for a clear intellectual map for teaching reading. A map should give the teacher a design for diagnosing the reading performance of students and for planning instruction. The Harris-Smith model is an intellectual outline or map that teachers can use. It is a logical description of the reading process and moves from simple to complex operations. Included in the model are the cognitive operations of decoding, perception, concept formation, recall, analysis, judgment, and extension, as well as the essential influence of background and attitudes.

The authors have also discussed the integration of reading instruction with all the other components of the language arts, especially writing. As more and more attention is focused on the need for students to be able to read *and* write fluently and effectively, teachers will want to apply the principles discussed in this section in order to help students master these two related and vitally important skills. As you read the following chapters on methods and procedures for teaching *reading,* keep in mind the guidelines presented here and always think about ways you can help students see the connection between *reading and writing* as complementary modes of communication.

Discussion Questions

1. In what ways do you see that a model of reading will help you observe children as they read?
2. If you accept the Harris-Smith model, how would you define the act of reading? If not, tell why you don't accept it.
3. Parents often ask about their child's progress in reading. Explain how you would use the Harris-Smith model in simplified form to describe reading to a group of parents.
4. Develop a set of sample discussion questions that would cover at least four levels of comprehension.

Recommended Readings

Bagford, Jack. (1981, January). Evaluating teachers on reading instruction. *The Reading Teacher, 34*(4), 400–404.
    Bagford lists characteristics that one might use in evaluating teachers.
Ekwall, Eldon E. (1981). *Locating and correcting reading difficulties* (3rd ed.). Columbus, OH: Charles E. Merrill.
    This is a handbook that provides specific practices for classroom teachers.
Guthrie, John T. (1982 March). Effective Teaching Practices. *The Reading Teacher, 35*(6), 766–768.
    Guthrie reviews research on the correlates of effective teaching.
Moffett, James. (1983, March). Reading and writing as mediation. *Language Arts, 60*(3), 315–322.
    Moffett describes ways in which reading and writing alter our stream of thought, our inner speech. In reading, our thought is altered because it is directed by the thoughts of another. In writing, it is affected because we direct inner speech to achieve a goal.
Schell, Leo M., & Hanna, Gerald S. (1981, December). Can informal reading inventories reveal strengths and weakness in comprehension subskills? *The Reading Teacher, 35*(3), 263–268.
    The authors show that commercially available informal reading inventories do not provide reliable information about students' mastery of subskills of reading.
Smith, Carl B., & Dahl, Karin L. (1984). *Teaching reading and writing together: The classroom connection.* New York: Teachers College Press, Columbia University.
    The authors give numerous classroom strategies for teaching reading and writing together, especially in the area of critical thinking.
Smith, Nila Banton (1967). *American reading instruction: Its development and its significance in gaining a perspective on current practices in reading.* Newark, DE.: International Reading Association.

This book gives a historical overview of the evolutionary progress of reading instruction in this country and the varying historical definitions of reading.

Weaver, Constance (1980). *Psycholinguistics and reading: From process to practice.* Boston: Little, Brown.

Weaver provides insights into the reading process by involving the reader in experiments with his or her knowledge of print. The first two chapters are especially helpful in developing a definition of reading.

Zintz, Miles V. (1980). *The reading process: The teacher and the learner* (3rd ed.). Dubuque, IA: Wm. C. Brown.

The author gives an overview of reading instruction. Chapter 3 on linguistic foundations for reading instruction provides valuable information on linguistics, terminology, and a comparison of phonics and linguistics.

Part II

Basic Components of the Reading Process

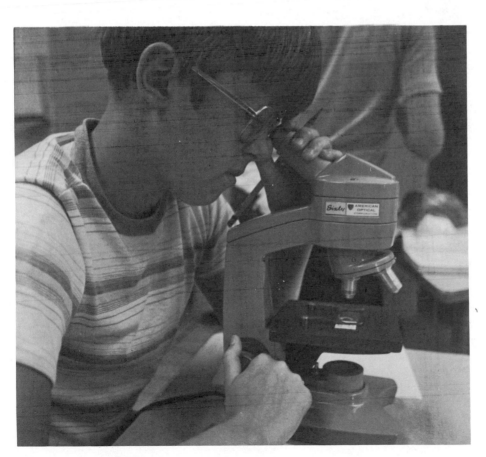

3

Language and Reading

Have you ever turned down the volume on your television set so low that no sound could be heard at all as you watched a program? This may have happened to you, as it has to us, when receiving a telephone call while watching TV, for example. If so, you may have noticed that oral communication between people in the absence of sound has a strange, even bizarre, appearance. Try the situation just described as an experiment. Watch Johnny Carson and Ed McMahon, for example, as they banter back and forth without voice sounds. What becomes obvious is that the ability of humans to communicate by the manipulation of air as it is expelled from the lungs is wondrous, yet rather simple mechanically speaking. As simple as spoken language may be in a mechanical sense, it is the ability to use oral language and its written counterpart that distinguishes humans from other forms of life. Yet we are so accustomed to the use of language that we often take it for granted. The experiment with the TV forces us to look at oral language in a novel way.

When children enter school, there are obvious differences in their ability to use language. Some know and use many more words than others, for example, and some use longer, more complex sentences than their peers. In an absolute sense, these differences are insignificant, however, compared to the accomplishment of all children in acquiring basic competence with their native language. If one considers that a boy, let's call him Billy, entering school at the tender age of five or six speaks and understands his native tongue well enough to converse with a person he has never met before, the accomplishment is staggering. Without formal study and despite the apparent inconsistencies of the English language, Billy can communicate with and understand others who use the same language.

As a language-based process, reading is related in a direct way to other uses of language—speaking, listening, and writing. In this chapter we will examine language development to provide a basis for understanding how children may be helped to learn to read. You should look for answers to the following questions as you read this chapter:

- *How do children develop oral language?*
- *How are language abilities important to reading?*
- *In what ways is learning to read like learning to speak?*
- *What are the special needs of children who are not native speakers of English in learning to read English?*
- *How can dialect differences interfere with learning to read?*
- *How can children who speak a nonstandard dialect of English be helped to learn to read Standard English?*
- *How can a teacher encourage language development?*
- *How can reading instruction be based on the child's personal language?*

Children Develop Language Facility at an Early Age

As a typical six-year-old, Billy has an impressive vocabulary (usually exceeding 20,000 words), an intuitive understanding of the grammar of English, the ability to hear and pronounce all or nearly all the sounds in the language, and a history of successful verbal interactions with others. He may be shy and confused by the newness of his school surroundings to the point of being temporarily "nonverbal," yet he has excellent control of his language. In fact, he has already learned something far more significant than virtually anything the school may be able to teach him in the next twelve years—how to talk.

Obviously schooling can nurture and expand the child's language skills, but the hard part is already done. For example, the child knows that the order of words in an utterance (*syntax*) is important to meaning. Most English-speaking six-year-olds can tell which of these statements "makes sense": (1) The dog barked. (2) Dog barked the. They can tell whether an event has already taken place or not from the form of a sentence—for example, We *saw* the fireworks. They know that words have various meanings (*semantics*) depending on their use in a particular sentence—for instance, a *bat* is both an animal and a wooden club used in playing baseball. Many other examples of what is known about language by even an "unschooled" six-year-old could be given. The point, however, is that children bring language skills to school; they are equipped, so to speak, with a basic capacity for learning through language.

If children do indeed have sufficient language for learning, why make a special point of it here? The explanation is simple: Often class-room activities neglect what children know about communicating and how they acquired that knowledge, and impose many fragmented, me-chanical activities to teach them to write and, of special concern here, to read. Reading instruction should take advantage of children's language skills building on what they know, relating word recognition and comprehension activities to that base of competence. Teachers should also be aware of how language facility is achieved, so that, wherever possible, reading can be learned in a similar way.

How Language Is Important to Reading

It is almost too obvious to state that reading is a language-based process. At a superficial level this seems evident because the printed page is made up of symbols that stand for words. Words are combined to form sentences; sentences form paragraphs; and so forth. Words, sentences, and paragraphs are language. Therefore, reading is language-based. But the fuller meaning of this statement requires exploration.

Reading is a form of communication. Information and ideas are exchanged between writer and reader in the act of communicating. Writers express their thoughts on paper with language, using whatever skills and style they have developed personally. Readers attempt to retrieve meaning from the printed page. Contrary to commonsense explanations that have persisted over the years, it is not the letters on the page or even the individual words that provide the only significant cues to the *competent, fluent* reader. The ability to construct meaning is based on the reader's previous experiences with a topic, familiarity with key concepts, and knowledge of how language works. The fluent reader searches the page for cues to meaning. The searching is not a precise, letter-by-letter, or even word-by-word process but rather one of predicting and anticipating meaning.

To illustrate, a reader who has had experience with football can predict what might go into the following blank: "The quarterback passed the ball to the _____." Experience helps the reader predict reasonable alternatives, such as *end, receiver, halfback,* and *fullback.* The reader may predict incorrectly if the written message is unusual or unpredictable (for example, "The quarterback passed the ball to the waiter.") But the reader's experience enables him or her to reduce the possible number of alternatives and predict with a high degree of certainty.

The reader's knowledge of language is also important in anticipating the author's message. The previous example is again useful. Knowledge of syntax helps the reader to predict that the sentence: "The quarterback _____ the ball to the receiver," will be completed by a verb. Whether they can verbalize that condition or not, speakers of English know intuitively that *table, cat, blue,* and *slowly* do not fit meaningfully into the blank. Readers predict, using their knowledge of syntax. It is not necessary for them to look at every letter of every word or even to look at every word to make this prediction.

Similarly, the reader's knowledge of semantics enables him or her to determine that in this case *passed* has a specific meaning. An appropriate synonym here would be *threw. Passed* has various other meanings that are inappropriate in this context. The reader recognizes this fact and predicts on the basis of the meaning that makes the most sense.

Because they are reading for meaning, an unexpected message will cause readers to retrace their steps to locate the source of confusion. Erroneous predictions are cast aside, new predictions made, and the search for cues to meaning continued. Often the pace becomes slowed, and more visual cues are sampled in an effort to gain understanding following a false prediction. If necessary, individual words and even parts of words may be scrutinized as the reader attempts to reconstruct meaning once again. But this careful study of cues interferes with meaning if it reduces the pace to a word-by-word reading. Understanding occurs best when phrases and sentences can be gulped in large, meaning-bearing units or chunks. This is possible when readers rely heavily on their knowledge of a subject, syntax, and semantics, and less on their ability to identify individual words. As a reader grows in proficiency, this transition from heavy reliance on individual words to assimilation of phrases and sentences occurs.

Frank Smith (1978) describes the reading act as one that involves both visual and nonvisual information. Reading obviously has a visual component in that the reader attends to printed symbols on a page. This information comes from in *front* of the eyeballs. As the reader scans the page, the eyes pick up cues that are transmitted to the brain. Reading also involves nonvisual information, or information that comes from *behind* the eyeball. The reader brings concepts, attitudes, and knowledge of how language works to the reading act. This behind-the-eyeball information permits the reader to sample visual cues as a

The child begins developing an understanding of language at a very early age by interacting with people and objects in the immediate environment.

Basic Components of the Reading Process

means of triggering his or her own nonvisual information. All visual cues on a page are not, indeed cannot be, sampled without overloading the brain with information. Meaning is not obtained by identifying the letters and adding them up in a left-to-right summation process. In fact, letter and word identification is very much dependent on meaning.

A mechanical view of reading suggests that the reader first identifies letters in words, then whole words, then sentences, and so forth until meaning is obtained. In this view the significant feature of written language is what appears on the page. It follows then that early reading instruction would begin with those visual elements. This emphasizes the mechanics of reading. Children learn to associate sounds with letters. Words are sounded out letter by letter, and sounds are blended to pronounce words. With this approach we believe reading may become a word-calling process. Meaning can get lost with this approach, for the task fails to draw on children's language or their background of experience.

Using Language Clues in Identifying Words

1. Experiment with your ability to identify what word has been deleted from a sentence. Ask a friend to pick five sentences from a newspaper and delete one word from each sentence. See whether you can determine the missing word by using the clues provided by the remaining words.
2. Compare another person's predictions for the missing words in the task just described with your own. Discuss with that person the strategies he or she used especially where that person supplied a word different from yours.

Meaning Is Conveyed by Personal Language

Meaning is not conveyed by the purely physical aspects of language, that is, sounds or printed symbols. Obviously, meaning of individual words is dependent on the shared understandings of those who speak the language. *Chair* refers to what we sit on only because that is our unspoken agreement; it is not any inherent quality of the object that makes *chair* its rightful label.

The order of words is also important to meaning. (For example, dog bites man versus man bites dog.)

Sounds or printed symbols alone represent only the *surface structure* of a language. Meaning is carried by the *deep* or *underlying structure.* Syntax, the set of rules or generalizations underlying language usage, links the surface and deep levels of language to permit the exchange of meaning. The receiver of a message must utilize the set of rules to get the meaning of a message. The words alone can be ambiguous and unclear to one who lacks an understanding of syntax. Fortunately, it is unnecessary to teach the rules of syntax, for children have learned them in the process of acquiring language.

The implications of the child's language competence for learning to read are all too often ignored. Thinking that reading is primarily a visual task, involving the identification of individual words (or letters), we have traditionally presented beginning readers with material that is devoid of the rich syntactic and semantic clues they so badly need to make sense of the printed page. Stark sentences—such as "A fat cat sat"—force the child to rely heavily on visual clues to identify words. Teaching strategies that treat each word as a goal to be conquered individually strip children of their most powerful strategies for dealing with language and meaning—syntax and semantics. Words in isolation or near isolation lack contextual clues that permit children to use their knowledge of language, background of experience, and store of concepts.

Viewed as a process of predicting meaning, reading becomes an act that is only incidentally visual. As has been said, the words on the page are not ends in themselves but rather cues or clues that help the reader search for meaning. Syntax provides the reader with valuable information even if every word cannot be pronounced. As readers gain experience and as their concepts grow, they sample fewer cues in order to predict meaning accurately. As their command of language increases, they employ more powerful strategies and understands more complex relationships in print. Instruction that leads children to predict and anticipate meaning, draw on their own experiences, and experiment with language contributes to reading competence. Suggestions for accomplishing these objectives will be provided throughout this book.

Words Are Identified More Easily in Context

This description of reading as a process of predicting does not negate in any way the importance of identifying words. Especially in the beginning stages readers must learn to identify words or they will never be able to put them together into sentences so that they can predict meaning. Therefore, it is necessary to spend some time helping children acquire strategies for recognizing words. More will be said about this in Chapter 6. But it is important to take a fresh look at word recognition when reading is considered as a language-based operation.

The major factor to remember in decoding instruction is simply that word identification should be related to meaning. This can be accomplished most easily by always dealing with words in phrases, sentences and paragraphs or in context. It is only in context that words have any specific meaning. The simplest words—*man, store, house, can*—have various meanings. We can *store* our winter clothes, buy food at a *store,* or be a *store* of knowledge on some topic. In addition to this semantic consideration, words should be presented in context because of the clues to identification provided by syntax. As was stated earlier, the reader who is gaining meaning from the printed page seldom needs to look carefully at all parts of a word. Readers predict words using a minimum of clues. Occasionally they will predict incorrectly and find it necessary to look more carefully at a word. An unknown word or one predicted incorrectly requires a systematic attack, and readers may need analytic skills to gain meaning (for example, phonics and structural analysis).

The key point to remember is that word identification does not lead to understanding; but understanding leads to word identification. And that is as it should be, for reading is a meaning-getting process not a word-calling process.

How Language Is Learned

The remarkable thing about language acquisition is that no one formally teaches a child how to talk. In a completely natural, self-directed process (which we will describe a little later), children master the language of their culture. This process is worth considering for several reasons. First, there are implications for how children might learn to read in the way they learn to talk. Second, the language so necessary for effective reading cannot be taken for granted. Children can and should engage in classroom activities that further develop their language skills and, in the process, their reading skills. Knowing how language develops can be helpful in understanding how and where to begin with further language development.

Reflect for a moment on how a child from birth to five years learns to talk. The descriptions given will make more sense if you can relate them to actual observations. It would be worth your effort to visit a nursery school to gain some personal impressions of child language growth. Even if your observations are informal and unsystematic, watching a child experiment with language can be quite revealing. Described in conventional terms the process is one of gradual expansion and refinement of language.

Initially, the infant produces sounds that are not language but merely random noises. Babies in all cultures make essentially the same sounds, and no single sound is used to signal meaning. Noise gets attention, but any noise does the job in this early babbling stage.

Later (by six months), the infant begins to make sounds intentionally. Sounds foreign to the baby's environment are dropped from the babbling. During this period certain sounds become associated with objects or situations. Parents often urge the infant to produce certain sounds and reinforce their production (for example, da-da-da).

As the infant's sounds become associated with specific needs or situations, recognizable speech begins. At first only single syllables may be produced—or single words. The tendency on the part of many adults is to believe that the child learns a word and then begins to search for ways to use it. In fact, the process is probably just the opposite (Halliday, 1977a, 1977b). The child is a thinking, feeling being with ideas to communicate. Rather than searching for the meaning of words, the child searches for words to convey his or her meaning.

Limited physical ability (for example, the ability to articulate), limited vocabulary (What should I call that thing put in my mouth?), and lack of knowledge of grammar (Do I say, "Me drink" or "Drink me" when I'm thirsty?) cause the twelve-month-old child to use *holophrases*, or one-word sentences, at first. The simple, single-word sentence represents complex meaning. "Ball" may mean, "Where is the red ball I had before?" Or "Throw me the ball." Or "The red ball just hit me in the head." In other words, the surface structure of the child's language is a rather stark representation of an elaborate, deep structure.

Gradually children begin to produce a more complete surface structure, as they acquire an understanding of the grammar of language. The earliest grammatical rule used by the child is one adults do not use in their own speech. Two- or three-word sentences are produced that clearly communicate meaning—for example, "Want down." Parents assist in language development by expanding the child's efforts at communication.

Robin: "Want ball."

Parent: "Robin wants the ball. Here, Robin. Catch the ball."

Eventually, the child's grammar evolves to that used by the parents.

The growth of the child's grammar is evidently not simply a matter of imitating adults. At various points the child seems to overgeneralize the rules of grammar and to apply them in "incorrect" ways. For example, the child who says, "Grandpa comed to my house," has probably never heard an adult use that form of the verb *come*. Yet many verbs are put into past tense by the addition of *-ed*. The explanation seems to be that the child experiments with languages. By testing the system,

Children seem to develop a sense for how the grammar of language works by experimenting with language and receiving feedback from those who are more skilled in the use of language.

Basic Components of the Reading Process

children learn how grammar works. F. Smith (1973) likens the acquisition of language to learning about cats. "In order to learn what it is about cats that makes them cats, the child needs to examine positive and negative examples" (F. Smith, 1973, p. 145). The child learns to generalize about how language operates but also learns to discriminate among proper and improper applications of these generalizations. It is important that a child get feedback about incorrect use of language in order to learn how the system works. The child actually learns as much from being wrong as from being right. Simply imitating adult language would fail to help the child learn what features of the language are significant.

Language Learning Holds Implications for Learning to Read

There are obvious differences between learning to talk and learning to read. It would be simplistic to equate the two and argue that children can learn to read in *exactly* the same way they learn to talk. Yet there are interesting parallels between the two that at least deserve consideration in our discussion of language and reading. These are discussed a little later. The authors believe that recognition by teachers of the similarities between these two aspects of communication will provide some guidance for instructional activities.

Errors Are a Necessary Part of Learning

The most significant principle of language learning, insofar as reading is concerned, has to do with the importance of making errors. It has just been pointed out that children make many errors in learning language. Errors are a necessary part of learning how the language system works. Certainly there is an implication here for reading instruction. Whether the activity is one of learning sound-symbol associations or searching for an author's main point, children should be supported by adults when they make errors.

Both teacher and child need to understand that reading involves prediction and that prediction involves error. One way to reduce error in reading is to approach word symbols strictly on a visual level. Careful processing of letters and words with great attention to detail will result in accurate word-by-word reading. But reading for meaning necessarily involves less attention to visual cues or clues, and more attention to nonvisual ones. Errors are a natural consequence of a search process involving anything as complex as retrieving meaning from the printed page. Neither the teacher nor the child should expect word-perfect oral reading or letter-perfect word identification.

This statement should not be interpreted to mean that errors are preferred to accuracy in reading. Accuracy in word identification and comprehension are important, but they are the result of effective prediction (which risks error), not the result of precise word-calling. In fact, in our opinion, the real test of a reader's skill is whether he or she corrects those errors that interfere with meaning, not whether the reader avoids errors altogether. Just as in learning to talk, the child who is learning to read must be allowed to make errors as a natural consequence of learning the written system of communication.

Learning from Errors

Play the popular game *Master Mind.* Note the importance of errors in solving the puzzle. Being wrong provides valuable information in narrowing down the possibilities.

Language Grows from the Needs and Interests of a Child

Another aspect of learning language has implications for learning to read: Both language and reading should grow from the needs and interests of the child. The child who grows up in an environment where almost every need and wish are anticipated and fulfilled typically is retarded in semantic development. In the absence of a need to communicate, children simply don't learn to communicate. In a normal environment children learn to ask for a drink because they will be thirsty if they don't. Language develops around a child's needs.

Carried a bit further, the child who becomes interested in rocks develops an extensive vocabulary and set of concepts around that interest. Or a child may be devoid of language and experiences related to ballet if he or she has no need to learn about, or no interest in, ballet. Language also develops around a child's interests.

The language of children is personal. It represents their experiences and in many ways enables them to label and manipulate their environment. Their language is adequate to their needs, or they learn new language to meet those needs. Remarkably, their language develops without the aid of formal instruction.

Building on this principle, reading instruction might profit from greater attention to the needs and interests of the child. Whereas language develops naturally around an interest, for example, frequently the reading program (unfortunately often) ignores the child's interests and brings topics to him or her in the form of stories. Often the language needed for success in learning to read is also missing when interest is lacking in a topic.

Particularly in beginning reading the needs and interests of the child should be used by the teacher to make reading meaningful. Stories can be read and discussed on topics children enjoy. This would obvi-

Through book sharing at home, caring adults help the child see relationships between spoken and written language.

ously involve individualization from the outset, for each child has different needs and interests. It is also possible to have children write (or dictate) their own stories on topics they enjoy. The story dictation approach, called the language experience approach, is described later in this chapter. Other techniques for building reading instruction around the child will be described throughout this book, as in Chapters 8 and 9.

Language Reflects a Person's Interests

1. Identify the popular sport where these terms are used: crease, net, cross-check, blue-line, icing. (Answer: ice hockey) If you get the answer correct, you have had occasion to watch the sport. If you did not get the answer, it's probably because of lack of interest in the sport or opportunity to learn about it. Most language reflects our interests in just this way.
2. Think of an activity you enjoy that many of your acquaintances do not. Try the identification game described in task one. See how many terms associated with the activity you can give without revealing the answer. (Suggestions: skiing, knitting, repairing automobiles, guitar playing, and gourmet cooking.) This also illustrates how our interests are reflected in the language we know. Children's language can be evaluated in much the same way.

Language Is Related to Meaning

A third aspect of language learning that has implications for learning to read relates to the central role of meaning. Most people can remember getting trapped in a situation such as a receiving line where language was exchanged more as a matter of custom or ceremony than as a way of exchanging a meaningful message. Even in such cases, words are strung together in a conscious way, not at random. This points up the obvious fact that the use of language always involves meaning.

The infant who is just learning to talk uses language in an effort to communicate ideas. Emphasis is on the use of whole words in some context that involves meaning. Oral language is not normally broken down and analyzed into its separate elements, not even by the child who is just learning to use it. To be sure, individual sounds may occasionally be isolated and taught to a child who has difficulty, for instance, saying, "Rabbit," Say, "R-r-r-r-r." But these instances usually occur in context, and the sounds do not become ends in themselves. Individual sounds are important only as they relate to the pronunciation of a word, which is typically part of a sentence intended to communicate meaning.

By the same token reading activities should always be in context. Meaning should be the overall concern. Words and parts of words should be seen against a backdrop of meaning. Attention to the mechanics of reading should not become an end in itself.

Approached in this way, reading will not become an abstract, memorization process with great attention to individual parts. The child who is learning to read is able to use the powerful semantic and syntactic strategies that have already been learned in acquiring language. Phonics and other forms of word analysis are taught and learned in a reading program that focuses on meaning, but they are not the starting points, and they are not important in and of themselves.

Children with Language Differences

Reading has been presented as a language-based process. Kim, an immigrant child who speaks Vietnamese, faces a serious handicap in learning to read. Not only does she lack the necessary vocabulary to read English, but the syntax of her native language is also different from English, and certain sounds of English do not appear in her tongue. Often economic and physical deprivation accompany her basic language problem, and in some cases she also meets prejudice and discrimination in her community and school.

A detailed discussion cannot be given here of how English can be taught to the non-English-speaking child, nor is that the purpose of this book. (Several references that address the larger issues involved in teaching English as a second language are listed at the end of this chapter.) Nevertheless it is well established that a second language for making the child bilingual can best be learned when the child is young. It is also clear that the language-learning process is not substantially different for the young child acquiring a second language from that for the child learning a first language (DeStefano, 1978). Stimulation from the environment, coupled with oral interaction with speakers of a second language and feedback concerning incorrect attempts at using the language, usually enable a child to master language use. Typically, the bilingual child occasionally mixes vocabulary and sentence structures of two languages, but maturity and experience normally eliminate this tendency (Downing, 1984).

From the standpoint of reading instruction, there is little point in even beginning until or unless Kim has the ability to express her thoughts spontaneously in English speech. Until Kim uses English easily and confidently in conversation, time spent teaching her to read English will be better used teaching her to speak it (Ching, 1976). Time lost from reading instruction in acquiring facility with the language will quickly be made up once the bilingual child has control of English.

Some programs first teach the non-English-speaking child to read in his or her native language. The special advantage of this approach is related to the pride children can acquire in their own heritage. They gain confidence in their ability to succeed at learning to read a native language, which may carry them through the difficult moments of learning to read English later on. Ultimately they must make this transition, however, and, in order to do so, must acquire English. Because that is unavoidable, the better approach is probably to delay reading instruction in favor of learning English from the outset. This approach eliminates the often difficult tasks of finding teachers who speak, write, and read the child's native language and finding appropriate materials for the child to read in that language. The wide variety of languages spoken in the United States makes the approach of learning to read in a native language impractical in many classrooms.

Suggestions for improving language skill are offered in a later section of this chapter and in Chapters 8 and 9 on reading comprehension. Although directed primarily to English-speaking children, the suggestions given are also appropriate for helping the non-English-speaking child acquire the language skills needed for learning how to read. Chapter 15 of this text deals further with the special needs of bilingual children.

Another Language Difference: Dialects

It comes as no great surprise that the English language is spoken by people who represent a large number of *dialects*.[1] One need not be a linguist to realize that a native Minnesotan speaks a different variety of English from a native South Carolinian. Yet two people who have dialect differences can usually communicate without great hardship because their English is more alike than it is different.

With only a little analysis of the matter it is possible to conclude

[1] A dialect is the form or variety of a language spoken in a region, community, social group, or occupational group. Dialects of a language often differ with regard to pronunciation, word meaning, and grammatical rules.

that differences in pronunciation and word meaning usually arise from differences in background experience. Someone who grows up in an environment where *pen* and *pin* are pronounced exactly the same (as in southern Indiana) will probably learn to pronounce those words accordingly. Someone else will pronounce them differently because it is a distinction made by important speech models in his or her environment. Likewise, the meaning attached to a word such as *dinner* varies from group to group (for example, for some it is a meal at the end of the day whereas for others it refers to the noon meal).

Differences in grammar are due to variations in background and may show up in inflections or in syntax. Some groups are inclined to report that "Jimmy *dived* into the water" whereas others say, "Jimmy *dove* into the water." "We could play tag" contrasts with "We might could play tag."

There are some obvious implications for the teacher of reading when dialect differences exist in the speech of children in the classroom or when the teacher's dialect is different from the children's. Certain sound-symbol associations will be different in various dialects. Thus, phonics instruction must reflect the relationships as children speak them. This can be tricky if several dialects are present, but not necessarily difficult. The teacher must also watch for discrepancies in word meaning, so that understanding does not falter on account of vocabulary differences. These adjustments, important as they may be, are not really the crucial issue insofar as teaching children with divergent dialects to read is concerned. The greater problem is simply one of attitude. Dialects often tend to evoke negative attitudes if they are not understood as an anthropological phenomenon (Laffey & Shuy, 1977).

Dialects Are Often Misunderstood

The problem with regard to dialect differences is related to the human tendency to label as wrong or inferior traits or characteristics of others that are different from their own. Sociologists have a label for such attitudes; they call them *ethnocentrism*. The teacher must constantly guard against ethnocentristic thinking, especially with regard to language differences. Even teachers who understand that "Southerners (or Northerners) talk as they do because that is the norm in their environment" may have a tendency to add consciously or unconsciously, "But it's wrong" or "It sounds ignorant." Such attitudes interfere with effective teaching by diverting attention from *what* is said to *how* it is said.

The teacher who lets an attitude about "correctness" of language creep into classroom procedures will typically reject the child's "incorrect" attempts at communicating. The rejection may be done kindly, but the consequences are the same: The children begin to wonder about their ability to communicate. Because reading is a language-based process, any reluctance on the part of children to use language will ultimately interfere with their success at learning to read. The preferred approach in such cases is to accept and reinforce the child's use of language at the time whatever its form, so that he or she gains confidence in communication skills. Later, instruction can be provided to teach Standard English because society expects and wants schools to do so.

Most teachers can accept this argument where matters of pronunciation and vocabulary are concerned. The most misunderstood aspect of dialect, however, is difference of grammar (including usage). Such differences seem harder to accept probably because dialects are not adequately understood. Many "enlightened" people appreciate that President Jimmy Carter's speech was "correct" even if it sounded "different," but do not understand that in the black dialect, "Momma, she be at the store," is "correct" or grammatical. The ethnocentricity of some people is better concealed, but it exists nonetheless. Teachers should realize any dialect of English is a complete language system having all the elements necessary to permit communication. No dialect is "better" than any other when the purpose of language is considered. Some dialects may have more prestige than others because of social factors and people's attitudes, but every dialect is linguistically acceptable.

All Dialects Are Functional

Language is an invention of humankind. It is a constantly changing invention that evolves to keep up with the need to exchange ideas and thoughts. Outdated or antiquated features of language die out because they no longer serve a function. Ambiguous or confusing aspects of language usually evolve or change in order to eliminate misunderstanding. Language systems do not harbor or support anomalies because such irregularities do not facilitate sharing of ideas. This is true of dialects as well, for they are simply special forms of language; dialects do not retain features that obscure or confuse a meaningful exchange of ideas.

From the ethnocentric point of view, a statement such as "Momma, she be at the store" may seem incorrect. Against some forms or standards of English, it is ungrammatical. But viewed within the context of a cultural dialect, the dialect of the black American, it is correct, it is grammatical and it communicates. It communicates more to the speaker of the dialect than is apparent to the unknowing observer. "Momma, she" is effective communication if reduction of uncertainty is the goal. The subject of the sentence is clearly identified twice. Is that necessary? Perhaps. But "standard" English has similar redundancies not characteristic of black English. (For example, in black dialect, "three girls," would be said as *"three girl."* Why not? *Three* has already indicated the plural condition; the plural marker, *s,* on *girls* is redundant. Black English would economize. So-called Standard English economizes in other usages. Who is to say which is right?) "Momma, she be at the store," indicates that Momma is where she usually is. "Momma, she at the store," would indicate that this is an unusual occurrence. Standard English has no parallel use of the verb *is.*

Without exploring any specific dialect further, the point is that no dialect is superior to any other (Wolfram & Fasold, 1974). Differences in dialect exist. Each dialect is complete and functional. Children may actually need to be skilled in using more than one dialect *eventually* as when they attempt to get a job. (Ching, 1976) But when children first arrive at school, their dialects represent their cultures, their homes, their self-worths. To reject the child's language is to reject the child. To insist that such children converse in another dialect is to rob them of their ability to communicate. The six or so years they have spent learning the intonation, syntax, and semantics of their dialect are stripped from them. The language tools needed to talk or read are denied to them.

An example of common occurrence will help illustrate this point. The child who speaks a divergent dialect will quite naturally translate the symbols on the printed page into his or her own language. The black child may read the sentence "Tom and Mary are out playing" as "Tom and Mary, dey out playing." The teacher who regards black dialect as an inferior language will probably indicate dissatisfaction and regard the reading as inaccurate. Yet the child has drawn on the language that has enabled him or her to communicate successfully with others for a number of years. Confused, the child may then pronounce each word in the teacher's dialect but will do so haltingly and probably without complete understanding. The child's own language competence is denied, and he or she is forced to approach reading as a highly abstract decoding task that has no relationship to his or her own experiences or concepts. A discussion of ways to build on the child's language competence is presented later in this chapter.

Language Differences

1. Identify traits in your own language that are regionally or culturally linked. This might include pronunciation of certain words, special expressions, figures of speech, or grammatical constructions. Discuss these differences with colleagues whose background is different from your own. Guard against ethnocentric thinking.
2. Role-play a situation in which you are a parent whose child is being penalized in school for speaking non-Standard English. (Your son says, "He don't know nothing," and "I can't hardly stay awake," for example.) The teacher takes the position that the language of the home is wrong. As a parent you believe your child is suffering unfairly merely for talking as he learned to at home. Attempt to resolve your differences.

Start with the Child's Language

By accepting the child's dialect, the teacher begins with the tools the child needs to acquire more effective communication skills. One goal may be to make the child a skilled user of a more prestigious form of English—a status-conscious culture may leave no other choice. But

Basic Components of the Reading Process

even that goal is not achieved by insisting that the child speak "proper" English in discussing a story or when reading aloud. The standard spelling in a book will be no handicap if the child is reading for meaning. Children will translate the visual symbols into their dialect as their personal language and experience are triggered. And the argument that they will be reinforced for using "poor" language fails to recognize that their language is functional and adequate to their needs.

Often the mislabeled "nonverbal" child is one who has learned that if he or she cannot speak "correctly" it is best to keep quiet. The teacher may have rejected the child's dialect as improper. Such a child's resulting silence and nonparticipation in school can easily be misunderstood as ignorance or even uncooperativeness. And so the vicious cycle continues as the language-different child fulfills the teacher's prophecy and fails in reading and other language-related activities. How much better it would be if such children felt confidence in their ability to express ideas in their dialect. Armed with the confidence gained from numerous successful attempts at sharing their thoughts, these children can learn to read using their language as a tool for retrieving meaning from the printed page.

Teachers Must Encourage Language Development

It is beyond the scope of this book to present a thorough and complete classroom program for language development. Other sources have addressed this task (Smith, Goodman, & Meredith, 1976). In the context of the present discussion it seems important to recognize that reading instruction cannot occur in the absence of, or separate from, a conscious language program. To do otherwise ignores the significant relationship between language and reading presented in this chapter.

One important aspect of a language program is the continued stimulation of natural language growth. Clearly, school-aged children have mastered the rudiments of their language inductively but still have much to learn in order to use their language abilities maximally. The school can nurture the more effective use of language in part by creating opportunities for experiences, facilitating interaction with others, stimulating and broadening personal interests, and generally supporting children in their experiments with language. In other words, many situations that encourage the use of language can be created.

Here are several examples illustrating the kind of opportunities that are appropriate. Children can be encouraged to participate in a regular sharing session. Important personal news, hobbies, topics of local interest, current events, interesting books, class projects, and other similar matters can be discussed. No specific content is organized for study in sharing sessions, nor are any specific aspects of language growth pursued. Children are simply given the opportunity to interact orally with their peers in a free-flowing exchange of ideas. Personal philosophy should dictate whether a sharing session includes the presentation of new possessions via the "show and tell." This is not a necessary feature of a sharing period that primarily focuses on stimulating language.

Children can gain in general language growth from excursions. A class walk to a nearby park to search for signs of spring or a field trip to a distant museum provide stimulation and the need to communicate. Inviting a parent or member of the community into the classroom to talk about a hobby, vocation, or personal experience broadens children's horizons and generates language opportunities. One simple but highly effective activity for promoting language growth has the teacher reading aloud on a regular basis from books that employ language skillfully. These and other activities immerse the children in language. From such experiences, continued expansion and refinement of language occur.

The school has a responsibility for *influencing* language growth to some degree. Whereas many open-ended activities are helpful in continuing the child's inductive language learning, other structured or controlled situations should be created to focus attention on specific, predetermined aspects of language development. Even here evidence suggests that didactic lecturing or drilling on language skills will be largely ineffective. Children need to generalize for themselves from specific exercises and activities that the teacher has planned and structured in keeping with some overall curricular design. Specific examples are needed to help make the point.

One goal might be to sensitize children to the importance of words that describe or qualify. An activity that involves children in expanding basic sentences might be introduced. The teacher can put a statement on the chalkboard; for example: "A tree fell." The children are then invited to discuss how the sentence could be made more descriptive. Questions such as "What kind of tree fell? What did it look like? Where did it fall?" can be asked to elicit specific details. An expansion like the following could occur.

> A tree fell.
> A maple tree fell.
> An old maple tree fell.
> A tall, old maple tree fell across the road.

Follow-up activities could be developed to involve children in adding descriptive words to a newspaper article or to one of their own creative-writing efforts. A contest could be held, with several small groups trying to add the most descriptive words to a kernel sentence.

Another specific instructional goal might be to interpret figurative language correctly. Expressions such as "lost his head," "mended his ways," "take your time," "stick your neck out," and "none of your lip" can be discussed and explained. Children can record the use of such expressions in daily conversation, on television or radio, and in newspapers over a period of time. A dictionary of figures of speech could be developed by the class.

A Language-Based Approach to Initial Reading: Story Dictation

The child's initial experiences with reading have the best chance of being successful when the language and ideas expressed in print are familiar. One way of guaranteeing this familiarity is to have the child dictate stories or narratives, then read them along with the teacher or aide. Many parents without formal training in teaching employ this approach instinctively at Christmas or birthday time, for example, when a thank-you letter for a gift is dictated to Aunt Bess or Grandma. Many kindergarten and first-grade teachers use this approach as a way of introducing children to the relationship between speech and print. Some teachers make the story dictation approach an integral part of their instructional program throughout the school year even in grades two and above.

Called the language experience approach (LEA), story dictation has been described in detail by various authors such as Lee & Allen (1963), Mallon & Berglund (1984), Reimer (1983), Veatch (1978), Hall (1981), and McCracken & McCracken (1972). Later in this book (Chapter 12), LEA is described as one alternative system for teaching reading. We discuss this approach here in the context of this chapter because of its strong link to the child's language.

Using Language Experience in a Classroom

Melinda Perdue uses language experience in her first-grade classroom on a daily basis. One day in the autumn Melinda pointed out that the leaves on many trees were beginning to change colors. She suggested that the children make a point of observing the trees on their way home from school to notice the number and variety of colors. She also asked each child to bring at least one leaf that had changed color to school the next day with the information concerning what kind of tree it was from if possible.

The next day after the early morning tasks associated with getting the school day started were behind them, Ms. Perdue asked the children to bring their leaves to the front of the classroom and sit in a semicircle on the floor. Gina was asked to show her leaf to the group and tell what she could about it.

"My leaf is red," Gina began. "It's from an oak tree."

"Where did you find it, Gina?" Ms. Perdue asked.

"In my front yard," Gina replied. "We have lots of trees and leaves."

"Who else found a red leaf?" Ms. Perdue asked the group. Five hands went up, each holding a reddish leaf. "What kind of leaf did you bring, Chuck?" she questioned.

"A red one," Chuck offered.

"Yes, it is," Ms. Perdue noted supportively. "Do you know what kind of tree it is from?"

"Nah," Chuck responded.

"Where did you find it Chuck?" Ms. Perdue asked.

"In the gutter," Chuck offered.

"Near your house?" Ms. Perdue persisted.

"Nah. Over at the park," Chuck ventured finally.

"Good. Chuck found a red leaf near the park," Ms. Perdue summarized. "Which leaf is larger—Gina's or Chuck's? Are both of these leaves from an oak tree? Are they shaped the same?" Ms. Perdue asked.

Using a similar strategy, Ms. Perdue helped the children note differences among the various red leaves brought by the other children. She pinned the leaves as a group on a bulletin board with the name of the child who brought them written beneath each leaf.

Next she invited someone who had brought a yellow leaf to describe where the leaf was found and, if known, what kind of tree the leaf was from. Again, the leaves were pinned on the bulletin board; and the contributors' names, noted.

After fifteen minutes of sharing the leaves, comparing and contrasting them, Ms. Perdue told the group they were going for a short hike to see what kinds of leaves they could find near the school. She suggested they look for colors and shapes that had not been shared in the discussion thus far. The children quickly put on their coats and lined up at the door for the hike.

While the group circled the school grounds, Ms. Perdue pointed out the various types of trees and reminded the children to look for new varieties of leaves. With the help of the children, she gathered eight or nine new additions for the bulletin board display.

Returning to the classroom, the children again gathered in a semicircle at the front of the room. Ms. Perdue indicated she would like the group to dictate a "story" about the discussion and hike to add to the collection of experience charts hanging on a rack near the sink.

"What would be a good title for our story?" she began. Suggestions included Leaves, Colored Leaves, Autumn Leaves, Finding Leaves, and Different Kinds of Leaves. Ms. Perdue suggested that the selection of a title be made from among those suggested after the story was done but wrote *Leaves* on the chalkboard as a way of focusing comments and suggestions. Before asking for the first sentence of the story, she led the group to think about the various ideas that might be included. The children remembered the hike, the trees they saw on the hike, the leaves they found at home and brought to school, the many colors and shapes of leaves they had found, and the names of the trees they had been able to identify at home and on the hike.

Ms. Perdue guided the group in dictating their story by suggesting they think of how they might describe their experience to someone who had not been a member of the group—their parents, for example.

"What would we want to say first to help someone who reads our story know what we've done?" she asked. "Alison?"

"We learned about leaves in school," Alison suggested.

"That's a good start, Alison," Ms. Perdue replied as she quickly wrote Alison's statement on the chalkboard. "What would come next? Leroy, what have we learned about leaves?"

Basic Components of the Reading Process

"They're red and orange and yellow and brown and green" Leroy responded.

"Yes, that's right, Leroy. Our story says 'We learned about leaves in school.' How should we add your idea?" Ms. Perdue prompted.

"We learned leaves are red and orange and yellow and brown and green," Leroy suggested.

Ms. Perdue added Leroy's statement and asked another question that guides the children's thoughts. "What else did we learn? Olaf."

"Leaves get a different color in the fall," Olaf said.

"Right," Ms. Perdue responded as she writes the suggestion on the board. "Anything else? Bonnie."

"I don't know," Bonnie answered.

"Look at our bulletin board, Bonnie. We've said leaves are different colors. What else did we see when we compared them?"

"Leaves are different shapes," Bonnie remembered.

With the teacher's assistance, the dictation went on. As an experienced user of story dictation, she walked the tight line between telling the group what to say and letting the ideas pop up haphazardly. As the children grow more experienced in story dictation, she exercises less leadership and lets the comments emerge more naturally. It should be noted that Ms. Perdue did not ignore or reject comments that seem to be inappropriate or illogical at any time. She accepted all contributions and wrote them as given without editing for grammar or usage. This was done to avoid discouraging children who may not contribute if there was a chance they will be corrected. The teacher did question contributions that were incorrect from the standpoint of content, however. She would not include a statement that some leaves are purple, for example, but would ask the child to bring one for her to see before adding that thought to the story. This is necessary to keep the children alert in their observations and to encourage the idea that evidence is needed to support one's ideas.

The story finally dictated was as follows:

Different Kinds of Leaves

We learned about leaves in school.

We learned leaves are red and orange and yellow and brown and
green.

Leaves get a different color in the fall.

Leaves are different shapes.

We found leaves from oak trees, hickory trees, dogwood trees,
and ash trees.

We found leaves from locust trees and walnut trees.

Some leaves are big.

Some leaves are little.

Some leaves are round.

Some leaves have points.

We rake leaves in the fall.

Leaves are fun to jump in.

After the story was completed, Ms. Perdue read it aloud and asked the children to read with her. This was repeated several times. The children then returned to their desks with instructions to draw a picture of whatever they would like so long as it somehow included autumn leaves. Ms. Perdue wrote whatever caption the artist dictated on each picture and displayed the captioned pictures on the bulletin board with the leaves.

The next day Ms. Perdue reread the story (now transferred from the chalkboard to a piece of tagboard) and then had the children read it as a group. Different children then took turns reading a sentence at a time.

Next Ms. Perdue pointed out individual words of high frequency in the story and asked the children to read them (leaves, some, we, fall, found). Other words that begin with the same letter/sound were then produced by the children. An experience story on another topic dictated earlier was reread, and words that began with the same letter as the high frequency words (leaves, and so on) were found. In this way, Ms. Perdue helped her pupils increase the number of common words they could recognize at sight.

Ms. Perdue also shared a book with the children that related to the topic of leaves (*A Tree Is Nice,* Udry, 1956). Discussion produced several insights concerning trees and leaves. The question of why leaves turn color in the fall was raised, and several theories were advanced by the children. Ms. Perdue promised to find a book that would answer this question for class the next day.

Each child then shared his or her drawing with the class and read the caption. A mimeographed copy of the "Different Kinds of Leaves" story was given to each child. These papers were sent home to be shared with the child's parents so that additional practice with the words could be gained and so that the parents would understand what their child was doing in reading class.

On the third day Ms. Perdue wrote several of the sentences from the narrative on strips of tagboard. She then cut the sentences into individual word cards. With some of the more advanced pupils, Ms. Perdue initiated an activity of shuffling the word cards and having the children recreate the sentences by putting the cards into correct order. Again, the recognition of these words was being practiced.

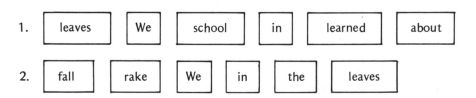

1. | leaves | We | school | in | learned | about |

2. | fall | rake | We | in | the | leaves |

She also asked the children to transform the sentences to communicate the same meaning with different word order. The sentence "Leaves are fun to jump in" became "Jumping in leaves is fun" and "It's fun to jump in leaves." The main purpose of this activity was to focus attention on how each word contributes to the meaning of a sentence.

Basic Components of the Reading Process

With another group of children, Ms. Perdue initiated a matching activity using the same word cards. The children put the cards in correct order by looking at the original narrative and matching the word order found there. In this way, visual discrimination was being learned by the children who could benefit from this activity.

Having spent parts of three days' reading periods on the topic of leaves, Ms. Perdue moved on to another subject, this time favorite television shows, as a means of generating another experience story. Many of the same reading/language abilities were practiced in dictating and reading the story.

Over time Ms. Perdue introduces and reviews many of the same skills she would teach using a more traditional approach to instruction. She prefers language experience, however, because it is based on concepts and experiences the children explore together using the language they produce themselves. The program has structure, but it is one Ms. Perdue creates according to her judgment of the pupils' abilities and needs.

Communication Skills Must Be Integrated

Just as there is danger of divorcing reading instruction from language, there is equal danger of divorcing language instruction from speaking and writing. All these communication skills are interdependent. None should be pursued in isolation from the others. It is important to keep classroom language activities closely linked to children's experiences and interests. Language flourishes around experiences, which, in turn, create and broaden interests. More will be said about the interdependency of all these variables as they relate to reading in Chapters 8 and 9 on reading comprehension.

As subsequent chapters deal with various aspects of reading, there may be a tendency to think of it as a separate, self-contained curricular area. Nothing could be further from the truth. Reading, once again, is a language-based process.

Summary

This chapter argues that reading is a language-based process. Language is learned inductively by children as they receive feedback concerning their attempts at communication. Efforts to teach reading should build on the language competence the child brings to school.

Reading involves more than adding up the words in a sentence or page to arrive at meaning. Understanding is important to word identification and helps the reader predict the author's message. Meaning must be emphasized from the outset of reading instruction.

Language differences can interfere with learning to read. The bilingual child must learn to speak English before trying to read it. The child who speaks a divergent dialect must be permitted to translate the printed page into his or her natural language.

Reading must always be viewed in its proper perspective—as one aspect of communication. Efforts to teach reading should be integrated with instruction in the areas of listening, speaking, and writing. The LEA is one approach to integrating the various language skills.

Terms for Self-Study

syntax
semantics
surface structure
deep structure
bilingual
dialect

Discussion Questions

1. How would language that is unnatural and stilted make the child's task of reading a book written in this way more difficult?
2. Ms. Petrie teaches seven-year-olds. She makes a special effort to find books on topics that are of personal interest to her students. What is the basis for her concern? Why is it well founded?

Recommended Readings

Britton, James. (1970). *Language and learning.* New York: Penguin.
This book discusses the development of language from the perspective of the learner with special attention to how speech is important in organizing and shaping experiences with people and objects in the environment.

Ching, Doris C. (1976). *Reading and the bilingual child.* Newark, DE.: International Reading Association.
The author provides practical ideas for teachers of bilingual and bidialectal students, including the development of motivation and self-concept, auditory discrimination, vocabulary, and oral language.

DeStefano, Johanna S. (1978). *Language, the learner and the school.* New York: Wiley.
This book raises awareness of the effect on learning and reading instruction of language variations such as dialect, social class, sex-difference usage patterns, and usage for different audiences.

Tough, Joan. (1973). *Focus on meaning: Talking to some purpose with young children.* London: Allen and Unwin.
Here is a description of the early stages of child language development and demonstration in a practical manner of how adults can positively influence the process.

Veatch, Jeannette, et al. (1979). *Key words to reading: The language experience approach begins.* Columbus, OH: Charles E. Merrill.
This is a practical guide to starting and implementing a reading program based on the language experience approach. It describes story-starting situations, motivating devices, and skill development activities.

4

Creating Interest in Reading

With the growing presence of computers in our daily lives, we are beginning to hear about the potential these technological wonders have for making routine tasks easier and more convenient. For example, bank customers in some cities already have the option of paying bills and transferring funds between accounts through a telephone link between home computers and a bank computer. In a similar manner, investors who want the latest information about the value of their stocks and bonds can arrange to have their home computers linked to a stock exchange for up-to-the-minute price quotations.

It will soon be possible to search for and read a particular book housed at the local library without leaving the comfort of your own home. The technology to make such service available is at hand right now; all that stands in the way is the funding to computerize public libraries. Of course, home computers are not yet common enough to make this service practical either, but that day is rapidly approaching. Think of the potential such a system would have for increasing the access of all people to information. The resources of an entire library, even a distant library such as the Library of Congress, would be accessible from your easy chair.

When we peek into the future like this and see the potential that will exist for those who can read in an information-rich society, we sometimes wonder whether the lives of people will really change all that much. Will people read more when it becomes possible to open almost any book at will? Perhaps, but the record suggests that those who actually read in any habitual way are rare. The typical citizen still fails to read even a single book in the course of an entire year.

As a teacher, you will face the challenge not only of helping children learn to read but also of building the reading habit as well. This chapter addresses the topics of how to create an interest in reading that becomes habitual and of cultivating personal tastes that lead children to seek out and appreciate the best literature available. As you read, look for answers to the following questions:

- *In what ways does the home environment affect interest in reading?*
- *What can a teacher do to encourage the habit of reading?*
- *What does research say about the interests of children at different ages?*
- *How can children's interests be expanded?*
- *How does the study of literature fit into an elementary school reading program?*
- *How can book reports contribute to a program of the study of literature?*

The teaching of reading in schools focuses primarily on the development of basic reading skills. The importance of a large sight vocabulary and effective word-recognition techniques is usually understood by teachers and emphasized by various instructional systems. Comprehension is central to the purpose of reading and thus receives a great deal of attention. Yet in the teaching of fundamentals of reading, another requirement is too often overlooked or given only passing attention. This essential component is a genuine *interest in reading,* a lifelong commitment to acquiring information and enjoyment through the act of reading.

The first major section of this chapter discusses the home as the origin of interest in reading and describes what parents can do to encourage children to read. Next, the role of the school in developing reading interests is considered, with special attention being given to the importance of a classroom atmosphere that encourages reading. Some research on children's interests is reviewed, and implications for classroom instruction are presented. Several means available to the teacher for assessing children's interests are also described. The second major section of the chapter discusses techniques for helping children develop personal standards to guide their selection of books. Special attention is given to book reports and children's classics.

Creating an Interest in Reading

Interest in reading does not develop in a vacuum but is founded on personal interests. For example, the girl who enjoys collecting insects will probably enjoy a good book on this topic. A boy who loves and cares for a pet husky will surely have a special interest in a book about grooming huskies for show. It may be much more difficult to create reading interest for a child who has few personal belongings, hobbies, or special interests. The first step in arousing interest in reading is to stimulate children with life and the world around them. The home is a potent factor in this process—a factor that can predispose children negatively or positively in their attitude toward reading.

The Home: Origin of Interest in Reading

Most children enter school with a broad variety of interests born of rich experiences during their earlier years. Typically, they have enjoyed a circus and are looking forward to additional trips to the zoo. Their backgrounds may include a vacation touring Disneyland or exploring the wonders of Mammoth Cave. The vocabulary and concepts gained from such experiences are fundamental to readiness for learning to read. Perhaps even more important is the desire created by these experiences to read about other vacation spots. Growth in reading interests is almost spontaneous with children of this sort. Other children do not fit this description and require special efforts on the part of the teacher. Suggestions in this regard are provided in the section of Chapter 8 that discusses building background experiences (p. 235).

The parents of children with a wide variety of background experiences are frequently anxious for their youngsters to learn to read. Usually, there are many books in their homes, books owned by the child and shared frequently with the parents. The parents themselves probably read occasionally. The child often sees a parent turn to the evening newspaper before dinner, read a book occasionally, and refer to the atlas when seeking information.

Reading is viewed as a desirable tool by the youngster from a background as rich as this one. Significant people in such a child's life read, and the child associates enjoyment with books. An interest in reading is as natural to this child as watching television.

The recollections of one of our elderly well-read friends are helpful in describing the role of the home:

> My early days at home are a warm memory to me. I can remember well the winter evenings when the wind would tug at our roof and shutters while newly fallen snow drifted against the tool shed and animal shelters. My mother would wrap an afghan around her shoulders and invite me to squeeze with her into a big stuffed chair near the Ben Franklin stove. From that port we ventured off together on many journeys. We hunted with our young comrade in Prokofieff's tale of *Peter and the Wolf,* drifted over sleepy villages far below with *Peter Pan,* and scratched for our existence alongside *Robinson Crusoe.*
>
> Often, in the spring of the year, I would tag along with my father in the evening as he took our small herd of cows out to pasture. We shared the sight of geese heading north and bluebirds building their nests in our orchard. Later we might hunt in the *Audubon Handbook* for the name of a new bird we saw perched near the creek. Sometimes I sat on his lap listening to the late news broadcast on the radio wondering at how he could know so much about world events. He listened carefully when I ventured a comment and sometimes helped me look at another point of view.
>
> On Friday evenings we went to town for shopping and visiting. The county library stayed open until 8:00 P.M. and I worried every week that we would be too late to get in. Somehow we always made it in time. I was permitted to search for new treasures while my parents completed their errands.

Grandpa Knippling was the best storyteller who ever lived, it seemed to me in those days. He always claimed to be fresh out of new stories, but remembered one when I begged him. I even loved to hear the same stories again and again. Later in life I discovered in books tales like those my grandpa told. It was like visiting an old friend to read them, but not quite the same as hanging on every word, hoping Grandpa would not run out of chewing tobacco and have to stop in the middle of an old favorite.

Those early days had a great deal to do with my fondness for literature and reading.

The rich background enjoyed by this individual was a significant factor in building his interest in reading. Today the opportunities for extending a child's horizons are even greater.

The experiences that sensitize children to their surroundings are certainly not limited to middle-class homes. (Indeed, in some middle-class homes parents are so involved with their own pursuits that their child is as deprived of enriching experiences as the child from a poverty-stricken home may be.) A trip to the Grand Canyon may be impossible for most children, but the opportunity to see and experience the wonder of a constantly expanding world can be theirs. A walk around the block or through the park with a parent who explains, discusses, and listens can serve the same purpose as a trip to a distant place. A parent with limited financial resources can take a child to the public library and share a book they select and borrow. Without a positive attitude toward reading, which such experiences provide, the child enters school with a severe handicap. Five or six years of influence in the home, the child's first and most powerful influence with regard to creating an interest in reading, have transpired before the youngster enters school.

The importance of early childhood experiences as a prerequisite to success in school has been underscored by programs such as Head Start. Children only three and four years of age are placed in an environment designed to provide the stimulation that may be lacking in their own homes. Teachers and trained parents read to these youngsters, listen to their ideas, teach them simple skills and concepts learned at home by many children, and generally enrich their backgrounds. Whether such programs are a satisfactory substitute for a varied and stimulating home environment is difficult to determine, but certainly they are a desirable alternative to no stimulation at all. The teacher who tells the class a story or takes the class on a field trip is providing valuable experiences insofar as reading interests are concerned. Although each child reacts individually to specific enrichment experiences, a variety of activities offers something to spark the interest of every child. One mechanically minded boy may be enthralled by a visit to the fire station, where shiny trucks with chromed engines wait. How eagerly he will listen to the story of *Engine No. 9* (Hurd, 1961). Later, his maturing reading skill can open many paths to enjoyment and information, paths that might not beckon to a youngster who regards reading and life in general as a dreary imposition. A little girl may be fascinated by a film about raising horses in Kentucky. Through

Basic Components of the Reading Process

discussions about horses and looking at picture books, as well as other techniques, the girl can develop an interest that leads to the writings of someone as good as Marguerite Henry. The joy of knowing literature of such quality might mean for this girl an understanding love for an animal.

What the Parent Can Do to Encourage Reading

Although this text is not written primarily for the lay public and, therefore, is not likely to be read by many parents, a program for building a powerful home environment for reading will be described for two reasons: First, many teachers are parents and are eager to know what steps they should take to help their children succeed in school. Second, and more important, teachers often have the opportunity to influence what goes on in the homes of their students. Many parents would gladly help their youngsters prepare for school if they only knew how. The teacher can be a supportive consultant in this regard.

Books are an individual matter, and the parent who wishes to encourage children to read should know something about books before beginning. Learning about books cannot be done overnight. Even before the child is born, the parent can begin to explore what is available. A local bookstore or library is the logical place to start.

In deciding what kind of children's book to choose, the parent should keep several points in mind. First, the child can be read to long before he or she can talk. Nursery rhymes and other short rhythmic

The child's attitude toward reading is influenced greatly by the importance of reading in the home environment.

pieces will be enjoyed by a child, who understands only the swing of the words and the beat of the language. Second, parents should select children's books that they enjoy. The pleasure conveyed by the adult's voice and feeling is an important factor in determining the child's response.

The child's first books should be attractive ones that contain accurate and colorful pictures. Children usually prefer uncluttered drawings that stress familiar objects, such as animals and activities that they enjoy. Cloth books that can be handled by the child are an excellent investment because small, uncoordinated hands are not likely to tear them. It is not possible or desirable to give a comprehensive list of recommended books for beginning readers, for personal taste should dictate the actual choices. However, the titles given in Table 4.1 may serve as point of departure.

TABLE 4.1 Recommended Books
for Beginning Readers

Author	Title
Leslie Brooke	*Ring o' Roses*
Beatrix Potter	*The Tale of Peter Rabbit*
Ezra Jack Keats	*A Snowy Day*
Aileen Fisher	*In the Middle of the Night*
Robert McCloskey	*Make Way for Ducklings*
Wanda Gág	*Millions of Cats*
Nonny Hogrogian	*One Fine Day*
Marie Hall Ets	*Gilberto and the Wind*

A Parent's Guide to Children's Reading by Nancy Larrick (1982) and *The Read-Aloud Book* by James Trelease (1982) are both excellent references. Several copies of these books should be available in the school library so that parents can borrow them. You can serve an important function by recommending them to parents who are seeking direction for their efforts to support and help their child in learning to read. You, too, should be familiar with their contents, of course.

Parents should learn something about their children's interests by carefully observing the children's reactions to stories that are read aloud and by their choice of play activities. An appreciative response to a rhythmic poem, such as "There Was a Crooked Man," calls for more of the same. Naturally, a solid diet of this fare is undesirable, but the child's favorable reactions provide a clue for future selections. Similarly, the child's attachment to stuffed animals may suggest stories that contain such characters (*The Velveteen Rabbit,* for example).

As young children become acquainted with picture books, their taste in books and in other things will develop. Their personal likes and dislikes will become evident. Opportunities for familiarity with a broad variety of books and topics are necessary to expand the child's horizons. The alert parent will not attempt to force classics or books on certain topics on the child if he or she shows a dislike for them.

Basic Components of the Reading Process

As a general rule, it is advisable to stop reading a particular book to a child when attention or interest lags. Put that book aside and begin another if it has not gained the child's interest after a time or two.

It is most important that books be available for children to look at and "read" on their own. If possible, they should have personal copies of their favorite books. While they must be taught to treat books with care and respect, their fear of damaging books should not interfere with their desire to handle them. It seems better to risk a torn page than to keep books in perfect condition on a shelf inaccessible to the child.

Children who grow to school age in an atmosphere where books are a respected and familiar commodity usually have an early interest in reading. They often have the necessary attitude and readiness to conquer the demands of reading in first grade. With this background, some youngsters, such as those described by Durkin (1966), Lass (1982), and Mason (1984), go far beyond acquiring a few sight words to the point of actually reading second- or third-grade material before they enter school. The stimulating home environment facilitates early reading when the child is ready to do so. Most children will not and should not be expected to read before entering school. The home that provides an atmosphere of interest in reading and familiarity with books has done as much as the school can ask. Further suggestions for involving parents in positive ways are described by Vukelich (1984), Sartain (1981), and Monson & McClenathan (1979).

The Role of the School in Promoting Interest in Reading

Children enter school with a broad range of home backgrounds. These include the fortunate youngsters who have their own books, parents who read to them, and a wealth of enriching experiences, as well as the child who has never seen anyone read a book for enjoyment. The classroom teacher has a responsibility for capturing and stimulating the interest of children in reading regardless of their home environments. In all instances, experiences similar to those provided in stimulating home environments are useful in school as well. Books can be shared, trips taken, discussions held, games played, poetry recited, and numerous other enrichment activities undertaken in the classroom.

The same experiences will not be appropriate for all children in a classroom. Differentiation of instruction to meet individual needs must begin immediately in the kindergarten and first grade. The child who lacks even fundamental knowledge about books, their use, and the wonder they can provide requires a program of experiences designed to build the background a more fortunate child has received at home. The youngster who owns a personal library and already reads a few isolated words may rebel at participating in some of the activities designed for a child without his or her background. The interest in reading the child has gained at home can easily be dampened by too much

Interest in reading is influenced by the availability and attractiveness of book displays in the classroom and school library. Here a unique display is both eye-catching and functional.

repetition of preschool activities that have already been shared with parents. Such children are ready for new experiences that take them from their present level and broaden their world.

Some experiences are worth repeating. Most children desire and enjoy the retelling of a favorite story or hearing a familiar book read time and time again. There is little danger of destroying interest in reading under these circumstances. In fact, good literature wears especially well. However, there is a real possibility that exposure to certain picture books, loved in the past but now regarded disdainfully as "baby books" by the mature child, will turn him or her away from reading. The youngster without early reading experiences undoubtedly requires exposure to such material. Therefore, the solution lies in differentiated instruction. Although some children are sharing a picture book such as *An ABC Book* by C. B. Falls with their teacher, those with a fuller background can independently read a book more suitable to their levels.

This is not to say that whole-class activities that benefit each member of the group are impossible. Listening to the teacher read *The Biggest Bear* by Lynd Ward (1952) is an experience all children in any primary-grade class could share with pleasure. Each child brings his or her background and reaps personal benefits from participating in this activity. However, activities related to a story must take into account the range of backgrounds represented in a group. For example, during a discussion the teacher cannot assume that every child has been to a zoo or museum and has actually seen a bear. A comment about *The Biggest Bear* that assumed such knowledge would only confuse

Basic Components of the Reading Process

some children. An adjustment must be made for the range of the children's backgrounds. The rich experiences of some youngsters may be used to increase the understanding of others. Johnny, who has seen and touched a bear, can share his experience with the class. Johnny benefits from the opportunity of sharing an experience, and others learn from his description and personal reactions.

A field trip is another example of a whole-class activity that can benefit each child by broadening background. Suppose a class of second-graders visits a local construction site. Juan may never have seen large machines, such as a bulldozer and steam shovels, at work. The opportunity to watch and listen to their operation may arouse his interest in learning more about them and what they do. A book, carefully chosen by the teacher or found by Juan with the teacher's guidance—*Mike Mulligan and His Steam Shovel* (Burton, 1939), for instance— might be the key to a new world for Juan. A girl in the same class may be very familiar with construction machinery but be intrigued by the scientific principles that enable a steam shovel to lift heavy loads. Again, a book on simple machines may be found, or the opportunity provided for her to make models of such machines with an erector set. In each case, the broadening experience of taking a field trip is valuable for the child. The follow-up to such a trip adds to its value from the standpoint of stimulating reading interests. Only alert teachers can know the distinct needs of their students and adjust their teaching accordingly.

Promoting Interests

1. Suppose you are the teacher of children in an inner-city school. What could you do to stimulate and broaden the children's interests in animals? Differentiate between direct, firsthand experiences that are easily accessible and vicarious experiences.
2. Locate several books in a children's library on the topic of animals that you could share with children. Focus on the age level of children you prefer to teach. Decide how you would share them with your class.

The Classroom Atmosphere Must Make Reading Attractive

Just as the parents' attitude toward reading is instrumental in molding the child's disposition toward reading, the teacher's attitude is also a significant factor. Children tend to imitate the attitude they perceive important adults displaying toward reading. The school environment, like the home environment, is a direct outgrowth of the adult's attitude. The parent who honors reading will buy and personally use books; teachers must also procure, use, and respect books if their example is to be positive. The parent who wishes to encourage reading will make books available for the child, as will the interested teacher. Both the parent and teacher must take time to share books at first hand with children. A parent can respond one-to-one; the teacher usually must share with a group. In short, the classroom environment must make it *easy* to read, and the classroom atmosphere must make it *important* to read.

The Availability of Books Is Crucial

It is a well-known fact that people tend to do what is convenient. The nearest market is usually the one where we shop; the closest gasoline station gets our business (provided we have the credit card they accept—and this is another convenience factor). The same is true of reading. People are more likely to read if it is convenient for them to do so. A book must be close at hand. This accounts in part for the popularity of paperback books, which are displayed conveniently in nearly every drugstore and supermarket.

Burger, Cohen, and Bisgaler (1956) succeeded in tripling the amount of reading done voluntarily by a large sample of urban children. Their approach was simply one of making books available. Books were placed in classrooms, and during reading instruction periods children were encouraged to read books outside of school. A follow-up check noted that after a year the children were still reading voluntarily.

Bissett (1969) worked with a suburban sample of fifth-grade youngsters who were reading on the average only one half of a book a week despite numerous advantages such as libraries, well-trained teachers, librarians, and reading specialists. When interesting books were added to the classrooms, the number of books voluntarily read by the children increased by 50 percent. A program of stimulating reading through recommendations by teachers and peers was then instituted, and the number of books read was tripled.

The habit of reading is founded in large part on simply that— reading. The availability of books is crucial in determining whether the habit will ever be acquired. (*See* Appendix A for a listing of book clubs for children.) An excellent means for making books available is by developing a reading corner in the classroom.

A Reading Corner Can Attract Children to Reading

The reading corner is a place in the classroom where books and other reading materials are conveniently and attractively displayed for children's use. Ideally, the reading corner should be in a quiet and private location so that youngsters can enjoy reading without being interrupted by regular classroom activities. Classroom procedures should be instituted that encourage children to visit the reading corner freely whenever their time permits.

The selection of a suitable location for building a classroom reading corner involves finding a quiet, relatively isolated area. Often a corner of the room provides these requirements. Low room dividers, shelves,

Basic Components of the Reading Process

or even tables may be used to shape the physical environment of the reading corner, helping to establish an atmosphere of privacy for young readers. A good light source is an equally important consideration. The area may be made more inviting with plants, colorful book jackets hung on the walls, book displays, and child-sized chairs. Some teachers prefer a rug or mats, so that the children may sit on the floor as they read. Books on many levels of difficulty and covering a wide range of subjects should be made available. Children with free time or those pursuing special interests are then able to find books expressly to fit their needs.

Class projects and reference work will be aided by a well-planned reading corner. Children who have had a part in the planning will be eager to add their stories or poems to class collections which can be shared, enjoyed, and reread as part of the classroom library.

The children can adapt and employ a simplified cataloging system for their books and stories. Children who finish a book can complete a card, reporting the title and author and adding a short annotation and recommendation for others. If books are brought from home, they may be cataloged also, perhaps including the owner's name.

Dioramas, posters, and attractive book displays should be a part of the reading corner. They can be changed frequently to reflect current units and incidental occurrences that have influenced class interests. The reading corner can contain filmstrips and a filmstrip previewer, a tape recorder and headphone set, a boxed reading laboratory, and literally dozens of other items. The creative teacher will think of many ways in which to make reading enjoyable and will use the reading corner as a marketplace for enticing activities.

Ms. Dale, a second-grade teacher, found a likely place for her reading corner directly beneath the windows in the back of the classroom. With low dividers, she separated the area from the rest of the room. Because no bulletin board was available in the reading corner, she fastened brightly colored corrugated cardboard to the wall and developed the first display: "Look, New Books!"—a collection of book jackets. The school librarian helped her make a general selection of books geared for the interests and reading levels of second-graders at the beginning of the school year.

Ms. Dale decided that later on more specific selections could be included and that the children in her classroom could add and request books for their class library. She also planned to use the public library as a resource, especially for supplementary and enrichment materials for classroom units.

One child brought a rug from home for the corner and Ms. Dale added two small rocking chairs and a table. The children placed plants on the window ledge and began to take responsibility for the display board. Soon books were being brought from home to be shared in the free reading time. A shoe box covered with adhesive-backed paper became their card catalog. The children took turns being librarian.

Ms. Dale made a "look it up" game for the corner as the year progressed. As some of her second-graders were beginning to use encyclopedias in conjunction with a social studies unit developed around

Creating Interest in Reading

"Our Country," she supplemented this activity with a question box. Cards drawn from the box by the children contained one question that directed them to a specific volume and page in the encyclopedia—for example, "What man became our sixteenth president after losing a race for senator?" Look under *L,* page 1435.

The children who found the answer wrote it on a separate piece of paper to be checked by Ms. Dale. Later, this activity was changed to reflect the growing independence of the children—only the volume was given.

All through the year the reading nook was a source of pleasure, information, and a storehouse for creative writing. Ms. Dale's children learned to use it efficiently and with enjoyment.

Forgan (1977) gives specific suggestions for creating a reading corner.

A Reading Corner

1. Draw a simple sketch of the reading corner you would create in your classroom. Make a list of items you would need, and identify a source where they might be found free or inexpensively.
2. If you had $200 to spend on materials to put in your reading corner, what would you purchase? Why?

Reading Should Be Made Important

Too often reading for recreation is permitted in the classroom only after all other work is finished. This unfortunate policy discourages recreational reading by making it the last thing to be done—almost a last resort. The policy is shortsighted because other work is often hurriedly and poorly completed when this requirement is in force. Furthermore, many children who are slow to complete their work may never get to read for recreation.

There must be regular and lengthy opportunities to read for enjoyment *in the classroom.* It seems incongruous to urge children to read or to make books readily available and then not treat recreational reading as an activity worthy of valuable class time. As we said earlier, an excellent grasp of reading skills is nearly worthless unless they are *used* by the reader. It seems appropriate that some class instructional time also be devoted to recreational reading (a better label might be *practice reading*). The daily, sustained silent reading (SSR) activity described by Berglund (1983), and McCracken and McCracken (1972) is an excellent means for providing needed practice reading. Several studies reported by Farrell (1982), Pikulski (1984), and Schaudt (1983) demonstrated positive achievement gains when children participated in SSR programs.

Basic Components of the Reading Process

McCracken and McCracken offer the following guidelines for SSR:

1. *Begin with the whole class.* Groups of ten or fewer children sometimes can't get started. Children in small groups tend to break the rules for SSR—to ask the teacher for help and expect a response. (Heterogeneously-grouped classes are easier to start than homogeneously-grouped classes.)
2. *Each child selects one book.* (No book-changing is permitted.) Kindergarten and first-grade children may choose a book from a pile. Older children select books at the library prior to SSR time and have their books in the classroom. If a child forgets to get a book or for some other reason does not get one, the teacher should be able to offer a wide selection from within the classroom. (No child should be chided for selecting a book that is too easy or too hard.)
3. *Each child must read silently.* He must interrupt no one. The implication of this rule is that "I, the teacher, believe and know that you can read silently, so don't pretend that you can't."
4. *The teacher reads silently.* The teacher selects something very interesting to read and remains engrossed in it until the SSR time comes to an end. The teacher must set a good example. She must permit no interruption of her reading if *all* of her pupils are to respond to the group compulsion to read.
5. *A timer is used.* An alarm clock or minute-timer (such as is used for cooking) is set and placed where no child can see its face. A wall clock does not work initially; the reluctant readers become clock watchers. Nor can the teacher act as the timer; children will interrupt to ask if time is up. Start with two to five minutes. When the timer rings, the teacher says, "Good. You sustained yourselves today. Continue reading silently if you wish." Most classes will choose to continue, and the children will maintain themselves for twenty to fifty minutes more. The teacher notes the class's sustaining power and the next day sets the timer forward so that it almost reaches the sustained reading time of the first pupil who quit[s] reading.
6. *There are absolutely no reports or records of any kind.* The children do not even keep a list of books they have read. Book discussions, writing, and record-keeping develop naturally later on as sustained silent reading becomes a habit. Initially, they are simply an unnecessary obstacle that encourages reluctant readers not to participate [McCracken & McCracken, 1972: pp. 152–153].

We recommend that at least once a week children be given the equivalent of a full reading period for recreational reading (not necessarily at one sitting). A logical time for providing some of this allotted time is immediately after the class has returned from the school library. Most elementary schools with a library arrange a schedule that reserves the facilities for each classroom for about a half hour once a week. Book selections are made by the children when they are in the library, and some skill instruction on using the library may be provided by the teacher or librarian. When they return to the classroom, the children's interest in a book just selected should be at its highest. What better time to provide twenty or thirty minutes for free reading? This brief period of time permits children to get a good start on a new book and thus increases the probability that the book will be read in its entirety.

Classroom Activities

1. Recreational reading is an excellent independent activity for children not working directly under the supervision of the teacher during the reading period. Several times a week each reading group can be given a fifteen- or twenty-minute respite from workbooks and other written exercises to enjoy the use of their growing skills through recreational reading.
2. Another activity that emphasizes the importance of reading is oral reading by the teacher. At opportune moments during the day the teacher can share a poem with the class or continue a story. The enjoyment in a book evidenced by an enthusiastic teacher and the personal satisfaction gained by each child when a selection is shared orally emphasize the contribution reading can make to one's well-being.

What Is Known About Children's Interests

Sebesta (1968) suggests that the reading interests of children are greatly influenced by the reactions of adults to "perceived" interests. For example, parents and teachers think Marie enjoys mystery stories, so they encourage and reinforce this perceived interest with discussions and books on the topic. Marie, who may or may not be especially interested in mysteries, responds to the expectations of those around her—not unlike the subjects who responded to teacher expectations in *Pygmalion in the Classroom* (Rosenthal and Jacobson, 1968). It is clear that differences in interests for the sexes are in part a product of fulfilling society's expectations.

The unfortunate aspect of this self-fulfilling prophecy is that children may read avidly on only those topics that teachers think interest them. Sebesta (1968, p. 21) states, "Interest studies generally describe preferences of the majority, while the child himself is a minority." The implications of this statement for teaching are important. Although it is helpful to know that intermediate-grade girls in general enjoy horse stories, a fifth-grade teacher cannot assume that Jessie or Heather has either an interest in or the background for enjoying *Born to Trot* (Henry, 1950). Generalizations about children's interests are simply that—generalizations. Each child is an individual who may or may not fit the usual pattern. Weintraub (1969) concluded from an extensive review of the literature on reading interests that no single category of books will supply all children of the same age with what they want to read. He suggests that each teacher identify the unique reading interests of children in his or her classroom and then try to supply the materials required. The October issue of *The Reading Teacher* each year reports the results of an annual survey conducted by a joint committee of the International Reading Association and the Children's Book Council in which children report their favorite books. This summary is an excellent resource for teachers who want to find specific books that children enjoy.

Are we to conclude then that research findings such as those reported by Leibowicz (1983) and Greaney & Neuman (1983) on children's interests are not useful in the classroom? Not at all. A librarian or classroom teacher should build a book collection with an awareness of general interests. Research says that primary-school-age youngsters are more likely than sixth-grade boys to be interested in fairy tales. A school library should have fairy tales on the shelves, and a first-grade teacher should display fairy tales in the classroom collection. But both the librarian and the classroom teacher should obtain many other types of books for youngsters who do not fit the pattern. More will be said later about the importance of broadening reading interests by making a variety of books available. Because individual youngsters may not have reading interests that coincide with those identified by research, some means for assessing children's interests are needed.

Assessing Interests

The best way to assess a youngster's interests is to learn more about this child as an individual. We know well the interests of our best friends and close relatives. Almost unconsciously we decide that Aunt Mary would enjoy seeing the latest play by Arthur Miller, but that Uncle Alex would prefer to see the Yankees play the Orioles. Or we may realize that our roommate will not appreciate hearing the latest folk-rock record album. An understanding of a friend's interests is

---

Classroom Activities

1. The pupil-teacher conference is an excellent way to get acquainted and a good source of information on interest. It is a technique that should be employed as often as possible. Later in this text (Chapters 12 and 14), specific suggestions are given for conducting conferences that reveal the child's interests and personal reactions to books the child has read. The teacher can learn valuable information about pupil interests by asking questions such as "What did you do for fun this past weekend?" "Tell me something about how you spend your spare time." "If you could have three wishes come true, what would they be?" The child's response to this type of question reveals personal preferences the teacher can incorporate into instructional plans and activities.

2. An informal questionnaire developed by the teacher can also gather information on pupil interests. An example of such a questionnaire, which provides highly useful information, is provided in the following "Like to Do" checklist. Another interest inventory is presented in Chapter 14 (page 471). The teacher can easily keep current on student activities with such data for each youngster. Providing the right book at the right time is accomplished more readily by having up-to-date information about interests. For example, Jerry may report on an interest questionnaire that his hobby of collecting insects has taken a slightly different direction and now focuses more specifically on bees. The alert teacher makes direct application of information about Jerry's leisure-time activity to recommend an appropriate book or reading activity.

Name _____   Date _____   *"LIKE TO DO"*
Age _____.   Class in School _____   *CHECKLIST*

Directions: This is a list of things that some boys and girls like to do in their spare time. If you never do the thing shown, leave the line blank. If you like to do it, put one check on the line; if you like to do it very much, put two checks. If you put a check on the line, and a question is asked about it, please answer the question in the space provided.

Watching TV _____   Repairing things _____
Writing letters _____   Drawing and painting _____
Sewing or knitting _____   Driving a car _____
Dancing _____   Cooking _____
Hunting _____   Fishing _____
Loafing _____   Teasing _____
Singing _____   Playing a musical
                                  instrument _____
Playing cards _____   Playing chess _____
Playing other
games _____   What other games? _____
Collecting things _____   What do you collect? _____
Making things with   What do you like to
tools _____   make? _____
Experimenting in   What kind of
science _____   experiments? _____
Going to the   What kind do you like
movies _____   best? _____
Going for a walk _____   Where? _____
Talking _____   What do you like to talk
                                  about? _____
Listening to the   What programs do you like
radio _____   best? _____
Working with computers _____

Basic Components of the Reading Process

based on familiarity with his or her likes and dislikes, our knowledge of his or her disposition and personality. Much the same is true of a teacher's ability to identify students' interests.

Another type of information the teacher will find useful in assessing interests concerns the child's background of experiences. This information can also be obtained by a questionnaire completed by either the child or the child's parents (see Chapter 8, p. 234 for an example). Much the same information may also be obtained by asking the child to prepare an autobiography. Or the teacher can get valuable information about the child's background from the cumulative record folder. Regardless of how the information is obtained, the teacher can use this knowledge to recommend books that he or she believes the child will enjoy. For example, a boy who has just moved into a community can be introduced to *Roosevelt Grady* (Shotwell, 1963), a story about a family that has just moved. Or a youngster who has lost a parent might profit from reading *Rascal* (North, 1963), a story about a child who faced and overcame a similar tragedy. Tway's (1980) *Reading Ladders for Human Relations* is a valuable resource for teachers who are seeking books with special themes.

Through daily observation the alert teacher can obtain continuous information about a child's interests. The daily reading period offers an excellent opportunity for using the child's reactions to stories, characters, and topics. A story about a dog may elicit an enthusiastic reaction from Bill. The teacher should note his response and take the appropriate steps to introduce *Big Red* (Kjelgaard, 1945), *Silver Chief, Dog of the North* (O'Brien, 1933), or similar books. The teacher can also note special interests in other subjects, particularly social studies. For example, *Johnny Tremain* (Forbes, 1944) or *My Brother Sam Is Dead* (Collier & Collier, 1977) are excellent books that relate directly to United States history.

Classroom Activities

Children often reveal much about themselves and their interests during informal "show and tell" or group discussions. The teacher who watches for such information can do much to individualize the assistance he or she provides in selecting books. Aids for selecting children's books are listed in Appendix C.

Assessing Interests

1. Administer the "Like to Do" checklist to a child. Identify at least two areas of interest that you could pursue in locating appropriate books for that child.
2. Add items to the "Like to Do" checklist to make it more suitable for children in your area. Make appropriate adjustments in view of recreational and other leisure-time opportunities available to these children (for example, skiing, skin diving, motocross, and so on).

Creating Interest in Reading

Expanding Children's Interests

It has been said by Dora V. Smith that when children enter school, their reading interests are the teacher's opportunity; when they leave school, their reading interests are the teacher's responsibility (Smith, 1964). The teacher has the responsibility for broadening and deepening the child's reading interests and making him or her more fully aware of what books are available. The surest method of achieving this goal is by creating a classroom environment that arouses the child's interest.

When the question "How will Mafatu survive?" appears on a bulletin board in the reading corner, the curiosity of an intermediate-grade child is sure to be stimulated. An illustration of Mafatu fighting a wild boar to defend his dog further stimulates interest. The final touch is to place a copy of the book *Call It Courage* (Sperry, 1940), on display with the recommendations of several classmates attached. Another excellent technique for advertising a book is to read an exciting passage aloud to the class and display other books by the same author in the reading corner. By carefully "setting the bait," a creative teacher can tempt many youngsters into trying a book.

Many teachers have found it helpful to keep some record of each child's recreational reading choices. With guidance, older children can easily do this for themselves. Younger children may copy the title of the book or simply sign their names on a sheet attached to the book. Another approach is to fasten slips of paper imprinted with the name of the author and title to the book. When a child has finished reading, he or she can simply remove one of the slips and place it in his or her record folder. In any event, a record of the books each child has read enables the teacher to tell at a glance what kind of reading is being done. A steady diet of one type of book may prompt the teacher to instigate a "sales campaign" on another category for a child.

A chart like the one in Table 4.2 is often helpful in tabulating the reading choices of children. Concentration of titles in one section of the circle may signal a need for greater variety in book selection.

Occasionally, a child will read only books of one type. Such a youngster was Daniel, who refused to read anything except nonfiction science books, usually on rocks and minerals. When urged to try good fiction, he responded, "I want to learn something when I read." How should a teacher react to this attitude: Daniel's motive for reading was certainly beyond reproach even if it was a bit limited. An older child of junior or senior high school age might be shown what can be learned about human nature from a well-written novel. Daniel might have been persuaded by this approach, too, but a different tack was taken by his teacher. The highly effective technique of *gradually broadening* Daniel's current reading interests was used, and he was led to try other subjects. The teacher first suggested nonfiction science books similar to those Daniel usually selected, but the subject matter was on plants rather than on rocks and minerals. Next, a biography of a well-known botanist was recommended. After reading several biographies about scientists, Daniel was ready to read some historical fiction that enabled him "to learn something" in a fictional setting. Eventually

TABLE 4.2

Directions: Write the title of your book in the space below and place the identification number in the proper category above

Date	Identification Number	Book Title	Author
1.			
2.			
3.			
4.			
5.			

he began to read other fiction stories and soon had a well-balanced reading diet.

Daniel's case is interesting for several reasons. First, we see how interests can be broadened gradually by finding topics related to the child's main interests. Second, the question of how much reading of one type should be permitted is implicit in Daniel's case. What if he had steadfastly refused to budge from reading about rocks and minerals? We believe that reading, even of a singular nature, is preferable to no reading at all. There is always the chance that a habitual reader will change his or her interests, but far less chance that a "nonreader" will pick up the habit of reading.

Another point to remember is that some of our most "unbalanced" citizens—insofar as interests are concerned—have been major contributors to society through their intense dedication to one pursuit. Einstein is an obvious example, but others can easily be cited. Anne Roe (1961) discovered that the vast majority of eminent scientists she studied were regarded by others as unbalanced and not well rounded in their youth. This is not to say that a balanced reading fare is unnecessary for most children. But we must keep in mind that there are youngsters who rebel at external demands placed on their reading. If well-planned guidance is ineffective in broadening the child's interests, it is advisable to stop short of badgering such a child to read more widely. He or she may be another Einstein or just a very persistent child; in either case, we should be pleased that the child reads at all.

But what about the child who will *not* read? For example, Mark, a boy we know, reads very poorly and flatly refuses to take a book out of the library. Teachers frequently ask how they can get a boy like Mark to read. There is no simple answer. One sure-fire way to fail with Mark is to threaten or coerce him into reading. Nothing is gained, for Mark will never read outside the classroom if he is literally forced to do so in school.

Often refusal to read is simply the child's way of avoiding a highly frustrating experience. Nobody seeks out an activity in which he or she constantly fails. The first step, then, is to help a child like Mark succeed in reading. This usually means finding a book that the child can read without difficulty. Perhaps this means going as far back as a preprimer to locate a book. It would be better if we could find an easy library book because the preprimer-primer route is often partially responsible for a child like Mark's lack of interest. After all, the failure to read probably started with these or similar materials.

Level of interest is a second factor to be considered in selecting a book for the child who refuses to read. Many easy-to-read books are now available on a variety of topics. Spache's *Good Books for Poor Readers* (1974) lists hundreds of them. Mark may be fascinated by submarines. The Harr-Wagner Deep Sea Adventure Series has a book titled *Submarine Rescue,* which is written at a low level of difficulty and may meet Mark's need.

It is also important to remember that Mark may need help even with easy books. A friend or teacher's aide may have the time to read through the book with him. The teacher or Mark's parents may even be able to help him read it.

The key with most reluctant readers is helping them find success in reading. Until the pattern of failure is broken, interest in reading is unlikely. Quandt & Selznick (1984) provide greater detail on the approaches we have described here as well as other practical plans you may find useful for helping children overcome negative concepts of themselves as readers.

The Elementary School Literature Program

We have seen how the home and school environments are related to children's interests in reading and have considered various ways of stimulating and assessing such interests. Most teachers would agree

Basic Components of the Reading Process

that without an interest in reading, such skill instruction is largely futile. Wanting to read and having the skills needed to read and comprehend are not enough; one additional element is missing—taste in reading.

Literature is the vehicle that carries young and old alike through doorways they may never personally encounter. It has the capacity to give sheer enjoyment, to provide new perspectives and vicarious experiences. Literature can develop one's insight into human behavior and transmit the accumulated wisdom of humankind. Good literature provides beauty and inspiration for the reader. Because literature has much to offer, it is essential that taste be encouraged, so that young readers will select the best that is available.

Classroom Activities

	B	P	N	E	W
Dogs					
Horses					
Mysteries					
Outer space					
Rocks					
Dinosaurs					
Music					

1. Challenge the children to find a nonfiction book in the library whose title or whose author's last name begins with the letter of the alphabet given at the top of the column and whose main topic corresponds to the subject on the left. Allow a certain length of time in the school library (for example, thirty minutes) to work on this task. (Probably no one will fill all the spaces; some squares may even be impossible to fill.) Five points can be earned by filling in one of the squares with a title or author not reported by anyone else. Three points can be earned if only one other person reports the same information. One point is earned for all other correct responses. The person with the highest point total wins. (*Suggestion:* Stagger the thirty-minute periods in the library throughout the day so that resources are not overburdened.)

2. Vary this activity by changing the topics and using different letters of the alphabet. You might also limit the source of data to the encyclopedia, almanac, atlas, or other reference volume and then vary the task accordingly. For example, if an atlas is used, the topics might become rivers, countries, cities of at least 100,000 in population, mountain ranges, and so on. Children can also work in teams on such a task to promote peer instruction and interaction.
3. Have the children bring parts or all of their hobbies to school. Give each child an opportunity to tell about how he or she became interested in the hobby, when and what he or she likes to do with it, and how it has changed over time. Ask children to think about how they would help a person get started who wanted to pursue the same hobby. Instruct children to develop a general outline for a hobby that would guide them in helping a beginner. Have children share the results. Offer suggestions for improvement. Have children add details to the general sections of the outline. Post the final products on a bulletin board.

This activity is appropriate for most children in grades three to five and for advanced readers.

Reading interests determine what will be read—for example, fairy tales or sports stories. Reading taste determines the quality of what is read—for example, *Sport* magazine or *All American*. Taste in reading grows from the opportunity to read materials of varying degrees of quality. Without adequate guidance, children's choices of books may be based on superficial and fleeting elements that have little connection with good literature. But the teacher is not a censor deciding what a child will or will not read. Only the child's parents have the right to provide such supervision—and the child, of course. Neither should the teacher sit in judgment of what is and what is not good literature. It is the teacher's responsibility to help youngsters develop their own standards (Huck, 1979).

Literature Instruction Can Be Initiated Early

Perhaps because of the difficulties involved in defining exactly what constitutes a total literature program at the elementary school level, no research has been done on the extent of such programs. We know that the senior high school curriculum usually provides for the study of literature in English classes. Some junior high schools have formal literature study also. However, several factors operate to limit the amount of time devoted to literature at the elementary school level. First, a surprisingly large number of elementary schools in this country are without libraries. Without adequate materials, the literature program is often limited to basal readers, not always a good source of literature of quality. Second, the emphasis on teaching basic reading, writing, and computational skills in elementary schools is so great that little time remains for other pursuits. It is our firm conviction that

Basic Components of the Reading Process

Children who are shown that reading is valued by parents have an excellent chance of being successful with reading in school.

instruction in literature cannot be separated from the effective teaching of reading. The basics of literary analysis and evaluation can be introduced early in the primary grades regardless of the instructional system employed.

Given a scheme for analysis and a basis for making judgments, primary-grade youngsters can begin to evaluate basic elements in literature. Indeed, they *must* be taught these skills or become nondiscriminating consumers of trivial writings that do little more than take up their leisure time.

The Teacher Can Encourage the Development of Personal Reading Standards

Our purpose in helping children develop a taste for good literature is not to make snobs of them but to enable them to sort the meaningful from the empty, the rich from the bland. Whatever reading is done should be put in proper perspective. This is possible only through accurate analysis and evaluation of literature.

We all read material that is not great literature. It would be folly to suggest that we hold up for the elementary school child the unrealistic ideal of reading only great literature. Yet, by studying the elements that comprise good literature, we provide children with means for making their own assessments. Good literature causes "the reader to perceive characters, conflicts, elements in a setting, and universal problems of humankind; it will help the reader to experience the delight of beauty, wonder, and humor; or the despair of sorrow, injustice, and ugliness" (Huck, 1976, p. 4). Good literature helps readers to understand

Creating Interest in Reading

themselves better, those around them, and their surroundings. Good literature is also rich in semantic and syntactic structures that help readers develop strategies for understanding what they read.

If he or she has judged a book as one written without real purpose, the child can still devote as much time to its consumption as desired; the child does so by choice, however, and not out of ignorance. In many ways, such reading corresponds to the interest some adults have in a James Bond. Ian Fleming hardly regarded his supersleuth as a Hamlet, yet millions have enjoyed *From Russia with Love* and *Thunderball* in books and movies. Adults who find Fleming's characters more real and more significant than Steinbeck's Jody in the *Red Pony* apparently lack sufficient skills to evaluate critically what they read. We believe that the classroom teacher has a responsibility for guiding the child in the development of skills necessary for making evaluative judgments.

The Teacher's Role in Evaluating Books

Teachers have two primary roles with regard to evaluating books. First, they must generally appraise a book and decide for which child the book is suited. In this process they use the traditional criteria for literary assessment that will be described in this section. Second, they are responsible for teaching skills of literary analysis so that the child grows in the ability to apply personal standards of taste independently.

Criteria for Evaluating Children's Books

Authorities in the field of children's literature classify books into a variety of categories, for example, fiction, picture books, biographies, and informational books. There is by no means complete agreement among experts on which classification scheme is best. It is important to note that regardless of the scheme used, different criteria are required for evaluating different types of the books. It is beyond the scope of this text to present criteria for all types of books. For purposes of illustration, we will discuss the evaluation of books of fiction as an example. The reader is referred to *Children's Literature in the Elementary School* by Charlotte Huck (1979) and *Children and Books* by Zena Sutherland, Dianne L. Monson & May Hill Arbuthnot (1981) for a more complete discussion of evaluating all types of children's books.

Even within the category of fiction, a number of criteria are required to evaluate the various forms. Historical fiction, for example, cannot be judged according to the same standards as fairy tales or mystery stories. Evidently, the first task of the teacher and the child is to identify the kind of book being evaluated in order to apply appropriate standards. Again, the reader, is referred to Huck and to Sutherland, Monson & Arbuthnot for a discussion of the various types of children's books.

We suggest consideration of these factors in evaluating books of fiction: theme, plot, setting, and characterization.

1. The theme of a book is the *idea* of the story; the author's reason for writing is revealed through the theme. Some themes may amount to little more than presenting a moral; others focus on the meaning of friendship or courage. For children, the theme will have meaning only as it relates to their experiences. Cervantes' *Don Quixote,* which reveals that high ideals are the only goals in life worth pursuing, has little meaning and, therefore, appeal to children in the primary grades. Yet the idea or theme of *Don Quixote* is a powerful one and is most appropriate for older children.

   A theme must be judged on at least two counts: its worth for presentation to children and the age level for which it is most appropriate.

2. The plot is the *plan* of the story. We can identify it by asking what happens in the story. What is the thread of events that carries the action forward? Good plots grow out of good themes. Actions in a plot normally progress in an interrelated fashion, leading to a climax.

   For purposes of evaluation it is important to consider the credibility of the plot. It must not depend on coincidence or contrivance but must grow logically and naturally out of previous events in the story.

   The plot of *Black Stallion* (Farley, 1941), for example, concerns a teenage boy who is marooned on a deserted island with a wild Arabian stallion. The boy tames the horse, is finally rescued, and returns to New York City with his horse. A special match race is arranged by a New York newspaper between the year's two greatest horses. The wild stallion is entered as a mystery horse and wins the race.

   Some stories, such as Mark Twain's *Tom Sawyer,* succeed with practically no plot. In this instance, a series of incidents is related in loose fashion. But most books require a strong plot to be successful.

3. The characters in a story must be *believable.* The author's ability to create individuals who possess strengths and weaknesses, who act in a manner that is consistent with their natures determines the success of characterization in his or her stories. Children can identify with believable characters. A story is carried by and comes alive through these characters.

   In addition to determining the authenticity of characters, we should also assess their depth. To be true-to-life, characters must be complex. Some facets of character will become apparent only after getting to know these people in the story very well. Seldom will a person be all good or all bad. These principles also apply to animal characters, such as Charlotte, the spider in *Charlotte's Web* (White, 1952), and humorous characters, such as Homer in *Homer Price* (McCloskey, 1943).

   Effective characterization is also dependent on growth and development. As events occur, realistic characters often change in the course of a story. To be believable, change will be gradual rather than instantaneous. Mafatu, for example, in *Call It Courage* (Sperry, 1940) grew in bravery as he proved to himself that he was capable of assuming the responsibilities of a man.

4. The *background* against which a story is told is called the setting. The time and place of the story comprise the physical setting; the religious, moral, social, and psychological conditions comprise the emotional or spiritual setting. All aspects of the setting should affect a story in an authentic way or not at all. *The Yearling* (Rawlings, 1944), for example, is set in the scrubland of Florida. Physically, the isolation of Jody from other youngsters his own age is an important factor in creating the boy's longing for a pet. The poverty of his family is instrumental in making the destruction of a new corn crop by his pet deer a genuine catastrophe. The time of the story is insignificant, for the events and characters have almost no relation to the outside world.

Some stories, such as *Mountain Born* by Elizabeth Yates (1943), have a physical setting of an almost incidental nature. The story revolves around a shepherd and his flock; it can be generalized to almost any setting, given these two necessary elements.

Two additional factors may be considered by the teacher and perhaps by older students: *style* and *format.* When books are being selected for a school or classroom library, these matters are of some importance because a variety of selections should be available for children to read.

Style is the author's particular way of expressing his or her ideas— his or her selection and arrangement of words. Just as different people speak in a unique manner, writing styles also vary. Older children, perhaps in grades five and six, may enjoy contrasting the descriptive style of Mark Twain with the terse presentation of Armstrong Sperry. Huck (1979) suggests oral reading as an effective means of studying an author's style. Though children may not be able to identify the specific aspects of style that appeal to them, they often prefer reading one author to another because of style.

Format concerns all physical aspects of the book itself, including size, shape, typography, quality of paper, durability, illustration, and length. Today's books for children are especially attractive in appearance. The teacher will want to evaluate matters of format primarily to decide on the appropriateness of a book for a particular child. A reluctant reader may require a book that looks "easy," with numerous illustrations and ample white space on a page. A more able student may insist on books that have more of an adult book appearance.

Because children often choose a book by its cover if left to their own means, the teacher must also devote some attention to overcoming this tendency. Obviously, the value of an attractive format must be balanced against the other factors mentioned. A good book in terms of theme, plot, setting, and characterization may lack a striking appearance. In this case, children need to discover that it is necessary to

Basic Components of the Reading Process

look inside to judge the book's value. A striking-looking book full of stereotyped characters and dull action cannot be saved by an attractive cover or glossy illustrations.

These criteria can be used by children in both the primary and intermediate grades. The kind of analysis and the depth of understanding will vary from grade to grade and among children in the same grade. Most younger children cannot be expected to discuss how the setting of a story influences the lives of the characters and thereby the plot. However, many older children in grade six, for example, could handle this relation—*Tom Sawyer,* set in the middle of a large city, would greatly change the events if not the actual personality of the main character. Speculation concerning the effect this totally different setting would have on Mark Twain's classic is both plausible and instructional for most sixth-grade children.

Yet even first-grade children can be expected to tell what happened in a story (plot). They can also identify who is in the story (characters) and report where the story took place. Some evaluation is also possible. "Could this story happen?" "Could you ever take a trip such as the one the boy in the book took?" "How did you feel toward the man in the story? Why?"

A planned program of literary criticism is an essential facet of the total reading program. An early start at identifying and evaluating the various aspects of a story is necessary for developing active, knowledgeable readers who evaluate literature rationally. One possible approach to organizing a program of library criticism is described in Table 4.3 in the next section.

Developing Children's Book Evaluation Skills

The purpose of helping children analyze and evaluate books is to increase their appreciation, deepen their understanding, relate literature to their lives, and improve their ability to read for meaning. By providing a system for studying the elements of a story, the teacher leads the child toward gaining as much as possible from reading. If the analysis of a story detracts from the child's enjoyment, the program of literary criticism has gone wrong. Analysis just for the sake of pseudointellectual discussion has no place in the elementary school—or any other school for that matter.

Developed with the proper perspective, literary criticism permits the child to compare and contrast one selection with others by the same author, with other similar works, or with literature in general. The criteria suggested here or those developed by others are helpful in considering specific aspects of literature in an objective fashion. For example, the development of a character can be studied for authenticity and consistency.

Some aspects of literary criticism are reserved to each individual reader. Children should be encouraged to develop their own standards for assessing literature. The opportunity to explore books with the teacher and other students is instrumental in helping an individual

TABLE 4.3 Sequential and Cumulative Literary Analysis Skills

Grade Level	Skill
1	Name characters; identify setting; retell story; identify conflict; tell solution
2	Identify beginning, middle, and ending of plot
3	Describe characters; identify climax
4	Discuss characterization; note cause and effect
5	Discuss mood through choice of words
6	Discuss style through sentence patterns and approach

arrive at personal criteria. The object of literature instruction is to encourage the *development* of standards, not to make children's standards uniform.

The Place of Children's Classics in the Literature Program

Certain children's books become classics because they have withstood the test of time; generation after generation of youngsters have enjoyed some of the same books. *Alice in Wonderland* is an example of a children's classic, as is *Heidi.*

Teachers often feel compelled to require children to read these classics. Others remember being bored by some so-called classics and are determined not to make the same mistake their teachers made. What is the place of classics in the elementary school literature program?

The fact that some books remain popular with children over long periods of time is a significant recommendation for them. Teachers should be familiar with such books and stand ready to suggest *The Jungle Book, Peter Pan,* or other classics to a youngster who is searching for something to read. But not all youngsters will enjoy these books. This reaction is understandable and should be acceptable to the teacher, who should not attempt to force a child to read *any* book, including a classic. Instead, the teacher must work very hard at enticing this student to select quality books.

The magnificence and enduring quality of *Treasure Island, Robinson Crusoe, Swiss Family Robinson, Tom Sawyer, Huckleberry Finn, Hans Brinker, or the Silver Skates,* and *The Secret Garden* guarantee that most youngsters will probably enjoy some, if not all, of these books. The teacher should read several such books aloud in order to be sure that all youngsters have some exposure to them, for the enjoyment these books provide should be experienced by all youngsters. Familiarity with children's classics is also important from the standpoint of giving children a means for assessing other books. In a sense, children's classics can serve as a measuring device. For example, other books can be compared to *Charlotte's Web* for effective character development. Or the plot of *Trea-*

sure Island can be taken as a measure of excellence that is useful for assessing other literature. The greatest danger in this approach is that dull, uninteresting books will be called classics and held up as exemplars. Unfortunately, "Award Books," chosen by adult judges, are sometimes misused in this way. If children's classics are judged strictly on the basis of children's reactions over a long period of time, the danger is minimized.

Sharing of Books Can Encourage Exploration

Like children's classics, considerable difference of opinion surrounds the matter of book reporting. Properly handled, book reports can play a significant part in the literature program. Because a major goal of the reading program is to develop critical readers, the opportunity to analyze and evaluate books must be provided. Book reports that focus on this goal can be productive of growth in critical reading skills.

Unfortunately, in their desire to interest children in reading, teachers occasionally conduct contests to see who can read the most books. They often require book reports as evidence of children's accomplishments. Under these circumstances, book reports, as well as reading books, can get badly skewed. No book report should ever be prepared simply to prove that a child has read a book. Contests involving the number of books read are ill-conceived. The means and ends have become confused in cases where either of these activities occur.

The purpose of reviewing, analyzing, and evaluating a book is to increase one's appreciation and understanding of its contents. A book report should contain the reader's appraisal of a book according to some previously chosen guidelines. The goal is to maximize learning, not to satisfy an external requirement. Book reports should be written to provide some evidence of the child's response to a book. The teacher should regard them as a means for evaluating the child's reading growth. A child's reading tastes and interests are reflected in the type of books he or she selects and how he or she reviews them. A child's understanding and appreciation are also evident in a book report.

In actual practice, book reports often contain little that is analytic and nothing that is evaluative. Typically, book reports are either written or oral summaries of the plot. The characters and the setting are mentioned if a teacher insists. The results of this approach are often not happy. Teachers decry the inability of youngsters to think; youngsters moan about the necessity for rewriting every book they read. If anything, *less* reading and *less* study of the literature probably result from this procedure. Therefore, several suggestions for improving book reports are in order.

First, teachers should encourage children to report on books through a variety of means. They can be permitted and even encouraged to use various art projects for reporting on books. For example, dioramas, maps, murals, models, table displays, bulletin boards, and posters can take a book as a source. Or puppet shows, flannel board presentations, mock radio broadcasts, and interviews with stand-ins for actual authors can be created. Book reports should be regarded as a means of encouraging children to *respond* to books. The more enjoyable they are for the reader and for an audience, the better the chance that these reports will encourage and reinforce reading.

Second, some skills of literary criticism should be taught. Skill teaching can be initiated in a group setting after children have heard the teacher read a story aloud. The teacher can encourage critical thinking and direct the children's attention to specific elements of the story (M. Olson, 1984). Characters can be evaluated for consistency. The plot can be studied for conflict. Later, children can be asked to study many of these same factors in a story they are reading independently. The technique of comparing books can also be introduced and encouraged by the teacher.

Third, a report on every book that a child reads should not be required. Some books should simply be recorded by the author and title in the child's record. The child should have the option of choosing not to report on a book.

Fourth, a standardized book report form should not be used unless the youngsters have helped design it. Even then, only a few specifics—such as author, title, characters, and setting—should be included on the form. Other information should be reported voluntarily, for children's responses to books should be as individualized as possible.

Sharing Books

1. As a part of an interview for a teaching position, a school principal indicates that her district is considering a proposal to require a minimum of ten book reports per year from each child. She asks what you think of such a proposal. How would you respond?
2. Sketch a bulletin board idea you think would encourage children to read and share books.

Classroom Activities

1. Children may be asked to prepare a book jacket for a book they have read recently. Examination of an actual book cover will reveal the need for cover illustration, an inner flap summary to appeal to prospective readers, and possibly a written sketch about the author on the back cover.
2. The children can be told that they are in charge of distribution and sales for a favorite book. They may be assigned the responsibility of writing an advertisement for newspapers or magazines offering the book for sale. Remind them that this is an appeal to buy the book that should emphasize its unique features.

Basic Components of the Reading Process

Fifth, whenever possible, book reports should be used to arouse other children's interest in a book. Reports can be displayed in the reading corner or on a bulletin board. One interesting approach is to have several oral reports given simultaneously. The teacher can announce what books are being reported on and then permit each child to attend the session that interests him or her the most.

Book reports are primarily a means for encouraging children to respond to books. But they are only a means to this end and must not be regarded as an end in themselves. It is especially important that children be encouraged to respond to literature because both interest and taste in reading are predicated on the personal involvement of the reader.

Summary

Chapter 4 has made a case for the belief that lifelong reading habits are as important to a good reader as the ability to decode word symbols or comprehend an author's message. An interest in reading determines whether an individual will read with any frequency by an individual.

The home is the origin of interest in reading for many children. Parents who value reading in their lives and take the time to provide stimulating experiences for their children facilitate their children's reading progress in school and promote healthy attitudes toward reading.

The school must build on whatever disposition toward reading the child brings to school. For some, interest need only be maintained and broadened. For others, a remedial program is necessary to build the attitudes and interests that were not created at home. The classroom atmosphere must make reading important and books accessible. A reading corner is recommended as providing these features.

Research abounds on the identification of children's reading interests. Though some general sense of direction is provided by such evidence, the classroom teacher must still assess each child's interest individually. Both providing appropriate reading materials and encouraging broadened reading interests are the responsibility of the teacher.

The elementary school literature program is designed to help children learn to establish personal standards for guiding their selection of reading materials. Analysis of literature is helpful to the extent that it permits children to make rational judgments about reading selections. Book reports should also be regarded as a means to the end of selective reading but not as an end in themselves. Children's classics should be available to children but should not be assigned as required reading.

Terms for Self-study

interest inventory
reading corner
children's classics

Discussion Questions

1. "If I had one wish," said Cleo Harper, a first-grade teacher, "it would be that all six-year-olds came from homes with books." Why do you think Cleo made this statement? What would your wish be for entering six-year-olds? Why?
2. How does censorship practiced by the teacher interfere with a child's development of reading taste?

Recommended Readings

Graves, Michael F., Boettcher, Judith A., & Ryder, Randall A. (1979). *Easy reading: Book series for less able readers.* Newark, DE:

Here is a reference volume that presents a summary of forty-three high interest/low vocabulary ("easy" reading) book series and six periodicals along with descriptions of supplementary materials available from the publishers of the series and an evaluation of whether students are likely to find the materials interesting.

Meacham, Mary. (1978). *Information sources in children's literature: A practical reference guide for children's librarians, elementary school teachers, and students of children's literature.* Westport, CT: Greenwood Press.

This book provides a bibliographic resource guide on book lists, sources in special fields, illustrators, authors, and award winners. It also suggests how to develop a basic collection of children's books.

Monson, Dianne L. & McClenathan, DayAnn K. (Eds.). (1979). *Developing active readers: Ideas for parents, teachers, librarians.* Newark, DE: International Reading Association.

This book presents a series of essays devoted to helping children find books that are well suited to their interests and abilities and to involving children with literature in personally meaningful ways.

Roser, Nancy, & Frith, Margaret. (Eds.). (1983). *Children's choices: Teaching with books children like.* Newark, DE: International Reading Association.

Here are a compilation of books selected by children as their favorite choices since 1973 and informative articles about how to use those books in an effective classroom reading program.

Spiegel, Dixie Lee. (1981). *Reading for pleasure: Guidelines.* Newark, DE: International Reading Association.

The author describes a variety of approaches teachers can use to promote a desire in children to read as a leisure-time activity.

Basic Components of the Reading Process

5

Readiness
for Reading

Any observant adult who has been present in an elementary school on the first day of class in the fall is sure to remember the montage of people, objects, and events that mark the beginning of a new school year. Even in the oldest of school buildings, the beginning of a school year is characterized by a pervasive freshness. The freedom of summer has been enjoyed, but nearly everyone is secretly glad to be back at school for a new start. An upbeat, optimistic mood prevails. There is much to be done, and today the process begins.

Included in this scene are a special group of participants: those children who are starting school for the first time. Some teachers may be new to this school, too, of course. Some other adults may be volunteers or aides who have not been in a school since their own days as a student. Some children may also be new to the building. But all these people have some previous experience with schools—some basis for building a set of expectations. The truly uninitiated, the fledglings in the schooling process, arrive full of innocence and fears. On the surface they exhibit obvious similarities and differences. Most are dressed in clean, perhaps even new clothes that have been chosen and prepared thoughtfully for this special occasion. Most carry the supplies they will need: paper, pencils, eraser, crayons, ruler, and so forth. Some are shy; and others, boisterous. Many are nervous. One child is shortest—another tallest—another fattest.

Suppose you had the responsibility for teaching this group. What are the factors that would concern and interest you on this, the first day of school? What would you attempt to teach these beginners? How would you adjust to the differences that are bound to exist from child to child? How would you help them learn to read?

One important principle confronting a teacher every day regardless of the age of the students being taught is that of readiness to learn. Readiness is a factor in all learning whether the topic is reading or aeronautics and whether the learners are six, twenty-six, or fifty-six years of age. In this chapter we will examine the topic of readiness with special emphasis on readiness for learning to read.

- *Why aren't all children ready to read when they enter school?*
- *What can parents do to help their child get ready for reading instruction?*
- *What behaviors indicate a child is ready to read?*
- *Why is readiness for reading dependent on the method of instruction employed?*
- *Why is predicting success in reading of such interest to educators?*
- *How can a classroom teacher assess readiness for reading instruction?*

A previous chapter told briefly about a six-year-old named Billy who was just entering school for the first time. Let's suppose you are the first-grade teacher who meets Billy at the classroom door that eventful day in September.

You greet Billy warmly, introduce yourself, and ask him his name. He replies cheerfully and without hesitation, "Billy Turner."

"He seems like a confident, outgoing child," you think. "I wonder how well he'll adjust to school?"

To Billy you say, "I've written your name on a piece of tape on one of the desk tops, Billy. Let's see if I can help you find your seat."

"I can find it," Billy says, and he starts down the aisle looking at the names on the desks.

"Here it is," he announces.

Before you have time to ponder the fact that Billy is surprisingly self-reliant and can recognize his own name on the first day of school, you hear a commotion in the hallway and hurry to meet another youngster whose harried mother is tugging him through the door.

"Come on, Alvin," she is urging. "I've got to get to work."

"Good morning," you say. "It's nice to have you here this morning, Mrs. . . . ?"

"Mrs. Morris," the woman replies gruffly. "I'm late for work, but Alvin insisted I bring him to school. Said he wouldn't come unless I brought him. I'm glad he's you're problem now. I told him he wouldn't be able to act in school like he does at home. You *will* straighten him out won't you?" Mrs. Morris asks threateningly. She glares at the retiring Alvin, who hangs his head and sniffles.

"Oh, we'll get along just fine, won't we Alvin," you offer, hoping to soothe the overwrought mother and unhappy child. "Let me help you find your seat, Alvin. Thank you for bringing him in, Mrs. Morris."

By coincidence Alvin's seat is directly behind Billy Turner's, and you find yourself wondering at the apparent differences in these two beginning first-graders. Alvin seems uncertain and immature compared to the self-possessed Billy. Will this initial impression hold up as we get to know the boys better? How will the other twenty-three boys and girls you're expecting this morning compare with Alvin and Billy? How many will be reading confidently by the end of the school year? You wonder.

Basic Components of the Reading Process

Entrance into School Is Based on the Child's Age

Billy, Alvin, and their classmates enter grade one at the age of six having little in common except their chronological age. Why? The laws of their state require school attendance at age six.

It may not have occurred to you that the determination to start school might be made in some other fashion. Consider these alternatives if you will: All children could enter grade one at age seven (or five or whatever); all children who have reached a certain mental age could enter grade one; or all children who can perform certain tasks might be admitted (e.g., count to ten, say the letters of the alphabet, tie their shoes, and so on). In British primary school, children enter whenever they reach their sixth birthday. Thus, children begin school throughout the year, not just in the fall.

You may wonder why entry into school is an issue here. The reason is quite straightforward: Children entering grade one differ widely on many factors commonly regarded as good indicators of "readiness to read." For example, some children in a typical first-grade classroom may be able to recognize a few words whereas others may not even understand that words can be represented in print. Some children may have extensive vocabularies rich with descriptive terms and abstract concepts whereas others employ only common nouns and verbs. Some are curious about letters and words, but other children of the same age show no interest in print at all. Some may have attended Head Start, Follow Through or kindergarten or all three whereas others may have been kept at home. Some have probably watched *Sesame Street* and *The Electric Company*. If this is so, shouldn't school admission policies be revised to admit only children who are ready to read? Wouldn't this reduce the range of differences the teacher must address and, in turn, improve the children's chances of success in learning to read?

We answer these questions in the negative for a number of reasons. First, and most realistically, that change is not one the public and state legislators are ready to make. Schooling starts at age six. We must live with that system if past history on attempts to alter it are any guide. But just as important, children who are not "ready" to read according to certain indicators can be gotten ready to read if we admit them to school and make readiness an important pursuit. Left at home, children are not likely to get ready through sheer maturation. Additionally, first grade is concerned with much more than reading, so it would be unwise to admit children strictly on the basis of potential for reading success. Finally, readiness for reading is not an absolute state that can be measured fully and accurately. This assertion is explained more fully later.

Readiness for Reading Is a Relative Matter

Readiness is a relative matter depending greatly on *what* is to be learned and *how* it will be presented. Reading can be defined in a number of ways, thus making various learning tasks more or less appropriate depending on what is valued. To illustrate, if beginning reading is equated with sound-symbol decoding, the child must be able to differentiate among isolated sounds of the language and relate them to printed symbols. A child who is not "ready" to deal with sounds and symbols might be able to recognize words of high personal interest such as his or her name. This suggests that readiness for reading can only be thought of in terms of what the child is to learn. One is not simply ready or unready to read, but ready for some things and not ready for others. Children are ready to learn knowledge and skills that make sense to them and to build on what they know and can do. There are other things that don't yet make sense to some children and do not relate to what they know. The difficult challenge for the teacher is to determine which tasks fall into which category and to make this determination correctly for each child in a classroom, since no two are probably at exactly the same point at the same time.

Readiness is also relative in the sense that various approaches to instruction can be employed using materials that are vastly different. Thus, the child who is introduced to reading via experience charts as described in Chapter 3 is asked to use certain skills and abilities. In another classroom a child uses other skills to do a paper-and-pencil task calling for discrimination among geometric shapes. In each of these classrooms a teacher has designed learning tasks that reflect this teacher's notions about the reading process. Likewise different materials are used depending on how the teacher approaches instruction. Some use work sheets, others use games or manipulative devices, and others use experience charts or trade books or a combination. How is readiness

Early exposure to books on familiar and interesting topics contributes to readiness for reading.

Basic Components of the Reading Process

ascertained in any absolute sense, given these important variations from classroom to classroom? It simply is not possible.

Background Experiences and Readiness for Reading

We have made the point previously that readiness is a factor in all learning. Whether the situation involves a five-year-old learning to tie shoelaces or a graduate student learning a sophisticated computer programming technique, the learner must be "ready" to relate new knowledge to what is known already. Frank Smith (1978) uses a familiar phrase in describing the learning process—he calls it "making sense" of a task or piece of information. The learner either makes sense of what he or she is to learn or it remains nonsense—not understood and not learned.

A person's background experiences are powerful in determining what will make sense. For example, the first time a person watches a sporting event, the action is confusing and even bizarre. The new sport might be racquetball or ice hockey. The sequence of events in a game is nearly impossible to sort out unless or until someone who knows the game helps the learner focus on certain events and actions, ignore other events and actions, understand the intentions of the participants, appreciate the purpose of the game, understand the rules that structure the pursuit of the purpose, and generally teach the learner about the game. A good teacher finds the most meaningful point of contact when attempting to explain the game to a novice. In essence, the teacher seeks to find a referent for the learner. "Do you know how to play handball?" the teacher may ask someone who wishes to learn about racquetball. "Yes." "Well racquetball is *like* handball in that . . ." and much is understood immediately because of similarities. The learner's prior knowledge or script based on experience with a similar game is used as a starting point.

If the learner doesn't know how to play handball, another frame of reference is sought. "What about ping pong? Badminton? Tennis?" If the learner has no previous experience with racquet games, the teacher must use a different tack. The learner may know a game as far removed from racquetball as volleyball, but at least the notions of competition among participants, use of a ball, scoring of points, and so forth, are understood by the learner and can be used by the teacher as a point of reference. "Racquetball is *different* from volleyball in that . . ." Because adults are older and have more experiences on which to draw, finding a point of reference that will enable the learner to understand is usually not terribly difficult. Children, on the other hand, have fewer experiences on which to draw, thus making readiness a much more elusive factor. Fewer assumptions can be made about what the child will find meaningful or, put another way, what the child knows.

Readiness for any learning experience is greatly dependent on making sense of what is to be learned. Things make sense only when they fit into the learner's frame of reference. This involves seeing similarities between something new and what is already in the learner's head. What is already in the head got there through interaction with people and things in the environment. What the learner can relate past experience to is meaningful; what is confusing or apparently haphazard is not meaningful.

Reading involves scores of items and activities that can appear meaningless and nonsensical to the child who lacks previous experience with books, printed symbols, paper-and-pencil tasks, sitting as a member of a group, being quiet, following directions, and so forth. The information contained in books will be meaningless to the child who has no previous experience with the topics, characters, events, and places described therein.

The readiness program will be useful to children if it broadens their background to introduce new topics and new information in a way that builds on their previous knowledge. The readiness program can also deepen children's understanding of topics they already know about and correct misconceptions that inevitably accompany initial learning. Depending on what the child has seen and done before entering school, such experiences might include learning what a fire fighter does and how the community is kept safe from fires. For another child it may include learning about farms and food production. Concepts may include *little* and *big, dark* and *light, up* and *down,* and so forth. The identification of basic shapes and forms such as circles, squares, and rectangles and the ability to name colors, certain objects, and even the letters of the alphabet are often included in readiness programs for the child who lacks the background to understand these and similar basic concepts.

Preschool Experiences That Build Reading Readiness

In building children's readiness for reading, we must discover what they know and can do well already. This enables us to start where we find the child rather than insisting that the child conform to a structured curriculum and instructional schedule that may be most inappropriate for him or her. In determining or assessing what certain key things a child brings to school, we are recognizing that preschool experiences are powerful factors in building readiness for reading. We are also acknowledging that where readiness is lacking or not yet fully developed, we must provide activities and experience in school that prepare the child for reading instruction.

In the chapter opening we met two boys, Billy Turner and Alvin Morris. From our initial contact with Billy and Alvin, we begin to suspect differences between them that will prove to be significant in determining how and what we will do with them insofar as reading is concerned. How can two boys of the same age be markedly different? A large part of the answer lies in their home environments. Although we cannot generalize from only two cases, it is instructive to look at the home environments of these two boys to gain some appreciation for the factors that influence their preschool development.

Billy Turner is the middle child in a family of three children. His father is a police officer, and his mother works part-time as a clerk in an apparel shop. A neighbor cares for the three Turner children on a few occasions when Billy's parents must both be at work at the same time. Both parents are high school graduates who liked school and want their children to go further than they did, perhaps earning college degrees. Mrs. Turner is active in PTA, and both parents make a point of participating in parent-teacher conferences at school each fall and spring.

Billy shares a bedroom at home with his older brother, Mike, who is nine. Mike is a collector of rocks, model cars, and assorted curiosities such as an old radiator cap, a rusty spring, and several steel roller bearings used to play marbles at school. Billy marvels at Mike's possessions and has himself started a collection of nails and screws found around the neighborhood. Mike has a collection of paperback books that Billy likes to handle, but the words are too hard and the stories too long for him. Billy has a few books of his own that Mike reads aloud to him once in awhile although it is usually Mom who does the reading from library books each night when the boys go to bed. Billy has learned to recognize a number of words by following along in the book as his mother reads aloud. He can print his own name and understands that words can be written down from the experience of dictating to his mother letters of thanks for Christmas and birthday gifts.

Billy has a large vocabulary for a child his age and expresses tentativeness and conditional relationships in his conversation. He has learned to do this through interactions with his parents in which such understandings were important. "We can't go the grocery *until* I get the workshop cleaned up," his father might say, or "These nails may be long enough *if* I drive some in from both sides." Billy's presence in his dad's workshop is welcomed and even encouraged. By patiently answering Billy's questions and giving him simple tasks to do such as sorting nails or pieces of wood according to length, Mr. Turner has involved Billy in language and thinking activities that promote growth. In addition, Billy has learned that he can perform tasks successfully and communicate his ideas to others. He has a healthy self-concept and a feeling of support from people who are important to him.

Not every effort on Billy's part has been successful. He didn't make the starting line-up on his park board T-ball team and hasn't learned yet how to ride a bicycle. But his attempts at these goals are supported by his parents, who understand that failure is occasionally a part of trying. They encourage Billy to be independent and self-reliant by giving him room to explore and build on his mistakes. A birdhouse Billy put together from scraps of lumber was proudly installed atop a clothesline pole in the backyard even though it was rather unsightly and probably not a safe haven for any bird. "Next time you may want to draw a plan before you build to see how the parts fit together," Billy's dad said, "But it's a good job for a beginning carpenter."

Alvin Morris is a month younger than Bill Turner, but this slight difference in age hardly accounts for the fact that Alvin is far behind Billy in general development. Alvin also has an older brother, and, unlike Billy also has an older sister. Alvin's parents are high school graduates, but never cared much for school themselves and seldom get involved in PTA, parent-teacher conferences, or other school activities. Mr. Morris is a car salesperson, and Mrs. Morris works as a part-time secretary. The children are often left home alone with the oldest child, twelve-year-old Jennifer, in charge. Mr. Morris is frequently gone, particularly on weekends playing fast-pitch softball, flag football, or basketball in a town recreational league. Sometimes the whole family goes along to an out-of-town tournament, but because of the expense, this happens less and less.

Alvin is very much interested in sports, and whatever time he spends with his father is usually sports related. He has acquired a knowledge of sports jargon, but otherwise shows slow language development. His sentences are usually short declarative statements. His vocabulary is limited by infrequent contact with adults in stimulating settings. Alvin's parents typically ignore questions he asks or send him packing with the suggestion that he "Go watch TV." There are no books in the home, and Alvin has never seen either of his parents read anything other than a newspaper.

Alvin tries to join his brother and friends in sandlot baseball and football games, but is usually left out because he's "too little." When he does get to play because one side is short a player, the older children complain that he performs poorly, can't catch the ball, or doesn't know the rules of the game. Even though he's a pretty good athlete for his age, his self-concept suffers from the abuse he receives. His father has tried to teach him some fundamentals, but lacks patience and adds to Alvin's low self-image.

Though Alvin is not stupid, he has limited associations for many objects and events in his environment. He shows little curiosity partly because his questions are so often ignored and partly because so much of what he sees is not meaningful. He has come to believe that there is no explanation for many aspects of the world and what is unexplained is best ignored. The result is little understanding on Alvin's part of relationships that many children his age have mastered. For example, the connection between words and printed symbols on cereal boxes, in fast-food restaurants, and on soft-drink labels is missed by Alvin completely.

Because he has not had the repeated experience of listening to a book being shared aloud, he has almost no sense of what makes a story. The closest experience he has in this regard is watching cartoons and situation comedies on television. He also finds it difficult to sit still for any length of time, not having had this experience often.

Basic Components of the Reading Process

These brief descriptions of Billy and Alvin are incomplete but can give us some insight into where to begin and how to begin our reading instruction. In addition to Billy's important strengths in language and cognitive development, the most significant areas of readiness are his healthy self-concept, positive attitude toward reading, and general awareness of the relationship between printed symbols and spoken words. If we are careful to select materials that draw on Billy's interests and relate to his personal experiences, we should be able to introduce him to book reading almost immediately. Whatever areas of readiness require further development or refinement can be addressed in Billy's case as part of the reading program. No purpose is served by delaying the introduction of book reading to learn the letters of the alphabet, for example. He can learn the names of whatever letters he has not yet mastered by meeting them in the context of the story.

In Alvin's case, the most important work to be done has little to do with reading in a direct sense. Unless or until he can be helped to make sense of his environment, learn the meaning of common words, and gain confidence in himself, encounters with book reading may be unsuccessful. The teacher can play an active role in accomplishing these ends by providing some of the same type of experiences Billy was fortunate to have in his preschool years. For example, Alvin needs to have the experience of listening to a book being read aloud. He needs to spend time holding books, paging through books, looking at pictures, and describing what he sees. He has much to learn from exposure to events and places in the company of a caring adult who will point out interesting facts and relationships, supply words, refine concepts, and ask and answer questions. He needs to play games that call for attention to visual and auditory clues.

Suggestions for Parents

The classroom teacher can enlist the aid of parents by recommending ideas such as these:

1. Encourage the child to describe something exciting, interesting, or unusual that happened today. Prompt by narrowing the focus to one part of the day, for instance, on the way to school, on the playground, during reading class, at lunch, and so on.
2. Play "I Spy" on the way to the grocery or when driving to church or to Grandma's house. "I Spy something green" is a signal to the child to focus on green items in the visual field. This game can be varied to focus on sounds, size, shape, texture, and so forth.
3. After sharing a story with a child, identify two events that happened in the story. Ask which happened first. View a television program together, and discuss the order of key events as a variation on this activity.

4. Give a set of two, three, or four directions that the child is to perform in the order named. Begin with simple tasks. Example: I would like you to find a pencil, sharpen it, and put it on the kitchen table.

5. A deck of playing cards can be used in recognizing letters or numbers. SNAP is an easy card game for children to learn. Each player turns up a card at the same time. It is agreed beforehand that whenever a certain color, number, or letter appears, the child is to say SNAP as fast as possible. If the child does it before the partner, he or she collects all the cards that have been played up to that point.

6. Most children enjoy helping in the kitchen. Successful participation in making a dish builds self-confidence. Children can make their own pancake in the shape of a letter that has been discussed. Or Mother can simply present a plate of ready-made letters, possibly including the letters in the child's name, and the child could put them in order before pouring syrup on them.

7. Traveling in a car can often provide a rich setting for teaching or reinforcing such concepts as shapes, colors, letters, numbers, and so on. In a given time period, the child looks to see how many circles or other things can be found.

8. Small children usually like to listen while the parent reads a nursery rhyme. Most young children love to think of words that will rhyme with words they hear in the verses. Have the child provide other rhyming words (nonsense or not). The rhyme can then be read again. Familiar songs can also be sung with children using their own new words.

9. Tell an original story without an ending. Ask the children to draw a picture of the most important part of the story as well as a picture to finish the story. Then have them tell about their ending to the story.

Background Experience

1. Outline a presentation you could make to a group of parents indicating what the importance of the home environment is in building readiness for reading.

2. Add two or three additional activities to the list of suggestions for parents on page 117. Indicate what abilities the activities foster.

3. Identify preschool experiences that were important in your own readiness for school (or the readiness of a child you know well).

Much of what Alvin needs, the classroom teacher will try to provide. Because of the teacher's limited time to help each child individually, however, Alvin's parents need to be involved in building the basic understandings and attitudes that lead to success in reading. The chances of gaining Mr. and Mrs. Morris's cooperation and support may seem remote given the description we read earlier of the home environment. If they fail to respond, Alvin will continue to work at a disadvantage. But most parents *will* help if they are not made to feel defensive about the way they have raised their child. They *will* help if they are given simple, clear-cut directions for activities they can participate in easily and without disruption of their own daily routines. (See Smith, 1984; and Sittig, 1982 for additional suggestions.)

Factors Associated with Readiness to Read

Although it is difficult to disregard any aspect of a child's development in determining his or her readiness to read, some specific areas of development are often regarded as more important than others. Differences in opinion exist among experts in reading concerning which areas of development are most fundamental, and research on the matter is helpful only in a limited sense. Even though it is impossible to make unqualified statements about what abilities indicate a child is ready to read, we would be remiss not to offer some specific guidance to you in this important area. Accordingly, we now turn to a consideration of key factors associated with readiness.

Cognition as a Factor in Readiness

We know that authors communicate information to readers by selecting words that capture the meaning they intend and arranging them in phrases, sentences, and paragraphs that express that meaning. The readers, in turn, draw on their own language and thinking abilities to construct meaning. Preschoolers engage in numerous activities prior to their first attempt at reading a book that prepare them to engage in this construction of meaning. From infancy onward children are faced with the task of organizing their perceptions of the world in a fashion that enables them to make sense of what they encounter. Some experts hypothesize that the child begins almost immediately after birth to categorize information according to a structure in which some objects or events are alike and some are different (Neisser, 1976). In so doing, children prepare themselves to deal with future events and keep themselves from being overwhelmed by each confrontation with the world.

This system of concepts or categories that enables the child to handle stimuli from the environment has been called the child's "cognitive map of the world" (Neisser, 1976) or "theory of the world" (Smith, 1978). Information seems to be organized in the human mind according to *schemata* or outlines that are continuously being expanded and refined as the individual tries to make sense of the world (Anderson & Pearson, 1984). Experiments on the nature of memory suggest that the schemata are important in the storage and retrieval of information (Rumelhart, 1980). Associations are made and relationships established in such a way that new information is not filed away in isolated bits to be recalled as needed. Instead the new information is meaningfully integrated with previous information in the schemata (Piaget, 1963; Waller, 1977).

Some children who enter school are already familiar with the names of letters of the alphabet. This is often a good sign of readiness for reading instruction.

From the standpoint of reading readiness, the child who has a wealth of schemata on which to draw is better able to respond to reading-related tasks. Schemata develop as a result of interaction with people and events. The child who has had limited opportunity to confront the kinds of tasks and demands associated with beginning reading will lack readiness. The teacher will need to build the child's cognitive abilities through opportunities to explore ideas and topics in a low-risk setting. The child will need to manipulate objects, ask questions, offer observations, and receive feedback and helpful suggestions. The teacher will serve as a guide and resource in this exploration by directing and redirecting the child's attention, pointing out relationships, and asking questions. Once the child is actually reading from a book, it will be very important that he or she be able to draw on cognitive structures that "match" those of the author in order to understand the ideas communicated.

Language as a Readiness Factor

The entire content of Chapter 3 of this book, "Language and Reading," is devoted to establishing the importance of language to reading. As we saw in that chapter, language usually develops naturally as the preschool child interacts with people and the environment. Appropriate labels for objects and events are learned as the need and/or opportunity arises. The child who has been to Mammoth Cave probably knows the meaning of *stalactite* and *stalagmite.* The child who has no similar firsthand experience is less likely to know those words. The child who has not been inside a cave may instead know terms associated with the waterfront or the forest if that has been that child's experience, however. It would be normal for each entering first-grader to know or use different terms or both because experiences of each are unique.

The fact that almost every entering first-grader has a good working vocabulary is significant. This provides a starting point for whatever learning activities the teacher wishes to provide. The terms a child understands give some clue to the child's background experiences and some indication of what he or she is ready to learn. Words already "known" can be discussed and nuances of meaning explored. Related terms with similar or opposite meanings can be introduced. Altogether new topics and words can be introduced and made meaningful by relating them to terms already known. Through continued vocabulary development the child grows ready to deal with terms and ideas when they are met in printed material.

As with vocabulary, the child's use of sentence structure also develops naturally as he or she interacts with people. Without formal instruction the child learns how words work together to deliver meaning. By age six the child understands and uses complex sentences. The teacher's task in the readiness program is to encourage the continued development of language competence by creating numerous opportunities for the child to share orally and listen to others share. Cullinan (1974) found that the teacher can effectively stimulate the child's language growth by reading literature aloud. Both vocabulary and understanding of complex sentence structures are enhanced by opportunities to hear and discuss the language used in books.

Auditory and Visual Aspects of Readiness

Most districts require that children entering school undergo a physical examination by a medical doctor. Through this practice the general health of all students is protected and conditions that might interfere with learning are identified and corrected whenever possible.

Although a routine physical examination may provide some assurance that the entering five- or six-year-old is free of contagious diseases or general malnutrition, additional information about the child's vision and hearing is needed to be sure that there are no physical impediments to reading readiness. Specifically, near-point and binocular vision must be assessed to determine whether the child is able to handle reading-related tasks (Jobe, 1976). Likewise, the child's hearing must be assessed in a more precise manner than is generally employed in a physical examination (G. Spache, 1976.) Fortunately many schools now screen vision with a telebinocular instrument capable of determining that a child can see print clearly from a distance of twelve to eighteen inches. Many schools also screen hearing with an audiometer that measures hearing ability at various sound frequencies (pitch) as well as at different levels of volume. Children who indicate abnormalities on these tests are referred to specialists who are trained to determine the exact nature of the problem and correct it if possible.

If screening of the type just described is not provided, it is possible that children who do not see or hear well may have these handicaps to overcome in learning to read. The possibility of reading difficulties is increased when problems with auditory and visual acuity go undetected and/or uncorrected (Spache, 1981).

The classroom teacher should argue for the necessity of providing vision and hearing screening. Beyond that the teacher can watch for signs of vision difficulty in the classroom such as those listed later and explore the possibility of acuity problems if a child has difficulty with reading tasks.

It is particularly important to realize that in the normal development of the eye, children are often farsighted when they enter school. This means they are better able to see objects at a distance and will often perform well at reading wall charts, such as the Snellen Chart, yet have difficulty seeing objects close at hand. Obviously, reading is a near-point task requiring a vision check that assesses this ability. The ability of the eyes to work together giving the brain one clear image is likewise important. Near-point and binocular vision can be checked by a trained nurse, reading clinician, or optometrist using a telebinocular instrument such as

Keystone Visual Survey Tests
Orthorater
Professional Vision Tester
Spache Binocular Reading Test
Stereotests

Signs of Visual Problems

1. Cocking the head so as to read with only one eye.
2. Holding the side of one's head when looking at the book or board.
3. Rubbing the eyes during reading.
4. Red eyes, watery eyes.
5. Holding the book too close to the face.
6. Holding the book at arm's length.
7. Complaints of headaches.
8. Squinting or other indications of strain.
9. Complaints of haziness or fading of printed symbols.

Two publications of the International Reading Association that explore the visual aspects of reading in greater detail are *Screening Vision in Schools* by Fred W. Jobe (1976) and *Some Perceptual Prerequisites for Reading* by Uta Frith and Juliet M. Vogel (1980).

Hearing or auditory acuity naturally plays a role in auditory discrimination. A child with defective hearing may not be able to identify certain kinds of sounds. For example, some hearing loss reduces or eliminates the reception of high-frequency sounds. Those sounds asso-

Basic Components of the Reading Process

ciated with the consonants *f, s, k* and similar sounds would go unnoticed or be effectively obscured with a certain kind of hearing handicap. An individual with this kind of hearing deficiency needs reading instruction that emphasizes visual techniques instead of a strong auditory-visual relation (Rosenberg, 1968).

In some instances, the teacher may notice symptoms of a hearing deficiency in a child. If the child turns the head as if to listen with one ear or cups an ear or does not respond to fairly low-volume instructions, these are clues to a possible hearing problem. Other symptoms are listed later. In the light of these symptoms, the teacher may want to conduct a rough screening test of her own. This can be done by having two or three children sit with their backs to their teacher, who then whispers their names or their birth dates or other key words. The children are to raise their hands when they hear the words that apply only to them. If such an exercise adds evidence to what the teacher has previously observed about hearing difficulties, the child with the problem should be referred to the school nurse for further testing. Again, instructional techniques should be adjusted to enable the child to function as well as possible with the disability. For example, such a child can be given a seat close to the teacher.

Signs of Auditory Problems

1. Inattention during listening activities.
2. Frequent misunderstanding of oral directions or numerous requests for repetition of statements.
3. Turning one ear toward the speaker or thrusting head forward when listening.
4. Intent gaze at the speaker's face or strained posture while listening.
5. Monotone speech, poor pronunciation, or indistinct articulation.
6. Complaints of earache or hearing difficulty.
7. Insistence on closeness to sound sources.
8. Frequent colds, discharging ears, or difficult breathing (Bond, Tinker, & Wasson, 1979, p. 81).

Visual Acuity

1. Visit a reading clinic, optometrist's office or other facility that has a binocular vision screening device. Observe someone who is trained in using the instrument; test someone's vision (perhaps your own).
2. Examine materials designed for use in reading instruction. Compare the size of type and length of line used in materials intended for beginning readers with materials intended for later grades.

Auditory and Visual Discrimination

It seems obvious that a basic prerequisite to reading is the ability to discriminate or differentiate between printed symbols. Any confusion on the part of a child over whether printed symbols such as *boy* and *toy* are the same or different could result in serious difficulty with reading. The label *visual discrimination* has been used widely to identify the ability to differentiate among visual objects.

Somewhat less obvious, but equally important to reading, is the ability to discriminate or differentiate between sounds. Again, confusion about whether *boy* or *toy* are the same or different when spoken could cause a serious difficulty when learning to associate the printed symbol for these words with the right spoken word. The label *auditory discrimination* is commonly used to refer to the ability to differentiate among sounds.

Any child of five or six years of age is skilled in making both auditory and visual discriminations. The learning of any concept is based on the child's ability to determine that some objects are the same or highly similar and can be assigned to a category. For example, a five-year-old can easily identify green growing things that belong in the class *tree* and not confuse those examples with green growing things that belong in the class *grass* or *weeds*. Except for borderline cases, the five-year-old can usually distinguish trees from shrubs or bushes—a feat many adults cannot perform any better. This illustration involves visual discrimination and requires the child to generate a "feature list" or list of characteristics that causes some vegetation to be called trees and some to be called something else. The feature list is typically an unconscious set of criteria the child cannot verbalize but has evolved over time with experience. Another example can be given to demonstrate that any five-year-old has learned to make auditory discriminations. A child who responds to his or her own name has learned to differentiate between that word and the name of a sibling, for example.

The child learns to discriminate initially on the basis of gross differences. With experience, differences among visual and auditory stimuli become more refined. The child's feature list can become quite detailed in matters where an interest is pronounced. To test this assertion, buy a substitute for the particular doll or toy truck a five-year-old wants for Christmas and you'll see how readily he or she can note minute differences.

Children entering school and being exposed to reading will usually learn to discriminate among symbols and sounds only after the importance of doing so is understood. We can give the difference between the symbols *b* and *d* importance artificially by giving a gold star to those who do a work sheet correctly or by letting the child's natural desire to communicate ideas cause him or her to dictate a story about a big steam shovel digging a hole in the neighborhood (*b* and *d* are used in a meaningful context and must be recognized to be read). One approach assumes that children do not know much about discriminating or discriminate only when forced to do so. The other approach

Basic Components of the Reading Process

acknowledges that discrimination is a normal part of learning and will occur when a need is felt (or created by the teacher).

Auditory and Visual Perception

The term *perception* is one used in a number of ways by specialists in varying fields and even within the field of reading. Often it is used synonymously with vision and occasionally in a neurological sense. We use perception here to refer to the meaning one associates with whatever is at issue. One can see a tree—this involves acuity. One can distinguish one tree from another tree—this involves discrimination. One can perceive a tree—this involves having an association for the object with something that is meaningful in the cognitive structure. For example, a tree can be shelter from the sun or rain, fuel for a fire, part of a large forest, or an element in a landscape plan for a yard.

Perception relies on accurate discrimination, but a learner perceives from many different vantage points. Perceptions reflect the socioeconomic, emotional, linguistic, and motivational resources of a person. The teacher can use this diversity of perceptual response to show children that reading can be quite personal and yet have some general

A child's relationship with others and experiences of the world around him are preparation for learning to read.

group meaning as well. When reading, children will use those perceptual cues they need in order to understand and interpret the printed page.

Physical Factors in Reading Readiness

In addition to auditory and visual acuity, several other physical aspects of readiness merit attention. Vernon (1958) reviews a number of studies that have explored the relationship between poor health and difficulty in learning to read. She reports that poor health and illness are seldom major causes of reading difficulties, but serve as minor or predisposing causes in over 50 percent of cases.

General health appears to be an important factor in reading readiness. Pertz and Putnam (1982) reviewed a number of studies that examined the relationship between nutrition and learning with the conclusion that poorly nourished children are less likely to achieve their academic potential than their well-nourished peers. The child who is malnourished, tired, or ill frequently is less attentive to the environment and, therefore, less responsive to opportunities to grow and learn. Clearly, the child who misses school when the class listens to and discusses an exciting book or visits a local dairy farm has fewer opportunities to develop the concepts and language such experiences afford. Children who participate in such experiences without a good breakfast may profit less from the experience if they lack energy or general alertness. Some schools provide breakfast for children from low income homes to offset this handicap. The school can do little for the child who stays up late watching television, however, other than instruct the parents on the importance of sufficient rest for growing bodies.

The wise teacher will consider the possibility of poor health, nutrition, and inadequate sleep in diagnosing the possible causes of a child's state of readiness. This may have to be accomplished by a home visit and may need to involve the school nurse.

A second physical factor related to readiness for reading is motor coordination. At first glance, it might seem that how well a child can bounce a ball or skip rope would be unrelated to an ability to recognize words and reconstruct intended meaning. There is an indirect relationship between these divergent areas, however. Because some who write in the field tend to overemphasize this relationship, in our opinion, we will look briefly at the underlying issues in the interest of putting the matter in better perspective.

First, let us say that all human abilities seem to be related to some degree. In studying gifted individuals over a lifetime, Lewis Terman (1959) found that his subjects tended to be healthier, happier, better coordinated, and generally superior in all areas of development than the average person. This suggests that children who enter school with an advantage in language and cognitive development will often have an advantage in motor development as well. Remember that this is a generalization, not a rule that necessarily applies to each individual case. Remember also that the relationship found is not necessarily causal. That is to say, excellence in motor coordination does not necessarily

Basic Components of the Reading Process

cause readiness for reading. What is more likely, from our perspective, is that the child who does well in motor activities probably has a better sense of well-being, more self-confidence, and a stronger ego, all valuable assets in any undertaking (including, or can we say, most especially, reading). In other words, children who have a history of success in games on the playground are more likely to persist in academic activities because they feel good about themselves as a result of those experiences. We doubt seriously that the neurological development promoted by physical activities helps "organize" the brain for reading tasks.

On the other hand, training in physical activities as advocated by Kephart (1960) and Getman (1968) may help some children gain a better sense of accomplishment. Balow (1971) reaches this conclusion after reviewing the relevant literature. We are inclined to agree. However, neither Balow nor the authors of this book believe that motor development activities should replace reading activities as a way of promoting success in reading.

Emotional and Social Adjustment as Readiness Factors

The fact that reading is a cognitive operation requiring the child to draw on a variety of intellectual abilities can cause us to lose sight of several other important areas of development, namely, emotional and social adjustment. To be ready to read, children must have a healthy self-concept that permits them to persist in the face of some adversity. They must be able to tackle a job independently and see it through to completion. And, given the number of children in nearly all classrooms, they must be able to function as members of a group—taking turns, respecting the rights and views of others, and cooperating in joint problem solving.

We have considered in this chapter how children enter school at all points along a continuum ranging from self-reliant to totally dependent on others (usually the parents). Depending on the opportunities provided during the preschool years to grow emotionally, a six-year-old may still view the world from the egocentric perspective of the toddler. A child accustomed to getting his or her own way is not well equipped to sit quietly as a member of a group, share ideas and objects with others, consider the views of others, take turns, follow directions, and so forth. These abilities are usually developed through interaction with other people, often peers, in a setting where cooperation is encouraged. The child who has had little or no contact with other children in an unstructured environment will find school a confusing place, as will the child who has not had to live with rules guiding his or her behavior. Likewise the child who has been dominated by others who have made all decisions and structured every minute of the day will find the school situation upsetting.

Grade-one teachers realize that school imposes a whole new set of expectations on children and create activities that foster emotional stability, independence, and cooperativeness. From the very first day of class the alert teacher makes sure each child knows what is expected. Tasks that are suited to the child's level of development are given to provide opportunities for success. Activities are chosen initially that require only a few minutes to complete. Gradually more complex tasks that require longer periods to complete are introduced. Allowances are made for the natural spontaneity of the child's responses until he or she learns to wait to be called on, and so forth. In other words, the skilled teacher is prepared to build on the emotional and social abilities the child brings to school. Problems could develop when the child is particularly insecure and self-centered. The wise teacher recognizes in such cases that reading instruction must be delayed or adjusted so that the activities provided promote emotional and social development rather than requiring these abilities as prerequisites.

Emotional and Social Adjustment

Observe a group of preschoolers at play. What evidence of cooperation and taking turns do you see? How will the differences you see in self-centeredness affect these children's readiness for reading?

Classroom Activities

1. Involve children who are just entering school in activities that require taking turns. Examples are telling about a favorite television program, describing a favorite pet, sharing a drawing, and walking on a balance beam.
2. Play games that require the child to listen carefully to directions. Examples include "Simon Says," "I Spy," "Bingo," and "Hot and Cold." Begin with easy tasks and gradually increase their difficulty.
3. Practice group problem solving by introducing an issue and encouraging the children to brainstorm. Invite all ideas and suggestions. Delay convergent and evaluative thinking until all new ideas are produced. Once all possible solutions have been generated, discuss the possibilities identified. Select two or three answers favored by the group. Sample topics are ways to improve a toy teddy bear to make it more fun to play with, new and different equipment for our playground, and gifts we could make in school for our parents at holiday time.

Attitude Toward and Interest in Reading as Readiness Factors

Children sometimes return home from the first day of school disappointed that they did not learn to read on this "day of days." Such incidents illustrate that the importance of school in acquiring reading

Basic Components of the Reading Process

ability is widely understood among children. With few exceptions, children see reading as important if only to make them more grown-up. Relatively few six-year-olds probably realize how basic reading ability is to acquiring knowledge and finding gainful employment. In any event, most children want to learn to read.

The teacher will need to seize on this initial predisposition toward reading, nourish it, and give it substance, for the commitment of many children to acquiring reading ability may waver in the face of instructional demands that involve attention to detail, completing paper-and-pencil tasks, and so forth. Beginning reading activities need not be tedious, but regardless of how enjoyable we make them, learning to read is an intellectual task. The child who has had the advantage of seeing parents and older siblings read for enjoyment and needed information is more likely to persist when the teacher puts limits on his or her freedom in an attempt to teach reading. The child's positive attitude is founded in personal experience with the value of reading, an attitude probably acquired over a long period of time in direct contact with books and people who read. Other children who think it would be great to know how to read, but lack direct experience with the value of reading, may be inclined toward disillusionment with reading once the teacher structures activities that limit their freedom.

What a teacher must do for such children, of course, is show the enormous potential reading has for providing enjoyment and supplying interesting and useful information. This can be done most directly by sharing books immediately and often with the intent of demonstrating the value of being able to read. Six-year-olds are not going to be enchanted by the notion that reading ability will get them a good job, of course. That long-term goal is simply too abstract. But even the most disadvantaged child can find enjoyment in the books of Ezra Jack Keats, Dr. Seuss, and Bill Martin, Jr., or be fascinated by facts about whales, dinosaurs, and turtles.

Every child comes to school with interests. The teacher can build positive attitudes toward books and reading by seizing on those interests, demonstrating that books are relevant to those interests, and making early instruction as meaningful as possible. The youngster who likes animals will enjoy books such as *Clifford the Big Red Dog* (Bridwell, 1966), *Frog and Toad Are Friends* (Lobel, 1970), and *Little Bear* (Minarik, 1957). The teacher will find that sharing these and other books with children causes them to want to be able to enjoy such books independently.

If initial instructional activities are not devoted exclusively to the mechanical aspects of reading (that is, alphabet memory work, sound-symbol memorization, paper-and-pencil work sheets, and the like), happy experiences with books will give the child purpose in learning to read. The language experience approach is an excellent way to ensure that reading is seen in context as one aspect of communication.

Finally, the teacher's own attitude toward reading is of paramount importance in building children's attitudes. The enthusiastic teacher who enjoys books and helping children discover the enlightenment they contain will infect his or her students with that enthusiasm. The same enthusiasm is communicated to the children's parents who can, in turn, be a strong influence in making the child want to read (Sittig, 1982).

In short, the child is predisposed toward reading by virtue of the value a literate society places on this ability. We must demonstrate to the child that reading can be valuable to him or her as an individual and that people around him think reading is important.

Attitudes and Interests

1. Make a list of topics that interest you. Exchange it with a colleague or class-mate. Visit a library or bookstore to see if you can locate a book that might appeal to your partner. Discuss your choice with the intended person to assess how well you succeeded in making a wise choice.
2. Read a book to a child. Discuss the characters and events in the story. Help the child develop a simple book jacket that conveys some important idea about the book.

Print Awareness as a Factor in Reading Readiness

Preschool and primary age children possess varying degrees of knowledge about written language, or print (Downing & Oliver, 1974; Mason, 1980). Even very young children are aware, to some extent, of print in the environment. The prereader who recognizes a Burger King sign, picks out his or her name from others in a T-shirt display, informs his or her mother when she leaves out a part of "The Three Bears" storybook, knows that *A* is a letter but "☆" is not, writes "messages" on paper to others, and can name the *E* in an EXIT sign is demonstrating a number of understandings of the ways in which written language has significance.

The term *print awareness* may be used to incorporate a range of concepts, including the following:

There is a process called reading.
The purpose of reading is to convey meaning, and printed symbols (letters and words) within the environment carry meaning.
Words and not pictures contain the real message heard when one listens to a book or story being read aloud.
A written word, or configuration of letters bound by white spaces, corresponds to a spoken word (word-in-print).
To read, in English, it is necessary to move in a certain direction: from left to right across a page and from top to bottom. It

Basic Components of the Reading Process

is also necessary to read the left page before reading the right page.

Words have a beginning (at the left) and an end (at the right).

There are certain terms used when talking about written language, for example, *word, letter,* and *sentence.*

These concepts do not appear to be acquired in a hierarchical fashion, with one naturally preceding another in a set sequence, but do develop gradually as children grow older and are able to engage in more and more meaningful experiences with print (Hiebert, 1981). Generally, children with rich preschool exposure to print (seeing, listening to, and talking about books and words) tend to develop a fuller awareness of print and its uses at an earlier age and are better prepared for the transition to literacy than are those children whose preschool experiences reflect a lack of focused interaction with written language. Almost all children will have many incidental encounters with print around them: they will see and recognize the KROGER sign when shopping, will ride in a car when it pulls up to a STOP sign, will look at the CHEERIOS box on the breakfast table. However, some will not have the advantage of being shown the relationships of their knowledge of reading. These children may have few conceptions of what reading is all about, of the connection between printed symbols and spoken language, and of the purposes and uses of books.

It is often a false assumption that an entering kindergarten or first-grade prereader knows absolutely nothing about print and reading. A similarly frequent but opposite assumption is that the beginner automatically understands the process of reading and the meaning of abstract terminology such as *word, letter, sound,* and *sentence* (Downing & Oliver, 1974). In either instance, such suppositions are questionable. Attempting to uncover what a child does understand about the purposes and processes of reading is an important task. The concepts about print discussed earlier are pertinent indicators of a child's preparedness for reading and are rarely dealt with in standardized readiness tests. Providing opportunities for a child to engage in "real-life," meaningful activities involving text offers a teacher a great deal of information in this area. Prereaders may not be able to respond to the question "What do people do when they read?" They may, however, be quite capable of holding a familiar storybook correctly, turning the pages from left to right, and retelling the story in their own words as they utilize some of the actual written phrases. This behavior reveals a substantial preliminary knowledge about how to approach printed material.

A fairly complete assessment of a child's print awareness may be accomplished by using Marie Clay's CONCEPTS ABOUT PRINT (CAP) Test (Clay, 1972). This instrument attempts to determine understandings about print such as

Orientation to books (front, back, top, bottom).
Reading print versus pictures.
Directionality (left-right, top-bottom) of print.

Word-by-word matching (concept of a word-in-print).
Beginning and end of a word.
Upper- and lowercase letters and simple punctuation.

An alternative assessment can be made using any simple trade book and a checklist compiled by the teacher. Determining whether or not the ability to recognize a word-in-print has been acquired can be undertaken easily by using a language experience story. After the story, group or individual, is written, have the child read what he or she dictated, pointing to the words as he or she goes along. A more extensive, one-to-one procedure for the same concept is voice-pointing, a technique that involves the initial memorization of a simple verse and subsequent "reading" of the written verse by the child, who points to the words as he or she says them. The type and quantity of spontaneous writing done by a child are valuable sources of information on that child's ideas about written language. Does the child have a purpose in writing and use real letters or other symbols? Are there distinguishable words or groups of letters separated by spaces? Is there any sound-symbol correspondence? Does the child talk about his or her writing and what it's for?

A prereader acquires understandings about print through exposure to written text and through actually writing. These understandings continue to develop, in quantity and sophistication, throughout the primary years. It is important to discover what concepts a child possesses and to build on those understandings.

The Kindergarten as a Component of the Reading Readiness Program

Up to this point in our discussion we have focused on grade one. Yet kindergarten is increasingly becoming a component of public education. Gutek (1983) estimated that nine out of ten preschool-aged children are enrolled in preprimary grade programs (including kindergarten) before entering grade one. This figure is up from less than eight out of ten just a decade ago. In the face of this trend, we must address the question here of how kindergarten programs fit into the topic of reading readiness.

In an earlier period (pre-1957) the importance of maturation to reading readiness was emphasized almost to the exclusion of concern for the environment. Many professionals were of the opinion that a mental age of 6.5 years was necessary for success in learning to read. Children who had not yet reached that level of development would do so eventually, so the reasoning went, and until that time efforts to teach reading were unproductive. As a result, kindergarten programs devoted time to activities that taught cooperation, sharing, taking turns, following directions, coloring, painting, and so forth. Although kindergartens were not merely playpens, play was an important part of the program and socialization was the principal goal. Children were pre-

Basic Components of the Reading Process

pared for grade one primarily by learning to become part of a group and follow a routine, obvious prerequisites to the formal learning that would be encountered. During this time children may have learned the alphabet and certainly would have heard stories read aloud by the teacher, but these were informal activities for the most part. Given the idea that normal maturation had not yet made most five-year-olds "ready" for reading, little effort was made to build readiness.

In the late 1950s the importance of the child's environment as a factor in learning and his or her readiness to learn became emphasized. The notion that development could be hastened by instruction that was suited to the child's level became popular. Special attention was given to improving the environments of children from "disadvantaged homes." Publicity was given to successful efforts to teach children of five and even four and three years of age to read. The result was that kindergarten programs began to take on a more formal instructional role. Particularly in the area of reading, specific skills thought to be important in getting the child ready to read were taught explicitly. Workbooks flourished containing exercises devoted to auditory and visual discrimination, left-to-right directionality, recognition of letters, and phonics. In reality, the readiness programs from first grade were simply moved downward and used with kindergartners. Many, and we include ourselves, would argue that most commercial readiness programs of the 1940s and 1950s were simplistic, mechanical, and unsatisfactory for preparing children to read. They were even less appropriate for younger kindergarten children.

Over time the importance of differentiating instruction for children, building concepts and cognitive abilities, promoting language development, and building positive attitudes toward reading was recognized and replaced the isolated readiness workbook in most kindergartens. A good readiness program in kindergarten is not much different from a good readiness program in first grade. Obviously, children who have been through kindergarten will enter grade one with a more solid base for learning to read, and the teacher must adjust accordingly. Some children may already be reading as a result of their kindergarten experiences. The teacher must take them on from there, not force them into irrelevant "readiness activities." Other children will not be at all ready for book reading despite the best of kindergarten experiences. They, in turn, will profit from extended readiness activities not unlike what they did in kindergarten.

To return to the initial question, how does the kindergarten program fit into the topic of reading readiness? It ought to dovetail with the first-grade program. In the absence of a good kindergarten program, the first-grade teacher will find entering pupils in need of more readiness instruction. In the presence of a poor kindergarten program (that is, one that approaches reading readiness from a mechanical, narrow viewpoint), the first-grade teacher may have remedial work to do at the outset, especially on children's attitudes toward reading. If the kindergarten program is a good one, the first-grade teacher can build on this start.

Predicting Success in Reading

The body of professional literature dealing with reading readiness is large and far-ranging. One type of study addresses the issue of predicting which children will be successful in learning to read (Bond & Dykstra, 1967). One reason for looking at how successful readers performed on an array of tasks administered before instruction begins is to identify the factors that seem to be associated with success. Once these are determined, future groups of children can be tested with those tasks for the purpose of (1) beginning instruction immediately for the children who are ready to read (according to the tasks) and (2) delaying reading instruction for those who are not ready in favor of instruction that builds readiness.

Studies of the type just described seek to find a relationship between some factor (A) that is hypothesized to be important to readiness (for example, mental age, ability to distinguish between visual symbols, listening ability, and so on) and a second factor (B), reading achievement. The relationship between two factors is often quantified by means of a statistical procedure called correlation, which yields a coefficient ranging from ± 1.0 to 0. Coefficients at or close to ± 1.0 show high relationship between variables A and B. Coefficients near 0 show little relationship.

Many readiness factors have been studied as predictors of reading achievement in an attempt to identify the "best" predictor. From an administrative or management standpoint, having a few accurate predictors shortens the time needed to identify the children who are ready for reading instruction. In this sense, the search for a "best" predictor has some merit. Unfortunately, even children who are "ready" according to their performance on certain tasks often find themselves being put through a "readiness program," apparently on the assumption that it can't hurt to be even more ready. Thus a boy like Billy Turner spends his first few weeks or even months in school covering materials that are old hat instead of getting on to the exciting business of reading books.

The attempt to find the "best" predictors of reading achievement also has another unfortunate side. The myth has developed that by concentrating attention on the tasks that the "unready" children did not do well on the readiness assessment, they can be gotten ready to read. This diagnostic use of readiness assessment is particularly misguided when the devices used for assessment are commercial readiness tests (Dykstra, 1967), but can be unproductive even when less formal measures are used. Let's look at the problems inherent in the practice of teaching unselectively specific readiness skills that correlation studies indicate are related to reading achievement.

Suppose that our friend Alvin Morris does poorly on naming the letters of the alphabet, a task known to be correlated with reading achievement at a $+ .5$ level (as high as any variable studied in attempts to predict reading achievement) (Dykstra, 1967; Silvaroli, 1964; Durrell, and others, 1958). Alvin's performance might be measured on a reading readiness test such as the *Metropolitan Test of Reading Readiness* or the

Basic Components of the Reading Process

Harrison-Stroud Reading Readiness Test or on an informal measure the school district has developed for local use. Following a diagnostic-prescriptive rationale, as Alvin's teacher we would teach him the names of the letters directly *to get him ready to read.* This might be done with tracing techniques, the use of sandpaper letters, making letters of clay, or even introducing each letter by means of a hand puppet. By making the activities varied and fun, we could probably bring Alvin along nicely. But are we getting him ready to read? Maybe so, maybe not. Depending on how we teach reading later, Alvin may not need to know the letters *before* beginning to read. He might learn them along with actual reading activities from a book. How can this be so if studies say children who know the letters usually learn to read and children who don't know the letters usually don't learn to read (as well)?

The fact that performance on a task (often a subtest of a readiness test) is associated with success in learning to read does not mean that the first causes the second. Correlation coefficients demonstrate that two variables are related, not that one causes the other. In fact, when two things are related, the distinct possibility exists that a third, unidentified factor accounts for the correlation between the two. Thus performance on a test of alphabet knowledge may correlate with readiness to read, thereby leading some to conclude (without real support) that by helping a child whose knowledge of the alphabet is low learn the letters, he or she will become ready to read. This conclusion may be true, but the possibility exists that general intelligence (a third factor) or background experience (another third factor), for example, is responsible for success in learning to read and for knowledge of the alphabet. Efforts to improve the child's knowledge of letters may increase his or her score on tests of the alphabet, but may not increase his or her readiness to read. Only by improving the child's intelligence (or background experience depending on which of these hypothetical third factors is the "real" causative one) do we affect his reading readiness.

The real implication of this discussion is that teachers ought to be cautious about planning readiness instruction for a child on the basis of his or her poor performance on a task "highly correlated with reading achievement." This is just too simplistic and ignores what we know about correlation studies.

Another difficulty with predicting success in reading has to do with the scope and nature of the tasks employed. Often children are asked to perform tasks that have not been clearly tied to a well-conceived, well-supported view of the reading process. Correlational data may indicate that those who read well perform well on a task and those who fail in reading perform poorly on this task. When children perform poorly on that task, the conclusion is drawn that readiness for reading can be improved by concentrating on that ability. The danger here is that zealots who are convinced that failures in reading are because of inadequate attention to some particular skill often succeed in diverting classroom time away from activities that might be devoted to abilities that have better support for their importance. Programs that cause children to creep and crawl as a way of helping them get ready to read fall into this category.

The important point to remember here is that any task included in an assessment of reading readiness ought to be obviously related to the reading act as you, the teacher, perceive it. This is particularly important in reading readiness tests where subtests without a clear connection to reading are sometimes included. For example, sentence copying provides an example of fine motor control but is not directly related to any aspect of reading itself.

One must also be careful to see that a readiness assessment task actually requires the child to perform the skill or ability suggested by the label given to the task. For example, a listening test may not assess the child's ability to understand what is said as much as it assesses his or her culture or background experience or tell you whether the child was paying attention. This would be true if the task draws on knowledge some children lack because of their home environments. A listening test should assess only the ability to understand directions or descriptions that any child has had the opportunity to learn.

Commercial reading readiness tests are plagued by one other limitation that seriously erodes their usefulness as "diagnostic" devices—subtest unreliability. Any assessment device that samples only a few behaviors in any "skill" category, such as vocabulary or auditory discrimination, has limited reliability. Consequently, the results must be viewed with caution and should be corroborated by other evidence. The *Murphy-Durrell Readiness Test* (1965), for example, yields a score that ostensibly represents the child's ability to hear differences among sounds by testing only ten behaviors. Since there are about forty-six sounds in the English language, such a score has very little diagnostic value. One could not plan an instructional program with any confidence that certain sounds are "known" and others not "known" on the basis of such limited information.

Another problem with the practice of identifying those who need readiness instruction on the basis of performance on good "predictors" of reading achievement, is the fact that method of instruction must be considered. Study A may find auditory discrimination to be a good predictor of reading achievement. This may be true because the children in Study A were taught to read in first grade using a program that emphasized sound-symbol. If another approach to teaching were used, auditory discrimination might not be such a good predictor.

Predicting who will be successful in learning to read is in many ways similar to predicting the order of finish in a horse race. Prior to a horse race, bettors have access to a wealth of information that they may have used successfully on other occasions to predict a winner. For example, the racing program reports the sire and dam for each horse. Using this information one can employ a system of betting on bloodline. Some bettors pay attention to the jockey or trainer of a horse or both. Others watch the horse's actual time in previous races. Needless to say, no system is 100 percent effective. Why not? Because horse racing, like reading readiness is complex. Uncontrolled factors can intervene to keep the fastest horse from winning. The track may be muddy, the horse may be in a poor running position in the gate or in the stretch, the horse may have an off day, the jockey may fail to pace the horse properly, and so forth.

How does this compare to predicting success in learning to read? Prior to instruction a wealth of information can be gathered on each child. We can ascertain the mental age or IQ, assess knowledge of the alphabet, measure visual discrimination, check motor coordination, and so forth. Various unknown factors may interact to cause a child who seems ready according to commonly used indicators to perform poorly in reading. These may include the instructional method employed, the child's attitude toward the teacher, the teacher's attitude toward the child, the amount of time spent on readiness activities, and so forth.

Assessing Reading Readiness

Most of us have had the experience of shopping for a new pair of shoes. Unless we are interested in endless browsing, we must decide ahead of time what features we want in the shoes we finally select. By studying our wardrobe and shoes already owned, we can determine the color, style, and price range that suits our needs. As a result, on entering a shoe store, we have specific criteria on standards to apply in evaluating the shoes on display. We can quickly narrow the many choices in the store down to a few that are appropriate. This process gives us a way to focus attention rather than aimlessly examining the many pairs of shoes in a store.

The shoe-shopping scenario is given here as an analogy for assessing readiness for reading. When selecting variables to study or assess in determining readiness, we confront a veritable "storeful" of possibilities. We decide what factors are important, then focus on them—much like examining our wardrobe to see what we need in the way of shoes. The specific information we gather depends on the standards we apply. In the case of readiness, we can judge what is important only if we have a clear conceptualization of the reading process and what skills or abilities are basic to success in learning to read. Thus, a view of reading that considers background experience to be important will focus on that variable in any assessment of readiness for reading. Other views would emphasize other variables such as knowledge of letter names or good hand-eye coordination.

Standardized Readiness Tests

Readiness is commonly assessed with standardized reading readiness tests such as the *Metropolitan Readiness Test* (1976), the *Murphy-Durrell Reading Readiness Analysis* (1965), the *Lee-Clark Reading Readiness Test* (1962), and the *Clymer-Barrett Readiness Test* (1983). These instruments represent the views of their respective authors concerning which variables are basic to reading readiness. On the one hand, teachers may be inclined to feel that these experts are well qualified to decide what to assess and gladly accept the test results as accurate. Developmental effort has certainly gone into these tests, and they should not be dismissed lightly. On the other hand, standardized tests are prepared for a national market and, therefore, represent a series of compromises. The tests do not reflect the conditions that exist in a local school or classroom and consequently have limited value in making instructional decisions. For example, background experience cannot be assessed with such instruments because test authors recognize that children growing up in rural Wyoming will normally have different experiences from children who grow up in New Orleans. No nationally marketed test of background experience could adequately sample the vast range of possibilities.

Furthermore, the skills and abilities that are important in a classroom where reading instruction will focus on phonics clearly result in different test content from the skills and abilities needed in a classroom where sight words will be emphasized. In other words, a readiness test is usually general in nature, which limits its usefulness in a particular teacher's classroom. The authors of reading readiness tests may or may not favor one approach to readiness instruction, but in either event dare not construct a test that is tied to a single approach.

In the previous discussion about predicting success in reading, other cautions concerning readiness tests were raised. We pointed out that subtests are often included because they correlate highly with success in reading. This may or may not indicate that instruction on those skill areas will result in improved readiness to read because cause-effect is not signaled by correlation. We also pointed out that subtests are sometimes mislabeled. Careful examination is needed to determine that the test measures what it claims to measure. Finally, subtests are typically too brief to give reliable measures of performance in a skill area.

Because of the limitations of standardized readiness tests, we are cautious about their value to teachers. Certainly diagnostic use of these instruments is not justified (Dykstra, 1967), and only limited use can be made of total scores (overall performance). The teacher can gain a sense of the development of general readiness for a group of children from standardized readiness tests. A tentative judgment can be made from readiness test results concerning which children are most likely to benefit from an extended readiness period and which children are most ready to begin book reading. Even here the danger of stereotyping children is great. All those labeled *ready* by a test are not alike. Some may succeed in a basal program, if that is the teacher's intent, only with careful attention to reading preparation prior to each story. Others may not need much guidance.

A Representative Readiness Test:
The Clymer-Barrett

Although an inspection of popular reading readiness tests will reveal that differences exist from test to test, there is also a high degree of similarity among them. All, for example, include a subtest involving letter recognition that requires the child to mark the letter named by the teacher from among several alternatives. We can gain a better understanding of readiness tests in general by looking at one more closely.

The *Clymer-Barrett Prereading Battery* is published by the Institute for Reading Research, Inc., Santa Barbara, California. It consists of six subtests and a Prereading Rating Scale, which is a checklist for the classroom teacher. The manual accompanying the test suggests that the results obtained can be used for two purposes:

> The results give a diagnostic picture of the skills needed by individual pupils. Also, along with other data, the results may be used for screening and grouping (Test Manual, p. 2).

The *Clymer-Barrett Prereading Battery* consists of six subtests as follows: Test 1: Recognition of Letters—the child selects, from among five alternative letters, a letter named by the teacher (thirty-five items). Test 2: Matching Words—the child matches a stimulus word with one of four alternative choices (twenty items). Test 3: Beginning Sounds—the child selects the picture from among three alternatives that begins with the same sound as a stimulus picture, as the teacher pronounces each name (twenty items). Test 4: Ending Sounds—this is the same as Test 3 except the ends of words are noted (twenty items). Test 5: Completion Shapes—the child finishes an incomplete drawing by copying a complete drawing of the same item (twenty items). Test 6: Copy A Sentence—the child copies a seven-word sentence.

The Readiness Survey asks for teacher judgment in eight areas: (1) facility in oral language, (2) concept and vocabulary development, (3) listening, (4) thinking abilities, (5) social skills, (6) emotional development, (7) attitude toward learning, and (8) work habits.

The entire battery can be administered in a total of ninety minutes and yields "diagnostic subscores" in these areas: visual discrimination (Test 1 and Test 2), auditory discrimination (Test 3 and Test 4), and visual motor coordination (Test 5 and Test 6). A total of ninety-five samples of behavior is obtained (not including the copying tests). The manual provides norms so that performance can be converted to percentile ranks and stanines (common standard scores that represent how well a child did in comparison to a reference group). With several important qualifications, including those we have made here regarding the use of such tests, the manual then recommends that the results be used to rank children for purposes of organizing instructional groups.

Informal Assessment of Readiness

The teacher's view of reading and readiness can easily be reflected in assessment procedures or devices or both that the teacher makes or selects. To use an earlier example, a questionnaire can be developed or found that gathers information on the child's previous experiences. (Has the child been to a public library, a circus, a rodeo, a train depot, an airplane terminal, a swimming pool, and a shopping center?) If the teacher considers independence and self-reliance to be basic compo-

FIGURE 5.1 Reading Readiness Checklist.

Always
Sometimes
Never

Cognitive Development

1. Does the child understand basic concepts of size (big-little), direction (up-down), and sequence (first-last)?
2. Does the child understand simple classification?
3. Can the child complete simple analogies involving opposites (e.g., hot: cold:; big: _____)?
4. Can the child make reasonable predictions for how a story might end?

Experiential Background

5. Has the child traveled out of state?
6. Has the child been to a zoo?
7. Has the child been to a library?
8. Does the child play regularly with other children?
9. Does the child have a hobby or special interest?

Language Development

10. Does the child have labels for concepts related to his or her environment (e.g., objects, actions, and places)?
11. Can the child tell a story or describe a personal experience accurately?
12. Does the child articulate clearly?
13. Does the child recognize that words often have multiple meanings?
14. Does the child understand common figures of speech?
15. Does the child recognize the connection between an anaphoric term and its antecedent (e.g., John is tall. *He* is also fat.)?

Emotional Development

16. Does the child seem happy in school and well adjusted?
17. Can the child accept a setback?
18. Does the child begin and finish a task without constant supervision?
19. Does the child adjust well to new tasks or changes in daily routine?
20. Does the child have a positive self-concept?

Social Development

21. Does the child take turns with others?
22. Does the child share when appropriate?
23. Does the child listen without interrupting others?
24. Can the child submerge himself in a group activity?

Physical Development

25. Does the child show evidence of visual problems?
26. Does the child show evidence of auditory problems?
27. Can the child sit quietly for a reasonable length of time when appropriate?
28. Can the child do simple exercises and related motor tasks (e.g., jumping jacks, skipping, and bouncing a ball)?
29. Does the child seem alert and well nourished?

FIGURE 5.1 (*continued*)

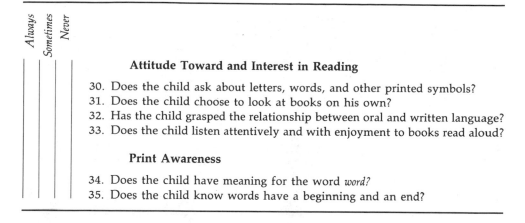

Always *Sometimes* *Never*

Attitude Toward and Interest in Reading

30. Does the child ask about letters, words, and other printed symbols?
31. Does the child choose to look at books on his own?
32. Has the child grasped the relationship between oral and written language?
33. Does the child listen attentively and with enjoyment to books read aloud?

Print Awareness

34. Does the child have meaning for the word *word?*
35. Does the child know words have a beginning and an end?

nents of readiness to read, a checklist can be developed that helps in cataloging relevant behaviors. (Does the child carry tasks through to completion, work well alone, try to solve problems before seeking the teacher's help, and so forth.) If the teacher believes visual discrimination is important, daily performance on paper-and-pencil tasks can be examined. (Does the child complete work sheets correctly that require matching identical letters or choosing the dissimilar letter from a series?) In such examples, the teacher has judged that these are important indicators of readiness as he or she perceives it and intends to teach it.

We feel much more positive about the use of teacher observation and trial teaching as ways of assessing readiness than we do about the use of readiness tests. The teacher who knows what to look for and how to interpret observed behavior has a constant source of useful information over an extended period of time. Because many factors compete for the teacher's attention, it is imperative that observation be systematized and recorded for thoughtful reflection. We believe a teacher-made checklist is an excellent way to achieve these ends. We have prepared a sample checklist to help you visualize what one looks like (*see* Fig. 5.1). This checklist reflects our view of reading and how we would approach beginning instruction. It would not fit all teachers or classrooms, nor is it as complete as one made for a particular group of children.

Trial teaching, another form of teacher observation, is nothing more than instruction that is provided in the interest of seeing how children respond. Tasks that are done easily and well signal that instruction can move forward. When children experience difficulty, the teacher recognizes that the task must be restructured, often with more concern for building prerequisite skills and/or understandings.

Several of the areas identified in this chapter as important to readiness are extremely broad and complex. As a consequence it is not practical to speak in terms of making specific assessments for the purpose of diagnosing needs in the areas of cognitive development, experiential background, language development, and emotional and social development. Teachers will need to be sensitive to how children are developing in these areas, of course, and provide learning activities as appropriate. Observation on a daily basis can be a valuable source of information for assessment in this regard. (In Chapter 9 on reading comprehension, specific suggestions for assessing needs in several of the above areas are provided, e.g., language and background experience). These suggestions can be adapted to readiness assessment if the activities are undertaken orally, thus eliminating the need for the child to read as in the case of a questionnaire or cloze procedure.

Here we provide specific procedures that are suitable for assessing visual and auditory discrimination—both skill areas generally regarded as unique to readiness.

Assessment of Readiness

1. Examine several reading readiness tests. Compare the subtests included in the tests to the *Clymer-Barrett Prereading Battery.* What differences and similarities do you find? Decide whether the abilities measured are basic to reading readiness as you view it.
2. Administer a readiness test to a child. Score the test and consult the test manual for information on interpreting the results. Discuss the errors made with the child to learn why he responded as he did.
3. Observe a kindergarten or first-grade classroom. Using the checklist on pages 140–141 or one you prepare yourself, identify children who seem to be ready for book reading.

Developing Readiness for Reading

The fact that some children come to school ready to read or already reading might cause us to wish that this were true of all children. The wish itself is understandable, if forlorn. What must be avoided is the trap of believing that children arriving at school who are not "ready" to read have somehow subverted the schooling process or that the homes these children come from have supplied us with inferior prospects. The obvious danger in assuming this attitude is that we excuse ourselves from helping such children because they have not gotten an adequate start. Regardless of the difficulties unready children represent for the teacher, they have a right to expect help and ultimately to succeed in learning to read. The challenge is formidable and the path to success varied, but the responsibility clear: All children must be helped at whatever level we find them.

Research evidence and expert opinion alike emphasize the importance of an effective readiness program. Studies by Bradley (1956), Blakely & Shadle (1961), and Powell & Parsley (1961), have demonstrated that delay of reading instruction in favor of a readiness program for children who demonstrate a lack of readiness is usually productive. Typically children who are given readiness training reach and even surpass in reading achievement children who begin book reading immediately on starting school. This general finding does not mean, of course, that all children profit equally from readiness instruction or that a uniform readiness program is appropriate for all. In this section we will explore the nature of readiness training and how adjustments can be made to accommodate differences among individuals.

A Classroom Scene

Jan Sante teaches first grade in a rural coal-mining community in the Appalachian Mountains. She plans and creates a variety of learning activities, ranging from sharing time to field trips that contribute directly and indirectly to the development of her students' readiness for reading. Some activities focus specifically on an ability Jan wants to develop; others are more general in nature and offer the opportunity to develop a number of abilities in an integrated fashion. The overall

A good kindergarten or first grade program include the kinds of experiences many children have at home such as listening to an adult read aloud.

goal of Jan's program is to encourage the growth of language and thinking abilities through exploration of topics and ideas.

On a typical day Jan begins class by involving the children in attendance taking; collecting milk and lunch money; and writing a summary of the day, date, month, and year; and a description of the weather on the chalkboard. Early in the school year each child begins the school day by claiming a name tag from a table so that Jan can determine who is absent. Besides providing practice in name identification, this activity gives Jan the opportunity to call the children's attention to similarities and differences among names, identify other words that begin with the same letter (or sound), and build the self-confidence of each child. Later in the school year the attendance-taking responsibility is delegated to a pair of children who gain practice in recognizing the names of their classmates by passing out the name tags and noting who is absent.

The milk and lunch money collection gives the children practice in counting, classifying (coins), one-to-one correspondence, and related number concepts. By involving children as helpers in such routine tasks, Jan promotes concepts of sharing, taking turns, self-reliance, carrying a task through to completion, cooperating, and being a member of a group.

The dictation and transcription of a daily summary and description of the weather on the chalkboard demonstrate the relationship of oral and written language; reinforce sound-symbol correspondence; illustrate left-to-right directionality; and introduce capitalization, punctuation, and other conventions of written communication. Many opportunities for social and emotional development are also provided by the story dictation. Again, taking turns, being a member of a group, and the like are practiced. Additionally, cognitive processes are encouraged through attention to the weather. The children might say, for example, "Today the sky is cloudy. It is colder than it was yesterday. We think it might snow soon. Wear a warm coat and keep it buttoned up if you play outside tonight." Here children are gathering observations, classifying, making comparisons, predicting, and so forth.

Jan usually follows these opening exercises with a brief sharing time. Children are encouraged to share their observations, special events, news, and ideas, as opposed to new or treasured possessions (although this, too, is permitted). As teacher, Jan herself also makes a point of sharing something unusual or interesting with the class each day. This might be a new book received in the library (that Jan will read aloud to the group either now or later) or an interesting item from the newspaper. A stuffed owl once led the group to seek information on birds of prey. This culminated in the construction of papier-mâché models of various hawks, owls, and eagles. Through skillful questioning and discussion techniques, Jan uses sharing time to stretch children's concepts, make new connections, see relationships, and broaden interests. New vocabulary is introduced when appropriate and words of interest written on the chalkboard at the suggestion of the class. Later these words are copied on index cards and filed alphabetically in a class recipe-box "dictionary." The meanings of entries are

Basic Components of the Reading Process

illustrated with pictures that class members can use in looking up words.

Jan recognizes that variety is important in the activities provided for her students. Most activities are planned so that children can participate at various levels of complexity depending on their stage of development. Letter-recognition activities, for example, allow some children to handle plastic letters, fit them into a frame according to correct sequence, group pictures together that begin with a particular letter, match capital and lowercase letters, and perform similar introductory activities. Other, more advanced children work with letters at the same time, but at a higher level of understanding. This might include the creation of a poster for a letter of the alphabet—all items shown on the poster beginning with the letter w—or writing the alphabet from memory.

No matter how busy the schedule, Jan makes a point of sharing at least one book orally with her students each day. By noting the children's reactions to an author's work and from past experience with books and children, Jan selects literature she thinks the children will enjoy. A second criterion used in selecting books to be shared concerns the quality of the language used. Jan seeks books with natural language that communicates effectively. On occasion she repeats a part of a selection and invites the children to study the way an author has selected words and combined them to express a thought. She also encourages creative, divergent thought by pausing at appropriate points and asking for predictions. Characters and story line are analyzed with an emphasis on seeing how a book compares with a book read previously or with real life. Sometimes a book is used as a springboard to art or drama activities. With the help of a scribe, children "write" their own sequel or alternate ending to a story. Some of these are typed and shared with the group by the teacher, an aide, or the proud child who created the new story.

Jan recognizes that short field trips provide numerous opportunities to stimulate cognitive and language growth. Following good teaching principles, she discusses the trip ahead of time with the children to arouse curiosity, guide observations, establish general purposes, and heighten anticipation. In some instances, she has children predict what they might see on their trip as a way of activating thought and focusing attention. During the field trip, whether it be a hike through a nearby meadow or a visit by bus to a museum, Jan asks questions, points out interesting features, reminds the children of their predictions, and supplies useful information. After such a trip she involves the class in discussion that clarifies relationships, reveals misunderstandings, and generally helps the children analyze and evaluate their experience. Jan also leads the class to dictate experience charts describing their trip. Later these charts are used for reading activities such as word identification, letter recognition, and phonics instruction. New or unusual vocabulary terms or both learned in connection with a field trip are reviewed and incorporated into ongoing instructional activities such as work sheets, games, and experience stories.

Jan also uses an excellent activity for involving children in classification. It requires that the teacher gather together an array of objects that can be grouped in several ways. Buttons, for example, or screws and nails of various sizes, shapes, and colors can be used. Individuals or small groups of children can be instructed to organize the items into a scheme they create or a scheme the teacher specifies (for example, nails grouped by length (*see* Fig. 5.2). Because the children have experience at forming groups according to more obvious attributes, they can attempt to show differences of a more subtle or abstract nature (nails grouped by shape).

In another useful variation, the teacher gathers objects that are quite dissimilar in nature and asks children to group them into a limited number of particular categories (no more than five or six, for example). Thus, a pocket comb, piece of chalk, ruler, pencil, shoe, piece of paper, bookend, ashtray, pocketknife, thumbtack, soft ball, eyeglasses, tape cassette, and the like are grouped first by size, then by texture, by weight, by normal place of storage, by place where used, and so forth. The fact that objects can be grouped in various ways depending on the scheme used is an important insight for young children to develop. Classification schemes involving *several* dimensions at once are sometimes described by Jan to challenge more advanced thinkers, but she recognizes that most six-year-olds do not understand this complexity (nails grouped by size *and* shape or buttons grouped by color *and* size, for example).

Pictures of objects cut from magazines are used by Jan for classification activities, as are letters of the alphabet (classify by shape, height, sound, and so on), winter coats and boots (classify by style, size, length, and so on), kitchen utensils, and teacher's jewelry. Jan recognizes the importance of *discussion* of the categories created and the rationale underlying each decision to assign an item to a category. She helps children clarify their thinking and introduces alternative strategies as a way of stimulating growth. Classification activities are often extended to areas such as sounds, events, places, and occupations.

Jan sometimes explores concepts well known to the children to sensitize them to the classification process they have already engaged in while learning to deal with their world. Animals and vehicles are

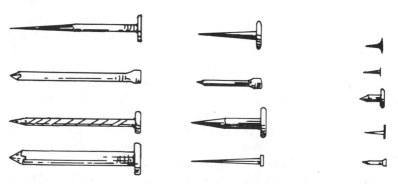

FIGURE 5.2 Nails Grouped by Length.

two categories most children have evolved, for example. What refinement of the category animal have they managed? Are all dogs merely dogs, or have they created subcategories? What do all dogs have in common? Vehicles are analyzed in a similar fashion. Depending on their background, children may have evolved complex systems of classification for trees, cows, trucks, city workers, or snowmobiles. Jan believes exploration of what they know already gives the children a sense of pride and accomplishment, in addition to helping them realize how the classification process works.

Dice Roll

Use a large pair of dice, or make a cube from a sheet of construction paper as follows:

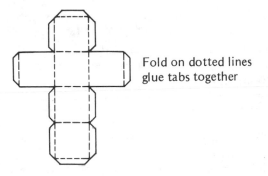

Fold on dotted lines
glue tabs together

Write letters of the alphabet, or draw geometric shapes on each face of the dice. Put the same items on the second dice.

In the game the child rolls the dice, names what comes up, and tells whether the items showing on each dice are the same letter (or shape) or different. A point system can be added, if desired, so that each player tries to earn a set number of points. The game can be varied so that a player must give a word that begins with the letters that come up. For more advanced children, words can be written on the dice; the task is to match words or even pronounce them aloud.

Jan recognizes that many of the concepts and abilities basic to readiness for reading require regular practice spaced over a period of weeks and even months. One approach she has found worthwhile is the use of games. Ideas for some of the games she uses were taken or adapted from resources such as E. Spache (1976), Russell (1951), Platts (1960), and Cooper et al. (1972). Several of Jan's games are described here.

Penny Toss

Make a large game board with letters, geometric shapes, or colors occupying sections of the board as follows:

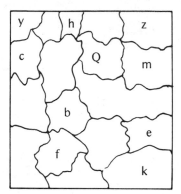

Place the game board on the floor. Players stand several feet away from the board. Each player tosses a penny (or other marker) on the board surface. The task requires the player to identify the letter (or shape, or color) of the section the penny lands on. Points are earned for each correct response. Extra points can be awarded for saying words that begin with the letter (optional).

Group Storytelling

Participants sit in a circle. The first person starts a story with a statement such as, "I remember the time I was almost scared to death." The person to the left adds a sentence to the story and so on around the circle until each child has contributed. The process is then repeated with another child starting the story. The teacher can furnish story starters, or they can be created by the participants spontaneously.

Word Pairs

A stack of picture cards is created using common objects such as a cat, a dog, a bicycle and so forth. The cards are shuffled and placed face down. In turn, each player draws a card, tells what the picture is, gives another example from the same group (category), and explains the relationship. For example, if a picture of a cat is drawn, the child might say, "This is a cat. A *lion* is another kind of cat."

Classroom Activity

Collect a variety of discarded magazines and catalogs. Let children each select two or three that have special personal appeal. Instruct children to page through the material for the purpose of cutting out pictures of scenes or objects they would

Basic Components of the Reading Process

like to read aloud. Have children paste the pictures they choose on a large piece of butcher paper or tagboard.

At this point a number of alternatives exist. Beginning readers can be helped to label the pictures they select. At various odd moments during the next few days children can then be asked to tell why they selected their pictures and can read the printed labels.

Primary-level readers can be helped to find books or stories related to the pictures they selected. When the children have finished each book or story, they can write the author and title, along with several words they found interesting or challenging, beneath the appropriate picture. Again, odd moments of the school day can be used to have children share their posters with others, giving brief comments about the book or story. Special attention can be given to the words selected.

This activity is designed for beginning readers and for those who are reading at the primary level. Children can work alone on this task or in small groups. In either case, sharing as described earlier benefits all children in the class.

Ms. Sante also makes use of several commercially prepared reading readiness programs though she is careful to adapt the materials to her curriculum rather than merely following the teacher's guide blindly. Her pupils respond enthusiastically to *Alpha Time* (1970), a program designed to teach letter names and basic phonic principles using games, songs, riddles, and colorful inflatable dolls for each letter of the alphabet. Jan also uses the Encyclopaedia Britannica Press program called *Language Experience in Reading, Level 1* (1970) as a way of structuring language development and story dictation activities. The *Peabody Language Development Kit, Level 1* (1965), is also used to stimulate language production and cognitive development. A multimedia program called the *Goldman-Lynch Sounds and Symbols Development Kit* (1971), involving the use of hand puppets, audio cassettes, and various visual stimuli published by the American Guidance Service is also available in Jan's school. In many cases Jan can and does make her own teaching materials, but she finds that commercial materials enable her to expand and enrich her instructional program and save her time and energy. Using the principles discussed in Chapter 12 of this book, she carefully evaluates the programs available against her notions of what her children need, before buying or using commercially made instructional materials. Through selective use of the suggested activities, Jan creates a well-rounded readiness program that can be adjusted to the individual needs and strengths of her pupils.

Summary

Readiness is an important factor in any learning situation. Unless the learner is ready to make sense of a new skill, concept, or piece of information, it is not meaningful and consequently not understood.

Readiness is the result of interaction with the environment and maturation and must be considered in terms of what is to be learned and how it will be taught or presented. Readiness to read is usually expected to occur when a child enters school. Factors discussed in this chapter that are basic to readiness for reading include background experience, cognition, language, auditory and visual acuity and discrimination, perception, physical development, emotional and social development, and positive attitudes toward and interest in reading.

In schools, readiness is often assessed by means of standardized tests. Informal procedures are also appropriate including teacher observation guided by a checklist. The readiness program of one classroom teacher was discussed in detail to illustrate various activities that promote readiness for reading.

Terms for Self-study

acuity	perception
discrimination	correlation
schemata	readiness checklist
binocular vision	visual screening
auditory screening	

Discussion Questions

1. Why is it not possible to say that a child is ready or not ready to read unless something is known about how instruction will proceed?
2. Why is the child's home environment considered to be an important factor in getting her ready to read?
3. Why is it not satisfactory simply to wait for normal maturation to get a child ready to read?

Recommended Readings

Butler, Dorothy, & Clay, Marie. (1979). *Reading begins at home: Preparing children for reading before they go to school.* Auckland: Heinemann Educational Books. This volume is written for parents who are interested in preparing their preschoolers to succeed in beginning reading instruction. It describes specific learning activities that can be undertaken one-to-one at home.

Clay, Marie M. (1972). *Reading: The patterning of complex behaviour.* London: Heinemann Educational Books. This book describes an approach to beginning reading instruction in which particular emphasis is given to the visual aspects of reading and preventing failure by attending to the errors that children make. It takes the point of view that children learn how to teach themselves to read during the first two years of instruction.

Durkin, Dolores. (1982). *Getting reading started.* Boston: Allyn and Bacon. A reading methods textbook, this volume is focused especially on the preschool, kindergarten, and first- grade years. It demonstrates that readiness for reading instruction is dependent on what is to be taught and how it is to be taught.

Basic Components of the Reading Process

Mason Jana M. (1984). Early reading from a developmental perspective. In P. David Pearson et al. (Eds.), *Handbook of reading research.* New York: Longman.

This book reviews and summarizes research studies that have examined how children first learn to read, including those who learn early (before entering school).

McDonnell, Gloria M., & Osburn, Bess E. (1978, January). New thoughts about reading readiness. *Language Arts,* LV, 26–29.

Here is a useful readiness checklist based on Marie Clay's research on the stages of readiness. It stresses the importance of the child's interacting with books and print at the readiness stage.

Ollila, Lloyd O. (1977). *The kindergarten child and reading.* Newark, D E: International Reading Association.

This book presents a general structure and specific suggestions for helping young children experience a successful start with beginning reading.

6

Word Recognition
for Beginning Readers

Suppose your instructor printed the following symbols on the chalk-board:

ΔΗΚΩΔΙΝΓ ΘΙΣ ΜΕΣΕΓ ΙΖ ΛΙΗΚ ΛΕΡΝΙΝΓ ΤΥ ΡΗΔ.
ΡΙΗΤΙΝΓ ΙΖ Α ΚΩΔ ΦΩΡ ΣΠΗΧ.

Then suppose the instructor said, "What I have written on the board is a message in English, but I have used Greek letters instead of the Roman alphabet to write it. How would you go about knowing what the message says?" Can you decode it?

Write your answer here:

What skills must one have in order to decipher this message? A beginning reader is in a similar situation. Things an adult reader takes for granted must be explained to the beginner:

The conglomeration of symbols stands for a message.
There are ways of identifying the beginning and the end of individual utterances (punctuation and capitalization).
There is a relationship between the sounds and the symbols of
speech.
The reader must know which sound or sounds each symbol represents.

The pattern or arrangement of the symbols gives some hints as to how they will be pronounced. Those generalizations that can be drawn from the most frequently used patterns of consonants and vowels will be discussed later in this chapter.

The decoding process is not simple. It requires much background knowledge in addition to the ability to translate individual visual symbols into speech sounds.

Now decipher the coded message using the symbols that follow. Each Greek letter is matched to the corresponding letter of the English alphabet.

| Alphabet Symbols | A B G D Ĕ Ē TH I K L M N |
| Code Symbols | A B Γ Δ E H Θ I K Λ M N |

| Alphabet Symbols | O P R S T U PH CH PS O Z |
| Code Symbols | O Π P Σ T Y Φ X Ψ Ω Z |

As you can see, the code is not too different from the regular English alphabet, but the original message looked quite confusing. Can you decode the message?[1] Do you agree with it?

This chapter will help you answer the following questions:

- *What skills does a beginning reader use in making sense of new words?*
- *What role does context play in word-recognition techniques?*
- *How does one teach sound-symbol relationships analytically?*
- *How does one teach sound-symbol relationships synthetically?*
- *What role does word meaning play in decoding?*

Building on Language Skills

Reading is the process of learning to understand the meaning of printed symbols. A number of researchers (Bransford & Johnson, 1973; K. Goodman, 1970; Rumelhart, 1977; F. Smith, 1977) have shown that many different language "cues" can be used in this process. Three of these are of particular importance to the skilled reader:

1. *Graphophonemic cues* are provided by the relationships between symbols and sounds. Knowledge of letters (*grapho*) and the sounds they represent (*-phonemic*) enables the reader to decode the letters into sounds and words. (More information on *graphemes* and *phonemes* will be given later in this chapter.)
2. *Syntactic* cues are suggested by the patterns into which words are arranged to form phrases, clauses, and sentences. Knowledge of syntax (word order within sentences) and of grammar (word functions and relationships) enables the good reader to know that a noun will probably follow the word *the* in a sentence, for example. This knowledge allows a reader to predict what an unknown word might be when it is first encountered.

[1] "Reading this message is like learning to read. Writing is a code for speech."

3. *Semantic* cues are given by the *meaning* of each word. Knowledge of how meaning is expressed through language enables a reader to know, for example, that *night* is probably the missing word in this sentence: He worked hard all day and slept all

_____ .

Anyone who uses a language (in speaking or listening) has already developed skills in using the syntactic and semantic cues; these are about the same in written and spoken language. Beginning readers can recognize many syntactic and semantic cues, and they can build on this ability whenever they examine a word in its grammatical or syntactic context. Some young children work diligently to use memory and pictures to pretend that they are reading stories that have been read aloud to them. Some clinicians have found it necessary to get these children to focus on individual words in order to bring them to real reading behavior (Ganschow, Weber, & Suelter, 1984).

The example given at the beginning of this chapter demonstrates that it is not enough simply to rely on context in order to decode a message, particularly with beginning readers. Although you, the adult reader, have a wealth of knowledge about the syntax and meaning of language, you still could not read the message until you had first deciphered the code and then decoded the message. Skill in decoding, then, is necessary for a child to be able to make sense of print. That is why most beginning-reading programs and most basal readers place heavy emphasis on this area. Children need some decoding skill before they can begin to apply their knowledge of syntax and meaning to print and, therefore, before they can understand a printed message.[2]

Although the word *decoding* has been used here, it is not meant to focus the attention of the beginning reader on a narrow type of activity such as sounding out one letter at a time. That is not what is meant at all. The beginning reader needs to understand that English spelling makes use of an alphabetic code: a system of letters that approximate the sounds used in speech. But the reader also needs to know that the English alphabet is often used in various arrangements to represent the spoken word. For that reason, early instruction in deciphering the printed page includes various word-recognition skills such as language cues, direct visual memory, the decoding of sound-symbol patterns, and some unique ways that individuals use to identify and remember certain printed words. In a sense, those skills are all part of the decoding game a beginning reader plays when presented with a new page of text.

Underlying the beginning reader's attempt to transform the printed page into speech sounds and into coherent messages are all the activities and learning discussed in the preceding chapter on reading readiness. The reader's ear, eye, and mind are discriminating, categorizing, and constructing as they attempt to put together a message that makes sense. Therefore, word recognition for the beginning reader entails a

[2] Some researchers (LaBerge & Samuels, 1974) suggest that a reader needs to be able to decode words automatically (without thinking) before he or she can attend to other language cues and to meaning.

combination of decoding, language-processing, perceptual, and cognitive skills that enable the reader to decipher and pronounce for a basic understanding of the words seen on the page. Chall (1983) refers to this stage of the child's development as "becoming glued to the print." In this stage, the child becomes fascinated with the printed word as a kind of passageway that opens up books as a means of discovery. In terms of the Harris-Smith model (Figure 2.3 earlier), word-recognition skills fall into the decoding and perceptual-image categories. Looking again at the model, one can see that a major interference in decoding and perception would prevent concepts from being triggered and thus prevent the author's message from being identified or retrieved. Facility in these skills, therefore, stands as a crucial starting point for the entire reading process. That accounts for the great stress on word-recognition techniques shown in primary-grade books even though these techniques are only means to an end. They help the reader understand the message.

Decoding and Phonics

A child who has read a mystery story or deciphered a coded message on the back of a cereal box knows that decoding means translating visual symbols into ideas, usually into word sounds that represent ideas. Beginning reading instruction helps students see the regularity of the alphabet code and thus helps them approach and decode new words independently.

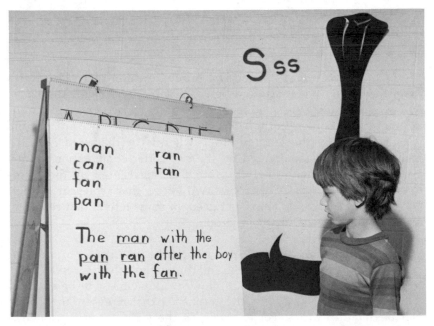

Children learn sound-spelling patterns by noting similarities and differences in words as in this simple story.

One type of word-recognition activity is called *phonics*. Although the term is based on the Greek root *phon*, meaning "sound" or "speech," it is important to stress that, in actual practice, *phonics* refers specifically to the *relationship* between word sounds (phonemes) and the written symbols (graphemes) that represent those sounds. For the teacher of reading, *phonics* means the systematic, organized presentation of the sound-symbol patterns that make up the English language. "The purpose of phonics instruction is to provide the reader with the ability to associate printed letters with the speech sounds that these letters represent" according to Heilman (1981, p. 14).

Terms Relating to Decoding and Phonics

Before discussing phonics instruction in more detail, we must define a number of terms that are important to the subject. Some of these should be familiar but may need review, whereas others will probably be new to you.

Phoneme. The term *phoneme* has been mentioned before but requires elaboration here. A *phoneme* is a single speech sound, the smallest unit that can be used to distinguish one word from another. In the words *bog* and *fog*, for example, the letters *b* and *f* represent two distinct sounds; the phonemes /b/ and /f/ constitute the only difference in the pronunciation of the two words. (Phonemes are enclosed by slanted lines, as explained later in the section on phoneme-grapheme correspondences.)

There are approximately forty-four or forty-five phonemes in the English language. Because there are only twenty-six letters, it is obvious that a number of phonemes comprise two or more letters. For example, phonemes are represented by the letters *sh* in *shall*, *tch* in *watch*, and *ough* in *through*.

Grapheme. A grapheme is a printed symbol that represents a phoneme. Many phonemes can be represented by single letters (*b*, *d*, *t*), but other phonemes require combinations of two or more letters, as pointed out earlier. In the word *kind*, for example, the initial sound is represented by the letter *k* alone whereas in the word *block* the final /k/ sound is represented by the two-letter combination *ck*, and in the word *unique* the final /k/ sound is represented by the three-letter combination *que*. Clusters of two letters that represent a single phoneme are called "digraphs"; clusters of three letters that represent a single phoneme are called "trigraphs."

Phoneme-Grapheme Correspondences. In order to show the relationship between word sounds and the symbols that represent them, the following procedure will be followed: Phonemes will be enclosed within slanted lines (/ /), and the graphemes that represent that sound will be given in italics. For example, in the word *car*, the phoneme-grapheme correspondence for the initial sound would be given as

/k/*c*, meaning the sound /k/ written as the letter *c*. In the word *rock*, the correspondence would be shown as /k/*ck*, meaning the same /k/ sound is here indicated by the digraph *ck*. As a rule, the examples will show the phoneme followed by the grapheme, but it is equally possible to show the grapheme first, followed by its corresponding sound (for example, *g*/j/ means the letter *g* pronounced as /j/ in the word *gem*).

The wide variety of graphemes that can represent the same phoneme is illustrated by the sound /f/, as shown in the following examples: /f/*f* (*fish*); /f/*ff* (*off*); /f/*gh* (*laugh*); /f/*ph* (*phone*); /f/*lf* (*half*). Some phonemes, such as /j/, /k/, and /s/, can be represented by an even greater variety of graphemes.

Vowels. The letters *a, e, i, o,* and *u* represent vowel sounds in the English language. In addition to these, the letters *w* and *y* can represent vowel sounds when they appear at the end of a word or syllable (*blew, flow-ing, fry, dy-nam-ic*).

Vowels are considered to be *long* when they are pronounced as they appear in the alphabet. The long sound of the vowel can be indicated by the *macron*, a dash placed over the letter (*āpe, ēven, īce, ōver, ūse*). The term *glided sound* is also used to refer to the pronunciation of long vowels. *Short* (unglided) vowels are sometimes indicated by the *breve*, a curved line placed over the letter (*ăt, ĕgg, ĭt, ŏperate,* and *ŭp*).

Vowel digraphs are formed by two adjacent vowels that represent a single phoneme. In some cases, the vowels in the pair may be the same (*oo* in *foot, ee* in *meet*), but in other cases two different vowels form a phoneme (*ea* in *bean, ai* in *maid*).

Diphthongs are formed by pairs of vowels that are so closely blended in speech as to form a single unit. Unlike the vowel digraph, the diphthong retains some of the sound of each individual vowel, but, when spoken, the vowels create a sound that is not exactly the same as that of the separate components. Examples: *ou* in *out* and *oi* in *boil*.

Consonants. The remaining twenty-one letters (other than the five basic vowels) are called *consonants*. These letters act as interrupters and modifiers of the vowel sounds. The letters *w* and *y*, mentioned earlier as vowels in certain situations, can function as consonants when they appear in the initial position in a word or syllable (*water, yellow*).

Consonant blends are clusters of two or more consonants that retain some of the characteristics of their individual sounds while joining to form still another sound that results from their pronunciation as a unit. The letters *bl* and *nd* in the word *blend* are examples of this, as are the letters *str* in *strike*.

Consonant digraphs are formed by pairs of consonants that form a completely new sound and do not retain distinct characteristics of their individual sounds. Examples are represented by the letters *ch* in *chop* and *sh* in *show*.

Phonics and Basal Readers

Accompanying most basal reader textbooks are practice materials, often in the form of workbooks. These workbooks usually present a wide variety of exercises in word recognition and comprehension. Some of the pages may carry a "phonics" or "decoding" label, especially in grades one and two. They are designed to help the beginning reader learn how to figure out and remember the sound-symbol patterns seen in words. A teacher must be aware, however, that the terms *decoding* and *phonics* are sometimes used to mean different things. In the six or seven basal reading series that are used most frequently, the term *phonics* is used as defined earlier: a program of instruction for helping children identify and pronounce the sound-symbol patterns as they are seen in complete words. But there are also basal programs and workbooks that isolate the letters of the alphabet, assign sounds to them, and ask children to identify and pronounce these sounds individually rather than within a word. In this book, the term *phonics* will be used to represent instruction that relates sound-symbol patterns in complete words. Where necessary, the concept of *isolated letter-sound learning* will be described separately.

The word *decoding* will be used to encompass more than phonics. The authors' definition of decoding includes grasping sound-symbol relationships and also using other print and language cues that relate the printed page to spoken language. Inflection, dialect pronunciations, and pauses cannot be fully represented in print although punctuation helps the reader to grasp the meaning of the printed message. Professionals in the field of reading have not yet adopted a universally accepted definition for the term *decoding,* so we will use the term broadly here to mean deciphering a printed utterance through a combination of phonics and language cues.

This chapter deals with those word-recognition skills that are usually developed first in order to help a child begin reading. They include letter-sound relations as they appear at the beginning and end of a word; certain major spelling patterns (phonics generalizations); writing

---

Speech Written Down

Some beginners read in a singsong fashion or in a monotone. Most teachers have had students who would read the sentence "LOOK OUT! Jack yelled" with no expression. Such students may not understand that printed language often represents spoken language, or they may not relate the meaning of the word *yelled* to the rest of the sentence. By reading a passage silently before reading it aloud, students can gain some idea of the underlying meaning (semantics). The teacher might also read the passage aloud while the students follow the printed words so that they can get a sense of how written dialogue becomes real speech. Reading plays aloud and using the teacher as a role model for expressive reading are also helpful.

Basic Components of the Reading Process

conventions such as periods, commas, and capital letters; and the use of context or sentence meaning.

Written symbols do not communicate as fully as oral language does. Gestures, inflections of the voice, and volume are three components of oral language that are not easily represented in written language. The wise teacher will constantly encourage learners to use *all* the language-processing cues (sound-symbol relationships, syntax, and semantics) to understand meaning and to discover various relationships between printed and spoken language. Children should be encouraged to interpret the action and emotion suggested by words that they read.

Analytic and Synthetic Phonics

At one time the debate about the best approach to use with beginning readers focused on whether to place all the emphasis on having children recognize words as complete entities (*sight words*) or to stress the sound of individual letters considered without reference to context (the *letter-to-sound* approach). The issue today is quite different. Most theoreticians now acknowledge the need for a variety of approaches to word skills. What they now debate is whether phonics instruction should unfold through a gradual, analytical (*inductive*) process based on a comparison of words the student already knows or should be intensive and synthetic (*deductive*) based on a given generalization with examples provided by the teacher. (An *inductive* process is one in which observation of several specific instances leads to a broad conclusion; a *deductive* process is one in which a general hypothesis is used as the point of departure, and conclusions about specific instances are based upon this initial generalization.)

In the gradual, analytic approach, the students first learn words by visual memory and context. When they know several words that begin the same way—*boy, bat, bird,* for example—students can be asked to describe the way in which these words are similar. That question leads to the generalization that words that are spoken with a beginning /b/ sound are spelled with *b* as their first letter. As other comparisons become possible, they are approached in the same way. Over the course of several years, students will have analyzed a large number of sound-symbol patterns and will have learned a phonics system (*see* Fig. 6.1).

In the intensive, synthetic approach, a predetermined set of phonics generalizations is selected, and matching words are built into the instructional program (the skills program). This means that the phonics program is not wholly dependent upon the words that may appear in a given story; instead, it introduces specific words for the purpose of illustrating the generalization. Thus, in order to teach the sound of /b/ in the first lesson, it is possible to use many other words (*bed, bit, big,* and so on) even if only one word in the first story began with the letter *b*.

As is often the case with issues involving different methods of instruction, a worthwhile solution is to merge the procedures instead of adhering rigidly to a single one. As any experienced teacher can testify, many methods must be used in order to assure the success

FIGURE 6.1 Sample Analytic Approach to Introducing New Words (Smith & Arnold, 1983).

The following exercise is designed to help children learn new words (given in boldface) that they will encounter in a story about a boy who is disgusted with his new baby sister because she can't *do* anything. The words and sentences to be used in this exercise should be written on cards before beginning work. This example is from a first-grade basal reader.

baby Display word cards for the new word *baby* and the known word *bed*. Elicit from the children that both words begin with the same initial consonant sound and letter, /b/b. Have the children read the sentence "You gave the baby a ride" while a volunteer frames the word *baby* by placing his or her hands on either side of the word so the class can focus on it.

isn't Display the word card for the new word *isn't* as you read it. Elicit that the new word is a short way of saying "is not." Have the children read the sentence "Baby isn't as big as you are" and frame the word *isn't* so the class can focus on it. Ask the children for additional sentences using the word *isn't*.

anything Display the word card for the new word *anything*. On the chalkboard, write the two words *any* and *thing* that make up the new word. Help the children recall the known word *thing*. Read the sentence "I can't have anything" and run your hand under the word *anything* as you read it. Ask for additional sentences from the children using the word *anything*.

disgusted Display the word cards for the new word *disgusted* and the known word *did*. Elicit from the children that both words begin with the same initial consonant sound and letter, /d/d. Elicit that the *-ed* ending shows that something has happened in the past. Help the children read the sentence "Nicky looked disgusted" while a volunteer frames the word *disgusted*. Elicit from the children the meaning of the word *disgusted*.

In order to reinforce new vocabulary and concepts, display the word cards for the new words in the story and give a clue for each word. Have a child find that word card and hold it up. Ask the children to find the word that fits each of the following definitions:

1. Is a short way to say *is not*. (isn't)
2. Means a newly born or very young child. (baby)
3. Has the word *thing* in it. (anything)
4. Begins the same as the word *did*. (disgusted)

Have the children use as many of the new words in one sentence as they can.

---

of all members in a widely diversified group. Some students learn best from an analytic (inductive) approach and some from a synthetic (deductive) approach. It is therefore helpful for the teacher to have materials that reach all students in the ways they learn best.

Basal Readers and Word Recognition

It is estimated that more than 90 percent of the primary classrooms in the United States use basal readers to guide their reading curriculum and instruction (Ingersoll & Smith, 1984a). Because such a large majority use basal readers and their accompanying teachers' guides, we should see how word-recognition skills are taught in basal texts.

Basal reading programs are published by approximately fifteen different companies. Each program consists of a series of books that provide content and a skills framework for reading from kindergarten through grade eight. The vocabulary and content are expanded lesson by lesson over the years so that children are assured exposure to an ever-increasing reading vocabulary and an ever-widening experience with poetry and prose. Teachers' manuals offer lesson-by-lesson guidance in teaching and reviewing the word skills and the comprehension

FIGURE 6.2 Sample Lesson-Plan Outline. The outline shows the manner in which word skills fit into the total teaching plan for a story in the child's first reader.

Objectives

Major teaching objectives are listed for a story. The activities in this lesson are planned to help develop the following:

Word Recognition
Review the phoneme-grapheme correspondences for initial /h/*h*, /k/*c*, /r/*r*, /g/*g*, and /b/*b* (p. 78).
Identify medial *a* as /a/ (p. 80).
Identify final *d* as /d/ (p. 79).
Review the plural ending -*s* (p. 80).
Review the verb ending -*s* (p. 80).

Comprehension
Draw conclusions (p. 78).
Find the main idea (p. 78).

Language
Review the question mark (pp. 76, 78).
Read with expression (p. 78).
Note sentence patterns (p. 81).
Write stories (p. 82).

Listening
Note details in a poem (p. 82).

Attitudes
Realize that problems can be solved (p. 78).

Resources

Workbook, pp. 38–42.
Story card No. 7.
Word cards
New words: *dog, hill, look, call, calls.*
Known words: *dogs, big, house, like, can.*
Phonics picture cards: /h/*h*, /k/*c*, /r/*r*, /g/*g*, /b/*b*.

Word Recognition for Beginning Readers

and study skills associated with the reading curriculum. As the philosophy or approach of each series is unique, there will be differences in the content and techniques used to teach various skills. The presentation of decoding skills for beginning readers will vary, some leaning toward an analytic approach to phonics instruction and some toward a synthetic approach.

Because the research on approaches and sequence of skills for beginning reading is far from definitive, the way is open to considerable interpretation. Nonetheless, the basal readers most frequently used by school systems in the United States have certain characteristics in common. These readers often provide readiness activities involving oral language, visual and auditory discrimination, and dictation of stories by the children. Then students are taught a group of words that are used in the first few stories in their books. After children have begun to "read" in that limited sense, most of these basals introduce the sound-symbol correspondence of consonants in the initial position (for example, the sound /t/ as represented by the letter *t* in the word *top.*) Consonants in the final position are taught next, followed by the sound-symbol correspondence of vowels.

The basals do not all teach consonants and vowels in the same order, nor do they necessarily teach all the initial consonants before moving to all the final consonants and then the vowels. Most introduce a few consonants and then a vowel or two that enable students to gain immediate control over a number of words. For example, the letters *b, c, t, m,* and *a* are sufficient to permit an analysis of *bat, tab, mat, cat,* and *cab.*

In first-grade basal readers, certain word-recognition skills are identified in each lesson. They are included in a list of objectives presented near the beginning of the teacher's manual. An example of such a list is given in Figure 6.2. No matter what the order of presentation, word-recognition skills are developed in order to move beginning readers toward independence as quickly as possible. With practice, readers will soon recognize words instantly; the more automatic the procedure becomes, the less a reader will need to employ specific word-recognition techniques. Consequently, *all the exercises in word recognition have the primary aim of achieving fluent, skilled reading.*

Teaching Activity

Most teachers' guides organize their lesson plans and directions around three major steps: preparation, reading and discussion, and teaching skills.

1. *Preparation for reading.* Students are aided in comprehending and enjoying the story they are to read. Background information and use of key vocabulary are included in the directions and suggestions. As new words are introduced, teachers may use the opportunity to teach word-recognition skills for that lesson.
2. *Reading and discussion.* Included are suggested purposes for read-

Basic Components of the Reading Process

ing, comments and possible questions about the pictures and the text on each page of the children's book, and discussion questions for literal comprehension and critical evaluation.

3. *Teaching skills.* Each of the lesson's objectives that can be organized into a skill activity is taught, practiced, and evaluated.

Sequence for Learning Analytically

We must constantly show the child how word-recognition skills fit into the reading program. The long-range goal is to provide a word-solving strategy that the child can use to get meaning from print. The procedure should be to try context clues first and then move on to the most direct decoding clues available. Context clues are those meanings in the sentence that help a reader predict the meaning of an unfamiliar word. If the word has still not been deciphered, the next step would be to consult a dictionary or other convenient resource. This might be called a context-phonics-context strategy.

If we assume that the child has the prerequisite background, including auditory and visual discrimination skills and an adequate vocabulary, and knows the names of the letters of the alphabet, the sequence followed by most gradual analytic programs in introducing skills is similar to that in the following list. (You may want to review the list of terms given near the beginning of this chapter.)

1. Match rhyming words such as *cat* and *mat*.
2. Identify the sounds of beginning consonants and their letter symbols. Initially, the consonants should be presented in an order that ensures a marked contrast in sound: /b/, /s/, /t/, /k/, /p/, /w/, /h/, and so on. These sounds and their symbols should be developed within the context of complete words, not in isolation: "You can hear the sound of /b/ at the beginning of the word *bat.*" It appears that children rely most on beginning consonants to identify words (Bertrand, 1976).
3. Identify the sounds of consonants at the ends of words, and relate each sound to its letter symbol: "You can hear the sound /b/ at the end of the word *tab.*"
4. Identify short vowel sounds in words such as *cap, bet, pit, cot,* and *but.* As a general rule, in three-letter words made up of the consonant-vowel-consonant pattern (CVC), the vowel is short.
5. Identify consonant blends at the beginnings of words and then at the ends of words (*br* in *bread, nd* in *sand,* for example).
6. Identify long vowels in words that fit the CVCe pattern (consonant-vowel-consonant plus silent *e*). As a rule, in four-letter words based on this pattern, the first vowel is long (*make, bite, rope, cute*).
7. Identify consonant digraphs at the beginnings and ends of words (*ch* in *church, ph* in *digraph*).
8. Identify the long vowels in words that have a double vowel (*meet, tool*) or that fit the consonant-vowel-vowel-consonant

(CVVC) pattern (*maid, seat, boat*). Generally, in four-letter words fitting the CVVC pattern, the first vowel is long, and the second vowel is silent.

The sequence just outlined would normally be spread over the first year of instruction for the average child. For a longer list and more technical information about phonics and linguistics skills, there are short texts devoted specifically to this subject (Forgan, 1978; Heilman, 1981; Hull, 1981).

By itself, the sequence indicates very little about strategy and instructional techniques. Various combinations are possible within the sequence to make instruction clearer and more interesting. As mentioned earlier, there is no reason why one vowel and a few consonants cannot be combined to form a number of short words.

Minimum Phonics Knowledge

Teachers who use the gradual analytic approach need to have many ready answers and instructional directions about decoding words. They need to be thoroughly acquainted with phonics generalizations and the sound-spelling patterns of English in order to establish their own decoding sequence when the needs of a particular child suggest special adjustment. Some of this basic information was given in the listing of terms near the beginning of this chapter, especially in the discussion of characteristics of vowels and consonants. Phonics generalizations attempt to organize the various sounds of the vowels and consonants into coherent patterns that can be used to guide students as they encounter unknown words in their reading.

Following are generalizations with which every teacher should be thoroughly acquainted in order to guide students through their first decoding experiences.

1. *Short vowel rule:* When there is only one vowel in a word or syllable, that vowel usually has a short sound if the vowel stands at the beginning or in the middle of the word (*at, met, it, hot, but*).
2. *Long vowel rule 1:* When a two-vowel word or syllable has a silent *e* at the end, the first vowel in the word usually is long (*made, ride, hope, tune*).
3. *Long vowel rule 2:* When there is a double vowel in a word or syllable, the first vowel is usually long, and the second vowel is silent (*maid, beat, toast*).
4. *Murmur rule:* when a vowel is followed by the letter *r*, it has a modified sound that is neither characteristically long nor short (*car, hurt*).
5. *Diphthong rule:* Certain double vowels have linked sounds that make use of both vowels, such as the *ou* in *house,* the *ow* in *now,* the *oi* in *oil,* and the *oy* in *boy* (C. Smith, 1967, p. 21). See additional generalizations in Table 6.1.

Basic Components of the Reading Process

One way to get children to practice a phonics generalization, once it has been introduced or discovered through class work, is to have them search the daily newspaper for words in headlines or in the stories and mark those that fit the rule or rules they have just learned. Beginners will be restricted mostly to one-syllable words.

Along with knowledge of the more common phonics generalizations, each teacher should have in mind a sequence for teaching phonics skills and should be acquainted with materials and techniques for giving children practice in decoding (phonics) skills. With that knowledge, the teacher is prepared to observe and test students in order to determine what skills they already have and how well they are learning the new ones which are taught in class.

Learning Decoding Skills

Presented here are several ways to assist beginning readers in learning the decoding skills listed in the sequence given earlier. The examples should also help teachers in diagnosing children's needs or in constructing appropriate training exercises. They will also help teachers know what to look for in the materials available in the classroom.

1. Alphabet Sequence

Have children match plastic letters with other letters written on paper. Then scramble the plastic letters, and have children put them in alphabetical order. Children can learn the lowercase letters by tracing a set of printed letters. Then they should write the letters in sequence (if they have learned to write them) or use cutout letters to place them in sequence.

2. Rhyme Sounds, Auditory Discrimination

Recite the following jingle. Ask the children to tell which word rhymes with *Joe*. Then ask them to make up a two-line poem using the rhyme.

I know a boy named Joe
Who froze his little toe.

Later, when rhyming seems easy for the children, ask them to supply a rhyme word that has been left out of a poem of two or more lines:

There's a big black bunny
That looks very _____ (funny)

3. Associating Sound and Symbol

At first, each letter of the alphabet should be given a regular sound value (*z* as in *zip*).

Sound Values for Letters of the Alphabet
(Used at the Beginning of Words)

Consonants	Vowels	(long)	(short)
b—bed	a	made	mad
c—cat	e	Pete	pet
d—dog	i	bite	bit
f—fish	o	hope	hop
g—goat	u	cute	cut
h—hot	w	know	
j—jump		now	
k—kite	y	cry	gym
l—lip			
m—mud			
n—nose			
p—pop			
q—quit			
r—red			
s—sun			
t—top			
v—vat			
w—wish			
x—X ray			
y—young			
z—zip			

To develop a sense of beginning consonant sounds, the children might use a list of consonants and sample words. They might then cut pictures from newspapers and magazines of objects whose names begin with those sounds. The pictures should be of things other than those used as cue words.

Using Phonics Generalizations

The underlying theme of most phonics instruction—in fact, of most decoding activity—is that the English language and spelling system have considerable regularity. By learning the regular sound-symbol patterns and the regular order of words, readers can build a storehouse of generalizations that enable them to make fairly accurate predictions about words encountered in reading. By the time the child comes to the first-grade classroom, many generalizations about the order of words in sentences and about their contextual meaning have already been developed. Beginning phonics instruction expands the child's power over words by providing generalizations about sound-symbol correspondences.

The objective of phonics instruction is the ability to *use* phonics generalizations, not the recitation of rules about sound-symbol relationships. The way children learn to generalize will depend upon the method of instruction. Some basal readers proceed gradually and analytically. They may not try to elicit a verbal description of the generalization from the student, although some do. The true test is the student's ability to use the generalization. The intensive, deductive method puts a generalization into words, gives examples, and then has the student practice it. The student may not be required to memorize the generalizations (although some deductive programs encourage memorization), but a verbalization has been heard when it was introduced. Here, too, the true test is its use.

Research Reports

The effectiveness of the gradual analytic approach versus the intensive synthetic (deductive) approach has been debated and researched for years (Chall, 1967; Perfetti & Lesgold, 1980).

In a nationwide first-grade study (Bond & Dykstra, 1967), the majority of the twenty-seven research projects included (synthetic) phonics or linguistics materials as one alternative method. Comparison between methods showed generally that children taught by a synthetic phonics system achieved higher scores in word recognition and paragraph meaning (comprehension) at the end of the first grade than children taught by a gradual analytic phonics approach. A second-grade follow-up on these children showed similar advantages on word-recognition tests for those who received early and intensive teaching of sound-symbol relationships. They did not, as a rule, demonstrate superiority in reading comprehension in the second grade (Dykstra, 1968b).

Chall's *Learning to Read: The Great Debate* (1967) focused critical attention on the teaching of reading. Following her review of research from 1912 to 1965, Chall concluded that a code-emphasis method using intensive synthetic decoding produces better results than a meaning-emphasis method using gradual analytic decoding. She cited other related studies that showed a significant relationship between the child's ability to recognize letters and their sounds on the one hand and reading achievement on the other. She noted that this knowledge appears to be more essential for success in the early stages of reading than are other factors such as intelligence and oral language ability. Chall stressed the need for a systematic method of introducing decoding skills rather than leaving the acquisition of these skills to chance, haphazard practice, or inductive learning.

In an earlier study, Chall and Feldman (1966) found that four factors were particularly significant in accounting for reading achievement, including an intensive phonics emphasis and a thinking approach to learning. Any systematic method of teaching phonics, then, should not be so rigid as to undermine the development of a thinking approach on the part of the child. A thinking approach emphasizes using the context of the sentence to build meaning.

The research evidence is not strong enough to convince every reading authority that intensive synthetic phonics is the way to begin reading instruction. There have, however, been demonstrable changes along these lines in the beginning reading materials that are being published. Forman (1977) found that major basal series have doubled their emphasis on phonics in the last forty years and that these series increase this emphasis with each revision. Recent editions of basal readers have introduced more phonics earlier and have sometimes provided supplementary phonics workbooks. These workbooks often give a synthetic, intensive presentation alongside the gradual analytic approach of the basal readers they support. At the same time, the new basal readers are also increasing their emphasis on language and experience story activities, thus helping children approach reading with many alternative techniques.

Some theorists (K. Goodman, 1969; Hoskisson, 1975; F. Smith, 1978) feel that teaching phonics actually hinders the child. A review of the research by Fulwiler and Groff (1980), however, does not support this negative view. On the contrary, their findings reaffirm earlier views that phonics instruction brings greater achievement in both skills and comprehension in the early stages of reading.

Teaching Initial Decoding Skills

From the preceding discussion it should be clear that the relation of symbol to sound can be demonstrated for students either analytically or synthetically. Initially, a teacher should emphasize one method or the other in order to keep the learning technique fairly simple, but later both techniques should be used to expand the development of word-analysis skills. Both initial approaches have been proved effective as is attested by the many mature readers today who once learned decoding skills by these means.

Story dictation activities can introduce phonics in a gradual, analytic manner. In such activities, the teacher uses words found in stories dictated by the children (experience stories) to provide the basis for analysis. The teacher might wish to wait until a child has included several *m* words in his or her story before leading the child to discover the sound-symbol correspondence of *m* and to apply the sound to other words. Proponents of the analytic method contend that this approach retains phonics as part of the reading process because sounds are taught in context and never isolated.

In contrast, the synthetic method advocates teaching letters and their sounds in an intensive manner. Some programs, such as those published by Lippincott and by Economy Co., introduce letters and sounds before having children begin to read stories. Sounds are then combined (synthesized) into words. For example, the pupils have learned the sounds of the letters *c, a,* and *t,* either in isolation or in words. The teacher writes the word *cat* on the board and asks children to synthesize these known sounds into a word. The process might develop as follows: "What is the sound of the letter *c?*" "The sound is /k/." "That's correct." The same procedure is followed for the remaining letters in the word. The three separate sounds are then combined or blended into the word *cat.*

Some commercial reading programs isolate letter sounds, and some programs identify the association of sound and symbol only as they appear within whole words. Some linguists (Fries, 1962; R. Hall, 1960)

Basic Components of the Reading Process

deplore the total isolation of letter sounds because they say this total isolation tends to distort the sounds. Experience with remedial reading has shown that some children fail to discriminate the sounds within a word and may be able to learn best if these sounds are presented in isolation. The teacher, therefore, must adjust the procedure to fit the needs of each child.

Some linguists seem to favor the intensive phonics approach when they advocate beginning word-recognition exercises using words that are spelled with regular features (only one letter to represent one phoneme). Some linguists (Bloomfield & Barnhart, 1961; Fries, 1962) state that the phoneme-grapheme system itself is fairly regular and can, therefore, be more easily taught through its regular forms. The words to be identified are set up according to principles of regularity, simplicity, and frequency.[3]

Their general procedure would be as follows:

1. First teach the children to respond to all the regular sound-spelling patterns; then teach them systematically to respond to the irregular sound-spelling patterns. For example, the letter *k* could be introduced in its regular and irregular forms using the following words:

Regular	Irregular
kid	knit
kin	knife
kit	knee

2. Overpractice the regular patterns. Once the base of regularity is established, the deviations will not cause trouble.
3. Develop automatic recognition responses to words by identifying graphic contrasts within a pattern and graphic contrasts between patterns:

CVC	CVCe	CVVC
mad	made	maid
met	mete	meat
bit	bite	tied
hop	hope	boat
cut	cute	dues

These recommendations might take the form of the workbook page shown in Figure 6.3.

[3] More recently, linguist Ronald Wardhaugh (1975) has suggested that reading material for beginners should reflect the natural language of speech and should not be artificially controlled except perhaps in skills exercises.

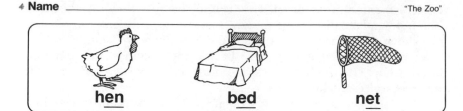

hen   bed   net

Choose the right word to finish the sentence.
Write the word.

1.

Nan ___fed___ the dog.

              fed
              red
              bad

2.

The _____ see the big dog.

              men
              man
              pen

3.

I see _____ little dogs.

              tan
              ten
              den

4.

I like the little _____ .

              pet
              met
              pat

5.

I like to read in _____ .

              bed
              bad
              red

FIGURE 6.3 Sample Workbook Page to Practice a Limited Number of Sound-Spelling Patterns (Smith & Arnold, 1983). The objective of this exercise is to teach students to recognize the short vowel /e/e with the CVC pattern and the graphemic bases *-en, -ed,* and *-et.*

Pattern Words

Words that are introduced should have only minimal differences in their sound and spelling patterns (*hit, bit, sit, fit*). By pronouncing a variety of word pairs with minimal spelling differences, the student is led to discover the contribution that a particular letter makes to the sound of the word. Through pairs such as *hit-bit* and *cat-bat,* the student discovers what the letter *b* does to the sound of words. This system encourages teachers to avoid isolating letters and asking, "What does this letter say?"

A number of linguistic readers are available, such as DISTAR (published by Science Research Associates) and a series published by Lippincott. Some of their stories use a limited number of pattern words.

A Fat Rat

A fat rat has a hat.
A cat has a hat.
A fat rat ran.
A cat ran.
A cat has a hat and a rat.

Suppose a child could not decode the word *fat* in the story. How would you help that child?

Try writing a story using the CVCe pattern limited to the vowel *a* (*lake, stake, snake, fake*) as well as words that fit the CVC pattern (*mad, bet, hop, hit, gum, fat, pot*).

Classroom Activities

1. Spelling Patterns

Fries (1962) identified two spelling patterns of particular importance: consonant-vowel-consonant (CVC) and consonant-vowel-consonant-vowel (CVCV). In the latter case, the final vowel is usually silent *e*, yielding the pattern (CVCe). Whether or not the program is linguistically based, the teacher should help students recognize these important patterns.

Vowel Generalization

The teacher and students can make lists that demonstrate the patterns or generalizations that are being introduced. Children should be encouraged to list as many words as they can to fit a given pattern.

	Pattern I (CVC)	Pattern II (CVCe)
Teacher Chart:	mad	made
	pet	Pete
	bit	bite
	hop	hope
	cut	cute
Student Chart:	had	
	cap	cape
	pad	
	can	cane
	ham	

2. News Heads

Newspapers provide a valuable source for practice in word identification. After a pattern has been introduced in class, have the children take one section of the newspaper and mark all headline words that fit this pattern. The children will quickly see that their efforts with word patterns pay off in daily reading.

3. Teacher—A Playful Story

To construct an exercise based on the regular words that match the phonics elements introduced in class, the teacher might write a simple story such as this as an exercise:

A Cat and a Rat

Can a cat bat a rat?
A cat can bat a rat.
Bam! Bam! Bam!
Bad cat.
Sad rat.

A child should read the story aloud, applying the consonant-vowel-consonant pattern. The teacher observes the child's recognition of each word and supplies guidance for individual sounds or for the complete pattern as needed. Questions might be asked to check on meaning: "What did the cat do?" With a story such as this, however, the subject matter has been covered after one or two questions. The children might be encouraged to write their own stories following a similar pattern. By exhanging them, they would gain practice and personal satisfaction at the same time.

Words that do not fit a pattern (*the, there, is*) are learned by visual memory techniques. They are developed as sight words and should be taught in context ("Tony *is* a tiger").

Emphasizing Regularity

Most methods for teaching initial decoding skills try to give students some generalizations about the regular English spelling system and its relation to word sounds. Students then see that there is a considerable regularity within the English spelling system, and they come to understand that this regularity can assist them in applying sound and symbol patterns as part of the decoding process (Hanna, Hodges, & Hanna, 1971).

To avoid confusion, many commercial methods limit the first lesson on the sound-symbol relationship to words that have a consistent one-to-one correspondence: Each sound is represented by a single letter. Words such as *man, bet, pop,* and *cup* have this one-to-one correspondence

Basic Components of the Reading Process

FIGURE 6.4 The CVC Pattern.
This pattern can easily be demonstrated and practiced on the chalkboard.

		CVC Pattern		
mad	bed	did	rod	bud
hat	net	sit	mop	rut
pan	pen	pin	dog	gun

between phoneme and grapheme in the CVC pattern and are, therefore, good examples to use in early lessons. After providing instruction on the sounds related to the letter-symbol *t, p, c,* and *a* and after discussing the sound of *a* in the CVC pattern, the teacher can present words such as *cat, tap, cap,* and *pat* and expect students to pronounce them.

After the phoneme-grapheme relationships for several letters of the alphabet have been established, patterns are introduced containing these phonemes and graphemes. Initially, the patterns should be simple ones. Many of the phonics and linguistic reading programs begin with the CVC pattern containing the short sound of the vowel (*bat, bet, bit, but*). See Figure 6.4.

Utility of Phonics Generalizations

Modern reading programs give the learner certain rules or generalizations to help in analyzing words. Several researchers have shown the usefulness of some phonics generalizations (Bailey, 1967; Clymer, 1963; Emans, 1967; Hanna, Hodges, & Hanna, 1971). Of the forty-five phonics generalizations examined in these studies, some seem to be quite useful for elementary school children whereas others are of limited value. Clymer examined materials from the primary grades, Emans looked at materials above the primary grades, and Bailey took samples from the six most popular basal readers of the 1960s for grades one through six.

These researchers first asked whether a phonics generalization fitted at least twenty words from a 2,000-word sample. They then applied the generalization to see if it gave the reader accurate pronunciations of those twenty words. If the generalization applied to only 30 to 50 percent of those words, the student would have at least that much assistance in deciphering them. This does not mean that a student need memorize all of these rules; most of them should become operational through practice with words in context (C. Smith, 1966). It is the application, not the terminology, that counts (Rosso & Emans, 1981; Tovey, 1980).

Emans (1967) identified eighteen phonics generalizations that were particularly applicable in reading materials produced for students in the middle grades (see Table 6.1). These generalizations will serve no purpose, however, if they are used without regard to meaning in context. If children are taught to identify words exclusively by means

TABLE 6.1. Phonics generalizations of high utility

Generalization	Percentage of Utility
1. The letters *io* usually represent a short *u* sound as in *nation*.	86
2. The letters *oo* usually have the long double *o* sound as in *food*, or the short double *o* sound as in *good*. They are more likely to have the double *o* sound as in *food*.	100
3. When a vowel is in the middle of a one-syllable word, the vowel is short except that it may be modified in words in which the vowel is followed by an *r*.	80
4. When the vowel is the middle letter of a one-syllable word, the vowel is short.	80
5. When the first vowel in a word is *a* and the second is *i*, the *a* is usually long, and the *i* is silent.	83
6. When the first vowel in a word is *o* and the second is *a*, the *o* is usually long, and the *a* is silent.	86
7. The vowel combination *ui* has a short *i* sound.	79
8. The two letters *ow* make the long *o* sound or the *ou* sound as in *out*.	100
9. When *y* is used as a vowel it most often has the sound of long *e*.	92
10. The letter *a* has the same sound (o) when followed by *w* and *u*.	84
11. One vowel letter in an accented syllable has the short sound if it comes before the end of the syllable and the long sound if it comes at the end of the syllable.	78
12. One vowel letter in an accented syllable has the short sound if it comes before the end of the syllable, and the long sound if it comes at the end of the syllable, except when it is followed by an *r*.	97
13. When *y* of *ey* is seen in the last syllable that is not accented, the short sound of *i* is heard.	97
14. A *-tion* at the end of a four-syllable word indicates a secondary accent on the first syllable, with a primary accent on the syllable preceding the *-tion*.	95
15. Taking into account original rules 5, 28, 29, 31, and 41,* one sees that if the first vowel sound in a word is followed by two consonants, the first syllable usually ends with the first of the two consonants.	96
16. Except in some words with a prefix, if the first vowel sound in a word is followed by a single consonant, that consonant begins the second syllable, and the vowel sound in the first syllable will be long; *or* if the consonant ends the first syllable, the vowel sound will be short.	84
17. A beginning syllable ending with a consonant and containing a short vowel sound is likely to be accented.	95
18. When a word has only one vowel letter, the vowel sound is likely to be short unless the vowel letter is followed by an *r*.	78

* 5. The *r* gives the preceding vowel a sound that is neither long nor short. 28. When two of the same consonants are side by side, only one is heard. 29. When a word ends in *ck*, it has the same last sound as in *look*. 31. If *a, in, re, ex, de,* or *be* is the first syllable in a word, it is usually unaccented. 41. When the first vowel element in a word is followed by *th, ch,* or *sh,* these symbols are not broken when the word is divided into syllables and may go with either the first or second syllable.

Source: Robert Emans. (February 1967), The usefulness of phonics generalizations above the primary grades. *The Reading Teacher*, pp. 419–25.

of a pronunciation guide, their daily lessons may well degenerate into little more than word-calling.

There is a wide variety of spelling patterns (graphemes) for the same sounds (phonemes) in the English language. This fact makes it necessary for teachers to guide students in finding generalizations and applying them. In some cases, words cannot be deciphered by phonic analysis. About 8 per cent of all words are of this type, according to Hay and Wingo (1960, p. 13) and Fries (1962). These must be learned by the whole-word method through visual memory techniques and the syntactic clues in a sentence.

A teacher will recognize many of the generalizations even if they have not been previously formulated and articulated. It will be helpful for teachers to memorize certain generalizations, particularly those with a high-usage potential. They could then be recalled readily in order to assist students who are having difficulty. (See the phonics test for teachers given later.)

Phonics Games for Classroom Use

1. Card Sort (This can be used for a variety of skills, including practice in sorting words according to vowel sounds.)

Clip pictures of a variety of common objects from old magazines and catalogs. Mount each picture on a three-by-five-inch index card. These cards can be used with beginning readers to practice auditory discrimination. Have children sort the cards into groups of words that begin with the same sound. Later, when initial sounds have been mastered, the cards can be sorted by ending sounds and then according to vowel sounds.

Children can be helped to check their own efforts at grouping if you write the word on the back of the card. When they have finished sorting the pictures, they simply turn the cards over to see if they have grouped words beginning with the letter *b* together, words ending with *p*, or words with a short *a* (this would require that vowel sounds be marked long or short). Having the words on the back of the cards also makes them useful for building sight vocabulary. The association of the printed word *cat* with a picture of a cat may help beginning readers learn to recognize the word.

The cards can also be used to practice alphabetizing. Begin by having children put the cards in order according to the first letter of the word. Then words beginning with the same letter can be put in order according to the second letter, and so on.

Children can do these activities while working alone. The activities are particularly appropriate for beginning readers.

2. Phonics Bingo

Bingo can be adapted to help students recognize the various phonics generalizations mentioned earlier. Make up a set of bingo cards, and in each box write a word that follows one of the generalizations you are teaching. In the example that follows, rules for the short vowel and for two long vowels are used.

hit	cake	lean	feet
seat	cat	rate	sit
ten	eat	boat	line
lead	tin	time	nut

Prepare a list of other words that follow these same rules. Either say these words (for listening discrimination), or write them on the board one at a time. The children place a marker on any word on their cards that has the same sound (or follows the same rule) as the word the teacher has given. The first child to complete a line across, down, or diagonally shouts, "Bingo!" Go back through the words, and ask for an explanation of each marked word. This will further clarify the phonics generalizations for all the children.

Phonics Test for Teachers

For diagnostic purposes, all teachers should be able to identify the more commonly used phonics generalizations. You might try the brief phonics test that follows and then discuss the answers with others.*

Place a circle around the item that does not belong with the others. Give a reason for your choice.

1. pr, gl, tw, sh, st _____
2. l, r, o, t, z _____
3. gh, ch, ph, th, tr _____
4. gnat, wrap, pneumatic, knee, press _____
5. a, e, m, i, y _____
6. can, red, pill, boat, rug _____
7. sh, sp, ch, th, ph _____
8. ci, ai, ea, oa, ee _____
9. cot, road, doe, soul, mold _____
10. thin, thing, thick, those, thought _____
11. pro, re, ness, in, ab _____
12. can, cup, cot, cone, cent _____
13. able, ly, ship, age, mis _____

* Answers to teacher's test:

1. sh	5. m	9. cot	13. mis
2. o	6. boat	10. those	
3. tr	7. sp	11. ness	
4. press	8. ci	12. cone or cent	

The Need for a Multiskills Philosophy

Decoding can be taught in a number of ways. The use of context clues and language-processing cues can be encouraged as means of unlocking new words. Whole words can be taught, and children can

Various classroom activities can provide the child with opportunities to discover how sounds and symbols are related.

be led to analyze the words and apply these analyses to new words. Sounds can be taught, and children can learn to blend the sounds into words. Any and all of these skills are appropriate for beginning readers.

It is not physically or psychologically possible to develop all reading skills simultaneously. No one expects competency after one week in school, but there is psychological and instructional value in letting children know that reading requires more than one skill and that these skills will be developing continuously over the months and years ahead.

While children are learning that their own speech can be written down and read, they are also learning to recognize visual-memory techniques and are being taught the rudiments of decoding. These three elements seem best interwoven in the initial stages of teaching. Children want to build a large storehouse of words that can be recognized instantly, but they also know that for those words that cannot be so readily recognized they can use the letters of the alphabet as well as spelling patterns (generalizations) to assist them in identification. It is a reasonable success story: "Reading makes sense, and I have a system for decoding words that helps me to get the message."

Assessing and Diagnosing Word Skills

Ordinarily, primary-grade teachers assess pupil progress and diagnose problems by observing the daily work of their students. That is as it should be. Teachers also have available to them the various tests pro-

Teacher's Resource Book

1 Initial /kw/qu ▶ Tell children to look at the picture of the queen and to say *queen* to themselves. Have them circle each word in the row that has the same initial sound that they hear in *queen*. Have them underline each word that does not have that sound. *Do not pronounce the response words in tests 1–5 and 7.*

2 Initial /bl/*bl* and /tr/*tr* ▶ Tell children to look at the picture of the tricycle and to say *tricycle* to themselves. Have them circle each word in the row that has the same initial blended sound that they hear in *tricycle*. Have them underline each word that does not have that sound. (Repeat procedure for *blimp*.)

3 Final /st/*st,* /ngk/*nk,* /nd/*nd,* ng/*ng,* and /ch/*ch* ▶ Tell children to look at the picture of the fist and say *fist* to themselves. Have them circle the pair of letters under

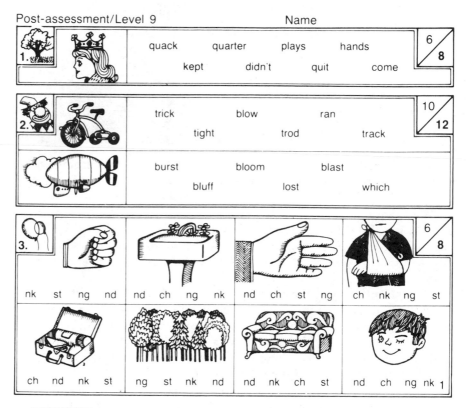

FIGURE 6.5 Sample Pages of a Criterion-Referenced Test (Smith & Wardhaugh, 1975).

vided by their basal readers. Almost all such readers have criterion tests that check the specific word skills taught in that reading series. Thus, classroom teachers can observe daily work and can help students improve; they can also administer the basal reader criterion tests to confirm their observations and to keep an official record of progress.[4]

Sample pages from a criterion-referenced test are given in Figure 6.5. The numbers in the small boxes to the right of each test item indicate the criterion for successful performance on that particular word

[4] Criterion-referenced tests are available on spirit masters or in separate test booklets. Some basal series reproduce these tests in their teachers' manuals.

Basic Components of the Reading Process

the picture that represents the final blended sound that they hear in *fist*. Have the picture items identified. (Repeat procedure for rest of section.)

4 Final /ī/y ▸ Tell children to look at the picture of the fly and to say *fly* to themselves. Have them circle each word in the row that has the same final sound that they hear in *fly*. Have them underline each word that does not have that sound.

5 Medial /ē/ee, /ē/ea, /ā/ai ▸ Tell children to look at the picture of the seat and to say *seat* to themselves. Tell them to circle each word in the row that has the same vowel sound that they hear in *seat*. Have them underline each word that does not have that sound. (Repeat procedure for *beet* and *sail*.)

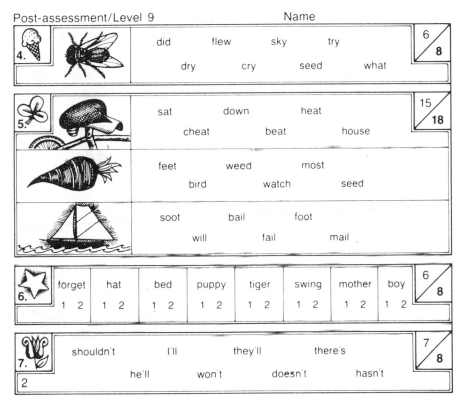

Post-assessment/Level 9   Name

4. did   flew   sky   try   dry   cry   seed   what   6/8

5. sat   down   heat   cheat   beat   house   15/18

feet   weed   most   bird   watch   seed

soot   bail   foot   will   fail   mail

6. forget 1 2 | hat 1 2 | bed 1 2 | puppy 1 2 | tiger 1 2 | swing 1 2 | mother 1 2 | boy 1 2   6/8

7. shouldn't   I'll   they'll   there's   he'll   won't   doesn't   hasn't   7/8

2

Figure 6.5 (*Continued*)

skill. For number one, a child must correctly identify six of the eight choices in order to meet a satisfactory criterion in identifying the sound-symbol correspondence of initial /kw/*qu,* as in *queen.*

Formal standardized tests, also available for testing word skills, are discussed in Chapter 14.

Teacher-made Tests

As a spot-check or as a means of diagnosing an individual's ability to perform a specific blending or pronunciation skill, teachers may want to construct word tests of their own. It should be noted that tests of word skills often examine words and generalizations in isolation. Although the teaching strategy places new words in phrases or sentences, a testing strategy may deliberately isolate words. In this way, the test can better control the type of response to be examined. Suppose, for example, that the teacher wants to know if a child can identify the /kw/*qu* correspondence, as in the word *queen.* If the test word is read in this sentence, "The king and queen came into the room," the student may say the word correctly because of context and not because he or she can respond correctly to *qu*/kw/. Thus, the list of isolated words is used for testing or diagnosing, but is not used for teaching. Several sample test items on decoding are given later. All can be administered to groups or to individual's, and teachers can use them to judge a student's competence with specific decoding skills.

Nonsense Words

The use of nonsense words to check on certain skills in decoding eliminates the possibility of visual memory being employed to provide the correct response in a test of a phonics generalization. Give the following instructions:

Here are some nonsense words. They are not real words at all, but I'd like to see if you can say them as if they were words.

fis	lort	faim
tope	kim	hin
bute	keat	vin
gud	muts	hife

Give a copy of the test to each child. The teacher pronounces each pair of words, asking pupils to listen to the beginning sound of each word. Pupils are to find the letter that represents the sound and circle it on their answer sheet.

Sample Test Items: Initial Consonants

Teacher: "Look at the first row. The words are *wagon* and *window.*" (The students should circle the letter *w* on their answer sheet.)

1. wagon   window
2. girl   gate
3. lion   leaf
4. tail   tent
5. carts   car
6. met   map

Pupil Answer Sheet

Name _____

Grade _____ Date _____

1. r   w   l   m
2. c   j   p   g

3. r	w	l	f
4. d	h	f	t
5. g	n	r	c
6. n	h	m	w

Sample Test Items: Vowels, Vowel Digraphs, and Diphthongs

The teacher pronounces each pair of words. Pupils circle on the answer sheet the vowel or vowel combinations that represents the vowel sound heard in the word.

1. cake	tail		7. for	more
2. bad	cat		8. up	just
3. hot	top		9. play	day
4. fur	turn		10. wait	tail
5. tie	kite		11. sound	about
6. farm	barn		12. boy	toy

Pupil Answer Sheet   Name _____

Grade _____ Date _____

1. e	a	i	o		7. ir	or	ar	
2. u	o	i	a		8. u	o	e	a
3. e	u	i	o		9. ay	ea	ew	oy
4. ar	er	or			10. ea	ou	oi	ai
5. e	o	i	u		11. oi	aw	ew	ou
6. ar	ur	ir			12. ay	ou	oy	aw

Sample Test Items: Initial Consonant Cluster

Review if necessary the principle that consonant blends represent more than one sound whereas consonant digraphs represent only one speech sound. The teacher pronounces the two words that begin with the same consonant sound. Ask pupils to circle the letters that make that sound.

1. cherry	chicken		4. truck	train
2. grass	green		5. crowd	crow
3. step	stairs		6. flag	floor

Pupil Answer Sheet   Name _____

Grade _____ Date _____

1. cl	ch	sh	th		4. th	dr	tr	fr
2. cr	gr	ch	bl		5. cr	dr	ch	wr
3. sl	fr	cl	st		6. ph	fr	gr	fl

Sample Test Items: Consonant Cluster and Digraph Phonograms

Have students look at the three phonograms that follow the first two letters in each example. One of these phonograms can be added to the first two letters to form a word that the children know. Direct pupils to circle the phonogram that forms the word, and then write the complete word in the blank.

1. bl	ame	ate	ay	_____
2. bl	urch	ock	im	_____
3. br	ud	ool	ing	_____
4. br	ick	ank	out	_____
5. cl	ab	ock	ine	_____

Summary

Decoding the printed page involves using language cues, visual memory of words, and sound-symbol generalizations. Although authorities do not agree on *when* to start sound-symbol decoding (phonics) or on *how* it should be taught, all believe that it *should* be taught and that it is an extremely important tool for analyzing words.

Some educators believe that phonics should be taught gradually and analytically from a meaningful context (that is, as the opportunities for using a skill arise in the normal course of reading). Others believe that an intensive and synthetic approach to phonics should be used in the early stages of reading instruction. Research results seem to favor the intensive, synthetic approach at the end of the first grade. By the end of the second grade, however, many of the differences have disappeared. What seems essential is that students see that practice in word skills provides them with a means for making sense of the printed message. In order to teach children well, teachers must themselves know the generalizations and patterns that help in decoding English spelling. They should also have in mind a procedure for diagnosing the competencies of their students and for planning instruction that will enable their students to read independently. The teacher's manual and tests provided by most basal readers contain a wealth of resources to help them.

Terms for Self-study

analytic phonics	grapheme
synthetic phonics	consonant clusters
linguistics	diphthongs
phoneme	spelling patterns

Discussion Questions

1. In what ways could nonsense words be used to teach or to test decoding skills?
2. Where do phonics skills fit into a broader strategy for decoding unfamiliar words?
3. How can a teacher combine analytic phonics and synthetic phonics in daily teaching?
4. What role does meaning play in beginning decoding activities?

Basic Components of the Reading Process

Chall, Jeanne S. (1983). *Stages of reading development.* New York: McGraw-Hill.
Chall describes learning to read as a process which varies depending on the child's stage of development.

Goodman, Kenneth S. (1976). Reading: A psycholinguistic guessing game. In H. Singer & R. Ruddell (Eds.), *Theoretical models and processes of reading* (2nd ed.). Newark, DE: International Reading Association.
Goodman hypothesizes that reading is a guessing game, not an exact science. Good guesses lead to success; bad guesses, to failure. Both lead to increased knowledge of how to read better.

Heilman, Arthur W. (1981). *Phonics in proper perspective* (4th ed.). Columbus, OH: Charles E. Merrill, 1981.
Here is a practical guide to decoding, with numerous classroom activities.

Hillerich, Robert L. (1978). *A writing vocabulary of elementary children.* Springfield, IL: Charles C Thomas.
This book serves as a ready reference for writing and reading instruction. It provides a listing and frequency ranking of words used in children's writing. These words can also be emphasized for word recognition in reading.

Hull, Marion A. (1981). *Phonics for the teacher of reading* (3rd ed.). Columbus, OH: Charles E. Merrill.
This is a programmed text designed to present the content of phonics and to provide practice in using the principles of this word-recognition skill. It is intended for use within the context of a college methods course.

Ives, Josephine P., Bursuk, Laura Z., & Ives, Sumner A. (1979). *Word identification techniques.* Chicago: Rand McNally.
This language-based text provides explanations and exercises covering a wide variety of word skills.

7

Growth in Reading Vocabulary

Have you ever noticed what children do with a new word they have learned? They test it out. You will see primary-grade children skipping down the hall repeating a new word just to get the taste of it: "Cauliflower, cauliflower, yea! yea!" At home that night they will use it in front of the family. Middle-grade children are more grown up. They use new words in sentences: "There is too much cacophony in this room!"

Children are fascinated by words—their sounds, their meaning, their power. Vocabulary accounts for more than 50 percent of the score on reading comprehension tests (Davis, 1972; Thorndike, 1974). And where do students get most of their new words? From books. Once children have moved beyond their early reading books, vocabulary growth is nurtured primarily through reading, not through listening, watching television, or conversing. Few people use the word *penultimate* in conversation, but a book will refer to "the penultimate experience."

It may be assumed that readers regularly test themselves as they read. Do they recognize a certain word? Do they know what it means?

Everyone who reads extensively is occasionally faced with a word that has not been encountered before or has not been seen often enough to be recognized instantly. For the adult, it may be a new technical term such as *multivariate analysis;* for the elementary school child, it may be as common a word as *subject*. Both adult and child foresee that they may well encounter these words again, and the next time they would prefer to respond *automatically*. How does one go about analyzing a word and then fixing it in memory so that it becomes a part of the reading vocabulary? How does one teach a child to do this?

Phonics is an invaluable aid to identifying new words, but students will need a number of additional word-recognition skills and techniques as well. Some of these skills must be taught, but others will be developed independently by each child according to individual experience and ways of learning. The teacher should offer direction and provide the opportunity for both to occur.

Many kinds of cues are available to the reader who knows how to use them. The more readers know about language and word cues and the more skilled they become in using techniques for identifying such cues, the more likely they will be to enjoy reading because less time will be spent on mechanics. The child who can utilize a knowledge of language and context clues will often recognize new words by understanding the sense of the sentence. The reader who has been trained to study an unknown word by seeking word cues that can be used to analyze it will quickly be able to decode the word *subject*. It immediately becomes evident that there are two parts (syllables) to the word because there are two separate vowel positions, *u* and *e*. The next step is to look for familiar word parts; there are two in this word, *sub* and *ject*. Each of these word parts has been learned separately in previous reading, and blending the two parts yields the word *subject*.

What about a more complex term such as *multivariate analysis?* How would an adult reader determine its pronunciation and meaning? This chapter provides a number of possible solutions as it considers these questions:

- *How can a reader's knowledge of language cues and thinking process be used to recognize new words?*
- *What are the word-recognition skills used by a competent reader?*
- *What is meant by context clues, structural analysis, and association skills?*
- *In what order should word-recognition skills be taught?*
- *By what means can the classroom teacher assess the word skills of students?*
- *In what ways are word recognition and word meaning related?*

In elementary schools, no area of reading instruction receives more attention than does the question of how readers analyze and recognize words. A system for teaching children to recognize words is so crucial to the reading process that most of the pedagogical controversies in recent years have focused on the various word-recognition techniques that can be employed. As previously stated, reading involves many skills other than word recognition, but the learner starts by identifying words because the message being conveyed is composed of these visual units. Even though word recognition is only one of the many skills a competent reader uses, it is usually thought of first when reading skills are discussed.

Good readers either recognize words instantly, or they follow analytical procedures that enable them to grasp the writer's meaning. By definition, the competent reader can rapidly, almost simultaneously, employ all the techniques needed to solve word problems: syntactic and semantic knowledge, context clues, phonics, syllabication, sound-spelling patterns, structural analysis, association, and picture clues.

During the years in which these skills were being learned, a strategy for applying them was also being developed; the beginning elementary school reader, on the other hand, needs assistance in developing a word-analysis strategy.

Most mature readers probably use context clues as the initial skill for word recognition. If such clues are not sufficient, they then apply other techniques depending on the cues evident in the word. Perhaps using the beginning and ending consonants along with context will reveal what the word is. If that fails, then the reader may try dividing the word into syllables, analyzing its components, or trying to associate it with other words or objects. Although context may provide the first clue for mature readers, the beginner often cannot start with this alone, particularly when there are several unfamiliar words on a page.

Developing Word-Recognition Skills

Beginning readers need to be taught how to approach new words systematically. They must learn how and when to apply each of the skills that a mature reader uses automatically. Generally, these skills can be categorized as

> visual memory and association
> use of context
> sound-spelling pattern identification
> analysis of structure
> use of external resources such as dictionaries

It is possible that all the skills and techniques to be discussed in this chapter could be taught in the first grade depending on the level of development of the child. These techniques are, however, particularly applicable for older children. Along with the previously discussed sight-word and decoding skills, the rudiments of word-recognition techniques may be introduced in the first year: context clues, structural analysis, some sound-symbol techniques (syllabication and syllable phonics), visual memory, and association. Most reading curricula introduce a variety of word-recognition techniques in the first year and then expand, refine, and reinforce those techniques in succeeding years. Consequently, the teacher has a variety of means available with which to help each child find the best way to learn to read.

Vocabulary Development

The Meaning of Words

The various techniques presented here and in the preceding chapter are designed to help students develop the ability to understand the meaning of words. The teacher's primary responsibility is to show students how to use a variety of word-recognition skills in order to comprehend word meaning. Teachers should create an attitude of appreciation for the importance of word meaning while building skills that enable students to grasp that meaning for themselves.

In beginning reading selections, most words have meaning for the child as soon as their sounds are recognized. Thus, when the word is pronounced, it is also understood. The textbook writer deliberately uses words that are part of the average child's listening and speaking vocabulary and uses them in stories with a familiar setting. If children can understand the meaning of words that they hear and speak, then they should have little difficulty in transferring that knowledge to print. As the reader advances into more difficult selections, the vocabulary and concept load become heavier. Perceiving meaning, therefore, will demand more and more instructional time and student attention.

In order to keep the understanding of meaning as the primary goal of reading, both instructional and practice reading materials must be coordinated with the background and performance skills of the child. Disregarding this precept would thrust children into frustrating and unhappy reading experiences and could result in their focusing attention primarily on pronunciation rather than on meaning.

Providing materials of an appropriate reading level will not of itself guarantee that children are reading in order to grasp word meaning. The importance of reading for meaning can be illustrated to the child by teaching vocabulary in context. Combining recognition skills with word meaning is a reliable method of checking the child's understanding.

The relationship between *pronouncing* (identifying) a word and *under-*

FIGURE 7.1 Sample Prereading Vocabulary Development.

New Vocabulary: sterilization, tranfusions, pericardium, sac, racial, interracial, prejudice

Remind children that less than 130 years ago the practice of medicine was relatively crude. Techniques of sterilization were unknown, anesthesia was limited to alcohol and opium, and X rays had not been discovered. With these and other advances, the physician became a true scientist.

Ask children to describe what they know about the way discoveries are made in the field of medicine. Discuss the importance of experimentation and research. Ask why it is important that doctors constantly try to improve their techniques and extend their knowledge. Point out that it is more than idle curiosity that prompts medical research and that discoveries in medicine are particularly important because they may cure thousands of sick people and save hundreds of lives. Explain that today's story is called "A Medical Pioneer." Have children discuss what this title means. Explain that the pioneer in this story is Dr. Daniel Hale Williams, a surgeon. Introduce the words *transfusions, pericardium,* and *sac,* using the sentences provided (sample sentences follow).

Explain that Dr. Williams was a black doctor. Have the children discuss what special problems a black doctor might have faced in the 1890s. Introduce *racial, prejudice,* and *interracial,* using the sentences provided. Explain that Dr. Williams was a pioneer of medicine in many ways.

standing its meaning can be shown during any reading lesson. For example, prior to reading, words that may be unfamiliar or that consistently cause difficulty can be extracted from the reading selection for purposes of analysis. After the appropriate word-analysis techniques are used, the process can be reversed by placing the words back into context to show their function in developing the meaning of the passage. In addition to this procedure, exercises similar to those discussed later in this chapter (for context clues) are appropriate for demonstrating the relationship between word recognition and word meaning. See Figure 7.1 for an example of prereading vocabulary development as presented in a teacher's manual for a middle-grade book.

Expansion of Vocabulary

Expanding the child's vocabulary is an important goal at every grade level and should be emphasized constantly. There is evidence that an increase in vocabulary leads to an increase in comprehension (Yap, 1979). Most children are interested in words and are eager to try out new ones that they hear. They realize intuitively that words are power, that a large vocabulary is a sign of maturity. Consequently, teachers may find that they can have children practice word-recognition skills by capitalizing on their desire to expand their listening and speaking vocabularies.

By establishing a "word-for-today" routine, teachers can encourage students to learn new words on a regular basis, as by saying, "Jennifer, it is your turn to provide a new word."

"*Astronomy.* Astronomy is the study of the stars."

"Now who can write it on the board for us? Can someone use it in a sentence?"

With such an approach, teachers can lead students to look at a word and use their word-recognition techniques to fix the word in their memories, asking, "How many syllables does the word have?" "How is each syllable pronounced?" "What other words have similar beginnings?" (*Astronaut, astronomer, astronomical.*) Vocabulary exercises help children recognize words for reading and encourage efforts toward self-improvement and growth.

Some students may enjoy keeping a vocabulary notebook, or the notebook idea can be expanded to include a vocabulary bulletin board for the whole class. The teacher reserves bulletin-board space for new words for a week. Words might come from class reading or from supplementary reading done by various students. Each day the children display a new word they have discussed. The word, its definition, and a sentence using the word are then mounted on the board. At the end of the week, the children enter the words from the bulletin board into their notebooks so they can review them and be motivated to keep vocabulary notebooks of their own. The bulletin board can be cleared at the end of the week for a fresh supply of words the following week. See Figure 7.2 for a sample page from a vocabulary notebook or note card.

Basic Components of the Reading Process

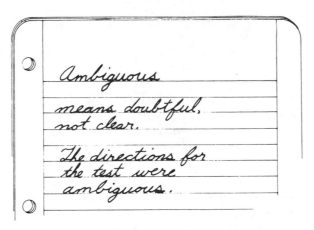

FIGURE 7.2 A Vocabulary Notebook Page.

Vocabulary Development (Activities)

1. Have each child write a new or interesting or appealing word on an index card (computer cards also work well). When the child is able to recognize the word and use it in a sentence, the card can be put into a packet marked "Words I know." Challenge each child to add a word a day to his or her packet. Occasionally, pair up children for a review of words in a packet. Any word that has been forgotten is removed from the packet and studied until it is "known" again.

   More advanced readers can use this same activity to increase vocabulary. In addition to saying the word aloud and using it in a sentence, they can be asked to give one or more meanings for the word, as well as synonyms and antonyms.

2. Show children how a crossword puzzle works. Discuss how such puzzles are created. The whole class can develop a simple crossword puzzle on the chalkboard with the teacher's guidance. Have children make their own cross-word puzzles around some familiar theme such as a season of the year, a popular book, a sport, or a chapter from their science book. Let the children exchange and solve the puzzles.

   With younger children it may be desirable to provide a crossword puzzle that has been partially constructed by the teacher. The children can then add more word squares and clues to those items already provided.

   More advanced readers may be interested in trying to work commercially prepared puzzles such as those found in most daily newspapers. With more difficult puzzles, children will probably experience greater success when working in teams than when working alone.

Vocabulary Development: A Continuous Process

Vocabulary expansion and related word-analysis exercises are not limited to the early grades. In fact, they are even more important in the upper grades as work in content areas becomes more complicated. From the primary grades through secondary school, teachers and students alike should consider vocabulary development an important part of their lessons and their conceptual growth.

In the early years of school, more emphasis is placed on expanding ideas through firsthand experience than through vicarious means. Students should be involved as directly as possible so that words and concepts in stories and in class composition activities can have a clearer and more vivid meaning. As trips to factories, museums, libraries, and zoos become slightly less important to children, teachers can begin to involve them more in projects, experiments, and exhibits such as building scale models of towns, collecting seashells, and so on. For

Vocabulary development is a continuous and wide-ranging activity. Real-life experiences usually provide the most powerful opportunities to expand word meanings.

Basic Components of the Reading Process

example, a teacher who guided an experiment in the speed and direction of the wind might add these words to students' reading vocabulary:

direction	measure	intensity
pressure	anemometer	instrument

It is not always feasible for the teacher to provide children with real experiences. Happily, much worthwhile experience and vocabulary can be gained vicariously. Secondhand experiences can be obtained from films, pictures, maps, radio and TV programs, recordings, and stories.

Simply providing children with experiences will not in itself expand their vocabularies. It is conceivable that a child could go to the zoo and not learn a single new word. There must be conversation, new words must be heard and recognized, and the child must then be encouraged to use the words repeatedly until they and their meanings are integrated into a working vocabulary. The teacher's task is to present words visually for analysis and storage in the reading-vocabulary bank.

One of the most effective ways to enrich a child's vocabulary is to encourage wide reading. In this way, many new words from different fields are encountered, and the child becomes familiar with different meanings of words in a variety of contexts. Also, adults (particularly teachers) should read aloud to children and discuss new vocabulary.

Vocabulary can be further enriched by providing experiences with "figurative language." For example, sentences using figurative language can be studied in order to determine their meaning:

The water laughed its way across the rocks.
His face fell.
Don't throw your money away on that.
He threw himself into his job.

Finding synonyms, antonyms, homonyms, and homophones for words that are already known provides another way to enrich vocabulary.

Synonyms:	words that are similar in meaning (*often, frequently*).
Antonyms:	words that are opposite in meaning (*hot, cold*).
Homonyms:	words that are the same in sound and spelling but that have different meanings (*block* [noun]: a solid mass of wood or stone; *block* [verb]: to obstruct by placing obstacles in the way.)
Homophones:	words that are pronounced the same but are different in meaning and usually in spelling (*wait, weight*).

The techniques described in this chapter deal primarily with words the reader can already recognize when they are spoken. A frequently neglected way of getting children to learn and remember words for reading is to teach words that are new to their vocabularies. At the same time the new word is pronounced and defined, it should be spelled out and written on the board or on a piece of paper so it can be analyzed and discussed as a word to be recognized and read. *Hearing, saying, seeing, and analyzing words will help the child recognize and remember them.* The technique used to commit words to memory may be an individual word-recognition method or a combination of methods, but the motivation for learning is provided by the fact that children are noticeably expanding their vocabularies.

The average child is interested in learning new words, and the teacher can use that interest to relate a general-meaning vocabulary to an analysis of a word for reading purposes. Once interest is focused on a word, only the teacher's imagination will limit how the word can be presented for visual analysis.

Developing Vocabulary: Seeing Relationships

Direct, structured instruction is a necessary and meaningful development in the vocabulary building of the elementary school child. Exercises such as the following may be helpful:

1. Underline the word in each row that has the opposite meaning from the other two words:

   a. grasp   drop   hold
   b. calm   angry   upset
   c. gigantic   large   undersized

2. Underline the words in the following paragraph that mean the same as *hungry.* Circle the words that mean the opposite of *hungry.*

It was well after six o'clock, and John was famished. He had worked all day on the construction site and hadn't had a chance to eat. He had stuffed himself at breakfast, hoping he would be full enough to skip lunch. But by lunchtime he was starved. He kept working even though his stomach growled. Finally at seven o'clock he feasted on a huge dinner.

3. What is the relationship between the first word and each of the other words in the line?

   illness: disease doctor absent hospital
   freedom: patriot jail speech police

Vocabulary Development: Diagnosis

There are a number of ways to evaluate vocabulary development. Orally administered standardized tests of word meaning can give an indication of a child's relative development. Work sheets and exercises

Basic Components of the Reading Process

(such as those used with basal readers), oral reading, and observation by the teacher can also be used. Information from all these sources can be used to answer these key questions:

1. *Can the child write or say the correct word when the definition is given?*
2. *Can he or she give the meaning of a new word?*
3. *Can he or she use new vocabulary words in reading, in writing sentences, and in conversation?*

Teaching Vocabulary

Association Techniques

Association techniques provide ways of relating an unknown word to another stimulus—visual, tactile, or auditory. This association between the word and a stimulus helps the reader recognize the word when it is encountered again.

Teachers often use association techniques to teach words to children, and reading tests use these techniques to evaluate reading vocabulary. Words that represent concrete objects (*truck*) and sensory impressions (*fire*) lend themselves well to associative learning techniques. The senses of touch, smell, hearing, sight, and taste can be exploited to impress a word on a reader's memory (for example, *garlic:* "The smell of *garlic* filled the gourmet restaurant"). Braun (1969) found that children more readily learn those words that are associated with things in which they are interested. Jorm (1977) found that words that bring to mind strong images are easier for poor readers to read. A popular book, Sylvia Ashton-Warner's *Teacher* (1963), reported success with words that were associated with deep emotion (for example, *mother, shark*).

The association process is often used in conjunction with other word-analysis techniques, but it is often difficult to determine where one technique ends and another begins.

Associations made by one person may differ greatly from those made by another because such associations are interwoven with each person's own experience and language. The connection that is made, therefore, is a highly individual one, and the value of this technique is that it allows each person to form his or her own personal, unique image of a given word. The teacher's task is to develop each child's powers of observation so that personal images can be associated with the written word.

Here are several examples of the personal images some individuals have associated with words in their reading lessons:

Sarah associates *whistle* with the noon factory whistle she hears every day during recess. (*hearing*)
Rhoda remembers the word *chocolate* because she visited a candy factory and was given some samples to eat. (*taste*)

Tony's reading lesson contains the word *walrus*. He recalls pictures of walruses that his father showed him. (*sight*)

Obviously, associations work only if there is a word or phrase in the passage that will trigger an image. The teacher can encourage the use of association as an aid to remembering words by providing materials and experiences in the classroom. One teacher presented new words by showing a filmstrip about a farmer. The picture of the barnyard was projected onto the chalkboard, and the teacher then wrote the names of objects in the picture (*barn, tractor, silo, fence*) directly on

Associations and Relationships

Development of the associative process can be encouraged by the use of games and exercises that put the written word and the associated stimulus together:

1. For beginning readers: The child is asked to match words with pictures on a bulletin board or flannel board.
2. For readers at any level: The child is asked to demonstrate (or see demonstrated) the differences between words that are close in meaning. For example, a child may first *walk*, then *ramble, totter, tiptoe,* and *stride* across the room, thus associating these words with such actions.
3. For readers at any level: Relationships among words are shown in diagrams that help the child make associations:

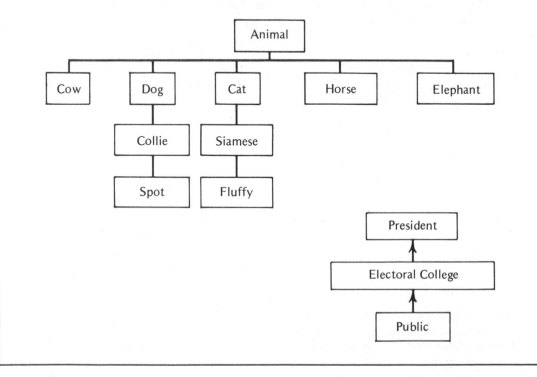

Basic Components of the Reading Process

the board, pronouncing each word as it was written. The children were able to associate the words with the pictured objects. When the teacher turned off the projector, only the words remained on the board, but the residual memory from the film continued to help the children identify the words. The position of each word on the chalkboard was related to the location of objects on the film, which could be shown again to reinforce the association.

The teacher's role may be compared to that of a guide. While ready to point out the association that can be derived and used to remember the new word, the teacher is also ready to stand back and allow children to bring their own interpretations and associations to the written symbol.

Association Techniques: Appraisal

In an evaluation of the child's use of association, it is important to ask if the child can do the following:

1. Match the printed word with the visual, auditory, or tactile stimulus symbol used in instruction.
2. Recognize the word when it is seen again.
3. Demonstrate associations through actions, diagrams, stories, and so on.

Using Context

Suppose a child is reading an article in the library and comes to a place where the page has been torn, obliterating a word in the selection. The news commentary that follows illustrates such a dilemma.

The Mideast

The superpowers have been deeply involved in the course of events in the Middle East. This area not only has the world's largest _____ of oil, but it is also a strategic land bridge connecting three continents. What happens in the Middle East greatly affects the rest of the world, and so all the superpowers are interested in becoming major influences in the area.

What will the student do? Abandon the article? Probably not. More likely, he or she will provide a word that seems to fit meaningfully into the pattern of the sentence. Perhaps the student will insert *supplies* or *reserves* or *quantities;* any of these words would make sense in the context of the sentence and allow the reader to complete the passage.

In order to use context clues, the reader must study the setting of an unknown word for assistance in identifying it. Use of context as an aid is not limited to a deleted word on a torn page. The reader can also use context to identify a printed word that is not known.

Using context to aid in word recognition is a necessary and valuable technique for both beginning and mature readers. Any unknown word must fit into the thought pattern of the sentence or paragraph. In order to use context clues, the reader must *think* while reading. Context will always provide a check for the other word-recognition techniques used by the reader. Most reading authorities agree with Tinker and McCullough (1962), who cite context clues as being "one of the more important aids to word recognition" (p. 150).

In the passage on the Mideast given earlier, the reader used context to select an appropriate word. A mature reader frequently uses the same skill to "guess" at the meaning of a new word. Some readers learn to use context clues on their own, but the successful acquisition of a skill should not be left to chance. All children will benefit from direct, well-planned, and sequential instruction geared to developing awareness and the use of contextual aids.

The use of context clues can be promoted in class. For example, during story time the teacher can stop momentarily at an appropriate place and ask, "What word do you think should come next?" The children will provide words that make sense to them. The words they contribute can then be checked by inserting them into the actual sentence. The children can decide if their words are suitable. Such an activity can be introduced in oral reading in kindergarten ("And then the squirrel climbed a _____ ") and can be continued throughout the elementary grades ("And that is how penicillin was _____ ").

"Perhaps the best way to develop contextual sensitivity and ability is to make the most of each functional opportunity while the children are reading," writes N. B. Smith (1963, p. 184). The teacher can give help in identifying unfamiliar words by stressing the use of context clues whenever the opportunity arises. This process can be further enhanced by the use of predictable story lines.

Instruction should not rely on the teacher's coaxing—"Guess the word." Such guidance may, in fact, be misguidance. Instead of leading the children to think, it may lead them to make wild guesses. Therefore, the teacher should ask, "What word do you think would make sense here?" If the word doesn't snap into place with that question, then the child should be encouraged to use other decoding skills in systematic order until a satisfactory match is obtained. Through repetition of a standard set of questions, the teacher helps the child use context and other clues to solve word problems.

The following set of questions can serve as a guide, helping the student use the smallest possible number of clues to figure out an unknown word:

1. After reading the whole sentence or paragraph, can you think of a word that would make sense in that spot?
2. Using context and the sound of the first part of the word, can you figure out what the word should be?

3. Using context, the first part of the word, and the sound of the last part of the word, can you figure out what the word should be?
4. Using context and applicable sound-spelling patterns across the whole word, can you figure out what the word should be?
5. If you still don't know the word, go to a dictionary to look it up, or ask someone.

Context: Types of Clues

As children move through the grades and master reading skills, they should be taught various types of context clues:

1. *Definition.* The definition of an unknown word is provided by the sentence in which that word appears: "Jane and Susan live next door, so they are my *neighbors.*"
2. *Experience.* Children must rely on their own backgrounds to predict the unknown word: "The mouse *gnawed* a hole in the box with its sharp teeth."
3. *Comparison.* Words in the sentence that compare or contrast with the unknown word give the clue: "Owls are *nocturnal* hunters; they sleep during the day."
4. *Synonym.* A synonym for the unknown word is included within the sentence: "They examined the various strata, or levels, of rocks."
5. *Familiar expression.* A knowledge of everyday expressions is necessary for clues to be received from this type of context: "He had such an *abundant* harvest because he had a green thumb."
6. *Summary.* The unknown word provides a summary of the ideas that preceded it: "They all marched in line, just like a *procession.*"[1]

Often context alone will indicate the appropriate word although there are times when context clues do not work. Because this possibility exists, other word-analysis skills are needed to check the accuracy of the word chosen or to identify it in the first place.

The identification of an unfamiliar word through context clues is not a matter of chance. The reader should carefully consider the meaning implied by a sentence or paragraph as a whole and, in the light of this meaning, deduce what the unrecognized word is.

Context clues are widely used by mature readers. This does not imply, however, that they are used to the exclusion of other word-recognition techniques. Instead, context clues are most successful when used in conjunction with other techniques, and children should be instructed to utilize them in this way. Figure 7.3 gives an example of a workbook exercise emphasizing context clues.

[1] Constance McCullough (1945, January). Recognition of context clues in reading. *Elementary English Review, 22,* 1–5.

Read each sentence.
What does the underlined word mean?
Fill in the circle by the answer.

1. After walking around, Ginny and Carmen decided to sit on the river <u>bank</u>.

   The word <u>bank</u> means ____.

   ⓐ a place where people keep money

   🔘 the land along a river

2. "Let's <u>pitch</u> a tent right near the river," said Carmen.

   The word <u>pitch</u> means ____.

   ⓐ to put something up
   ⓑ to throw

3. "I hope you don't <u>mind</u> what I'm going to say," said Carmen.

   The word <u>mind</u> means ____.

   ⓐ part of a person that has thoughts
   ⓑ to get upset about

4. "But I think we should move the tent <u>back</u> from the water a bit."

   The word <u>back</u> means ____.

   ⓐ away or to the other side
   ⓑ part of a person or animal

5. "This way, the wind won't <u>batter</u> us all night."

   The word <u>batter</u> means ____.

   ⓐ a baseball player
   ⓑ to strike or beat

6. "I can't <u>bear</u> the sound of wind on a dark night."

   The word <u>bear</u> means ____.

   ⓐ a big, fuzzy animal
   ⓑ to put up with

Macmillan Publishing Co., Inc.

FIGURE 7.3 Workbook Exercise Emphasizing Context Clues (Smith & Arnold, 1983). The objective of this exercise is to have students identify unfamiliar meanings of familiar multiple-meaning words by using context clues.

Cloze Technique

It is not necessary to rely exclusively on experience stories for material with which to construct context exercises. The teacher can also make use of paragraphs that were written specifically for the occasion or that were selected from books.

There were sixteen _____ on the bus. As it swerved around
the _____ , six people tumbled out of their _____ .
Fortunately, no one was _____ . The driver got
out to see if there was any _____ .

This concept can be adjusted by the teacher to leave blanks where
key vocabulary words would appear or where specific types of words
(such as adjectives) are used. Thus, the teacher can bring the students
to focus on the particular kind of vocabulary being emphasized.

Exercises such as this incorporate a technique known as the *cloze
procedure.* (This procedure is discussed at greater length in Chapter 14.)
Based on psychological studies of the gestalt idea of *closure* (the impulse
to complete a structured whole by supplying a missing element), the
reader completes the sentence by filling in the missing word or words.
Practice to develop the ability to use contextual clues can be given
with isolated sentences, each requiring the addition of one word to

Use of Context (Practice Exercises)

Each sentence that follows demonstrates one type of context clue. Determine the
meaning of each nonsense word, and identify the type of context clue provided.

1. There was a time when she would have greeted him with *hoylub.* Now all
   he got was a curt "Hello."
2. He picked up his *frinkle* and forced the hubcap off.
3. He was home as quick as *dulkjam.*
4. Social *typgyicles,* or levels, are often measured by income.
5. Shrimp and lobsters and all other *btergils* are becoming harder to catch.
6. *Hiolhil* grows abundantly in the Midwest, so the Midwest is covered with
   pastureland.

Context and Experience Stories

1. A suitable instructional technique for beginning readers is to take stories
   from the children's own experience or stories that are familiar or predictable
   and write them on the chalkboard with several words left out, as in these
   examples:

   We have a hamster in our _____ .
   Her _____ is Lori Blackberry.
   She lives in a _____ .
   She likes to _____ the place.
   We like our _____ .

2. Have the children keep a set of "context cards." Every time they come across
   a word they don't know, have them write the word on one side of the
   card. On the other side, have them write the *sentence* in which the word

was used. Then have them guess what the word means based on context and then write their guess below the sentence. This will encourage them to analyze the context carefully. If they feel their guess was wrong, let them look up the word and write the definition below their guess. These cards can then be used to reinforce the new words in two ways: by flashing the word and having the children supply the meaning and by showing the context and having them give the word.

The children might also circle prefixes and roots on the front of the card to give additional information. Also have them write what the prefix means. A "context card" might look like this when complete:

front

back

complete the meaning. Pupils are asked to supply words that fit the blanks and thereby complete the sentence. When using the cloze procedure, the teacher can ask, "What word do you think should go into the blank to finish this sentence?" The word or words that are volunteered by the children are checked by using them in the sentence. In some cases, several words may be correct.

Often in exercises using isolated sentences, the number of words that the children think of can be quite large. For example, take the sentence: "Dick _____ home after school." Conceivably, any of the following words could be used: *came, ran, walked, went, skipped, called.* If appropriate, the teacher could then utilize other word-recognition techniques to narrow the choice to one word. For example: "All these words could be used, couldn't they? But now I want you to tell me what the word is if it begins with the letter *r.*"

Skill in the use of contextual hints can also be strengthened by having pupils select the correct word from a group of words:

Jeff played ball for the _____ .
(violins, horses, champions, baseballs)

Supplying several possible choices may be very helpful for beginning readers. Once they have become accustomed to the idea, the cloze technique will make them conscious of the variety of clues available to them.

These and similar exercises should develop the child's ability to use context clues as an aid to word identification. Frequently, the teacher will provide informal guidance in context clues by telling the children to read the remainder of the sentence or paragraph or story and then to come back to the unrecognized word.

The cloze technique can also be used to determine how appropriate a book is for a child. Rankin and Culhane (1969) found that a child could read a book *independently* if he or she was able to replace correctly at least 61 percent of the deleted words. If the child had 41 to 60 percent correct, he or she could read the book *with* some instruction. If less than 40 percent of the words were replaced correctly, the child would probably have considerable difficulty with the book (Keller, 1982; Lange, 1982). The teacher may find it beneficial to analyze the kinds of errors made on a cloze exercise (semantic versus syntactic

What About High Cloze Scores?

What should a teacher do if 50 percent of the cloze items are passed? If 30 percent are passed?

There are no simple answers to these questions, but an adjustment in the level of difficulty of the books would seem appropriate when tested materials are too easy or too difficult for the child.

Percent of cloze items passed	Level of performance
61–100%	Independent
41–60%	Instructional
0–40%	Frustration

Cloze Technique

Make duplicate copies of experience stories the children have written or dictated themselves, but put a blank in place of every tenth word. Have the children fill in the blanks, using the context of the story and the sentences to determine what is missing.

With older children, creative writing stories can be reproduced the same way, but with every *fifth* word deleted. Encourage the children to discuss their answers and compare particular instances in which different words were supplied for the same blank. Readers at all stages of development can benefit from this.

errors, for example) and use that information to build instructional exercises (Legenza & Elijah, 1979).

Context and Meaning

Linguists maintain that longer utterances (phrases and sentences of which individual words are a part) provide keys to word meanings and also determine word usage (Wardhaugh, 1975). The meaning of a given word depends on the other words with which it forms a sentence as well as on its position within the sentence.

A word does not simply exist independently within a sentence, but instead it joins and interacts with other words. This interaction determines the exact meaning of the word. A word may have a certain meaning in one sentence, but in another sentence it may have a very different meaning. The range of possible meanings for a single word is reflected in the definitions given in a dictionary.

Take, for example, the word *nut*. In many dictionaries you can find at least six definitions:

1. A dry fruit or seed having separate rind or shell and interior kernel or meat; also, the kernel or meat itself.
2. Something likened to a nut (sense 1) in the difficulty it presents (i.e., having a hard shell which cannot be penetrated easily).
3. A perforated block (usually of metal) with an internal or female screw thread used on a bolt for tightening or holding something.
4. Slang: (a) the head; (b) a fellow—used disparagingly; (c) one whose thinking or conduct is eccentric; (d) a crank.
5. Botany: an indehiscent, polycarpellary, one-seeded fruit, with a woody pericarp, as an acorn, hazelnut, chestnut, etc.
6. Music: in stringed instruments, the ridge on the upper end of the fingerboard over which the strings pass.

A very real problem exists here as is made clear by the many varied meanings of this one word. If the word *nut* is heard in isolation, it is not possible to know which meaning to apply. Ascribing the appropriate meaning to the word *nut* is possible only when it is used in a larger unit such as a phrase or a sentence. This concept is illustrated in the following sentences:

1. That math problem was a hard *nut* to crack.
2. They bought some *nuts* and bolts at the hardware store.
3. Stop acting like a *nut*, you clown!
4. We're going to the woods to gather *nuts*.
5. The violin strings were not properly fitted across the *nut*.

When the same word can fulfill so many different functions, it is even more apparent that the larger utterance vitally affects the meaning of a word. For example, here is a word that is used first to denote an object (noun) and then to show action (verb):

1. He sat on a *chair*.
2. Harry will *chair* the class meeting.

Basic Components of the Reading Process

Demonstrations such as this—using a word in several ways in different sentences—can be understood by second-graders and even by many first-graders. As early as possible in school, the teacher should make children aware of these variations in order to emphasize the need for a variety of skills in deciphering the printed page.

Diagnosing Context Clues

Because of the nature of context clues, a connected communication must be provided as a testing device in order to evaluate a student's use of context. You may want to determine whether or not the children understand that they must *think* as they read in order to use the context-clue technique.

Probably the most direct method for determining a child's ability to use context is to ask what the child does when an unfamiliar word is encountered. The child may respond that he or she *thinks* while reading and gets a good idea of the word from the total context of the passage.

In order for the teacher to be able to evaluate a student's ability to apply context clues, some reading exercises should be provided that will help to answer the following questions:

1. *Can the child supply a reasonable substitute for the blank in the sentence?*
   "Henry dropped the egg, and it _____ all over the floor."
2. *Can the student use internal word cues in addition to context to find the correct word?*
   "The drowning man gr__ped for the log."
3. *Can the child infer meanings of words from context?*
   "Being fired from his job was Henry's *Waterloo*, for it was a defeat from which he never recovered."

Sound-Spelling Patterns

Syllabication

Syllabication may be considered an extension of the phonics skill presented in the preceding chapter. As a reading skill, syllabication involves the separation of longer words into pronounceable units (syllables). An individual syllable is a word segment that is pronounced with a single pulse of air pressure from the lungs and that contains one (and only one) vowel phoneme. Some words contain only one syllable and one vowel grapheme (*hat*) whereas others contain a single syllable in which the vowel phoneme is represented by a double vowel (*heat, boot*). As the syllables are recognized and pronounced, they are synthesized to yield the pronunciation of the entire unknown word. Being able to locate the accented syllables (those that receive the greatest emphasis, such as the first syllable in the word *EM-pha-sis*) is an integral part of this skill because that emphasis (accent) makes the word recognizable to the ear of the reader.

The teaching of syllabication usually comes relatively late in the sequence of word-recognition techniques. Syllabication was originally developed for use by printers, and, as a result, rules for syllabication are more applicable to writing (dividing words at the ends of lines) than they are to reading instruction. Even so, there are certain aspects of syllabication that relate to reading and can aid the learner in the discrimination and pronunciation of words.

Instruction in syllabication usually begins with auditory discrimination, which is designed to help children hear the syllables within words. An understanding of syllables and their function can be nurtured by using the following procedure: "The word *sun* has one syllable, or part. The word *sunny* has two syllables. What do you think a *syllable* is?" Responses may include the notion that a vowel sound is needed for a syllable or that one can tell the number of syllables by the number of *beats* (rhythmic units) in a word. In this way, the teacher moves the children toward a definition of *syllable*.

Eventually, the children should be led to an awareness that a word has as many syllables as it has *sounded* vowels. We should also point out that some syllables contain *only* a vowel (the *i* in *hes-i-tate*, for example), and others contain double vowels pronounced as a single sound (*boat, meet*).

Vowels and Syllables

In order to develop an understanding of the vowel–syllable relationship, the teacher should provide a list of words in which children are to identify the following:

1. The number of vowels.
2. The number of vowel sounds.
3. The number of syllables.

For example:

	Vowels	Vowel Sounds	Syllables
fact	1	1	1
summer	2	2	2
float	2	1	1

Accent

Awareness of accent in words is helpful because accent affects the sounds of vowels. For example, "the vowel 'a' has the long sound when accented in *able*, but a different sound when unaccented in *apart*. The vowel principles apply to accented syllables but they usually do not apply to unaccented syllables," according to N. B. Smith (1963, p. 235). Children should be aware of accent so that they can use it to determine the correct vowel sound of each syllable. In words of

Basic Components of the Reading Process

two or more syllables, one syllable is usually pronounced more forcibly than the others. Teachers can explain *accent* by saying, "In words having more than one syllable, we usually pronounce one syllable more forcibly or loudly than the others. This loudness, or stress, is called *accent*."

A feeling for accent can be further cultivated by instructing students to tap or beat the accents with their fingers or with pencils as they pronounce lists of words. They should tap harder for accented syllables than for unaccented ones.

One difficulty in the application of vowel-sound rules is that unaccented syllables usually have a muted sound known as the *schwa*, which is represented by the symbol ə in the dictionary. No matter what vowel letter is used to represent it, the unaccented syllable sounds rather like the short *u* sound in the word *hut*. The schwa sound is represented by the *a* in *about*, the *e* in *system*, the *i* in *easily*, the *o* in *gallop*, and the *u* in *upon*. Furthermore, in words that contain a syllable comprised of consonants plus silent *e*, the schwa sound is implied (as at the end of the word *syllable:* sil-ə-bəl).

Experience has shown that students learn to adjust fairly quickly to the various spellings of the unaccented syllable because the syntax of the sentence aids recognition of the word. Accurate spelling of unaccented (schwa) syllables requires different learning from that used to work with the more usual vowel sounds.

The ability to divide written words into syllables is greatly facilitated if the child knows some generalizations (principles). These principles should be taught inductively: The child should analyze many words that fit one generalization and then, with teacher guidance, reach a conclusion about the nature of the overall procedure. For example, the child might be given words such as *can-dy, aw-ful, pic-ture, mon-key*, and *al-so*. After determining the proper division of each word into syllables, the child should see that each two-syllable word contains medial consonant letters; the break comes between the two consonants (generalization 1 in the following list).

Syllabication Generalizations

Syllabication should be used as an aid wherever it is suitable. The teacher must determine which guidelines will be helpful in the application of spelling patterns. The following generalizations may be useful:

1. When two consonants fall between two vowels, the division of syllables is usually between the two consonants (*rab-bit, sis-ter*).
2. When a vowel is followed by a single consonant, the consonant usually begins the second syllable (*be-fore, to-ken*).
3. When a word ends in *le* and a consonant precedes the *le*, that consonant goes with the *le* syllable (*ta-ble, fum-ble*).
4. If the word contains a prefix, the division comes between the prefix and the base word (*view, re-view; form, con-form*).
5. If the word contains a suffix, the division comes between the suffix and the base word (*like, like-ly; fool, fool-ish; long, long-er, long-est*).

6. Consonant digraphs and blends are never divided (*part-ner,* not *par-tner; eth-ics,* not *et-hics*).

The recognition of a word's pronunciation does not stand or fall entirely on the child's ability to know exactly where the breaks between syllables occur. Knowing whether the division of syllables in the word *amble* comes before or after the *b* does not assure correct pronunciation of that word. For that reason and because these principles of syllabication do not apply to *all* words, they are recognized as being *generalizations,* not rules. They are merely helpful clues that can be used to aid in dividing words into syllables; these words must still be subjected to phonic or structural analysis in order to arrive at proper pronunciation or identification.

Correct division of a word into syllables will facilitate the child's correct pronunciation because open and closed syllables affect the vowel sound. A syllable that ends with a consonant is termed a *closed* syllable (for example, both syllables in the word *tăc-tĭc*). The vowel sound in a closed syllable is short. Syllables that end with a vowel are called *open* syllables, and the vowel sound is long (for example, the first syllable in the word *nū-mer-ous*). The correct division of a word into syllables will, therefore, yield clues for determining the word's pronunciation.

In evaluating the understanding and use of syllabication, ask these questions about the child's reading activity:

1. *Can the child identify the number of syllables he or she hears in a word?*
2. *Does the child know that the number of sounded vowels in a word indicates the number of syllables?*
3. *Can the child apply syllabication generalizations when dividing words into syllables?*
4. *Is he or she aware of the location of accents in words of more than one syllable?*
5. *Can the child apply common accent generalizations?*

Structural Analysis

Many base words undergo changes in meaning and pronunciation because of prefixes, suffixes, inflections, and compounding. Making use of such factors in order to determine the meaning or pronunciation of a word is called *structural analysis.* For example, the preceding sentences contain a number of words made up of clearly discernible structural components: *under/go, mean/ing, pre/fix/es, clear/ly,* and so on. Utilization of the techniques of structural analysis by mature readers is the result of instruction and practice. Children must be taught to use these analytical techniques, too. The visual learner—the child who learns best when he or she can look at and "figure out" a problem—will find them particularly helpful, for the reader is searching primarily for visual cues to help in identifying significant word parts. Auditory skills are also operating, especially with regard to inflectional endings such as *-s* or *-er.*

The teacher must lead the children to separate words into meaningful components in order to recognize and understand the words. This

Basic Components of the Reading Process

is not an easy task, for the elements that are included within the term *structural analysis* are many and varied. Here are some of these:

Base word: a word element that is not compounded or modified by a prefix, suffix, or inflectional ending and that retains the same spelling when such additions are made (bound*ed,* *re*-bound, bound*less*).

Prefix: an affix (something joined or added) placed *before* a base word, thereby changing that word's meaning (lucky, *un*lucky; possible, *im*possible; port, *re*port, *de*port, *im*port, *ex*port).

Suffix: an affix placed *after* a base word, thereby changing that word's meaning (express, express*ion,* express*ly;* like, like*ly;* work, work*able*).

Inflectional endings: endings that change base words grammatically by indicating case, gender, number, tense, person, mood, or voice (boy, boy*s;* men, men*'s;* produce, produce*s,* produce*d,* produc*ing*).

Compound word: two or more base words that are combined to form a single word. Sometimes the compound word retains essentially the same meaning conveyed by the original words (*class-room*), but in other cases the compound word may have a meaning that is different from any of its components (*broadcast, airplane*) or that suggests a different connotation or a more narrow interpretation than found in the individual base words (*seashell, lifetime*).

Contraction: a shortened form of two words that have been combined into a single word by omitting one or more of the letters (usually of the second word). An apostrophe (') is used to indicate that letters have been omitted (can not, *can't;* I will, *I'll;* he would, *he'd*).

Instruction in the use of structural analysis can begin as soon as the child's reading material begins to contain words fitting the six categories just discussed. The teacher can use the child's existing supply of sight words to form the basis for teaching these analytical techniques. In the early stages of instruction, the teacher should make students aware of structural components by simply pointing them out briefly in passing; formal instruction should wait until the child has mastered more basic skills.

The following passage might appear in a child's book:

The moon was shining brightly. Its light was reflected on the water.

An exercise in structural analysis might select the two simple, familiar words *moon* and *light* from these sentences in order to introduce the compound word *moonlight.* Identifying the two parts of the compound word and labeling an appropriate picture would assist in introducing the children to the idea that words are changed by adding parts.

By drawing upon the child's supply of sight words, the teacher can develop an understanding of what a *base word* is. This understanding

FIGURE 7.4 As children grow, so do the number and flexibility of their word skills.

must be taught early because it is the *base word*—the fundamental word unit—that is subjected to modification. If a child can identify the base word in a modified version (*read*/ing) or can recognize the components of a compound word (*foot*/*ball*), then a basic concept in the use of structural analysis has been mastered.

Structural Analysis: Sequence

As with other kinds of reading skills, structural analysis should not be tied to a specific grade level but should be taught as the child develops (Fig. 7.4) and can assimilate or has a need for new skills. Following are structural-analysis skills listed in a sequence that can be used to guide the teacher who is working with a nongraded or individualized curriculum:

> **Meaning-Structure Sequence**
> 1. Base words (*boy, run*).
> 2. Inflectional endings (*-s, -es, -ed, -ing*).
> 3. Compound words (*sail*/*boat, air*/*plane*).
> 4. Identifying root words (*phono*graph, tele*phone*).
> 5. Prefixes (*mis*match, *un*fold).
> 6. Suffixes (hope*less*, wonder*ful*).
> 7. Contractions (is not, *isn't;* we will, *we'll*).

Most basal readers specify the order in which specific inflectional endings, prefixes, and suffixes are introduced.

Inflectional Endings

Inflectional endings are encountered frequently in all extended reading. In fact, the addition of endings such as *-s, -es, -ed,* and *-ing* to known words may often be the first use a child makes of structural analysis. Instruction in inflectional endings should be relatively simple. The child is asked about the meaning of the word while his or her attention is called to the ending. The teacher can use the same technique whenever the child encounters words having these endings and ask, "What happens to the meaning of the word *walk* when we add *-s, -ed, or -ing?* Read the new word."

The child already knows and uses inflectional endings in speech. Relating speech sounds to the written symbols may be quite helpful in teaching the concept of inflectional endings. The goal of instruction is to lead children to *read* the endings that they automatically use when speaking. See Figure 7.5 for a sample workbook page that provides practice in certain plural endings.

As children become familiar with inflectional endings, they can begin to make some generalizations about the spelling and, therefore,

---

Name _____ "The Ghost Catcher"

A. Finish each sentence. Fill in the circle by the answer.

1. My grandmother took me to see an old ____.
   (a) house   (b) houses

2. There was one big ____ in the yard.
   (a) tree   (b) trees

3. The big house had two ____, one in front and one in back.
   (a) porch   (b) porches

4. "Two ____ came to stay in the house," said my grandmother.
   (a) princess   (b) princesses

5. But they left because there were ____ inside
   (a) ghost   (b) ghosts

6. I told my grandmother that this was a silly ____.
   (a) tale   (b) tales

B. Finish each sentence. Underline and write the word.

1. Two ____ came to the door.
   women   womans

   women

2. Grandmother, Aunty Alice, and Aunty Kate lived in the house when they were ____.
   childs   children

   _____

3. Grandmother said, "We have been for a long walk. Our ____ are tired."
   foots   feet

   _____

4. Aunty Kate said, "Come in. I love to have ____ come to see me."
   peoples   people

   _____

Macmillan Publishing Co., Inc.

FIGURE 7.5 Workbook Page Giving Exercise on Plural Endings (Smith & Arnold, 1983). The objective is to recognize irregular plural forms of given singular nouns, and to identify plural forms of given nouns ending in -*es*.

Growth in Reading Vocabulary

about the pronunciation of these endings. These spelling generalizations include the following:

1. When inflectional endings are added, there is very often no change in the spelling of the base word (walk*ing*, match*es*, call*ed*, girl*s*, go*ing*).
2. If the base word ends in *e*, the *e* is usually dropped when adding an inflectional ending that begins with a vowel (hope, hop*ing*; take, tak*ing*).
3. When a base word ends in a single consonant following a single vowel, the final consonant is usually doubled when an ending is added (run, run*ning*; drop, drop*ped*).
4. When a word ends in *y* preceded by a consonant, the *y* is usually changed to *i* before adding the ending (cry, cr*ied*; pony, pon*ies*).
5. If the final *y* is preceded by a vowel, the ending is added with no change in the base word (buy, buy*s*; monkey, monkey*s*).
6. If the word ends in *f*, the *f* is usually changed to *v* before the addition of an ending (wolf, wol*ves*; scarf, scar*ves*).

Inflectional Endings

Here are sample exercises and procedures for developing an understanding of inflectional endings:

1. Write the words *want* and *kick* on the board. Have the children pronounce the words, after which the teacher adds the endings -*s*, -*ed*, and -*ing*. The children frame the base word in each example and then speak a sentence using the inflected form: want s, kick ing.
2. Written exercises similar to those just given can be provided:
   a. Circle the base word in each of the following examples:

plays	playing	played
walked	walks	walking
planting	plants	planted

   b. Draw one line under the base word and two lines under the part that has been added to it:

raining	played
throws	asking

   c. Write the correct word in the blank:

   John is _____for his hat.
   (looked   looking   looks)

Compound Words

Compound words may be used to give children an early introduction to the additive properties of words. When they see two familiar words joined to represent a new concept, they realize that they do know

Basic Components of the Reading Process

enough to analyze some words, to pronounce and make sense of them. When the known words *work* and *book* are joined to form *workbook,* children begin to develop a strategy for looking at longer words, and they begin to realize that they possess powers for unlocking the meaning of some words that may seem quite formidable at first glance. Teachers often use mix-and-match columns of words to help children learn how to put compound words together and, therefore, to recognize them in running text:

bed   shine
foot   room
sun   ball

Compound Words

The following tasks will illustrate compound words and assist children to become adept at identifying them:

1. Auditory perception of the two or three words within a compound word may be cultivated by having the children listen to the teacher say a new compound word (*aircraft,* for example). They must then say the two words they hear. All compound words should be written on the board and each component identified visually.

2. The teacher writes the compound word on the board and then covers one of the component words. A child is asked to identify the part of the word that is not covered. The teacher then proceeds to cover the other part of the word, and another child identifies the visible portion. This leads the children to see the elements in a compound word.

3. The familiar game of tic-tac-toe can be turned into any number of interesting and worthwhile reading games. For example, a large block of nine squares is drawn

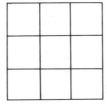

and a word card is turned face down in each square. The words written on the cards are those frequently used in compound words (*some, earth, every, where*). Before a player can place either a cross or a circle in a square, a compound word must be created using the word on the card. You may also ask children to use the word in a sentence if you like.

Make the game more challenging by requiring each player to create *two* compound words containing the same base word on his or her first turn. For subsequent turns, the number of compounds can be increased.

Prefixes, Suffixes, and Roots

A technique similar to that used in recognizing words with inflectional endings may be employed to identify words with affixes such as prefixes and suffixes. The base word is first identified; then the affix is isolated.

In order to develop an understanding of prefixes and suffixes, have the children draw lines or brackets around the affixes, and tell how the meaning of each base word is changed (for example, [ab]sent, hope-[ful]). Knowledge of the meanings of the more common prefixes and suffixes will help students recognize the derived word and its proper meaning. Tables 7.1 and 7.2 list some of the most frequently used prefixes and suffixes.

Knowing the exact meaning of prefixes and suffixes is not always possible because some of them have more than one meaning. However, by first presenting those affixes that *are* fairly consistent in meaning, the problem will be lessened. Most basal series and commercially prepared reading materials include a logical sequence of affixes that can be used for instruction. Figure 7.6 gives a sample workbook page designed to develop an understanding of prefixes.

TABLE 7.1   Common Prefixes

Prefix	Meaning	Example
ab-	away from	absent
ad-	to, toward	admit
co-, con-, com-, col-, cor-	together, with	contest
de-	away, down, out of	depart
dis-	not, opposite	dislike
ex-	out of, formerly	extend
in-, im-, il-, ir-	in, not	immoral
pre-	before	precede
pro-	forward	proceed
re-	back, again	review
un-	not, opposite	unhappy

TABLE 7.2   Common Suffixes

Suffix	Meaning	Example
-able	capable of, worthy of	lovable
-ance, -ence, ancy, -ency	act or fact of doing; state, quality	allowance
-er, -or	person or thing connected with; agent	teacher
-ful	full of, abounding in	helpful
-less	without, free from	helpless
-ly	like, characteristic of	saintly
-ment	state of, quality of	amazement
-tion, -sion, -xion,	action, state, result	election

Basic Components of the Reading Process

Write one of the prefixes at the right before each underlined word to make the word fit in the sentence.

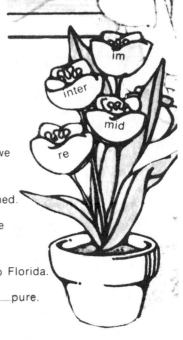

1. The table was ___im___ movable because it was so heavy.

2. Our school is having an ___inter___ class basketball game for the fourth grade.

3. We had to ___re___ paint our fence because the first time we painted it the rain washed the paint away.

4. The picture is ___im___ perfect because it has been scratched.

5. Even though we woke up early, we did not leave the house until ___mid___ day.

6. There is an ___inter___ state highway that goes from Maine to Florida.

7. You'd better not drink the water, because it may be ___im___ pure.

FIGURE 7.6 Example of a Prefix Exercise from a Basal Workbook (Smith & Wardhaugh, 1975).

Many prefixes and suffixes are derived from foreign languages, especially Latin and Greek, and many of the words that we commonly use in English are also based on *roots* that are borrowed from other, older languages. In earlier discussions, we referred to *base words*—English words that can be modified by affixes and compounding (*need, needs, needy, needless, needed,* and so on). *Root words* are those portions of English words that originate in other languages and that may be modified in spelling (depending on the particular context) and may also be altered in meaning by the use of affixes and compounding.

The Greek root *phōn* (sound, speech) has already been mentioned in connection with *phonics* and *phonemes;* it also forms the basis for *phonometer* (a device for measuring the intensity of sound), *phonoscope* (an instrument for making visible the motions of a sounding body), *phonograph,* and *telephone,* to mention only a few of the words having to do with *sound.* In fact, many "English" words are formed by combinations of two or more Greek or Latin roots. For example, the Greek word *tēle* refers to "distance" or "transmission over a distance," and its combination with *phone* yields a word rooted in antiquity but used to identify a relatively recent invention. The Greek word *metron* (measure) obviously provides the root for *meter* and can be combined with any number of other terms to provide names for measuring devices (*altimeter, speedometer,* and so on).

Words based on Latin roots can be combined and altered just as the Greek examples were. The Latin verb *capěre* (to seize, take, or con-

Growth in Reading Vocabulary

213

tain) provides the root *cap* found in words such as *capture, captive, captivate* and can be seen in even more elaborate words such as *encapsulate*. The Latin verb *audire* ("to hear") yields a familiar word in its first-person singular form *audio,* and the verb *videre* ("to see" or "to look at") gives us the word *video*. Together they have provided the name for those familiar twentieth-century technological devices, *audiovisual* aids for the classroom.

The ability to use and understand the meaning of prefixes, suffixes, and root words borrowed from other languages becomes an important part of word-identification skills for older students. Beginning in the intermediate grades, common root words (especially from Latin, Greek, and French) are introduced. These roots, together with prefixes and suffixes, provide a foundation for continuing vocabulary growth because many of our larger and more complex words are constructed from these smaller units.

When words using a particular root are encountered in a reader or a content text, the teacher should use the opportunity to isolate the root and explain its meaning. Other words that use the same root can then be suggested by the teacher or students, and examples can be given to show how a root word affects the meaning of the larger word. Students often remember the meanings of roots more easily if they link them to known words that use these roots. For example, students will be more likely to remember that the Latin verb *spectare* means "to observe, watch" if they relate that root and meaning to words they already know such as *spectator* and *spectacle*.

The number of English words based on roots borrowed from Latin, Greek, and other languages is enormous. There are, for example, a relatively small number of root words and prefixes—about fourteen of each—which provide the basis for more than 14,000 words commonly used in the English language (Brown, 1965, pp. 3–4). In addition to those given in Table 7.1, the more important prefixes include *inter -* (between), *sub-* (under), *mis-* (wrong), and *trans-* (across, beyond). A few of the most frequently used roots are the Latin verbs *tĕnēre* (to have, hold: *tenable, tenacious, tenant*); *mittĕre* (to send, launch: *message, missile, missive*); *făcĕre* (to do, make: *fashion, artifact, manufacture*); and *scrĭbĕre* (to write: *scribble, scribe, script*). For a more extensive discussion and listing of roots and the words derived from them, see C. B. Smith (1978, pp. 197–201 and 216–228).

The spelling and pronunciation of some of these roots have changed over the centuries, and, therefore, the use of root words to recognize new words may sometimes be confusing. However, a knowledge of roots can reveal the meaning of a great many new words, and it can also help the child to remember a new word by suggesting an association with a known word based on the same root.

Armed with a knowledge of prefixes, suffixes, and roots, the reader has a considerable body of information to bring to bear on unfamiliar words. It must be noted, however, that knowing the meanings of the *parts* of a word does not necessarily give a student an understanding of the whole word. Word meanings change from their original usage,

Basic Components of the Reading Process

and thus structural analysis alone can help with translation but not always with definition. Structural analysis combined with context can usually give the reader enough clues to enable him or her to determine the meaning of a word. By relying on structural analysis and context, the reader can usually decipher an unknown word without interrupting the flow of meaning while reading.

Prefixes, Suffixes, and Roots

How do word structure and context help you to understand the italicized words in the following sentences?

> He was very careful as he wrote so that he would not
> be accused of *mistranscribing.*
> In *retrospect,* I can see I made a mistake.

Prefixes and Suffixes

Exercises such as the following will enable children to practice analyzing words that contain prefixes and suffixes:

1. When a child encounters a word such as *unlike,* the teacher should draw a line under *like* and ask if the child recognizes that word and knows its meaning. The child should then identify the prefix and combine it with *like* to form the compound *unlike.*
2. Have the children make a list of common prefixes (*dis-, im-, ir-*) along with words in which these prefixes appear (*dislike, impossible, irresponsible*). Do the same with suffixes.
3. Use the following written exercises:
   a. Add the suffixes in Column 1 to the words in Column 2. Use the complete word in a sentence.

Column 1	Column 2
-ness (state of being)	1. cold 2. happy 3. kind
-er (one who does something)	1. labor 2. view 3. play

   b. In each of the following rows, draw a line through the word that does *not* have a prefix or a suffix:

1. dislike   will   react
2. knee   enclose   unlock
3. boundless   wonderful   book
4. recount   real   return

c. Underline the root word, and write the prefix or suffix (or both) in the correct column.

	Prefix	Suffix
indirect	(in)	
regardless	(re)	(less)
useful		(ful)

d. Read the following sentences, and supply the missing word:
   A farmer is a person who _____.
   A helper is a person who _____.
   A reader is someone who _____.
   What suffix is added to all these words?

e. Draw a line under the prefix in each of the following words, and tell how it changes the meaning of the base word:

   unhappy   dislike
   displease   retake
   unknown   mistreat

4. Have the children cut articles from the newspaper, and ask each child to find a word containing a prefix. Discuss the meaning of the prefix and how its removal would affect the meaning of the sentence. Challenge the children to find as many other prefixes as they can. List on the chalkboard all the words found in the articles.

   As a follow-up activity, construct a poster that lists common prefixes, the usual meaning of each prefix, and examples of the prefixes in use.

   As often as possible, these exercises should be used in conjunction with the reading of sentences and paragraphs. Unless they are applied in a meaningful context, such activities will remain sterile.

Contractions

Contractions are used frequently in everyone's speech. Few would say, "I do not want that"; instead, they would be more likely to abbreviate the statement to "I don't want that." The contraction is a shorter way of saying two separate words. Because these words are often contracted in everyday speech, reading and writing them in their shortened form is a logical step. Explaining this logic to a child may help with a sometimes troublesome analysis, for contractions do not always sound like either of the words they are replacing—such as *don't* for *do not.*

   The teacher can write the words *let us* on the chalkboard, and

Simple charts are useful in helping students learn to recognize common words at sight.

after them the contraction *let's* is also written. It is explained that *let's* is a short way of saying *let us*. The teacher can explain as follows: "This mark [pointing to the apostrophe] shows that some letters have been left out. We call this mark an 'apostrophe.' In the word *let's,* the apostrophe tells us that one letter has been left out. What letter is it?"

As with other instruction in word-analysis skills, the instructional sequence should proceed from simple to complex. Words in which single letters are left out (*is not, isn't*) should be taught first. Later, words in which two or more letters are omitted (*I will, I'll; he would, he'd*) should be introduced.

Contractions

The following exercises can be used to practice working with contractions and related spelling concerns:

1. Draw a line from each word in the first column to the correct contraction in the second column. Use each contraction in a sentence.

does not	can't
is not	doesn't
can not	isn't

2. Rewrite the following sentences, substituting a contraction for the italicized words.

He will go to the house. _____

I *do not* want to go. _____

You will have to do it. _____

3. Write the words that each contraction stands for:

I'll _____   you've _____

we've _____   can't _____

we'll _____   it's _____

In all exercises involving structural analysis, the reader should be encouraged to search for the largest possible unit that can be recognized and then to figure out how the other part or parts of the word change the pronunciation and meaning of the basic unit. The reader should not feel compelled to look first for the root and then the affixes in a word such as *reconstruction* if he or she instantly recognizes the first part, *reconstruct,* and knows that it means "to build again." Structural analysis is not mental gymnastics, but a tool to assist the reader in determining the pronunciation and meaning of words that are not recognized at first glance.

Structural Analysis: Diagnosis

A series of evaluation questions can be asked about the word-analysis skills discussed in this chapter. It is not absolutely necessary that every child be able to articulate the generalizations behind the skills although it is reassuring to the teacher if the child remembers the generalization. The important point is to determine whether or not the child can apply the skills by asking questions such as the following:

1. Can the child recognize roots in derived words? (*information*)
2. Can the child recognize compound words? (*cupcake*)
3. Can the child analyze and define words made up of familiar roots, prefixes, suffixes, and inflectional endings? (*predated*)
4. Can he or she add necessary prefixes, suffixes, and inflectional endings to give words the appropriate meaning and form needed in the sentence? ("Can't stand it!" *un* + *bear* + *able*)

A number of standardized tests are available that can help the teacher assess word-analysis skills, and criterion tests found in several basal readers are also helpful. For information on such tests, see *Reading Tests and Reviews* by Oscar Buros (1969).

A Strategy for Word Recognition

The ultimate goal of reading is *to get meaning from print.* The flow of meaning in a passage or story is really more important than the individual words.

Even beginning readers have a working sense of the syntax (grammatical functions) and the semantics (the way meaning is conveyed) of their language. In speaking and listening, users of the language rely on these two cuing systems in order to process language and understand meaning. These same language cuing systems will often allow a reader to understand the meaning of a sentence even if a particular word in the sentence is unfamiliar. For example, a reader might use a knowledge of syntax and semantics to understand the meaning of the following sentence even if he or she did not know (or could not decode) the italicized word:

> Because he loaded trucks all night, his main *diurnal* activity was sleeping.

If the reader was able to understand the sentence without directly decoding the word *diurnal,* the immediate purpose for reading—to get meaning—was achieved. Part of word-recognition instruction, then, should be to encourage children to use their already developed language skills and their thinking skills.

At the same time, reading instruction should help children develop skills that will enable them to recognize and know the word *diurnal* when it is encountered again in a different context. One way to do this is to present the word *diurnal* in a number of meaningful contexts and thus lead children to apply their own idiosyncratic skills in order to recognize and remember the word. (In fact, many commercial controlled-vocabulary materials have this as a primary goal.) A second way is to teach the various word-recognition skills and techniques as well as a strategy for using them so that the children can apply them each time a new word is encountered until the response becomes automatic. The optimal practice session would combine word-analysis skills, language cues, and thinking skills in order to help children learn how to understand the meaning of what they read.

After years of training and of reading experience, a child will learn how to use these skills automatically, but deciding how to employ the skills in the beginning will require some guidance. Isn't there some pattern that will help so that children do not apply these skills at random? Each child wants to make sense of the thinking and word-recognition skills he or she has, and the teacher can provide a strategy for using these skills simply by asking the same set of questions each time a word problem is discussed in class. For example:

1. *Do the words around the problem word give an idea of what it is or what it means? (context clues)*
2. *Do context clues and the sound of the first part of the word tell what the word is? (context clues plus initial sound)*
3. *If the first two steps do not produce the word, does it help to add the final sound in the word? (Context plus initial sound plus ending sound)*
4. *If the first three steps do not produce the word, can it be understood by looking for sound-spelling patterns (CVC: bat; CVCC: back; CVVC: book) or by analyzing the structure (prefixes, roots, compounds, and so on)?*

5. *If the first four steps do not produce the word, ask someone or look it up in a dictionary (or skip it and read on).*

This set of questions will remind students to move systematically through their word-recognition skills whatever those skills may be at each child's stage of development. Initially, the child will go through the entire repertoire of skills, searching intently for the one that will solve the problem at hand. Later, after much practice and repetition, the search is more automatic. Through the five-step pattern, the child learns to use the smallest possible number of clues in solving word problems, stopping after any one of the steps when the word is identified. It is conceivable in the following example that the unknown word could be identified after step 1 or step 2, depending on the individual child's background and skills:

The quick brown fox $\underset{2\quad 4\quad 3}{\overset{1}{\rule{2cm}{0.4pt}}}$ $\overset{1}{\text{over}}$ the lazy dog.

Step 1. Context: The fox *does something* over the dog.

plus Step 2. Initial sound /j/.

plus Step 3. Ending sound /t/*ed.*

plus Step 4. Sound-spelling pattern CVCC = short *u* plus /j/ plus /t/*ed.*

plus Step 5. Ask someone or consult a dictionary.

The system emphasizes the additive or combining features for solving word problems.

Using New Words

1. Children should be helped to develop all their language-processing skills in order to decode words and understand their meaning. *Strategy lessons* use the child's existing language strengths as the basis for developing new strengths and can be written either for individual children or for groups so that they may develop their use of language cues and discover their own miscues. A teacher, for example, might want to help a reader use his or her strengths in order to discover what the word *entered* is. The teacher could write a strategy lesson such as the following:
   a. Construct a story using the word *entered* several times.
   b. If possible, use familiar words in the rest of the story.
   c. Give syntactic and semantic cues in each sentence to help the child decipher the new word:

   When I was six, I entered the first grade. I was frightened, but my mother took my hand as we entered the classroom. My friend Joe entered

Basic Components of the Reading Process

at the same time. The teacher wasn't there when we arrived, but she soon entered the room. She was a nice teacher and we had fun.

After school, I had to take the bus home. I entered the bus in back of Joe. We rode home together. When I got home, I entered the kitchen, where my mother and father were cooking dinner. I told them all about my first day at school.

By the time children have read such a story, they usually know that the new word is *entered* and that it means "went into." Such a strategy lesson stresses the importance of comprehending meaning. It also helps children develop a thinking approach to reading, and it encourages them to use their language-processing skills.

2. Have the children identify unfamiliar words in their reading. They should put these words on cards, together with the context in which each word appeared. Then have the children work in groups of two or three to analyze each other's words, using the five-step system discussed earlier. Have the child who can identify a word in the smallest number of steps explain to his or her teammates how the answer was arrived at. This will both reinforce the *system* and allow for valuable peer tutoring.

Diagnosing Word Skills

The child's ability to use word-recognition skills should be evaluated soon after such skills are taught. Because word-recognition skills are developed gradually over five or six years and because it is generally assumed that these skills build on one another, it is important to let the child know whenever he or she is successful and to discover and correct any problems as soon as they appear.

The teacher has four general approaches that can be used to evaluate each child's strengths and weaknesses in reading: informal testing, observation, introspection, and formal testing. Depending upon the situation, one or all of these general approaches will be used. Table 7.3 indicates typical classroom activities and applies the four procedures for assessing word recognition to them.

After teaching a specific word-analysis skill, the teacher may ask individual children to read a word list aloud. As a child pronounces each word, the teacher notes whether or not he or she is applying the skills that have just been taught. The teacher also looks at the child's practice exercises, whether on work sheets or on the chalkboard. If several errors are repeated, the teacher should schedule additional instruction time in the skill for that child.

A more valuable type of informal testing takes place when a teacher listens to a child read aloud. A better idea of student mastery can be gained by hearing how a child reads words in context than by hearing the child recite a list. The teacher can note how well the child uses context and his or her own language cuing systems and can determine whether or not the child is using recently taught skills. The teacher

TABLE 7.3 Means for Assessing Word-recognition Skills

Materials Activities	Ways to Observe			
	Informal testing	Observation	Introspection	Formal testing
Oral reading				
Word lists				
Workbook exercises				

can also ask the child to explain exactly what he or she does when encountering a new word that requires analysis.

Workbooks and reading texts often contain tests to determine mastery of a given skill. Teacher-made tests and tests provided by publishers for specific achievements in reading should be used as diagnostic instruments. Their purpose is to isolate a specific skill such as using initial and final consonants as clues to word identity. Because tests are constructed to examine specific skills by asking students to perform specific tasks, the teacher should examine these tests to see whether or not children can perform these tasks. The pattern or regularity with which the child applies the skill or fails to use it is the point of the observation.

In the case of each word skill discussed in this chapter, the teacher should try to determine two things:

1. *Does the child know the generalization and the way in which it will assist in analyzing words?*
2. *Can the child apply the generalization to a variety of situations: reading aloud, doing a workbook exercise, taking an achievement test?*

Specific appraisal questions and suggestions are included in this chapter for each word-analysis skill. Any evaluation of pupil performance in these skills should have the direct effect of indicating to the teacher which skills should be taught again in subsequent instruction. If the child has mastered the skill, the teacher can continue to present other skills in the sequential program. If evaluation indicates that the child is not able to use a certain skill satisfactorily, the teacher should then schedule further teaching and practice.

Summary

Chapter 7 has discussed word-recognition and word-analysis techniques beyond the initial skills of visual memory (sight words) and sound-symbol decoding. A variety of word-perception skills is needed by a reader who wishes to cope with the printed page efficiently and competently. In addition to the visual memory and decoding skills discussed in preceding chapters, a reader needs to be able to analyze words on the basis of syllables (sound structure), on the basis of meaningful structures such as roots and affixes (meaning structure), and on the basis of context clues (thought and syntactic structure).

Syllabication and structural-analysis techniques are usually taught after visual-memory and phonic techniques. At first, the child needs to understand the symbolic code and to decipher the parts and patterns that words exhibit. As soon as several techniques for analyzing and responding to words can be used almost automatically, the student can pay more attention to the message that words carry in context, which, in turn, helps him or her to understand individual words.

Linguists have recently reinforced a dictum from reading education—that word-recognition exercises should always end in a meaningful utterance such as a complete sentence or a paragraph. Words are only hollow sounds and hollow shells when they stand alone; it is the whole utterance that gives them meaning.

Terms for Self-study

word recognition   syllable phonics
word analysis   phonics skills
visual-memory skills   picture clues
syntactic skills   context clues
association skills   cloze procedure
structural analysis   figurative language
syllabication skills   analytic skills

Discussion Questions

1. In the grade level at which you are teaching (or plan to teach), what terminology would you use to help children develop a word-analysis strategy?
2. If you were to use a language-experience approach to the teaching of reading, how would you provide instruction in structural analysis, syllabication, and the other techniques discussed in this chapter?
3. How could a teacher build and organize a repertoire of teaching activities related to word recognition?

Recommended Readings

Bortnick, Robert, & Lopardo, Genevieve S. (1973, January). An instructional application of the cloze procedure. *Journal of Reading, 16*(4), 296–300.
This article provides practical suggestions for developing instructional material using the cloze procedure and describes how to use this procedure to teach word identification as well as the structure of the language.

Ives, Josephine P., Bursuk, Laura Z., & Ives, Sumner A. (1979). *Word identification techniques.* Chicago: Rand McNally.

Here is a thorough review of the various types of word identification clues such as picture clues, syntactic clues, semantic clues, phonic clues, and spelling clues. There is a good section on syllabication and accenting principles.

Johnson, Dale D., & Pearson, P. David (1978). *Teaching reading vocabulary.* New York: Holt, Rinehart and Winston.

This volume suggests the importance of providing direct vocabulary instruction because of the positive correlation between fluent reading and vocabulary development. It also presents a way to teach word identification skills and develop vocabulary simultaneously.

Kaplan, Elaine, & Tuchman, Anita (1980, October). Vocabulary strategies belong in the hands of learners. *Journal of Reading, 24* (1), 32–34.

The authors show how to make students responsible for their own vocabulary development.

Pikulski, John (1976, March). Using the cloze technique. *Language Arts, 53* (3), 317–318, 328.

Pikulski explains how to use the cloze technique as an instructional tool for reinforcing or extending reading skill and encouraging writing skills. The article provides excellent guidelines and gives illustrations of use of the cloze technique.

Ribovich, Jerilyn K. (1979, December). A methodology for teaching concepts. *The Reading Teacher, 33* (3), 285–289.

The author discusses the nature of concepts, the trends in concept development, and a four-step procedure for teaching concepts.

8

Reading Comprehension: Experiential and Language Factors

Sometimes everyday events have the power to reveal rather meaningful lessons. For example, a colleague recently told us of an incident she witnessed at a family reunion that illustrated the importance of comprehension in reading. Apparently two of her relatives were describing the school-related successes of their children in a familiar one-upsmanship fashion.

"My daughter, Greta, is reading in the top group in third grade," one parent volunteered.

"My girl, Alice, had the highest score in her class on the SRA reading test," the second parent responded.

"Greta reads books her older sister brings home from the library," the first parent countered.

"Alice can read the *Wall Street Journal*," the second parent claimed with fervor.

"The *Wall Street Journal?*" Greta's advocate repeated slowly and with obvious disbelief.

"Yes. I'll prove it to you. Where is Alice? Alice! Alice, come here for a minute. I want you to read for your Uncle Walter," the proud mother said with determination.

What followed was a revealing demonstration. Bewildered nine-year-old Alice was first asked to read from the local newspaper (no *Wall Street Journal* was available), then from *Time* magazine, then finally from an encyclopedia. She read haltingly at first as curious relatives listened, then more confidently as she lost her self-consciousness. A few words were mispronounced, but her ability to read even rather difficult passages amazed everyone, including the storyteller, our colleague.

"See," Alice's mother closed the experiment triumphantly.

"That's impressive," Uncle Walter admitted, "but does she understand what she reads?"

With this inquiry the argument gained new intensity. What should have been a pleasant Sunday afternoon was well on its way to ruin. Uncle Walter insisted that Alice should answer questions about the material she had "read" to prove she was really "reading," and Alice's mother refused to let her do so on the grounds that she had just demonstrated her reading ability. The standoff was interrupted by a welcome announcement that dinner was ready and a resulting evacuation of the living room.

Our friend confessed to being relieved that, as a resident "expert"—so named because she is a university professor—she had not been called on to settle the family disagreement. She knew that Alice and her mother would be deflated if she agreed that "saying the words" was not truly reading, yet she, too, had been impressed by Alice's ability to handle difficult reading material. For that Alice deserved recognition, not failure. There was little doubt that Alice was a good reader who could comprehend material within her range of personal experiences, but no nine-year-old can be expected to understand much of what appears in the *Wall Street Journal.* In any case, we agree with our colleague that family arguments over whose child is the more gifted should be resolved in a way that permits everyone to win. Family reunions are not likely settings for lectures on the reading process.

On the other hand, the incident just described is especially useful to us in helping to identify some of the complex issues to be explored in this and the next chapter on reading comprehension. We will examine the answers to questions such as these:

- *What are the major factors that contribute to reading comprehension?*
- *How are background experience and prior knowledge important to comprehension?*
- *How are language abilities related to comprehension?*
- *How can background experience and language abilities be assessed?*
- *What can be done to help students overcome comprehension problems due to limited background or language or both?*

The improvement of reading instruction is an important undertaking that has captured the attention of people all over the world. The pursuit of better strategies and techniques for teaching reading has taken different people in a variety of directions. It is probably an understatement to suggest that disagreement may be found on many aspects of learning to read. Despite disagreements on particulars, however, there is widespread recognition of the primacy of comprehension. Even advocates of intensive decoding approaches to reading explain that once a word is pronounced, it will be understood (comprehended) by the reader.

Despite the importance of comprehension, relatively little is known about how it takes place or why some children comprehend well and others don't. It is not lack of attention that causes this state of ignorance about comprehension, for many researchers and theoreticians have addressed themselves to the question. (See, for example, Anderson, Spiro,

Basic Components of the Reading Process

& Montague, 1979; Gutherie, 1981; and Spiro, Bruce, & Brewer, 1983.) Rather, it is the abstract nature of comprehension that makes it elusive. Any mental operation that cannot be observed or measured directly is slippery. Certainly the results of comprehension, the *product,* [1] can be observed and analyzed; but the *process,* the hidden mental operation, cannot.

The consequences of this uncertainty about the process of comprehension are real and far-reaching. Without a clear and accurate model of the process, classroom instructional activities tend to focus on the products of comprehension. Inordinate attention is given, for example, to answering questions about a story on a test or in a discussion (Durkin, 1978–79). Some time *should* be spent with the products of comprehension, for they often involve the application of ideas gained from reading. But attention to only the products of comprehension fails to deal directly with the process itself—the thinking operations underlying comprehension. The child who has difficulty finding the main idea of a selection, for example, is often given extra practice in discovering main ideas. The hope apparently is that by concentrating on the product, we can somehow positively affect the process. A better approach would deal directly with the process.

The authors believe that a conceptualization of comprehension helps the teacher deal with the process by identifying key components and describing how those components interact. By focusing instructional activities on the key components, the teacher is able to improve comprehension by attention to its basic elements. In this way, attention is given to the process as well as to the product of reading comprehension. With some conceptualization of the basic components of comprehension, the teacher is also much better able to locate the source of any difficulty in comprehension. Rather than attacking an amorphous mass called comprehension, the teacher can deal with recognizable components, but must keep in mind that comprehension is more than the sum of these parts.

Factors Affecting Comprehension

Figure 8.1 presents the authors' idea of the major factors that enable a person to comprehend the printed page. It necessarily involves some simplification of a highly complex process. Nonetheless, it serves as a map of comprehension and is intended to be helpful in organizing the information presented in this chapter. It has implications for instructional activities, as well as for the assessment of student needs.

Five factors internal to the reader are identified as the primary determinants of reading comprehension in the figure: background experience, language abilities, thinking abilities, affection (interests, motiva-

[1] A product of comprehension would be the result of understanding. Some results might be observable (such as a written answer to a question); other results might not be (such as a change in opinion). Other examples of products include an illustration, model, or diorama based on a story, retelling the story, and giving a puppet show based on the story.

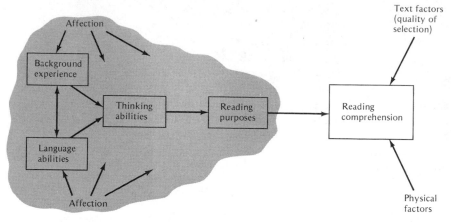

Figure 8.1 A Reading Comprehension Model. The major factors affecting comprehension interact to bring about comprehension.

tion, attitudes, beliefs, feelings), and reading purposes. The reader draws on these internal resources in order to understand what he or she reads. A sixth factor, external to the reader, is the nature of the text to be read. In recent years, our knowledge about the role of text in comprehension has grown at a rapid pace as research into this domain has increased. The seventh factor shown in Figure 8.1 (physical factors) relates to such items as proper lighting and room temperature, legible reading matter, and a well-rested learner. We will not deal with those matters in this chapter. To illustrate how these factors interact, consider the following situation. Malcolm has been given this story to read.

Soap Box Derby

Charlie had waited for this day all his life. As he pushed his soap box racer to the starting line, memories came flooding back. He had spent days and weeks and months drawing sketches and building models of this red beauty.

When he was only five years old, he had watched his oldest brother win a derby. Two years later his cousin won a race. The next year it was his sister who crossed the finish line first.

"Now it's my turn to carry on the Hansen tradition," Charlie thought.

In the last two weeks he had won races in his hometown and state. Now Charlie would have a chance to win the national soap box derby.

At last his race car reached the starting line, and Charlie pushed it into place. He put on his helmet and adjusted his goggles. The announcer began to tell the large crowd the names of the drivers and their hometowns. Charlie climbed into his car and crouched forward.

"Watch the man with the flag," Charlie reminded himself.

They were off! The racer to Charlie's left dropped back slowly, but on his right a green car stayed even with him. This was going to be close. As they coasted down the hill, the cars picked up speed.

Suddenly Charlie's red racer began to weave. He swayed left and then right. The steering wheel wiggled in his hands.

"Oh, no! This is no time for problems," Charles whispered.

The green car pulled ahead and beat Charlie to the finish line.

Putting on the brakes Charlie slowed to a stop. The boy in the green racer smiled and waved. Tears of disappointment filled Charlie's eyes. A man came forward and helped the winning driver from his car into a wheelchair.

Disappointed as he was, Charlie was glad the green car had won.

First we should acknowledge that understanding of this or any selection is typically not an absolute matter. A reader often grasps some of an author's message but not every nuance of meaning. To return to our illustration, Malcolm will understand this story only if certain conditions are met.[2] First, if Malcolm has never seen a race, he will find the story hard to follow. If he has never heard of a soap box racer, the story will be mostly nonsense to him. If Malcolm has never felt compassion for someone with a physical disability, he will certainly not understand the ending of the story. Malcolm must have experiences in his background that enable him to bring personal meaning to the events and feelings of the story. His understanding will be greater the more his own experiences are like Charlie's. Clearly, not all children can comprehend this or any other story in exactly the same way because each has different background experiences on which to draw.

A second dimension of understanding this story is related closely to the first. The story involves language that must be meaningful to Malcolm. The most obvious language requirement is one of semantics, or word meaning. Malcolm must know what a *soap box racer* is. He must have the appropriate meaning for words such as *place, even, picked up,* and *race,* as they are used in the context of this story. Expressions such as *crossed the finish line first* and *they were off* must be understood. Understanding of semantics comes from experience with words in various, personally meaningful settings. If Malcolm has built his own racer, discussed racing with other children, or seen races on TV, he has probably acquired the depth of semantic understanding he needs to give meaning to these terms. If such personal experiences are lacking, comprehension suffers because of a language deficiency.

Another language ability that Malcolm needs in order to comprehend the story is a grasp of syntax. The order of words has much to do with the message that the author intends to share. Malcolm must be able to retrieve the flow of ideas as they are communicated by words working together in a sentence. For example, "Two years later his cousin won a race" involves any number of elements that must be correctly related to each other for accurate interpretation. Malcolm

[2] We will assume Malcolm can identify the words. Earlier chapters of this text discuss that matter in detail.

must know to whom *they* refers in "They were off!" Malcolm's ability to understand the story depends on his ability to recover the deep structure of the language. This requires that Malcolm have a mastery of syntax, which links deep and surface structure.

A third aspect of comprehending the story concerns Malcolm's ability to think. Depending on his intellectual development and the opportunity he has had to engage in various types of reasoning, Malcolm will be able to deal with the events and concepts in the story to a greater or lesser degree. For example, if Malcolm has not yet developed the ability to keep a series of events in correct sequence, important aspects of the story may be missed. Charlie's reminiscing on the way to the starting line may confuse Malcolm and interfere with his understanding. Malcolm will be unable to make inferences or engage in critical thinking about the story unless opportunities have been created for him to develop such thought processes in the past. He must also have a sense of story that guides him in the search for elements such as setting and event.

Another factor that could cause comprehension problems for Malcolm is related to his ability to understand his own emotions. Perhaps the most easily recognized affective factor is Malcolm's personal interests. Common sense suggests that Malcolm will attend better to a story about a topic he finds personally interesting and, in the process, will comprehend it better. The cause of greater understanding may also lie in the reader's attitudes and beliefs. Interest, attitudes, and beliefs are usually closely linked. A reader understands material better when it matches his or her own attitude on a topic. Malcolm will comprehend the soap box derby story more fully if he is interested in the topic and positively inclined toward such competition.

Malcolm could also have problems understanding the story if he reads it with no particular purpose in mind. Or understanding can be a problem if the story is read for one purpose and then analyzed or discussed relative to some other purpose. To illustrate, Malcolm might read the story because it is assigned by his teacher. With no specific purpose in mind to focus his attention, Malcolm will probably wander aimlessly through the story passively processing words. Unless he establishes his own purpose before reading or commits the entire story to memory, he will recall little if any of what he has read. Most people have the general purpose of following and enjoying the story line even if no other purpose is established. Yet in the absence of specific directions that have been consciously established by either Malcolm or his teacher in this situation, subtleties may be missed. The feelings of the handicapped boy driving the green car could easily be overlooked, for example. This would clearly be truer when the selection is longer and more complex than in this story.

The clarity of the story itself is another factor that affects how well Malcolm understands what he reads. The author's skill in choosing words that convey the ideas intended and weaving them into a coherent whole that is easily apprehended plays an important part in the comprehension process. The appropriateness of the overall structure created by the author and his or her ability to reveal that structure to the

Basic Components of the Reading Process

reader can facilitate or impede comprehension. The author's use of metaphor, analogy, and advance organizers are just three examples of variables that influence the difficulty of written text. Malcolm must be able to make sense of the story using his knowledge of how text is structured; the more obvious the clues, the better the chances that understanding will occur. Even physical clues to meaning such as page format, headings, and typeface can play a part in making the reading selection easier or harder to comprehend.

This overview attempts to identify the key factors that affect comprehension. Subsequent sections of this and the next chapter deal with each of these factors in more detail. This chapter deals with experience and language factors. Chapter 9 deals with intellectual and emotional factors. Included will be descriptions of ways to assess and develop children's performance in these basic areas. All the factors mentioned are internal to the reader, thus making them subject to the effects of instruction. We will also examine text-related factors briefly in Chapter 9 and discuss how teachers can determine possible sources of confusion in what a pupil is asked to read. It should be pointed out that there is great interdependence among the factors singled out for discussion here. Because each factor is individually presented, it does *not* mean that they are in fact separate. Indeed, it is impossible to discuss language without discussing background experience, for example. Purposes for reading are closely linked to thinking skills. Thinking and feeling are obviously related, and both grow from personal experiences, and so on. With the caution that *the factors affecting comprehension are interdependent,* each is now considered.

Background Experiences Build Concepts

In simplest terms, experiences supply children with the raw materials they must organize and manipulate as they go through life. From infancy onward, children are constantly bombarded with stimuli from the environment. They learn to cope with those stimuli by classifying and cataloging them for future reference. Through a process of noting similarities and differences, they develop concepts and an understanding of relationships between and among concepts. As this organization of environment develops, so does the children's understanding of the world and their place in it (Rumelhart & Ortory, 1977).

As they read, children decode symbols on the printed page that trigger understandings they have developed about life. Those understandings are the result of firsthand and vicarious experiences. When the printed message relates to experiences they have not had, children fail to comprehend. They may even be able to pronounce every word on the page, but if the experiences that give personal meaning to the topic or idea are lacking, children cannot bring understanding they do not have to the reading.

Suppose a group is about to read a story about the circus. Let's say two children in the group have vastly different backgrounds. Tony is the son of a farmer. His home is far out in the country. All members of his family help with the chores, and so there has never been time to see the circus. Sarah has a relative who works for the circus. Whenever the circus is in town, she sees every performance. She has also met the clowns and even eaten with them in their tent. Who will have the best chance of understanding the story? Even if Tony is the better decoder, Sarah has an enormous head start. Certainly, Tony may follow the series of events in the story and be able to answer basic questions. But obviously his depth of understanding is limited by inadequate experience with circuses.

This does not suggest that one cannot learn by reading. Everything a person reads about need not be experienced in order to understand it. But there must be a reservoir of relevant concepts to draw on, or a reader cannot interpret the printed page adequately. A person reading a description of a roller coaster ride may have no closer point of reference than an airplane flight or an automobile ride on a hilly road but still can get an approximate understanding of the author's meaning. But clearly the best experience for understanding the description is an actual roller coaster ride.

Reading instruction, especially as it is embodied in basal reading programs, has a strong tradition of building background (along with introducing key vocabulary) before children read a story. It has been our experience that these activities often become routine, even ritualistic, and may even be omitted after a period of time with the final result being an unfortunate loss of opportunity to enhance children's understanding of what they read. Too often a story about a topic that could be explored in a variety of interesting ways is introduced

Family trips such as this visit to a museum broaden children's horizons beyond their own immediate experiences.

with a shortened preview such as, "What is a circus? Let's read the story on page 73 about a circus coming to town."

Durkin (1984) reported the findings of a study that makes even the one question just asked about a circus seem commendable. She discovered in a study designed to learn to what extent teachers followed the recommendations of basal reader manuals that "not even a minute in any classroom was used to develop or review background information." As if to clinch the matter, she tells of an instance in which a teacher she observed failed to take advantage of a space shuttle launch from Cape Kennedy on the same day a group of children was about to read a story involving a flamingo living in Florida who confused a rocket with a farm silo. In follow-up conversations with the teachers in her study, Durkin found that the press of time caused teachers to omit background-building activities. We can only lament this practice and point out that comprehension depends to a large extent on what the reader brings to the printed page.

The really significant point is that many children often have rather limited background on which to draw. Some children have seen and done far more than others, and differences will exist from topic to topic. But if there is to be the greatest understanding of any given story, the teacher will help children recall whatever experiences they may have had that will help them relate to the events or ideas in a reading selection. Where possible, experiences that build understanding should be provided prior to the reading, ideally at firsthand, but at least vicariously. The discussion of building background will be continued later.

Although a more complete consideration of the matter will be presented in the next chapter, it is appropriate to point out that a person's experiences have a great deal to do with one's interests, attitudes, beliefs, and feelings about a topic. Having tried snow skiing, for example, one may be more interested in reading about snowplow turns and stem christies. Later these factors of affect will be explored as they relate to comprehension.

Assessing Background Experiences

In order to maximize the chances that children will understand what they read, it must be determined what relevant background experiences they have or will need to have before reading a selection. As was stated earlier, no amount of effort will make all children alike insofar as readiness to comprehend a story is concerned. Nevertheless, it is necessary to know how much preparation is needed for a basic level of understanding and which children require such preparation.

The classroom teacher can employ informal assessment techniques to identify specific background limitations. Standardized tests and other formal instruments only generally indicate that a youngster has difficulty with comprehension. To determine whether limited background is the factor particularly responsible for comprehension difficulties, teachers have several means at their disposal.

Questionnaires Can Provide Information on Background Experience

One of the primary advantages of teacher-constructed questionnaires is that special concerns can easily be incorporated in their design. The teacher can write certain questionnaire items to obtain information relevant to a special topic or theme. For example, suppose a group of second-grade children is about to begin a unit on pets in their developmental reading program. Recognizing that understanding is greatly dependent on familiarity with concepts, teachers could construct a questionnaire like the one that follows to assess their students' backgrounds.

Questionnaires can be developed so that even younger children, who cannot write, can provide the information a teacher needs. In this case a first-grade teacher might read the questions to his or her students and ask them to draw or find a picture in a magazine for their answers. A questionnaire can also be used individually with a child in a conference, with the teacher jotting down the child's responses. Questionnaires can be designed to gather general information on a child's travel experiences, hobbies, interests, play activities, or other topics relevant to classroom activities.

Name_____

Interest Questionnaire

1. Do you have a pet?_____
*2. What kind of pet do you have? (Or what kind of pet would you like to have?) _____
3. What other pets have you had before? _____
4. Where does your pet sleep? _____
5. How do you care for your pet? _____
6. Does your pet get a bath? _____
   How do you give the pet a bath? _____
7. What does your pet like to eat? _____

* *Note:* Children who indicate in Item 1 that they do not have a pet can answer subsequent questions for a former pet or the pet they would like to have. Their answers still provide the teacher with a knowledge of the child's background and understanding.

A Questionnaire on Background

1. Develop a questionnaire that would help you learn useful and important information about a child's background. Ask a colleague to complete the questionnaire as a trial run. Discuss the results with your respondent. Determine whether the items are clear and appropriate and how they might be improved.
2. Ask a child to complete your revised questionnaire. Prepare a statement for the child's teacher indicating what interests your questionnaire indicates would be good points of departure for classroom activities.

Basic Components of the Reading Process

Observations Reveal Valuable Information on Background Experiences

Classroom discussions and informal conversations before, during, and after school provide the teacher with an excellent opportunity to note a youngster's background and understanding. Contributions and comments that show misunderstanding or general ignorance about a topic should alert the teacher to the possibility of poor background in that area. For example, a first-grade child who does not know the difference between a helicopter and a jet airplane may never have been to an airport or seen a helicopter hovering overhead. This lack of understanding could be troublesome if the child were going to read *Helicopters and Gingerbread* from the Ginn Series.

At the same time a child's unwillingness to contribute to a group discussion might *not* indicate a lack of background. Shyness or boredom can also explain silence, so additional evidence must be obtained in this case.

In time the teacher will learn which students require further background experiences on most school-related activities. It would be dangerous to label a child limited in terms of background categorically; constant assessment is necessary. Nevertheless, teacher's observations can be guided to a degree by past experiences with the class.

Conferences Help the Teacher Assess Background Experiences

One of the best means for assessing background experience is through a personal conference with a child. Whether a pupil-teacher conference is structured by the completion of a questionnaire or is simply an informal chat, the alert teacher can gather valuable information about a child's experiences by this means. A technique recommended by Strang (1968), introspection by the child, can be employed in a conference. Strang suggests that the child be invited to describe his or her thinking process while reading a selection. The teacher may ask the child how he or she managed to know the meaning of a word or arrive at the meaning of a sentence or paragraph. The child may be asked to explain a specific difficulty as he or she sees it. Given the opportunity, even young children may be able to explain where their comprehension begins to falter. Breakdowns in understanding caused by lack of background can also be revealed with this approach.

Building Background Experiences

The reason for assessing background is to provide experiences the child lacks. This might occur on two levels: The teacher can plan and create numerous opportunities for enriching the child's background generally, or the teacher can often build background for understanding a specific reading selection. Suggestions for dealing with both situations are given next.

Helping Children with Limited Backgrounds

We must be especially careful when talking about children with limited backgrounds. Nearly every child comes to school with a wealth of experiences. However, poverty and lack of mobility often limit some children to a certain type of experience. They may not have had such experiences as visiting a museum, a park, or a lumberyard. A strong cultural bias can creep into a teacher's thinking if the experiences a child might have had in the inner city or in the hollow of some mountain are disregarded in favor of a typical middle-class experience. Schools and teachers might well respond with more sensitivity to the experiences every child has by building on what children bring to school. The language experience approach (discussed elsewhere in this book) attempts to do just that. New curricular materials do a better job of reflecting a variety of backgrounds, so that every child need not fit into a white, middle-class mold.

Limited background, as defined here, does not refer to children from poverty areas alone. For example, children from the inner city or the suburbs may have no conceptualization of events and things on a farm. Their experiences frequently have not exposed them to a tractor, a hayloft, a litter of pigs, or an apple orchard. The word *tractor* may cause some children from suburbia to think of the seven-horse-power miniature used to mow the lawn and plow snow. When Farmer Jones uses his tractor to pull a truck from a ditch, their experience may not square with the description.

A person's understanding of a topic can seldom be called complete.

The opportunity to visit a firehouse allows children to feel part of their community, provides them with new information, and helps expand their world beyond home and school.

Basic Components of the Reading Process

Adults as well as children learn daily and broaden already rich concepts. One's concept of a word like *river* is constantly growing as new experiences provide new information. Understanding the role of waterways in the development and settlement of the United States is a complexity not easily grasped. A concept of outer space is another, dynamic example of an ever-growing field of study. Except for very simple writing, it is safe to say that understanding of a selection is seldom completed. As the appropriate concepts deepen and expand, greater comprehension of a selection previously read is increased. The point is that no matter how many advantages children have had, they can expand their concepts to increase understanding of what they read.

With this broad definition of background, it is clear that nearly anything the teacher does to involve children in a world of ideas is helpful as a way of stretching their experiences. This, in turn, contributes to reading comprehension by building concepts needed for ready reference during reading. Obviously, some activities are more fruitful than others. Concrete, firsthand experiences nearly always have a more lasting impact than vicarious experiences. Active experiences that involve children are preferable to ones in which they are passive observers. Experiences that relate to personal interests or have relevance to children's lives are especially meaningful. It is important to remember that differences in cognitive development may permit some children to get more out of a common experience than another, less mature child will.

A specific example might help illustrate the application of these principles. Suppose Judy Crawford, a primary-grade teacher, decides her students need a better understanding of pollution. This conclusion might be the result of general observations of the children's lack of understanding, a consequence of some classroom incident, or related to an upcoming unit of study. Ms. Crawford might plan a series of active, firsthand experiences that focus on how pollution affects children's daily lives. This could include a walking excursion to a nearby shopping center to observe littering, a field trip by bus to a water filtration plant, a cleanup hike around the neighborhood, a visit to the classroom by an environmentalist, and individual exploration by children to identify sources of pollution in the community. Discussions can be held, letters written for information and to protest pollution sources, interviews conducted, and so forth. Displays might be arranged, and objects handled by the children. All these activities can be done in such a way as to broaden children's backgrounds and introduce or enrich concepts.

Though this example is long-term and fairly involved, simple, onetime experiences can be valuable. A lesson can be planned, for example, to sensitize children to various textures. Common objects in the classroom environment can be touched and compared. Items can be classified into groups and labels found to describe their textures.

These firsthand experiences certainly do not rule out the possibility of vicarious experiences, such as watching a film or listening to a record. These and other, similar activities are more abstract and consequently are not so easy for children to relate to. Nevertheless, concepts and the language related to those concepts can be explored via audiovisual means as ways of building general background.

Building Background for a Specific Reading Selection

In a reading program where the teacher frequently assigns the same selection to a group of children it is feasible to spend some time building background for a single story. If children are selecting their own stories and reading them independently, it is nearly impossible to build backgrounds for every child and every story. In that case the child's interest in the topic has probably guided his or her choice of the story or book, and so he or she often has some background experiences that account for interest and facilitate comprehension. If understanding falters, the teacher should be alert to the need for background experience and supply it if at all possible. The language experience approach automatically builds on the child's background, for in such cases children usually write their own stories.

When a group is about to read a story, the teacher is obliged to determine what background experiences are basic to understanding the story and supply those experiences wherever possible. Here is an example.

Suppose a group in a second-grade class is about to read "The Airport," a story about two boys who take their first plane ride. Well in advance of the day the group will read the story, the teacher should begin to assess background experience and gather resources for overcoming limited backgrounds among the children. The teacher can prepare a questionnaire that explores each child's familiarity with airports and airplanes. The teacher may have noticed youngsters with a special interest in airplanes, who can be asked to share a book or models that may be built. If the school district has an instructional materials center that stores or obtains films and other teaching aids on various topics, the teacher can request materials on airports and airplanes. In some instances, it might even be profitable to arrange for a trip to an airport as a means of building necessary background. The extent of the teacher's efforts in gathering materials and arranging background experiences depends on the readiness of the youngsters to proceed to read the story without this special preparation. It also depends on the amount of time the teacher can devote to such activities. A balance must be struck between giving adequate time to building background and making an unjustified production out of such activities.

On the day the reading group is ready to begin "The Airport," the teacher can introduce the topic and make use of the resources that have been gathered. The teacher can initiate a discussion by asking questions and relating experiences of his or her own. For example:

> Boys and girls, today we are going to read about Ben and Matt's trip back to their home. How do you suppose they will travel? (Children offer ideas.)

Basic Components of the Reading Process

You will see that they are flying by jet airplane. Have any of you ridden in a jet? Tell us about it. (Sharing takes place.) What was the airport like? What interesting or unusual things did you see there? (Comments by children.) What happens to your luggage at the airport? (Suggestions are given; the teacher tells about losing luggage on a recent trip because this is an important element in the story to be read.)

The discussion should be guided by the teacher to cover topics that are important in the story (handling of luggage in this case). During this period the teacher can introduce some vocabulary items orally and sometimes on the chalkboard, as well to be sure they have meaning when they appear in the story. (All "new" vocabulary probably should not be introduced, for children need opportunities to employ their word identification skills.) A model airplane might be shown; and a child, asked to tell about a hobby of flying models with a parent.

These activities are designed to create interest in reading the story, as well as to build vocabulary and related concepts. The goal is not to guarantee that every child knows the same amount about airplanes but rather to provide sufficient information for every child to predict meaning and understand the story. Because of past experience, a pilot's son will find much more personal meaning in the story than another child, George, whose experience with airplanes is negligible. Nonetheless, George will be better prepared to comprehend the story, having heard and seen the planned activities before reading. Keep in mind that on another topic (for example, fishing) George may be the expert; and the pilot's son, the inexperienced one. The alert teacher will capitalize on student's strengths and try to use stories that are related to their personal experiences.

When children fail to understand some aspect of material they have read, consider the possibility that insufficient prior experience with the topic, issues, or events may be at fault. It is only by taking the time to build necessary background that the teacher can ever expect children to gain sufficient experiences to read subsequent materials with understanding. Adequate time spent on exploring a variety of topics should result in improved reading comprehension.

Building Background for a Story

1. Suppose you were going to have a group of children read "The Three Billy Goats Gruff." What activities would you plan to enhance their comprehension?
2. Describe how you could follow actual reading of the story in 1 with activities that would broaden the children's backgrounds.

Comprehension Is Dependent on Language Abilities

To state the obvious, one must have a basic knowledge of the English language in order to read it. *Semantics* and *syntax* are important to the delivery of meaning. As a reminder, the semantics of a language refers to the meanings of words; syntax refers to the way words work together. Semantics and syntax as they related to reading comprehension, as well as suggestions for assessing student language abilities and overcoming deficiencies, are given in the next section.

Semantic Meanings Grow from Personal Experience

Teachers and publishers have for decades recognized the importance of semantics in reading instruction. Typically, their concern has been identified as one of controlling vocabulary. When the printed page presents too many "new words" the vocabulary load overburdens the reader and comprehension falters. Try reading this paragraph, which contains a high percentage of "hard" words:

> A neoteric car can egress anyplace. This exiguous car has six wheels. It egresses on promontory and in the paludal. Fishermen desiderate this neoteric car. They can egress into the paludal with it. Farmers desiderate this neoteric car, too. They can egress into barnyards and variform lieus without roads.

Put more simply:

> A new minicar can go anywhere. This little car has six wheels. It goes on land and in the water. Fishermen like this new car. They can go right into the water with it. Farmers like this new car, too. They can go into barnyards and other places without roads.

Obviously, unfamiliar vocabulary can interfere with comprehension. (So there is no mistake, let us reemphasize at the outset that vocabulary itself is merely a surface representation of underlying concepts. Comprehension involves seeing relationships among concepts, not simply "knowing words." A program that builds vocabulary in a meaningful way is actually building concepts.)

The burden of vocabulary is a relative matter. What is hard for you may not be hard for someone else. A second dimension of this matter has been mentioned previously: Each person is an "expert" on a different topic. You are undoubtedly more knowledgeable than your friends in a number of areas and, consequently, have in your vocabulary many terms they may not know (for example, ballet terms, fencing terms, sewing terms, physics terms, and so on).

The explanation for vocabulary differences is relatively simple. People normally have the vocabulary that accompanies their experiences. Younger children have fewer experiences than older people;

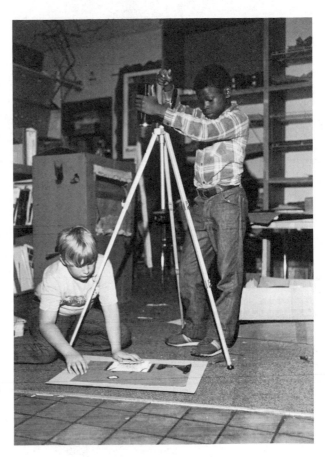

These boys are learning new concepts and the terms needed for the equipment and procedures related to their hobby of photography.

consequently, their vocabularies are smaller on the whole. The best way to increase vocabulary is to engage in stimulating experiences that are accompanied by language. Thus, each of the activities suggested earlier for building background will also build vocabulary provided they include discussion, asking and answering questions, and general conversation with people who know the language related to a topic (for example, a teacher, a guide, a visiting expert).

Programs that attempt to build vocabulary by teaching the meanings of selected words are not well founded. Dictionary meanings are not learned by memorizing; they grow from using a word in a context that is important to meaning. Having students look up "new" words in a dictionary before reading a story is typically not productive. Those terms should be embedded in an interesting discussion or activity about the topics treated in the story. In other words, vocabulary must be met in context.

Context is important to word meaning in several ways. First, the clues of surrounding context help readers make specific applications of the intended meaning. To illustrate, if you are told a *gasket* is "a piece of rubber, cork, or other material placed around a joint to make it leakproof," you have an abstract description of the item. If you meet the term in this context: "The *gasket* on this dripping faucet needs to be replaced," its meaning becomes much more vivid through application. Second, as most terms have a variety of meanings, context is needed to know which particular meaning applies. For example, the word *rule* can mean (1) something that usually happens (e.g., we eat around 8:00 A.M. as a rule); (2) a regulation (e.g., one rule we have is no running.); (3) a measuring device (e.g., I'll get a rule and measure it.); (4) the reign of a government (e.g., it was during the *rule* of Queen Victoria). The intended meaning is clear only in context.

Semantics

Invite five people to give you immediate word associations for these terms: frog, typewriter, asteroid, altruism. Make a list of their responses. Determine what similarity and dissimilarity there is for each term across participants. Discuss how personal experiences influenced the associations given. (Frog: Slimy—I hate them. My brother put one down my back once.)

Syntactic Clues to Meaning

When children first learn to read, it is the semantics of their language that typically gets the greatest attention. The fact that word meaning varies and, in turn, affects the meaning of a sentence or paragraph is so obvious that it cannot be overlooked.

Just as obvious, but not so readily understood, is the importance of syntax, which refers to the "rules" or sentence structure people use unconsciously when they speak a language. Consider the following sentence: "The jurd sumped dooly to the rem." Most of the words in this example do not have lexical or dictionary meaning. They do have structural meaning, however; that is, they contribute to meaning by their places and function in the sentence. Persons who are familiar with English can readily determine that the subject of the sentence is *jurd*. Furthermore, the structure of the sentence enables us to tell what the *jurd* did, how it was done, and where it was done.

Meaning is signaled through the structure of English in three ways:

1. By patterns of word order.
2. By inflectional endings.
3. By function words that have little or no meaning of their own (Goodman, 1963).

The words in the nonsense sentence example follow a common pattern for American English. Even without semantic cues, any speaker of English can specify that this alteration of the previous sentence is not grammatic: "Jurd dooly sumped rem the to the." Word order is one important carrier of meaning.

242   Basic Components of the Reading Process

In this example the inflectional ending *ed* on *sumped* tells us that

1. *Sump* describes an action.
2. Whatever action occurred took place in the past.

In the same way, *dooly* is evidently an adverb telling how the *jurd sumped*. We also know that only one *jurd* was involved in the action; the inflectional ending *s* would be used to indicate more than one *jurd*. Meaning is also carried by variations in word endings.

Finally, *the* serves as a *function word* in the nonsense sentence, marking *jurd* and *rem* as nouns. Examples of other function words are *very, not, there, when, yes, no,* and *well.*

One does not add word meanings together in a left-to-right sequence and arrive at meaning when the end of a sentence is reached. Meaning is delivered by the interaction of words. It is the meaning delivered by words working together that must be retrieved so that the reader understands. This is accomplished according to generative-transformational grammar theory by means of a series of transformations.

Transformations are essentially rearrangements of phrases in a sentence that make its underlying meaning more explicit. Transformations are conducted according to the rules of syntax. These are the rules that every speaker of English has learned inductively despite the fact that all the rules cannot be specified. Some linguists believe that humans are born with a predisposition toward acquiring these rules. Meaning is gained from reading by recovering the deep structure of language using the rules of syntax. Authorities have not yet agreed on the exact nature of *deep structure,* but it is thought to be a basic grammatic form that serves as a point of reference for understanding the relationships among meanings.

In effect, a sentence is read at the surface level (the printed page). Readers understand the ideas communicated by the author by engaging in a series of transformations that take them to the deep structure. For example, all three of the following sentences have different surface structures, yet two have the same meaning. Therefore, those two sentences have the same deep structure. The third sentence has a different meaning, hence a different deep structure.

1. He drew a brown bear.
2. He drew a bear brown.
3. He drew a bear that was brown.

In order to gain meaning from the printed page, the reader must be able to recover deep structure. In Chapter 3 we described the language acquisition process briefly. We pointed out that formal instruction in language typically does not occur, and yet children learn the rules of syntax. The question to be asked, then, is, Should reading instruction focus on syntax as a means of improving comprehension? Different authorities answer that question in different ways. Some writers, such as Hoskisson (1974, 1975), argue that children can learn to read much as they learn to talk—by being immersed in reading. Hoskisson's strategy, called *Assisted Reading,* is described thus:

> Assisted reading is the natural extension of what many parents already do—read to their children. Many children ask to know what the words are that they see on signs, in advertisements, and on television. Parents extend this curiosity or develop it by reading to their children and having the children repeat the words after them. Words, phrases, or sentences may be read by the parent and repeated by the child. Thus, the visual or graphic configurations are presented to the children in an informal but pleasant situation. The child can look for the significant differences that will eventually lead him to establish the graphic features he needs in order to become a fluent reader. He begins to learn to read by reading, much as he learned to talk by talking [Hoskisson, 1975, p. 313].

Though Hoskisson would not avoid discussions about word endings, for example, these would occur only as the child initiated them. The parent or teacher would not systematically teach certain inflections, specific sentence patterns, or the like in a formal manner.

Other authorities believe certain aspects of syntax should be taught consciously and systematically. For example, Deighton (1966) cites four separate ways that words can be related to each other.

1. Subject-predicate relation.
2. Coordinate relation.
3. Complement relation.
4. Modifier relation.

The complexities involved in sorting out a sentence so that words are correctly related to one another prompts Deighton to recommend that reading instruction include the study of how sentence structures deliver meaning. As a first step in this direction, he suggests that it is helpful to note the direction of word flow in a sentence. The flow is not, as we might suppose, consistently from left to right—it is not always additive. Although some sentences have a left-to-right flow of meaning—for example, "Tom hit the ball"—in a great many English sentences the flow is circular: "Tom is the president." The verb in the second sentence, a form of *be,* is called a linking verb. The words following the verb refer to the word preceding the verb. Thus, the flow of thought is from left to right and back to the beginning, or circular. To comprehend the sentence, the reader must hold meaning in abeyance.

Deighton states that all linking verbs—such as *look, remain, stay, sound,* and *get* and *keep*—in certain constructions deliver meaning by identification, characterization, or description. They attribute specific features to the subject of the sentence and, therefore, transmit information in a circular pattern.

Children's reading comprehension can be improved, according to Deighton, by planning instructional activities that call attention to different sentence patterns. For example, children can be taught that the presence of a linking verb in a sentence signals the circular flow of meaning described earlier. The teacher can provide exercises in which linking verbs are circled. Later the object of the sentence can be underlined; and an arrow, drawn showing the flow of meaning. Such activities focus the children's attention on those aspects of syntax that are important to reading comprehension. Similar exercises can make young readers aware of other sentence patterns.

Weaver (1979) undertook an experiment to determine whether reading comprehension could be improved by providing instruction about sentence organization. The results were encouraging. Third-graders performed significantly better on several comprehension measures after being taught a strategy for arranging a jumbled set of words into a meaningful sentence. Similar findings have been reported by Cromer (1970), Gibbons (1971), Gibson and Levin (1975), Greenewald and Pederson (1982), and Resnick (1970).

Sentence-combining exercises that teach students to read two or more short, simple sentences and combine and rewrite them into one, longer, more complex sentence have also been shown to improve reading comprehension (Combs, 1977). Similar findings have been reported by Fisher (1973), Hughes (1975), and Straw (1978).

Pearson and Johnson (1985) present a number of practical suggestions for involving pupils in activities that build on various syntactic abilities. They organize their discussion around nine types of relations that exist between propositions (clauses) in written discourse: (1) paraphrase, (2) association, (3) main ideas, (4) comparison, (5) figurative language, (6) ambiguous statements, (7) cause and effect, (8) sequence, and (9) anaphoric relations; but they caution that overlap is inherent in their scheme. The types of teaching suggestions they recommend range from asking questions to instructional games and make use of common materials such as cartoons, and newspaper articles. We recommend that you examine the Pearson/Johnson book for detailed suggestions concerning the teaching of language (and thinking) operations applied to reading.

Many other teaching ideas and procedures are being developed by those interested in the application of linguistics to reading instruction to help children deal with syntactic clues to meaning. We expect continuing research in the area of linguistics to provide further direction for these efforts in the future.

Assessing Language Abilities

Classroom teachers have various formal and informal means at their disposal for assessing children's language abilities. Measures of semantics will be discussed first, then measures of syntactic ability.

Measures of Semantic Abilities

It is quite common for the achievement batteries and reading survey tests used in schoolwide testing programs to include a vocabulary subtest. Tests such as the *Stanford Achievement Tests* and the *Gates-MacGinitie Reading Tests* give children a series of tasks in which a term is presented, often in a short phrase, along with four alternatives. The children are asked to select the one alternative that is closest in meaning to the term given. The children demonstrate their knowledge of word meaning by matching synonyms. Some tests of vocabulary call for the child to match words of opposite meaning. Typical vocabulary test items are

Directions: Select the word that has the same or nearly the same meaning.

1. the *illumination* was poor
   a. lighting   b. furniture   c. discrimination   d. destination
2. a *magnificent* view
   a. terrible   b. frightening   c. pleasing   d. narrow

Many basal reading programs used by schools today include vocabulary tests with the preceding format that enable the teacher to determine quickly and easily which words included in a story may not be familiar to the child. Basal reader tests often use a format in which the child places words in sentences containing a blank. For example:

Directions: Write the word that best completes the sentence in the blank provided.

joyful   wonderful   awful   restful   useful

1. The _____ crowd cheered as the excellent show ended.
2. Jack thanked Peter for the _____ gift.
3. The quiet vacation we spent at the lake was very _____ .
4. I have a _____ gift for your birthday.
5. Hitting that boy was an _____ thing to do.

You as a teacher may want to develop your own vocabulary tests using a format similar to those just described.

Vocabulary can also be assessed through the use of pictures. In tests such as the *Peabody Picture Vocabulary Test* (PPVT), the child is asked to select a picture that best describes a word from among several alternatives. Such tests measure the child's experiential background and opportunity to learn and consequently can contain substantial bias. Nevertheless, they do assess the child's familiarity with vocabulary he or she is likely to encounter in many reading programs. A teacher can counteract this cultural bias in commercially prepared tests or in the development of teacher-made vocabulary tests by including pictures known to be appropriate for the students. Other pictures that are relevant to the materials the children will read in the instructional program can also be included.

Classroom teachers who need information about the semantic abilities of their students will find any number of opportunities to observe children's performance on a daily basis. The child's use of words in attempting oral and written communication give a clear indication of semantic ability. Misuse of words or the child's failure to understand

Basic Components of the Reading Process

a word's multiple meanings gives the teacher specific information useful in planning language development activities. Through observation the teacher can identify vocabulary that children understand in receiving information (that is, *receptive vocabulary*), but do not use in their own communication efforts (that is, *expressive vocabulary*).

Teacher-made tests can be developed to determine children's understanding of vocabulary from the basal reader; from the content areas, such as science and social studies; from classroom discussions; and from other classroom activities. Tests can reveal the child's understanding of compound words, roots, word origins, prefix and suffix meanings, and multiple meanings. The importance of context should be reflected in tests you develop. Several examples are given on page 247 to illustrate how teacher-made vocabulary tests can be developed. The distinct advantage of such tests is that you can include whatever words are important for the instructional program in your classroom.

The cloze procedure described on page 480 can be used to assess the child's semantic ability. A cloze passage can be prepared by deleting either every fifth, eighth, or tenth word or words of a certain type (for example, nouns, adjectives). The child's ability to supply the deleted words provides a direct and clear measure of his or her knowledge of words. Obviously, the cloze procedure does not measure semantic ability alone, for the reader is heavily dependent on syntactic clues when supplying words that have been deleted. Despite this complication, the teacher will be able to gain a picture of the size, as well as the maturity level, of a child's vocabulary.

Sample Teacher-Made Vocabulary Test

Compound Words

Combine words from List A and List B to form compound words that fit into the blanks that follow.

earth	body
pan	worm
some	where
every	cake

1. I put an _____ on my hook and dropped it into the lake.
2. Mary looked _____ for her lost book.
3. We can make a _____ for breakfast.
4. Did _____ borrow my pencil?

Prefixes

Write the usual meaning of the prefixes in italics in the following sentences:

1. Dad had to *relight* the fire. *Re* means _____.
2. A *multicolored* rainbow followed the storm. *Multi* means _____
_____.
3. Our new car is a *subcompact*. *Sub* means _____.

Substitute a word for the italic word that makes the meaning just **Antonyms** opposite in the following sentences:

1. It will be *frigid* outside tomorrow.
2. We were *elated* at the way the football game ended.
3. This *enormous* box can be put near the door.

Measures of Syntactic Abilities

The cloze procedure provides valuable information regarding the child's understanding of syntax. His or her ability to supply deleted words gives an indication of ability to see the relationship among words.

Asking the child to identify an incongruent sentence among three with different surface structures (when two have identical deep structures), as described earlier in this chapter, is also a useful measure of syntactic understanding. For example, which sentences below would the child identify as having the same meaning?

1. I like to eat fish.
2. Fish is something I like to eat.
3. Something I eat likes fish.

A variation of this approach requires the child to complete sentences that have words missing in such a way as to give them the same meaning:

1. _____ is something I like to _____ .
2. I like to _____ _____ .

Another way to measure syntactic ability is to present the child with a sentence in which the order of words has been scrambled. The child uses his or her knowledge of syntax to recreate a sentence with a meaningful message. For example, *"dog up the stairs ran the"* is reordered as *"The dog ran up the stairs."*

Teachers can gain a sense of the child's knowledge of syntax by observing use of language in oral and written communication. Children who consistently confuse word order may have a language deficiency that can interfere with reading comprehension. Children who have difficulty understanding oral communications may have similar problems.

Expanding and Refining Language Abilities

Efforts to expand and refine children's language abilities should acknowledge the fact that language is acquired initially without formal, carefully sequenced instruction. The child learns language inductively by being immersed in language. Classroom activities can promote language development most effectively by creating many and varied opportunities to use language. Activities that actually involve children and build on their personal interests usually result in greater enthusiasm and participation. The child who is motivated by an intrinsic desire to communicate will develop the necessary abilities to do so over a period of time. Naturally, the availability of skilled users of language to provide feedback to children about their efforts at using language is important. The teacher's role becomes one of creating a stimulating environment and assisting children as they experiment with language.

Encouraging Language

1. Many teachers find dramatic play and role-playing to be especially good ways of encouraging language production. Props are often helpful in creating the right conditions, but they aren't absolutely necessary. Two children can be asked to pretend that they are going fishing or on a hike. Their conversation can center around preparations for the coming event, collecting equipment, planning a schedule, and so forth. Younger children take to such play without self-consciousness; older children may need more help in getting started. This is where personal interests can be useful. A scene involving a topic several children enjoy automatically encourages involvement and participation. Two eleven-year-old boys might pretend to be scouts who are hoping to recruit a basketball player for their team, for example.

2. Puppets and a puppet theater help children overcome their stage fright and use language more freely. As it is the puppet "talking," not the child, spontaneity is encouraged. Flannel boards and shadow theaters can also be used to add variety to language activities. Children enjoy retelling favorite stories using these devices and making up their own stories.

3. Language can also be expanded and refined through group discussion. Topics for these sessions can range from current events to sharing of hobbies and avocations. Children often profit from class interactions following the reading of a story when these are not turned into testing sessions in which dissecting the story is the main goal. Freewheeling discussions can lead off into numerous byways, and topics and subtopics generate interest and stimulate sharing of children's related experiences. Vocabulary grows naturally in this and other, similar activities not because it is the subject of study but because it occurs in a context where ideas are examined and meanings are exchanged.

4. On occasion it is appropriate to make language the object of deliberate study. Children enjoy playing with words in games such as password, charades, scrabble, and so forth. Crossword puzzles often provide an enjoyable word-centered activity. Linguistic word blocks that are spilled and arranged to form sentences focus attention on a number of language elements. Bulletin boards that introduce unusual words or point out oddities about language encourage language study. Word origins can be investigated, and the evolution of words or expressions can be traced in an historical context.

5. The cloze procedure can be used as a way of encouraging children to study language. A discussion among a small group of children concerning what terms might fit into a blank and how the use of different words affects sentence meaning can be most revealing. A transparency can easily be made of a cloze passage so that an entire class can work on the same exercise at one time, discussing and considering how the language in the passage functions.

6. Present the following synonym game based on the familiar game of dominoes. Draw two connected squares on the board. Write *jump* in one square and *slow* in the second square. Draw two more squares on either end of the original pair (as in the following diagram).

		jump	slow		

Have a volunteer write a synonym for either of the words in the middle squares in the adjacent square and use the word in a sentence as a check on meaning (e.g., place *hop* next to *jump*). Have the volunteer choose another word for the next square (on the same side). For example:

run	hop	jump	slow		

Another volunteer now adds two squares to the left and fills in a synonym for *run,* as well as another new word in the square to the left; or this volunteer can write a synonym for *slow* in the square to the right and add a new word in the next square to the right. In other words, each player adds two squares to one end of the chain. The first word is a synonym for the adjoining word; the second word is the volunteer's choice.

hurry					
dream					
run	hop	jump	slow	slack	wait
					stop
					turn
					spin
					round
				chair	circle

Once children understand the principle, have them pair up and play the synonym domino game on a piece of paper for a specified period of time. (Squares can be added above or below a previous square to conserve space. See page 250.)
If one player cannot think of a synonym for either end of the chain, the other player gets to add a synonym and another word. Keep track of the number of squares each player adds. The winner is the player who adds the most squares.

Developing Language

1. Make a flannel board by covering a three-by-five-foot piece of cardboard with flannel. Cut characters for a story you enjoy from flannel (*Peter Pan* or *Mary Poppins,* for example). Practice telling the story without a script in front of a mirror. When you feel ready, present the story to a friend.
2. Present your story to a group of children. Involve several children in retelling the story by giving them a part and a flannel character to manipulate. Avoid learning lines. Follow a general plot, and let dialogue emerge spontaneously.

Studying Language Used in One Selection

One of the oldest traditions associated with reading instruction is the practice of introducing "new" words before a group of children reads a whole selection. The intent of this procedure is laudable—to guarantee that children will understand the language they encounter in the story and thereby maximize everyone's chances for successful reading. In practice, the procedure often falls far short of its goal, for this approach to vocabulary is merely a cosmetic one. The pronunciation and meaning of the word are introduced. Often the word is not presented in a sentence context, and the obvious limitations of this have been cited earlier. Even when the words are presented in context, however, the procedure is inadequate. Words are not objects to be strung on a neck-lace. They have true meaning and are integrated by the learner only when they help label some object, idea, or concept. One does not start with a word and look for a meaning in the normal course of events. Meaning evolves, and words are found to label or express that meaning. Words for a reading selection should be met in the context of a discussion that focuses on the key concepts in a story. If courage and loyalty are the important elements, for example, discussion before and after reading the story should help children remember and draw on their own experiences relevant to these elements. It doesn't help much to write those words on the board and "introduce" them prior to reading. Such an approach treats words as the most important factor in reading. The words are important, but only as they *reveal meaning.*

As a side issue we should also point out that the practice of teaching new words prior to reading as a regular routine relieves the child of the need to apply word-identification skills when meeting those words in the context of the story. A good approach is to introduce irregular, hard-to-decode words if they seem to jeopardize understanding. Otherwise, key concepts can be dealt with, and important vocabulary can be extracted from an introductory discussion. When children use a word or when the teacher can introduce it in the context of preliminary activities, the word becomes tied to personal experience and has meaning.

The story "Earthquake" describes a major quake that occurred in Alaska in the mid-1960s. This description of a teacher in the classroom indicates how vocabulary can be extracted from an introductory discussion that focuses on concepts rather than merely memorizing word meanings in isolation.

An Approach to Introducing Vocabulary

Arrange the children in a circle or semicircle so that visual contact and discussion are facilitated. Begin by showing the group a picture of a large building, bridge, or other structure made by humans that has been heavily damaged by an earthquake. Invite the children to describe what they see in the picture. Ask for speculation concerning how the damage shown in the picture may have occurred. Group their suggestions into categories, such as "natural events" and "events made by humans." Invite descriptions of personal experiences with tornadoes, hurricanes, fires, explosions, earthquakes, floods, mud slides, tidal waves, and other catastrophes. Draw out examples of the powerful forces involved in these events (for example, moving heavy objects, destroying buildings and homes, redirecting rivers). Introduce *collapsed* in this context by writing it on the board in this phrase: "The bridge collapsed during the flood."

Ask the group to think about how people react during such events. Encourage expression of personal feelings of fear, alarm, panic. Introduce *terror, screamed, fright* in this context by using the words in sentences on the board.

Explain that today's story is about one of nature's most powerful forces—earthquakes. Determine whether any of the children have experienced an earthquake. Discuss the cause of earthquakes and their usual locations (in or near mountains). Go to a map of North America, and ask individual members of the group to point out places where earthquakes might be expected to occur in North America.

Point to Alaska on the map. Ask whether it is likely that earthquakes would occur there. Invite speculation. Call attention to the mountainous nature of Alaska's landscape. If possible, locate the more mountainous areas of Alaska on the map. Show a picture of snow-covered mountains. Introduce *glistening* and *craggy* in sentences on the board.

Ask what danger there is to life in an earthquake. How might people or animals be injured or killed? Suggest the possibility of drowning as a cause of death due to earthquakes. Describe a tidal wave. Give a concrete referent for the size of a tidal wave (forty to eighty feet) by comparing its height to something familiar to the children (a building, water tower, or other local landmark). In this context introduce the terms *swell, ebb, tidal wave* in sentences on the board.

252   Basic Components of the Reading Process

Summary

Efforts to help children understand what they read often focus on the products of comprehension and ignore the process. Teachers who can remember a particular conception of comprehension stand a better chance of improving comprehension because they can pay attention to its basic components and thereby affect the process.

A model of comprehension is presented in this chapter. Two major components, background experience and language abilities, are discussed with regard to the role they play in helping a reader gain meaning from a selection. Background experiences provide the reader with a repertoire on which to draw when searching for an author's meaning. Language abilities grow around background experiences when the learner has an opportunity to discuss his or her reactions and questions with someone who uses language effectively. Meaning is communicated by semantic as well as syntactic clues.

Teachers must first understand how background experiences and language abilities are important to reading comprehension. They must also have strategies and techniques for assessing the child's experiential and language base. Where deficiencies that interfere with understanding are found in these areas, the teacher must create opportunities and provide instruction that helps the child bring adequate resources to the reading task so he or she can understand better.

Terms for Self-study

assisted reading	function word
cloze procedure	transformation

Discussion Questions

1. What experiences that children would ordinarily have in their first nine years of life would enable them to find meaning in the story of Cinderella?
2. How is it possible for a child to "read" and understand a word in story and not be able to pronounce that word?

Recommended Readings

Flood, James (Ed.). (1983). *Understanding reading comprehension: Cognition, language, and the structure of prose.* Newark, DE: International Reading Association.
This volume includes papers that focus on three aspects of comprehension: the cognitive ability of the reader, the linguistic ability of the reader, and the structural organization of the text.

Goodman, Yetta M., & Burke, Carolyn. (1980). *Reading strategies: Focus on comprehension*. New York: Holt, Rinehart and Winston.

This book provides reading strategy lessons in a workbook-type format and presents a theoretical framework for stressing the use of semantic and syntactic cues. It also provides actual reading material and lesson plans as examples.

Pearson, P. David, & Johnson, Dale D. (1985). *Teaching reading comprehension*. New York: Holt, Rinehart and Winston.

The authors take the view that comprehension is teachable and provide a theoretical base along with numerous activities that illustrate the kinds of instruction teachers can provide to enhance understanding.

Spiro, Rand J., Bruce, Bertram C., & Brewer, William F. (1983). *Theoretical issues in reading comprehension*. Hillsdale, NJ: Lawrence Erlbaum Associates.

Here is a collection of twenty-four papers by noted scholars, who explore reading comprehension from a variety of perspectives, including cognitive psychology, linguistics, artificial intelligence, and education.

Strange, Michael. (1980, January). Instructional implications of a conceptual theory of reading comprehension. *The Reading Teacher, 33*(4), 391–397.

Strange develops the idea that reading instruction should be based on an interactive model of reading and emphasizes the importance of the reader's prior knowledge in constructing meaning from text.

Tierney, Robert J., & Cunningham, James W. (1984). Research on teaching reading comprehension. In P. David Pearson et al. (Eds.), *Handbook of reading research* (pp. 609–656). New York: Longman.

This is a review and summary of research studies that have examined how reading comprehension can be enhanced through instruction.

9

Reading Comprehension: Cognitive, Affective, and Text Factors

One of the most interesting parts of a daily newspaper, in our view, is the editorial page, including most particularly the section containing letters to the editor. At times the appearance of an editorial will provoke a spate of letters to the editor—some challenging the editor's position on a topic and others supporting the editor. What we find fascinating and especially revealing occurs when the letters from some readers interpret an editorial one way and other letters indicate just the opposite interpretation. We are not speaking of differences in interpretation that reflect shades of meaning here, nor are we thinking of occasions when an editorial is not clearly written and is, therefore, ambiguous. Rather, we have in mind those occasions when absolute and diametrically opposed interpretations are made of an editorial that seemed to us, at least, to take a clear position on a controversial topic.

What amazes us is that some readers can miss what we take to be the intended meaning of the editorial so completely. Having watched for such misinterpretations over a period of time, we note that these responses often come from someone who has a strong emotional investment in a topic. A member of the National Rifle Association may believe an editorial has supported registration of firearms, for example, when many other readers who bothered to respond to the editorial evidently got an entirely different meaning. What these cases of differing interpretation demonstrate is the strong influence one's beliefs and attitudes have on reading comprehension. Although some differences in the interpretation of an editorial are to be expected, all interpretations cannot be equally appropriate. Among the most severe challenges a teacher of reading will face is that of helping children apply their thinking and feelings in appropriate ways as they read. This chapter will explore important issues having to do with cognitive and affective influences on comprehension. Look for the answers to the following questions as you read:

- *How are thinking and comprehension related?*
- *How do thinking abilities develop, and how can they be assessed?*
- *How are feelings and beliefs important to comprehension?*
- *In what ways does having a purpose for reading affect comprehension?*
- *When is poor writing to blame for comprehension problems?*
- *How can comprehension be assessed?*
- *What instructional strategies are helpful in improving comprehension?*

In discussing Figure 8.1 in Chapter 8, we looked at two of the factors identified as major components of reading comprehension (background experience and language abilities). Four additional major components of comprehension also shown in the figure will be discussed here: thinking abilities, affective factors, purposes for reading, and text factors.

Thinking Is a Basic Component of Comprehension

As you read this text, you are in the process of thinking. We have asked you to see relationships while you are reading, to make comparisons, to follow sequences of ideas, and to engage in any number of similar mental operations, so it should hardly seem necessary to persuade you that reading involves thinking.

As a teacher of reading, you will want to involve children in activities that help them think as they read. To do that, you need some understanding of how thinking abilities develop and what the teacher can do to assess and help develop children's thinking.

How Thinking Abilities Develop

A child, from the time of birth, is constantly bombarded with stimuli. Events and information gathered by the senses and impressions are fed to the brain. A great deal of speculation and research has been done to explain how the child begins to deal with the flood of data the environment provides. It seems fairly certain that each individual event or piece of information cannot be handled as a unique and novel incident. Apparently, the child, even as an infant, begins to develop some structure for ordering his or her perceptions. Mental categories develop, and stimuli are assigned to those established categories. New stimuli are encountered, and categories grow to include these data. Eventually new categories are created as the type and number of stimuli require them and as the child's growing understanding of the environment permits this. Through a process of generalization and discrimination, children bring some order to their world. Their structure for dealing with the world orders their perceptions (Rumelhart & Ortony, 1977).

As children grow and mature, their way of ordering their observations changes. More and broader experiences with objects and people explain this change, in part, but children also grow in ability to deal with abstractions. They are able to move from the here and now to the past and to the future. They can move from the concrete to the abstract and from the specific to the general. It appears that every child reaches these more advanced stages of thinking via the same route. That is, the child goes through the same stages of intellectual, or cognitive, development. According to the cognitive psychologist Piaget, these stages cannot be hurried. Information and events are interpreted or perceived by the child within his or her mental structure (called "schema" in the current literature). When the child is ready to evolve a new structure the same information or event will be perceived or understood differently. Teaching that does not take the child's level of development into account will be unsuccessful (Piaget, 1963).

To illustrate, children operating at Piaget's preoperational level—away from self-centeredness but not yet logical—are prone to see everything from their own viewpoint. Their thinking is self-centered, or egocentric. The "Soap Box Derby" story introduced in Chapter 8 would be interpreted by such children from a strictly personal perspective. It would be fruitless to argue with a preoperational-level child that his or her interpretation of the story is illogical or that it is only one of many possible interpretations. Later—because of interaction with objects, peers, and adults and because of maturation—the child will be ready to compare his or her thoughts with others. But formal and systematic instruction will not cause this change before the child is ready to make it.

Certain conditions can facilitate cognitive growth. These include an environment that encourages exploration, manipulation of objects, and "play"; peers and adults who interact with the child; and curricular goals that are organized in a hierarchical manner, from logical step to bigger logical step. Learners must actively interact with the physical and social environment. Their interactions with the environment should provide an opportunity to encounter cognitive conflicts that, in turn, will facilitate growth at the time they are ready to expand or refine their conceptual framework.

Assessing Thinking Abilities

The most commonly used and best-known formal measure of thinking abilities is the intelligence test. Individually administered IQ tests, such as the *Stanford-Binet* and *Wechsler,* and group-administered IQ tests, such as the *Kuhlman-Anderson* and *Otis-Lennon,* are based on the principle that more advanced levels of thinking enable a person to perform more difficult and more abstract tasks. It was assessment of intelligence with such tests that first led Piaget to become interested in intellectual development.[1]

IQ tests measure cognitive ability by comparing a person's performance on certain standard tasks to the performance of a number of other people. One's "mental age" is determined by the number of such tasks successfully completed. You are probably aware of the hazards associated with this procedure and the frequent misuses of the results of such tests:

1. IQ tests are nearly always biased in favor of some culture.
2. Emphasis is usually placed on producing one "correct" answer rather than many possible answers.
3. Tasks often reflect the opportunity to learn rather than the potential to learn.
4. A time-limit factor tends to discriminate against deliberate, contemplative thinking styles.
5. Such tests fail to allow for differences in answers that are related to the child's level of cognitive development.

Despite these and other limitations, intelligence tests can provide some index of a child's thinking abilities. This is particularly true if steps are taken to minimize the limitations (for example, a test that is as culture-free as possible can be chosen, a timed and an untimed score can be obtained, and so forth). Teachers can also employ Piaget's strategy of studying the child's answer on IQ tests to determine what stage of development it represents.

In all likelihood, teachers can learn more about children's thinking abilities by observing their behavior, noting their contributions to a conversation or discussion, and studying how they solve a problem or complete a task than from an IQ test. For example, Josette may not be able to classify objects using more than one attribute at a time. She can group a pile of large and small objects according to size or function but not according to size *and* function. The teacher notes Josette's inability as a factor to be considered in assigning tasks to her. Difficulty with classification on a physical task signals a lack of readiness to classify in a more abstract process, such as reading. Josette might be able to classify characters in a story according to one trait (for example, age). But she should not be asked to identify characters in a story according to age and disposition if her cognitive development does not permit it. She would likely confuse characters who are kind and elderly with those who are kind and young or mean and elderly. A discussion would have to focus on one character trait at a time in order to fit Josette's level of understanding. Observation can reveal such information to the alert teacher.

---

[1] Piaget was intrigued by children's "incorrect" answers. This led him eventually to the conclusion that children's answers make sense to them because they respond from the perspectives of their stages of cognitive development.

Basic Components of the Reading Process

Promoting and Developing Thinking Abilities

As information comes to a person, it must be processed. Various experts have developed explanations concerning how the child develops a scheme for dealing with the environment. The application of a theory of learning to classroom instruction is not a simple matter. Yet the classroom teacher needs some understanding of how thinking abilities are applied in reading so that instructional goals can be established, appropriate activities can be developed, and assessment of student progress can be made.

It is common to describe the application of thinking to reading by means of comprehension skills. Lists of such skills are often detailed and lengthy. Typically, they include a mixture of procedures for teaching comprehension, uses for comprehension, and psychological processes involved in comprehension (Simons, 1971). The result is often a conglomeration that confuses the teacher more than it helps. Long lists of skills also tend to overwhelm anyone who takes seriously the job of teaching each item.

We believe the needs of teachers and children can best be met by seeing the thinking process in terms of four operations: *identifying, analyzing, evaluating,* and *applying. There is an obvious interdependence among all thinking operations,* but for purposes of discussion and to help the teacher keep a clear conceptualization in mind, let's ignore that reality for the moment.

At the most basic level a reader must be able to *identify* the ideas on the printed page. To do this he or she must draw on immediate memories or perceptions. Apparently one's perceptions are very much dependent on the person's stage of cognitive development. At the next higher level of understanding the reader must *analyze* the message. This means examining the parts, studying the organization, and seeing the relationships. At a third level the reader must *evaluate* the ideas gained from reading. This involves the use of standards in arriving at judgments. The reader determines the authenticity or quality of an idea or point of view. Finally the reader *applies* what he or she has read to solve a problem or answer whatever question(s) were raised prior to reading. Information may also be rejected or stored for use at some later time.

Each of these thinking processes overlaps with and builds on previous levels. A reader cannot analyze or evaluate information, for example, if it has not been identified correctly at the outset. The development and effective use of these thinking processes in the reading act are dependent, in part, on practice. The teacher's role is one of creating opportunities for children to engage in activities that call for various kinds of thinking. Interaction with peers and adults who employ various thinking processes is a necessary condition of such activities. This underscores the importance of having children engage in exchanges with others to see what interpretations and reactions other people have to what has been read. The kinds of questions teachers ask and encourage children to ask also seem to be important to the kind of thinking children will practice. We believe teachers who have some fundamental idea of comprehension and thinking—one that is simple enough so that the major parts can be remembered—tend to ask and encourage better questions and set classroom conditions that promote a higher level of thinking.

Stimulating Reasoning and Problem Solving

1. Invite children to imagine that they are going to join an expedition that intends to explore a newly discovered river in South America. This river is thought to begin high in the Andes and flow into the Amazon River. Discuss and speculate about what such an adventure would be like.

    Ask the children to decide what equipment they would need if their expedition were to be taken by helicopter to the mouth of the river. Instruct them to develop a list of necessary items, the weight and cost of the items, and the places where they could be obtained. Make catalogs and telephone books available to the children, and give them several days to work on the task.

    Have children share their findings. They can compare their lists for the purpose of deciding which items are absolutely necessary and which are not. If a parent or other persons in the community is experienced in wilderness survival techniques, invite them to visit the children and lead a discussion. Encourage interested children to read fictional and nonfictional accounts of people and expeditions that have survived extreme conditions.

    This activity is most appropriate for advanced readers but can also be adapted for primary grades.
2. Set up a cooking center in the classroom. Display a variety of cookbooks, or make selected recipes available in a card file. Encourage children to locate a recipe that appeals to them, bring the necessary supplies to school, and make the dish. (This can also be a homework assignment.) Be sure to remind the children about the safe use of a hot stove, knives, and other equipment.
3. Locate and clip short articles from children's magazines or the daily newspaper. Remove the title or headline from the articles. Put the articles in one envelope and the titles or headlines in a second envelope. Invite children to spill the contents of the two envelopes on a table, read the articles, and locate and match the correct title or headline with the article. Normally

four or five articles are enough to avoid mere guesswork, but more can be added to make this task more difficult. Roman numerals or letters on the backs of the pieces can provide feedback on whether the task has been done correctly. Advanced students can be asked to write their own titles or headlines for comparison with the original.

This activity is most appropriate for a child working alone. If the difficulty of the articles is adjusted the activity can be made appropriate for all but the beginning reader.

Applying Thinking Operations to Reading

The usual approach to the challenge of helping children think as they read is to grill them on what the chicken said to the fox or what the boy loaded into his wagon. Questions that require children to recognize and recall details constitute 78.3 per cent of those asked in second grade, according to a study by Guszak (1968). Even in grade six, the teachers in Guszak's study primarily asked questions calling for the lowest levels of thought. Questions requiring inference or evaluation were usually framed as yes-no questions. More recent studies by Durkin (1978–79) and Duffy and McIntyre (1980) support and extend the findings of Guszak with respect to the nature of classroom interactions. Durkin's study indicated that teachers depend heavily on asking questions that focus on factual recall. Duffy and McIntyre found that teachers seem to be more concerned about keeping a flow of activities going than in causing reflection and thought on the part of learners.

The rationale seems to be that we teach children to understand by making sure they "get it." If they didn't "get it" we go back, reread that part of the story, and point out their errors. Later we gnash our teeth because children believe "whatever they read," yet we fail to look in a mirror for the culprit.

Because the questions teachers ask and the tasks they assign play a large part in determining what thought processes children will apply to reading, it is crucial that these opportunities not be squandered. Classifications by Barrett (1972), Pearson and Johnson (1985), and others are useful as a means for analyzing and classifying questions and tasks to determine what level of thinking these questions and tasks require. Although such classifications are not empirically based, they do offer a logical description and organization of various thinking operations.

We believe the four thinking processes (identification, analysis, evaluation, and application) can be used effectively as a means for classifying questions and instructional tasks. Although less specific than the classifications of Barrett and others, you can easily keep the four categories in mind. The details of intricate classification schemes are more difficult to remember.

The four thinking operations are now described in a way that should help you decide where a question or task fits:

1. *Identification* requires the reader to recall or locate information stated by the author. The author's ideas are understood.
2. *Analysis* requires the reader to examine the parts according to a scheme or structure. Information not stated is reasoned from what is given.
3. *Evaluation* requires the reader to judge information against a standard to determine its value.
4. *Application* requires the reader to do something with the information.

It is not possible to equate the use of certain key words in questions (for example, *when, how*) with any given level of this scheme, for an author may say *when* explicitly, or it may only be implied. For example, a teacher might ask, "When did the ducks begin to fly South?" The reader may be able to find an explicit statement in the story such as this: "In early October the ducks started their long journey South." Or the reader may find: "As the leaves began to turn, the ducks headed South." Pearson and Johnson (1985) make a useful distinction in their classification scheme between three kinds of question-answer relations. *Textually explicit* questions have obvious answers "right on the page." This parallels the identification level in our scheme. *Textually implicit* questions also have answers "on the page," but the answers must be inferred. *Scriptually implicit* questions require that readers draw on their own prior knowledge or script to produce an answer. Whether the earlier question about ducks heading south draws on the text or on the reader's experience depends on how explicit the text is. Our four-level scheme incorporates Pearson and Johnson's textually implicit and scriptually implicit types of questions into the second level: analysis. The distinction they make about the source of the inference that must be drawn is an important one that you should keep in mind.

Try to classify the questions and tasks that follow for the "Soap Box Derby" story in Chapter 8 (p. 228), and fit them into the four thinking operations listed earlier:

1. What color is Charlie's racer?
2. Why does the driver of the green racer need a wheelchair?
3. Who do you think deserved to win the race? Why?
4. How old was Charlie when his brother won the race?
5. Draw a picture of Charlie's racer.
6. Estimate Charlie's age.

Items 1. and 4. are level 1 (identification). The story states explicitly that Charlie's racer is red and that Charlie was five when his brother won the race. Items 2. and 6. are not answered explicitly, so they are level 2 (analysis). Item 3. involves a judgment, so it is level 3 (evaluation). Finally, item 5. falls at level 4 (application), for it involves extending the story and doing something with the information given. You might want to write a question or develop a task related to this story for each level of the classification scheme. Discuss your results with a classmate or with your instructor. Don't be discouraged if some of

Basic Components of the Reading Process

your ideas don't fit neatly into one category. The scheme is only a means to an end. By using it, you can concentrate on developing questions and tasks that encourage children to use various thought processes as they read.

To illustrate further the use of this classification scheme, let's consider what questions and tasks might be appropriate for college students concerning the first four sections of this chapter. At the lowest level (identification), basic factual questions could be asked:

1. What factors are thought to cause the child's cognitive structure to change?
2. What technique can the classroom teacher use for assessing thinking abilities other than IQ tests?

The answers to both of these questions are given in the text and require only that the reader remember exactly what the authors wrote.

At the next highest level (analysis), the reader must use reason to answer a question. Questions that require analysis might be these:

1. How would the child's cognitive growth be affected by an absence of stimulation in the environment?
2. What inaccuracies in intelligence assessment could result from comparing the performance of children with distinctly different backgrounds on an IQ test?

These questions relate to ideas presented by the authors but require the reader to go beyond what is stated explicitly to see relationships and make inferences.

At the third level (evaluation), the reader is asked to apply criteria in arriving at judgments. For example:

1. Which of the hazards associated with the use of intelligence tests listed by the authors is most pertinent to this discussion on thinking and comprehension? Why do you think so?
2. Do you agree with the premise that a teacher's questions affect the kind of thinking children engage in? Why, or why not?

Both of these questions require the reader to make a judgment and explain the standard used in arriving at that judgment.

The fourth level of question or task (application) requires the reader to do something with the information. These tasks involve application:

1. List three things parents can do to help their children develop the thinking processes necessary for reading.
2. Write out questions that involve analysis that children could be asked to answer after reading a story.

The reader is asked to use the information gained from reading to solve some need or problem.

The four-step scheme can be used to classify questions you intend to ask in story discussions, written assignments, group activities, enrichment activities, workbook tasks, and so on. Depending on the age level you teach, the evident needs of the children, the type of material being read, and the objectives of the instructional program, you can adjust instructional activities to emphasize the application of thinking to reading.

The program should pay attention to all four thought processes regardless of grade level, but some developmental sequence should be planned. Logically, you would emphasize the more fundamental processes with younger children but not ignore higher-order processes. Even beginning readers are ready and able to make inferences within the realm of their experiences and cognitive levels. Older children should concentrate more on higher-order thought processes, but not to the exclusion of identification. Depending on the topic and the child, individual differences suggest that certain thought processes may be more appropriate than others at any point in time. On the topic of whales, for example, eight-year-old Bruce may be able to analyze and evaluate a selection effectively whereas twelve-year-old Terry may find identification of meaning a chore.

Normally, the increasing complexity of the reading material children can handle as they become more fluent readers provides a natural developmental sequence for applying thinking processes in reading. In other words, Sandra will be able to engage in all levels of thinking to some degree in the second-grade reader when she is seven years old. By grade four the selections have become more difficult, so similar thought processes applied to stories in the fourth-grade reader continue to challenge and stretch Sandra's comprehension abilities.

Constructing Questions

1. Select a chapter of this book you have read previously. Write several questions at each of these levels: identification, analysis, evaluation, application. Ask a classmate to judge whether your questions call for the intended level of thought.
2. Prepare a teaching plan for the grade level of interest to you based on the use of a story of appropriate difficulty. Include questions at all levels of the scheme presented on page 262.

Classification

Have children draw vertical lines on a piece of paper to form five columns. Label the columns *Who, What, When, Where,* and *Why.* Demonstrate how to put relevant information in each column using a well-known fairy tale or fable for purposes of illustration (e.g., the story "Jack and the Beanstalk").

Basic Components of the Reading Process

Who	What	When	Where	Why
Jack	Trades cow for magic beans	One afternoon	In the village	To become rich

Have children fill in the columns using information from a story they have just read. Discuss the children's responses. This activity is appropriate for readers at all stages of development and can be used with groups or individuals.

Children's Knowledge of Story Structure

One thing that characterizes U. S. society is the periodic emergence of fads. For example, we remember the fifties for Hula-Hoops and Davy Crockett coonskin hats. The sixties saw long hair become faddish, and in the seventies it was jogging. Presently, aerobic exercise is widely popular.

We also note a tendency for jokes that people share to run in trends. Knock-knock jokes were once the rage, but now seem passé. Jokes that poked fun at an ethnic group were common a few years ago (the group under attack being different depending on where one happened to live). The most recent fad in jokes, it seems to us, is this: "How many _____ s does it take to change a light bulb?" (Fill in the blank with whomever you want to lampoon—university professors, politicians, or what have you.)

Jokes of a particular type or genre seem to follow a standard pattern. For example, when knock-knock jokes were popular, it wasn't necessary to prompt a friend with anything more than "Knock, knock" to get the expected, "Who's there?" response. Much the same is true with "changing a light bulb" jokes today. What happens very quickly when a new type of joke emerges is that people learn the structure by hearing jokes that follow the pattern. Comprehension requires that we know the structure, so we learn it if we want to be sociable.

We invoke the "structure of familiar jokes" notion here because it provides a meaningful way of illustrating another type of cognitive structure that people develop—story structure. Early work with folktales revealed that certain patterns of stories existed within a culture (Meyer & Rice, 1984). This phenomenon may indicate something about how human thinking and memory work, but, in any case, it suggests that identifiable story patterns do exist. We will go into greater detail with respect to the nature of story structure later. Here it may be helpful simply to say that stories of the Western culture typically involve a setting and one or more episodes; episodes normally have a beginning, middle, and end that involve the resolution of a conflict or problem. Decades ago, in research on people's memories for stories, Bartlett (1932) found that recollections of stories tended to be closer to idealized stories than to the original version. This suggests that

Children begin developing a sense of what makes a story very early in life through repeated exposures to well-formed stories.

people store and retrieve information using story schemata that have been developed through previous experiences with stories.

Much as children develop a sense of how their native language works by interacting with facile users of their native language, people seem to develop a sense of how stories are structured through exposure to stories. They soon learn by listening to stories that certain elements are included. Evidence collected by Brown and Murphy (1975) and Poulson, Kintsch, Kintsch, and Premack (1979) indicates that children have some knowledge of story structure as early as age four.

It is important for a reader to have a sense of story as a way of anticipating and processing an author's ideas. The existence of a cognitive framework or schema for stories in the reader's mind is thought to enhance comprehension and facilitate remembering by giving the reader a way to sort and organize information. When the internal structure of a story is highly predictable, the reader can assign main ideas to the appropriate slot in a schema and group supporting details under those headings.

Building on the work of early researchers such as Bartlett (1932), Propp (1958), and others, a number of researchers have attempted to develop systems for analyzing narrative text (as opposed to expository text, a type we will examine later in this chapter and at greater length in Chapter 11—about content area reading) according to what is commonly known as story grammar. A story grammar is "a set of rules that will define a text's structure and an individual's mental representation of story structure." (Whaley, 1981) Through careful specification, a story grammar can be used to parse a story much as structural grammar enables one to parse a sentence. Whereas the main elements of a sentence include the subject and predicate, the main elements of a narrative include a setting and at least one episode.

Mandler and Johnson (1977), Rumelhart (1975), Stein and Glenn (1979), and Thorndyke (1977) have developed story grammars that have been used in much of the recent research on story structure. Story grammars have been used to study the development of children's awareness of story structure, for example, and to learn that good readers show more awareness of story structure than poor readers (Rand, 1984).

The Teacher's Knowledge of Story Grammar

Tierney, Mosenthal, and Kantor (1984) argue that a teacher has no immediate need for the sophisticated story grammars that researchers such as Rumelhart have developed. They do indicate, however, that a teacher needs a general framework for analyzing stories for at least two reasons. First, by using a relatively simple system such as the one shown in Figure 9.1, teachers can gain greater insight into material they ask their students to read. This insight enables the teacher to determine ahead of time the extent to which a story deviates from the "idealized form." The decision can then be made not to use a story if it will present children with special difficulty. Second, the ability to analyze a story in general terms permits the teacher to prepare children for a deviation. A story that uses flashbacks, for example, will be understood better if the teacher spends some time discussing techniques that authors use to signal a departure from a chronological presentation of events.

Marshall (1983) describes another approach that requires the teacher to have a general understanding of story grammar. She suggests that comprehension questions that draw on the structure of a story be asked by the teacher and offers the following description of story elements as a guide to developing appropriate questions:

1. Stories are made of a theme and a plot.
2. The plot is made of an episode or series of episodes.
3. A complete episode contains a setting and a series of events.
4. The setting describes time, place, and the central character.
5. The series of events include:
   a. An initiating event that sets a goal or problem.
   b. Attempts to achieve the goal or solve the problem.
   c. Goal attainment or resolution of the problem.
   d. Reactions of characters to events. [Marshall, 1983, p. 616]

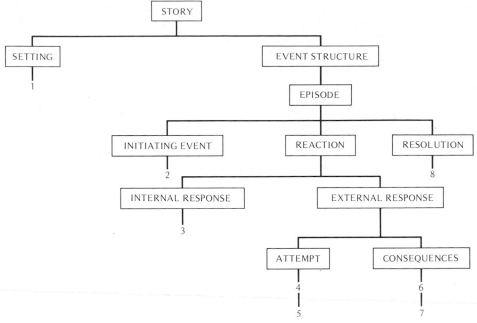

Text
1. Merle was a farmer in Minnesota.
2. One morning he discovered a terrible blizzard had arrived.
3. He knew his cattle in the field would be hungry.
4. He got a wagon
5. and filled it full of hay.
6. But the snow was too deep.
7. He couldn't reach his cattle with the hay.
8. Some cattle died before a path could be plowed.

* After Tierney, Mosenthal, & Kantor, 1984.

FIGURE 9.1* Tree Diagram of a Simple Story

Though the very brief story analyzed in Figure 9.1 offers limited opportunity to develop questions, we will use it to illustrate Marshall's approach. Where information is not given explicitly, the reader must infer the answer.

I. Identification (literal level)
    A. Initiating event
        1. What is Merle's problem?
        2. What must he do to solve his problem?
    B. Setting
        1. Where did Merle live?
        2. What kind of weather had occurred?
    C. Attempt
        What did Merle do first to solve his problem?

D. Resolution
  1. What kept Merle's plan from working?
  2. What happened when his plan failed?
II. Analysis (inference level)
  A. Setting
    1. At what time of the year does this story take place?
    2. Why were the cattle in the field?
  B. Attempt
    1. Why did Merle think his cattle would be hungry?
    2. Why did he use a wagon?
  C. Resolution
    How did the snow ruin Merle's plan?

Sadow (1982) offers a slightly different set of guidelines in the form of the following generic questions:

1. *Where and when did the events in the story take place and who was involved in them? (Setting)*
2. *What started the chain of events in the story? (Initiating Event)*
3. *What was the main character's reaction to this event? (Reaction)*
4. *What did the main character do about it? (Action)*
5. *What happened as a result of what the main character did? (Consequence) [Sadow, 1982, p. 520]*

Sadow cautions that teachers should not use these generic questions directly with children, but as "frames" to guide them in analyzing a story. With the outline of events clearly in mind, teachers can develop questions that reflect that outline.

In contrast with the question-asking scheme suggested in an earlier section of this chapter on promoting various thinking abilities (i.e., questions at four levels: identifying, analyzing, evaluating, and applying—p. 262), here we are oriented toward the development of text awareness. Over time teachers can sensitize children to the important features of story structure through the nature of questions asked.

Enough is known about story structure as an aspect of cognitive development to suggest to us that teachers must be prepared to respond in several ways. One set of responses has to do with helping the child develop a sense of story structure; and the second set, with selecting instructional materials. Here we will focus on matters related to the child. Later in this chapter when we discuss external factors that affect reading comprehension, we will focus on instructional materials.

Aiding in the Development of Children's Sense of Story

In Chapter 8 we explored the question of whether children need to be taught explicitly about syntax (how words work together to deliver meaning) in order to promote better comprehension. As we saw, the evidence on that is mixed at best. A similar situation exists with regard to teaching story structure in an overt way to improve comprehension. Many children, especially good readers, probably develop a sense of story just as they learn the syntax of language: through experience. Nevertheless, the question remains as to whether comprehension instruction should take the form of teaching the application of rules and strategies that concentrate on story structure or simply provide more experience with stories or both. Let us explore each of these alternatives a bit further.

Teaching Rules and Strategies That Focus on Story Structure

It seems obvious to us that overt instruction can take many forms ranging from one extreme of having children memorize definitions for story elements such as *setting* and *character* to the other extreme of merely modeling the use of a tree diagram that provides slots for certain story elements. We reject the drill type of activities as having no useful application to comprehension. It does make sense to us, however, that overt instruction of some sort that encourages students to examine story elements can be helpful. Unfortunately, little research has been done to date on the effectiveness of comprehension instruction that focuses on story structure. Studies that do show positive results tend to be rather narrow in focus, thus making it difficult to judge how well the results would generalize to a normal instructional program.

Bowman (1980) employed a questioning strategy linked to story structure with sixth-grade students in an effort to improve reading comprehension. A control group exposed to conventional questions at three cognitive levels showed less improvement. McDonell (1978) taught fourth-grade disabled readers to recognize the parts of a story (i.e., setting, characters, problem identification, and episode—including beginning, middle, and end). She found that, after training, the experimental group outperformed the control group on an immediate retelling task, but the two groups performed at about the same level on delayed recall of the same story two weeks later.

Sebesta, Calder, and Cleland (1982) found that the comprehension of classroom teachers on a pretest-posttest recall measure improved significantly by learning to analyze stories using an adaptation of Applebee's true narrative diagram. Applebee's system (1978) can be used to represent graphically main events, sequence, cause-effect, and their relationship to theme or focus. In a second experiment, fifth-grade readers did not perform better on a pretest-posttest comparison of retelling scores after four treatment sessions of ninety minutes each. Again, the Applebee system was taught, but comprehension performance did not improve. The researchers thought the relatively brief training period may have explained their results. Fitzgerald and Spiegel (1983) also found that training on story structure transferred to a subsequent measure of comprehension.

Many ideas for improving reading comprehension by focusing on story structure have been described but not subjected to experimental testing. For example, Smith and Bean (1983) describe several strategies designed to help students learn to predict events and outcomes and to make up their own stories. Story patterns are emphasized in one approach that has the teacher sketch scenes that portray the key events in a story in a vertical sequence (top to bottom on a page). Using the sketches to focus on the story structure, children then create their own story as the teacher draws new sketches adjacent to the original story. This approach would work best when a story with an obvious pattern is used in step one. For example, in one story, a farmer feeds his horse, but some grain is left behind. The amount left feeds a smaller creature, who in turn leaves some even smaller pieces of grain behind for yet a smaller creature, and so forth. Using the sketches as a guide, children can create their own story with this pattern.

Smith and Bean also suggest that certain stories be analyzed in a visual diagram that is in the shape of a circle. This is appropriate when a main character starts at a given location, then goes through a series of adventures with the story, eventually returning to the original location. A circle is divided into whatever number of sections it takes to provide space to sketch something depicting each episode. When children can use the pattern to write their own story, the key elements of that type of story have evidently been learned.

Another approach described by Smith and Bean uses a tree diagram similar to the one in Figure 9.1 to keep track of simultaneous story lines. Initially, a familiar story is diagramed with information put on the tree telling *who, where, doing what, story begins, does what,* and *end.* After analyzing and diagraming other stories using these frames, children write their own story using the tree diagram to help them organize their ideas.

Providing Experiences with Stories

We indicated earlier that we were inclined to favor overt instruction on story structure of a type that avoided merely memorizing and drilling on story elements. At the same time, it seems just as appropriate to us that teachers devote a fair amount of energy simply to locating and sharing good literature with their children as a way of developing a sense of story. We support regular oral reading by the teacher to children (see Chapter 4). We also support recreational reading by children as a regular classroom event (see Chapters 4 and 13). And we stress the importance of using literature as a basis for numerous creative experiences in Chapter 10.

We believe strongly that it is important to provide frequent exposure to good literature to develop a sense of story. We are not sure that exposure is sufficient in and of itself, however. It seems so natural to engage in a little literature study in such situations that we would find it hard to resist. In Chapter 4, for example, we emphasize the importance of book sharing as a way of deepening the reader's understanding of a book and stimulating the interests of other readers in that same book. Sharing activities are bound to touch on story structure. We see no harm in using the terms appropriate to these activities (e.g., setting, character, episode, and so on), and we would even encourage it. We also believe good literature should be discussed to be fully appreciated, and discussion requires the use of vocabulary that goes with key concepts.

Assessing Sense of Story Structure

The most obvious way to get an idea of what sense children have of story structure is to have them read a story with strong structural features and then retell the story to you. Using an outline that you have developed ahead of time that breaks the story down into its key elements, you can check off the features that the children include in their retelling. Parts that are left out can be probed, with specific questions developed along the lines of Marshall's (1983) scheme described earlier in this chapter. We also describe a system later on page 477 for scoring retellings developed by Goodman and Burke (1972).

The main advantage of having children retell a story is that they create the structure and thereby reveal their sense of story without intrusion. You can also assess sense of story structure without first asking for a retelling by questioning the child about specific aspects of the story such as setting (e.g., Who is the main character? Where did the story take place?), initiating event, attempt, consequence, and so forth. However, in this approach you are providing the structure for the child and consequently may not get a true picture of the child's own sense of story.

Other approaches you might use include (1) adding incongruous words, sentences, or parts to a story (i.e., ones that don't fit into the story) for the child to identify; (2) scrambling parts of a story for the child to place in correct order; and (3) pulling out certain parts of a story for the child to reinsert (e.g., number or otherwise signal places where parts have been omitted, and then list the omitted parts at the bottom of the page or at the end of the story—the child identifies where each part belongs).

It might have occurred to you that these assessment ideas would also be good for instructional purposes. We think so, too. By using simple stories at first, children can experience success in identifying incongruous parts, for example, and then move to more complicated stories. Instructional situations often offer the best opportunity to assess student progress.

Creating a Classroom Atmosphere for Thinking

We have seen how different kinds of thinking are related to reading comprehension. Evidently one way of promoting children's thinking is through asking questions. But the problem of promoting thinking is too complex to be resolved so easily. Because thinking is a mental function not subject to direct assessment, we are almost forced into a process of elimination to determine whether poor thinking or some other factor is causing a child's comprehension difficulties. If a child's language skill, background experience, and intelligence are adequate for a reading task, poor thinking may well be causing the problem. In addition to asking good questions, what other alternatives are open to the teacher?

One is simply to wait for the child to mature. Some thinking processes apparently are not hastened by instruction, as we have seen. In practical terms this means that the child should not be asked to comprehend material that requires thinking processes he or she does not yet possess. An accurate time sense is an example of a thought process that requires some time for development. Thus, most second-graders cannot study historical fiction with any true understanding of events occurring within fixed periods of time. The best alternative for the teacher may be to wait for the process of maturation to overcome this limitation.

A second alternative is to give direct instruction on the thinking processes. Authorities on children's thinking agree that instruction will not hasten maturity, but it can maximize learning once the child is intellectually ready. Demonstrations on the constancy of matter, for example, can help a child who is ready to understand this concept. Experiments with liquids, clay, and beads can be conducted to illustrate that a quart of milk in a tall, thin beaker is exactly equal to a quart of milk in a short, squat beaker. Other concepts, such as cause and effect, can also be demonstrated for the purpose of maximizing growth.

A third alternative is for the teacher to read aloud and discuss with the class the thought processes implicit in a selection. A good lesson can often be learned by listening to others explain their thoughts on a topic—teacher and classmates alike.

Perhaps even more basic to the matter of promoting thought is organizing a classroom that really allows thinking to occur. Whether by design or by accident, many classrooms place an emphasis on following directions. Children are given little freedom to choose or pursue topics of personal interest. Little problem solving or inquiry learning is permitted. Memorization and acquisition of knowledge for its own sake dulls children's natural curiosity and rewards them for *not* thinking.

The classroom should be an environment that stimulates exploration and discovery. Children should be active agents in that environment, pursuing questions that have relevance and meaning to them personally. In such a setting thinking is encouraged and rewarded. Divergent thinking is given equal time, and the child's level of cognitive development is acknowledged in the classroom that is child-centered. (See Stephens [1974] for a detailed discussion of how to create classrooms that promote thinking.) Chapter 13 of this text gives suggestions for organizing a classroom that respects the child's individuality. We also find the products of Midwest Publications Company, Inc. (P.O. Box 448, Pacific Grove, California 93950), extremely useful for promoting higher levels of thought. One series of booklets called *Mind Benders* provides numerous exercises for using deductive thinking skills. Other materials focus on cause-effect reasoning, solving analogies, and critical thinking.

Affective Factors Are Important to Comprehension

We have presented the view in this chapter that children need guidance in learning how to respond to a printed message. So far we have focused on cognitive responses to information. No one would argue that intellectual processes are unimportant to understanding, yet by virtue of neglect we often seem to believe that emotional responses are unimportant. Certainly, much of what literature offers is as much emotional, or affective, as it is cognitive. The teacher needs strategies for helping children respond to affective factors in order to maximize comprehension.

One of the most encouraging trends in the elementary school curriculum is that greater attention is being directed to the affective domain. Educators and parents are increasingly recognizing that the child's interests, motivations, attitudes, beliefs, and feelings are important factors that cannot be taken for granted or ignored in the educational process. Though they are significant matters in their own right, we will consider affective variables here as they relate to reading comprehension.

Let's begin with the premise that reading comprehension is improved when children read about a topic that interests them. Whether this observation is true because interest in a topic normally grows from experience, and it is experience that actually explains greater understanding, or because readers attend better to material that interests them is hard to determine. In any case, the fact remains that a child who is excited about rock collecting will better comprehend material on that topic than, let us say, on tea-leaf processing. Teachers often find that a child will persist in and gain much from reading material that is "too hard," when that child is keenly interested in a subject. You will want to capitalize on this by creating numerous opportunities in the reading program for children to read about topics of their own choosing.

Children's attitudes and beliefs are frequently closely linked to their interests. Attitudes and beliefs are learned and usually reflect background experience, and they play a role in comprehension. Material that expresses a viewpoint similar to one held by the reader is comprehended best whereas opposing views are easily misunderstood, disregarded, or even ignored. Education is not intended to indoctrinate but rather to help individuals arrive at conclusions consciously. The teacher's task is not one of imposing certain ideas but one of helping the child recognize his or her own attitudes and beliefs and to be aware of the need to consider new evidence that may cause a change in attitudes and beliefs. The age and maturity of the class, the community setting, and the willingness of parents to support a teacher are important factors to be considered in deciding what issues to raise with students. The topics chosen are probably not so important as the act of helping children recognize the influence their personal attitudes and beliefs can have on their understanding of an author's message.

Basic Components of the Reading Process

Having a personal interest in sailing ships makes reading about that topic more rewarding and interesting to this boy.

Affective Influences on Comprehension

1. Find a newspaper editorial or letter to the editor that you find bothersome. Summarize the author's main points. Cite evidence that contradicts the points made. Write a rebuttal. Share the original article, your summary, and rebuttal with someone who is neutral on the topic at issue. Ask that person to decide which side of the issue is most persuasive and why.
2. Make a list of five issues that are emotionally loaded for you, thus influencing your comprehension of material written on the topics. Describe how you can guard against distorted comprehension as you read.

Encouraging Personal Responses to Literature

1. Have the children write an epilogue to a story they have read.
2. Exciting episodes from a story can be developed into short dramatic vignettes.
3. Have children turn a story into a comic book. Illustrations and dialogue need to be planned to summarize the story accurately. Less important detail can be left out. The final product can be bound and placed in the reading corner for all to enjoy.

Assessing Affective Factors That Influence Comprehension

Chapter 4 of this text is devoted in large part to children's interests, assessment of these interests, and ways to capitalize on them in a reading program. Interests must be assessed almost exclusively with informal devices. Questionnaires, conferences, and teacher observations are excellent ways of identifying topics that appeal to individual children.

Attitudes and beliefs can be assessed in exactly the same ways as interests. It is a relatively straightforward matter to determine what a child's attitude or belief is concerning Santa Claus, for example. You need only ask children how they feel. Feelings on a more complex topic can be discovered by means of a simple inventory. Suggestions follow for using this information in the classroom. This survey form can be adjusted to gather information on many topics and for older or younger children:

Topic: Energy Conservation

	Strongly Disagree	Disagree	Don't Know	Agree	Strongly Agree
1. People should be able to buy as much gasoline as they want.					
2. New houses should have a certain amount of insulation.					
3. Gasoline should have a 15¢ per gallon tax added to discourage people from buying it.					
4. The countries who produce oil are wrong to raise oil prices.					
5. Most people waste energy.					
6. Electric companies should be allowed to burn soft coal even though it's dirty.					

Developing the Affective Domain

Classroom activities can be planned to make children aware of their feelings. Once awareness has been gained, activities can be conducted to cause children to analyze and evaluate their feelings, compare them with the feelings of others in the class, and recognize the influence their feelings have on their interpretation of what they read. This strategy is offered as a way of helping children deal with their emotions consciously, not as a way of eliminating emotions or totally objectifying the world.

Emotions are a fact of life. Feelings develop early when infants find some things pleasant and others unpleasant. Most people grow up with the full range of emotions. Schools do not literally need to teach emotions, but it is probably a good idea for schools to help children understand these emotions to the end that *some* control over them can and should be gained by each individual. Obviously, the school cannot accomplish this goal by itself, but neither can the home, the church, or any other social organization. If the school fails to participate in the task of helping children master their emotions, one major source of input is eliminated.

Life would be very dull without emotions. Countless books have been written, movies made, and television shows produced about a stereotyped, supercontrolled individual who approaches life unemotionally. Invariably such a person experiences a catharsis that makes life more meaningful and more fun. The lesson such tales tell is that some spontaneity is important to life. But society expects individuals to have some control of their emotions.

Another common theme presented in popular entertainment is uncontrolled rage, hate, passion, or other emotion. Individuals who lack restraint menace the existence of others and are often institutionalized or isolated. Evidently some middle position is endorsed by society. People are expected to have feelings, but not in the extreme, and they certainly are not expected to express feelings violently. Because literature helps define the type of behavior society will tolerate and ways that emotion can be expressed constructively, some attention to this aspect of literary content seems necessary. Even if this were not the case, full appreciation of good literature requires that emotions be understood as an important story element.

The teacher's fundamental technique for dealing with affective variables is again to ask questions. Through questions the teacher helps the child come to grips with an emotion or an issue relative to an emotion (for example, "How did Wilbur feel when Charlotte died?" in a discussion of E. B. White's book, *Charlotte's Web.* "When someone is grieving over a death, how can another person show concern?").

The classification introduced earlier for the cognitive domain can be used to plan questions that focus on the affective domain. At first children will need to deal with basic tasks, such as identifying the emotions in a story. Later they can analyze and compare emotions in a story to ones they have experienced themselves. Next they can be led to make judgments about the appropriateness of an emotion in a specific context. At the highest level, application, children gain a better understanding of emotions as these apply to their lives. Children are able to bring principles learned from literature into actions of their own.

Referring again to the "Soap Box Derby" story in Chapter 8, discussion of the affective domain might take the following form:

1. *Identification.* How did Charlie feel before the race? How did he feel after the race?
2. *Analysis.* When have you felt as Charlie did after the race? How was your disappointment different than Charlie's? How does this story make you feel? Why?

Reading Comprehension: Cognitive, Affective, and Text Factors

3. *Evaluation.* Was it right for Charlie to feel glad about the other car's winning? Why? What feelings that Charlie had before the race were inappropriate in your opinion? Why?
4. *Application.* Why is it important to be able to accept disappointment? How can envy change a person?

Many teachers find that by reading a book aloud to their classes they create opportunities for a discussion of feelings and emotions. Certain books—*Charlotte's Web* or *The Yearling,* for instance—are touching stories that involve many emotions in a natural, unforced way. A heightened sense of feeling is often introduced by an effective oral reading.

Dramatizing a story is another good way of focusing on emotions. Good stage directing calls for a discussion of the emotions contained in a scene and how they should be portrayed by an actor. Pantomine and dance are also excellent techniques for expressing the feelings contained in a story.

Purposes for Reading

Mature readers vary their approach as their purpose for reading changes. This ability to adjust reading behavior according to different purposes takes on special importance when we consider the wide variety of reasons for which people read. Consider the difference between reading a newspaper report of a football game and following a recipe for making fudge. The newspaper story may present a considerable amount of detail, but we usually read such material for the main ideas— the final score, who scored the touchdowns, the team's record, and so on. Occasions arise when main ideas are not enough and a more thorough reading of any kind of story is desirable. On the other hand, one normally reads a recipe for quite another purpose—to follow step-by-step directions for preparation. Nothing less than a careful word-by-word reading will enable us to achieve the purpose of correctly following a recipe.

Purposes for reading have been regarded as important for comprehension because they help the reader focus on the specific aspects of a selection. Common sense and research evidence have long supported this view (Beaucamp, 1925; Distad, 1927; Shores, 1960).

As there are a host of purposes for reading, it is common for the teacher who wishes to help children become better readers to plan lessons where reading for a particular purpose is emphasized (for example, to identify a cause-effect relationship). On other occasions other purposes are established, and over time many purposes for reading are practiced. Many sets of instructional materials claim to "teach" children to read for lengthy lists of purposes. There is great variance among such lists and practically no explanation of how one purpose is different from another on the same list (for example, How is reading to draw conclusions different from reading to make generalizations?).

Some research has brought into question the practice of having

The excitement of working with a computer gives real purpose to this boy as he reads the instructions that accompany a software package.

children read for specific purposes (Brady, 1974; Goudey, 1970; Wiesendanger & Wollenberg (1978). Goudey and Brady (in separate investigations) used procedures that contrasted the reading comprehension of children who read with a specific purpose assigned prior to reading with the achievement of children who read only for the general purpose of understanding. The researchers found that specific purposes for reading actually seemed to interfere with comprehension. Wiesendanger and Wollenberg reported similar findings. Certainly, further research with children needs to be done before drawing final conclusions on this matter. One possible explanation for these findings, however, is consistent with the view of comprehension presented in this textbook. It seems reasonable to hypothesize that purposes for reading assigned by someone other than the reader may not aid comprehension because such purposes assume a state of readiness and a frame of reference that are inappropriate for the given reader. (Anderson & Armbruster, 1984a). For example, a teacher might ask a group of children to read "Soap Box Derby" for the purpose of identifying Charlie's motive for entering the race. That purpose may help some children focus on a key issue and as a result better understand an important aspect of the story. The same purpose may be inappropriate for other children, however, when they lack experience with family traditions or for egocentric children who perceive all human behavior as self-serving.

Whereas a purpose for reading may seem logical to an adult, the child's stage of cognitive development and experiential background may undermine that logic.

If we believe purposes for reading are important, as we do, but that the teacher can seldom successfully determine these purposes for children, what are we proposing should be done with respect to reading instruction? The answer is that we should lead children to establish their own purposes prior to reading. Some research (Duell, 1978; Frase & Schwartz, 1975; Schmelzer, 1975) supports the value of student-generated questions—an approach that can be used to cause establishing purposes for reading. However, other studies have found student-generated questions to have no effect (Bernstein, 1973; Morse, 1975; Owens, 1977; Pederson, 1976).

Suppose some beginning readers are going to read a story about a pet dog that gets into trouble by digging in a neighbor's yard. If asked without preparation to decide why they are reading the story, typical six-year-olds or even nine-year-olds would have little success establishing their purposes for reading. By involving children in a discussion concerning their pets or ones they know about—how pets can cause trouble and what can be done to keep pets from being a nuisance—a teacher can help those youngsters generate some ideas of their own around the topic. They can then come up with questions such as, "What kind of trouble could Rex, a dog, cause in the story?" Or "How is Rex like my pet?" The teacher's task is one of leading children via a preliminary discussion into recalling and drawing on relevant personal experiences and concepts so that questions are raised that the story may answer for them. Obviously, the kinds of issues and questions the teacher introduces during these preliminary activities are most influential in determining what purposes the children will finally have for reading the story. Not all children will or should develop the same questions, but a follow-up discussion after the story is read can incorporate a range of responses to the advantage of all in the group. Here again the issues and questions raised by the teacher in a follow-up discussion are critical in terms of stimulating the child's level of thought. This, in turn, affects the purposes the child might bring to a future reading task.

The teacher may seem to be a rather passive actor insofar as purposes for reading are concerned. But quite the contrary is true. The scope and nature of the introductory activities that are planned by the teacher promote the kinds of questions children will want to answer as they read. A stimulating debate on how dinosaurs became extinct stands a good chance of pulling every child into the discussion. Models of dinosaurs that appeal to several senses, pictures that create visual images, open-ended questions that create opportunities for speculation, and the like lead children quite naturally to a state of anticipation. They are anxious to learn what position the author takes on the topic or to see whether events in the story bear out their *predictions*. We use the word *predictions* because as children ask questions (set purposes), they can be helped to anticipate what they believe to be the answer to the questions. Reading to verify predicted answers makes reading

Basic Components of the Reading Process

an active search process that improves comprehension. And that is just the point of setting purposes for reading—to improve comprehension.

In Chapter 8 a detailed description was given (p. 238) concerning how background might be built for the story entitled "The Airport." As the children tell of their experiences with jets, air terminals, handling of luggage, and so forth, the teacher is attempting to build a state of readiness for reading the story. As George recalls a trip he took across country by airplane, he begins to wonder whether the characters in the story have experiences similar to his. Are Ben and Matt frightened by the roar of the jet engines? Do they hit an air pocket, as he did, and drop like a roller coaster? What do they have to eat on the plane? These are questions the teacher cannot pose for George, for every child's experiences are different. Yet they are real and meaningful to George because of where he is in a developmental sense. The teacher can help George formulate these and other, more significant questions by planning introductory activities that trigger his memories and arouse his curiosity.

Initially, it may be wise to have each child share aloud his or her purposes for reading or to write them on paper to reinforce the notion that one begins a selection with a specific purpose in mind. Later the procedure may be less formal—less artificial—as the children develop the habit of setting their purpose for reading. Certainly, there are no rules that must be adhered to rigidly. Teachers can offer what they think is an appropriate purpose for reading to a child, to see how well it is handled or to broaden the child's thinking. What should be avoided is the teacher routinely making the determination of what purposes children will pursue as they read.

The teacher must study a selection ahead of time to determine what purposes might successfully be pursued by youngsters in the class when they read a story. The teacher can then set the stage via appropriate introductory activities. Even then children may occasionally be disappointed that their purpose for reading is not satisfied by the selection. That is a reality the mature reader must face also, and the fact that it occurs should in no way discourage us from having children take the lead in setting purposes for reading.

Obviously, purposes for reading must be established before a selection is read. Only through this procedure can readers properly direct their attention during the reading. Afterward, the stated purpose can be used as a basis for discussion to determine whether the readers have achieved their goal.

Adjusting Reading Rate to Purpose

Just as readers must adapt their reading to meet various purposes, they must also adjust their reading rate. The answer to a specific question concerning supporting detail will require the reader to skim for the right section and then read that section carefully for the correct answer. Following directions calls for slow, careful reading, as does reading an account of a scientific experiment. Recreational reading and newspaper reading often call for a rapid rate but usually not as fast as skimming.

Generally, readers should read as fast as possible and still achieve their purpose. It is widely accepted and often demonstrated in practice that good readers tend to read faster than poor ones. In some respects, rapid reading accounts for good comprehension, for thoughts and phrases are more easily gathered into wholes in this way. Slower readers sometimes miss the point of a sentence or paragraph because they concentrate so intensively on individual words that synthesis of thought becomes difficult.

The teacher has two primary tasks with regard to reading rate:

1. Demonstration of the need to adjust reading speed according to purpose
2. Encouragement of maximum speed for all reading.

(A more complete discussion of improving reading rate is given in Chapter 11.)

Text Factors in Reading Comprehension

Up to this point we have focused primarily on the reader in our discussion of how background experience, language abilities, and cognitive and affective factors influence reading comprehension. We acknowledged earlier that even these factors, which we call internal to the reader, overlap and affect each other; yet, for purposes of clarity, we discussed the topics separately. We will now turn to factors in comprehension that are external to the reader, but we want, once again, to acknowledge the artificiality of discussing this matter as though it is separate from factors internal to the reader. We have noted at various points in this and the preceding chapter that reading is an interactive process between reader and text. As we now examine factors in the text that influence reading, it will be important that you not lose sight of the interactive nature of reading.

What is it that makes printed matter difficult to comprehend? Conversely, what is it that makes some things easy to comprehend? In a word, the answer is *clarity*. An author who writes clearly makes the comprehension process far easier for the reader than one who does not.

Clarity in Writing

Clarity in writing is a complex matter. We can illustrate particular techniques and devices that contribute to clarity, but it is beyond our means and not central to our purpose here to be totally comprehensive in that regard. We can begin with the assertion that good writing is well organized. The writer has a plan that guides his or her presentation of ideas, and that plan is shared explicitly with the reader. Moreover, the plan is typically one that suits the topic and the author's purpose, and it is one the reader has encountered in print before. Main ideas are placed in prominent locations in the text as in topic sentences and headings if they are used. Supporting details or other information relevant to main points are grouped with the main ideas. Relationships among main ideas are described explicitly for the reader and illustrated with examples. Analogies are used to make unfamiliar ideas understandable. The intended referents for terms such as *it, they, he,* and so forth, are clearly identified (linguists would say that anaphoric relationships are clearly stated). Advance organizers, summaries, and transition statements are provided to give a selection coherence and cohesion. Technical terms are defined and may be set off in a special typeface such as italics or boldface. More could be said about what constitutes clarity in writing, but this serves to illustrate the point.

It is probably easier to say whether a sample of written matter is clear or not than it is to say why. Researchers in a number of fields are working to develop text analysis systems that attend to the elements of text structure we mentioned earlier and to other elements as well. We saw in an earlier section of this chapter that story grammars have been developed for specifying the internal structure of narratives. Similar text analysis systems have been developed for expository text by Fillmore (1968), Frederiksen (1972), Grimes (1975), Kintsch (1974), Meyer (1975), and Schank and Abelson (1977)—to name a few. At the root of any system for analyzing the clarity of written text is the notion of predictability. Any feature of text that helps a reader predict or anticipate an author's message enhances its clarity. Where readers are left without clues that enable them to predict meaning, ambiguity sets in.

Unfortunately, children are often asked to read material in school that is written poorly—meaning it lacks clarity. We are convinced that the classroom teacher needs to be just as aware of text factors in planning and conducting comprehension instruction as of background experience, affective factors, and the like. The story grammar and expository text analysis systems mentioned earlier can be helpful to a teacher in determining why a text is unclear or unpredictable, though probably in an indirect way. (We say indirectly because it is unlikely that teachers will have the time to parse (analyze) a text completely, using Meyer's [1975] or one of the other text analysis systems, but will instead gain a general sense of how the systems work and look for a few key factors such as the hierarchal organization of a selection, for example.) Ultimately better instructional materials will be written for schools, we believe, in part because of the research and development being done with text analysis systems. Publishers may be able to use these systems to improve the clarity of their textbooks. Unless or until this happens, however, the teacher confronts a situation where reading problems can be caused or exacerbated (or both) by poorly written textbooks. Next we will look at ways the teacher can address this problem.

The Problem of Difficult Textbooks

In 1984, Commissioner of Education Terrel Bell complained that the textbooks used in U. S. schools had been "dumbed down," meaning they had been simplified by publishers to such an extent that they no longer challenged students with significant content. Publishers of textbooks responded to Bell's complaint, in large part, by "blaming" teachers and other school officials for insisting on books that yielded lower estimates on readability formulas. Teachers' organizations responded by complaining that textbooks are often too difficult for many of the slower students found in classrooms. If anyone had bothered to ask the students, it is likely they would have said that their textbooks are boring and poorly written. We are inclined to think that there is some truth in each of these assertions.

Textbooks are a dominant force in U. S. schools today (Anderson, Osborn, & Tierney, 1984). That situation is unlikely to change in the immediate future, thus making it crucial for teachers to be sensitive to what makes textbooks difficult. What should a classroom teacher consider when judging the difficulty level of a textbook? In recent years, readability formulas were used to estimate difficulty level. Vocabulary and sentence length are the key factors in such formulas (see Chapter 11, p. 336, for a description of readability formulas and their use). As a result of recent research on text structure, we realize that factors such as those mentioned earlier (e.g., prominence of main ideas, use of advance organizers, and so on) make text more or less difficult to comprehend. Readability formulas do not tap many of these factors (Kintsch & Miller, 1984; Klare, 1984).

The Structure of Stories

We saw earlier in this chapter that written narratives follow certain discernible patterns. Children develop an awareness of these patterns as they mature. Stories that deviate from familiar patterns are less easily understood and remembered. Consequently, the teacher must be concerned about story structure with respect to how it affects comprehension from two standpoints: (1) the child's sense of story and (2) the structure of the story to be read. We examined this topic from the perspective of the child earlier; we will now look at the same topic from the perspective of the text.

In an ideal world, a teacher would have time to analyze every story used for instruction according to the specifications of a story grammar such as those by Stein and Glenn (1979) or Thorndyke (1977). We predict that such analysis would enable the teacher to identify ahead of time story elements that have the potential to confuse or mislead children. In the real world, busy teachers will do well to read and reflect on a story with the intent of doing a less formal analysis concerning its clarity and predictability before their pupils read it. We believe even this simple step would do much to facilitate better planning on the part of the teacher with respect to preparing students to read and in conducting follow-up discussion of a story.

Basic Components of the Reading Process

A practical way to undertake this informal analysis is to prepare questions using Marshall's guidelines presented on page 267. Even if you do not have time to ask your pupils every question you prepare in this analysis, the act of writing down questions to focus on theme, setting, initiating event, attempt, and resolution for each episode will cause you to dwell on the key elements of the story. As you decide how each question should be answered, you will become aware of what information is stated explicitly and what must be inferred from the text or from the child's own experience.

We invite you to develop such a set of questions right now for the "Soap Box Derby" story (p. 228) to gain practice. Write down your questions and show them to a classmate. Discuss the value of this activity in causing you to examine the story for key elements.

The Structure of Expository Text

Not all reading matter children encounter in school is in the form of stories. Some textbooks have as their primary purpose providing the reader with basic information about such topics as health, geography, history, earth science, and so forth. The structure of the written matter in these textbooks is not narrative, but expository in form. The authors of such texts want to identify and describe the basic concepts underlying their academic discipline, relationships among those concepts, and the ways in which new knowledge is added to the field. As a consequence, textbooks take a variety of forms depending on which field of knowledge is being presented.

Children, in turn, often find textbooks written for a particular field (usually called a content area) to be difficult to understand because the books are unlike the stories they met when learning to read. An entire chapter of this textbook, Chapter 11, is devoted to the complex topic of reading in the content areas with special attention being given there to the ways in which a teacher can help children meet the special demands expository texts place on readers. In view of the extensive treatment of that topic elsewhere in this book, here we will limit our discussion to the more general concern of what can make expository test difficult to understand.

The text analysis systems of Frederiksen (1975), Meyer (1975), and others, like the story grammars we mentioned earlier, do not serve the classroom teacher well on a daily basis because of their inherent intracacies (nor should they because they were designed for other purposes). Yet those systems can serve to help us identify the major features of expository text to which a classroom teacher should be alert. The key text features identified by such systems include the main ideas presented in a selection, the details that support those ideas, the cohesive relationships among ideas (e.g., comparison, cause-effect, and so on), and the emphasis given by the author to the various ideas presented. (Meyer, 1984)

Based on their understanding of text analysis systems, Tierney, Mosenthal, and Kantor (1984) suggest that an analysis of text clarity by a classroom teacher include examining (1) the ideas in a text, (2) the relation between the ideas, and (3) the structural qualities of a text. With respect to identifying the ideas in a text, they recommend a subjective analysis by the teacher involving intuition: "The teacher will have to rely on intuition. Intuitive, subjective judgments should be based on the teacher's knowledge of the subject matter *in combination with* the teacher's knowledge of the common experiences of children" (emphasis theirs, p. 147). For those who doubt that subjective judgment is sufficient with respect to identifying which ideas in a selection are most important, Piché and Slater (1983) determined that first-year university students were able to identify the most important segments of text with brief and quite nonspecific instructions. Students in their study who used the Meyer text analysis system were less successful in identifying the ideas that would be recalled after reading a selection than were those who used a simple gist approach (i.e., subjective judgment).

With respect to the second task, examining relationships between ideas, Tierney et al. again recommend that teachers use their own sense of whether relationships between ideas in a text are clear. Tierney et al. identify several types of relationships as ones the teacher might examine. These include text features such as pronominalization—the use of *he, her, this, those,* and so on—and conjunctions—the use of *and, but, yet, or,* and also *therefore, however, for example,* and *so forth.* These two aspects of text contribute to cohesiveness by clarifying to whom or to what reference is made (the referent for *he* is unclear in this sentence: John likes Dan. He thinks he is reliable) and by specifying how ideas are linked or connected (e.g., the link between these two thoughts changes when a different connective is used: (1) John likes Dan; *therefore,* Mary likes Dan, too. (2) John likes Dan; *however,* Mary likes Dan, too).

To determine how cohesive a selection is—that is, how well ties and connectors are communicating the author's intentions—Tierney et al. suggest that "it would be reasonable for teachers to examine those ideas within a text which they deem important and then determine the extent to which the ties used render the text obscure, ambiguous, unduly implicit, or just generally indeterminable" (Tierney, Mosenthal, & Kantor, 1984, p. 149). If a teacher sees that ties do not work in a text, confusion on the part of students can be anticipated.

The third aspect of expository text structure that teachers can monitor is the structural qualities of a text. Tierney, Mosenthal, and Kantor described Meyer's system (1975) as a tree diagram that places ideas in a hierarchal (superordinate-subordinate) arrangement that also depicts the nature of the relations between ideas. Seven fundamental relationships are identified: (1) concept and example, (2) concept and properties, (3) concept and definition, (4) temporal succession, (5) cause and effect, (6) conditions, and (7) comparison. In a general sense, the process of identifying key ideas for which a text is to be read and placing subordinate ideas under those ideas are akin to outlining the passage. Text analysis systems add one important element not easily shown in an outline, and that is a specification of the relationships between ideas. The most practical approach a classroom teacher can take may be examining the structural qualities of expository text by outlining the content according to key ideas and supporting detail and then specifying the relationship between ideas, using the seven types of relations listed earlier. To the extent that an outline is difficult to generate, the text should be regarded as complex. Of special importance in developing an outline is the purpose or purposes for which the teacher wishes to have the material read. After an outline of the text content is completed, it should be obvious whether the information (e.g., facts, concepts, or relationships) the teacher wants to emphasize is sufficiently clear in the text to make it worth reading.

Reconciling the Author's Purpose or Purposes with Your Own Purpose or Purposes

One thing that can make a text particularly difficult for someone, especially a child, to understand is incongruity of purpose. That is to say, if a text is written for one purpose, but used by a teacher to achieve an altogether different purpose, the child who is still learning to read may get squeezed from both sides. The historian who sets out to describe the military strategy involved in a great battle must make certain assumptions about his or her audience. This historian may, for example, assume that the readers already have a sense of what led up to the battle and even what significance the battle had in the course of a war. Given the historian's purpose (describing military strategy) and assumptions about the audience (knowledgeable about that period of history), he or she writes in what seems a suitable manner to him or her. A reader who does not fit the author's assumed audience may come to the author's essay with other purposes in mind. The result is often unsatisfactory. A teacher can help prevent such mismatches by seeking to identify what purposes a selection can be expected to serve (even purposes different from what the author may have intended could be quite appropriate) and what assumptions the author seems to make about the prior knowledge expected of the readers.

Like so many of the other factors we have discussed in this section on text factors that affect comprehension, there is no formula or recipe available to guide the teacher. Instead we are suggesting that a teacher who is sensitive to the factors we have described make a subjective judgment about how well a given text fits a group of students and a particular set of instructional objectives. Furthermore, when children fail to understand as expected, the possibility should be considered that the fault lies in the text or the purpose(s) for which the text is being used or both.

Implications of Text Analysis for the Teacher

If the suggestions just made for judging the difficulty level of a textbook are followed, the teacher has several options once a book is judged to be difficult. One possibility is to use alternate materials that are less demanding. This is likely to be the most appropriate solution for students with reading problems. In the basal reading program, this probably means using an easier reader in the same series. In the content areas, this may mean using a different text or other nontext material such as magazines, trade books, pamphlets, or newspapers.

When appropriate alternative materials are simply not available, the teacher can make the use of difficult reading material tolerable by taking special pains to prepare students for a reading assignment and by supplementing the textbook with ancillary instructional aids such as study guides, inserted questions, or content outlines. The teacher can also adjust expectations for what students will gain from a textbook—recognizing that the author evidently had a different audience or purpose in mind or both when the text was written.

Promoting Reading Comprehension

One message that should stand out clearly is that no simple or easy solutions are available for solving comprehension problems. You will need to work continually on many fronts with children in the classroom to promote and develop the ability to understand the printed page. Numerous factors alone or in combination can stand in the way of comprehension. In addition to the ideas already presented in this chapter, here is one general strategy for minimizing comprehension problems: the guided reading lesson.

In a guided reading lesson, the teacher organizes and plans a number of activities that lead children through a selection. This involves a minimum of six steps and provides a format that helps the teacher address the major factors affecting comprehension. It is no panacea and is not intended to become a ritual that takes on a worth of its own. It is merely a means to an end and requires adaptation and variation.

The guided reading lesson has six steps:

1. Building and activating relevant background.
2. Setting purposes that focus attention for reading.
3. Independent reading.
4. Follow-up discussion.
5. Development of related skills.
6. Extending and applying ideas from a selection.

Building and Activating Relevant Background

The section of Chapter 8 on background experience demonstrated how important it is for a person to have some familiarity with a topic before reading about it. Vocabulary, concepts, and, in large degree, interests, attitudes, beliefs, and feelings are based on background experience. The teacher's first task is to help children recall background experiences they will draw on to understand a story and, at the same time, to create an interest in the topic by showing its relevance to the child's life. Learning theory suggests that, for maximum effect, these introductory activities should be as concrete as possible and involve the child as an active participant.

Setting Purposes That Focus Attention for Reading

Once the teacher is satisfied that adequate background is in place, the child should come to have some purposes for reading. If the introductory activities have been effective, the child, even at an early age, should be able to identify purposes that logically grow from those activities. A discussion of volcanoes, for example, might lead the child to ask how they come to exist. The story can be read to find the answer. Naturally, the purposes for reading must be keyed to the content of a story, as well as to the abilities of the children. Imposing a purpose that is ill-suited to a story's content or inappropriate for the child does not improve comprehension or provide useful practice.

As children set about the task of reading, they should have easy access to whatever purposes for reading have been agreed on. They can write these down on a piece of paper, or the teacher can put them on the chalkboard. This point of reference helps children to remember why they are reading.

With younger children, the teacher may at first need to play a larger role in setting purposes. Gradually, more of this responsibility should shift to the child, for that is where it resides ultimately for the mature reader. This can happen only if the introductory discussion arouses interest and helps create an attitude of anticipation in the child.

Independent Reading

The teacher should be available to help when children read a selection independently, but the emphasis should be on having children conquer difficulties themselves whenever possible. This does not mean the teacher must remain with the group, but it is not a good idea for the teacher to be completely removed from the area. Most children even beginners, can read silently and without page-by-page discussion if materials of appropriate difficulty are selected and if the introductory activities have been satisfactory.

Follow-up Discussion

Whereas introductory activities lay the groundwork for comprehension, it is the follow-up discussion, we believe, where the teacher has the greatest opportunity actually to teach comprehension. Particularly through the kinds of questions asked, the teacher directs the application of thinking operations. This is an excellent time to reenter the story to study the topic being emphasized in a lesson. Questions must focus on various levels of cognition and yet not neglect the affective domain.

Schedules do not always permit the ideal, but, whenever possible, the discussion of a story should follow independent reading immediately. The story is fresh in the children's minds at this time, and confusion or misunderstanding can be cleared up while a problem is still vivid.

The discussion should not be a time for testing whether each child

Discussion of a story often helps clarify meaning and enables children to gain appreciation for the interpretations of others.

remembers every detail of the story. Instead, it should focus on the purposes established ahead of time and permit children to share their reactions to the story. It may be necessary to return to certain passages of the story for clarification. Different interpretations of incidents are natural and should be taken by the teacher as an opportunity for studying the author's wording or plan of organization.

The teacher's role during the follow-up discussion is that of a diagnostician. Evidence of misunderstanding can be obtained from children's comments. These responses can provide the insight for planning additional instruction later on.

Written responses to questions can occasionally be asked for so that evidence of each child's understanding is available. Discussions sometimes limit the number of responses that can be heard, and the ideas of some quiet children may go unnoticed.

Skill Development

One of the most important aspects of teaching comprehension begins once a reading group has completed a selection and discussed it. When children don't understand what they have read, it is for cause, and the teacher must begin to deal with those causes. The ideas in this chapter should direct the teacher toward a sense of what might be done.

Skill instruction can often be based effectively on the story a group has just completed. By returning to a passage that caused some pupils difficulty, the teacher can demonstrate the application of a principle. For example, comprehension may have faltered because a figurative statement—"Jack was up a tree"—was taken literally by the children. To overcome this problem, several other figures of speech might be cited by the teacher and discussed by the group. A practice exercise could then be assigned on interpreting figurative phrases.

Basic Components of the Reading Process

This example illustrates the important role of the teacher in actually providing instruction. Resource material, such as a teacher's manual, can be highly useful, but the teacher is still responsible for guiding a learning experience in the classroom. If sequence of ideas is the skill causing difficulty, a demonstration of following a sequence might be given by the teacher, or the teacher may guide the group in identifying a sequence of events. The actual teaching technique used will vary from teacher to teacher and from group to group. What must be avoided is the notion that children learn to overcome difficulties simply by being given a workbook assignment or similar written activity or that they will understand what they read by being encouraged to "think harder" or "concentrate."

Extending and Applying Ideas from a Story

Unless the story is to serve as an end in itself (which may happen on rare occasions), the interests generated, the topics explored, the related topics identified—all lead the child naturally to further reading, writing, speaking, and listening activities. Some stories are better in this regard for some children than for others. The diagnostic teacher should attempt to detect how each child reacts to a story and what various possibilities it offers for extension and then adjust his or her expectations for each child accordingly.

The teacher should also attempt to adjust as much as possible to the learning style of each child. The child who enjoys art activities can easily capitalize on this strength in extending a story through drawings or illustrations. The youngsters who read widely can read library books on a given topic. Naturally, some variety ought to exist, and each child should try new experiences occasionally. Indeed, group activities should be pursued frequently.

The goal of enrichment activities is to broaden and deepen the child's understanding of a world of ideas and thus stimulate communication. Through dramatizing, role-playing, and other expressive acts, the characters and ideas in a story become more real and useful to the child, and the desire to communicate is kindled. Chapter 10 of this text provides many suggestions for helping children extend and apply what they read.

Extending a Selection

1. Have children read part way through a story or book, stopping at some predesignated point. (All children can read the same or different material, as you prefer.) Discuss the characters and events as they have developed up to that point. Make a special effort to help children identify the conflict involved in the story they have read ("What problem do the characters try to solve in the story?"). Ask the children to predict different ways the story might end. Seek explanations for the endings they suggest. Encourage children

---

to consider what the personalities of the characters are and how these will affect the outcome, the likelihood of unusual intervening events, and so forth.

Ask each child to write on paper the ending he or she finds most plausible, with a brief rationale for the answer given. Have each child seal the predicted ending in an envelope with his or her name on the front; collect the envelopes and keep them in a safe place for later reference.

After finishing the book or story, have each child open his or her own envelope and share the prediction it contains by reading it aloud if willing. Discuss the predictions made and what clues the children used in making the forecast. Identify clues in the story that were missed initially but seem more important with the advantage of hindsight.

Repeat the process later with another story, encouraging the children to apply the insights they gained from their first attempts at predicting outcomes. Be sure to point out that more than one ending is plausible for most stories.

This activity will be most successful when used with groups of children because of the interaction this involves. However, it can be used with individuals in a conference setting. Advanced readers in the upper grades will normally profit most from this activity because they can better deal with the personalities and events in a story. Younger children can and should engage in activities of this type, but the analysis they are expected to perform must be adjusted to their level of sophistication.

2. As a follow-up activity in predicting outcomes, cut popular comic strips from the daily newspaper. Snip off the last frame of each strip. Have children read the first three frames and draw the final frame, including dialogue. They can then compare their endings to the original. No answers should be considered wrong; however, some will probably be quite similar to the original, which will indicate the child's ability to predict the outcome. Use simple comics with beginning readers and more complex ones with primary and advanced readers.

Assessing Comprehension

In these chapters on reading comprehension, we have looked at a variety of ways to assess children's performance in areas basic to comprehension. We have seen, for example, how vocabulary can be assessed using formal and informal measures. However, the matter of assessing overall reading comprehension has not yet been addressed. Let's turn to that topic now.

Four approaches to comprehension assessment seem practical and worthwhile to use for us on a daily basis. They include use of cloze passages, asking questions, retelling, and constructing creative products.

The *cloze procedure* is discussed at length earlier in the preceding chapter (p. 247), and in Chapter 14, (p. 480). As a simple-to-construct, easy-to-interpret device, the cloze procedure is probably the classroom

Basic Components of the Reading Process

teacher's most effective means for determining how well children understand what they read. Many samples of behavior are collected quickly and conveniently, yet the possibility of qualitative analysis is retained (in other words, the child's answers can be examined for quality, not merely counted right or wrong).

Asking questions has traditionally been the teacher's main approach to ascertaining pupil understanding. Despite the potential tyranny inherent in a "guess what I'm thinking" approach to assessment, a teacher's questions have great value in determining understanding. On pages 261 to 265 of this chapter specific suggestions were given for asking questions that go beyond mere rote memory. This is extremely important if children are to learn that reading involves active processing of print. A second related issue, raised on page 258, is that of recognizing the child's frame of reference in formulating a response to any question. Again, the notion of qualitative assessment is relevant here. The child does not normally give "wrong" answers to reasonable questions. The answers given are right from the child's perspective, considering what he or she knows. Classroom teachers must try to get behind the answer itself to seek an understanding of why a "wrong" answer made sense to the child. (For example, why does the child say that water makes a sailboat move? Clearly, that is wrong, but why does the child give that answer?) By learning why children answer as they do, the teacher discovers where and how misunderstandings can best be addressed.

The third approach to assessing comprehension involves having children *retell* what they remember of what they read. This approach, first used by Donald Durrell in the *Durrell Analysis of Reading Difficulty* in 1937, permits children to structure their understanding according to what makes sense to them. The teacher can note what is remembered, what is remembered incorrectly or in an altered form, the relative importance of what is remembered, and what is not remembered at all. Follow-up questions can be asked to determine whether ideas not remembered were simply overlooked or were not understood.

The *Reading Miscue Inventory* (Goodman and Burke, 1972) employs a retelling approach to measuring comprehension. That particular procedure is described in Chapter 14 (p. 477). As we have discussed under text factors earlier in this chapter, currently some reading research is using new tools for text analysis that permit the specification of the content of the author's intended message. Meyer (1975), for example, developed a discourse analysis procedure that provides for the delineation of each of the idea units contained in a passage and for specifying the hierarchy of relationships among propositions. That is, her procedure enables a user to scale propositions as main ideas, primary details, and supporting details. Her procedure can be used to identify what a reader might include in a retelling. A promising area of investigation related to discourse analysis in general is the identification of specific types of inferencing behaviors that readers must use to reconstruct the author's intended message (Frederiksen, 1975).

Just now it is not apparent what application these tools have in the classroom. Eventually, they may be useful to the teacher in determining: (1) *what* a reader can understand from reading a selection, and (2) *how* that understanding occurs. Another application may lie in the area of materials preparation. That is, children's texts may be written to conform to guidelines that discourse analysis research reveals to be important to improved understanding.

Comprehension can also be assessed by having the child *construct a creative product* that involves the use or application of ideas encountered in reading a selection. To illustrate, a child who reads *Album of Dinosaurs* might model clay replicas of several dinosaurs. Or a small group of children might follow the directions given in, "Building a Soap-Box Racer," from the *Macmillan Reading Program,* Series r, and actually construct a racer. The final product represents the child's interpretation of what he or she understands and affords the teacher an opportunity to assess progress. For example, children who have difficulty identifying the main idea when they read might be asked to make illustrations of what they believe to be the author's primary concern in a selection. Through discussion or by asking specific questions, the teacher can determine what the child comprehends. Other examples of creative ways to demonstrate understanding include the following:

> Drawing or painting a mural.
> Making a diorama.
> Preparing a bulletin board.
> Preparing and giving a flannel board presentation.
> Writing a sequel.
> Preparing appropriate sound effects.
> Drawing scenery and designing costumes for a dramatic oral reading.
> Developing a map.
> developing a time line.
> Constructing a small scale model.
> Portraying a story character in a skit.

Additional ideas for creative responses to books are given in Chapter 10, "Critical and Creative Reading" (see pp. 318 to 327).

Guided Reading Is Only One Component of a Total Reading Program

Not all reading should be in groups, nor should reading always be done with the teacher's guidance. Without question the child should have numerous opportunities to select materials of personal interest and read them independently. Every well-balanced reading program will include nonguided reading activities that place the child in control. Only by selecting and reading materials without introduction by the teacher will the child learn to become a self-reliant reader. This observation in no way negates the value of the guided reading lesson. Your task is not to choose between group or individual reading and between guided or unguided reading, it is to find the proper balance for students, given their level of development and ability.

The results of an achievement battery, reading survey test, or informal reading inventory often indicate a level of comprehension for a child; this is a fallacy we must address. Every person is actually a composite of *many* levels of comprehension, depending on the topic. The child who has been to the circus many times, toured the performers' quarters, fed the elephants, smelled the atmosphere of the animals' quarters, and talked with a clown has a vivid, rich personal field of reference to draw on when reading a circus story.

Another youngster, who "reads equally well," may not have had such meaningful experiences with circuses, and his or her comprehension naturally suffers in consequence. Change the topic to soap-box racers, and one child's strength becomes another child's weakness. Obvious? Perhaps, but classroom practices belie that such a basic principle is really understood.

Too often children reading at the same "level" are expected to read and comprehend all stories pretty much equally. Moreover, it is typically the teacher's level of understanding and enthusiasm for a topic that determines how much all children should "understand." That is, unless children can answer those questions *the teacher* feels are important, their comprehension is often judged wanting.

Because differences in background dictate differences in understanding on almost any topic, such differences should be accepted and respected. Everyone can remember reading something a second time, months or years later, and finding meaning that one missed before. What has changed? Certainly not the story. Obviously the reader has changed.

Yet we are often unwilling to accept this phenomenon among children. As a result we too often rework a story to be sure everyone "gets" it. Gets what? What the teacher got? The teacher is older, more experienced, a different person from the child. Why should the teacher set the arbitrary standard of minimum comprehension? To avoid this trap, we must regard comprehension as a personal matter and make provisions for "levels" of comprehension within each person.

Improving Comprehension

The concerns discussed here lead us to offer these guides for improving comprehension:

Build background before reading.
Create interests and develop concepts with real objects that children can see and handle.
Develop vocabulary in the context of a discussion or activity.
Follow up reading experiences with discussions that explore the main as well as related issues.
Show how topics children read about are relevant to their lives, thoughts, and feelings.

Use a reading experience as a springboard to many exploratory activities.

Integrate reading with all curricular areas.

Expect different levels of comprehension, depending on the child's background and interests.

Encourage independent reading on topics of personal interest.

Form interest groups that facilitate interaction among children.

Provide for sharing of reading experiences through diverse means and varied media.

Establish a youth-tutoring-youth program.

Encourage children to set their own purposes for reading.

Expect children to think, especially along divergent lines.

Recognize opportunities to emphasize comprehension in all curricular areas.

Avoid expecting everyone to understand a story exactly as you, the teacher, understand it.

Use parents, local people, and the community as learning resources.

Encourage children to stimulate and learn from each other.

A classroom that follows these guidelines approaches reading comprehension as a part of a general concern for communication. The teacher is a facilitator, one who creates a stimulating environment. The classroom is rich with displays, manipulative devices, learning centers, and unusual objects. Children interact with each other frequently as their interests carry them into topics that overlap. Much individual, independent learning occurs in such a classroom, but grouped instruction also takes place, as common needs and interests are identified by the teacher.

Skill instruction is provided, but not according to a rigid, arbitrary sequence recommended by a publishing company. The child's needs dictate, when skills are introduced, a need the teacher consciously creates by the kind of environment he or she cultivates. Thorough and accurate records enable the teacher to monitor each child's progress and to individualize instruction accordingly.

In a total communication program, reading comprehension grows as the child's awareness of the world grows because it is not torn from its roots. In this type of classroom, comprehension is viewed as a thinking process, not as the sum of the separate, isolated skills listed in a teacher's guide.

Nothing suggested here is inconsistent with using a basal reading series occasionally or even regularly. However, adjustments to the basal routine are necessary. First and foremost, not all stories in a basal series will necessarily be read, and clearly the sequence of stories will be altered. Not all suggestions for skill activities will be followed. The preparation before reading will be expanded and made more concrete. Vocabulary will grow out of discussion where key concepts in the story are explained. Follow-up discussion will range far beyond the suggested questions and will encourage children to think critically and creatively about topics and characters in the stories.

The stories will be viewed as springboards that launch the group

Basic Components of the Reading Process

into many related topics for further exploration—each perhaps following a different course.

Unlike the more mechanical aspects of reading, comprehension cannot be broken down, logically sequenced, and practiced until the child has mastered it. Comprehension must be viewed against a backdrop of the total child. Adjustments must be made for the background and interests of the individual. This makes instruction more complex—and more demanding—but ever so much more enjoyable for teacher and learner alike.

Summary

Four important factors in reading comprehension are identified: thinking, feeling, purposes for reading, and text factors. The teacher plays an active role in causing children to apply their thought processes to reading by the kinds of questions that are asked and the types of tasks that are assigned. Often neglected, the affective domain plays an important part in influencing what is understood by the children. Purposes for reading help the reader focus on information that is most relevant at a given time; consequently, such purposes are most effective when established by the reader. Some texts are not written in a way that gives the reader sufficient help in constructing meaning. Techniques and strategies for assessing student status with regard to these components are given in the chapter, as well as suggestions for strengthening the student's resources in these areas.

The guided reading lesson is described as a useful six-step play for helping children understand a story. The steps are as follows:

1. Build and activate relevant background.
2. Establish purposes for reading.
3. Read independently.
4. Discuss.
5. Develop skills.
6. Extend and apply ideas from the story.

Reading instruction must take into account the differences among children that make comprehension a personal matter involving not only what the author says but what the reader brings to the page. Efforts to improve comprehension will be most effective in a classroom environment where reading is viewed as one aspect of helping children explore a world of ideas.

Terms for Self-study

guided reading lesson	affective domain
cognition	analysis
identification	application
evaluation	

Discussion Questions

1. How should a teacher respond to a child's interpretation of a story when it is clearly "wrong" from the teacher's perspective? What is the reason for your answer?
2. A visitor has complained to teacher Jackie Phillips that too much time is spent on follow-up activities that extend stories and not enough time is spent making sure the children really understand the stories. How should Jackie respond?

Recommended Readings

Flood, James (Ed.). (1984). *Promoting reading comprehension.* Newark, DE: International Reading Association.
The authors examine the effectiveness of various approaches to reading comprehension instruction and recommends practices that appear to have value.

Gordon, Christine J., and Braun, Carl. (1983, November). Using story schema as an aid to reading and writing. *The Reading Teacher, 37*(2), 116–121.
Here is a description of an instructional procedure for enhancing children's reading comprehension through the use of diagrams that focus on the main elements in the structure of the story.

Johnston, Peter H. (1983). *Reading comprehension assessment: A cognitive basis.* Newark, DE: International Reading Association.
Johnston presents a model of reading comprehension, then identifies factors that influence its assessment. He also describes various approaches to comprehension assessment from the standpoint of what can and should be measured.

Raphael, Taffy E. (1982, November). Question answering strategies for children. *The Reading Teacher, 36*(2), 186–190.
The author presents an instructional strategy that focuses children's attention on the source of information needed to answer comprehension questions that are explicitly stated in the text, implicit in the text, or in the reader's own experience.

Stauffer, Russell G. (1975). *Directing the reading/thinking process.* New York: Harper & Row.
Here are a discussion of reading as a thinking process and a proposal of a directed reading-thinking activity plan for group instruction.

Wood, Karen D. (1983, January). Vocabulary, language and prediction: A prereading strategy. *The Reading Teacher, 36*(4), 392–395.
Wood describes several prereading strategies that focus on vocabulary, language, and prediction that teachers can employ to enhance children's reading comprehension.

Part III

Approaches to Teaching Reading

10

Critical and Creative Reading

Do you consider yourself to be a critical thinker? How about a creative thinker? As you are both, does that automatically make you a critical and creative reader?

The terms *critical* and *creative* carry high positive connotations. You want to be a critical and creative thinker. Parents want their children to be taught critical and creative thinking. Obviously, these are desirable traits, but what exactly are they?

In class, a teacher may ask, "Did you like that story?" One child responds, "Yes"; another, "No." No explanations are offered.

The teacher will probably categorize the "no" answer as representing critical thinking and the "yes" answer as uncritical. Why? Isn't it too often the case that we associate critical thinking and reading with giving a negative evaluation? Both children in our example gave one-word answers: yes, no. Each may have had good reasons or no articulated reasons for giving one-word answers, but the teacher, nevertheless, assumed that the negative evaluation was sparked by critical thinking—an untested assumption and, therefore, an uncritical reaction by the teacher.

In a similar misconception, many people believe that creative reading is merely reading with expression. In fact, creative reading falls into two major categories: (1) the dramatic interpretation of reading and (2) the application of reading to some other situation that includes an artistic representation such as drawing or dancing.

Dispelling false notions about creative and critical reading constitutes one instructional task, but an even more important objective is for the teacher to develop a clear concept of what critical and creative reading really are in order to be able to describe them and to help students learn how to use these skills. That task may not be simple.

301

If you had to answer right now, what would your concepts of critical and creative reading be?

- *How does critical reading differ from identification and recall?*
- *What kinds of questions would you ask a student in order to determine whether or not that student is reading critically?*
- *Are certain students incapable of reading critically?*
- *Are there valid ways of teaching a child to read critically?*
- *What is creative reading?*
- *Where does dramatic reading fit?*
- *Does the creative emphasis shift between primary and intermediate grades?*
- *How do children become involved in creative reading?*

In order to read critically and creatively, one must analyze and judge reading material and then respond to it. Critical and creative reading are closely allied; the instant a reader makes judgments (critical reading), it almost invariably becomes necessary to decide how to use or synthesize the information gained (creative reading). In its most useful sense, the information gained from the reading experience has been applied or organized for some purpose. Creative reading extends far beyond utilitarian application, but it certainly can begin there. We will discuss critical and creative reading separately in the hope of achieving greater clarity and enhancing understanding.

Critical Reading

The diagram given in Figure 2.3 (see p. 31) shows where critical reading fits into the Harris-Smith model in Step 7 (Analyze) and Step 8 (Judge). Critical reading begins with analysis and includes judgment or evaluation. It would be more precise to speak of teaching children to read for analysis and evaluation than to speak of critical reading, but the term *critical reading* is used frequently, though often vaguely, in educational literature. Therefore, it is used here as a link to that broad usage that refers to most higher-level comprehension activity as "critical reading."

What Is Critical Reading?

Robinson (1964) states that critical reading is the ability to apply relevant criteria in evaluating a selection. It is the judgment of the "veracity, validity, and worth of what is read, based on criteria or standards developed through previous experience" (p. 3).

Russell (1956) suggests four conditions essential for critical reading:

1. A knowledge of the field in which the reading is being done.
2. An attitude of questioning and suspended judgment.
3. Some application of the methods of logical analysis or scientific inquiry.
4. Taking action in the light of that analysis.

Neither teachers nor their students will meet all these conditions at all times. Neither adults nor children can possibly be armed with background knowledge in every field in which they must read. Today's world is too large, and human knowledge is too vast for that to be possible. It is necessary, therefore, to equip students with an attitude of general awareness so that they can detect unsupported statements, sweeping generalizations, and conclusions that do not necessarily follow from the evidence given. Even then, an attitude of suspended judgment may not always be possible. Earlier biases and prejudices affect one's ability to read critically at a later period, as do factors such as age, sex, home background, and sociopolitical attitudes. Students should be taught to recognize their biases and deal with them as factors in the way they react to the printed or spoken word. Teachers should foster an attitude of inquiry when presenting the techniques of critical reading. Against such a background, children will develop high standards for judging what they read.

Critical reading, then, is one of the many operations that make an effective reader. It involves analysis and judgment in evaluating written material. Although there are a number of factors that influence a reader's ability to be critical, the processes of analyzing and evaluating can be taught in the reading program.

Neglect of Critical Reading in the Classroom

Instruction in critical reading does not receive sufficient emphasis in the schools. A study of teaching time and emphasis in the United States showed that more than half the teachers questioned devoted "little or no time" to critical reading in the first or second grades (Austin & Morrison, 1963). The National Assessment of Educational Progress (1976) showed that critical reading skills were already low and were continuing to decline. The study found that 50 percent of high school students could not respond correctly to questions that required them to read critically. If practice makes perfect, it would seem that the concepts and practice in critical reading are being neglected all along the way. Durkin (1984) found that teachers spend most of their time asking simple recall questions even when their basal reader teacher's manual recommends more challenging questions.

This does not mean that children at any grade level are *unable* to analyze and judge. Research has indicated that even first- or second-grade readers or those who were reading as much as two years below their grade level were capable of reading critically in materials at their level (McCullough, 1957; Covington, 1967).

It appears, then, that critical reading skills, though often ignored, can and should be developed gradually from the early grades. Perhaps with a better understanding of what is involved in analyzing and evaluating, teachers would devote more time to teaching critical reading in the elementary grades.

Steps Toward Critical Reading

Before higher-level mental processes can function, a student needs an understanding of the facts and ideas presented by the author. An assessment of the student's ability to identify the main idea of the content and to recount important details is a check on literal comprehension. Basic comprehension skills were treated in Chapters 8 and 9. One task of the critical reader is to interpret the writer's message accurately, a process sometimes described as "reading between the lines," a process involving analysis.

Analysis

In the Harris-Smith model (Fig. 2.3, p. 31), the operation *analysis* involves an attempt on the part of the reader to understand the logical unity of a presentation. At this point, the reader begins to manipulate the author's ideas mentally in order to perceive relationships and to visualize such things as the structure of the selection. The reader asks: "What is the author's main thesis?" "How are the main points supported by detail?" "How do major points within the selection relate to each other?" "Has significant information been overlooked?" During this period of questioning, the reader forms a mental outline and weighs points for their relation and strength.

Children are analyzing the material they are reading when they underline key words and phrases, ignore irrelevant passages, or select appropriate titles for stories. Skill in analytical interpretation requires both *practice* (guided by the teacher) and *practical illustrations.*

Inference is an attempt on the part of the reader to understand what the author has left unsaid or what has been expressed only through implication. It is a process involving deductive leaps from what is literally stated to what is actually intended: "This is what the author has said, but what does he actually mean?" An example of this type of reading is found in Marc Antony's funeral oration in Shakespeare's *Julius Caesar.* Marc Antony continually repeats the phrase "But Brutus is an honorable man" while clearly implying the opposite—an effective strategy.

The inferences made will depend on a reader's background and intuition. It is necessary to put several clues together in order to predict possible occurrences or behaviors, and readers must become adept at using context as a sounding board against which inferences can be tested. In addition, more information may sometimes be needed about the author: Is the author a satirist? Does the author try to manipulate the readers? The reader tries to bridge the gaps in an author's observation by gathering clues as a springboard and then making the inferential leap.

Evaluation

How valuable are the author's ideas? The reader is called on to make judgments as to the worth of the message. Evaluation depends not only on literal comprehension and interpretation skills but also on the reader's ability to appraise the truthfulness, validity, and accuracy of the material. The reader attempts to determine the accuracy of presentation, the author's professional competence, and the relevancy of the author's thoughts.

Students who are asked to make judgments while reading will occasionally need external guidelines or other references and sources. Pupils who have had no previous experience with a subject should suspend judgment until a frame of reference can be established through the application of criteria obtained from outside sources. When asked about the quality of a short story and having no sense of how to respond, students must seek information from sources outside themselves (books, teacher's advice, and so forth).

Internal standards may be all that are necessary for students with a strong basis of experience in the area. Their task is simple. Difficulty may occur, however, when a pupil's internal criteria—the products of his or her culture—are strongly in conflict with the prevailing outside sources. Because of an emotional reaction, the reader may not be able to suspend judgment until a sufficient amount of evidence is presented on a given subject. For example, Quakers who are reading a plea in favor of expanded offensive power for the military are influenced by their beliefs to reject this argument, regardless of its logic or its persuasive rhetoric.

It is the teacher's responsibility to aid students in clarifying the assumptions they bring to the reading task, in analyzing and determining the assumptions of the author, and in broadening the background of information from which more unbiased standards of judgment may come (DeBoer, 1967).

Judging the literary value of a poem or prose selection is another aspect of evaluation that has come to be included within the definition of *critical reading*. We usually call this "literary appreciation" because it is treated in courses on literary criticism, but it is actually a kind of critical reading, using criteria arising from the literary form and from the nature of the experience being described.

The Art of Questioning

When teachers ask questions in order to promote critical reading, they not only present students with a type of problem but also lead them to ask their own questions and to set personal purposes for reading. Questions from the teacher that require analysis or evaluation can serve as models for the students and can help them approach other materials with the same critical attitude.

Critical thinking does not happen automatically. Well-formed questions can give students an inquiring attitude. If the teacher's questions require nothing more than immediate recall, however, then only reading for detail is reinforced, and critical reading skills are neglected.

Wartenberg (1969) lists three qualities involved in the construction of critical questions. Such questions should do the following:

1. Relate new ideas to the student's experiential background and personal involvement.

2. Develop critical thinking and the correct assessment of statements.
3. Integrate the structure of disciplines so that future learnings and past experiences can be encompassed in the structure.

By choosing questions that require analysis or evaluation, a teacher can promote the development of critical reading and thinking skills.

The Art of Questioning

What questions might be asked about the following selection from a children's book? Formulate three questions a teacher might ask a second-grade child concerning this story:

> Susan and Billy watched Billy's new airplane sail through the air.
> "Look at it go, Susan!" Billy called. "It's as fast as lightning."
> "Let me fly the airplane," begged Susan.
> "No, you're too little," answered her brother.
> "Please?" Susan asked again.
> Billy handed the airplane to his sister. "Be careful," he warned. Susan raced across the yard. Gaining speed, she threw the plane into the air. It made a sudden turn and dropped to the ground in a nose dive. One of the bright red wings lay beside the plane.

Formulate critical thinking questions:

1.
2.
3.

If a teacher asks questions such as this: "What did Billy say when Susan asked to fly his plane?" or "What color was Billy's airplane?" then the reader is asked simply to recall or restate facts. If the child is asked: "How do you think Billy feels toward his sister now?" or "What do you expect Billy to do now? What makes you think so?" then it is necessary to move beyond literal comprehension.

Tapping critical judgment would require questions like this: "Would it have been better had Billy not shared his toy?" or "Could a toy plane fly as fast as lightning?" Questioning can also lead the child to see the application of the story to real life: "Have you ever had to share with younger brothers and sisters? How did you feel about it?"

The Teacher as a Critical Reader

A mature reader should be prepared to detect devices designed to influence a less perceptive reader. What kinds of questions might arise from the following passage?

Approaches to Teaching Reading

You know that I was born and raised in Austria. Do you know that there are no remedial reading cases in Austrian schools? Do you know that there are no remedial cases in Germany, in France, in Italy, in Norway, in Spain—practically anywhere in the world except in the United States? Do you know that there was no such thing as remedial reading in this country either until about thirty years ago? Do you know that the teaching of reading never was a problem anywhere in the world until the United States switched to the present method around 1925? This sounds incredible, but it is true.[1]

A competent reader might ask: "How is *remedial reading* being defined by this author?" "Does the author refer to remedial cases or to classes designed to handle such readers?" (Refer to the fourth sentence in the passage.) "What is the cause against which the author is building his case—his purpose for writing?" "What is his professional field of interest, his specialization?" "Where are the facts supporting his assumptions?

Although a reader may have no immediate knowledge with which to substantiate or refute this author's statements, it is still possible to detect some sweeping generalizations and a rather hastily drawn conclusion. Note the last statement: "This sounds incredible, but it is true." The author appears to have foreseen disbelief on the part of his readers and uses rhetoric to validate the argument. The mature reader knows that statements are not necessarily true simply because someone says they are true. Children can be led to a similar type of intelligent inquiry by teachers who are critical readers themselves and who ask questions which encourage evaluation (Meehan, 1970).

Teachers become academic role models for their students not only by the way they ask questions but also by the way they read. When teachers talk about the books they have read, they give their students a message: Adults read and think while they read. If teachers discuss books in a manner similar to that shown in the preceding paragraph, then students begin to become aware of the mental activity involved in reading critically. Teachers are more likely to read critically themselves and to stimulate critical thinking in their students if they have a schema, a mental outline of what critical reading means (Meehan, 1970). The Harris-Smith model (Fig. 2.3) presents an instructional schema that may foster classroom questioning and thinking.

Critical Reading Techniques

Technique: Truth Versus Fantasy

In the primary grades, one of the first critical reading skills that teachers attempt to develop in students is the ability to distinguish truth from fantasy. They are careful, however, not to discount the importance

---

[1] This selection was taken from *Why Johnny Can't Read* by Rudolf Flesch (New York: Harper & Row, 1955), a book that stirred much controversy in the late 1950s because of its indictment of United States schools for their lack of attention to phonics.

of stories that are fictional. Teachers realize that tales of fantasy can spark imagination and elicit creative thought. Even first-grade children, however, can learn to distinguish fact from fiction. They become aware of fantasy signals such as "once upon a time" beginnings and of stories incorporating traditional fantasy motifs such as the beautiful princess, the aged king, the triumph of the younger brother or sister, and reliance on magic powers and objects.

To initiate awareness, the teacher may wish to start with isolated statements and have children respond with a yes or no, depending on previously established criteria as to the truth or falsity of the statements. For example, the following statements might be used:

The moon is made of green cheese.
A dog can fly.
A boy can run.

By indicating agreement or disagreement, children can become aware of printed statements that are not based on fact. Later, they can discuss the fantasy elements within stories that take a "could this have happened?" approach.

Could the prince really have climbed up on Rapunzel's hair? Why or why not?
Could a body be as small as Tom Thumb's?
Could the cabbage leaves actually have grown as large as a barn? How do you know?

Very young children can detect the difference between fantasy events and those that are plausible or might have happened. Children can be directed to listen to two accounts of an event, one of which is more true-to-life than the other. Discussion as to which really could have happened can then be encouraged.

The puppy shivered from the cold. No one seemed to notice him on the sidewalk as last-minute shoppers hurried home with arms full of Christmas packages. He huddled against a tall building to avoid being stepped on.

Oliver Puppy shivered from the cold. "Oh dear," he sighed, "don't any of those people want a puppy to take home? I do *so* want a people." Just then he had an idea. "I'll ask one of them to belong to *me*!"

Truth Versus Fantasy (Classroom Activity)

Children enjoy changing a factual presentation to one of fantasy by incorporating talking animals, magical events, or other elements of fantasy. Lessons of this type enable children, when they are older, to recognize specific incidents in works of fiction that make the story depart from realism.

Have the children read a factual account of something from their basal reader, from a school paper, or from some other source. Demonstrate various ways in which the factual incident could be retold as a fantasy. Then have the children tell or write their own fantasy stories based on another factual account.

The Connotative Power of Words

Awareness of the power of words is a crucial factor in reading critically. Words can comfort, coax, convince, and deceive. A first step toward intelligent and profitable reading can be taken when the reader scrutinizes a passage to determine what reaction the author is attempting to elicit through the use of words that appeal to the emotions, arouse sentiment, evoke sensory images, or incite action. A competent reader can distinguish between the dictionary definition of a word—its *denotation*—and the images and implications suggested by the word—its *connotation.*

Advertisers are aware of connotations as they market a product, appealing to the vanity, desires, and weaknesses of the public. Editorials that take a decisive stand on a controversial issue are rich with loaded words that may either flatter readers by appealing to their highest virtues or may awaken fear and distrust of an issue that is new or different. Appeals for worthwhile charities make full use of connotative language for good causes. Election times provide an abundance of campaign material that carries loaded words that seek to win public approval for a cause or a candidate. In descriptive writing, words that appeal to the senses, evoke mental images, and provide literary effectiveness and vividness are used extensively.

Connotative Power of Words (Discussion)

Briefly describe your immediate reaction to each of these words:

child
death
disease
poverty

Each has a certain denotation, but you may have found that your reaction to the words went far beyond their denotative meanings. For example, although *child* simply means *offspring,* the connotative implication may have called to mind the sum-total of your experiences with children, or it may have reminded you of certain specific instances—your childhood memories or thoughts about the children you teach. Each of the words just given is an example of a "loaded" word because, whether you react positively or negatively, each has triggered a stereotyped response within you. Awareness of the techniques of connotative language makes readers far more critical than they would otherwise be. How would you make children conscious of the connotative values of these four words?

Connotative Power of Words (Classroom Activities)

1. For Primary Grades

Children who can recognize evocative language are better equipped to read critically and to make rational judgments about what they are reading than they would be without such awareness. Exercises in the primary grades can be used to identify words with strong imagery. A teacher guides the children to spot such imagery through specific direction:

Find the words that make you almost able to feel the kitten: (*fuzzy, warm, rough tongue*).

Find words that give clues to how Mrs. Hill's farm may have smelled: (*fresh-cut hay, newly painted fence*).

Similarly, children can find examples of words that appeal to sight, sound, and taste. Many words appeal to more than one sense. Children with limited experiences develop fewer connotations. Those that *do* develop first center around sensory impressions. The teacher should look for opportunities to build on a child's storehouse of personal connotations: "Tell me what comes to mind when I say a word." "Describe what you see or think about." (Use words very close to the child such as *home, mother, love,* and so forth).

2. For Intermediate Grades

It should not be the teacher's purpose to stress analytical reading to such a point that students scrupulously examine every word in a selection for an expected connotation. Literary works are sometimes better appreciated as a *gestalt*—the sum of the parts. Newspapers, advertisements, and political speeches provide excellent opportunities for working with connotative language in the intermediate grades.

For example, have children underline the loaded words in a political speech such as this one:

Long have I been a citizen of our beloved community. I have watched my children grow up here. But now I am deeply disturbed. Never have I witnessed a more tragic upheaval than our city has suffered under my opponent, Major Davis. Taxes have skyrocketed, yet children lie awake at night too hungry to sleep. Our once fair city streets are littered and gutted. Graft and corruption have encamped at City Hall. But, my friends, there is hope. Beckoning us is a bright new horizon, involving us all as free Americans who want desperately to stop decay and begin anew. With a dependable team we can aim toward a better tomorrow. Continuing down the same path can lead only to certain civic death. The judgment is yours.

Lead children to note generalities, words with fuzzy meanings, and the ways in which words can be used to skirt issues and to embellish empty statements.

3. For Intermediate Grades
   a. In an advertisement, look for words that try to appeal to the senses:

   Hair that shines like the sun . . . soft and perfect all the time. (*shampoo*)

   With all the sassy flavor, tender garlic, and mild sweet peppers . . . oozing with twenty-three herbs and spices. (*salad dressing*)
   Seeks out and eliminates cooking odor, musty odor, all kinds of household odors—leaves a fresh, clean scent, but never a telltale odor of its own. (*air freshener*)

   b. Discuss some words that advertisers avoid. See if you can determine why some words are chosen rather than others (*scent* rather than *smell,* for example).
   c. Try to determine why a particular brand name was selected for a product (*Joy, Thrill, Halo,* and so on).
   d. Write advertisement or editorials incorporating as many loaded words and words with strong imagery as possible.

4. For Intermediate Grades
Think of words that have recently gained second connotations (*liberation, détente,* and so on). Which of these words has a general connotation (eliciting similar responses in the total populace) as opposed to a personal connotation?

Fact Versus Opinion

Often it becomes necessary for the reader to distinguish between statements of fact and statements of opinion. Factual statements are objective and can be verified by using procedures that can be replicated by others. The truth of the statement "Johnny is seven feet tall" can be determined by anyone using a measuring instrument such as a yardstick. On the other hand, the statement "Johnny is extremely tall" is not verifiable but rests on one's interpretation of the words *tall* or *extremely,* which may or may not coincide with another's viewpoint.

Altick (1969) clarifies the difference between fact and opinion by stating the condition for factual presentation: "Where there is no commonly accepted measure of truth, there can be no objective fact; everything that is judged by the individual on the basis of personal standard is subjective."

That is not to suggest that we should not express an opinion unless facts are obtainable. Opinions are an important part of life. We depend on the commentaries of experts and on their opinions, which are based on facts. We expect a senator to interpret economic developments, for example, and we expect an editor to editorialize. The mature reader attempts to maintain critical awareness of the issues so that these can be weighed in relation to the opinions of others.

At times, however, facts are a necessity. We demand facts about daily occurrences in straight news reporting, for example. We demand this same kind of factual presentation from textbooks.

Distinguishing fact from opinion is not always simple, especially when one's experience and background in a subject are weak. In such cases, the reader must make use of outside criteria. An author giving an opinion often sends signals to indicate this. Children can be made aware of these, just as they can be made aware of fantasy signals. Opinion signals include the following: "It seems to me," "Although not necessarily proved," "In my opinion," "As I (we) see it," and so on. These indicate that the author's expert (or inexpert) opinion follows.

Fact Versus Opinion (Classroom Activities)

1. For Primary Grades
Children in primary grades can work with fact and opinion at a simple level. If the teacher makes sure that children have assimilated criteria for assessing the truth of one statement, they can then be taught to watch for an obvious signal in another. A teacher can prepare a list of sentences such as the two that follow and ask the class to indicate which are opinions by underlining the signal words.

A dog is an animal.
I think dogs should be kept outdoors.

2. For Intermediate Grades
At an intermediate level, isolated statements of fact and opinion may progress to materials taken directly from the content areas. Truths should be rewritten as opinions, and vice versa. The teacher should help children understand the importance of factual presentations in texts. For example, speculate as to how social studies books would reflect different points of view if written by strong-minded Republicans, Democrats, segregationists, English people, and so on. The teacher can offer statements such as the following and ask students to indicate which are facts (verifiable) and which are opinion:

Asia is the largest continent.
Asia is the most beautiful continent.
On June 13, 1967, Thurgood Marshall became the first black person to be appointed to the Supreme Court.
Thurgood Marshall deserved the honor of being appointed to the Supreme Court.

Judging Author Competence

Children who have learned to evaluate the printed word critically will be guarded in their acceptance of an author's right to speak as an authority on a given topic. Again, judgments of this sort need not be delayed until the intermediate grades.

Approaches to Teaching Reading

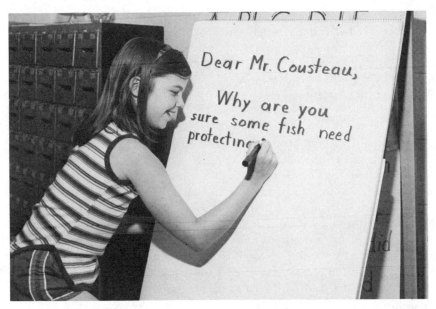

Reading comes alive when the author is viewed as a person with whom to communicate. One way students can gain a sense of involvement with an author is to write a letter.

Two third-grade boys in a summer corrective reading class were having an animated discussion concerning the amount of gear needed by a deep-sea diver:

> "But I read it in a book!" Paul protested, when his argument was disputed.
> "Yes, but books say different things sometimes," David retorted.
> "But Jacques Cousteau wrote my book!"

The point was won, both boys resting their cases on their assessments of the competency of this authority.

A mature reader notes both the source of a publication and the author's background. Knowing about an author's professional training and bias enables a reader to discern and evaluate the author's viewpoint.

Judging Author Competence
(Classroom Activities)

1. For Primary Grades
Children in primary grades can be asked the following:
   Is this author writing about something or someone he or she really knows?
   How can we find out? (Lead students to the jacket flaps of books, to reviews, to the librarian.)
   Where might we look to check some of these facts? (Encyclopedias and other references.)

Critical and Creative Reading

2. For Intermediate Grades

Children in intermediate grades can be taught to use a number of resources in judging an author's competence. They can be shown how to use *Who's Who in America* and *American Men of Science* for biographical data. They can learn to check the card catalog in the library and the *Reader's Guide to Periodical Literature* in order to determine the scope of an author's work. Additional lessons for the intermediate grades might include the following:

a. Having the children write to publishers to obtain information about an author.
b. Having the children use sources such as the *Junior Book of Authors* or sections of the *Horn Book* or *Elementary English*. (A school librarian can provide assistance in helping children learn about various references and how to use them.)
c. Having children critically compare different authors' backgrounds, education, reputations, and professional positions. For example, two blurbs about authors of science books could be presented. One author might be the head of a science department and director of research studies at a university and might have worked as a consultant on several science textbooks. The second author might be interested in science, might have read extensively, and might be primarily an author of books for children. Ask students: Which of the two might have more background for writing a book on leaf identification? What is the standard for selecting one author over the other? Can you determine whether people who write publicity copy for publishing houses have any reason to exaggerate an author's expertise in a particular field? This may result in evaluating the source of the author's expertise.

Determining Author Purpose

Determining the intent of the author enables the reader to evaluate the author's message more carefully. Is the purpose to inform, amuse, convince, or arouse? Does he or she wish to state facts, deprecate, or dispel doubt? The purpose of an author's work determines where it is published. If the author wishes to contribute to an increase of knowledge in a certain field by reporting the results of his or her research, then a scholarly journal with limited readership may be chosen. On the other hand, an author who wants to appeal to a wide audience might choose the *Reader's Digest.* Similarly, the *Congressional Record* probably carries a more direct account of a Senate bill you are following than does the editorial page of your local newspaper. The purpose for which each piece is printed is different.

Children can learn to become aware of how author purpose may affect a presentation. For example, Robert Lawson's delightful book *Ben and Me* is a fictionalized account of the scientific achievements of Benjamin Franklin as "told" by a mouse who takes full credit for Franklin's discoveries. It can be compared with the D'Aulaires' book *Benjamin Franklin,* a biography of this famous inventor. The totally different approach and purpose of each book are evident in this contrast.

Children can be taught to discern differences in presentation because of differences in purpose.

Determining Purpose (Classroom Activity)

Stories can be analyzed for author purpose. A simple classification scheme such as "fun" or "information" may provide a good starting point for such work. Newspapers and magazines may be used by students in the intermediate grades. Other activities include the following:

1. *Reading selected paragraphs with readily determined purposes.* For example, one paragraph may inform the children about the new school cafeteria—size, cost, seating capacity, and hours it is open. Another may urge students to take care of the cafeteria, stressing the rules while appealing to school spirit.
2. *Writing articles with different purposes.* Using the same subject matter, have each child write a piece with a specific purpose in mind that is different from other children's pieces. The purpose can be to amuse, to inform, to frighten, and so on. Compare the articles.
3. *Comparing several newspapers for different accounts of the same event.* Also, contrast articles that are written in straight news style with those that are feature presentations. Determine the slant of each article, the author's purpose, and the way this purpose can be determined.

Identifying Propaganda

In 1937 the Institute of Propaganda Analysis reported seven techniques commonly used to influence the unwary reader. Since then, the identification of propaganda has been emphasized by teachers more than any other area of critical reading. The original list of techniques has since been expanded, interpreted, and repeatedly redefined. Basically, the list includes these:

1. Bad names.
2. Glad names.
3. Transfer.
4. Testimonial.
5. Plain folks.
6. Stacking the cards.
7. Bandwagon.

Bad names is a method by which readers are encouraged to make a negative judgment about someone or something without examining the evidence carefully. The writer intends to provoke an emotional reaction through the use of words with unpleasant connotations. Avoidance behavior is sought by name-calling: "Relieve irritating itching" or "the situation is a rotten-smelling mess."

Critical and Creative Reading

Glad names is a method that is also dependent on the connotative appeal of certain words. In this case, the propagandist appeals to our senses, our noblest ambitions, our feelings of love and of loyalty. "Lovers of justice," "seekers of truth and honor," "dedicated to democracy," and "delicate, demure beauty" are examples of "glad names" used to arouse a pleasant response and to ensure acceptance or approval without scrutiny of the evidence.

Transfer involves the utilization of long-standing feelings of admiration for one thing in an attempt to evoke the same feelings toward a different product or issue. Politicians cite their church affiliations, hoping for the transfer process to work its magic. Beauty queens extol the merits of different products, and the public is led by its desire to emulate the beauty who is selling the products.

Testimonial involves an authority or well-known person who endorses or rejects a product, service, or issue. The propagandist attempts to play on the name and fame of the individual in order to convince the public to react in the same way. Testimonial is similar to transfer: for example, "Janie Jansen, famous screen star, uses *Tress,* the shampoo for beautiful women."

Plain folks is the title given to the attempt—often by public speakers such as politicians, ministers, and businesspeople—to gain favor and win confidence by imitating the speech patterns, dress, and interests of those whom they seek to impress.

Stacking the cards is a method of withholding some element of truth. Omission of truth or slanting of judgment may make truth appear to be falsehood and vice versa. For example: "You know that Roosevelt was betraying us because he made secret deals with the Communist boss Stalin."

Bandwagon is the "follow-the-crowd" approach. All are urged to join with the masses and to team with a winner. For example: "More doctors use_____," or "_____ is the number-one selling brand."

Because there are so many types of propaganda, it is more important for teachers to help children become aware of the technique itself rather than to become expert in classifying the various types. A ready source for classroom work with propaganda is found in the advertisements sprinkled abundantly throughout newspapers and magazines. These are easily obtainable and are usually interesting to students in the intermediate grades.

The ability to recognize propaganda does not guarantee the ability to resist it in its varied forms (Nardelli, 1957). Therefore, the teacher should strive to give as many concrete examples as possible and to give applications to actual experiences.

Evaluating Critical Reading

Children who become critical readers can judge the veracity, worth, and validity of what they read. They can judge the author's work by distinguishing fact from fantasy, by determining the author's purpose and competence, by taking note of the use of evocative language, and by utilizing outside resources to check facts. They become aware of propaganda and the effect it can have, and they can successfully analyze arguments, grouping the points made and evaluating the conclusions. Critical readers make use of their skills in newspaper reading, incidental reading experiences, and reading for pleasure. They are likely to become more intelligent voters, citizens, and consumers as a result of these skills.

By using the ideas and exercises described in this chapter, teachers can develop their own tests for critical reading. One of the surest ways to evaluate performance in this area is to ask a series of key questions. For each category of critical thinking that has been emphasized, select a question that channels the child's response. For example: "Is this passage an opinion or a fact? Give your evidence." Whether the response is in writing or through discussion, the teacher has an opportunity to determine the child's skill in making that kind of judgment. If the child has difficulty, the teacher has a very clear objective for teaching. A checklist similar to the one given in Figure 10.1 can be used to record observations about the critical skills chosen for emphasis.

Written responses to reading can be of great value in getting children to think critically. Many theorists see reading and writing as constructive acts. Writing requires a structuring of ideas that may give students a more critical sense of what they have read (Lehr, 1983).

FIGURE 10.1   Checklist of Skills in Critical Reading

	Always	Usually	Seldom	Never

Can the student do the following?
  Recognize the significance of the content.
  Find the main idea of a paragraph.
  Find the main idea of larger selections.
  Develop independent purposes for reading.
  Identify the author's purpose.
  Develop standards to determine the accuracy and relevancy of information.
  Draw conclusions from the author's interpretation of controversial issues.
  Evaluate concepts gained by contrasting and comparing them with facts and opinions from several other sources.
  Suspend judgment until sufficient data is gathered.
  Recognizing the inference implied by the author.
  Distinguish between fact and fiction.				

Creative Reading

If affective processes are involved in critical reading, it is probable that cognitive, critical-thinking processes are operating during creative reading (Newton, 1980). *Creative* is a term that evokes visions of sparkle, mist, or explosion. Because most people want to be creative and want to encourage creativity in others, the term is used endlessly to describe what teachers and students "ought to be doing" in the classroom. Yet the very personal nature of creativity suggests that we cannot measure a "creative" product.

Must we assume that any original activity or product merits the label *creative?* Must a discussion of creativity stop with a label because we don't have low-to-high criteria for creativity? Just how does one determine originality in the first place? Evidently, we can easily become entangled in the vague meanings of the word *creative.* But in this text we want to go beyond the vague statement that teachers and students "ought to be creative," a statement that is little more than a cliché.

Why, then, do we use the term *creative reading?* The term elicits many positive feelings in teachers and in those who train teachers, and positive feelings are not a bad place to begin. Creative reading will be defined here operationally in terms of what creative readers do.

Creative Reading: What Is It?

Creative reading occurs when the reader attempts to extend a passage beyond the limits set by the author (see the Harris-Smith model of reading, Fig. 2.3). The reader develops new ideas and feelings that can be traced directly to reading and can describe the relationship between the selection read and the extension that has been made from it—that is, how the reading has been applied. In that sense, a teacher can say that students engage in creative reading when they perform a dance, recite a poem, or draw a picture representing their reaction to something they have read. Hypothetically, children can trace the relationship between their reading and the feelings expressed by their artistic work.

This is not to say that extension activity must always be artistic or a representation of feelings. Quite the contrary! Most creative reading, as defined here, will probably be a cognitive activity. A typical extension of reading is to incorporate what has been read into some framework of knowledge or experience. The reader tries to organize or synthesize knowledge. By rearranging or filling in gaps in a conceptual scheme, the reader is using the reading selection to develop an expanded view of the world. Or it may be possible to predict what will happen next in the story—another cognitive and creative activity.

Creative reading is defined here as a unique personal expression stimulated by the reading material whether this expression is a thought, a composition, a dramatic presentation, or a work of art. The reading

Approaches to Teaching Reading

is transformed into something usable for the individual. On reading about Alice falling down the rabbit hole in Wonderland, one child may say, "Oh! How scary!" Another may draw a picture of Alice using an umbrella in the manner of Mary Poppins about to drift into the land of make-believe. Both responses flow from what is read and in that sense can be viewed as part of the continuous process of reading.

It is imperative for the reader to absorb ideas so that they exert an influence on thoughts and actions. In order to be successful, reading instruction must lead the reader to understand that what is read cannot simply remain on the page, but must have an impact that affects attitudes and perceptions (Torrance, 1969).

The creative extension begins when new arrangements, applications, and relationships are drawn. In a sense, the child actually enters into a form of coauthorship, so engrossed in the material does he or she become when encouraged by a teacher who also reads creatively. Thoughts and feelings spring up, ready to be channeled into a multitude of creative directions.

Readers can employ the experience as a foundation on which to fashion a unique superstructure. In that way, reflective thinking and the ability to react in the light of one's own experiences constitute creative reading. It should be emphasized that the desire to communicate through a creative product is a logical follow-up to any creative act. Indeed, the communication itself may be integral to the creative act, as in a child's spontaneous comment: "That poem makes me feel like a warm doughnut."

Preparing for Creative Reading
(Classroom Activity)

The satisfaction gained from extension develops feelings of worth and a sense of individuality for each child. Teacher alertness to the many opportunities for creative expression will help children *experience* reading and *expand* thoughts and feelings in a variety of ways.

Sparking creative expression involves "expectation and anticipation" as the reading task is approached, and it also requires "doing something" with the story. Suppose your class had just read "The Three Little Pigs." Prepare sample lessons that would lead to each of the following categories. How would you build expectation and anticipation for the activities before the children begin to read?

1. Oral activities.
2. Written activities.
3. Arts and crafts.
4. Dramatics.

Interpretive Oral Reading (Discussion)

Reading aloud gives students a chance to express feelings and to show that they have good vocal command of one kind of reading. In all the activities listed here, the intent is to create an atmosphere in which children can demonstrate their feelings and thoughts as they read a particular passage. The teacher must remember, however, that reading aloud tends to be a highly emotional experience for some youngsters. Each of us has experienced stage fright to some degree. The prospect of standing before a group as a performer is often intimidating, particularly for one who has difficulty with reading. Although a healthy attitude toward self-improvement is necessary, it should not be emphasized to such an extent that mistakes are feared. It is important that an atmosphere of support and acceptance be created for oral-reading activities. In this setting, a child can comfortably prepare for oral reading.

Oral Reading by the Teacher

We make the blanket recommendation that every teacher read aloud to students every day of the school year. This may be difficult to accomplish during busy periods such as parent-teacher conference time, but the value and importance of daily oral reading by the teacher are undiminished.

Oral reading by the teacher contributes in many ways to an effective reading program. It forms an integral part of the total literature-appreciation program (Huck, 1976), but oral reading by the teacher need not be limited to literary classics. In fact, a wide selection of books should be read to children in order to broaden their reading interests and build their backgrounds in unfamiliar areas. The teacher can actually stimulate children's reading by the type and breadth of reading shared with them. Children frequently read silently a book their teacher has shared or find another book by the same author after the teacher has read a book aloud.

Not to be overlooked is the therapeutic value of reading aloud to students. Books with a special theme can be selected to suit the needs of a group or can be chosen to match the events of the day. *Ladycake Farm* by Mabel Leigh Hunt (Philadelphia: J. B. Lippincott Co., 1952), a story of race prejudice, may provide the opportunity for some children to face their personal biases individually. The story can also provide the basis for group discussions, with an exchange of ideas encouraging reflection and self-analysis.

The skill of many teachers at oral reading can serve as an excellent model for students. The effectiveness of proper phrasing, clear articulation, and dramatic interpretation is readily apparent to children when demonstrated by their teacher. Special attention can be called to these factors, and the students can be helped to concentrate on each element in turn while the teacher reads aloud.

As not all teachers are effective oral readers and because of the need for a variety of models, recordings of others reading aloud may be used. Leonard Bernstein reading "Peter and the Wolf" can be a valuable listening experience for students, and boys in particular will benefit from the opportunity to hear male voices reading aloud.

Supplying Different Endings

In many classrooms it is too often assumed that a story is over when the final sentence is read. Instead, teachers should realize the end of a story provides an excellent opportunity for doing something new, for expanding on what has been read. Reopen the story, provide new solutions, let each child speculate about it according to his or her own creative urges. Instead of accepting the "happily ever after" ending, why not imagine what might have happened to the "Gingerbread Man"? A whole new series of adventures can be built on the repetitive sequence of the story's structure with the children becoming oral authors.

Modifying a crucial incident within the story may also lead to spinning off new ideas. The teacher who encourages divergent thinking of this sort is helping children to respond creatively. "The Valentine Box," a story by Maude Hart Lovelace, deals with the efforts of a lonely girl, new at school, to aid a classmate in recovering valentines blown from her hand by the winter wind. Children could speculate about a change in the new girl's decision: How would the story have changed if she had decided not to risk being late or losing her own valentines in order to help someone else? Several children can be given the opportunity to finish the story in different ways.

Even prereaders who are listening to a story can participate in creating a story ending. One first-grade teacher noticed a frown on the face of one boy in the story circle as the tale of "Peter Rabbit" came to an end.

"What are you thinking, Danny?" the teacher asked.

"Well, he shouldn't have left home in the first place!" Danny shouted defiantly.

Here is a chance to find out how Danny would reconstruct the story and make up new consequences. A lively discussion is certain to follow, and the result can be a new twist to an old tale.

Story Endings (Classroom Activity)

Have children read a story or a book. (All children can read the same thing, or they may choose their own material to read if you prefer.) Discuss the characters and events in the story. Make a special effort to help the children identify the conflict involved in the story they have read. ("What problems do the characters try to solve in the story?") Then guide the children to invent new endings for the story by having them:

1. Add an additional character (perhaps themselves).
2. Change one of the key events in the story.
3. Resolve the conflict, using the same characters in a new way.

With older children you can do the same activity, but have them try to write their new ending as if the original author had written it. Have the children read their new endings and try to decide whose ending is most similar to the author's style and why.

Dramatic Oral Interpretation

Oral interpretation helps children become sympathetic to the characters they portray. Reading parts can put life into a story, help children understand the characters' motives, and offer a more direct experience with the story itself. Prior class discussion about the kind of person a particular character is can lend a sense of reality to that character's life and may result in varied oral interpretations by students who view the character from different vantage points. Abraham Lincoln and one of his famous speeches (such as the Gettysburg Address) are favorites for dramatic interpretation in the classroom.

Poetry and Drama (Classroom Activities)

Poetry lends itself well to dramatic oral interpretation. The enjoyment of poetry is heightened when it is shared by reading aloud. All children can share in the experience of poetry through choral reading.

1. For Primary Grades
A teacher can take advantage of the rhythm of a poem by having young children provide accompaniment with simple instruments such as sand blocks, dowel sticks, seedpods, or bottles. Children begin choral speaking quite naturally as they chime in on the chorus or a repeated line of a favorite poem read by the teacher. From this simple beginning, the rudiments for choral reading are developed.

2. For Intermediate Grades
Older children can find natural divisions for high and low voices in favorite poems and can also locate parts of the poem that seem to require a solo voice or sound effect. In this way, the potential for enjoying poetry together is greatly enhanced. Children who are hesitant to read aloud by themselves may join in a group reading, thus gaining a sense of belonging. The satisfactions derived from choral reading should not be sacrificed for the sake of achieving perfect rhythm and harmony. The importance of choral reading lies in interpreting the mood of the poem and in gaining pleasure from group participation.

Students can give life to stories by *creating new endings* and by communicating such endings orally or in writing. Especially because writing enables children to make direct visual comparisons, the notion is fostered that stories need not be static but can involve fresh, dynamic thinking.

Children can also turn stories of all kinds into *plays* whether based on dialogue or presented as straight narrative. The impetus for writing plays stems largely from the desire to participate actively in a story that lends itself to action. The fables of Aesop provide a good starting point for novice playwrights: The action is simple, the characters are few, and the dialogue is straightforward. Fairy tales, legends, and the favorite stories of students themselves are easily dramatized.

Writing poetry and songs is also possible as a follow-up activity when the children are caught up in a story or event. When such activity is not assigned, but arises rather from spontaneous appreciation of a shared reading experience, the enjoyment is heightened.

A first-grade class finished a story about a snowstorm. Later that afternoon, big snowflakes began to hit against the classroom window. The children were excited to see the story coming to life. The teacher sensed this excitement and followed the repetitive rhythm of one child's chant—"It's snow, it's snow, it's snow"—on the piano. Soon other children joined in, and the result was a melody "composed" by almost everyone in the class.

It has been said that every child is a poet. Indeed, poetry arises ·

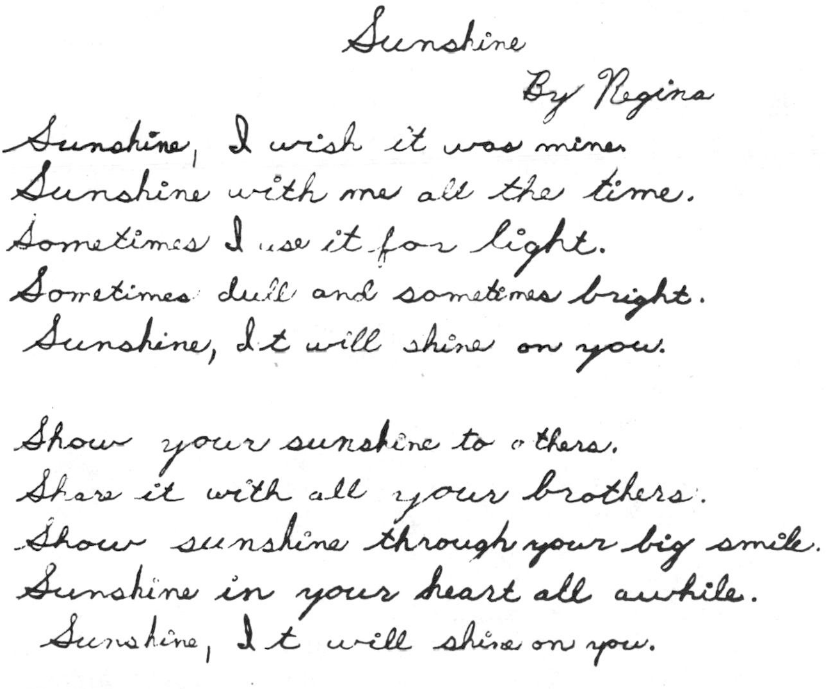

Sunshine
By Regina

Sunshine, I wish it was mine.
Sunshine with me all the time.
Sometimes I use it for light.
Sometimes dull and sometimes bright.
Sunshine, It will shine on you.

Show your sunshine to others.
Share it with all your brothers.
Show sunshine through your big smile.
Sunshine in your heart all awhile.
Sunshine, It will shine on you.

FIGURE 10.2   Children Enjoy Writing Poems.

Critical and Creative Reading

spontaneously from children who are deeply excited by an experience and are intent on communicating this excitement. To encourage the writing of poetry, the teacher should read poems to the class—lots of poems of all kinds—and should openly demonstrate pleasure in reading poetry. It is also important to be alert to the poetry in the language of children and to write down as many examples as possible. Children's poems need not rhyme but should reflect and express their innermost thoughts. Figure 10.2 gives an example of a poem written by a third-grade girl.

Letter writing can serve as an excellent extension of creative reading. It can be imaginary, as, for example, a letter Jane and Michael Banks might have sent to Mary Poppins after her abrupt departure. Children also benefit from writing letters to authors, expressing appreciation for a story they have read or suggesting alternate solutions or asking pertinent questions. Many authors respond to their young critics, and an increased interest in reading and an immeasurable sense of self-worth develop as a result of such communications.

Writing Stories and Poems
(Classroom Activities)

1. Parallel Stories

Parallel stories grow from the original plot but may follow a minor character into full development or fan out from an event mentioned only briefly in passing within the original story. They can develop from such discussions as "If I were Sarah . . ." or from speculation about what must have happened before the event took place. Expanding the role of a character provides opportunities for children to manipulate events and to assign characteristics, feelings, thoughts, and even environmental stimuli to enrich their reactions to the story. Children are often deeply drawn into discussions of two versions of a story prepared by their classmates. Sharing a story on parallel planes adds richness to the reading experience. Other opportunities for building parallel stories include the following:

1. Pretending to be a character who witnesses the action from a perspective different from that of the author. Write this new interpretation.
2. Describing the personality traits a character would probably exhibit if he or she could be met face-to-face.
3. Pretending to be a certain character and keeping a diary of that character's thoughts and feelings.
4. Composing a letter that one character in a story might have written to another, describing some event and that character's reaction to it.

2. Class Poetry

Writing poetry in response to a story makes an excellent class project. The teacher should recognize, however, that children's poems are sometimes lacking in those elements considered important in adult writing. Although children's poetry may appear rudimentary by some standards, those children who write poetry as a reaction

Approaches to Teaching Reading

to what they have read will gain confidence in their ability to communicate. When encouraging the writing of poetry, the teacher should stress communication far more than form.

Poetry starters for the class may include these:

1. Finding descriptions in stories that lend themselves to poetry. Have the children read these descriptions and then write their reaction to (or re-creation of) the passage in a poetic style.
2. Having the children respond poetically to the story by structuring each line. Begin each line the same way ("I feel . . . ," "The giant . . . ," and so forth, and have the children complete the line. After the first few lines, the children will probably have exhausted the obvious endings and will begin to be more creative.

Sample techniques for writing poetry are given in books such as *A Celebration of Bees—Helping Children Write Poetry* by Barbara Juster Esbensen (Minneapolis: Winston Press, 1975).

Arts and Crafts

The kinds of illustrations youngsters make for the stories they read can give a good indication of the things that appeal to children and that they remember and consider to be important. Furthermore, illustrating stories provides children with opportunities to express themselves in ways that do not rely exclusively on words. Finger paints can be used effectively to illustrate stories and poems of mood and mystery or those that draw on these elements for special effect. With splashes of blue and swirls of white, young artists can create wind and rain. A story that lends itself particularly well to this type of expression is *Plink Plink Goes the Water in My Sink* by Ethel and Leonard Kessler (New York: Doubleday, 1954). Encourage children to sweep their fingers and swirl their fists in the paint to create movement, excitement, and texture.

In books such as *Hide and Seek Fog* by Alvin Tresselt, the titles suggest the moods that the stories elicit. Watercolors can be used as background wash for illustrations of these books.

Children's Drawings

1. Crayon-resist is a method in which foreground figures are drawn in crayon before watercolors are applied to the entire picture, with the crayoned part resisting the paint. This method can be used effectively for depicting passages of graphic description.

2. Three-dimensional models are tangible interpretations of a shared story experience. Models can be sculpted from paper, clay, toothpicks, or odds and ends. Children involved in a unit of stories dealing with pioneers can fashion an entire village as a class project or can work on *dioramas*—miniature scenes reproduced in three dimensions against a painted background.

Dramatic Interpretation

When children respond to a story, they move wholeheartedly toward a reenactment of the tale and delight in re-creating the events in the lives of the characters. Through the imagination of children, the author's words are brought to life. Pantomiming, role-playing, playacting, puppetry, and shadow plays are all methods for creative interpretation.

Playing out a story through *pantomime* is one of the simplest forms of creative dramatics. Variations on the pantomime technique include acting the story while selected readers describe the events or freely interpreting favorite parts of a story.

Shadow plays—acting out a story behind a suspended sheet with a strong light directly behind the players—can be most effective in implementing pantomime because all attention is focused on bodily movements and gestures.

Puppets provide an excellent medium for expressing reactions to what children have read.

In *role-playing* the students assume the outstanding traits of the main characters in a story and play out imagined discussions or climactic scenes. Students from a third-grade class read with interest stories about the life of Christopher Columbus from boyhood to old age. Deciding to act out his life, they constructed his ships from tables and chairs, designated the chalkboard as Spain, and set sail. Similarly, other children followed newspaper and TV accounts of a lunar expedition and then enacted the roles of astronauts.

Playacting differs from role-playing in that parts are assigned and usually "learned" in one fashion or another. Often such plays are written, produced, and directed by students.

Simple *puppets* are a joy for most children. They are particularly good for helping shy children to project their feelings and to extend their verbal experiences. Activities with puppets spark language expression, broaden understanding, deepen feelings and emotions, and develop sympathy and relationships with the characters in the story. Puppets can be made from paper bags, from sticks, or with papier-mâché heads and cloth bodies. They may be as elaborate as time, energy, and skill permit. They serve the function of allowing children to play out stories in a projected role.

Creative dance and rhythms are techniques that can be used to enact entire stories or to demonstrate a portion of a story with movement.

Pantomime and Dance

1. *Pantomime.* Choose portions of the story that lend themselves to action and movement. Instruct the children to use only gestures and movements to convey their characters. For example:

Skip through the woods as Little Red Riding Hood.
Run home from the ball as Cinderella.
Be the crotchety grandfather or carefree Peter in "Peter and the Wolf."
As one of the seven dwarfs, discover the intrusion of Snow White.
Children can design their own pantomimes and challenge the class to guess what they are portraying.

2. *Creative dance and rhythms.* Prepare instructions ahead of time that will lead the children through a creative interpretation experience. Allow the children plenty of time to experience and act out the instructions. Sample directions could be these:

Move like the saggy, baggy elephant. Bend and sway slowly, slowly.
Be a tiny seed under the ground. Feel the warm sun on your back. Stretch to the sun. Grow. Grow.
Be the Indian, hiawatha. Greet the morning sun. Move to the beat of Indian tom-toms. Dance a joyful dance.

Summary

Critical and creative reading were discussed separately in this chapter although in reality the two cannot be clearly separated. *Critical reading* is concerned primarily with the reading-thinking skills that enable a reader to apply criteria to a selection and make judgments about it. The skills of *analysis* and *evaluation* relate closely to critical reading. *Creative reading* is concerned primarily with integrating the reading experience into the knowledge and feelings of the reader and with producing a response unique to each individual. The skills of *synthesis* and *extension* are closely related to our definition of creative reading; they involve a demonstration of the connection between the selection read and the way the reader uses that selection. Such a connection is characterized by both an objective, rational element and a subjective, emotional one.

The most important procedure a teacher can follow in helping students to become critical readers is to ask questions that lead students beyond simple recall and restatement. Students should learn to classify information or events and to apply criteria in this classification process. The teacher who is able to move the discussion systematically toward evaluation is most likely to help children become critical readers.

A key factor in developing creative readers is the teacher's attitude of encouraging, exploring, and valuing the extension or application of what is read by the child. Creative reading fosters divergent thinking whether the results are expressed orally, in writing, through motion, or through an art form.

The active involvement of children with print, whether through analysis, evaluation, or extension, is an important part of the reading process. Critical and creative reading foster this active involvement.

Terms for Self-study

analysis	extension
inference	pantomime
evaluation	synthesis
connotation	

Discussion Questions

1. Why is it important for a teacher to distinguish between literal and critical reading?
2. In what ways would the teaching of critical reading differ between the primary and intermediate grades?
3. In addition to asking questions, what other means does a teacher have for teaching critical reading? For teaching creative reading?
4. How can the Harris-Smith Reading Model from Chapter 2 help teach critical and creative reading?
5. What statements of objectives could be used to give teachers a sense of direction for developing creative reading?

6. How would a teacher determine whether or not a response to reading was an original one?

Recommended Readings

Cheyney, Arnold B. (1971). *Teaching reading skills through the newspaper.* Newark, DE: International Reading Association.

Cheyney provides practical suggestions for developing critical and creative reading skills by using the newspaper.

Hittelman, Daniel R. (1983). *Developmental reading, K-8: Teaching from a psycholinguistic perspective* (2nd ed.). Boston: Houghton Mifflin.

This book stresses the relationship between reading and writing and offers the premise that students of all ages gain in reading proficiency if they write or create their own texts.

Lehr, Fran (1983, November-December). Developing critical and creative reading and thinking skills. *Language Arts, 60*(8), 1031–1035.

Lehr offers practices for involving students in thinking critically.

McCaslin, Nellie (1974). *Creative dramatics in the classroom* (2nd ed.). New York: David McKay.

This book provides guidance on how to encourage creative dramatics. Chapters 6 and 7 suggest ways to develop plays from stories.

Newkirk, Thomas (1982, May). Young writers as critical readers. *Language Arts, 59*(5), 451–457.

Newkirk suggests writing as a means to spur critical reading.

Roser, Nancy, & Frith, Margaret (eds.). (1983). *Children's choices: Teaching with books children like.* Newark, DE: International Reading Association.

This text identifies books that children frequently choose and like to read. It also suggests that children will read more critically in those books they want to read.

Tiedt, Iris M., et al. (1983). *Teaching writing in K-8 classrooms.* Englewood Cliffs, NJ: Prentice-Hall.

Tiedt presents a model for teaching writing that includes actual lesson plans for using oral language, narrative writing, expository writing, sentence writing, word choices, and editing.

Zavatsky, Bill, & Padgett, Ron (Eds.). (1977). *The whole word catalog 2.* New York: McGraw-Hill. Published in association with Teachers and Writers Collaborative.

This is a novel collection of ideas and materials that can be used to stimulate creativity through writing, drama, music, art, and media such as film and television.

11

Teaching Reading for Life—Content Reading

When Tony was four years old, he brought home a pail of pond water in which there were some tadpoles. He was told to watch them to see what would happen. He watched the tadpoles develop through a number of stages, and two of them survived as frogs. The day Tony got up and found what had happened to his tadpoles, he commented: "Tadpoles make the nicest frogs."

What happened to Tony may provide some clues about reading in content fields. In a way Tony went through the kind of thinking a scientist engages in when he or she looks at nature and tries to make some conclusions about what he or she has observed. The pattern of observing nature, of making some inferences about the observations, of classifying the observations, and of arriving at conclusions may provide some important clues as to how to read content subjects. If the scientist's thinking is reflected in his or her writing, comprehending what is written could be aided by knowing about the scientist's typical thinking patterns.

Reading for real life plays an important part in most children's lives. They want to succeed in science, social studies, and math courses in school; and they want to enjoy reading magazines and newspapers at home. That's reading for life. It is different from reading in a basal reader. That is not a surprising statement, but it needs to be repeated because teachers do not often teach children how to handle expository writing, which is different from fiction and has a different purpose from the basal reader.

To determine what content reading is and how to teach it, think about these questions as you read this chapter:

• *What is the difference between reading content material and reading basal reader stories?*

- *Is there a visual difference in content material?*
- *What are the general skills needed to read content material efficiently?*
- *What special reading skills are used to read specific kinds of content, such as science and math?*
- *Are there instructional guidelines for teaching content reading?*

Content reading is receiving considerable attention these days. Professional organizations are discussing the topic, publishers are producing reading series that contain an increasing volume of expository material, and teachers are listening to speeches about it at state conventions. The term *content reading* sounds like someone's double talk. After all, if you do not read content when you read, what are you doing?

Content reading is a term used for the reading of expository (non-fiction) material, which is concerned with giving information. The term does not usually refer to the reading of a short story or a novel, that is, a selection that provides a vicarious experience or an emotional involvement in imaginative living.

One reason for isolating content reading in a text on teaching reading is that children need particular practice in reading content material. They have been systematically introduced to the short story, for they spend most of their first six years in school learning to read short stories. Teachers and pupils spend much time building a short story vocabulary, analyzing plots, describing characters, interpreting actions, and applying the morals stated in these stories to their own living.

A Problem of Vocabulary and Concepts

When it comes to information subjects, such as social studies, most instructional emphasis goes into recalling specific information and gaining concepts. Students have to read in order to get these facts and these concepts, but as this activity is not called learning to read, many teachers seem to feel that no overt transfer of reading pedagogy is necessary. Even though the content subject has a new vocabulary, often no effort is made to get children to analyze the vocabulary and develop automatic recognition habits, as is always done in "reading" lessons. Even though content is organized differently, the writing is not analyzed in class as those hundreds of plots in readers are. The attitude that creates a wall between learning to read and reading in content subjects reflects a failure to understand what reading is. It is a tool, or a process, whereby a learner communicates with an author.

Once the initial mechanics of learning the code of writing English are conquered, reading becomes a combination of reading and thinking—an inseparable union when an individual is reacting to a printed message. People have to read some content; they cannot simply read writing. The natural and relevant place for reading-thinking to take place is in conjunction with literature, science, math, and social studies. The question, then, is how does the teacher put the learner and the content author together so that the printed page communicates something. Communication involves, among other things, a common vocabulary between writer and reader, a common interest, and the ability of the receiver of the message to follow the thinking of the writer of the message. Because individual writers have different thinking patterns and because different content areas show different patterns of thought, the teacher has the responsibility of aiding students in identifying some of those patterns in order to open channels of communication.

Comparison of Material

Consider some samples of writing from various subject areas.

There is a story in one of the basal readers that is called "A Kitty for Kathy." It is a typical primary-grade story with characters and a situation or problem that the characters try to resolve. After students have read the story, they are asked: "Who are the characters?" "What are they trying to do?" "How do they do it?" "Did they succeed in what they wanted to do?" Those are typical questions because they indicate the organizational pattern of short-story writing.

"A Kitty for Kathy" is representative of that pattern. Kathy finds a kitty on her way home from the playground and asks her mother if she may keep it. Mother tells her that they cannot keep the cat because they are going to grandmother's house for a week. They cannot take the cat with them, nor can they leave it home alone. Kathy asks if she can keep the cat provided she finds someone to take care of it while they are away. Her mother consents to this plan. After a period of sitting on the door stoop, Kathy has an inspiration. She goes next door and asks Mrs. Henrietta if she will baby-sit for her. Mrs. Henrietta says that she will be happy to do this for Kathy anytime. Then Kathy explains that it is a cat Mrs. Henrietta is to sit with. Mrs. Henrietta, being a nice neighbor, accepts the kitty-sitting job for the week, and the problem is solved. This pattern is typical of the short stories in their basal readers that children continue to analyze for four, five, and six years.

The child has to read other types of material as well. In expository writing a character, a plot, a problem to be solved, or some interaction between characters may not appear in the piece that is being read. What do the children do? What kinds of questions do they ask when they approach the material and try to comprehend it? The structure of this selection is different from the short stories they had previously read. It is not sufficient to tell the children that they will have to discuss the topic and that they are to read the next several pages. It is not enough to tell them that they must answer several fact questions such as "What is a tadpole?" "Where do tadpoles live?" "How do tadpoles develop?" The child must recall many facts and details from the writing, but also needs suggestions on how to analyze the author's purpose and thinking pattern.

Through a series of analyses of science, social studies, and mathematics texts, students can see that there are different structural patterns or different organizational patterns in different kinds of texts. Science writing usually has an organizational pattern unlike that in social studies, for example. If students were alerted to these patterns they would have a way of organizing themselves so as to increase their comprehension (Meyer, 1984).

To understand a selection a reader must get the main idea, know the important details, and see the interrelation of the parts. To analyze scientific data, classify them, and find some conclusion or resulting law, a reader must begin with literal comprehension. Beyond that readers have to know what the various parts of the selection are, what relationships exist among the parts, and how those relationships lead to the conclusion. Even though that learning is very important, one wonders how often it occurs in schools where memorizing of content is stressed.

Readability of Content Texts

Children face many problems when they come to the task of reading science content. The teacher's guide for one book states that it was written for the lower track of junior and senior high school groups, but no specific grade or readability level is given. Evidently, it is meant to be read at some reading level below grade seven. According to the Dale-Chall readability formula, it has a 7.8 reading level.[1] Thus, it would appear that some of the people for whom the book is intended may have considerable difficulty with it.

Another selection taken from a popular elementary school science text is designed for grade five according to the publisher. In the teacher's guide the authors say they were deliberately conscious of writing on a simple level so that the book could be used by children whose reading skills are average or below. Using the Dale-Chall readability formula on that text produces a grade readability of 9.1.

Why should the readability formula indicate a much more difficult level than that the publishers and authors estimate? One reason is that the selections contain many difficult words, that is, words that do not appear on the list of easy words in the readability formula. The larger the number of difficult words, the higher the readability level will be. The list of easy words is composed of those that appear most frequently in basal readers. Through basal readers, children are trained to read easy words. Then, for example, they are asked to read *heredity, Austrian, monk monastery, differed, traits, cross-pollinated, resulting,* and *offspring* in an article about Mendel discovering the laws of heredity. All these words appear in one paragraph of the text and are considered difficult words because they are not commonly used. In the next paragraph are the words *generation, pure-bred, produced, tallness, dominant, shortness, recessive, depressed.* One out of every eight words in the article is not regularly used in basal readers or in language arts texts. Therefore, children are not expected to be able to respond to them automatically. They have to stop and analyze such words—provided they have sufficient word-analysis skills.

[1] Readability formulas include the number of difficult words and the length of sentences, combined with a mathematical formula to produce the grade equivalent of the material. The use of readability formulas is discussed later in this chapter.

Content area readers are often more difficult to read than indicated by the designated grade level.

Consider a word like *hybrid* in the sentence: "He prided himself in having both hybrid corn and hybrid chickens." What does *hybrid* mean? A child can analyze all day and not know what *hybrid* means unless he or she is from a farm region. Even then the child may not know precisely but only know that *hybrid* is a word associated with a kind of corn. Children have to have some way of relating words to their experience and some way of identifying words.

The paragraph that follows illustrates a young reader's difficulties in reading when key words are not known. What comprehension questions can he or she answer? Can you determine what goes in the blanks?

The Digestive System

After you _____ the food, it passes down the _____ into your _____ . Juices from the lining of your _____ mix with the food. The juices soften the food, and _____ in the juices break up _____ into even smaller ones.

Most food is not completely _____ in the _____ . When the food is _____ and soft enough, a _____ at the end of the _____ opens, a little at a time. The partly _____ food flows into a long, _____ narrow _____ called the small _____ .[2]

This selection on the digestive system was taken from a fifth-grade text that was rated 9.1 on the Dale-Chall formula. The first paragraph contains *esophagus, stomach lining, soften, chemicals,* and *particles*—all words

[2] Herman Schneider and Nina Schneider (1968). *Science in Our World,* Book 5. Boston: D. C. Heath; p. 185.

not found in the easy word list. Other difficult words in the paragraph are *completely, digested, moist, valve, coiled, tubes, liver, pancreas, intestine, glands, molecules, bloodstream, capillaries, gristle,* and *stringy fibers.* One out of six of the words in the selection is not in the easy word list. If you eliminate one sixth of the words in a passage, comprehension must suffer. Many words that are essential to comprehension cannot be identified by the reader. It is evident, therefore, that vocabulary and word recognition play key roles in reading content selections.

Content teachers need to know ways to teach vocabulary just as a reading teacher would. They have to build background so the child has concepts to work with, and they have to present vocabulary in terms of concept development, as well as in terms of word recognition.

In addition to difficult vocabulary in content material, there are diagrams, charts, and tables that often accompany the text and that must be comprehended. Usually, it is important to relate the text to the diagrams. How does a child learn to do that?

Using Illustrations

Here is the opening paragraph from a story entitled "From Tadpoles to Frogs,"[3] taken from a second-grade book:

> When I first put my tadpoles into the bowl they were funny little things, I had never seen anything like them before. They stayed under water all the time.

For those who can find tadpoles in ponds and creeks near their homes, this paragraph is no problem. But a student living in a large urban center might not know what a tadpole is. Children in Cleveland and New York City may never have seen a live pig, much less a tadpole. We know an eighteen-year-old boy from Brooklyn, New York, who took a train to go to school in the Midwest. When he arrived on campus, he told his counselor that on the trip he had seen his first live pig and his first live cow. It is not unrealistic to say, therefore, that many second-grade children do not know what a tadpole is.

That is the reason why teachers have to build concepts and relate a text to the illustrations. Look at the sample page from the "Tadpole" story (Fig. 11.1). The science text gives a diagram, a picture, or an illustration. A child reads: "I'd never seen anything like them before. They stayed under water all the time." Without illustrations, what image would the second-grade reader have? What has the child seen on television that stays under water and that he or she has never seen before?

The illustration demonstrates the growth of a tadpole. The teacher must explain: "Look at the pictures and go back to the text." This seems quite elementary, but for the child who has not had the experience, the teacher must show how to relate illustrations to the text.

[3] C. G. Stratemeyer and H. L. Smith, Jr. (1963). *Frog Fun.* Evanston, Ill.: Harper & Row.

The tadpoles are growing.
Oh how fast they grow.
They are turning into frogs.

Tell me, little frog,
what happened to your tail?

FIGURE 11.1   Illustrations from *Frog Fun.*

This is especially true when the illustrations are quite different from those in the basal readers.

The "Tadpole" story is from a second-grade science reader. In a fourth-grade science text the subject may be the operation of a refracting telescope. The conceptual problem is now compounded. Not only does the student not understand what a refracting telescope is, but the teacher must study diligently at night to relate an illustration of the telescope to the text that describes it. Relating the drawing to the text is a reading skill that is needed often with science, math, and social studies tests.

Children must be shown how to move systematically through a diagram by locating the point where the text explanation and the diagram correspond. Reading the illustrations will help children to visualize, conceptualize, and understand.

Estimating Readability

Basal reading series have long carried grade level designations for the various books they contain. One book or set of books is typically labeled grade two, for example; another is referred to as grade four level, and so forth. Promotional materials developed by a publisher often extol the virtures of their basal program in terms of the attention that has been given to control of readability or reading difficulty in its development. In recent years we have seen similar claims become commonplace for content area textbooks. A United States history book may be described as one "written at the tenth-grade level," for example.

It seems appropriate to spend some time here examining (1) the concept of readability, (2) ways commonly used to determine the "reading level" of a textbook, and (3) how a classroom teacher might respond to concerns about readability in selecting materials for pupils to read. First, let us examine the concept of readability.

Approaches to Teaching Reading

Some Books Are Harder Than Others

It hardly seems necessary to convince you that some books are more difficult to read and understand than others. Everyone who reads has had the experience of struggling with printed text that simply doesn't reveal itself with ease. Yet other material virtually sings a clear, sweet message. But have you thought about why this is so? On reflection, some factors seem fairly obvious: familiarity of the words used, length and complexity of sentences, descriptiveness of headings and subheadings, usefulness of illustrations, diagrams, charts, maps, and the like. A book that you find easy contains words you know, sentences you can follow, headings that help you organize your thoughts, and so forth. A book that overwhelms you is just the opposite: The words are unfamiliar, the sentences too complex, and so on.

On further reflection, you probably realize that some factors that determine the difficulty of a book are related to characteristics of the book itself, and some are related to your own traits. To illustrate, a book even on a topic you know something about may use many technical terms that are unknown to anyone other than an expert in the field. Another book on the same topic might cover the same material but use more common terms. One book is "harder" in the most common sense use of that term because of a factor basic to the book: vocabulary. On the other hand, a book may be about a topic that is entirely foreign to you. In this case, even the use of the most common terms may not enable you to comprehend because your prior knowledge simply isn't sufficient to the task. Another factor internal to the reader (rather than the book) is interest in the topic. Keen interest can be a powerful factor in making a "hard" book "easier." Conversely, when interest is lacking, comprehension typically comes harder.

Even in these examples it is obvious that no factor is entirely book-based and no factor entirely reader-based. The difficulty of a book or any printed matter is determined by an interaction between the text and a particular reader. What is easy for one person is not easy for another. Are we saying that no objective measure of reading difficulty is possible? Is it impossible to say in any absolute sense that *Hamlet* is "harder" than *Homer Price?* No, of course not. Our own experiences suggest otherwise. Some reading matter is harder than others by any measure. Procedures have been devised for estimating the difficulty level of printed matter. Called readability measures, these procedures yield a grade level that serves as a numerical index to reading difficulty. Used cautiously and with full appreciation for their limitations, readability procedures can serve a useful purpose (which we'll describe shortly). It is important to remember that they only estimate difficulty level, however, and do not take into account any of the very important factors that reside within the reader (Kintsch & Miller, 1984). Readability procedures are strictly attentive to factors in the text itself and even then take into account only a few text-based factors believed to affect readability and ignore many others (such as the usefulness of headings, illustrations, and the like).

How Readability Can Be Calculated

Readability level is normally reported in terms of grade level. Thus, a book may be given a grade five reading-level designation, for example. How is this number determined, and what does it mean?

Reading levels were first determined with the aid of a formula. Several formulas emerged in the middle of the twentieth century that are still used today (Dale-Chall, 1948; Flesch, 1948; Lorge, 1939; Spache, 1953). Of course, a formula is nothing more than a statement that calls for certain values to be supplied so that they can then be weighted as desired to arrive at a solution. Early experimentation attempted to refine these formulas by employing a number of grammatic variables (e.g., number of subordinate clauses). In this case, the use of complex text analysis proved to add little value. As a result, the best-known and widely accepted readability formulas are based on only two factors: (1) sentence length and (2) vocabulary (Chall, 1984).

To calculate readability using a formula such as the Dale-Chall, you must determine (1) the average length of sentences in at least three separate samples of text (every tenth page of a book should be sampled with at least 100 words in each sample) and (2) the number of words in each sample not on the Dale list of 3,000 most familiar words. Detailed guidelines are used to standardize these procedures. Numbers generated with these procedures are plugged into the formula, and a corrected grade level is obtained (e.g., grades five to six). The Dale-Chall approach is valid for grade four material and above only. Some formulas (e.g., Spache) are also valid for primary-grade materials.

The procedures involved in the use of a readability formula are tedious and time-consuming. Publishers often have the time, the means, and the desire to calculate readability levels for materials they publish using a readability formula. Recently software packages for microcomputers have made this task somewhat easier (see Mason, 1983, p. 177 for a listing of readability programs for microcomputers). Whether you do your own calculations or not, it would be well for you to know how readability formulas work so that you can interpret and make appropriate use of readability figures assigned to materials by publishers.

When doing a readability calculation, some variation in level may result depending on which formula is used. Clearly, there is more reliability among the levels calculated using one formula than there is among levels calculated using several formulas. Therefore, a book yielding a fifth-to-sixth grade level on the Dale-Chall is probably easier than one yielding a ninth-to-tenth grade level with the same formula. One cannot have as much confidence in comparing fifth-to-sixth grade Dale-Chall score with a ninth-to-tenth grade Spache score, however.

Because readability formulas are not quick and convenient to use, a variety of alternative approaches have emerged in the past ten to fifteen years. Procedures such as those developed by Gunning (1952), Fry (1969), McLaughlin (1969), and Raygor (1976) enable the classroom teacher to estimate a difficulty level for a book in a matter of a few minutes. The reading levels resulting from the use of these procedures have been validated against the scores yielded by the time-honored formulas. This step is satisfactory to the user of readability procedures only if he or she is confident that the formulas are themselves worthwhile and accurate. As McConnell (1982) observed, "validation studies were typically not performed in the development of readability formulas. Rather, the more recent formulas have been validated only in terms of the earlier formulas. In turn, the earlier formulas were validated in terms of practice exercises in reading that were never meant to be used to measure comprehension" (McConnell, 1982, p. 15).

It is important to bear in mind that the newer readability procedures probably have all the limitations of the older formulas. In our view, the limitations of readability calculations in general are such that it is better to arrive at a "quick and dirty" level using a procedure such as the Fry than to invest hours of time using one of the old formulas because both approaches yield little more than a crude estimate that has only limited value to the classroom teacher in any case. But before discussing how a readability level can be used, let us look more closely at one of the newer, faster procedures, the Fry graph for estimating readability.

Expanded Directions for Working Readability Graph

1. Randomly select three (3) sample passages and count out exactly 100 words beginning with the beginning of a sentence. Do count proper nouns, initializations, and numerals.
2. Count the number of sentences in the hundred words estimating length of the fraction of the last sentence to the nearest $\frac{1}{10}$th.
3. Count the total number of syllables in the 100-word passage. If you don't have a hand counter available, an easy way is to simply put a mark above every syllable over one in each word, then when you get to the end of the passage, count the number of marks and add 100. Small calculators can also be used as counters by pushing numeral "1," then push the "+" sign for each word or syllable when counting.
4. Enter graph (Figure 11.2) with *average* sentence length and *average* number of syllables; plot dot where the two lines intersect. Area where dot is plotted will give you the approximate grade level.
5. If a great deal of variability is found in syllable count or sentence count, putting more samples into the average is desirable.
6. A word is defined as a group of symbols with a space on either side; thus, "Joe," "IRA," "1945," and "&" are each one word.
7. A syllable is defined as a phonetic syllable. Generally, there are as many syllables as vowel sounds. For example, "stopped" is one syllable and "wanted" is two syllables. When counting syllables for numerals and initializations, count one syllable for each symbol. For example, "1945" is 4 syllables and "IRA" is 3 syllables, and "&" is 1 syllable.

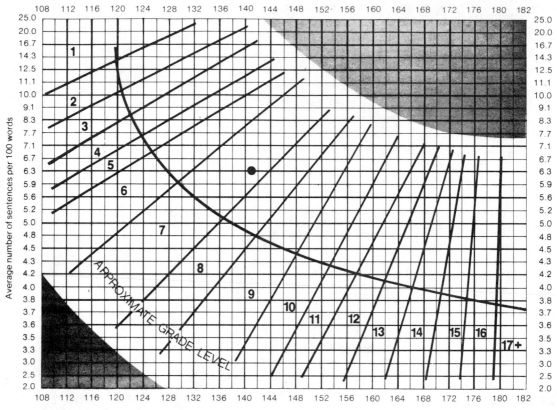

Average number of syllables per 100 words

FIGURE 11.2 Fry Graph for Estimating Readability—Extended, by Edward Fry, Rutgers University Reading Center, New Brunswick, N.J. 08904.

As you can see, the relative simplicity of counting syllables in three 100-word passages is much quicker than determining which words do not appear on a list of familiar words as required by the Dale-Chall formula. Furthermore, the Fry graph eliminates the necessity of making intricate mathematical calculations. These factors make the Fry procedure relatively easy to use. The McLaughlin, Raygor, and Alfie procedures are equally simple. As a consequence, a reading level can be estimated quickly for virtually any material the teacher wants to use. And therein lies the rub. Because reading levels can easily be estimated, the temptation is strong to employ the procedures widely and frequently. Such ease enables a teacher (or publisher) to assign a label to virtually every piece of reading material available. Once reading material is labeled, the grade level tends to stick, taking on a life and meaning altogether undeserved. One story or book is thought of as being harder than another as though the grade level designation is precise. Students may even be forbidden by some teachers from reading a book above their reading level (even though the readability estimate is based on factors entirely different from those

Approaches to Teaching Reading

normally used in determining a pupil's reading level). These and other misuses of readability estimates are much less likely to occur when teachers understand how they are derived and what limitations apply.

Using Readability Estimates in Decisions for the Classroom

One theme developed in this book is that the classroom teacher is constantly making decisions. Decisions must be made about how to group pupils for instruction, which skills to teach, which workbook exercises to use, and so forth. One of the most basic decisions a teacher makes is which reading material to use with each pupil. Leaving aside any number of important issues we have explored elsewhere in this book such as the quality of literature, the reputation of an author, and the usefulness of the skills program, we should discuss one dimension further here: matching the learner with reading material that can be read with adequate understanding. Readability estimates are of some value in making this match.

We have mentioned some cautions with respect to the accuracy of readability estimates. Clearly, the grade level designations generated by a readability procedure are imprecise and insensitive to a host of important factors affecting the comprehensibility of a text. They yield quantitative measures in an area where qualitative measures are desirable. Despite this, we see a place for readability estimates in the teacher's decision making when it comes to matching reader and book.

As we view it, readability estimates provide a useful starting point that must then give way to fine tuning based on experience and professional judgment. The teacher with six or seven pupils in a classroom who score at or below third-grade level on a standardized reading test knows that those pupils are likely to have difficulty reading a social studies textbook written for the average sixth-grader. The use of the Fry readability graph seems warranted in verifying that the textbook is indeed at the grade six level. This does not prove that the six or seven low achievers cannot read the textbook, but it indicates a need to watch for signs of difficulty.

It also suggests that it may be wise to look for other, "easier" material written on the same topic. Here again the Fry graph can be of some value. Another book may be found that produces a grade four Fry estimate. This seems to be closer to the level of the students. At this point, the teacher should examine other factors not taken into account by the readability procedure. Does the so-called easier book provide useful, helpful headings and subheadings? Is a typeface used to provide additional clues to meaning? Is a glossary provided? Have sentences been kept short by the questionable elimination of explicit connections among thoughts, thus requiring the reader to make more inferences in the "easier" text? Have important details been left out to make the presentation short and simple? What is the net impact of this abridging? Pearson (1975) and others have demonstrated that simplified text is not always easier because explicit clues to meaning may be lost when material is rewritten to satisfy the requirements of a readability procedure. If formulas can so easily be wrong in their estimates, why use them? If the teacher must still look at the factors mentioned earlier, what is gained?

Teaching will never be reduced to set patterns. Recipes and formulas will never yield absolute dictates for the teacher to follow. Tools such as the Fry procedure can supply data the teacher uses or rejects as the situation dictates. The book that looks too hard may get a second, more careful look because the readability estimate proves to be surprisingly low. Another book may yield a low readability estimate but fail to pass a more qualitative inspection performed by the teacher.

We hold no great allegiance to readability estimates and have little patience with those who treat them as gospel. We think they can help a teacher sort through prospective reading material, narrowing the possible choices down to a few that require more careful examination. Clearly, there is no justification for placing a pupil whose grade equivalent on the SRA achievement test in reading is 4.0 in a book simply because it yields a 4.0 reading level by using the Fry graph. Such a procedure assumes far too much in the way of accuracy and makes no allowance for factors idiosyncratic to the child. If we know anything at all about individual differences, it should make us unwilling to assume that background experience and interests, two powerful factors in reading comprehension, are uniform across learners. For this reason alone a book "written at the grade five level" on one topic may suit a child whereas another book "written at the same level" on another topic may not.

Reading Skills for Content Reading

The primary goal of content reading is to teach the child how to comprehend the totality of the selection. Children must comprehend what the science writer had in mind when he or she made an observation about nature. In a sense, the reader wants to know how the scientist thinks when he or she writes. That is an excellent "handle" to give children: Read like a scientist; read like a mathematician; read like a social scientist. By trying to identify the structure of the content discipline and typical patterns for presenting that information, the reader is prepared to comprehend.

If reading the expository material in content subjects needs a different approach, what are the skills required for efficient reading? Evidently, most of the same skills that are used in reading narrative will also be used in reading content selections. *Word analysis and word meaning skills and skills leading to a literal comprehension of the selection will be employed in all types of reading.* In addition to those elements, however, content reading requires other skills related to using materials and skills of analysis and evaluation.

The general skills that enable a person to achieve literal comprehension include a basic reading vocabulary; the use of context to help determine the meaning of words; and the use of phonics, structural analysis, the dictionary, and illustrations as aids in deciphering words.

The reader should ask these basic questions: "What is the main idea?" "What are the major parts of the selection?" "What are the important or supporting details to the main idea?" But in answering those questions, the reader often is faced with some of the problems that have already been identified as problems in content reading. *The vocabulary, format, references, point of view, and organization deviate from what he or she is familiar with.* Readers need to employ a number of procedural skills that will assist them in locating information, examining it efficiently, and adjusting their reading rate so that they can achieve their purpose for reading the selection. The common study skills—such as summarizing, outlining, using references, and organizing time—play a role in comprehending content subjects. Study skills are treated last in this chapter.

As readers grasp the basic meaning of a selection they can analyze and evaluate it. *Involved in the task of analysis are classifying, categorizing, and identifying the principles of organization. Evaluating requires the reader to formulate some criteria for judging the relevancy, utility, and validity of the information.* Readers have to make decisions about the content. If nothing more, they have to decide whether to remember it or not and whether or not to make it a part of their concept of the subject area. If their evaluation indicates that the selection yields little or no valuable information, they will decide not to store what may have read.

Teaching Skills for Reading in Content Subjects

Knowing that content subjects require general reading skills, skills for using the specialized material, and analytic and evaluative reading skills does not make those skills automatically usable. Fig. 11.3 indicates the variety and levels of skills incorporated in reading content material. Each of the areas will be discussed here in relation to teaching children how to read content material.

General Reading Skills
Many children have the general reading skills to read content material, but they often do not realize that is the case. The teacher should demonstrate how general reading skills can be transferred or applied to science, math, and social studies and should tell the students that reading con-

FIGURE 11.3 Skills for Reading Content Selections. Reading content subjects requires general reading skills, as well as other locational and thinking skills indicated by the format of the material and the presentation of the ideas.

tent material should be considered a continuation of learning how to read. In one sense, reading of content material can begin as the child acquires the basic reading skill of word analysis and the recognition of a simple vocabulary.

Because developing concepts and a specialized vocabulary are integral to reading, specialized content instruction for reading in the content areas can be said to be always occurring. An eclipse of the moon is discussed in class in anticipation of the event. When this happens, students read about it in newspapers and magazines. Because students pay more attention to the purposes for which they read they can more naturally and easily learn content reading skills. Instruction for content reading begins before children can "read," continues as they go through the process of learning to "decode," and progresses throughout their encounters with reading materials and other classroom activities.

Recalling Basic Information

The primary application of general reading skills is to assimilate the meaning of the passage. This is often called literal comprehension. In order to assimilate meaning, the reader must first have an understanding of the concepts contained in the passage and be able to identify the words used. The reader must also be able to follow the writing style and the organization of the writing—all of which sounds fairly simple until it is applied in reality. Earlier, a passage from a fifth-grade science test on the digestive system was used as an example. The completed passage from page 334 follows (you may wish to match your answers on the previous cloze test with the original):

The Digestive System

After you swallow the food, it passes down the esophagus into your stomach. Juices from the lining of your stomach mix with the food. The juices soften the food, and the chemicals in the juices break up particles into even smaller ones. Most food is not completely digested in the stomach. When the food is moist and soft enough, a valve at the end of the stomach opens, a little at a time. The partly digested food flows into a long, coiled, narrow tube called the small intestine.*

* Schneider & Schneider, 1968, p. 185.

The concept-development problems, definition problems, and word-identification problems in this selection are considerable.

Concept attainment is, in itself, a complex task. What is meant by a *system*, for example—a system for processing food? Vocabulary development (definition) is not necessarily a complete concept development. The meaning to be used in a particular context may not require recognition of the total complex of characteristics and relations making up the "true" concept symbolized by a particular word. In the classroom this is particularly true. Children's concepts develop over time and rely on their ability to perceive and understand the various components of a concept. The problem for the teacher is to identify the special

Approaches to Teaching Reading

words and the aspects of the total concept necessary for understanding the particular material being read in class. Those aspects can then be related to the knowledge the children already have to help them obtain adequate meanings from a text. For example, consider this sentence: "Landforms are closely and intricately related to people's use and occupation of the land." Special words to be defined and studied for recognition are *landforms* and *occupation*. The teacher may find it advisable to discuss *intricately* as well, not because of its special connotation but because it may not be part of the children's reading vocabulary. Depending on the age and education of the children, the teacher then works to establish and clarify the concept. Perhaps there are local examples or experiences that show that river valley land (landform) is used for cattle grazing or mining coal (occupation). By relating the words to the child's experience, the teacher enables the child to understand the sentence and probably the paragraphs that follow.

Developing Vocabulary and Concepts

A major problem with vocabulary and concept development is that the vocabulary assumes different technical meanings in different content. For example, *satellite* is a body orbiting around another body, a country whose government and control comes from another country, and an object made by humans revolving around the earth. This variety of meaning makes it difficult to preview material and select at a glance the words that need concept development. Questioning students about the material should also provide information concerning their grasp of the meaning of a single word. Questioning should be carefully planned by the teacher because reiteration of a statement in a book by the student is no indication of understanding. The question should elicit explanatory, definitional, or application responses. Restating or defining is relevant to certain concepts; for example, What does *satellite* mean in that passage?

The ambiguity of words is clearly illustrated in "story" problems in arithmetic. Children need to learn to translate words such as *is, more, less, times, greater* as computational signals and as indicators of relations between quantities. Direct and explicit instruction often assists in the acquisition of this skill. Another means of instruction is to use "headlines." A mathematical equation is presented as a "headline" ($2 \times 3 = 6$ or $2 + 3 = ?$) (Fig. 11.4). The students are asked to tell a story that could be represented by the equation headline. That procedure reverses the translation process. Once the relation between story and equation is understood, the translation difficulty, or the reading problem, decreases.

Students need experiences equal to their grasp of concepts, as well as experiences that expand the level of their understanding. If instruction is planned to draw on past experiences and concrete examples, vocabulary and concepts will usually develop routinely.

FIGURE 11.4 What Is the Story That Goes with This Headline?

$$2 \times 3 = 6$$

Vocabulary and concept development is critical across all grade levels. For some words a simple explanation in context will suffice; for others a special experience or set of experiences of varying degrees of "concreteness" is required. Picture dictionaries, flash cards, and word lists can be useful tools. If dictionaries and word lists are made, then occasional activities—even games—using the lists should be included in the curriculum. For a child to refer to the dictionary or word list on reencountering a word whose meaning has been forgotten is essential for several reasons: Meanings of words are usually forgotten until repeated encounters strengthen recall; repeated checking establishes the habit of relearning.

Words

Word meaning in content subjects, then, needs to be developed by using such activities as these:

1. Firsthand experiences.
   a. Real situations involving contact with names, concepts, principles.
   b. Dramatization of a real situation.
   c. Construction of examples or models representing the concept.
2. Relating to personal experiences or acquired concepts.
3. Exhibits.
4. Films, filmstrips.
5. Pictures.
6. Context clues.
7. Dictionary.
8. Word lists.
9. Flash cards.

Concepts

Concept development can be promoted by guiding a student's analysis of ideas. This analysis should include the following:

1. Comparing and contrasting instances and noninstances of the concept.
2. Extracting relevant criteria belonging to the set of ideas.
3. Identifying the relation of the concept to others and to the problem being considered.
4. Using the concept in the immediate and in extended situations.

Literal comprehension or recall of expository material also demands the ability to cope with the structure of the content and the style of the author. To aid learning, the most plausible approach for the elementary school teacher is to consider each reading activity as a relatively separate task and to make sure that the skills required for that task are available to the student. Comparisons are not possible without adequate familiarity with the characteristics of different types of materials. In general, the teacher is the decision-maker who determines how explicit the instruction is to be with respect to attention to concept

Developing Vocabulary and Concepts

Choose a hypothetical class. How would you help children in that grade level grasp the following words and concepts:

metamorphosis
telescope
declaration
foreign

How would you establish and clarify the concepts?

Children Select Words

Let the children decide whether they would prefer to work in a group that will explore math, physical science, biological science, history, geography, economics, health, music, or art. Form groups that honor the preferences as closely as possible. Give each group the task of developing two lists of words: The first is to include technical words that are important to the content and process of the field they are studying (for example: steppe, plateau, tree line, and so on in geography); the second is to include words that have a special meaning in the field they are studying and a different meaning in general conversation (e.g., beat, harmony, swing, and so on in music).

The groups can begin the search for words by consulting their textbooks. Encyclopedias and other reference books can also be consulted. The final product of each group's efforts should be two lists of words in alphabetical order with examples of the words in sentences.

or vocabulary development and to structure and style of the reading material.

Skills for Using Materials

The second general category of skills for reading in real life contains all the procedural skills one needs to handle efficiently the material one reads. Three sets of skills are found in this category:

1. Locational skills—those procedures for using books and other materials efficiently.
2. Study skills—those procedures that organize and direct efficient and effective learning from printed material.
3. Reading-rate adjustments.

Each of these sets requires a knowledge of the skills, a demonstration of when to apply an appropriate procedure, and the actual implementation of the skills.

Procedures can be explained to children, but they will never completely learn when to apply and actually use the skills unless a real opportunity is provided. Map reading, note-taking, or scanning material will not become practical skills for the reader who has few occasions to perform them in real situations. Having a variety of materials available will be of little use if the reader can answer all questions with one or two books and without using maps, charts, notes, and so on. Activities must be designed to include a variety of skills with a variety of materials. Efficient use of a skill such as note-taking requires practice and refinement. The student who can achieve a goal without using a skill or by using it poorly will never attain refinement in the skill.

Location Skills

Locational skills are the *skills one needs to find information.* There is a body of knowledge to be learned. The reader needs to know the kinds of information obtainable from different types of books and reference guides. They include these items:

1. Textbooks.
2. Dictionaries.
3. Encyclopedias.
4. Almanacs.
5. Trade books.

The reader also needs skills in locating and using these:

6. Bibliographic references (authors, *Who's Who in the United States,* and so on).
7. Table of contents.
8. Indexes of books, encyclopedias, and periodicals.
9. Card catalog.
10. Bibliographies.
11. Glossaries.

For using these resources, the following skills are needed:

1. Alphabetizing.
2. Use of multiple classification.
3. Use of pronunciation keys.
4. Use of titles and major and minor headings.

In a developmental sense the first content activities in the primary grades may begin with locational skills using:

1. Picture dictionaries for practice with alphabetical knowledge and skill.
2. Table of contents with all books consulted.

3. Glossaries.
4. Indexes in all books consulted.
5. Headings, titles.
6. Pictures and simple graphs and maps.

Dictionary.   The dictionary is a tool children can begin to use as soon as reading instruction starts. At this early date they can begin to learn the functions of a dictionary and how to look up the information it contains. Various publishers produce picture dictionaries—such as *My Little Pictionary* (Scott Foresman, 1964), *The Cat in the Hat Beginner Book Dictionary* (Random House, 1964), and the *Storybook Dictionary* (Golden Press, 1966)—that introduce the child to this reference. Picture dictionaries should be included in every first-grade book collection.

The organization and purpose of picture dictionaries is fairly simple. A picture is used to "define" each entry. The child knows what object is represented by a word from the picture that accompanies the printed symbol; *dog* is "defined" by a picture of a dog, *tree* by a picture of a tree, and so forth. Fig. 11.5 shows a sample page from a picture dictionary. In some dictionaries, guide words appear at the top of each page, and the entries are alphabetized. Children can learn their first lessons about the dictionary from these simplified editions.

Picture Dictionary

Picture dictionaries can also be made—by the teacher or by children—for primary science, social studies, and even math concepts. A "shoe box" of words and corresponding pictures on three-by-five-inch cards can be developed, or a loose-leaf notebook can be used. In addition to teaching children how a dictionary is developed, a self-made picture dictionary can be used by youngsters as a practice list of words they recognize at sight or as a resource for developing language experience stories.

As children grow in reading ability, other types of dictionaries can be introduced or developed. These more sophisticated dictionaries can include multiple meanings for words, definitions following a set format, and simple diacritical marks (symbols that indicate pronunciation). Children at this stage can be taught to use a commercial dictionary as well as to develop their own dictionaries for content subjects.

Encyclopedia.   In addition to the dictionary, primary-grade children should be introduced to the scope and use of an encyclopedia. Because of the reading difficulty of published encyclopedias for primary-grade children, the teacher may find it worthwhile to develop his or her own. Some authorities suggest that the primary-grade teacher create a picture file arranged in alphabetical order according to index words such as *animal, city, farm, transportation, weather,* and the like. Materials, especially pictures, relevant to each of the topics are then placed

acorn Patty found an **acorn** under the oak tree.

airplane The jet **airplane** flies above the clouds.

GOLDEN

album Anita is looking at a photo **album** with her grandfather.

allowance Chris gets an **allowance** every week.

FIGURE 11.5 *My Picture Dictionary,* compiled by Ellen Rudin and Marilyn Salomon, pictures by Elizabeth B. Rodger. This is page four of the dictionary. A Golden Book, 1984. Reprinted by permission of Western Publishing Company, Inc.

for future reference in the appropriate file. The children should be held largely responsible for finding useful items, classifying them, and filing them in the collection. Eventually, cross-references and other embellishments can be added as the need for them becomes apparent.

The value of such a simplified encyclopedia is that through its development children begin to understand what an encyclopedia contains. They learn how this resource is organized and how one analyzes a topic for entries of potential value. By asking, "What shall we look under to see what our resource file contains about animals on the farm?" the teacher initiates instruction at a fundamental level on a highly important aspect of encyclopedia usage.

As with the dictionary, in the intermediate grades, children's reading skills and general knowledge are sufficiently advanced to make systematic instruction on using the encyclopedia profitable. Instruction should be based on a solid foundation of established skills learned

Using the Encyclopedia

Direction to Children: A pictured set of encyclopedias follows. By looking at the letters on the spine of each book, an individual can decide which one contains information we might need.

Indicate in Column B which volume you would use to locate information about the topic in Column A:

Column A	Column B
1. Brazil	
2. baseball	
3. measles	
4. horses	
5. Colorado	
6. tropical fish	
7. beetle	
8. guitar	
9. knighthood	
10. Yellowstone Park	

in the primary grades and should proceed according to a sequential plan of skill development. A need to use the encyclopedia should be created in order to keep interest high and to give learning a goal. The teacher should demonstrate new skills and then provide for their immediate application in worthwhile projects. Exercises, such as the one that follows, provide an opportunity for the child to practice new skills. They also yield diagnostic information for the teacher.

Other Reference Books. The classroom teacher also has the responsibility for introducing children to other reference works—such as almanacs; atlases; *Who's Who;* index volumes, such as the *Reader's Guide to Periodical Literature;* newspaper and picture files; the telephone book; and special dictionaries. These and other reference tools will eventually be discovered by children as they mature and pursue varied interests. The teacher cannot possibly anticipate every resource that

---

Indexes

Exercises on the use of a particular reference material or locational skill can be devised by the teacher. Skill in using an index, for example, could be developed through activities like the following:

Listed as follows are topics found in an index to a book on Egypt. Use the index to answer the questions that follow.

Alphabet, 31
Art, 15–17, 75, 76
   ancient, 43–45
   recent, 113–115
  in tombs, 45
Cairo, 13, 19–21, 25
   burning of (1952), 70
   government of, 140
Customs, 5, 57–59
Food, 48, 51

Islam, 99
Moslems, 95–98
   creed, 97
   laws of, 101
Nasser, Gamal Abdul,
   117–121
   early life of, 117
   personality of, 123–125
Sports, 132–133
Villages, 17, 43, 83

On what page or pages in the book will you read about the following?
1. Islam _____
2. Moslems _____
3. Sports _____
4. Early life of Nasser _____
5. Food _____
6. Burning of Cairo _____
7. Customs _____
8. Moslem laws _____

How many pages are about the following?
1. Food _____
2. Ancient art _____
3. Customs _____
4. Nasser _____

---

will be used but must introduce the major references mentioned here and arrange for their use by the students. Once these are found, the next concern is helping children learn how to use them by applying *locational skills.*

As dictionaries, encyclopedias, and other reference books are introduced, children will need instruction in using them. In the primary grades, basic locational skills can be developed. Children can be shown how to use a table of contents to find the specific location of a topic or to preview the contents of a section. The use of glossaries, some indexes, headings, pictures, graphs, and maps can be developed as part of the basal reading instruction, as well as for the content curriculum. Index use, graph and map reading will need teacher guidance.

In the upper grades, as more reference material is required, formal instruction should cover the details. Exercises that clearly call for the use and practice of those details are essential. The desired skill should be called for frequently. The skill should also be demonstrated through use with a specific article. Most students need assistance in accomplishing a transfer of learning from practice during the reading period to actually using the skill on science or math. For example, it is usually necessary for readers to formulate the main idea of what they are reading. As a matter of habit, then, the teacher can ask for the main idea of a science selection, just as he or she would for a narrative: "You read the selection about Mendel and heredity. What is its main idea?"

Practice in specific locational skills can follow the same pattern: "Where in the book can I tell if there is a major section on heredity?" (*Table of contents*) "Let's look." "Where would I look for a definition of *heredity* as used by the author of this book?" (*Glossary*) "Let's see what it says."

The student's trained reaction to a new word, to scanning for an answer, to finding information on a chart, and so on depends on the patterns encouraged and developed by the teacher. No special tools are needed. Practice can be given with textbooks, for a table of contents, index, glossary, headings, pictures, graphs, charts, and maps are built into many texts. By employing these resources as they use the text, students discover the usefulness of skills for obtaining information quickly.

Using the Library

Skill in finding information in books and reference materials constitutes one part of location skills. The other part involves being able to find appropriate books and reference materials for a topic. The development of skills in using a library is an important component of the reading program.

As with reference materials, the best approach to teaching children how to use the card catalog is to create a need for its use. Careful attention must be paid to the importance of prerequisite skills, such as alphabetic and classification skills.

Library Work

Special exercises in using reference materials should be devised by the teacher to lend weight and reinforcement to skills introduced functionally. These exercises should be brief (able to be completed in fifteen minutes or less). They could include such problems as:

1. Pick a topic in early American history. What books does our library have on this topic? List their names and authors.
2. After you have selected a book to read, check the card catalog under the author's name, and list what the card tells you about the book. List other books written by the same author.
3. After you have selected a book to read, try to find some information about the author. Check the encyclopedia, the bibliographies of authors, and the book itself.
4. Select a restricted topic, and, using an index of three or four books, find the pages on which you find information about this topic.

Short problems such as these can be checked individually by the teacher. As each child indicates an ability to use a reference skill, he or she can go on to explore a topic of interest. Children can then use the skill as situations arise. The more frequently the need arises, the more important the skill becomes.

The Card Catalog

The library card catalog is a resource that children must learn to use. They need to know that the card catalog is a file containing the title, author, and subject cards for every book in the library. They must also know how to find books through its use. An excellent approach in grade two or three for developing this necessary knowledge is to construct a simple card catalog for the classroom library.

The books housed in the reading corner can each be noted by author, title, and subject on a three-by-five-inch card. As a first step students can be asked to decide how the cards might be arranged for easy retrieval. Alphabetizing the cards by author's name is a handy technique and entirely satisfactory as a first step. Later, students will discover that searching their card catalog for an author is satisfactory only when the author of a book is known. Occasionally only a title is known. The suggestion should be made—one hopes by a student—that a second card, alphabetically filed by book title, might be added to the catalog.

Subject cards can be added when students are ready for that kind of classification. The fact that several subject cards might be made for the same book is a significant discovery for children to make; this helps them understand the complexity of indexing. The suggestion can also be made—by the teacher, if necessary—that brief summaries or annotations added to the cards would be helpful to someone who finds an interesting title but wonders about the exact nature of the story or the difficulty of the book.

If this approach is used, a fairly sophisticated card catalog can be evolved by the children themselves by the fourth grade. Some children will then be ready to learn about the card catalog in their school and public libraries. (Some children may be ready for this step as early as grade two. This sequence of steps illustrates only one possible approach. Other approaches and especially other chronologies will be appropriate in a variety of situations.)

In connection with the card catalog, intermediate-grade children should also be given instruction on these points:

1. Specific abbreviations are used in catalog cards. For example: ©1964 represents copyright 1964; 96p illus means a book is 96 pages in length and contains illustrations.
2. Cross-reference cards direct the user to other potentially useful sources of information.
3. Call numbers, listed in the card catalog, are needed to find a book in the library.

Classifying Books

Several discovery techniques might be employed in introducing the concept of a library classification scheme to children. For example, the books housed in the reading corner could be cataloged with a system devised by the class. Nonfiction and fiction books might be separated and then alphabetized by author. All books written by authors whose last name begins with *A* could be numbered (1A, 2A, 3A, and so on); the same numbering system would be used for books by authors whose names begin with *B*. Or books might be grouped by geographic location of setting, type of story, or even reading difficulty. The number assigned to a book (1A, 3B, and so on) would also be written on appropriate cards in the catalog and would be noted on the spine of the book.

A presentation of the organization and function of the Dewey decimal system by the classroom teacher or librarian might be just as meaningful as a discovery approach provided children are later given an opportunity to study its application at firsthand. Typically, the major classifications and more commonly used subdivisions—such as fairy tales, reference volumes, and earth sciences—are introduced in the fourth grade. In later grades more specific categories can be presented.

A second aspect of library locational skills is understanding the cataloging system. One such is the Dewey decimal system. Few people have memorized even the main categories of this system. That is not a goal of the instructional program. Rather, children should learn the function of the system and how it is organized. They should also learn how the system has been employed in their own libraries so that books of special interest can be located.

Dewey Decimal Classification System

000–099 General works
100–199 Philosophy
200–299 Religion
300–399 Social sciences
400–499 Language
500–599 Pure science
600–699 Applied science, or technology
700–799 The arts
800–899 Literature
900–999 History

Study Skills

Study skills are those that enable a person to gather information and to organize it in such a way that recall, analysis, interpretation, and evaluation are facilitated. Although many skills could be discussed under this heading, it is possible to treat only a few major topics here. These include the following:

1. Outlining.
2. Summarizing.
3. Using a study strategy.

Outlining. The ability to prepare an outline is a fundamental skill useful to many youngsters in organizing and writing a report. At the same time, outlining is a complex task demanding careful instruction and guidance from the classroom teacher.

The first step in teaching outlining skills is to demonstrate how to use the headings of a well-organized factual or textbook. The teacher can place an outline of a selection on the board. After discussing the various elements of the selection and how they are related to each other, the teacher should direct children to read for the purpose of noting an author's organization of main points and supporting detail. A follow-up discussion can then focus on how the author builds a case by relating ideas to major points. It can be shown that the skeletal framework of ideas contained in the teacher's outline on the board have been expanded by the author in sentence and paragraph form. Outlining is merely the reverse of the author's process, that is, identifying main ideas along with supporting detail and properly relating them to each other.

This introduction to outlining focuses children's attention on the organization of a selection. The teacher must also call children's attention to outline use of Roman and Arabic numbers and of capital and small letters, as well as to how points are grouped together by indenting them under a heading.

Armed with an understanding of how an outline is organized and the mechanics of listing ideas in their proper relation, children are ready to try some outlining on their own.

Special care should be taken in selecting the first material to be outlined independently by children. First, it should be well organized.

Second, it should have sections that are clearly marked by headings. Finally, it should be fairly brief—probably not more than four or five pages in length. A chapter or part of a social studies or science book is usually suitable.

Children can be asked to complete only the details of an outline that has been organized and developed for them through several levels. The following exercise illustrates this approach. The teacher can then gradually withdraw the amount of assistance provided. For example, in the exercise that follows, the number of points under each heading (A, B, C) is left for the child to determine. Next, the wording of each head is omitted so that only the number of headings is provided, and so forth. Through this strategy the child is gradually asked to provide more and more of the outline until finally he or she can achieve the entire task alone.

Procedure for Teaching Outlining Skills *Directions:* Provide children with an outline that is complete through the first three levels. Their task at this stage is to compare the outline with the text, noting form and the relation among elements of the chapter.

Chapter 4 Ancient Cultures in the River Valleys
I. The Tigris-Euphrates River Valley
    A. Conditions in the valley promoted settlement
        1. Rich soil (silt) was provided by the flooding rivers
        2. Rivers provided moisture for dry land
    B. The Sumerians were first to live in the valley
        1. Developed good water control system
        2. Irrigated dry land
        3. Built cities of sun-dried bricks
        4. Food surpluses led to specialization
        5. A way of writing was developed
        6. The Semites conquered the Sumerians
II. The Nile Flood Plain of Egypt
    A. Physical features of the region
        1. Little rainfall in Egypt
        2. Flooding covered land with silt
        3. The Nile River begins in mountains of central Africa.

The second step in this procedure is to provide children with an outline that contains labels for major sections and a list of the number of points to be found under each label. Children must provide the information that is missing from the outline.

Summarizing. Anyone who has asked a child, "What is your book about?" or "What happened in the movie you saw?" knows how difficult the task of summarizing can be. Many youngsters find it necessary to relate every detail in order to answer such a query. At the opposite extreme some children can summarize the most complex story in astonishingly few words: "It was about a horse." Or, "Everybody gets killed." One of the problems confronting the classroom teacher is leading children away from such extremes to the point where their summaries include only pertinent information but in sufficient quantity to do a selection justice.

Outlining and note-taking are actually specialized forms of summarizing. Skill in selecting major points is required for each of these tasks. Placing ideas in proper relationships is also important when preparing an outline, taking notes, or writing a summary.

The child's first opportunity to summarize is provided early in the developmental reading program. For example, children may be asked in grade one to recount the incidents from a story in a basal reader. Teachers are constantly refining children's ability to summarize by discussing stories and daily events with them and through the teachers' own examples.

Formal instruction might well take advantage of the close relation between summarizing and outlining and note-taking. For example, a chapter of a geography book might be outlined. Next the sections of the outline might be translated into sentence form, thus producing a summary of sorts. Notes taken on the same selection could be used to expand the summary where needed. Such a procedure would effectively demonstrate for the child how a summary is made up of the main points from a selection. It also illustrates the similarity of summarizing, outlining, and note-taking.

Teaching Study Skills

According to Armbruster and Anderson (1981), "Studying—learning from reading—is probably the most important skill students acquire in school." There is little doubt that anyone who cannot learn from reading is seriously handicapped in the modern world. Unfortunately, teachers often have no idea of how to help students become more effective in their studying. Too often they merely exhort their students to study in order to do better on an upcoming test or so that they will do better in school the following year. Sometimes training is provided on note-taking, outlining, or previewing a selection; but this often takes the form of learning abstract rules or following directions in a rote, unthinking manner. It has been our experience that these approaches seldom work.

Many early techniques for studying did not deal with the significance of the information being learned. Rote recall was emphasized too often. Newer approaches to studying (e.g., self-questioning, categorizing information as it is learned, or elaborating the information) focus the child's attention on the strategy itself and why it is effective. As a result, an element of meaning is brought into the learning process as opposed to relying solely on rehearsal or repetition.

In our view, it is the teacher's duty to help children see some personal relevance in material they are asked to read, then to be quite specific about how mastery will be tested or otherwise assessed. Under these conditions, it is possible to provide some fairly specific help to children with regard to studying. Several important principles that can guide instruction in this domain have emerged from recent research.

Approaches to Teaching Reading

Brown, Campione, and Day (1981) offer the following summary: "Effective learning involves four main considerations: (1) the activities engaged in by the learner, (2) certain characteristics of the learner including his or her capacity and state of prior knowledge, (3) the nature of the materials to be learned, and (4) the critical task." They indicate that two classes of problems can impede effective studying: (1) inefficient application of rules and strategies and (2) impoverished background knowledge. Instruction must overcome problems in both of these areas but often focuses on only one and almost never addresses the interaction between the two.

The teacher can help children increase their effectiveness with studying in several ways. First, the nature of the event for which the child is studying (the criterion task) should be clear to the learner. The most effective studying occurs when learners know how their knowledge or skill acquisition or both will be tested. If a history book is being studied to the end of passing a test, for example, the exact nature of the test should be specified so that the most effective study techniques can be employed.

A second principle of effective studying has to do with the nature of the material being studied. The clues to meaning inherent in the material should be used to advantage by the learner. For example, if section headings summarize the main points, they can be used to guide memorization, if that is the goal, or to build a sense of structure if learning the gist is the goal. Relationships among important ideas can be studied by highlighting key words such as *because, if–then, next, first–second–last, therefore,* and so forth. Diagrams or concept maps can be developed to show how important ideas are related. Though we do not advocate having children actually learn the details of a text analysis system such as those developed by Meyer (1975) or Frederiksen (1975), teachers can look to them for some guidance with regard to identifying elements in text structure their students might examine for clues to meaning. We can illustrate this by noting that the Meyer's system organizes ideas in a hierarchy with supporting details gathered together under main ideas. Relationships among ideas are identified by looking for key words that indicate one of five patterns:

1. Antecedent-consequent (essentially cause-effect relationships).
2. Comparison (differences and similarities).
3. Collection (things grouped on the basis of some commonality).
4. Description (more information given about the topic).
5. Response (problem and solution).

Children can be helped to understand expository text by identifying and then studying the author's use of these structures.

A third principle of effective studying relates to the characteristics of the learner. Recent research suggests that self-monitoring of understanding may be the most important of these factors, but others include ones we examined in Chapters 8 and 9 such as the learner's background experience and motivation (Baker & Brown, 1984). Readers who monitor their own learning recognize when their understanding is inadequate and engage in one of several compensatory activities such as rereading, self-interrogation, rehearsing, or going to other sources of information. Children can be taught to monitor their own understanding, to use "fix-up" strategies when learning is not occurring, but this happens best in situations where the child has sufficient background experience and high motivation to learn (hence the material must be important or at least interesting to the learner). Furthermore, self-monitoring of learning is not achieved through simply learning a set of rules or procedures for studying. It also requires the opportunity to practice the desired approach over a reasonable period of time.

One study approach that deserves special mention is the SQ3R method. The name SQ3R comes from the first letter of the five steps included in this strategy: survey, question, read, recall, review. As a system, SQ3R has its merits; however, the steps sometimes become mechanical and thus lose their value.

A survey of a section of a book noting its headings, pictures and charts, and listing questions that may be answered in the section as a group activity will prepare children for reading and will provide an example of how to proceed when they are reading on their own. The same procedure with recall and review can be directed by the teacher in the early stages of developing this study strategy. After some time the actual stages can be identified and explicitly discussed and evaluated by the class.

The key elements of the SQ3R method appear to be setting purposes for reading and for reviewing what was read. These two aspects require stronger stress, and in some instances it may be more economical of time for the teacher to set purposes for reading and then to have the class set purposes for reading. To accomplish this, they will have to survey—asking for recall (or whatever relates to the purpose of the content) will lead to reviewing what was read when the children realize they have forgotten or overlooked content. Because there is evidence to suggest that recall is strongest for that material one looks for while reading, care must be taken to set purposes that shape the reading behavior in the desired direction.

Reading Rate

Just as there is no "normal" speed for walking to school, there is no predetermined rate at which children should read science or math selections. It is valuable, however, for a reader to change reading rate depending on the purpose and content of reading. Reading rate must be adjusted so that it is as rapid as one's skill and purpose for reading will permit. For example, a student should read faster in trying to detect the main idea of a social studies passage than in trying to savor each incident in a mystery. The description of a chemical process usually demands slower reading than an article on the sports page. But many children will not make these adjustments if they are not informed about them and if they are not reminded regularly.

Instruction in how to increase reading speed will enable children to adapt their speed of reading to various selections. A number of commercial speed-reading courses—often incorporating techniques such as SQ3R—have been developed. Generally, these courses help someone become an active reader—one who previews what he or she intends to read, notes section headings, reads the first and last paragraphs of a chapter, and mentally predicts what a selection will contain.

The classroom teacher can borrow certain aspects of speed-reading courses and adapt them for classroom use. For example, most people do not read as rapidly as they can simply because they fall into the habit of reading slowly. Speed-reading courses provide practice in reading at a faster pace, one that more closely approximates the reader's true potential. Various commercial pacing machines are available for pushing the reader along at a given rate. These machines teach nothing in the way of new skills; they merely help readers to realize their potential.

A much cheaper and equally effective procedure than any teacher can use in the classroom is simply to provide practice sessions during which children are asked to focus their attention on reading rate. Providing the opportunity for children consciously to try to increase their reading speeds can often lead to marked success. Each child should be given material to read that is written at his or her independent reading level. The teacher instructs the members of the class consciously to read faster than they normally do. At a signal the entire group begins simultaneously to read. The teacher stands at the front of the room noting the elapsed time and recording each ten-second interval on the chalkboard. When a child completes his or her selection (usually one page of material, 200 to 500 words in length), that child notes the last number the teacher has written on the board (a 6 would indicate that 6 ten-second intervals have elapsed). While other children are completing their selections this child can calculate his or her reading speed. The number on the board multiplied by ten reveals approximately how many seconds it took the child to read his or her selection. The number of words in the selection are counted and divided by the number of minutes to get the average words read per minute.

For example, suppose a youngster read a selection of 300 words in 15 ten-second intervals. The total time required would be approximately 150 seconds (15 × 10 seconds per interval equals 150 seconds). If we divide 150 into 300, the number of words read per second is found to be 2. Multiplying this figure by 60 (the number of seconds in a minute) gives us the number of words read per minute, found in this case to be 120.

Step 1: $15 \times 10 = 150$

Step 2: $150/\overline{300} = 2$

Step 3: $2 \times 60 = 120$ words per minute.

Each child could keep a chart of his or her own reading speed.

Comprehension questions can be asked by the teacher to make sure the children are actually reading the material and not just running their eyes over the page. This exercise can be practiced several times a week with an emphasis on surpassing the previous speed without sacrificing understanding. Materials of varied difficulty and content can be selected by the teacher to give a more accurate estimate of reading speed under several conditions and to provide practice in adjusting rate according to the type of material read. Children can often give themselves incentives if they know what to look for. A self-inventory on flexible reading can be such a stimulus.

The act of trying to read faster frequently causes an increase in speed. Success with a more rapid rate proves to the children that they can speed up. Regular practice increases the chances that they will read more rapidly when they are not being timed.

Analytical and Evaluative Skills for Content Reading

In addition to general reading skills and skills for using content materials, there are special concerns related to the analysis of concepts and organization of the selection prior to evaluating it—that is, determining its veracity, relevancy, and utility.

Ordinarily a content teacher in a departmentalized staff will expect a reader to spend a good deal of effort in the areas of analysis and evaluation. The problem is, how does the teacher instruct and test for those higher-level reading skills? Because content material usually contains a heavy concept load, less easily identifiable organization or theme, and more inaccessible criteria for evaluation and use, a restatement and evaluation of the material is quite difficult. The instructional conclusions are as follows:

1. The student needs special assistance in gaining the basic concepts—vocabulary identification and associations for concept development.
2. The student must be given demonstrations and practice in analyzing, expressing the organizational unity, and evaluating selections from content books.

In a certain sense this is equivalent to asking the reader to think like a scientist, to think like a geographer, to think like an historian. It might be more accurate to say, "to think like a science writer."

Given that kind of orientation, the reader or the teacher can first pose comprehension questions that draw forth a literal meaning. For example, ask about the following:

1. The main idea of a paragraph, section, or chapter.
2. Factual support for the main idea.
3. Sequence of ideas, events, acts.
4. Organization of the presentation.
5. Author's purpose, point of view, and style.

The opportunity to experiment with ideas found in content area textbooks makes facts and concepts more meaningful.

Studies with adult readers have shown that asking the same types of questions consistently (factual, recall, main idea) tends to produce greater facility in retention of that type of material. If instruction tends to be biased toward one type of thinking activity, that skill will be strengthened with little effect on the level of ability in the other skills (Meehan, 1970).

At the beginning stages one skill may be emphasized—such as that of identifying the main idea. Recalling details, then, will be overlooked if it is always underplayed in payoff situations in class assignments. The same will be true of the identification and recall of main ideas if detail is always rewarded. The development of each of the comprehension areas mentioned earlier should be made methodically and regularly in view of the content area goal. Students need to receive reinforcement and concrete satisfaction for each type of answer.

A second group of comprehension competencies include these typical activities of analysis and evaluation:

1. Relate past knowledge and/or events to present knowledge or events or both.
2. Distinguish similarities and differences, fact from fancy or opinion or generalizations or a combination of this.
3. Make predictions about the outcome of events.
4. Draw conclusions or inferences.
5. Organize the material obtained to suit the purposes for reading.
6. Judge the relevancy, adequacy, authenticity, and utility of the information.

Teaching Reading for Life—Content Reading

None of these abilities are mutually exclusive, and they presuppose the ability to isolate factors, discriminate among factors according to a variety of criteria, and apply new information through a set of criteria. In that way, readers prepare themselves to make judgments.

To develop these higher competencies, the reader has to be aware of the bases for analysis and evaluation. It is important that the criteria for making an analysis or evaluation be as clear as possible. For example: size, color, and weight may be criteria for analyzing and categorizing objects to determine similarities and differences; utility in an urban school may be a criterion for evaluating or judging a technique. Decisions for instruction have to be made according to the reader's abilities, the purposes of reading, and the necessary prerequisites for reading. Instruction should be tied to specific content and activity. No one should presuppose that transfer of reading skills will occur until the method of transferring the skill has been adequately demonstrated in one subject. This does not mean that the student will not recognize similarities between skills for reading narrative and reading content. But similarities will not be recognized without teacher demonstration. Research indicates that the process of thinking is modified by the organization of the material. Reading instruction in the content area, then, should take the form that will produce the objectives of that area. Once the reading and thinking processes of the subject discipline have been acquired, general reading skills will be more readily applied, with modifications to types of material.

Instructional procedures must look at both long-range goals—those that should be attained over the years—and at short-term goals—those to be attained within a particular unit of study. The short-term units must use a variety of activities, including consistent question patterns for the different reading and thinking skills. The reader should refer to the chapters on basic comprehension and on critical and creative

Developing Analytic Thinking

Involve the children in original research in one of the social sciences. Identify the kinds of questions a sociologist, political scientist, or historian might ask about children in a given school, for example. Arrange for students to interview other children in the school for the purpose of testing a hypothesis or reaching a generalization. Have children organize and study the information gathered from such interviews. End the experience with a report in written or oral form summarizing the findings.

Possible areas of exploration could include: the television viewing habits of children in different grade levels, the mobility of children and families in the school, career goals of elementary school children, political loyalties of ten-year-olds, how children earn and spend money, population trends in the neighborhood, how teachers happened to become teachers, customs and ceremonies practiced by the families, and so forth.

reading for guidelines on question patterns to be used for developing higher reading competencies.

Diagnostic Teaching in Content Subjects

The development of reading skills should be coordinated with the purposes and nature of the content material. The teachers of reading and the teachers of content areas should not operate separately as we have said. If they are two different teachers, they must work together to facilitate the student's progress. Reading skills are not independent of the purposes for which the material is being read, nor are the purposes for reading independent of reading skills. A basic consideration for instruction in reading content material is the coordination of the purposes of content and the reading skills.

This coordination of content with reading skills requires the identification of four factors:

1. The structure of the content material
   a. What concepts does the author assume the reader knows?
   b. What concepts, generalizations, or processes does the author develop?
   c. What style of presentation is used?
   d. What is the order of presentation?
   e. What assumptions does the author make about background knowledge of the subject?
2. The purposes for which the material is to be read
   a. What should readers be able to do when they have read the material?
   b. What concepts should they have (before reading)?
   c. What concepts should they develop?
   d. What are the readers expected to do with the material?
3. The skills of the reader
   a. Can the student read the material and grasp the meaning of the vocabulary, the concepts presented, and intent of the author?
   b. What concepts and reading and thinking skills should the reader have in order to read effectively and efficiently?
4. The conditions under which the material will be read
   a. Is the length of time adequate for achieving the purposes for reading?
   b. Are distractions minimized?
   c. What is the time lag between reading and implementation of the information gained?

Instructional decisions rest on a set of teaching principles, which may be stated thus:

1. The teacher has knowledge of the structure of the particular subject, as well as specific concepts and generalizations to be promoted in that subject.

Teaching Reading for Life—Content Reading

Thinking Skills

Browsing tables in the classroom can set conditions for exposure to trade books and provide an opportunity for students to become aware of a variety of books and materials. These activities help develop thinking skills:

1. Questioning the truth or fantasy of a situation.
2. Deciding if action is plausible in stories not labeled fairy stories.
3. Leading children to judge competence of the author.
4. Judging the fairness and justice of others.
5. Judging the characters as real or lifelike.
6. Appraising titles.
7. Judging pictures.
8. Judging likenesses and differences in books dealing with children of other lands.
9. Setting up various types of comparisons of sources of information: biographies of the same person, books versus filmstrips, books versus television.
10. Evaluating oral or written reports.
11. Detecting propaganda.
12. Being alert to figurative language.
13. Being alert to words that arouse emotion.
14. Selecting pictures according to preferences.
15. Listening to the teacher retell a story with incorrect information.
16. Looking at bulletin board displays of pictures with incorrect and correct titles and judging which are correct.
17. Writing summaries of poems and making selections of correct and incorrect ones for a critique.
18. Completing teacher-made exercises designed to develop selected thinking skills.
19. Selecting relevant and irrelevant facts in a story.
20. Interpreting character traits.
21. Differentiating fact and fiction.
22. Drawing conclusions and inferences from stories.

The primary-grade teacher has an opportunity to develop through many activities the skills the child will need in reading to learn. On a day when a youngster brings a caterpillar to school the teacher can ask: "Will someone read about the caterpillar and report to us on how he grows and develops? Where will you look for information? What kinds of things will help us understand the life of a caterpillar?" Whenever possible, the use of locational and study skills may be introduced and illustrated. Deliberately planned activities that demand the use of a particular skill are essential for learning. Singling them out for new learning gives them an importance that many children might miss if they are treated only incidentally. The art of directing questions and activities toward concepts, reading, and thinking skills must be included in the instructional repertoire of the primary-grade teacher (Meehan, 1970).

2. The teacher must grasp the concepts, their dimensions, or levels of abstraction and be able to break them down into components for learning.
3. The teacher must propose appropriate learning activities that are suggested by the objective for that selection.
4. The teacher needs to tie a set of varied experiences to the concepts being developed.
5. Reading should be used as a medium of learning when it is the most effective method for achieving the teaching purpose.
6. The material used should be appropriate for the teacher. The teacher needs to know the following:
   a. Reading ability as reflected by tests and observation.
   b. Nature and extent of the student's specialized vocabulary.
   c. Rate of the pupil's reading in different materials.
   d. Nature and extent of each pupil's reading experience.
   e. Interests, personal characteristics, and social adjustment factors that affect reading.
7. Competence comes with practice and application in a variety of situations.

The first problem of a teacher who must cope with content reading is to identify the purposes of instruction in the content area. Next the teacher must identify the reading and thinking skills required to achieve those purposes. Finally, the skills that require development must be identified. That information provides a basis on which to direct both the reading and the content instruction. If the skills are such that direct instruction and practice skills are needed for successful application to content purposes, then the teacher should work with those skills intensively. Other skills can be taught simultaneously with work in the content area. The development of a child's thinking skills for a content subject should be integrated with the books the child reads. Because so many trade or general books for young readers have been published recently, such coordination can be accomplished more easily than before.

Helping Children Who Are Having Trouble with Content Material

For a number of reasons—including the high reading levels of some textbooks and difficulty with new concepts—some children have considerable difficulty in reading and understanding content materials. A teacher then has three basic choices: change the materials, change the students, change the methods.

1. *Change the materials.* The teacher can find easier materials on the same topic. The teacher can provide audio or visual aids to help with understanding concepts.
2. *Change the students.* The teacher can help the children—over a

period of time—to develop the skills needed for the content material. But, in the meantime, what does a teacher do *today* with the children?

3. *Change the methods of teaching the content materials.* There are several ways to teach content materials that make them a little easier to read and that develop habits and skills in children which they can later use on their own in other subject areas.

Methods of teaching that help children to approach the particular type of content material and immediately develop the skills to read it independently are based mostly on the idea of modeling. Using a modeling approach, the teacher arranges the reading in such a way that the skills needed to comprehend the content are actually carried out as the child reads. A number of these techniques have been developed (e.g., structured overviews, Earle, 1969; Guided Reading Procedure, Manzo, 1975; and others). The techniques used most often, however, seem to be prereading questions that guide the child to find the most important information, and study guides that direct the children, while reading, in how to approach each paragraph and what types of information to look for. In both cases, the children are aided in reading and develop an idea about how their minds can work. They learn to ask the right questions or evaluate paragraphs because the materials show them how to do it; that is, the materials provide a model for reading that selection.

The prereading questions and the study guide provide structure for the students. This structure can be provided when the teacher has first carefully analyzed the reading selection and decided several things:

Which ideas are most important for the students?

How must the students read this material in order to grasp and develop ideas?

What concepts or vocabulary terms are likely to cause problems?

What part of the selection can be applied in figuring out the meaning of a concept or term?

At what points in the selection might the students be able to make extensions or applications of the ideas?

Once the teacher has determined the answers to these questions, the teacher chooses questions or directions that will direct the students to the information. Prereading questions may be used, or questions may be asked during reading (study guides). For convenience, study guides are usually reproduced and each student has one as he or she reads.

As an example, suppose a selection introduced the term *plateau.* As a prereading question, the teacher might ask, "What is a plateau?" or "Where would you find a plateau?" In a study guide, the teacher might write, "On the first page, the author explains what a plateau is. How does the author describe plateau?" Or "At the bottom of page 5 there is a map with plateaus on it. Where is the one nearest to us?"

Study Guides

1. Write out study guides for the children to help them focus on important issues, key words, and subtle relationships as they read a text or reference in a content area. Make the questions and tasks as personalized and relevant to the children's interests and backgrounds as possible. (For example: "In the section on the causes of the Civil War, three points we discussed in class are made. What are they?")
2. Provide children with a skeletal outline of material they have been assigned to read. Have them take notes by filling in the parts of the outline that are left blank.
3. Put difficult material on audiotape. Those who wish to can listen to the tape and follow along in their books or can simply acquire the information through listening. More capable readers can help make tapes for those needing this type of help.

Science: Simple Machines

Study Guide A

pp. 12–17

1. Read the first paragraph under "Simple Machines" carefully. Name four simple machines.
2. Look at the picture on page 13. What two machines are shown in the picture?
3. Read the first paragraph under the heading "Pulleys" (p. 13). Give an example of a pulley you use everyday.
4. Read the two paragraphs under the heading "Inclined Planes" (p. 14). Which of these inclined planes would require the *least force,* but the *most distance,* in pushing something up it?

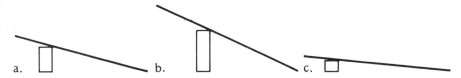

Study Guide B

pp. 12–17

1. Read the two paragraphs under "Simple Machines." Give an example of four simple machines you use every day.
2. Read the first paragraph under the heading "Pulleys" (p. 13). What is the advantage of using more than one pulley at a time?
3. Look at the picture on page 14. The human arm is one of the levers shown in the picture. What other parts of the body are also levers?
4. Read the paragraphs under "Inclined Planes" (p. 14). If you had to move a 75-pound rock up to a second story window, would you rather use a pulley or an inclined plane? Why?

Study guides also provide an opportunity to meet individual needs in content reading. Several different study guides for the same selection can be prepared. These study guides can stress different skills—finding main ideas, recalling information, or evaluating author purposes, for example. By matching the various study guides to student abilities, a teacher can provide individualized instruction for a wide range of students while still covering the same content material. An example of a study guide is shown below.

Although the development of prereading questions, study guides, and similar techniques are time-consuming, they are timesaving in the long run. Students often learn how to read content materials by using such modeling techniques.

Skills for Specific Content Subjects

Even if students had a repertoire of all the skills discussed in the previous sections they would still have to be aware of the unique qualities of the disciplines of science, math, and social studies in order to move through their content with ease and competency. A number of suggestions have already been given on how to cue students into content material so that they know how its structure differs from another subject. There are additional aids that are much more specific than the general admonition "to read as a scientist does." The items that follow list some of these specific cues for reading math, science, and several kinds of social studies.

The classroom teacher can use cues in a variety of ways. For example, the major headings under which cues are given may be models for asking questions about content: "What is the special vocabulary?" "What can you learn from the graphs or charts?" Or the teacher can take one cue at a time and demonstrate to students how they can use each cue for a clearer understanding of what they are reading. Following are sample selections on which you can try to apply some cues. Naturally, not all cues will apply to every written article. Children can be taught to look for these cues as aids in reading specific content subjects:

Math Cues
1. Vocabulary cues
   Essential key words or phrases help to determine operations or sets to be utilized:
   Additional: total, sum, add to, in all, altogether, plus
   Substraction: difference, left over, minus, subtract, minus
   Multiplication: total, times, how many times, product
   Division: how many times more, divided by, how many would
2. Typographical cues (locational cues)
   a. question mark (gives clue to the location of the question to be answered)
   b. charts and graphs (give essential information for problem on page; often located in another area of the page)

Math Cues

Read the math problem that follows. How many math cues can be used to help read the problem more clearly and so arrive at solutions?

Circumference of a Circle

The circumference of the circle is 6¼ inches. We often speak of the circumference of a circle as the "length" of the circle or the "distance around" the circle.

As we cannot wrap our rulers around a circle, as shown earlier, we will look for other ways to find the circumference of a circle. Try this experiment:

1. Draw on cardboard a circle with a diameter of 3 centimeters. Cut out the circle carefully.
2. Draw a line 30 centimeters long on a piece of paper.
3. Mark a starting point on the circle. Use a pin and roll the circle along the line, marking the place where the starting point touches the line again.

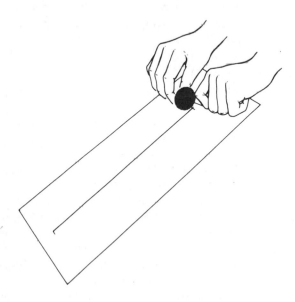

4. To find the circumference of the circle measure (to the nearest $\frac{1}{10}$ centimeter) the segment along which you rolled the circle.

5. Use this method to find the circumferences of circles with diameters of 4, 5, 6, 7, 8, and 9 centimeters. Copy the table and record your results in the circumference column.

Special Factor		Diameter (cm)		Circumference
a	×	3	=	
b	×	4	=	
c	×	5	=	
d	×	6	=	
e	×	7	=	
f	×	8	=	
g	×	9	=	

After you have found the circumference of the circles with the diameters given, divide to find the "special factor" for each equation in the table. (Give the factor to the nearest hundredth.)*

* M. L. Keedy, et al. (1970). *Exploring Elementary Mathematics, 5.* New York: Holt, Rinehart and Winston, p. 252.

    c. illustrations (may act as road signs or directionals for the problem)

    d. signs (percent, decimal point, operational signs indicate categories and math operations)

3. Kinds of readings—read for the following:
   a. skimming for the purpose and overall comprehension
   b. question asked
   c. key words or phrases
   d. operation or operations to be utilized
   e. key numbers (also eliminate extra numbers)
   f. write equation
   g. reread problems to justify equations; redo if necessary
   h. solve problem
4. Special considerations
   a. The same term is not always used to indicate the same operation (e.g., and, added to, and plus are interchangeable).
   b. The same term can indicate different operations (e.g., altogether could indicate either addition or multiplication).
   c. Several technical terms have different meanings in general conversation (e.g., square, mean, product, and so on).
   d. Mathematics involves the understanding of many terms that remind the student of absolutely nothing and must be learned by memorization (e.g., multiplier, divisor, radius, diameter, circumference).

5. Organizational guides
   There is no specific order, but certain sections appear in most math problems:
   a. A situation is given.
   b. A numerical question is asked.
   c. An equation must be formulated from information given.

Science Cues

1. Vocabulary cues
   a. There are certain words and related concepts that all pupils should know in order to read almost any science material above the primary level:
      i. Things "in common," "characteristics," "various," "classified," "similarities." An understanding of these terms is quite helpful in comprehending the data that follow the terms.

      ii. Common Latin, Greek, or other derivations:
         hydro
         electro
         photo
         un
         bi
   b. Every new science lesson requires the teaching of terms pertinent to that selection.
2. Typographical cues (locational skills)
   a. In most science textbooks there are good subtitles and chapter headings to use.
   b. Often there are good summaries at the end of chapters.
   c. Typographical cues are especially important in the first survey reading.
3. Kinds of readings—read for the following:
   a. Surveying the material.
      i. Attention to pictures.
      ii. How many main parts? Use the subheadings.
      iii. Read the first paragraph and the summary, if given.
      iv. Formulate questions for reading from the survey.
   b. Answering the questions.
      i. Appreciation of facts and objective data.
      ii. Critical reading—what are the criteria?
   c. Reviewing the material read.
      i. The discussion and evaluation of the reading is probably the most important part of the lesson.
      ii. Pupils should be urged to report exactly what they have read; precision.
         "*Most* kinds of bats are useful to humankind because they eat harmful insects."
         "*Some* scientists believe there is life in outer space."

4. Special considerations
   a. Ability to read symbols. AuH_2O = goldwater.
   b. Ability to follow diagrams; for example, a student must understand the idea of completeness, as in an electrical circuit or a chemical equation.
5. Organizational guides
   Various organizational approaches typical of science selections are these:
   a. Generalizations are given first, then the examples and data; deductive.
      i. All mammals have hair, bear young alive, and so on.
      ii. The different kinds of mammals are listed.
   b. Examples and supporting data.
      i. Information on different mammals—their size, speed, and so on.
      ii. In other selections—phenomena about light, heat, and so on.
   c. Classification of data.
      i. Different classes of mammals, stars, and so on.
      ii. Differences and similarities among the classes.
   d. Often the data are given first, then the science writer builds up to classifying and generalizing; inductive.

Geography Cues

1. Vocabulary cues
   a. Extend concept of a previously known word (e.g., *range, mountain range*).
   b. Homonyms (e.g., *plain, plane*).
   c. Refer to glossary.
   d. Develop vocabulary in context (e.g., Bananas are a *tropical* fruit).
   e. Use illustrations to create perception of vocabulary.
2. Typographical cues
   a. Chapter headings, main headings, and subheadings are given.
   b. The format of the book includes illustrations, glossary, appendix, and index.
   c. The book is generally set up with two columns to make reading easier because of the shorter line of type and to facilitate scanning.
3. Kinds of readings
   a. Survey for overview.
   b. Read to answer specific questions.
   c. Skim to find specific answers and make generalizations (e.g., "What are the natural resources of Manitoba? How does this affect the industries of Manitoba?")
   d. Detailed reading of charts, graphs, maps, and so on.
4. Specialized considerations
   a. Statistical reading: This type is developed through repeated use of statistics (e.g., present statistical data and provide an exercise for using the data, such as comparing the area in square miles of several given countries).
   b. Symbolic language of maps (e.g., a child's use of the map legend).
   c. Recognize that a map is a ground plan drawn to scale.

```
┌─────────────────────────────────────┐
│                                     │
│         **Political Map**           │
│                                     │
│     �֍  Capital                      │
│                                     │
│     •  Other City or Town           │
│                                     │
│     ▲  MOUNTAIN                      │
│                                     │
│        River                        │
│                                     │
└─────────────────────────────────────┘
```
A map legend

    d. Interpret different kinds of maps (e.g., population, political, rainfall, topographical).

    e. Reading graphs (e.g., the reader learns to interpret data of various types of graphs—circle, line, bar, and pictorial).

    f. Authenticating facts (e.g., the reader must verify the date of statistical information, such as the population of a given area).

    g. Readers cut across the author's organization and make their own groupings of factual material for a given purpose.

5. Organizational guides

The material in a geography book is generally organized in one of two ways:

    a. A specific area is given and all geographical aspects are examined (e.g., the New England states would be thoroughly discussed as to topography, climate, population, industries, and so on).

    b. A geographical aspect is considered as it is found throughout the world.

Biography Cues

1. Vocabulary cues

    a. Pronunciation skills

        i. Multisyllabic words (e.g., *as-tro-labe*)

        ii. foreign words (e.g., *apartheid*)

    b. Meaning skills

        i. technical words (e.g., *latitude*)

        ii. abstract words (e.g., *democratic*)

        iii. concepts; abstractions (e.g., *tolerance*)

        iv. general terms (e.g., *elevator:* grain or passenger)

        v. mathematical terms (e.g., *ratio*)

2. Typographical guides

    a. Headings and subheadings provide clues to location of responses to questions.

    b. Use the parts of the book as reference tools.

    c. Relate text and graphic content such as maps, graphs, and cartoons to corresponding text material.

3. Kinds of readings—read for the following:

    a. Main idea and supporting details.

    b. Use of key words, concepts, and literal facts.

Teaching Reading for Life—Content Reading

c. Read critically:
      i. appraisals
      ii. conclusions and inferences
      iii. propaganda
      iv. current events
   d. Organize ideas to recognize relations and sequence of events; identify central issues.
   e. Graphic skills (maps, graphs, charts, diagrams, and pictures).
   f. Related reference skills (table of contents, index, cross-references, footnotes).
   g. Related materials (periodicals and mass media, such as radio, television, lectures, and field trips).
4. Organizational guides
   General organization of the content:
   a. Material in the social studies area is usually organized by the initial statement of a selection (e.g., the current voter age limit), a practice (e.g., selection of the president by an electoral college), an event (e.g., passage of the Eighteenth Amendment), or a method (e.g., representative democracy).
   b. Often a point of view is presented, usually subtly (e.g., private enterprise is best for the country); in some cases, overtly (e.g., dictatorships are bad).
   c. A relation often presented is one of conditions surrounding an effect: condition-effect relation.
   d. Chronological order often meets the organizational needs of social studies material.

"Go-go" Reading

Not all content reading is performed with textbooks. After a child is finished with school most reading will be content reading that may not include the contextual aids found in textbooks. Road signs, labels on bottles, newspapers, and magazines all demand content reading. Magazine and billboard advertisements require reactions that involve many of the same skills that have been proposed for textbook reading and perhaps additional ones.

Tank trucks roll across the country bearing the red label *imflammable;* others, *flammable.* What is the difference between these two words? The Readers of these signs had better protect themselves by being able to read such signs.

Reading-on-the-go, or "go-go" reading, requires quick reactions. The reader must apply criteria in order to make immediate judgments. It is easy enough to decide not to drink a liquid when it has *Poison!* stamped across it (see Figure 11.5). But the parent with a sick five-year-old child must bring other criteria to bear on reading the label: "Take one teaspoon four times a day. For children under six consult a physician before administering this medicine."

Though "go-go" reading does not occupy much classroom time, examples from the world of signs, television, the newspaper, and magazines afford excellent teaching examples of what reading-thinking skills

FIGURE 11.5 Being Able to Read Can Be a
Life-Saving Skill.

must be used when examining content selections. Children will usually
respond vigorously to exercises in examining popular commercials:
"The computer confirms that Regi cigarettes give you whiter, brighter
teeth"; "Senator Fogbound comes from the Midwest and knows the
problems farmers face"; "Sandpaper tissue is so soft—buy the tissue
with more of what you're looking for."

Each of these statements makes assumptions; some of them are
quite misleading. In the first ad the reader must ask, "What do computers do?" They do not *confirm* anything. They simply report data. In
the second statement the reader should ask, "What does coming from
the Midwest teach you about farming?" A person could live his entire

No textbook can be as varied and up-to-date as a daily newspaper.
Children can be helped to begin the habit of staying current with
events by using the newspaper in content area classes.

Teaching Reading for Life—Content Reading

life in Indianapolis and not know how to milk a cow or disk a field. And in the third statement the reader should ask, "More than what?" There are other avenues to explore with these statements, but such brief comments indicate ways in which to show youngsters how to apply content reading skills to the "go-go" world around him. Short examples like these provide direct and pertinent demonstrations of some of the analytic and evaluative reading skills that are integral features of content reading.

Career Education. Many elementary and middle schools encourage youngsters to learn about careers through demonstrations, field trips, and through reading. Various alternatives gradually unfold especially through reading. Youngsters gain concepts about jobs and the work world by reading about them and see that many occupations use written directions for workers to follow. They see quite early, for example, that they must be able to relate a diagram to associated written explanations. When catalytic converters were installed on automobiles to reduce air pollution, the manufacturers sent complex instructions for maintaining and adjusting those converters to garage mechanics. A mechanic who could not read proficiently could not take care of these devices to make sure they continued preventing pollution. It would be very helpful to show children a sample of such instructions as one instance of real-life, on-the-job reading.

Reading is a continuing and growing factor in

1. The review of job skills and concepts.
2. The selection of an occupation (one cannot actually experience many careers except through reading about them).
3. The training for a specific career.
4. The updating skills to advance in a chosen profession.

Both career information and the incentive to read become linked as real-life activities. Reading increases in value as the child understands that it is a tool for adult life, as well as a way to experience pleasure.

Appraising Content Reading Skills

Chapters 8 and 9 discussed a means of asking graded questions in order to appraise the child's application of certain reading-thinking skills. The same method can be used in teaching the content material discussed in this chapter.

If the teacher expects a child to think like a scientist while reading science material, then the teacher should have some knowledge of the structure of that discipline. Teachers should know that what is called the discovery method in education is akin to the scientific method—there is observation of data, classification of the data, and a prediction of conclusion that follows from the relationships observed.

Part of the teacher's preparation for an appraisal of content reading skills is to make sure that the background of students warrants such an appraisal. In this case, the examiner expects to find some skills and is prepared to correct and develop those skills that need changing or adding to. The examiner might use a checklist similar to the one that follows to appraise his or her performance and the capability of the school system in carrying out a program to teach content reading skills.

These practices are often recommended for teaching special reading skills in various content areas. Teachers should check off the items that apply to their teaching and make an appraisal of what has to be done to prepare their classroom to teach these skills (see Figure 11.6 for an awareness checklist).

If we assume that the teacher has enough knowledge of the structure of the subject discipline, the next step is to get a broad picture of the skills children have for reading content selections with comprehension. As was recommended for several other kinds of reading skills, careful observation of children during content reading may provide a picture of what the strengths and weaknesses are. The broad categories in the checklist could guide the teacher in a general appraisal. A teacher could also construct a checklist with a different set of skills if specific skills were identified for individual achievement by the end of the term or the end of the school year. The kinds of observations indicated on the checklist are essential in order to differentiate instruction.

FIGURE 11.6 Checklist for Teacher Awareness of Content Reading.

1. Text material used is suited in difficulty to the reading levels of students.
2. Students are encouraged through assignments to read widely in related materials.
3. At the beginning of the year, adequate time is taken to introduce the text and to discuss how it may be read effectively.
4. The teacher is aware of the special vocabulary and concepts introduced in the various units.
5. Adequate attention is given to vocabulary and concept development.
6. Provisions are made for checking on the extent to which important vocabulary and concepts are learned, and reteaching is done where needed.
7. The teacher knows the special reading skills involved in the subject.
8. The teacher teaches the special reading skills in the subject.
9. Students are taught to use appropriate reference materials.
10. Adequate reference materials are available.
11. Plenty of related informational books and other materials are available for students who read *below grade* level.
12. Plenty of related informational books and other materials are available for students who read *above grade* level.
13. The teacher helps the poor reader to develop adequate reading skills.
14. Students are grouped within the classroom for differentiated instruction.
15. The teacher knows the reading level of the textbook or textbooks being used.
16. The teacher knows the reading ability of the students from standardized tests, other evaluative materials, or cumulative records or a combination of these.

In any fourth- or fifth-grade classroom the range of content reading skills is likely to be quite wide. Some children will have learned to respond to cues on their own. That they use the skills well, or at least know what to look for, will necessitate only a minimum amount of instruction for maintaining and improving what they already know. Others may not be consciously aware of cues. Students who have difficulty in using special skills may need additional practice with supplementary materials.

Teach and Test for Specific Criteria

In assessing content reading skills, we could easily slip into the practice of testing the child with a single selection and trying to estimate the child's use of all skills on the basis of a single response. Because so many factors are involved in demonstrating skills for reading content material, the teacher's assessment and the child's progress are more likely to benefit from several tests on specific criteria. For example, children should perform an exercise in which the teacher can observe their use of headings to determine the main parts of the article, or they should read a selection and then draw a map of what they have read to test visualization and following directions. In reverse, children could be asked to describe what a region or a city is like by looking at a map.

The major headings for which a teacher should test a child are *vocabulary, using heads, using charts, typographical cues,* and *organizational guides.* The test should include seeing if the child gets the facts straight, identifies the organizational pattern or principle of the selection, states the conclusion or prediction, applies criteria to evaluate the information and the selection, and uses the information to relate it to the life he or she knows.

On the basis of criterion tests of vocabulary, chart reading, organizational analysis, evaluation of information and procedure, and use of conclusions to make predictions or to integrate information, the teacher can form instructional groups, place some children with study kits, and give some demonstrations to the entire class. This is part of a continuing process of making children aware of the power they have over printed information once they develop a few key reading skills.

Summary

There is a difference between content selections and narratives, especially the short stories typically found in basal readers. Vocabulary differs with respect to the technical terms found in science, math, and social studies, but also because those disciplines have an organizational structure that often influences the way information about the subject is presented in an elementary school test. Thus, it seems important that teachers and children learn something about the way in which expository selections are written within specific subject areas.

There are various kinds of cues that a reader can use to assist in reading content material effectively. These cues relate to vocabulary, typography, expository writing patterns, and, in a sense, learning to read like the scientist or the mathematician who wrote the selection.

To teach content reading skills, the teacher and students together should make a task analysis of the kinds of skills that are needed by individuals in the class, then construct criterion exercises where they are needed. Content reading is a part of the idea of developmental reading. Content reading includes reading signs, ads, tables, editorials, and news reports. The skills that are needed for reading a content subject text must also be adjusted to reading on the go. Verifying information, reading directions, knowing a vocabulary are just as important in our daily lives as they are in the more formal textbook area.

Finally, an appraisal of content reading skills should start with the teachers' appraisal of their knowledge of the structure of a discipline. In this way, they can teach children to "read like a scientist," continue through an analysis of the capability of the school to teach content skills, and end with specific criterion tests—those to be used as a prelude to grouping and individualizing instruction in the skills of reading content selections.

Terms for Self-study

organizational pattern
readability formula
analysis
evaluation
expository writing

translation
locational skills
typographical cues
criterion tests

Discussion Questions

1. How could a teacher determine if the class text was too difficult for students to read?
2. What are several ways of demonstrating to children the differences between reading a story and reading subject-oriented content?
3. What means does a content teacher have for adjusting to the various reading abilities of students?
4. What instructional guidelines are there for helping children think through their content reading?

Recommended Readings

Anderson, Richard C., Osborn, Jean, & Tierney, Robert J. (1984). *Learning to read in American schools: Basal reader and content texts.* Hillsdale, N J: Lawrence Erlbaum.
    This book contains a collection of papers and responses to those papers given by noted authorities at a conference for educational publishers and researchers conducting studies on instructional materials.
Anderson, Thomas J., & Armbruster, Bonnie B. (1984). Studying. In P. D. Pearson et al. (Eds.). *Handbook of reading research.* New York: Longman.

This volume reviews and analyzes research on studying as a special form of reading.

Graham, Kenneth G., & Robinson, H. Alan. *Study skills handbook: A guide for all teachers.* Newark, DE: International Reading Association.

Here is a practical guide to help teachers at all grade levels understand the importance of various study skills and comprehension strategies. The book also provides specific suggestions to strengthen children's performance in those areas through classroom activities.

Moore, David W., Readence, John E., & Rickelman, Robert J. (1982). *Prereading activities for content area reading and learning.* Newark, DE: International Reading Association.

This book describes and provides examples of activities teachers can use to prepare students to learn from printed materials and emphasizes the need for review and enrichment activities for postreading situations.

Vacca, Richard T. (1981). *Content area reading.* Boston: Little, Brown.

Vacca presents a system for incorporating principles of reading instruction at the middle and secondary levels into the content areas.

12

Basal Readers and Other Approaches

Some people think that "teaching reading" means covering all the material and doing all the exercises prescribed in a given textbook. That attitude confuses the *materials* that are used for instruction with the *teaching methods* employed. This chapter will focus on the important distinction between *materials* and *methods* in order to help you determine what each contributes to an effective reading program.

You know that various instructional methods are used in the teaching of reading, but you may be unable to tell how they differ from each other or how they work in the classroom. You may also wonder if one method can possibly fit the needs of all children and, if not, how various methods can be combined effectively. These concerns will be discussed as well.

In this chapter you will find the answers to the following questions:

- *What methods are used for teaching reading?*
- *Which method is best?*
- *What are the advantages and disadvantages of each approach?*
- *Can all children learn by the same method?*
- *How are instructional materials selected?*

Educators have long searched for the best method of teaching reading. Recently this search has spawned countless investigations involving hundreds of teachers and classrooms, but the major finding of practically every such study is that *no single method of reading instruction is best for all children.*

A considerable amount of evidence indicates that people learn in different ways. It is, therefore, not surprising that studies that compare teaching methods are typically inconclusive. In fact, it is often found that there is a greater difference in achievement among learners taught by a *single* method than among those taught by different methods. Even when *group* achievement seems to be comparable with two different methods, *individual* learners still vary considerably, with some doing better with one method than with the other. The same is true for children who do less well: Each method is relatively ineffective for some students.

In view of this, we recommend that you make a careful study of the approaches that we will discuss and select one of them to serve as a starting point. Before making such a choice, however, we must look carefully at the various methods of reading instruction and consider the merits of each.

Choosing an Instructional System

Reading instruction must proceed according to some plan. Our analysis of the many available programs leads us to group them into these three systems:

1. Basal reader approach.
2. Language emphasis approach.
3. Personal interest approach.

None of these systems should be regarded as a cure-all; each should be viewed as a strategy with specific characteristics.

Because individual students have unique learning styles, one instructional system may be more appropriate than another for some children. The teacher must adjust to the strengths and weaknesses of each system. Because the one "best method" does not exist, it is necessary for each teacher to develop the procedures that he or she finds most effective.

The Basal Reader Approach

More than 90 per cent of American elementary school teachers use a basal reader to conduct reading instruction (Ingersoll & Smith, 1984). With that enormous majority, it is clear that almost every teacher will use a basal reader approach, and so it must be examined as to its purposes, methodology, and the power of its appeal.

Definition and Description

A basal reading program is a series of graded books usually spanning kindergarten through grade eight. Though an oft-mentioned feature of these books is their control over the reading vocabulary, they are characterized as well by the measured introduction of skills designed for learning to read and another set of skills designed for reading to learn (sometimes called study skills). The content of the four or five best-selling programs is planned to cover a wide range of classical

Group reading activities are an important part of the basal reader approach. Here a reading group discusses a story they have just finished reading.

literature and contemporary children's themes and to accommodate the state and local mandates that identify the types of characters and authors who must appear in books adopted by the public schools.

The characteristics of the basal reader approach (measured vocabulary, skills, and content) can be better understood when seen as a means for teaching a long-term curriculum. Most school systems now view their reading curriculum as a series of sequential experiences that starts in kindergarten and extends through grade eight and above. Reading instruction starts with introductory or "readiness" experiences and follows a developmental pattern for the subsequent eight to ten years. Both the skills and the story content of the basal reader progress year by year to match the normal developmental patterns of elementary school children—a concept used in all basic textbooks, whether math or science or reading.

Because most of what we read is composed of less than one thousand high-frequency words, those words are introduced into the content of the first three grades. Many of those high-frequency words are also used as the basis for introducing and practicing word-recognition skills. From the outset of instruction, however, both high-frequency words and valuable content words are introduced through the stories contained in the basal reader.

Writers of basal texts do not assume that children will limit their reading exclusively to the stories in their basal readers. Children will read about many other concepts in other books, but the purpose of controlling the vocabulary in this approach is to assure all students that they will learn well a highly usable reading vocabulary and that

Basal Readers and Other Approaches

they will not be threatened by having to respond to more words than the average student can tolerate.

In a similar manner, the skills program of the basal reader is measured across the years, being spaced to provide first those skills that have the most frequent application and then others as time allows. The intent of the skills program is to give children an orderly picture of the logic of the English sound-spelling system, the meaningful structure of words (their morphemic and semantic content), and a sense of how children can manipulate the concepts that they read, that is, the thinking skills that they may employ as effective readers. A sampling of those skills may be seen in the following chart.

Sample Skills, Grades K–8

	Word Skills	Comprehension Skills
K	Identify rhyming words	Identify setting
1	Sound-spelling patterns CVC, CVCe	Sequence of events
2	Compound words	Determine *main* idea
3	Common suffixes (*-ful*)	Find details to support main idea
4	Meaning of words with prefixes (*counter-*)	Paraphrase a negative sentence
5	Semantic rationale for hyphenating words	Demonstrate comprehension via cloze
6	Form antonymns by adding antonymous prefixes (*dis-*)	Form generalizations from details
7	Identify base words in words with affixes	Draw a conclusion to syllogism in a paragraph
8	Identify changes in meaning when affixes are added to roots	Identify different kinds of paragraphs

The skills in this chart are only samples of the kinds of items that appear in the skills programs of basal readers. But the purpose of the skills plan is to assure children (and the community) that they will be taught a wide variety of reading skills over the years. The skills are built into a planned sequence, a sequence that follows the developing mind of the child, a plan that does not leave the introduction of thinking skills to the vagaries of time and circumstance.

Content of Basal Readers

For years it has been the sport of adults to joke about the content of children's readers. The "Dick and Jane" variety of readers that were used in schools from the 1930s through the 1950s began with first-grade stories that read:

RUN, DICK, RUN.
RUN, JANE, RUN.
RUN, RUN, RUN.

Adults focus on the script; children, on the pictures and the total context. Millions of children learned to read through that type of text despite the apparent vacuous content. Children followed the adventures of Dick and Jane or Jack and Sally (another basal pair) from little children in grade one to adolescents in grades seven and eight. The content was home, neighborhood, city, state, country, the world—the adventures of Dick and Jane.

That safe, middle-class image was the kind of content required by the society of those decades. Since the 1960s, the content of basal readers has changed to reflect the social and educational concerns of current society. Classics from children's literature, a picture of the diversity of American society, the representation of the variety of roles that men and women play, the inclusion of the handicapped and the elderly, the point of view of writers from many nationalities—all these characteristics are now built into the content of contemporary basal readers.

Over three centuries of American education, reading instruction has received a determined scrutiny from the citizens. Reading has always been seen in the United States as a vehicle for protecting and promoting the fundamental interests of society. In their debate over methodology, educators often miss the emphasis that society demands—that the reading curriculum carries the burden of literacy and of values. From the first century of American education, when the purpose of literacy was to read the Bible and other religious tracts, to the present day, when cultural diversity and literary heritage are

Historical Changes in Content of Reading Series*

Date	School Purpose	Reading Content
1600–1700	Promote religion	Hornbook
1700–1776	Promote religion	New England primer
1776–1840	Morality and nationalism	Graded readers, moral life
1840–1880	Citizenship	McGuffey basals, responsibility
1880–1910	Acculturation	Cultural enrichment, child emphasis literature
1910–1925	Personal growth	Read beyond the basal
1925–1935	Practical education	Reality, extend experience
1935–1950	Advance through education	Realism and social relations
1950–1965	Live in a changing world	Experimental methods and content
1965–1977	Promote individual rights	Cultural diversity
1977– ?	Competence with discipline	Literary and social heritage

* Abstracted primarily from N. B. Smith (1965). *American Reading Instruction*. Newark, DE: International Reading Association.

uppermost on the minds of the community, the content of instruction has always been more crucial to the general public than the method of instruction (N. B. Smith, 1965).

The chart that follows indicates the shift in content of readers used in American schools. In each time period listed in the chart, the purpose for basic literacy changed, bringing with it a change in the content of the reading books that children used. From the mass introduction of the McGuffey readers about 1850 until today, the basal reader concept has remained the dominant type of material used for reading instruction. The content of those readers, however, continues to change with the needs of society.

Textbook and Curriculum Standards

Though there are practical management reasons why teachers use basic textbooks, there are more compelling reasons found in state and local standards. With more than two thirds of the states now requiring frequent competency tests, teachers need the highly organized skills activities in basal readers to prepare the children for those tests. Few teachers have the energy needed to prepare those kinds of exercises on their own. Even if they do, the reading content requirements are almost beyond the capability of any one individual. The range and specificity of content defies the resources of one teacher or of a school library no matter how elaborate the library.

State Standards

In 1984 the State of California published standards for reading and language-arts textbooks—standards that are reminiscent of those found in the curriculum statements of other states. They illustrate the guidelines with which teachers and publishers must comply. There follow several examples of these standards:

Student texts will contain selections that reflect the following content emphases:

- *A major inclusion of works that expose students to a rich literary heritage in continuous, connected prose with examples of such length that the discourse is not fragmented.*
- *Significant contemporary themes that broaden the vistas of today's students.*
- *Classical and contemporary works that represent the best in language.*
- *A systematic exposure to the various type of literature.*

Student texts will promote the concept of reading as being useful, desirable, attainable, and pleasurable:

- *Materials will stress the value of reading in today's society (reading has a payoff).*
- *Materials will model reading by presenting content and illustrations that portray readers in a variety of situations.*

Approaches to Teaching Reading

- *Materials will include a broad spectrum of print (signs, labels, posters, as well as narrative).*
- *Materials will direct students to conduct extended research using materials other than the basal and to read library and trade books.*

The state standards also stipulate that the total program must include applications of technology—that is, the microcomputer.

Local Standards

One large city school system listed the following characteristics for its reading program:

1. It should be developmental and sequential.
2. Special emphasis should be placed on comprehension skills.
3. Major competencies should be identified and tested.
4. Reteaching and retesting options are needed.
5. A wide variety of literature and content should be included, accommodating the diversity of American culture and content-area reading.
6. Children should have multiple practice opportunities for sustained reading and for sharing the same selections.
7. Parents need to be involved in the instructional process.

Those characteristics would then establish the major criteria for selecting the tools for teaching—the books and materials used in the classroom and in the home. Interestingly, those same items describe the characteristics of a number of existing basal reading series.

One of the most powerful curriculum tools that schools have is a basic text series, in this case a basal reader series. The purpose of a basal reader is to provide students and teachers with carefully structured skill development and literature that will lead them gradually to effective reading. If we assume that the major goals of the reading series match the major goals of the school system and that the reading series matches the instructional characteristics selected by the school system, the basal gives each teacher a clear curriculum plan with all the associated materials for teaching. To produce a similar plan would require many years and millions of dollars in development money were the school system to work out its own plan with matching materials.

What makes the basal reader such a powerful tool is its long-range organizational plan and the wealth of materials it contains to achieve that plan. But it is only a tool, one tool of many that a teacher may use. If used intelligently and consistently, positive results will occur. If used creatively, superior results will occur.

An example may help. Students in a small city in Oregon had average scores that were at least one year below grade level at each grade. The school system purchased a new reading series and at the same time formed a committee of teachers and administrators who worked to make sure that all teachers would use the series as it was designed, that is, as presented in the teachers guide. Within two years the scores for those schools averaged six months above grade level instead of one year below. It wasn't only the new reading series. The change was caused primarily by teachers actually using the program as it was designed. The basal can thus be an extremely powerful curriculum tool provided it is used as intended.

The Role of Guidelines

Though some teachers may see any standards or guidelines as an interference with intellectual freedom, these or similar guidelines represent the voice of the community. They constitute one of the few protections that the community has that its children will receive the kind of education that it desires. Such guidelines provide legal ways to set criteria for curriculum and textbooks. Recent guidelines from various states have influenced changes in the content of basal readers published in the eighties. For example, in the very first reading books that first-graders now see, there are well-known nursery rhymes to represent traditional literature and to develop oral language, rhyme sounds, and letter-sound discrimination:

> Hey, diddle, diddle,
> The cat and the fiddle,
> The cow jumped over the moon;
> The little dog laughed
> To see such sport,
> And the dish ran away with the spoon.
>
> Little Boy Blue, come, blow your horn!
> The sheep's in the meadow, the cow's in the corn.
> Where's the little boy that looks after the sheep?
> Under the haystack, fast asleep!

Many children know these nursery rhymes when they arrive at school. They thus see old friends in their books from the outset, and some of them can take a lead in using them for the purpose of better understanding the printed page.

Familiar children's stories such as "The Tale of Peter Rabbit," "Little Red Riding Hood," "Goldilocks and the Three Bears," and "The Little Engine That Could" grace the pages of first-grade basal readers. Not only do they represent the required traditional literature, but they also give many children an opportunity to use stories they already know and love in order to sense the repetitiveness of language, the setting and the sequence of storytelling, and the predictable character of language and storytelling. If the first-grade basal reader has changed that much from a "Dick and Jane" content, it is clear that the content at other grade levels will show comparable traditional literary selections appropriate for the age of the student.

Rationale of the Basal Reader Approach

The basal reader approach is built on the premise that reading instruction involves more than learning a few simple strategies for dealing with printed messages. Reading instruction includes a long-term curriculum with identifiable content as well as procedures or skills for gaining meaning. The basal approach assumes that consistent practice is needed in skills and in various prose types before a child becomes an effective reader. Though all children do not require this careful sequence of content and skills practice, a very high percentage do. Consequently, the process of learning to read is analyzed, and the significant parts are organized into a logical, coherent series of lessons. Content, in a similar fashion, is analyzed and organized over the years to match the age of the children and to communicate a mandated curriculum. Social and legal requirements by state and local boards now outline the concepts and types of literature to be included in a reading program.

Broad characteristics of the basal reader approach are these:

1. "Content should proceed from the known to the unknown."

    The basal reader approach is based on a principle commonly accepted by educators: Proceed from the known to the unknown. The content and setting of controlled-vocabulary stories reflect the same idea: Begin with what is familiar or interesting to the learner or both. Neighborhood scenes, with family and pets as the central characters, are frequently found in primary-grade stories. Fanciful and imaginative stories are common. This kind of story content is intended to help the child learn to read by reducing potentially troublesome factors such as unfamiliar concepts and story characters.

2. "Vocabulary should be systematically repeated."

    The principle of systematic repetition of words is another central element in the basal reader approach to reading. Frequent exposure to a word is necessary for it to become an automatic response (Samuels, 1979). A few words are introduced in each story, and each new word is repeated to provide practice and reinforcement.

3. "Reading selections should gradually become more difficult."

    The readability of stories gradually increases in difficulty from book to book. Vocabulary, sentence length and complexity, the number of characters in the story, and the length of stories all gradually increase. Subsequent books require more understanding of sequence and of making inferences. Learners are asked to accomplish more sophisticated reading tasks, but they are led to do so in a systematic, controlled fashion.

4. "Reading skills should be taught systematically."

    Reading skills are identified, organized, and taught. The principles of continued practice and movement from the simple to the complex are applied to skill development. Workbook and teacher-directed activities introduce and reinforce reading skills. Finding the main idea, for example, is introduced early and developed in more difficult stories across the grades.

5. "A 'complete' program is developed for teachers and learners."

   Materials are provided for the learner and the teacher. Teaching suggestions, tests, and other tools that have been developed by reading experts are provided for the teacher. References are given for supplementary and enrichment materials, such as filmstrips, books, and reading games. Many of these materials are included in the program itself as supplementary items.

The basal reader approach is not regarded by its proponents as a program that can solve all reading problems, but it does provide well-organized content and methods to meet complex demands on the teacher.

Limitations of the Basal Reader Approach

Though basal readers provide extensive coverage in content and procedures, they need to be examined in view of their limitations:

1. "Today's children need fewer controls."

   The controls on vocabulary, content, and skills organization are usually listed as strengths, but some argue that controlled-vocabulary programs destroy rather than create an interest in learning to read. The critics point out that today's youngsters are sophisticated learners. Television has catapulted four-year-olds into space, under the sea, and into the heart of a living man; fourth-graders can watch the proceedings of Congress or the United Nations in color.

   Technology, television, and microcomputers, the critics argue, have further expanded the horizons of youngsters today by making transcontinental travel a common occurrence among many. Families have more leisure time, rapid modes of transportation are available, and the means necessary for such travel are present.

2. "In the early grades, the language used in stories is stilted and unnatural."

   Although great strides have been made in recent years toward making the language of basal readers more like speech, the control and repetition dictated by a controlled vocabulary necessarily impose certain restrictions. Studies such as those by Strickland (1962) and by Loban (1963) demonstrate that today's six-year-old uses the basic sentences, including complex, compound, and complex-compound structures. A more recent study by Smith and Ingersoll (1984) raises some serious doubts, however, about the vocabulary level of elementary school children. They report a large decline in the diversity of vocabulary over the past forty years.

   It should be noted regarding the language of children's stories that educators have sometimes incorrectly judged the interests and reactions of children. The "dry" stories of the primary-grade reading program may well be entirely satisfactory from the child's viewpoint. Repetition of a word may be more of a blessing than a bore to the primary-grade youngster who struggles with each word encountered.

3. "Educators misuse the system."

One criticism of the basal reader approach is directed at the misuse of the system. Despite cautions to the contrary, many educators use the basal reader and nothing else. They have children do all their reading in the graded reader. The workbook is assigned without regard to individual need. Every suggested activity in the teacher's manual is followed. Under these circumstances, the child never reads a library book or a magazine. This criticism, of course, is directed at teachers rather than at the basal reader itself.

4. "Reading is taught in a stylized manner, unlike real-life reading."

Another disadvantage is that its structured nature makes the basal reader seem artificial when compared to the uncontrolled reading a child does for recreation or in locating information. In this sense, the important transfer of skills from the instructional program to application in everyday reading may be hampered. For example, seldom does the child begin reading a news item or directions for assembling a model airplane by studying the new vocabulary he or she will encounter. Yet the basal system introduces new words prior to reading as a regular procedure.

Vocabulary Controls

Most basal readers exercise vocabulary control by using a high-frequency vocabulary, but some of them use sound-spelling patterns to decide which words to include. A high-frequency vocabulary refers to those words used most often in oral and written language. Being familiar with high-frequency words enables a reader to recognize a greater percentage of the words encountered. Some word lists are developed from tabulations of children's written communications, such as the Smith and Ingersoll list (1984). Others are based on an analysis of the words used in popular basal reader programs, such as the Harris and Jacobson list (1983).

Some programs use phoneme-grapheme correspondences to determine the words that will appear in stories, especially the early stories in the first grade. Phonics programs (such as the Economy Program) begin with isolated sounds (for example, the sound of the letter *b*). Words included in early stories are selected to represent the sound-symbol correspondence that is being taught. Early learning tasks involve that reader in associating sound with individual letters and combinations of letters, blending sounds, and generally mastering the separate elements of the printed code.

Some sound-symbol programs begin with consonants and then move to vowels, consonant clusters, vowel clusters, syllabication, and so forth. Others begin with vowels and follow another sequence. Stories included in these programs emphasize and illustrate whatever sound-symbol relationship the children are learning in the skills program (for example, one story may feature words with the letter *w* in the beginning position).

Other programs such as the Lippincott Readers and the Merrill Linguistic Readers are organized around spelling patterns. Early learning tasks present the reader with words that are "regular" in pronunciation. Stories present families of words that follow a pattern (for example, "A fat rat sat on a mat"). When one spelling pattern has been mastered, others are introduced.

Programs (such as those of Harcourt Brace, Houghton Mifflin, and Macmillan) that use words of high frequency are not as easily identified as the other types of controlled-vocabulary programs. There is nothing very distinct about stories that employ words such as *will, run, boat, water, the, house,* and so forth except that no particular sound-symbol relationship or spelling pattern predetermines word choice. Words introduced initially are simply those that most children are expected to understand and use in their conversations.

Controlled Vocabulary

1. Visit a curriculum library or other center where elementary school textbooks are housed. Peruse a basal reader series by examining readers, teacher's guides, and workbooks. Determine how vocabulary is controlled in the series you examine.
2. Compare two different basal series. Note in particular the differences in vocabulary from series to series. Which series introduces the fewest words at a given grade level? What impact does the use of limited vocabulary have on story content?
3. Prepare a presentation that you would make to parents at a PTA meeting describing the reasons for using a basal reader approach. Try to anticipate questions the parents would ask and how you would answer them.

Summary

Basal readers include a methodology and a content. The methodology of the basal approach includes a long-range curriculum plan that systematically spreads content and skills practice over grades K to eight. The skills and content are distributed according to two logical principles:

Approaches to Teaching Reading

1. Content should match both the child's developmental age and the guidelines established by society.
2. Skills should be sequenced logically to accommodate the expanding language and thought of the elementary school child.

The content of basal readers has changed historically to reflect broader movements in society and in education. It is truly a people's curriculum. Basal reader selections in the eighties reflect societal demands for traditional values, cultural diversity, and emphasis on literary writing.

Language Emphasis Approach

A language emphasis approach is tied directly to the interests and needs of each individual child. This is not to say that structure disappears or that adults do not have to exercise judgment about the content of instructional activities, for that would be inaccurate. But a language emphasis approach tends to follow the lead of the child. Some define this approach as "The Child is the curriculum" (Harste, Woodward, & Burke, 1983).

A story or description dictated by a group of children has inherent interest and meaning for the authors. Here a teacher records her students impressions of a field trip to a nearby firehouse.

In a language emphasis approach, performance objectics, skills, and specific content are not given priority. The process of learning to read is given priority, especially the process of learning to read in an environment full of language. It is an attempt to make reading and writing as natural to learn as listening and speaking are. Thus, the setting for learning must include a wide array of books and combination of speaking, writing, and reading with little or no attempt to segment the learning. It is thought that when children need to learn certain vocabulary, they will ask or find a way of figuring it out. Frank Smith (1974), for example, says that the natural curiosity of children will lead them to make guesses and confirm their guesses about language. The child's own language capacity and personal drive, then, become the curriculum that a teacher follows. If a child wants to write before wanting to read books, the teacher encourages writing while suggesting the connection. Even though the first attempts at writing may be unintelligible to the teacher, he or she asks the child to read back the story the child has written. A curriculum designed in advance by adults is seen as artificial and unnatural by the proponents of this approach.

Language emphasis proponents direct teachers to use broad strategies in their teaching and to encourage children to develop strategies for handling reading. In a seminal paper on this approach, Kenneth Goodman (1976) called reading a "psycholinguistic guessing game" in which the primary strategy is to guess what is coming next in the text, confirming or negating the guess by the text that follows. It is through this guessing and confirming strategy that learners develop confidence and grow.

Rationale for a Language Emphasis Approach

The basic concept for a language emphasis approach resides in its belief that reading should be learned naturally, intuitively, as a child first learned to speak. Because it is assumed that no one carefully sequenced speech for the child, it is assumed that the child does not need a carefully sequenced program to learn to read because reading is a language activity, a natural extension of speaking.

1. "Language begins with the individual child."

   To carry out a language emphasis approach requires the teacher to seek wide language opportunities for each child, following the lead of the child to discuss, read, and write as the child-as-curriculum premise would suggest. The teacher surrounds the children with books, reads to them, and encourages them to read and to write as inclination dictates. Naturalness is a key concept. In the early stages, teachers read predictable books and encourage children to follow suit. Predictable books contain repetitive phrases and ideas that make it easy for children to develop a natural flow to their reading. Chicken Little keeps repeating: "The sky is falling. The sky is falling." Once

Approaches to Teaching Reading

they understand the pattern, children are able to simulate reading and gain a natural sense of rhythm.

2. "Growth occurs through wide reading."

    Growth in reading occurs through the student's use of library books, with difficulty increasing as the student gains confidence and competence. Skills are learned inductively; that is, as students see repeated instances of sound-spelling correspondences, they generate in their own minds the rules or generalizations that serve them. Skills lessons and workbooks are anathema to purists in a language emphasis approach. Because no set sequence must be followed, the teacher can use ongoing activities to introduce and reinforce skills as they are needed. The primary advantage of such an arrangement is its emphasis on reasoning and the utilization of skills as opposed to memorization.

3. "Writing activities are a corollary of speaking and reading."

    Teachers and children are encouraged to write often and to share their writing as a means of stimulating reading. The language experience story technique is a writing activity that fits easily into the framework of a language emphasis approach to reading.

Limitations of a Language Emphasis Approach

1. "Heavy demands are made on the teacher."

    Because of the lack of structure and prepared materials, the classroom teacher assumes far more responsibility with this system than in a basal reader approach, for example. Although the flexibility inherent in this plan encourages individualization, it also raises the risk of creating a haphazard, incidental reading program.

2. "Skills may not be sequenced or practiced adequately."

    The development of reading skills requires some organization in order to build readiness for subsequent skills. For example, following a sequence of events is a skill that depends on the ability to find main ideas and recognize transitions. Without instruction and practice on underlying skills, subsequent competencies may not be attainable. A skillful teacher is capable of developing such a sequence for individual children. Instructing thirty individuals properly, however, requires superior ability and organization.

3. "Most materials must be made by the teacher."

    The language emphasis approach does not eliminate the use of commercially prepared materials, but it does place primary emphasis on teacher- or child-prepared materials. Again, this feature of the system maximizes the opportunity to individualize instruction, but it also places enormous demands on the teacher. In the absence of a standardized text and workbook, the teacher must develop or find appropriate materials. The same is true of books written with a desirable reading difficulty, or filmstrips helpful in supplementing a story. The teacher must find or develop them.

4. "Vocabulary is not repeated."

The absence of structure with regard to vocabulary, sentence building, and concept development may be troublesome for some youngsters. The planned repetition evidently required by some children in order to learn to recognize a word at sight is difficult to achieve when books are chosen for content or interest rather than for controlled development. The large number of words introduced through talking about and writing about their experiences places an unfair burden on young learners. Although research evidence indicates that even young children have a broad grasp of oral language, it is not clear whether the same assumption can be made for written language. It is likely that concepts or sentence structures that a child easily grasps in an oral setting become much more difficult when the tasks of decoding and interpreting written symbols are added to that of understanding.

Language Experience Stories

One frequently used activity in a language emphasis approach is the language experience activity. In Chapter 3 we described a primary-grade teacher using a language experience activity (LEA) in her classroom (pp. 71–75). You may want to read that description again at this time. Though no hard-and-fast rules must be followed in using LEA, five steps are typically involved:

1. Children participate in a shared experience such as looking at a picture, examining an object such as an empty hornet's nest, or occasionally taking a field trip (a hike through a nearby woods, for example).
2. A description of the experience is dictated by the children (or by a single child) and written down by a scribe (the teacher, an aide, or an older child).
3. The story or narrative is read aloud by the teacher as the children follow along.
4. The children reread the story or narrative immediately and review it several times later in the day or week.
5. Each child receives a copy of the story or narrative.

Any number of variations and follow-up activities can be undertaken:

1. Word identification lessons can focus on sound-symbol relationships (finding words that begin with the letter *b,* for example), recognizing high-frequency words (*the, and, we, saw,* for example), or noting spelling patterns (consonant-vowel-consonant words such as *can, red, but*).
2. One way of directing attention to story structure would be to cut a story chart into sentences, scramble them, and then have children recreate the sequence of events.
3. Children can study syntax by putting into correct order the scrambled words of one sentence from the story.
4. Transformations of sentences in the original story can be developed as a further activity emphasizing syntax.
5. Students can attempt to substitute synonyms for words used in the original experience story as a way of studying semantics and changes in meaning caused by word substitution.
6. The teacher can develop cloze exercises by deleting words from the story and having children identify the missing terms.

As these examples illustrate, opportunities are almost endless for involving children in reading and language activities centered on experience stories they have created. An integration of all language modes—speaking, listening, writing, and reading—is achieved using a language experience activity. Children see how language is represented in print. Encoding and decoding activities occur in a context that is meaningful. Background experiences necessary for understanding what is read are provided as an integral part of the activity.

To illustrate our point, we will now consider an example of how LEA was used in a class with children of various ages. Before looking at that description, however, let us observe that story dictation does not always require exotic props or elaborate learning experiences. Stories can grow from everyday matters such as observations of the weather or reactions to a book or to a TV program. The examples we use here serve to illustrate how far one can go, but they should not discourage the teacher who wants to use LEA more modestly. In practice, the teacher probably runs the gamut from simple to extensive lessons using the learning-experience approach.

In connection with a Teacher Corps training program in Grand Forks, North Dakota, a group of children ranging in age from six to thirteen attended a summer school. Teacher Corps interns were asked to think of ways to make the summer school program interesting as well as educational, and many of the activities generated relied on use of the language experience approach. In particular, it was decided that the community offered several interesting possibilities for field trips, among them a potato chip processing plant and a railroad roundhouse.

The interns began laying the groundwork for field trips by having the children talk about how people in Grand Forks earn a living. Farming, railroading, and several other occupations were identified, and because farming is such a significant factor in the local economy, the children pursued this further by discussing what crops were grown.

Sugar, beets, wheat, and potatoes were all mentioned, and the children were thus led into a more detailed discussion of ways in which these crops are important in daily life and how they are turned into various types of food. All the children were drawn into this discussion as each had something to contribute, and they gradually came to realize that there were many things they did not know. Choosing potato chips as a subject with which they were all familiar, the children began to list questions on the board, including these:

1. How are potato chips made?
2. Why do some potato chips taste like tacos?
3. How do potato chips get put into bags?

The possibility of visiting the potato chip processing plant was viewed enthusiastically, and the children began to think in earnest about the questions they wanted answered on their field trip. A chart-sized tablet was made, and further discussion led to the addition of these questions to the ones already formulated:

4. What are the steps in making potato chips?
5. How are potatoes cut up to make potato chips?

On the day of the field trip, a guide led the group through the plant, pointing out the operations in the process and answering the questions the children had asked. One intern videotaped the visit, and follow-up discussions about the trip were tape-recorded over the next several days. All this would provide material for future reference and use in developing additional activities.

With the teacher transcribing on the chalkboard, the group dictated the following story about their field trip.

Our Trip to the Old Dutch Factory

We took a field trip to the Old Dutch Factory. They factory is hot.
Potatoes get washed in a machine. A machine cuts the potatoes. Hot
oil cooks them. We got a bag of potato chips to eat.

Older children who preferred to write their own stories were encouraged to do so. All drew pictures of some part of the field trip, and these were displayed on a bulletin board under the title "Making Potato Chips."

The next day the videotape of the trip was viewed, and the five questions were answered on the board. Small groups pursued various projects, such as preparing a narration to accompany the videotape and writing out in detail the steps involved in making potato chips. Some children consulted encyclopedias and other reference books for more information and others wrote for brochures on potato farming. Each child developed a booklet containing copies of his or her own stories and descriptions, as well as copies of stories produced by the group as a whole.

Skill instruction involved some children in learning sight words

Approaches to Teaching Reading

frequently used in the stories (*process, conveyor belt,* for example); others followed a sequence of ideas, reading critically and interpreting tables and graphs. Material used in teaching these skills was taken from the writing of the children themselves. Stories were cut into strips, with one sentence per strip, and young children recreated the story by putting the sentences in order. Similar activities could be developed using individual words and phrases.

A later trip to the railroad roundhouse was planned, and stories were written for less ambitious projects as well. A stroll around the neighborhood or a popcorn-making adventure can provide a worthwhile topic to use in getting children to write about their experiences.

Experience Stories

1. Think of an interesting site in your area that would generate student interest. Visit that site for the purpose of deciding how you might include it in a language experience lesson. Develop a lesson plan with a group of children.
2. Visit a nearby elementary school that uses language experience. Ask to see examples of stories dictated by children. Observe a teacher leading a group in story dictation.
3. Act as teacher for a group of peers. Lead them to dictate an experience story about an event they shared in common (a football game, TV show, or class lecture). Ask for feedback on your skill at guiding the group without controlling the input.
4. Ditto or mimeograph copies of experience stories the children have written or dictated themselves, but delete every tenth word, leaving a blank. Have children fill in the blanks using the context of the story and the sentence to determine what is missing. With older children, creative writing stories can be reproduced in the same way, with every fifth word omitted. Encourage children to discuss their answers, comparing particular instances where they each supplied different words for a blank.

Personal Interest Approach

It is possible to adjust instruction to the unique needs of individuals with either of the systems already discussed, but there is still another approach that makes personal interest the centerpiece of its methodology. A more descriptive name for this procedure would be a "free-choice" reading approach. A large body of literature can be found under the headings "individualized instruction" or "personal interest reading."

As the name implies, the personal interest approach teaches reading by permitting each pupil to work almost exclusively in books, magazines, or other material that the child selects. Conferences between

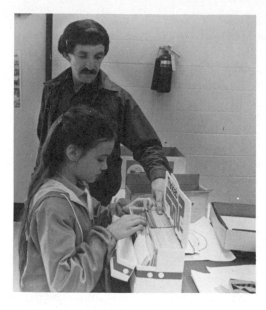

Teacher-pupil conferences can occur in many settings and often provide useful information concerning a child's progress.

A Suggested Format for Reading Conferences

(15-minute session)

1. *Greet the child and engage him or her in a brief conversation about a matter of personal interest, for example: How are you getting along in Boy Scouts or Girl Scouts? (30–60 seconds)**

2. *Ask the child what has been read since the last conference and what is currently being read. Invite a brief account of the material read. (60–120 seconds)*

3. *Have the child read a passage orally from the book he or she is presently reading. On occasion you select the passage; normally the child should anticipate that you will ask for a passage to be read and should be prepared to do so. Note reading fluency and the difficulty level of what the child is reading. Offer positive feedback and encouragement. (120 seconds)*

4. *Check a skill you reviewed or introduced at the preceding conference, and correct the assignment given (see Step 6). Praise the child for accomplishments. (120 seconds)*

5. *Review a skill or introduce a new one. (180 seconds)*

6. *Give a follow-up assignment to be checked at the next conference. (60 seconds)*

7. *Help the child set goals for what will be accomplished by the next conference (tell him or her when the conference will be, how much will be read, and what skills will be practiced). (60 seconds)*

8. *If a new book will be needed soon, make several suggestions, and describe one briefly. (60 seconds)*

9. *Compliment the child on progress made, then dismiss him or her.*

10. *Complete your record of what was accomplished during the conference before turning to the next child. (60 seconds)*

* Time estimates are approximate. Each conference is adjusted as necessary. Some steps may be skipped on occasion to make more time for other steps.

the teacher and the child are held regularly to check progress and to identify needs. Grouping is not the primary mode of instruction although occasionally interest groups are formed. Most skill instruction is provided during the conference or in small groups that meet for a short period of time after the children request help. Students may discuss their books as a means of sharing their experiences with classmates. Various publishers, such as Random House and Scholastic, produce packages of materials that encourage this approach.

In this approach, students select any book they care to read from

Sample Conference Record

Paul L.
_____
Child's Name

Date	Summary
9/27	Now reading _Paul Bunyan_ (p. 72). Finished _Homer Price_ on 9/21. Read incident on Babe the Blue Ox to me. Miscued on condition, action, puncture. Note: watch Paul on word endings. Paul will find 5 words for next time that end in common suffixes. Will finish this book by Wednesday. Suggested book on _Pecos Bill_.
10/8	Reading _Football Heroes_ (p. 15). Finished _Paul Bunyan_ on 9/30. Continues to have problems with word endings (e.g., vacation, seeking). Found 5 words assigned. Will make 5 word cards on those 5 plus 5 new words from _Football Heroes_. Check him on these in next conference.
	Gave Paul worksheet on rhyming — nonrhyming words. Suggested book on _Babe Ruth_. Didn't buy the idea. Will pick his own book.

the extensive collection in the reading corner, from the school library, the visiting bookmobile, the city library, or their own personal libraries. The books may be paperbacks that have been purchased by the children through a book club (see Appendix A for a list of children's book clubs and addresses).

Each morning during the scheduled reading period children read independently at their desks or in a comfortable spot that has been created around the room (for example, sitting on a pillow, lying on a rug, or sitting in an overstuffed chair in one corner of the room). The teacher meets with one child at a time and gains an idea of what the child is reading, what problems are being encountered, and how he or she feels about reading. Conferences may include a brief instructional activity. The teacher may also identify a need that is addressed later in a group that includes other children having a similar need. Conferences vary in length, but generally last fifteen minutes. A conference is scheduled with each child at least once every other week and more often if requested by either the teacher or the child.

Conferences

1. Conduct a reading conference with a child (or a colleague if you lack access to a child). Follow the format recommended on page 402, or adapt the steps as appropriate to your situation.
2. Develop a record-keeping system that will enable you to keep track of the individual progress of children as noted in a conference setting.

Rationale of the Personal Interest Approach

1. "The child's interests can be used to motivate reading."

    The idea behind the personal interest approach is that, given the opportunity to pursue their own interests, children will be eager and willing to read. This view is in contrast to some systems, which impose stories on the child. Self-selection of reading materials also provides the child with an opportunity to build a positive self-image. Interests and desires become an important part of the reading program. The close association between pleasant personal experiences and reading activities then acts as a powerful factor in developing lifelong readers.

2. "Self-selection is characteristic of real-life reading activities."

    A reading program based on self-selection closely matches the reading activities of a nonschool setting. Outside of school, adults as well as children usually read only what they choose for recreation or information. School reading programs emphasizing assigned reading, follow-up discussions, and related skill activities do not resemble the reading demands of adult life.

3. "Teacher and child meet on a personal basis."

The regular interaction that takes place between the teacher and learner facilitates instruction that meets the unique needs of each child and guarantees the child an undivided segment of the teacher's attention. As the teacher comes to understand the personality of each child, through such personal contacts the child grows both emotionally and educationally.

4. "Opportunities occur to adjust to individual needs."

The teacher assumes a great deal of responsibility for organizing the instructional program. The flexibility and freedom of such an arrangement enable the teacher to make any adjustments needed to individualize instruction. A premium is placed on being able to diagnose the needs of each student, and the opportunity to differentiate instruction is clearly available. Only the teacher's ability and the resources available to him or her limit the effectiveness of the instructional program.

Limitations of the Personal Interest Approach

1. "Many demands are placed on the classroom teacher."

Substantial demands are made on the teacher's time and energy. This system requires extensive planning, careful diagnosis and record-keeping, efficient organization, and a thorough understanding of the reading process. Unfortunately, not all teachers can measure up to these tasks, and others are not willing to try. Those who want to make the system work must be prepared to put forth extra effort. To illustrate, few commercially prepared materials are ideally suited to the individualized approach. Those that are useful are usually not packaged and organized into a comprehensive program. The teacher must create a coherent plan by conceptualizing a skills program and locating instructional materials to support that program.

2. "Knowledge of children's literature is needed by the teacher."

The very nature of the personal interest approach makes it important that the teacher be familiar with a wide variety of children's books and authors. This knowledge is necessary to carry on effective conferences and to help children locate appropriate reading materials. Even though self-selection of materials by the child is an important principle of this system, the teacher must guide and upgrade the child's reading tastes and interests.

3. "A large number and variety of books are required."

Some schools simply do not have sufficient numbers and varieties of books to implement a personal selection system.

In order to provide each child with an adequate opportunity to select reading materials on topics he or she enjoys and at a reading level that the child can handle over a period of weeks and months, the school must have a minimum of twenty books per child. In addition, a knowledgeable librarian who is available to students and teachers on a regular basis is important to the success of the system. Obviously, one important limitation of this approach is the amount of resources necessary for its operation. Many schools do not meet these requirements and should be cautious about attempting to teach reading with this system if the needed personnel and materials are not available.

Combining Systems for Effective Instruction

We have presented three distinct approaches to the teaching of reading, each having unique strengths and weaknesses. Because no single system has been found superior for all children, it is important to be pragmatic.

We may appear to be suggesting that every classroom teacher must use all three systems to meet the needs of all students, and with some qualifications we are doing just that. *The classroom teacher must initially select one system that he or she endorses and understands. As experience and expertness permit, the teacher should supplement the chosen system with elements borrowed from other systems.*

Typically, the basal reader approach is the system a teacher will employ as the basis for instruction. Because of its structure and well-organized teaching activities, this is a useful procedure. At first many new teachers will no doubt closely follow the teacher's manual. The sequence of skills and the variety of prepared materials that it offers are helpful to the beginning teacher. The background and character of students then dictate certain adjustments. The authors of materials cannot anticipate the tremendous variety of teachers and students who will use their products. Consequently, they usually admit that adjustment will be necessary.

The teacher can incorporate from each approach as it is appropriate. All children require the opportunity to read in a setting that corresponds to real life. Occasional self-selection of materials and individual pupil-teacher conferences merit special use. At the same time, computer materials can be an invaluable aid to students as we will point out later in this chapter. The teacher can draw on such a collection as the need occurs.

Materials That Assist in Implementing a System

A teacher can guard against relying too heavily on instructional materials by recognizing that no book, kit, game, or chart can possibly meet the needs of all students. The skilled professional selects materials to suit a particular need at a particular time.

Increase in Available Materials

Keeping abreast of new materials is no easy task. During the past twenty years, the variety and sheer number of materials produced commercially have multiplied rapidly. To illustrate, according to Ronald W. Mitchell, an official with the International Reading Association, a total of 99 publishers of reading materials exhibited their wares in 106 booths at the Dallas convention in 1966. In 1984 the number of booths required to display materials had increased almost fivefold to 501.

Similar growth has taken place in the publication of trade books for children. According to *Publisher's Weekly*, more than 2,500 new titles have been published every year since 1965. It would be nearly impossible to be familiar with all materials available for reading instruction. All of this means that a teacher must know where to turn for information on what is new and must sharpen evaluation skills so that appropriate items can be selected.

Sources of Information About Instructional Materials

There are a number of things teachers can do to keep abreast of the availability of materials for reading instruction. One approach is to request publishers to place your name on their mailing lists to receive flyers and other promotional materials. You may discover that your school principal or reading supervisor regularly receives such advertisements already. Those individuals or the district resource center may even have specimen sets of materials furnished by publishers who are interested in gaining adoptions.

Specimen sets of instructional materials are often available in the curriculum library of colleges and universities that have teacher preparation programs. In some states where an approved list of textbooks is developed, materials repositories are sponsored by the department of public instruction so that professional educators and the public at large can review materials being considered for approval. Publishers furnish materials for these repositories because they cannot be approved for adoption unless they have been reviewed. You can check with education officials in your state to determine whether or not a repository is within reach.

Instructional materials are often displayed at conferences and meetings sponsored by professional organizations. Representatives from various publishing companies display their wares at such exhibits and willingly explain their materials and answer questions. The opportunity to browse through many exhibits looking for specific items or merely gaining a sense of what is new and different is most valuable. Descriptive literature is available from each publisher, and, on occasion, sample materials can be requested at no charge.

You can also read descriptions and critical reviews in professional journals such as *The Reading Teacher* (International Reading Association,

800 Barksdale Avenue, Newark, Delaware 19711) and *Language Arts* (National Council of Teachers of English, 1111 Kenyon Road, Urbana, Illinois 61801). These and similar publications have a regular column devoted to instructional materials. In addition, advertisements for instructional materials in these journals help you become aware of what is available.

Another source of information is EPIE (Educational Products Information Exchange, EPIE Institute, 475 Riverside Drive, New York, NY 10027), an information center that periodically reviews, analyzes, and describes materials for reading instruction. Trained reviewers at EPIE examine materials according to specific guidelines so they can inform consumers about available programs. Evaluative judgments are left to the purchaser, but useful facts and figures basic to decision making are provided in publications from EPIE.

Evaluating Instructional Materials

The question "Will I really have a choice in selecting materials, or will they be selected for me?" may have occurred to you as we have been discussing the evaluation of instructional materials. It is difficult to say exactly what role you will have in selecting materials for purchase. This varies from school to school. As a general trend, it is our perception that teachers are serving increasingly as members of textbook selection committees. Twenty years ago such decisions were often made by administrators acting alone. Today the selection process often involves parents, community representatives, and even children in addition to teachers and administrators. For that reason, you should be prepared to sit on such a committee. The checklist given in Figure 12.1 may help you systematize your evaluations.

In some schools, you as teacher may have the opportunity to order materials for your own classroom. Perhaps you may be given only a small amount of money for supplementary materials, or you may be able to make a major expenditure for the materials that will form the backbone of your program. Should you be in such a situation, it is important that you be able to act responsibly.

Those who do make decisions can be influenced by a well-conceived argument supporting the purchase of certain items. You can and should be involved in persuasion of this sort. Second, the materials provided for you can be used selectively and supplemented by free and inexpensive materials gathered or made by the teacher. With the ability to appraise what the school district furnishes, you are able to determine what the strengths and weaknesses of the district-adopted materials are and how they might best be used.

Admittedly, universal standards for selecting instructional materials are difficult to establish. The standards that are appropriate for a classroom in Brooklyn, New York, are totally different from those that fit an Indian reservation in North Dakota. Experiences vary, as do values, beliefs, and attitudes. Teachers differ even in the same school, of course, as do parents.

FIGURE 12.1 Guidelines for Evaluating Reading Materials.

Always	Usually	Seldom	Never	Priority	Assigned*

A. General Considerations

1. Are the materials consistent with the conceptualization of reading embraced by the school?
2. Is the relationship among all communication skills (speaking, listening, reading, and writing) enhanced by the materials?
3. Do all activities keep the identification of meaning at the forefront?

B. Learner Considerations

4. Are the materials well suited to the background experiences and personal interests of children who will use them?
5. Will the children who use these materials find the language natural and familiar?
6. Does the content include motivational and interest factors suitable to the age and culture of the population?
7. Do the materials recognize and provide for dialect differences?
8. Do the materials reflect child development principles?

C. Instructional Considerations

9. Are objectives to be accomplished with the materials specified?
10. Is a systematic teaching plan presented for achieving the objectives?
11. Are the instructional tasks arranged in a logical order, or organized so that the structure is evident?
12. Are record-keeping devices provided?
13. Are tools and strategies provided for evaluating student progress toward goals?
14. Are suggestions given for differentiating instruction according to individual needs of learners?
15. Is adequate attention given to building readiness at all levels of instruction?
16. Are meaning and the identification of words developed together?
17. Is the importance of using word identification techniques in combination emphasized throughout?
18. Are suggestions given for extending a topic beyond the materials into related trade and reference sources?
19. Does a bibliography for further reading accompany each story?
20. Can the teacher and learner get clear directions from the materials?

D. Content Considerations

21. Does the content actually reflect the stated philosophy and purpose or purposes of the material?
22. Is vocabulary introduced in a meaningful context and related to known concepts?
23. Does content lead to appreciation of literature and a lifelong interest in reading?
24. Are stereotyped characters avoided?
25. Are women depicted in a great variety of roles?
26. Does content depict a pluralistic society?
27. Is attention given to the affective domain?

* Depending on local conditions, certain questions will be weighted more heavily or given greater priority as determined by the evaluator.

FIGURE 12.1   (*Continued*)

Always	Usually	Seldom	Never	Priority	Assigned*	
						28. Is there a balance of story content: fiction-nonfiction, fantasy-reality, humor-serious?
						29. Are the works of well-known children's authors included?
						E. Format Considerations
						30. Are the illustrations attractive?
						31. Do the illustrations contribute to reader anticipation of meaning?
						32. Is the print clear and legible?
						33. Is length of line and type size adjusted to the age of children who will use the materials?
						34. Are different typographical techniques used to help the reader understand the message?
						35. Are the materials durable?
						36. Is the cost commensurate with the instructional value the materials provide?

* Depending on local conditions, certain questions will be weighted more heavily or given greater priority as determined by the evaluator.

These differences mean that materials that may be ideally suited to one child or classroom are totally inappropriate in another situation. Consequently, there are no universal standards for evaluation. If materials are selected in or near the place where they will actually be used, the chances are increased that a good match can be made between learner and book (or game, chart, puzzle, or workbook).

To be sure, certain general standards can and should be applied. Materials that stereotype groups of people or fail to represent a pluralistic society have no place in any classroom.

The standards for materials selection used by Mary's teacher should evolve naturally from the determination of what goals are appropriate for Mary and her classmates. The first rule to keep in mind is this: "Evaluate materials in terms of your own instructional objectives." Before looking at materials, the teacher must determine precisely what the materials are supposed to do. An effective strategy is to describe for yourself what the children should be able to do once they have finished a course of instruction and then determine achievement.

It is not sufficient to take the word of a publisher or a publisher's representative that their materials teach a certain skill, ability, attitude, or concept. Anyone can claim that a series of work sheets enables the child to use context clues. The teacher must examine the materials to verify that fact. Another possibility is to try materials out on an experimental basis to determine whether or not they are effective.

Evaluating Materials in a Group Setting

Lest we falsely create the impression that a teacher must act alone in evaluating materials, let us point out that interaction among teachers who have children from the same background can be very beneficial. Each individual teacher must keep his or her own classroom in mind, but before any purchase of a new kit for supplementary instruction in study skills, all teachers who propose to use it should examine it. One individual may see a strength or weakness overlooked by others. The very fact that an item will be discussed may stimulate more careful examination.

These advantages explain in part why materials selection committees spring up at the district level. A group of trained individuals who know the needs of children and teachers in the district do their best to screen out inappropriate materials and select what fits local conditions. Yet all is not a net gain when a committee acts at the district or even state level. Compromise is necessary because the instructional goals must be generalized to suit a large number of classrooms. The individual teacher must still determine how a particular teaching aid can be used in the classroom.

Establishing Criteria for Evaluating Materials

We have pointed out that all teachers have the responsibility for establishing standards for materials evaluation that reflect their instructional goals. This does not mean that every teacher must reinvent selection criteria, however. Numerous sets of criteria are available, and appropriate ones can be chosen, weighted as desired according to personal preference, and even revised to fit the specific children in a classroom.

We present a set of criteria here that you can also use as a starting point. Depending on the age, the types of background and experiences, attitudes toward reading, the availability of other reading materials, and a host of other factors, you will need to add to your criteria and refine them.

Evaluating Materials

1. Using criteria given in Figure 12.1 (or any other criteria), evaluate a set of instructional materials for use in your classroom (actual or anticipated).
2. Develop your own criteria for materials evaluation.
3. Ask a teacher or administrator in a local school system to describe how materials are selected for purchase. If available, obtain a set of the selection criteria used. Compare them to your own criteria and those presented in this text.

Computer-Assisted Reading Instruction

The growth in the use of microcomputers in American schools has been phenomenal. In the 1980s schools have spent more money on microcomputers than on any other type of instructional material. Without question, microcomputers have become a force in elementary education, and their use is seen in almost all subjects. Among content areas, the microcomputer is used in reading instruction in the elementary grades more than for any other subject except mathematics (Ingersoll & Smith, 1984).

As this chapter is written, the use of the computer is peripheral to most instruction—that is, it is used as an activity or a supplement to one of the basic approaches to teaching reading. *Computer-assisted instruction* (CAI) is not yet seen as a method in itself. How long reading CAI will remain supplementary is difficult to say. It is clear, however, that CAI will occupy a more prominent role in the future than it does now. For that reason alone, teachers will need to review CAI just as they would any other instructional material.

The computer and CAI make possible a kind of individualized instruction not unlike that provided by a tutor. The child can be identified by name, a task is presented, the child responds, the answer is acknowledged and explained in context, a similar task or a new one is presented, and the computer congratulates and keeps track of the answers. Program designers refer to that kind of sequence as an *interactive environment*. The student must be involved; the computer will not proceed until the learner responds.

Many publishers of basal series offer CAI that can be used with a number of the better-known models of microcomputers. These programs provide extra drill on particular language skills, vocabulary development, story comprehension activities, and problem solving. The computer will permit endless repetition and immediate feedback and will allow the student to proceed at his or her own pace. In terms of the language emphasis approach, the word-processing capability of the computer is obviously helpful because it allows students to type stories and revise them easily without the need for retyping the entire story when changes are made.

Courseware

One of the major concerns for the use of computers in the schools has been the need for good-quality *software* (or, in educational circles, *courseware*)—the programs and instructions that make the machine function in the first place. The haste with which microcomputers were thrust on the schools, however, raises concerns about the forethought given to their application within the curriculum. Criticism of software designed for reading and language-arts instruction usually focuses on the fact that much of it is limited to rather simple drill-and-practice exercises, leading some critics to say that the microcomputer is little more than an expensive page turner, providing "electronic flash cards" and duplicating much of the material formerly found in workbooks.

Although this criticism would be justified if existing courseware stopped there, it does not. A wide variety of microcomputer programs has been developed and will continue to be brought into the educational marketplace. Some of the software is poor, and some is quite good, but the variety and quality are evolving naturally as educators and programmers work together on curriculum software. We must all remember, of course, that frequent repetition and drill are often appropriate, and the availability of a computer to perform these chores means that the teacher can attend to other matters.

Rationale of Computer-assisted Reading Instruction

1. "Objectives are stated as observable behaviors."

    Based on the work of behavioral psychologists, programmed instruction teaches by taking the student through a series of carefully planned steps, often in the form of statements or questions, culminating in some "predesignated response." For example, beginning readers can be led through a step-by-step procedure into recognizing a family of words that rhyme with *cat.* The children would demonstrate their newly acquired skill or knowledge by correctly picking from a list of ten words the five that have the same spelling pattern as *cat.*

2. "The learner makes a response at each step."

    Computerized instruction often requires a "series of responses" on the part of the learner. The steps in a program are arranged so that correct responses are practically certain. Clues are often provided to help the learner. For example, only the last two letters may be missing from the correct response to a question or statement in the program. As the program proceeds, the clues become fewer, and the learner must provide more of the correct word. Eventually, the learner supplies an entire word without the benefit of prompts.

    This process of gradual clue withdrawal is referred to as "successive approximation," and it is by a series of such approximations that the learner's behavior is "shaped."

3. "The learner receives immediate feedback and reinforcement."

    Most programmed instruction provides "immediate feedback" to learners concerning the correctness of their responses. After the learner supplies a response, the program provides the correct answer for comparison. Because each step is carefully designed to avoid retaining incorrect responses, the learner is afforded "immediate" reinforcement. Proceeding a small step at a time, learners can know their progress as it happens, and they are rewarded for each correct response. These features make learning efficient. An example of the interaction and feedback in CAI is presented in Figure 12.2.

FIGURE 12.2   Computer Tutorial Program for Reading.

Hello. I am Patient Tutor.
What is your name?   _____H-E-L-E-N_____
                                    (Type name)
                              <Press RETURN>

Helen, we are going to review some words that will help you in reading about the desert.
Have you ever seen a desert?   (yes/no) _____N-O_____
                              <Press RETURN>

Many people have not seen a desert, Helen. But you probably know some things that are found in a desert. Type some things that you might find in a desert.
1.
2.
3.
                    <Press RETURN when you are finished.>

Thank you, Helen. There are many things to see in a desert besides sand, aren't there?
I will show you a picture of something you might see in a desert. I will also give you some words. Type the one that you think matches the picture.

     horse   lizard   raccoon   mazooza
                    _____R-A-C-C-O-O-N_____
                    <Press RETURN>

No, Helen, a raccoon is a furry animal. This one has no hair, and it catches bugs with its tongue. Try again.

     horse   lizard   raccoon   mazooza
                    _____L-I-Z-A-R-D_____
                    <Press RETURN>

That's right, Helen. Lizards often live in the desert. A lizard catches bugs with its tongue.

                    <Press RETURN to continue.>

4. "The learner works at his or her own pace."

Self-pacing is another important aspect of CAI instruction. The able learner is not held back by slower classmates, and very slow youngsters can take whatever time they need with each step, or "frame." Slow learners make as many correct responses as the bright student and suffer fewer failures because they have more personal response time than they would in a typical classroom setting.

5. "Programs focus on specific skills."

Programs are often written to develop specific skills and concepts. Because children work independently, the teacher can easily match each learner with a program that meets his or her individual needs. A youngster who experiences difficulty with short vowel sounds, for example, can be assigned to remedial work in a program suited specifically to this need. Children who are absent and might not otherwise be able to make up important lessons are able to do so using CAI. A child simply begins where he or she left off before the absence.

6. "Skills are sequenced carefully."

Perhaps most important, the computer presents skills and concepts in a carefully organized, logically sequenced series of steps. Instructional goals are established ahead of time, and each step contributes to the eventual achievement of the objectives. Those responsible for developing programs are alert to possible confusion or errors and anticipate them, and systematic research is conducted to guarantee that a program leads to the desired behavior.

Limitations of Computer-assisted Instruction

1. "Computerized learning can become monotonous."

Such pains are taken to eliminate the possibility that the student will make an incorrect response that little challenge or interest may remain for the learner. Once the novelty of this approach has worn off, students may find it monotonous.

2. "All students do the same work."

The step-by-step sequence of many CAI materials tends to be extremely slow for some learners. The more able learner, in particular, may be bored by the repetition of what seems obvious. In a few programs an adjustment in sequence, often called "branching," permits those who need less background to skip ahead and work at a faster rate. When branching is not provided, however, every student, fast or slow, goes through exactly the same steps. One of the selection criteria for CAI, therefore, should demand an escape or a leapfrogging option for the learner.

3. "The teacher is less involved in instruction."

    The interaction between teacher and child is not completely eliminated by the computer. Indeed, freed from constant group work and paper correcting, the teacher may have more time for such interaction in a classroom using programmed materials. However, the impersonality of the instruction is an obvious limitation of this approach. Opportunities for discussion and exchange of ideas are decidedly reduced. The teacher is less responsible for instruction and, therefore, may know less about the needs of individual children.

4. "Emphasis is placed on one correct answer."

    At a time when students need freedom of thought and creativity in developing diverse thinking, CAI may not contribute much to our educational goals. Certainly, interpretive and creative reading are worthy components of an instructional program. Interpretation and creativity are usually shared in a group experience.

5. "Programs handicap poor readers."

    Ironically, in most CAI approaches to the teaching of reading, children must be able to read in order to respond. The child who has difficulty in reading is obviously at a disadvantage in such a program.

Evaluation of CAI

In evaluating CAI for reading, a teacher should ask two important questions beyond those asked when evaluating other instructional materials:

1. *Can the same results be obtained from books or workbooks at lower cost?*
2. *Does the CAI program take advantage of the capabilities of the computer? Those capabilities include self-pacing, interaction, tutorial functions, graphics/simulation, automatic record keeping, and diagnostic reporting.*

    Just as the basal reader is a tool for instruction, library books are tools, kits and games are tools, so is the computer a tool in the hands of the teacher. The teacher, then, must decide how CAI is to be used. It could be used, for example, as a reward (play a game when you are finished), as a pleasant means for introducing the computer to children, as a means for practicing skills, as a means for exploring comprehension of selections contained in the basal, as a means of developing vocabulary, as a means of writing about selections read.

    It should be clear from this list that there are computer programs for all sorts of classroom-related reading activities. To appreciate more fully how the computer can serve learning, you may find it helpful to recall that learner involvement and immediate feedback to the learner are powerful aids to effective learning. The computer handles with ease those two aspects of the learning environment. In the frames shown in Fig. 12.2 (p. 414), one can see a simple example of how the computer gets the learner involved and the type of feedback that is typical of a simple routine like this one.

That simple example represents CAI at a rudimentary level. The purpose of that particular exercise is to teach vocabulary for a specific reading selection. (The same format could be used to review vocabulary.) But the intent of showing it here is to demonstrate several simple yet powerful things that the computer can do to aid instruction. It requires the student to act, to make regular decisions. It not only will count right and wrong answers but gives hints as a live tutor might. And, like a tutor, the program calls the student by name—a quick way of personalizing, of holding the student's attention. Everyone, after all, likes to see his or her name on the screen.

CAI Review

Using criteria that you develop in class from your reading, review a CAI reading program. Share the results of your evaluation with your class members.

Higher-level CAI

Most teachers understand the use of the computer for traditional workbook or testing activities but probably are not as familiar with its capabilities to promote more advanced skills, for example, projective thinking while reading. Teachers are likewise justifiably concerned about the amount of time individuals can spend on the computer. Don't advanced skills require time to think and to construct, time better spent with a book and with other children in a discussion group?

Answering that question requires a reminder of our earlier discussion about classroom tools for instruction. Just as a book or a kit is not a method but merely an instrument for delivering instruction, so, too, is a computer program. Just as one selects a book for purposeful instruction, so one selects a computer program. One obvious purpose for using a computer is to motivate students. For certain reluctant readers, books conjure up failure and boredom; computers, excitement. The arcade games have given them allure. Teachers may use computers just to keep students on task.

We have already suggested the value of a tutorial monitoring function in CAI. Many learners benefit from the sense of a patient tutor. But as valuable as that learner-tutor interaction may seem on the surface, its greatest strength may lie in its potential for giving each student a sense of the process of reading and thinking. The built-in monitoring of the learner's responses prompts the learner to think about what is happening. Much of the skill development in reading instruction, for instance, is aimed at arriving at a generalization or a principle for effective reading.

In normal classroom instruction, it is difficult to concentrate on one individual as he or she works with a series of examples and tries to formulate a generalization about them. A computer program, however, can follow such a process with each individual and can allow that individual to go back and review the examples, discussing their similarities. At an appropriate point in the sequence, the computer can ask learners to construct their own generalization about what they see or think. While poking into the consciousness of the learner ("No, Helen, a raccoon is a furry animal. This one has no hair."), the computer can also record successes and failures, offering a diagnosis and a recommendation for continued learning. If the teacher wants a report about the learner's activities, the computer can record and report them to the teacher in an executive file, one available only to the teacher through a password. For the majority of the children, however, it is sufficient that the computer reminds them and gives them a report. The interaction with "Patient Tutor" and the summary report are often sufficient to motivate the student to try again.

Time on the Computer

Time available for students on a computer certainly influences the type of CAI that schools will purchase. Though computers will increase dramatically in schools in the 1980s, the average time per day was only five minutes per pupil in 1984–1985 (Ingersoll & Smith, 1984). Those numbers must be expanded by ten times before computers can be viewed as significant learning tools for the average in-school youngster. Those statistics, however, should not deter teachers from using computers, not even for using them for higher-level tasks. Statistics speak in averages. Many schools have enough computers to allow each student to use them one hour a day. Other schools, by contrast, may have no computers at all.

There are many fine programs that help students see reading and writing as constructive acts. *Microzine* (Scholastic Press), a magazine on a disk, features stories in which the reader makes choices at certain points in the story. Depending on the choices made, the reader follows a story line different from those associated with other choices. *Kidwriter* (Spinnaker Software) lets children construct a scene from a set of fixed images, and then they can type a brief statement or story about the picture they have created. This type of program stands alone (is not tied to a book or particular curriculum objective) and can be used for a variety of purposes as determined by the teacher or perhaps by the child.

CAI that accompanies basal readers offers options for relating reading and writing as constructive acts. One option has the students read a selection in the textbook under the usual conditions for teaching. At a prearranged page, the students stop reading and go to the computer. The program prompts them to type a new ending for the story they have been reading. Once they have written their new ending for the story, the computer raises such questions as these:

This kind of reflective process could be accomplished with every
student on a computer terminal—an extremely difficult, if not impossible, task for a teacher to accomplish face-to-face. The computer has
time; the teacher does not. This type of questioning, where the learner
is asked to be introspective about what has been done, and the revision
that it suggests could prepare students before they come together for
a sharing and discussion of the story and their endings. Without doubt,
live minds must meet to explore the full range of intellectual and
emotional responses that they can make to passages they have read.
That kind of interplay seems essential for exciting intellectual growth.
But with early computer prompting as just described, each student
comes to the live discussion with certain basic questions already attended to.

Summary

The search for one reading method that is best for all children seems
inappropriate. A more realistic approach is to recognize that different
learners benefit from different instructional system.

Three distinct systems of reading instruction were reviewed:

The basal reader approach.
The language emphasis approach.
The personal interest approach.

The rationale and limitations of each system were also discussed.

The basal reader approach is the most highly structured of the
three systems. Constraints are placed on the vocabulary, sentence
length, sentence complexity, and content in this system. The learner
uses a textbook written at a specified level of difficulty and a workbook
containing practice exercises. The teacher is provided with a guide
that contains teaching suggestions and activities. The careful control
of all aspects of the system is designed to make learning tasks manageable for the child. The complexity of the tasks gradually increases as
the learner grows in the ability to handle them. A major criticism of
this approach is that such a high degree of control is unnecessary for
today's sophisticated child.

The language emphasis approach builds the reading program
around the child's own stories and language. The interrelatedness of

the language arts is emphasized. Early reading activities are based on stories created by the child. Books are used to stimulate and create activities that grow into language-arts experiences. The major limitation of this system is its lack of structure in terms of skill development and sequence. In this approach, the teacher must assume a large measure of responsibility for providing structure.

The personal interest approach is essentially a reading program based on self-selection of library books. Each child selects his or her own reading material, reads independently, and regularly meets with the teacher for discussion and skill activities. Personal interests and genuine ego involvement make motivation appear extremely high with this plan. For schools able to supply the enormous amount of material necessary to implement it, this system offers definite advantages. The major limitation of this approach lies in the amount of responsibility placed on the classroom teacher for planning and executing the activities. In particular, the teacher must be capable of assessing and guiding a complete reading program for a whole class of children simultaneously.

Realistically, most teachers are likely to use the highly structured basal reader approach. Ideally, the best of each system is combined so that a teacher draws on the strengths of all systems.

The large quantity of material available today, both basic and supplementary, makes selection difficult. Guidelines for evaluating reading materials are listed under criteria for the following:

General considerations.
Learner considerations.
Instructional considerations.
Content considerations.
Format considerations.

All materials must first be judged on whether they can achieve the teacher's instructional objectives—that is, to teach at appropriate levels, to meet specific skills needs, and to provide continuing motivation for the child.

Terms for Self-Study

instructional systems
language emphasis approach
programmed approach
personal interest approach
sound-symbol emphasis
supplementary materials
controlled vocabulary

Discussion Questions

1. Why is it desirable for a teacher to adapt and deviate from the structure provided by the controlled vocabulary approach? How does teaching experience enter into making this adjustment?

2. In what sense is the language experience approach more child-centered than any of the other instructional systems?
3. On taking a new assignment in a school, how does a teacher get a realistic view of what materials are available for use?
4. In a practical way, how would a teacher match the characteristics of children with the characteristics of available books?

Recommended Readings

Auckerman, Robert C. (1981). *The basal reader approach to reading.* New York: Wiley.
  The author examines a number of well-known basal readers and their positive roles in carrying forward a consistent reading program.
DeStefano, Johanna S. (1978). *Language, the learner & the school.* New York: Wiley.
  DeStefano discusses the function of language in elementary instruction and offers specific classroom practices for promoting language development.
Geoffrion, Leo D., & Geoffrion, Olga P. (1983). *Computers and reading instruction.* Reading, MA: Addison-Wesley.
  This book gives extensive information on the use of computers in all areas of reading instruction (readiness, word identification, comprehension, remediation, and so on). It also gives information on evaluating and locating software.
Hall, MaryAnne (1981). *Teaching reading as a language experience* (3rd ed.). Columbus, OH: Charles E. Merrill.
  Hall presents a thorough description of the language experience approach and provides practical suggestions on how it can be used to develop vocabulary, comprehension, and word analysis. This text also provides a checklist useful for implementing a language experience approach.
Hoskisson, Kenneth, & Krohn, Bernadette (1974, September). Reading by immersion: Assisted reading. *Elementary English, 51,* 832–836.
  This article reports on a study in which basal instruction was supplemented by having the teacher read to the children and by having children read to each other. It suggests ways in which classroom teachers can use these strategies for positive results.
Mason, George E., Blanchard, Jay S., & Daniel, Danny B. (1983). *Computer applications in reading* (2nd ed.). Newark, DE: International Reading Association.
  This text provides brief discussions and extensive annotated references on applications of computers in the reading programs of various schools, sources of services, recommended uses of computers in reading instruction, and software.
Tierney, Robert J., Readence, John E., & Dishner, Ernest K. (1980). *Reading strategies and practices: Guide for improving instruction.* Boston: Allyn and Bacon.
  The authors present a variety of teaching techniques, strategies, and procedures used for reading instruction, including the cloze procedure, DRA, SQ3R, sustained silent reading, Fernald Technique, and Gillingham-Stillman Method.
Van Allen, Roach, & Allen, Claryce (1982). *Language experience activities* (2nd ed.). Boston: Houghton Mifflin.
  This text suggests ways to expand the language experience approach by developing learning centers for writing, language study, art, cooking, drama, and listening.

13

Organizing for Instruction

Recently while visiting a nearby elementary school, we overheard a conversation between a principal and an irate parent. The parent was registering a rather heated complaint about the fact that her second-grade son was being tutored in reading by a fifth-grade boy from another classroom.

The mother had two concerns, she said. "First of all, that fifth-grader is not a qualified teacher. I want my son to be taught by someone who knows what he's doing."

The principal jotted this concern on a notepad and prompted the parent, "What is your other concern, Mrs. Holloway?"

"My second concern is that Kevin doesn't need a tutor or special help in reading—at least no one has told me that he's having trouble—and I'm sure the other children will think he's a remedial case," she challenged.

"I see," the principal responded. "I think an explanation of how our youth-tutoring-youth program works would help you understand what is happening, Mrs. Holloway. We sent home a newsletter last month describing this new approach. Did you have a chance to read it?"

As the principal began an explanation, we left to keep an appointment at another school, but on our way out of the building, we noticed several pairs of children in various locations who also seemed to be a part of the tutoring program the principal was describing to Mrs. Holloway. As we walked down the corridor, we also noticed teachers working with small groups of children in several classrooms and one teacher conferencing with children individually in another classroom. It seemed clear to us that teachers in this school were organizing their classrooms for instruction by using a variety of approaches. What a sharp contrast, we found ourselves thinking, between this school and one we had visited recently, where the standard practice seemed to be whole-class instruction with everyone being on the same page of the same book for reading instruction. Happily, very few teachers settle for whole-class instruction but instead employ a number of means to meet the needs of each learner.

Few topics cause more anxiety among beginning teachers at the outset than the logistics of organizing books, desks, tables, children, and time for reading instruction. This chapter offers suggestions for resolving organizational concerns and will consider such questions as these:

- *How can grouping be used to meet the individual needs of learners?*
- *What kinds of groups can be used in a classroom?*
- *How can a teacher organize a schedule to meet with each group daily?*
- *What are the dangers of grouping for reading instruction?*
- *How can children not working with the teacher be occupied profitably?*
- *What are some good activities for children to pursue independently?*
- *How can a youth-tutoring-youth program be established?*
- *What is a management system, and how can one be created?*

Every teacher, experienced or not, must deal with the task of organizing children and materials for effective instruction. Easy solutions to problems of organization may satisfy the teacher who is not much concerned about differentiating instruction or meeting individual needs. For example, all children in a class can be given the same reading material, directed to stay on the same page all the rest of the children are reading, and do the same assignments. Organization becomes simple and routine with this approach, but differences among children are ignored. The more alert teacher will consider a variety of organizational schemes that permit children with varied needs, interests, and achievement levels to be better served.

This chapter addresses the issue of how reading instruction can be organized to facilitate individualization. Suggestions will be provided as to how independent activities can be planned and managed in a classroom of thirty or more children. Much of the discussion will relate to the effective use of groups, for outstanding teachers usually combine grouping and individual activities.

Grouping as a Means of Individualization

The advantages of independent work as a means of individualizing instruction are fairly obvious. Each child can be assigned a task that is especially designed for that child's needs. Not so obvious is the usefulness of grouping as a way of individualizing instruction. Yet for most teachers the effective use of groups will be their most important tool in differentiating instruction. Therefore, let us first consider the teacher's more common response to individual needs—grouping. Next, various independent reading activities will be discussed.

Groups Are Comprised of Individuals with
Varied Needs

In recent years the movement toward personalizing instruction in schools has sometimes given grouping a negative connotation. Teachers faced with the impracticality of managing a totally separate and different curriculum for every child have been placed in the uncomfortable position of using groups out of necessity but often feeling guilty about doing so. In one sense this guilt has some justification. Groups of children are comprised of individuals who are more different than alike. Yet this need not be a problem if groups are used simply as a way of scheduling time to ensure that the teacher and children will meet regularly in something other than a mass setting. The teacher's attitude is crucial. If children in a group are regarded as one in terms of instructional needs, grouped instruction can be a trap. If, however, the teacher remembers that every child in the group is an individual with unique background and interests, grouping can facilitate differentiation of instruction.

Clearly, the alternatives to grouped instruction are not altogether desirable as a single answer to organizational problems. Whole-class instruction obviously lumps children together in a gross manner totally ignoring individual differences. Yet independent instruction by itself neglects the value of interaction among learners and neglects the fact that the development of communication skills, including reading, involves the sharing of ideas.

It seems that the issue is not whether grouping as such is valuable and useful, but rather when and how groups should be employed. The next section will address these important matters.

Grouping Practices

One of the tasks facing a teacher is grouping children so that individual needs can be met in the most effective way. Let's look at three ways this can be done:

1. Achievement grouping.
2. Grouping by instructional need.
3. Interest grouping.

Each method has an important function in an effective reading program.

Georgia Talbot is an experienced teacher of nine- and ten-year-olds who uses all three types of groups at various times. Early in the school year Georgia collects information about her students' reading performances from a combination of sources. Recognizing that not all the children can successfully read the same level of text for basic instruction, she decides to create *achievement groups.* These groups are comprised of children who read at nearly the same level even though their skill needs are varied and different. In Georgia's classroom the children fall into roughly four groups:

1. Those able to handle an advanced book (Level 20 of the basal series she uses).
2. Those reading at their grade placement (Level 14).
3. Those who are unable to read "at grade level" (Level 8).
4. The slowest learners who range from nonreaders to those who read at a low beginning level (Levels 1–5).

Georgia recognizes that one important condition for effective reading instruction is matching learners with reading materials that are neither too difficult, thereby frustrating them, nor too easy, therefore unchallenging. Though actual skill instruction must be varied within each of the groups to provide for individual rates of growth on specific skills, the *achievement groups* enable Georgia to schedule time with groups of manageable size and to provide opportunities for practice reading in materials that are suited to each child's level of reading.

Although Georgia's achievement groups are flexible, so that children can move from one group to another as this becomes appropriate, they remain fairly stable throughout the school year. The main reason for the stability of achievement groups is that children reading at roughly the same level will normally advance together in reading and in sharing stories within the same books provided their individual needs are being met through differentiated skill assignments. If the teacher cares to individualize within groups to the greatest possible extent, the children in these groups need not share anything more than common reading experiences. Often children in an achievement group will profit from common skill instruction of a developmental or introductory nature, however.

When a child in any group does not advance at a rate similar to his or her fellow group members, reassignment to another group for basic instruction is called for. The key factor in making such shifts is determining that the difficulty level of the reading material being used with another group is more appropriate for the child than is the material being read in the child's present group. Skill needs cannot be satisfied by movement from achievement group to achievement group, for individuals within every group have unique skill needs.

Alert teachers such as Georgia make extensive use of another grouping pattern to avoid the shortcomings of achievement groups in meeting skill deficiencies, *instructional need groups*. Georgia frequently pulls children from various achievement groups to work on a specific skill. In this way, children with similar *instructional needs* form a short-lived group that may meet for only one session or at most for several sessions. Once the need has been satisfied, the skill group is disbanded. For example, efficient use of an index might constitute the focus of a specially formed skill group. Georgia would gather together children reading at Levels 20, 14, 8, and 1 to 5 who have misconceptions about the purpose and format of an index. Instruction is provided; children practice the skill until it is mastered; and then the group members return to their usual activities. Occasionally, the entire class might be regarded as a need group when a skill is being reviewed or a general misunderstanding corrected. More often, skill groups will be rather small, perhaps having fewer than five members.

Georgia also places children into groups according to their *interests*. Regardless of the reading level, children enjoy and can profit from meeting with others who like to read mysteries, sports stories, or jokebooks, for example. Whether these are related to hobbies, themes growing out of social studies and science units, possible careers, or passing fads, interest groups stimulate reading, deepen and broaden subject areas, and motivate all readers. Group projects around common concerns can give all children a chance to participate and make a unique contribution to the class based on personal experiences and individual reading tastes. Achievement levels can be forgotten in interest groups, and everyone in the group has a chance to succeed.

Because interests come and go—especially among children—Georgia reforms the interest groups often. In October the children form groups on sports heroes, current events, horse stories, humor, and stories of fantasy. By mid-November only one group, the one on sports heroes, continues. The horse story group broadens its base to animal stories, thus attracting new members from various other groups. A new group forms around the theme of science fiction, humor is replaced by historical fiction, and fantasy gives way to myths and legends. Seldom do groups contain the same members from beginning to end of the year although membership becomes firm while displays and reports are being prepared for sharing with the whole class.

The key to Georgia's use of groups is that all categories are employed at the same time. Depending on the day and the purposes that she hopes to pursue, the achievement, instructional need, and interest groups might all operate at the same time. Because of the ongoing nature of a developmental reading program, achievement groups often form the backbone of the organizational scheme, especially for beginning teachers. However, this need not be the case. The point to keep in mind is that each type of grouping between students in the class makes a unique contribution to the reading program. No single grouping pattern is sufficient for effectively adjusting the reading program to individual needs.

Regardless of the basis for the various formations, good grouping has several important characteristics. First, groups must be *flexible*. Membership in any group should be based on the child's potential for benefiting from instruction. If membership in another group is more likely to tap a child's potential, immediate action should be taken to move the child to that other group. Second, groups—particularly short-term groups—must have *specific objectives*. This means that a specific task or set of tasks must be clearly outlined and activities oriented to the accomplishment of the task. Related to task orientation is a third aspect of good grouping—*termination* of groups that have achieved their purposes. Even long-term groups should be subjected to this criterion. Groups must not be continued beyond the limits of their usefulness. Fourth, groups should be kept *small in size* whenever possible in order to maximize teacher interaction with each pupil. It is not possible or practical to define what is meant by small in this case. For some purposes, four children comprise a large group; for other purposes, ten children can be called a small group. Numbers are not the issue; the point is that groups should be small enough to maximize the opportunity for individualizing instruction.

A Plan for Meeting with Groups

Educational textbooks are sometimes criticized, as are methods courses, for an apparent failure to be specific. Prospective teachers badly want someone to describe exactly how to—in this case—group for instruction. The standard response to this request is that a recipe cannot be provided because different situations require vastly different solutions. Actually, there is much accuracy—if not much satisfaction—in this stock reply. A textbook or methods instructor cannot anticipate every plausible circumstance and provide a list of surefire remedies.

However, at the risk of being misinterpreted, we will be fairly prescriptive with regard to grouping for instruction. Only by working effectively with groups can most teachers begin to differentiate instruction and thereby take the first halting step toward individualized instruction. The plan suggested here is only a starting point. Considerable adaptation and refinement must be part of its application. Despite these limitations, it is a useful and workable approach to the task of grouping for instruction.

Before School Begins

Suppose the time of year is mid-August. The workshop before the opening of school is just getting underway. You have been assigned a third-grade class for this, your first year of teaching. You decide to group for reading instruction. How do you assign children to groups? How many groups should you have? What reading material should each child receive? In answering these questions, we will discuss the use of a controlled vocabulary system (basal reading program). Other systems could be chosen, yet many teachers are expected to use this approach or do so voluntarily.

Until the children arrive, you are limited to information that can be obtained at secondhand. If used properly, the cumulative record file, which most schools maintain on each child, is an excellent resource. You may have a chance to talk with the teacher or teachers who taught the youngsters in your class the previous year. Old workbooks and other samples of the children's work may be available. You can begin an anecdotal record file by entering the information gathered on each child in a notebook, with a full page or two reserved for each one. Included will be a summary of such data as standardized test scores, unusual attendance figures, the results of physical examinations, previous teachers' comments, and the reading level achieved the previous year.

It is best to regard all secondhand information of this sort as tentative. Surprising spurts or setbacks can occur over a summer. Personalities and attitudes can undergo enormous changes. Each child should enter your class with a clean slate insofar as academic and social behavior is concerned. Be cautious about letting the information gathered prior to the beginning of the school year bias or prejudice your appraisal. Instead, let it serve to support or point up significant information you obtain for yourself during the school year.

A September Reading Program

No reading groups need be formed for the first two or three weeks of the school year. Permanent groups should never be formed, but relatively stable achievement groups can probably be identified after several weeks of school, during which you should be actively assessing student needs. Children can be interviewed individually for personal conferences. Brief discussions and informal chats to assess interests, language facility, and attitudes toward reading and school are most valuable for getting information about students. A series of paragraphs graded in terms of reading difficulty, called an informal reading inventory (*see* Chapter 14), can be given to each child. Questionnaires and checklists can be administered.

The school and classroom libraries ought to be fully used during this period. The children should be encouraged to read independently during this time of data-gathering. Books read by each child can be noted and entered in your ever-expanding notebook of pertinent observations and information. Library books can be brought to personal conferences for discussion and for oral reading by the children.

You might take this unstructured period as a time to begin a program for sharing books. A variety of appropriate activities is presented in Chapter 4. From the standpoint of diagnosis, oral and written book reports by children provide valuable information for the alert teacher. Comprehension, the ability to summarize, skill in noting significant detail, facility with verbal communication, and poise before a group are only a sample of the kinds of behaviors that can be observed and noted through children's sharing of books.

Many school systems administer achievement tests during the fall. The results of reading and study skills sections of these tests can provide additional information that is valuable to the teacher in establishing groups.

Occasionally a structured reading activity can be conducted by the teacher. For example, a skill-development lesson might be given with appropriate follow-up exercises.

Forming Trial Groups

On the basis of all the information gathered, trial reading groups can be established during the first month of school. Assignment of children to groups should be based primarily on the child's instructional reading level. The informal reading inventory (IRI) or cloze procedure, discussed in Chapter 14, can be used to indicate what level of material is most appropriate for each child. Preferably the material to be used for instruction is incorporated into this assessment. Other information gathered during the initial three or four weeks of assessment is especially valuable in supplementing these devices. Because any measuring device has limitations, evidence from other sources can be used as well to make initial placements.

It may be a good idea for inexperienced teachers to begin with two groups. Experienced teachers who are not accustomed to managing more than one group may also want to begin slowly. We suggest these two kinds of reading groups be formed initially: (1) children able to handle the grade-level text and (2) children not able to handle the text. The main reason for this modest beginning is to protect the teacher. You may not be ready to administer the details of teaching more than two groups even though more groups may seem necessary. Increased experience and familiarity with your class will gradually enable you to add a third and perhaps a fourth group. But two groups will provide you with the experience of planning independent activities for some children while directing a lesson for the remainder of the class.

Trial groups are recommended so that obvious errors in initial placement can be quickly corrected. Early in the school year it is a simple matter to move a child into a different group for several days to give him or her a trial. As the year progresses, changes can still be made—indeed should be made—but the initial gap between groups is widened every day. Therefore, whenever possible, experimentation with group placement should be conducted early in the school year for the most part.

Each group should be given reading texts according to its level. Often the same series is used with an entire class, and two different levels of books in the series are chosen to provide material near the instructional level of each group. In some cases, two separate series are used so that each group has a different basal. This latter plan enables each group to read "fresh" stories and avoids the common dilemma of what to do with children who know a story because they once heard another group of which they were not members discuss it. The important point is that unless materials appropriate to the reading level of a group are located and used, much of the value of grouping for instruction is lost. Even at this early stage you will want to regroup children often into skill groups and interest groups in order to get a feel for this dimension of a balanced grouping program.

With only two achievement groups, a perfect match between the instructional reading level of each child and the reading difficulty of materials is not possible. It is necessary to aim for the middle of a group, choosing materials that are not too far removed from any child's reading level. The extremely high- and low-achieving youngsters are obviously missed when this approach is used. As you become more expert, you should begin additional grouping and individualization of instruction. Suggestions for expansion of the grouping program will be discussed later in this chapter.

Meeting with Two Groups

A specific plan complete with illustrations of classroom activities cannot be presented in a text unless several assumptions are made. First, a reading period of approximately sixty minutes for basic instruction will be described. Actual time allotments vary among various states and for each grade level. Again, you are reminded that considerable adaptation of this plan will be necessary before you employ it in your classroom. Second, children grouped in this manner must be capable of working independently. No magic spell can be cast to achieve this requirement. It is essential that clear and concise goals be established for children who are working independently. The goals or purposes should be readily available to the child on a chalkboard or a dittoed sheet.

When you divide your time among groups, it is necessary to consider the number of children in each group. Larger groups will require more time, for each child will need and is entitled to an equal portion of your attention. It frequently happens that more capable students are deprived of an equal share of direct teacher supervision. Such youngsters usually work well on their own. And most teachers seem to identify with the youngsters who struggle at learning to read, occasionally to the neglect of more able students. Each child requires direction, even the very capable. Often it is these youngsters who are most retarded in reading—if achievement is compared to potential. Therefore, in dividing your instructional time, you should consider the size of each reading group and make a genuine effort to work with all youngsters, not just those who obviously have problems.

To illustrate, here is a plan for meeting with two groups of comparable size. The total sixty minutes of instruction will be divided equally into two periods. You must schedule yourself with each group for about thirty minutes of activity and also plan thirty minutes of independent activity for each group. Figure 13.1 will help you visualize this assignment of time.

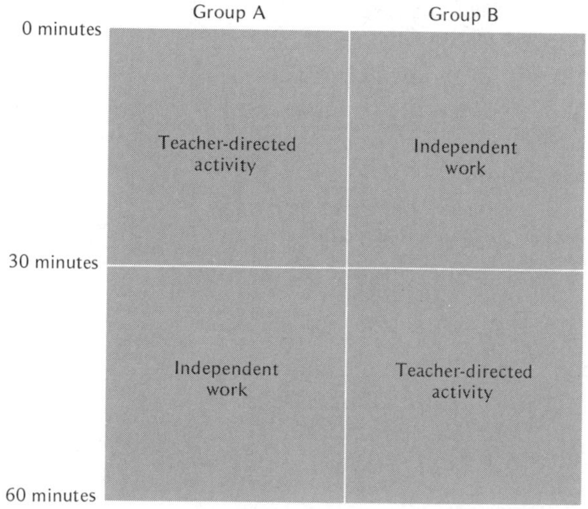

	Group A	Group B
0 minutes	Teacher-directed activity	Independent work
30 minutes	Independent work	Teacher-directed activity
60 minutes		

FIGURE 13.1 Meeting with Two Groups. This scheme represents one approach to organizing a reading period with two instructional groups.

Depending on what has transpired the previous day, various alternatives are possible. Suppose Group *A* has just completed the activities related to a story and is ready to move ahead to a new story. Group *B*, on the other hand, had completed a story the previous day but has not completed several useful skill-building activities suggested by the teacher's guide and needed by the group. In this case, the teacher might get Group *B* started on a work sheet he or she has prepared, which requires the children to find descriptive phrases in the story and rewrite them in their own words. Because this activity will require only ten or so minutes for some youngsters, but the entire thirty minutes for a few, the teacher suggests that any spare time can be spent on free reading at the reading corner with the purpose of preparing a selection for oral reading.

Under teacher direction, Group *A* is given an opportunity to preview its new story and discuss the pictures, title, and general topic of the story. Several words are introduced by the teacher in sentences on the board, and the children are asked to apply their word-attack techniques to them. When the teacher is satisfied that the group is ready to understand the story, he or she directs the children to read for specific purposes. As the children of Group *A* are reading silently, the teacher can circulate among the children in Group *B* to check on their progress. Those experiencing difficulty can be aided and a note made on the special corrective instruction required by some children. Then, returning to Group *A*, the teacher has the children discuss the story and checks their comprehension and tests their understanding of the new vocabulary. A workbook assignment can be given, and Group *A* is left to work independently.

Returning to Group *B*, the teacher discusses the descriptive phrases the children found in the story. All the children get to share some of their ideas and also compare the appropriateness of their responses to phrases that other children in the group share. The teacher can then collect the papers for further study and comment in order to individualize instruction where it is indicated. Next, the children might share their oral reading selections or immediately be regrouped for corrective instruction relative to the skill just used. Those needing no further instruction could go on to another activity—such as a reading game, a listening lesson, or a creative writing activity. To summarize, the teacher spends time by doing the following:

1. Starting Group *B* on the work sheet.
2. Previewing a new story with Group *A*.
3. Circulating among Group *B*, while Group *A* reads silently.
4. Discussing a story with Group *A* and assigning the workbook.
5. Discussing and correcting the seatwork with Group *B*.
6. Regrouping for immediate corrective instruction with Group *B*.

This very stylized plan gives a rough idea of how the teacher moves from group to group and also illustrates the planning that is necessary to carry out such a scheme. Useful and appropriate actions both for independent and teacher-directed activities must be identified ahead of time. Teacher-developed materials should be ready and designed to meet the needs of the particular youngsters in Group *B*. The suggestions in the teacher's guide should be studied and appropriate activities utilized; other suggestions are to be rejected. Special instruction is immediately provided for members of a group who show evidence of confusion; those succeeding with the tasks are not required to sit through an extra lesson.

You may want to add to this timetable a brief organizational period prior to reading and a brief summarization period afterward (*see* Figure 13.2). Only a few minutes are required to preview what activities are planned for the reading period before dividing into groups. Directions can be given then and questions answered in order to avoid confusion later. Again, it is important to have available a list of things to do and the goals or purposes so that students can refer to them easily. The brief summarization at the end of the reading period should be a positive experience for the children. With the help of your students, try to point up the progress that has been made by emphasizing the successes of each group and occasionally of an individual child. You might also discuss occasionally why some activities were less than successful and decide with the class how to avoid such problems next time.

Frequently, the amount of time allotted to a reading group should be adjusted according to the activity planned. For example, one group might be preparing a dramatization of a favorite story. In this case a twenty- or even thirty-minute period will be inadequate for making real headway. The teacher who is flexible will simply extend the length of time given to this activity. If this means spending forty or fifty minutes with one group while the second group works independently, this should be done. By all means occasionally circulate among the independent workers to check their progress or start them on a new

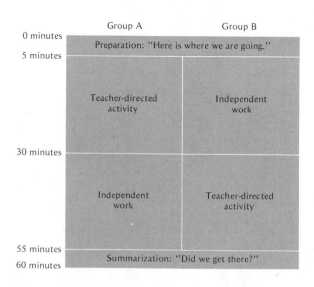

FIGURE 13.2 Adding Preparation and Summarization. A few minutes at the beginning of the reading period should be used to provide children with a sense of direction by clarifying the goals. A brief summarization near the end of the period can be helpful in evaluating progress toward stated goals.

activity. You might even allow those who finish their work early to watch the rehearsal of the other group.

Another important policy—essential to running a smooth, efficient, and flexible reading period—is to permit interruptions by members of Group *A* when you are working with Group *B* and vice versa. Some reasonable limit must be established, but a moratorium on questions from youngsters working independently is shortsighted. Given no opportunity to seek your help, a child having difficulty can soon disrupt a whole group or classroom. We suggest that children with questions be encouraged to stand quietly near you until you get a chance to help them. Then, while one youngster from the supervised group goes to the board or reads orally, you can turn to the child who is waiting and quickly provide the help that is needed. Any serious instructional problems in such circumstances must wait, but only by seeing and understanding the nature of a problem can you give the child something else to do and make a note to work with that child individually on his or her problem.

Another possibility is to encourage another member of the group to help a child with a problem. More will be said later in this chapter about how children can help each other.

Expanding to Three Groups

You will soon want to consider adding a third reading group to challenge those youngsters who can handle reading material above the grade level. Two factors should determine when a third group will be formed:

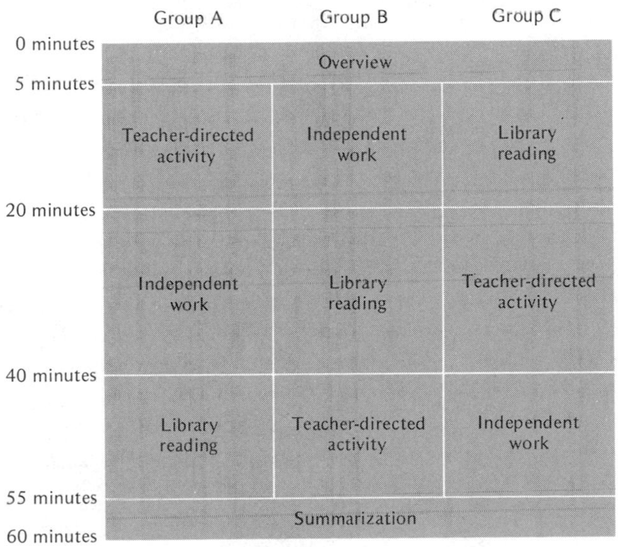

	Group A	Group B	Group C
0 minutes		Overview	
5 minutes	Teacher-directed activity	Independent work	Library reading
20 minutes	Independent work	Library reading	Teacher-directed activity
40 minutes	Library reading	Teacher-directed activity	Independent work
55 minutes		Summarization	
60 minutes			

FIGURE 13.3 Meeting with Three Groups. With experience, the teacher can expand and refine the basic scheme for meeting with instructional groups.

1. Your ability to plan for and meet with an additional group.
2. Specific evidence that certain members of the class need other kinds of attention or activity.

Because each teacher will encounter special problems when grouping for instruction, no definite timetable can be given for expanding to more than two groups. Most teachers will want to experiment with a third group on a temporary basis. Appropriate reading materials and the membership of the third group can be decided by what happens during the trial period. The teacher can also discover how much of a burden is added to the workload by forming the third group (*see* Figure 13.3).

Dangers of Overgrouping

Because of special circumstances where one or several youngsters fall considerably beyond the scope of three groups, complete separation from a group may be required. A child reading material considerably more difficult than that read by classmates will benefit very little from regular participation in group activities (occasional participation may be quite useful, however). Clearly, special provision must be made for such an exceptional youngster. At the other extreme, a child so severely retarded in reading achievement that participation in a grouped setting would be frustrating should be handled individually. It is hoped that a reading specialist can be asked to work with such a youngster. Expansion of the grouping plan to more than three groups will probably not be helpful in meeting the needs of such atypical learners.

Are more than three groups *ever* necessary? What is the largest number of groups a teacher can comfortably handle? It would be foolish to suggest that more and more groups enable the teacher to meet the needs of each child better. Three or four achievement groups should be adequate for most classrooms. Five or more achievement groups require so much preparation and scurrying about that only an exceptional teacher could operate effectively under such conditions. Teachers must be cautious about solving instructional problems with administrative juggling. Instead, a limited number of groups should be formed so that attention can be focused on individualizing instruction according to the varied needs of the children within each group. These guidelines for the number of groups do not apply to groups formed on the basis of skill need or interest. Such short-term groups can and should constantly vary in number and size.

Most teachers cannot tutor each child, nor do they want to teach only on a whole-class basis. A limited number of groups can be an aid to the teacher when arrangements are made for some sharing experiences for children. Too many groups defeat the purpose of grouping by requiring excessive time devoted to administration on the part of the teacher. The suggestion of two to four groups is intended only as a guide. The actual number of reading groups in a classroom is not significant; what matters is the individualization of instruction that occurs in the groups.

Approaches to Teaching Reading

Individualizing Instruction Within Groups

The point has been made several times in this chapter that grouping can facilitate individualized instruction. Grouping permits the classroom teacher to meet daily on a semipersonal basis with each child. Unless the individual children in a group are given differential treatment, however, grouped instruction is no better than whole-class instruction.

Differentiating Assignments

A number of techniques and instruments for gathering information on children's reading performance have already been mentioned. Included were formal reading tests, informal measures of reading, and teacher observations. Evidence for forming reading groups can be gathered with these tools. The same tools are vitally important for individualizing instruction within groups. For example, a basal reader test not only helps the teacher decide what a child's reading level is but also provides information on needed instruction. An informal reading inventory can be used to assess specific comprehension difficulties that require corrective instruction.

All information the teacher receives through observation, through test performance, or through written assignments is diagnostic data. The alert teacher translates such information into an instructional program based on the children's needs. Whenever an activity is undertaken by a reading group, the teacher can use the information required to differentiate instruction according to need. Youngsters in Group A who already possess a given skill—for example, matching sound and symbol—can be excused from a scheduled activity on that skill and can be given an appropriate alternative exercise. In many cases, all youngsters in a group may need the instruction provided by the teacher. Occasionally, only one or two youngsters will need assistance. Children can also be selected from various instructional groups and brought together for discussion and instruction. The ability to differentiate instruction as suggested here requires a knowledge of reading skills, the tools for assessing progress, a comprehensive record system that provides easy access to information on each child, and a teacher who is continually diagnosing.

Misuses of Grouping

Grouping is essential to good teaching. The practice is subject to some misuses, however, and these must be acknowledged and avoided. Some teachers, for example, use grouping as an excuse for regularly teaching a standard lesson to an entire group. In this case, membership in a group causes children to lose their identities and thereby the pinpointing of their individual strengths and weaknesses.

Another serious misuse of reading groups occurs when the teacher mentally assigns each child to a status in a reading group and then assumes that same placement for each child in all other subjects. Trait differences—that is, differences within one individual—should caution us as to the dangers of this practice. The lowest-achieving child in a class during the reading period may be an excellent mathematician or speller.

Related to this danger of unfairly giving a child a low-achiever label is the old practice of seating children according to reading groups. We strongly recommend that youngsters be thoroughly mixed when seating plans are drawn. Some teachers unconsciously ignore one side of the room during a social studies discussion because the top reading group sits together on the opposite side. It is both unfair and educationally unsound to identify a group of youngsters constantly as a collective body, especially outside of the purpose for that group.

Still another misuse of grouping occurs when the teacher fails to break up groups occasionally or to combine groups for reading activities. The whole class ought to participate in an activity from time to time. A play or choral reading can offer excellent opportunities for whole-class participation.

Although personal taste dictates actual choices, we are opposed to giving reading groups names that have implied status. The Robins, Bluebirds, and Crows are labels frequently used as humorous examples. Why not use the name of the book being read or the name of a child in the group? Although this seems a small matter, the stigma of group membership weighs heavily on some youngsters. The alert teacher will actively avoid contributing to this circumstance and seek to counteract it whenever possible.

Grouping is misused when all groups are not given adequate time. Although the high-achieving group can and should work independently more often than other groups, this does not mean that teacher direction for the group is not needed. Indeed, with adequate supervision, capable youngsters can use their skills to make exceptional achievements. Left to themselves, they are likely to do only what is specifically assigned.

Using Groups to Individualize

1. Suppose that at the first PTA meeting of the year a parent complains because his or her child is in the "low" reading group. What explanation would you offer to satisfy the parent's anxiety?
2. Plan a week's schedule that illustrates how you would meet with reading groups. Consider using interest groups and need groups to vary your program from day to day.

Children Should Also Work Independently

Our discussion of grouping places the teacher in a very prominent position. Much group instruction does center around activities the teacher plans and directs. Obviously, group activities can be developed and carried out without teacher direction, but the fact remains that one advantage of grouping is that the teacher can efficiently work with many children at the same time in this setting.

But it is also important to provide for *independent reading activities* in the classroom. In this case, independent does not necessarily mean alone, but it certainly means without direct teacher supervision. Independent activities are important for several reasons. First, reading is fundamentally something that people do of their own volition throughout their lifetimes. It is through their own initiative and by their own self-discipline that they read for enjoyment, for information, or to solve a problem. Consequently, the more artificial the classroom situation in which a teacher directs reading, the less chance there is of building lifelong reading habits. An independent situation controlled by the child probably leads to good future reading habits.

Another reason that independent reading activities are important is a very practical one: Grouped instruction is not possible unless the members of a class are capable of working independently. A teacher must be able to leave some children on their own for a period of time if he or she is to work intensively with a reading group.

On a more general level, independent activities offer children the opportunity to grow and mature as people by making them responsible for their own accomplishments. While this important educational goal obviously cannot be reached in the reading program alone, there are unique opportunities during the reading period to contribute to a strong, healthy self-concept.

The Teacher's Role in Planning Independent Activities

Most teachers are greatly concerned about finding worthwhile activities that children can do independently. We are often asked how children working independently can be actively involved. More often, teachers ask, "How can I keep the rest of the class busy when I am working with a group?"

The teacher who wants only to keep children busy is missing an important opportunity. A healthy, attitude toward independent work gives real emphasis to these pursuits. One of the major goals of reading instruction is making all the children independent readers who set purposes for themselves, organize their resources, and carry a task through to completion. Only by carefully planning and conducting independent activities as an important aspect of the reading program can the teacher realize this goal.

The first step in building independent work habits is deciding on appropriate activities. A work sheet assigned for the sole purpose of occupying children's time stands little chance of capturing their interest or enthusiasm. In such a case, even the most responsible and mature learner gains nothing from the experience. A work sheet or activity selected because it ties in closely with a newly introduced skill comes much closer to being worthwhile. Children can be helped to see the importance of such a task and are much more likely to put forth real efforts to complete it.

A second factor to keep in mind is that frequently members of the same reading group are different and so do not need the same assignment for independent work. The work sheet related to a new skill is probably more valuable for some than for others. Occasionally, the whole group *should* complete the same assignment. It is also possible to assign only part of a work sheet to some youngsters who require less drill and then plan a different activity for the remainder of their independent work period. Only teachers who know the needs and abilities of their students can effectively differentiate assignments in this manner. The decisions involved in planning independent activities require that the teacher choose from a variety of alternatives.

Independent Activities Growing from a Reading Selection

One excellent type of independent activity relates directly to whatever reading selection the child has just completed. For example, the child can choose word pictures from the selection or prepare a section for oral reading. A group of children that has read the same narrative might prepare a dramatization based on the story. The selection can be studied for evidence proving certain statements true or false or for answering specific questions. Often a workbook or work sheet assignment can be found or developed by the teacher to further understanding of the narrative and promote analysis. Vocabulary items from the story can be used in sentences that reveal the meaning of the words. A teacher's guide often contains numerous suggestions for such activities.

Independent activities can also lead children to make immediate use of ideas gained from their reading. Individualized and recreational reading, in particular, ought to draw on such suggestions. An obvious, but highly worthwhile, activity is to pursue additional reading material on the same or related topics. The child might construct a model that summarizes or highlights events from a reading selection. Developing an outline of the story or making a comic or film strip based on the story's main events can also be valuable activities. A book or story can be publicized to other members of the class with a pupil-made poster, flyer, or map. Other individual projects include making a scrapbook, writing an original selection similar to the story that has been read, giving the story a different ending, or conducting an experiment.

Group projects, such as setting up a special display, can be undertaken. A radio broadcast, puppet show, or mural can be developed by a group. Often an appropriate excursion relating to the story can

The teacher can work with a child needing special help while other children pursue independent activities.

be planned by a group and made with adult supervision. Developing a game show based on a selection can be a particularly effective group project.

Most of these activities may seem to be more appropriate for the intermediate than for the primary grades. However, with adjustment in the amount of teacher directions provided and the length of work periods, many of the same ideas can be effective with younger children as well.

Independent Activities That Give the Child a Choice

Some independent activities grow from the shared reading experiences children have in their groups. But other independent activities are "self-contained" in the sense that they stand on their own without reference to a story. Perhaps the greatest value of such activities is that they give the child a chance to make a choice. The following sections will describe some of these activities.

Learning Centers Give the Child a Choice of Activities

Many teachers give their students a choice of independent activities by employing learning stations, or *learning centers.* Also called activity centers, these areas consist of designated places within a classroom

Learning centers have natural appeal to children who seek variety and activity in their learning environment.

where children may go to do a specific thing that is related to some concept or skill the teacher wishes them to develop.

Learning centers are usually attractively set up to invite students to use them. Materials ranging from cardboard boxes to old window shades can be adapted in creative ways to encourage children to perform such interesting tasks as matching prefixes with their meaning, placing sentences into correct sequences, or performing literally hundreds of other reading-language-related work. Usually, each center is separate from others and may even be sectioned off from the general classroom space by room dividers, bookcases, shower curtains, or other means.

Although centers vary, they usually are based on certain common principles:

1. Self-motivation.
2. Self-pacing.
3. Self-selection.
4. Self-correction.

To be sure, many teachers use centers, prescriptively; that is, they assign some children to certain centers for appropriate practice of a skill. Nevertheless, centers provide children with many options and can be used to give them a choice of independent activities as well.

To the casual observer, learning centers may appear to be haphazard and random in nature. Quite the opposite is true; centers are usually created with some specific objective or set of objectives in mind. All activities in the center are then designed to address that objective.

By observing a child at a center or studying the written results of a child's efforts at a center, a teacher can identify skill needs, misunderstandings, and potential problems in a specific area. Used in this way, centers add a dimension to the informal diagnostic procedures available to the teacher.

Learning centers are usually popular with children because they make the learner an active participant. At one center used by a teacher in West Fargo, North Dakota, a child could spill a collection of five dice with letters printed on each side onto a table and then spell as many words as possible with the letters in three minutes. The child was required to write each word spelled on a piece of paper and was challenged to improve his or her own record on subsequent tries. An egg timer provided at the center added an air of urgency, and accuracy was encouraged. The timing device motivated children to do better each time. Bonus points were earned for writing a sentence that illustrated the meaning of the words. Students recorded their scores on a tally sheet and placed their notes in a box so the teacher could review their progress. With this activity, children are active and have a chance to manipulate concrete objects they can touch and see.

Learning centers are also valuable for children with different learning styles because they are not limited by one approach that all must follow. With dozens of centers available at any time in a classroom, children can find those that suit their interests and particular learning modes. The very nature of centers arouses curiosity and promotes experimentation. It is also possible to create a range of centers from simple to difficult and from concrete to abstract.

Numerous resources are available to assist teachers in developing

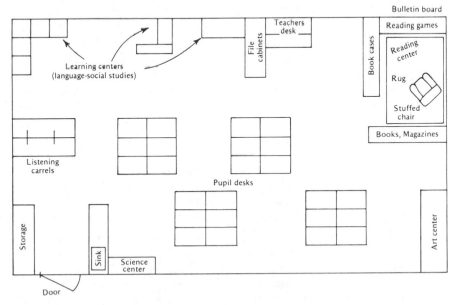

FIGURE 13.4 A classroom can be arranged to accommodate group, as well as independent, learning activities.

Organizing for Instruction

learning centers (Don et al., 1973; Fisk, Lindgren, 1974; Reeke & Laffey, 1984; Voight, 1971). It is important to introduce new centers regularly and to rearrange old ones so as to keep interest high and topics current. Often aides and volunteers can assist a busy teacher in creating and constructing learning centers. Teachers in several classrooms can also exchange centers to add variety (*see* Figure 13.4).

Cross-age Tutoring as a Means for Individualization

It is surprising how often techniques and methods are rediscovered in the never-ending search for better classroom procedures. What is discarded in one era sometimes resurfaces in another as an innovative practice. Cross-age tutoring is a classic example of how ideas recycle.

Simply defined, *cross-age tutoring* is having children teach other children. The familiar one-room rural school made extensive use of this technique decades ago when no other alternative was available to the teacher of grades one to six or one to eight. Rejected by many experts as recently as ten or fifteen years ago, as an example of teachers' shuffling their responsibilities onto others, youth-tutoring-youth programs are today seen as having special advantages for tutor and learner alike. The value of cross-age tutoring makes it worth considering as a way to individualize instruction and provide meaningful independent learning activities (Lehr, 1984).

Usually, cross-age tutoring means that an older child works with a younger child. The older child assumes responsibility for teaching or reviewing some concept or skill that a teacher has determined the younger child needs. This does not rule out the possibility of same-age children working in a tutorial relationship or even of having a younger child tutor an older one. Yet experience indicates that special considerations come into play in either of these latter arrangements.

Tutors—whether older, of the same age, or younger—must be well prepared to serve their function successfully. This is the first value of tutoring. Children who might otherwise tend to loaf or even refuse to practice some skill can be easily motivated to master it if they know they will be teaching it to another child. If care is taken in matching tutor and learner, as a matter of fact, older, low-achieving children often profit enormously from the experience of tutoring a younger child (Nevi, 1983). Freed from the stigma of doing "baby work," because they are preparing to teach a skill, they can and will work long periods mastering something well enough to teach it. A twelve-year-old boy, for example, can rehearse a Dr. Seuss story that he plans to share with his learner even though he could not justify to himself reading such as "easy" book on his own. The fact that this easy book is written at a level the boy can read successfully only with concerted effort is camouflaged by the tutoring program. Thus, a child practices needed reading skills without loss of ego.

Tutoring is also valuable from the standpoint of the intense personal relationships it promotes. Working one-to-one, each child has close contact with another person on a regular basis. Emphasis is on a specific task where the chances for success are great. Competition

442

with others is avoided. Cooperation is reinforced. Both tutor and learner come to respect each other and themselves in this kind of association when it works.

The ability of children to talk a common language is indisputable. A difficult task can often be explained by a child who sees it as a *child* and knows what makes it tough. Tutoring programs facilitate this type of exchange.

It is not always clear who benefits most from cross-age tutoring: the tutor or the learner. Evidently both can be happy winners. The tutor can build a strong self-concept of himself or herself as a worth-while individual with something to offer to others. The learner receives individual attention from someone who cares.

The teacher also benefits from a tutoring program in that additional human resources become available to meet individual needs better. Yet the teacher must expend some time and effort in meeting with tutors and guiding them in their work. Published accounts of successful tutoring programs indicate that an initial training program for tutors is advisable. Topics included in this training might range from how to reinforce the learner for correct responses to making flash cards. After initial training, tutors also require a teacher's time for general supervision to discuss specific problems, receive directions, provide feedback, and the like.

Dreyer (1973) suggests that teachers supervising a tutoring program should be prepared to do the following:

> Have materials and assignments ready and available for the tutor.
> Relate tutorial sessions to recent lessons through several kinds of activities.

An older child can gain confidence in her own reading ability by helping a younger child with various reading tasks.

Institute a spaced review system, thus providing tutors with a structured review method for each pupil.

Keep assignments within the time period and goals set by pupil and tutor.

Help tutor and pupil chart or otherwise record daily progress.

Assist tutors in developing motivation techniques—especially positive reinforcement.

Assign very specific tasks for tutors.

Teach tutors to make flash cards, using the particular manuscript form the pupil recognizes.

Provide the necessary level of positive reinforcement to maintain enthusiasm and a conscientious attitude on the part of tutors.[1]

Despite the demands it places on a teacher, youth-tutoring-youth programs give the teacher another viable alternative for independent activities. Various other resources are available if this brief description has stirred your interest. Gartner, Kohler, and Riessman (1971) describe tutoring plans in great detail in *Children Teach Children,* as do Smith and Fay (1973) in *Getting People to Read.* Various magazine articles describe experiences teachers have had with tutoring (Dreyer, 1973; Dickerson, 1982; Ellis & Preston, 1984).

Independent Work Can Be Organized into Contracts

Reading teachers can borrow a practice that has been used in the teaching of social studies for many years for independent work—*contracting.* With this approach, the teacher and child agree on a certain quantity and quality of work. Specific objectives, means for reaching those objectives, and a certain length of time for the activity are usually spelled out in writing and "signed," much as a legal contract is signed, by both teacher and student. In some cases, contracts are written for a certain letter grade if the teacher is required to give them. Often some product is developed by the child as a way of demonstrating the knowledge and skills the child has learned while fulfilling the contract.

To illustrate contracting, let's visit the classroom of Don English, who teaches ten- and eleven-year-olds. Mary is a ten-year-old in Don's class who enjoys reading horse stories. Don believes Mary needs special instruction and practice in recognizing compound words, so he suggests in a conference that Mary and he agree on a contract that will focus on this skill. Don recognizes that a large part of the value of contracting lies in the motivation Mary will gain from designing much of her own program. He, therefore, identifies his concern and asks Mary to suggest how she might proceed. He suggests that her interest in horses be reflected in her learning program.

Mary decides on the following activities:

1. Make a list of fifteen compound words related to horses (e.g., horseshoe).

[1] Hal B. Dreyer. (1973, May). Rx for pupil tutoring programs. *The Reading Teacher, XXVI*(8), 811.

2. Complete five work sheets on compound words.
3. Write a story about horses using at least fifteen compound words in a correct context.

A deadline is set for completing these activities (one week away), and Mary is ready to fulfill her contract. One copy of the contract is kept in Mr. English's folder, and one copy is kept by Mary.

Contracts prepared in this fashion can be designed jointly by the teacher and child to capitalize on unique learning styles. An active child, for example, can build a model or paint a mural to demonstrate competence. The great advantage of this approach is that children assume responsibility for their own learning. They decide how much they will do and how long it will take. Children can also work together on contracts when this is appropriate to their needs.

Teacher Aides Can Guide Independent Work

Most teachers have days when they seem to be needed in six places at one time. This is especially true if they are attempting to individualize instruction. One approach teachers seem to be turning to increasingly in order to meet the demands placed on their time is the use of teacher aides and volunteers.

Aides are valuable to the teacher in a number of ways. They can free the teacher from various routine tasks that require little or no training but consume inordinate amounts of time. Examples would be collecting milk money, taking attendance, mimeographing, typing, making reading games, cutting out bulletin board letters, correcting daily work, and so forth. Freed from these jobs, teachers are able to spend more time in planning, identifying, or creating appropriate materials and in working directly with children.

Aides can also work individually with children or in small groups by supervising and guiding their efforts. Usually, the teacher's select and structure the activities according to their judgment of the children's needs, and the aides carry out the task. For example, aides can write an experience story as it is dictated by children, listen to a child read orally, administer a test, play a reading game with children, read a book aloud, or organize a choral reading. Tasks such as these require some training but do not always need the teacher's skill. Other tasks require considerable training but might also be appropriate for some aides. Examples are calculating readability levels of reading materials, recording oral reading miscues, explaining a phonic principle, or leading a discussion of a story with a group.

If aides are parent volunteers, they can serve several other important functions. Parents who regularly participate in the school program come to understand and appreciate what a teacher is attempting to do in the classroom. They become a means for getting a complete and accurate picture of the school program to the community. Misunderstandings and fears regarding new techniques, materials, or procedures are often shortstopped by school volunteers who explain what is happening in school to concerned neighbors. Parents who speak the dialect of a region or subculture and understand the home environments of children can open a two-way communication between teacher and children (see Chapter 16, Parents, Partners, and Volunteers).

Perhaps the most important aspect of any teacher-aide program is careful specification of expectations. Aides must have a clear understanding of what they are to do and how it should be accomplished. Training programs for aides can be of great help if certain tasks commonly assigned to them are discussed and they are shown where supplies are kept. Aides should also be made aware of school policies that they must observe and enforce.

In a classroom that uses learning centers, aides can provide a valuable service by supervising children as they move from center to center. Someone is often needed, for example, to resupply a center with materials or assist a child who experiences difficulty.

Many communities have a ready supply of volunteers that frequently is overlooked—senior citizens. Elderly and retired men and women often have time on their hands, as well as the desire to remain productive. It may be necessary to arrange transportation for some of these people, but the benefits derived by child and adult make the extra effort worthwhile. Senior citizens can read to children, listen to children read, supervise independent work, and perform other useful tasks within their physical limitations. And there is an added value for children in getting to know older people in this way, especially when the children's grandparents are far away or perhaps no longer living. Even homebound people may be willing to tape-record stories, cut out felt board characters, and so on, if materials and directions are taken to them.

The national Right to Read effort seeks to overcome illiteracy in part by the use of volunteers. A 1973 statement by the International Reading Association describes how paraprofessionals should be selected, trained, and evaluated (*The Reading Teacher,* Dec. 1973). A helpful IRA publication is *Handbook for the Volunteer Tutor* (Rauch and Sanacore, 1985).

Independent Activities Can Be Organized into a Kit

We have known teachers who gathered their independent learning activities together and organized them into a kit. Although various schemes can be used, one approach is to group activities in the kit according to skills. All activities children can do independently and related to reading critically, for example, can be placed in a folder. Folders for various other skills are also developed, and the entire package is placed in a file drawer or box. Folders can be alphabetized by skill or arranged according to their order of presentation to children in the planned instructional program.

The activities in the kit might include work sheets and other paper-and-pencil tasks—such as crossword puzzles, riddles, and exercises from workbooks. Kits can also contain manipulative devices and directions for activities that require more participation. Some teachers type each activity on a card called a job card and give children the option of completing whichever "jobs" they choose. Obviously, specific jobs can also be assigned by the teacher as they are deemed appropriate.

A sample activity or job card is given here.

Job Card No. 51   1. Read an adventure story.
2. Tell something exciting that happened to the main character.
3. What caused this exciting thing to happen?
4. What was the outcome of this adventure?
5. What do you think the story character learned from this experience?[2]

Children enjoy adding their own ideas to a kit of this kind. Teachers can exchange ideas and adapt them to the programs. It is a good idea to have a range of difficulty within each skill area to accommodate children of various achievement levels.

Reading Games Are Excellent Independent Activities

Children respond especially well to reading games as another form of independent activity. Games are available commercially and may involve reading directly or indirectly. At the very least, the directions for a game, the cards needed to play the game, and the playing board provide practice in reading. Some commercial games are designed specifically as reading games; others require extensive reading incidentally.

Many teachers develop their own reading games or have aides and children make reading games the teacher has conceptualized. Basic game formats can be turned into literally dozens of skills activities. For example, dominoes (matching of tiles in a chain) can be turned into a reading game that requires the matching of geometric shapes, letters, words, synonyms, antonyms, or homonyms.

Not only do games provide a pleasant respite from the usual classroom routine, but they also provide skill practice, encourage children to interact and learn from each other, and appeal to several learning modes.

An example of a reading game follows. You may want to see Cooper et al. (1972), Platts (1960), E. Spache (1976), and Wagner, Hosier (1970) for suggestions on creating reading games.

Prefix   Directions:
Concentration

1. Make a set of playing cards using three-by-five-inch cards. Write a prefix on one card and the meaning of the prefix on another (for example, *pre* on one card and *before* on a second card). Make ten to twenty pairs of cards.
2. Two to four players sit around a table.
3. The cards are shuffled.

[2] *Language Arts Job Cards.* Vancouver, British Columbia, Canada: B.C. Teacher's Federation Lesson Aids Service.

Some games such as *Scrabble* offer the opportunity to practice and apply reading and vocabulary skills.

4. Place cards facedown on a table in regular rows and columns.
5. The players take turns turning over two cards at a time. A match between a prefix and its meaning entitles the player to keep those cards and turn over two more. Cards not making a match are turned facedown again in the same place, and the next player has a turn.
6. Continue until all cards have been matched.
7. The player with the most pairs of cards is the winner.

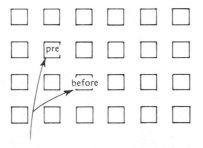

The Ideal Independent Activity: Free-choice Reading

The best way to acquire most skills is to begin early and practice them often. Champion athletes in sports ranging from golf to skiing acknowledge the importance of practicing their skills regularly and

Approaches to Teaching Reading

often. Obviously, reading is not a physical skill, but the parallel is illustrative. To become a proficient reader, one must read—regularly and often.

Attitudes die hard, and the attitude has persisted for a long time that free-choice reading is an occasional treat that should not be overdone lest children think school is all fun and no work. Little wonder that reading skills develop slowly and the reading habit fails to become internalized for children in this atmosphere. Happily, many teachers and schools see the fallacy in that attitude. Nothing could be better for reading instruction than having children read materials they select and enjoy. A program for encouraging independent reading, called sustained silent reading (SSR), is described in Chapter 4.

The ideal independent activity is simply having children read. A broad range of materials from magazines and comic books to encyclopedias and almanacs should be considered as appropriate fare. Opportunities for follow-up activities involving sharing of reading interests can also be regarded as excellent independent work.

Independent Activities
1. Create a learning center that gives children an opportunity to practice classification. As you plan, keep in mind the age level you want to teach. Provide easy, as well as more difficult, variations to accommodate individual differences.
2. Make up a form that you could use when contracting with a child for a particular piece of work. Remember to provide for the completion date, description of the final product, and a place for both teacher and pupil to sign.
3. Using the format followed in playing bingo, plan a reading game that helps children learn and remember the meanings of new words.

Managing Grouped and Independent Activities

Taken separately, each of the previous sections of this chapter seems reasonably simple and workable. Viewed as a whole, the many parts may begin to look unmanageable. It is for that very reason that many teachers develop a traditional, "safe" organizational scheme that keeps children locked into a dull routine. Children not working directly under the teacher's supervision must sit quietly doing a battery of workbook or dittoed papers that will keep them busy and out of "trouble." Perhaps a brief discussion on managing a system with many disparate parts will help you feel more comfortable in giving the ideas described here a try in the classroom.

The key to running a multifaceted reading program is a sense of direction. The teacher must know where each activity is headed and how it contributes to the overall plan. This means quite simply that clear, achievable objectives must be identified for each component of the program. These objectives must be related to the broad goals of the reading program.

Individual tastes and beliefs will play a large part in determining how objectives will be stated. Behavioral objectives are a controversial topic, and we do not propose to resolve it here. Regardless of their form, however, when objectives are not clearly formulated, the many components of a reading program can easily get lost in activity for the sake of activity. Learning centers can proliferate, for example, without contributing in a significant way to improving children's reading performance.

Once objectives have been identified and activities, such as those discussed in this chapter, have been developed to lead to those objectives, the next task is to identify where each child stands with regard to each objective. A complete and workable record-keeping system is needed for this task. Some teachers develop a master plan with individual checklists for specific skill areas. They establish a file folder for each child and record progress on the various checklists. Each objective can be given a code, and classroom activities can be keyed to that code. A learning center on using context clues, for example, might be identified as E4 to indicate Checklist E on Context Clues in the child's folder. The number 4 indicates that a specific subskill listed on the checklist, synonym clues, is featured in the learning center. By numbering the learning center (149) and noting this number on the checklist, the teacher has a simple cross-reference that identifies which activities treat a given skill (*see* Figure 13.5).

Whenever new skills are identified, they are simply added to the appropriate checklist, or a new checklist is created. When new learning activities are developed, the objectives are keyed to the code. In this way, the teacher has a handy system for seeing that all activities contribute to the goals of the program.

Using the various sources of diagnostic information available, the teacher can identify which activities are appropriate for which children. All those who need practice with the synonym type of context clues can be asked to visit center number 149, for example. Children needing help with skill A14 (finding roots of words) can be placed in a skill group for a review lesson.

Many of the newer basal reading series have a management system that accomplishes the purposes just described. Teachers may want to key their learning activities to such a system or adapt the system to their own uses, depending on how they utilize the basal.

A management system for classroom instruction consists of the following:

1. A list of objectives (skills and attitudes) to be achieved.
2. Criterion tests or observation cues that match the objectives.
3. A means for recording a child's performance on specific skills— a record that can be passed from teacher to teacher.

FIGURE 13.5   Example of a Learning Center.

Child's Name

CHECKLIST E

Using Context Clues

Is able to use the following:
1. Definition type of context clues.
2. Experience type of context clues.
3. Comparison type of context clues.
4. Synonym type of context clues.
5. Familiar expression type of context clues.
6. Summary type of context clues.

LEARNING CENTER 149

The purpose of this center is to provide practice in the following:
1. Using synonym type of context clues (E4).
2. Writing a creative ending to a story (G3).
3. Inferring the author's purpose (B8).

4. A class plan sheet or a sorting technique for grouping those who need similar instruction and practice.
5. A cross-reference chart and a file of materials that shows where in the classroom skills are taught and practiced, thus enabling the teacher to have immediate access to necessary lesson plans and practice materials.

Regardless of the system used, it is imperative that some management plan be designed if you want to conduct a reading program with many facets. Central to this effort is the importance of deciding what goals are to be pursued. With a large number of children and a variety of activities there are simply too many children and too many activities—too many variables—involved in a reading program for you to rely on your intuition alone. The alternative to a system of the kind described is to give every child the same program—hardly an attractive solution.

Organizing for Instruction

Summary

Children with common instructional needs are frequently grouped together for reading. Differences among youngsters, as well as differences within the same youngster, prevent the creation of truly homogeneous groups.

Grouping within a classroom is essential for meeting the needs of the individual. Effective groups are flexible in membership, are formed to accomplish a specific task, are terminated when a task is completed, and are kept small in size. Information needed for forming effective groups must be gathered by a variety of means and on a continuing basis by the teacher.

This chapter presented a stylized plan for meeting with groups. During the first few weeks of school, it was recommended that the teacher gather evidence on each child and encourage recreational reading. Teachers were urged to begin on a trial basis with two reading groups, splitting their time almost equally between the groups. Gradually, it would be possible to add a third and perhaps a fourth group as the need arose and the teacher's ability permitted. Reading groups are not comprised of youngsters with identical needs, and, therefore, instruction within groups must be differentiated.

Children also require the opportunity to work independently. Some independent work can flow from a shared reading experience. Opportunities can be created to give children a choice and some variety in their independent work. These alternatives were described: learning centers, cross-age tutoring, learning contracts, teacher aides and volunteers, learning kits, and reading games.

The need for a management system in a classroom containing various learning opportunities was identified. One suggested management system was described in detail.

Terms for Self-study

> need group
> interest group
> achievement group
> independent activity
> learning center
> cross-age tutoring
> learning contract

Discussion Questions

1. How can instructional groups help a teacher individualize reading instruction?
2. What is the value of giving children a choice among independent learning activities?

Barbe, Walter B., & Abbott, Jerry L. (1975). *Personalized reading instruction.* West Nyack, N. Y: Parker.

Here is a practical guide to implementing a personalized reading program that incorporates the principles of self-selection and individual conferences as the primary elements.

Cunningham, Patricia M., et al. (1983). *Reading in elementary classrooms.* New York: Longman.

This is a comprehensive textbook on reading instruction containing one special chapter devoted to organizing the classroom. It describes the movement of one class of children through the elementary grades with each teacher taking a somewhat different approach to reading instruction.

Johnson, Dale D., & Pearson, P. David. (1975, May). Skills management systems: A critique. *The Reading Teacher, 28* (8), 757–764.

This book describes skills management systems that break the reading act into myriad objectives for the sake of prescriptive-diagnostic instruction. It cautions teachers concerning the possible undesired consequences of using such systems.

Lapp, Diane (Ed.). (1980). *Making reading possible through effective classroom management.* Newark, De: International Reading Association.

This book describes and discusses both the theoretical and practical aspects of the management procedures needed to implement and maintain a personalized reading curriculum.

Otto, Wayne, Wolf, Anne, & Eldridge, Roger G. (1984). Managing instruction. In P. David Pearson et al. (Eds.), *Handbook of reading research* (799–828). New York: Longman.

This volume reviews and summarizes investigations that have examined the effects of various approaches to managing classroom reading instruction. It presents studies in three categories: those that deal with organizational plans, those that focus on classroom behaviors, and those that examine teacher's planning and decision making.

Part IV

Beyond the Fundamentals

14

Diagnosing Needs and Assessing Progress

Have you ever watched a contest on television in which a panel of judges is asked to rate the performance of contestants on some highly complex skill? Examples might include figure skating, dancing, diving, tumbling, or cattle showmanship. If so, you have probably wondered, as we have, how the judges can distinguish between performances that seem to us to be equally superb. When two world-class divers execute twisting full gainers from the low diving board, for example, there appears to be no discernible difference in their technique. Yet one diver may earn a score of 8.0; and the other, a 7.7 or 7.8. How can the judges decide what score to award, we wonder?

Whether the area being judged is diving, bronco riding, or showmanship, it is crucial that the judges in such events have a list of criteria or standards on which they can base their decisions. In diving, the position of the feet seems to be important, for example, and so is clean entry into the water that avoids leaving a splash. Judging in other situations is much easier to understand. To illustrate, there is certainly more to judging a high jump event than merely noting the height of the crossbar; but in this event, form is not a consideration: The jumper either clears a certain height or not. No points are awarded by the judge for style or form. The master of ceremonies for a television game show plays much the same role as a judge. A contestant either answers a question correctly or not. Judges in such situations have much clearer criteria to apply than does the judge in a diving contest.

Do you see any similarity between judging a child's reading performance and judging a diving contest, or is judging a reading performance more like judging a high jump event? Are the indicators of reading success more like those a judge uses in diving or more like those in the high jump? As a teacher of reading, you will be expected to judge a student's reading performance in order to provide help where it is needed. In this regard, you will be more like a student's coach than like the judge identified in the athletic events just presented. But many of the same issues facing an athletic coach or judge will confront you as a teacher when you attempt to determine how to help the students in your class make progress. In this chapter we will consider how a teacher diagnoses student needs and assesses progress. We will examine the following issues:

- *How should published reading tests fit into a teacher's assessment program?*
- *How should the results of assessment be used to plan instruction?*
- *What kinds of reading tests are available to a classroom teacher?*
- *What are the key differences between formal and informal measures of reading?*
- *What is an informal reading inventory?*
- *When should an oral reading miscue be ignored?*

Let us first build on the analogy of the teacher as coach a bit more. We have indicated that, like a coach, a teacher must be able to assess performance. Much like a track coach, a teacher employs observation techniques in deciding where instruction needs to be provided. The coach structures observations according to what training and experience have shown to be important and useful. Some of the observations are more objective than others. For example, a stopwatch or measuring tape can be used to get an accurate estimate of performance in a race or distance in a throwing or jumping event. Comparisons over time can indicate whether improvement is being made in performance.

With the advent of computers, athletic performance can even be translated into graphic representations on a monitor screen, then converted into data for analysis. An athlete's running stride can then be shortened or lengthened to study the effects of such a change on performance, for example, or the angle of an arm or leg can be altered for analysis.

Other kinds of observations can be employed as well. Blood can be drawn from athletes and analyzed for oxygen, lactic acid content, and so forth. All these examples involve instruments that are available to a coach that permit "scientific" measurement of important information.

Some of a coach's observations are less scientific and more judgmental, however. A judgment must be made about the effects of a particular training routine, for example. Is a particular routine adversely affecting an athlete's morale? Is performance going to peak at the correct moment by using a particular training schedule? Experience and training are extremely important to a coach in arriving at these less quantifiable judgments as well.

Like a coach, a teacher also must structure observations of a child's reading performance. Some techniques used are less judgmental than others; some involve more scientific rigor than others. The coach's task is difficult and important, to say the least. But because the coach deals primarily with physical matters, the observations can be more precise than the teacher's. The teacher is dealing with an extremely abstract matter—a cognitive operation. It is crucial that teachers understand the nature and limitations of the diagnostic means at their disposal.

Educators, parents, and even children tend to look for exact measurements in reading. The coach has a stopwatch, blood tests, measuring tape, and so forth. What similar quantified measure does the teacher have? The answer is none. Every reading measure—standardized or informal, published or homemade, extensive or brief—is nothing more than a means for gathering samples or observations of an abstract operation. These observations must then be interpreted in light of their limitations. But the situation is not hopeless. The teacher who has a mental map of the reading process and knowledge of the various means for assessing progress in acquiring reading competence is clearly better able to individualize instruction than someone who lacks these tools. Previous chapters have presented the mental map, or conceptualization, of reading. In this chapter student progress and needs are discussed.

Assessment Involves More Than Testing

Like all specialities, education—particularly reading education—is bedeviled by a surplus of terms. Some terms have very precise meanings; others are vague and imprecise. At times a variety of labels is applied to the same concept. Perhaps more than any other area, assessment is complicated and confused by the vocabulary game.

To avoid this problem, we must clarify some terms as they will be used here. *Assessment* refers to the far-ranging act of determining what a student can do and cannot do with respect to decoding, understanding, and appreciating the printed message. *Diagnosis* refers to determining a student's understanding in a specific skill area (for example, we diagnose a child's needs with regard to the understanding of main ideas). The term *testing* is often misunderstood; testing and diagnosis are *not* synonymous. Diagnosis might well include the use of tests and testing procedures because these refer to the practice of trying a person's ability to perform a task. Testing refers to more than paper-and-pencil tasks purchased from a publishing house, however. Let's pursue this matter briefly by separating tests into two categories: formal and informal.

Differences Between Formal and Informal Measures

It is hardly adequate to identify *formal measures of testing* as those you remember taking in a whole-class setting with a darken-in-the-box answer form, yet this description should cause you to recall a personal impression. Formal measures are those published tests that are given under strictly controlled conditions (for example, uniform directions to all, strict time limits). They are accompanied by information regarding their reliability and validity. (Reliability refers to the fact that the test will yield the same results every time it is given to the same subject; validity means that a test measures what it claims to measure.) Such measures have been "standardized" (a term often used synonymously with formal) and often include tables of norms that indicate how a large sample of children scored on the tests previously, so that comparisons can be made.

Informal measures are found in a variety of forms and differ from formal measures in several ways. First, it is the classroom teacher who decides the conditions under which measures will be used. In other words, informal measures are not administered under standardized conditions. Furthermore, informal measures have not typically been studied for reliability and validity and are not accompanied by norms for comparison of pupil performance. From a diagnostic standpoint, informal measures are valuable because they can be selected or created so as to relate in a direct way to what has been taught in the instructional program, thus providing a basis for immediate adjustments in subsequent instruction.

Johns (1982) identifies four major purposes for informal assessment:

1. Studying, evaluating, or diagnosing reading behavior.
2. Monitoring student progress.
3. Supplementing and confirming information gained from standardized and criterion-referenced instruments.
4. Obtaining information not readily available from other sources.

Informal measures include, but are not limited to, assessment devices the teacher makes. Examples would be teacher-made tests, work sheets, daily assignments, oral reading inventories, learning centers, reading games, and so forth. Many devices that are not teacher-made also qualify as informal measures. The workbook available with most basal reader series is prepared by a publishing company, but the activities in it require a child to apply various reading skills. Workbook exercises can be used without specified time limits as can literally dozens of other published devices that provide a teacher with informal assessment opportunities (for example, audiotapes with response forms, learning kits, games). It may seem strange to think of a game as a test, but, looked at in this way, games and other informal measures provide a steady flow of diagnostic information to the teacher.

We have said that assessment involves more than testing. But testing is one important part of assessment—perhaps the part that is most misunderstood. It is fashionable in some circles to reject tests and decry the value of testing. For example, critics cite the cultural bias built into many tests as one serious limitation (Fitzgibbon, 1974). It is impossible to refute many of these criticisms because, in fact, they are all too often true. Tests are not infallible measures, but tests and testing, especially formal measures, have attained an undeserved high status in the minds of some people—educators and parents alike. On the other hand, such critics are often also guilty of engaging in hyperbole when they dismiss tests, which are actually rather neutral.

It is the way tests are used and interpreted that often merits criticism.

One of our purposes will be to describe how tests can be used in constructive ways and to present alternatives to the easy misuse of published tests.

Assessment Is Central to Individualization of Instruction

Assessment is important to the teacher as a means of individualizing instruction, for it enables a teacher to identify a reading level where the child can work effectively on a daily basis, and each child's pattern of strengths and weaknesses.

Identifying the Child's Instructional Reading Level

As children gain competence in reading, they are gradually able to handle selections of increasing difficulty. Common sense suggests that we do not confront developing readers with materials that are so difficult that they cannot successfully decode and understand them. We would not ask even an advanced eight-year-old to read Steinbeck or Baldwin regularly, for example. At the other extreme, developing readers must have exposure to materials that stretch them, or they will find it hard to get beyond the easy-to-read "big books" on the bottom shelf in the library. Somewhere in between these extremes is a "match" of child and material that challenges children but doesn't overwhelm them.

The labels that reading specialists apply to *levels* of reading are worth knowing. The level that is "too hard" is called the *frustration* level; the level that is "just right" is the *instructional* level; and the level that is "easy" is called the *independent,* or *recreational,* level. Authorities do not agree on exactly how these levels should be specified in terms of actual reading performance. Opinions differ, for example, on how many word recognition errors on a given page indicate that a reader is operating at his or her instructional level. This complex and important issue is taken up later in this chapter under the subject of oral reading diagnosis.[1] Different reading levels do exist, and it is extremely important that teachers make an effort to match the children with materials that they can handle successfully for daily instruction.

As we saw in Chapters 8 and 9, it is important to note that all readers, young and old, will find the happy "match" of personal reading ability and difficulty of material occurring for them at different levels on different topics. High interest and rich personal background uniquely equip each individual to handle material in one area that is "harder" by some standard measure than they might handle in another area of little personal interest or experience. The discussion regarding

---

[1] A description of reading levels suggested by Powell is given on page 473.

the importance of identifying the child's instructional level needs to be read with this variable in mind.

The classroom teacher must plan and conduct assessment that helps to identify a general level of reading competence for each child. This determination is necessary in order to form groups of children that can profit from reading the same selections, as well as to assist all children in finding books they can read successfully on their own. Both formal and informal measures are helpful in identifying the child's instructional level.

Identifying Each Child's Pattern of Strengths and Weaknesses

Given the many variables that interact to enable a child to read, it is not surprising that no two children probably ever have exactly the same instructional needs at one time. Fortunately, children can adapt themselves to our organization and often profit from instruction that is less than optimum insofar as their own readiness is concerned. Yet all the adjusting cannot be done by the child; it is our obligation as teachers to individualize instruction whenever we can. The diagnostic data available from formal and informal sources are basic to making such adjustments for individuals.

Without information that indicates who needs help with following sequence, for example, there is a strong tendency to give everyone in a group the same dose. It is clear that assessment is most valuable when it helps the teacher set instructional goals.

Assessment Must Relate to Instructional Goals

Often we are asked by teachers to recommend a reading test. Sometimes it is possible to identify several reading tests the teacher might consider using if certain variables can be identified:

1. How old the children are.
2. What materials the teacher is using for instruction.
3. What other information is already available on the reading performance of the children.

Even more important than these variables in selecting a test is identification of the teacher's instructional goals. A test is worth little to a teacher if it does not tell how far children are from the objectives that have been established. This is true whether the assessment is made before, during, or after instruction begins or whether the test is a published one or is teacher-made.

Matching the objectives of a test and the objectives of instruction is very important. Testing is too expensive and too consuming of student and teacher time to be conducted for its own sake. Assessment of any kind, including formal testing, must provide a basis for making decisions that ultimately affect instruction. A test that measures reading rate, for example, when there is no intention to provide instruction in this area is nonproductive. Even worse, it steals from the time and money that might be spent on assessing a skill that is of higher priority from an instruction standpoint.

You may feel that reading rate is important and merits assessment. If so, it should be identified as an instructional priority and included in the objectives of your program. But every reading skill cannot be included. If reading rate ranks high, something else must be dropped from your goals and treated incidentally. Otherwise, you run the risk of pursuing all skills at once and achieving none successfully because your energies are not focused on the skills your students need most. Goal setting can be difficult when there is much that seems to need doing, but some decisions must be made early to give a program coherence and structure.

Determining what test is best in a given situation depends on objectives. What do you intend to teach? What does the test measure? Is there a match between the two? A test that measures performance in areas you intend for instruction should be used.

It is important to remember that individualization of instruction involves establishing different goals for different children. You will want seriously to limit the amount of testing you do of a whole class with the same measure. Your interest will be in finding measures that are useful with individuals or small groups because you probably want to set instructional goals on this basis. Criterion-referenced tests are particularly helpful in this regard.

Criterion-referenced Tests Focus on the Individual

A *criterion-referenced* test assesses the performance of an individual against a predetermined standard of "mastery." Only one skill or set of related subskills is included in a criterion-referenced test. For example, such a test could be developed to assess mastery of identifying root words. Twenty tasks could be designed that require a reader to underline the roots in a list of words. According to this approach, successful performance on eighteen of the twenty tasks (90 per cent) would indicate mastery of the skill. (See cautions below.)

On a criterion-referenced test the performance of an individual is not compared to the performance of others. When individuals are compared to each other, someone has to be low (or last), and someone has to be high (or first). Mastery of the skill gets lost in this comparison of people. Consider that in some situations everyone taking a test may do very poorly against a standard of skill mastery (for example, 90 per cent correct). But when individuals are compared to each other, the top achievers seem to be successful. The fact that everyone taking the test has performed unsatisfactorily (if mastery of the skill is the ultimate goal) is obscured. Carried to its logical conclusion, thousands of children could graduate from our schools without having mastered crucial skills while looking well-educated because they are consistently at the top by comparison with other children.

Tests that give meaning to performance by comparing individuals are called *norm-referenced* tests. These are not related in any direct way to mastery of skills. By their very nature, most norm-referenced tests survey many reading skills rather than assess mastery of any one skill. They are designed to create a range of scores; in fact, they require a range to rank individuals from high to low. Ideally, no one will score perfectly on a norm-referenced test; the average performer will miss about one half the items. These characteristics of norm-referenced tests limit their usefulness for the teacher who is looking for guidance in planning daily instruction. Norm-referenced tests are useful primarily for assessing the overall performance of a group (such as an entire classroom or school) and for classifying children into general achievement groups.

Criterion-referenced tests can assist the teacher in planning the specifics of an instructional program because they indicate who has "mastered" a skill and who has not. To reinforce a point made earlier, assessment with criterion-referenced tests can be tied to a teacher's instructional goals.

Recently, many criterion-referenced reading tests have flooded the market. Examples include these:

> *Competency Tests for Basic Reading Skills* (Center for Applied Research in Education)
> *Criterion Reading* (Random House)
> *Fountain Valley Support System in Reading* (Zweig)
> *Prescriptive Reading Inventory* (McGraw-Hill)
> *Wisconsin Tests of Reading Skill Development* (Interpretive Scoring System)

Most new basal reading series also include a set of criterion-referenced tests keyed to the "skills" program.

The teacher who wants to use criterion-referenced tests will find the task mainly one of knowing how to use and interpret them. *Two cautions should be raised here.* First, some criterion-referenced tests attempt to measure distinct factors that may, in fact, not be separate, measurable aspects of reading. The unsuspecting teacher may thus become unduly concerned about minuscle factors that will result in an instructional program that is abstract, unintegrated, and unrelated to reading as a language-based process. Second, the hierarchical arrangement of reading skills assumed by most criterion-referenced tests is questionable. The ideal sequencing of reading skills is unknown and probably nonexistent. The idea that one skill must be mastered before the next is begun, a notion criterion-referenced tests unavoidably reinforce, is inaccurate. Even the concept of mastery is one that can be challenged insofar as reading achievement is concerned. (See Chapter 16.)

Despite these limitations, criterion-referenced tests offer the teacher who is interested in individualizing instruction an important alternative to norm-referenced tests. We should point out that many

Comparing Tests

1. Compare a norm-referenced and criterion-referenced test. Note, in particular, the range of skills or knowledge assessed by the norm-referenced test and the specificity of the criterion-referenced test.
2. Write your own criterion-referenced test, focusing on some aspect of reading that you will emphasize as a teacher—map reading or finding main ideas, for example.

informal measures are criterion-referenced in the sense that they are task-oriented and provide evidence of skill mastery.

Evaluating Formal Reading Tests

For a good many years standardized tests have been the tail that wags the dog in reading instruction. Assessment of student progress has too often been limited to an annual administration of an achievement test. Reading groups have often been formed solely on the basis of grade equivalents obtained from standardized tests. Unfortunately, some teachers have regarded such tests as sacred measures of their own effectiveness.

Standardized tests have a definite place in a comprehensive evaluation program. They can provide gross measures of overall performance. School districts can use the results of formal tests to make judgments concerning the overall effectiveness of their reading programs. Teachers can use the results of standardized reading tests in conjunction with intelligence tests to determine whether an individual child is performing up to expectancy. Or children who are reading at approximately the same difficulty level can be identified for purposes of grouping (difficulty level is most often the level a child can attain with maximum concentration, not the level at which instruction should be provided). It is important that standardized tests be kept in proper perspective.

In order to understand fully the limitations of standardized tests, how to use them, and how to interpret them, teachers need some special training in educational measurement. We cannot provide that here, but we can make you aware of several valuable sources of information about formal reading measures. Several publications of the International Reading Association are useful references. These include *Reading Tests and Teachers: A Practical Guide* (Schreiner [Ed.], 1979) and *Diagnostic and Criterion-Referenced Tests* (Schell [Ed.], 1981). Other references of particular value are described later.

Buros Mental Measurement Yearbook

The *Eighth Mental Measurements Yearbook* (1978), edited by Oscar K. Buros, is a comprehensive source of information on standardized tests. One section deals with tests; a second examines books on measurement.

The *Mental Measurements Yearbook* contains reviews of commercially prepared tests. Here a teacher checks on the uses and limitations of a standardized test.

We are primarily concerned with the section on tests, where entries are classified by type. One major section is devoted to reading tests; subsections include oral reading, reading readiness, special fields, reading speed, study skills, and miscellaneous reading tests.

Each entry provides the following information about a reading test:

1. Title.
2. Description of the groups for which the test is intended.
3. Date of copyright.
4. Part scores (subtests).
5. Whether test is a group or individual test.
6. Whether test is machine scorable.
7. Forms, parts, and levels of test.
8. Reliability and validity.
9. Cost.
10. Time required for administration.
11. Author.
12. Publisher.

A test references section—which lists all known references, published and unpublished, on the construction, validity, use, and limitations of the test—follows each entry. Critical reviews of each test are also included. Some of the reviews are written especially for the *Yearbook;* others are published elsewhere and are only excerpted in the *Yearbook.* In either case, the views of experts concerning the value of each test are provided.

One can find reviews of achievement batteries, intelligence tests, and tests for certain content areas (for example, mathematics, social studies, and science). The entries on character and personality tests may be of special interest to elementary school teachers.

The purpose of the Buros *Yearbook* is to help those who use standardized tests to select the best of what is available and to interpret correctly the results obtained from the use of tests. Unfortunately, many teachers fail to use the *Yearbook,* perhaps because they do not know of its existence or because they do not realize the importance of doing so. It is clear from the reviews in the Buros *Yearbook* that the results of some tests are of practically no value—so great are the limitations of these tests—yet they are used and believed in. Classroom teachers must assume responsibility for obtaining the information needed for making judgments about the standardized tests they use.

Buros Volumes on Reading Tests

Buros has compiled information and reviews on reading tests in *Reading Tests and Reviews,* Volume I (1968), and Volume II (1975). These volumes aid in the task of checking on reading tests. As information has been taken from the first seven volumes of the *Yearbook,* the necessity for

---

Evaluating Formal Tests

1. Locate Buros' *Mental Measurements Yearbook* in the reference section of a library. Turn to the reviews of reading tests. Find a test that might be useful at your grade level, read the reviews of that test, and make note of the test's good and weak points according to the reviewers. Discuss your findings with colleagues or classmates.

2. Examine the manual accompanying a norm-referenced test. Find the reliability and validity coefficients reported for the test. How were these coefficients determined? What criterion was the test compared to for determining validity? To what extent does the test focus on skills and knowledge you believe are important to effective reading performance?

3. How were the norms established for the test you examined in task 2? Are children like those you teach or intend to teach included in the norming population?

4. Administer a standardized reading test to a child. Score the test, and consult the test manual for guidance in how to interpret the results. Consider what use the results have in helping you as a teacher plan appropriate instruction for that child. Share your conclusions with a classmate or your instructor.

Diagnosing Needs and Assessing Progress

following the cross-references used in the original yearbooks is eliminated. A copy of this reference should be available in every school district.

Informal Sources of Information

Although every classroom virtually teems with valuable information that can help a teacher identify individual needs, we will describe only eight in detail here. These will serve to illustrate rather than exhaust the possibilities for informal assessment. It is our view that the teacher should approach every classroom activity with assessment in mind. Presumably, lessons or activities are planned because they contribute to the achievement of some identifiable goal the teacher has consciously set and sought. Children's progress toward that goal can be measured in numerous ways. The work sheet, the written assignment, the discussion, the learning center, the reading game, the crossword puzzle, and so on, can all be informal measures if they are regarded as such.

Informal sources of information are particularly useful in providing continuous assessment of a student's performance, thereby providing the information necessary for prescribing day-by-day corrective instruction. Whereas most group tests measure broad skill areas, informal measures that assess specific skills can be selected and used with certain children. Furthermore, attitudes, tastes, and interests—all of which are difficult to assess by formal means—can be tapped by various informal measures.

Eight categories of informal sources of information will be discussed:

1. Workbooks and work sheets.
2. Conferences.
3. Checklists and inventories.
4. Cumulative records.
5. Oral reading inventories.
6. Teacher observation.
7. Cloze procedure.
8. Trial teaching.

Workbooks and Work Sheets Provide Diagnostic Information

Although they are usually regarded as exercises for practice and not as assessment devices, workbooks and work sheets can be extremely effective means for daily evaluation. For example, following the introduction of a new skill, the teacher can assign appropriate follow-up exercises in a workbook or provide work sheets on a topic. In addition to providing practice in using the newly learned skill, such a procedure enables the teacher to determine which children might be regrouped for additional instruction and which need individual attention. Teacher-prepared work sheets can be especially effective because the special needs of individuals within a class are considered as the instructor writes the exercise.

It should be remembered from the earlier discussion that workbook or work sheet exercises serve the diagnostic function described here only when they match the teacher's instructional goals. Unfortunately, paper-and-pencil tasks are often given to children for the purpose of keeping them occupied quietly in their seats while the teacher is busy with other children. No careful match is made between the needs of the child, the instructional goals, and the workbook task. When this match is absent, the exercise becomes busy work that does little to provide useful diagnostic information. You can avoid this unhappy situation by selecting or developing exercises that tie into your instructional program.

Teacher-Student Conferences Provide Opportunities for Assessment

The teacher can use conferences with individual children to gather information that is useful in planning daily instructional activities. Even teachers who depend heavily on grouped instruction should attempt to meet periodically and on a regular basis with each child. Interaction of this sort permits the teacher to know the child personally

Regular teacher-student conferences provide valuable information to the teacher and encouragement to the child.

and identify his or her needs as no other technique can. The conference is uniquely suited to assessing the child's attitude toward reading, reading tastes and interests, and strategy for gaining meaning from the printed page.

Conferences can be structured in various ways to serve different purposes. Activities can range from open-ended discussions of a book the child is reading independently to in-depth analysis of oral reading performance. Other examples of possible conference activities include checking skill development, reviewing previously learned skills, clarifying misunderstanding, and reinforcing progress. The teacher who enters each conference with specific objectives in mind will be in a good position to decide what should be done to accomplish those objectives. Although some activities may be strictly diagnostic, others may be instructional.

Not to be underestimated is the value of the child's coming to have a pleasant association between reading and working individually with the teacher in a relaxed conference setting. This alone can be instrumental in building positive attitudes toward reading. The tutorial setting of a conference is also well suited to helping the child be successful with reading tasks in that complete adjustment to individual needs is possible even if it is only for a brief period of time. Insights gained from a concentrated ten-minute session every second or third week can assist the teacher in adjusting to a child's individual needs within those group or assigned independent activities conducted between conferences. See page 402 for a sample conference format.

The frequency and length of conferences are open-ended matters that depend on various factors. Some teachers prefer shorter, more frequent conferences; others believe longer conferences are better even if they cannot be held as often. The teacher's use of groups, the materials selected for instruction, the age and ability of the children, and the experience of the teacher are all examples of factors that affect the scheduling and use of conferences. We suggest you start slowly and build up to a frequency that suits your style of teaching and the children's learning.

One useful strategy is to begin with conferences that are intended to explore personal interests and attitudes. A simple questionnaire such as the one shown on page 471 can be used to help you ask pertinent questions (for example, "What hobbies do you have?"). Later, a series of conferences can focus on the reading children are doing for recreation. Questions can be general and largely open-ended (for example, "Why did you choose this book? What did you like about the book?"). Gradually, you can add features to the conferences that supply needed information on skills growth. Comprehension questions can become more specific (for example, "Which character in the book would you want for a friend? Why?"). You can survey vocabulary and word recognition skills; the child can read a paragraph orally.

Conferences are extremely helpful as a means of gathering important information. Unfortunately, much of the information can slip away if it is not recorded. Although a narrative summary can always be written and dropped in a folder for each child following a conference, this is a time-consuming way to keep records. Teachers often employ another type of informal measure, the checklist or inventory, to record their findings and observations in a conference.

Checklists and Inventories Tie Directly to Instructional Objectives

Checklists and inventories are little more than lists of questions or skills that require a brief response or simple check to complete. They can be prepared for practically any aspect of reading instruction and may be completed by either teacher or child, depending on their purpose.

A sample inventory is now given to illustrate what can be done.

Interest Inventory Record

Name _____

What games do you like to play best of all? _____
What other games do you like? _____
What do you like to make? _____
Do you have pets? _____
What things do you collect? _____
What are your hobbies? _____
Suppose you could have one wish that might come true. What would it
  be? _____
What is your favorite television program? _____
What other television programs do you watch? _____
What is the best book you ever read? _____
What other books have you liked? _____
Do you have any books of your own? About how many? _____
Does anyone read to you? How often? _____
Do you go to the library? _____
Do you read comic books? What is your favorite comic book? _____
What magazines or newspapers do you like best? _____
What kind of work do you want to do when you finish school? _____
What school subject do you like best? _____
What school subject do you like least? _____

This inventory is completed by the child and provides the teacher with information that may be valuable in planning instructional activities. Obviously, books or stories can be found to capitalize on the interests revealed through this inventory. Children's attitudes, travel experiences, home background, and various other matters can be surveyed in this way.

Checklists can be developed that itemize the various elements in some area of reading instruction. This becomes, in effect, a statement of instructional goals. The child's progress toward mastery of each element can be noted on the checklist as a way of keeping records. The teacher can tell at a glance where work remains to be done or, by looking at a class summary sheet, who might be grouped together for a special lesson. A sample checklist follows.

_____ knows the meaning of the following prefixes:

Child's name

Yes	No	Comments
		un
		de
		re
		pre
		non
		tri
		bi
		post
		ultra

Checklists and inventories are valuable on a whole-class basis. Information gathered with these devices enables teachers to adjust their programs in a variety of ways in order to make the best of individualized instruction. Examples of checklists and questionnaires, as well as other informal measures, are presented throughout this text, and their use in special skill areas is discussed.

The Cumulative Record Can Be Useful

The cumulative record is a sometimes-useful source of information that has been compiled in previous years. The results of formal testing are normally recorded in the cumulative record. More important, the observations of the child's previous teachers are often reported, as well as pertinent information concerning health, attendance, and home background. The results of referral for special testing or training, if this has occurred, are contained in most cumulative records.

You should be careful about letting the observations of a child's previous teacher prejudice your appraisal. With the proper precautions, the cumulative record file can provide much insight, possibly even showing where one teacher's personal perceptions of a child may have had adverse effects on the child's classroom performance. An in-depth study of one child often begins with the information contained in the cumulative folder.

Assessment with the Oral Reading Inventory

Both tradition and common sense suggest that a child's oral reading performance is an index of reading ability. The reasoning seems to be that one who has difficulty reading aloud evidently has some problem that careful observation and analysis will reveal. There is some truth to this belief, but there is also much fiction.

Given appropriate training, a teacher can learn much about Curt's reading level, as well as his specific needs, by analyzing his oral reading performance. The procedure is far more complex than it appears at first glance, however. The time-honored custom of counting each "error" the child makes while reading aloud in order to calculate his or her success is under widespread attack—and deservedly so. Before getting into the details of how oral reading performance should be interpreted, let's look at the nature and content of oral reading inventories. Discussion elsewhere in this book deals with oral reading that is not primarily for purposes of assessment.

Paragraphs Increase in Difficulty

Oral reading inventories are all very similar. They include a series of paragraphs that begin at a simple level and gradually increase in difficulty. Grade designations are usually assigned to each level. The child's task is to read a paragraph aloud and then recall what he or she read in his or her own words, answer specific questions about what he or she read, or do a combination of both. This occurs in a conference setting, where distractions are kept to a minimum. The teacher's task is to record on a second copy of the material just what the child does while reading and how well he or she recalls the details afterward. With this technique the teacher tries to identify what level of material the child can handle successfully. Although criteria differ in their specifics, generally the instructional level is defined as that where comprehension and word recognition accuracy indicate the child is not overburdened. Powell (1968) recommends these specific criteria:

		Word Recognition Accuracy	Comprehension Questions
Frustration reading level	Grades 1–2	84% or less	50% or less correct
	Grades 3–6	90% or less	50% or less correct
Instructional reading level	Grades 1–2	85–95%	60–70% correct
	Grades 3–6	91–94%	60–70% correct
Independent reading level	Grades 1–2	96% or above	80% or above correct
	Grades 3–6	95% or above	80% or above correct

The most obvious application of this procedure is in identifying what level of material children should read in the instructional program. Caution must be used in accepting the level indicated by this procedure because the materials used for instruction may be graded differently from the oral reading inventory. A 3.0 level on a commercially prepared inventory may not equal a 3.0 level in the Macmillan, Ginn, or other reading program.

Skill Needs Can Also Be Identified

In addition to indicating something about the child's reading level, an oral reading inventory can be used to identify specific skill needs. The word recognition miscues[2] recorded by the teacher often follow a pattern. One child may consistently miss word endings, for example, or another child may skip words according to some discernible pattern (all words of three or more syllables in length).

The value of identifying patterns of miscues is that the teacher is alerted and begins to look for explanations for the behavior. Some oral reading problems are purely ones of fluency and do not signal an underlying reading deficiency. The solution is one of improving the child's skills of oral interpretation. Other oral reading problems should alert the teacher to genuine instructional needs. When this is the case, appropriate corrective instruction is needed. A third explanation of oral reading miscues is that they may simply reflect the child's attempts to match his or her language with the language of the author. It is this possibility that makes oral reading diagnosis complex and potentially misleading to the teacher who does not understand the relationship between oral reading miscues and the reader's search for meaning (Beebe, 1980).

It is not possible to explore the topic of oral reading miscues from a psycholinguistic viewpoint in sufficient detail here to do it justice. Some aspects of the relationship will be discussed in subsequent chapters, and this will provide some additional insight. We will discuss here the implications of psycholinguistics for oral reading diagnosis as it fits into the issues being raised on assessment.

Oral Reading Miscues Reveal the Child's Reading Strategy

Reading is a process in which the reader scans printed symbols on a page for the purpose of retrieving meaning. The reader, let's call her Betty, comes to this task with a lifetime of personal experiences to draw on and an intuitive understanding of how language operates. Drawing on her experiences and language, Betty uses cues from the page to understand the writer's message. As she scans, the reader predicts meaning. When she predicts well, she comprehends well. When her predictions are wrong, meaning breaks down, and she must reread to pick up cues she needs to predict correctly.

The reading process viewed in this way is not a precise, word-by-word processing of the printed page. Quite the opposite. It is an imprecise searching process involving educated guesswork on the part of the reader. Every word is not processed. In fact, the better Betty is at predicting, the fewer cues she needs to read with understanding. Her experience with the topic and her ability with language are more important than her skill at recognizing all of the individual words on the page.

The implications of this view of reading are many and far-reaching;

[2] A miscue is any oral response made by the child while reading that which differs from the expected response.

for the topic at hand, they are significant. As Betty reads aloud, the printed symbols trigger her speech. When the language of the reader differs from the language of the author, the result is a miscue. Often the reader who is gaining meaning will correct herself, thus indicating she knows her attempt was incorrect. Other miscues may not be corrected, yet they do not alter the meaning of what is read and in that sense are not wrong. An oral reading diagnosis that simply counts errors without regard to their nature fails to reflect what is known about language and reading. In effect, not all miscues are equal, and any diagnosis that seeks to understand truly what the reader is doing well and what she is not doing well must involve some miscue analysis.

Deciding What Constitutes a Genuine Error

Some disagreement over what should be counted as an oral reading error is apparent in the directions for scoring the *Gray Oral Reading Test* and the *Gilmore Oral Reading Test* (Harris & Niles, 1982). Table 14.1 contrasts the categories of errors for these two tests. General agreement is found for five types of errors: aid, omission, insertion, substitution, and repetition. Mispronunciation is an error according to either scheme; however, the *Gray* system differentiates between partial and gross mispronunciation. The *Gray* also calls an inversion a specific type of error; the *Gilmore* shows an inversion as a mispronunciation only. The *Gilmore* has special categories for disregarding punctuation and for hesitation.

Disagreement over what constitutes an oral reading error is not limited to the *Gray* and *Gilmore* tests. Other oral reading tests—such as subtests of the *Durrell Analysis of Reading Difficulty* and the *Spache Diagnosis Reading Scales*—contain other definitions of what constitutes an error. For example, the *Durrell* instructs the examiner to count as errors all words that are repeated. The *Spache* counts repetitions as errors only when two or more words are repeated. The *Durrell* counts any hesitation as an error; the *Spache* does not.

What causes this apparent confusion? When is an oral reading "error" really worth counting, and when is it only a momentary stumble, a speech pattern, or some miscue related to the stress of reading orally? This question can best be answered in terms of the purpose

TABLE 14.1 Comparison of Errors recorded on *Gray* and *Gilmore* Tests

Errors recorded in the Gray Oral Reading Test	Errors recorded in the Gilmore Oral Reading Test
1. Aid	1. Word pronounced by examiner
2. Gross mispronunciation	2. Mispronunciation
3. Partial mispronunciation	3. Omission
4. Omission	4. Insertion
5. Insertion	5. Substitution
6. Substitution	6. Disregard of punctuation
7. Repetition	7. Repetition
8. Inversion	8. Hesitation

of identifying miscues, namely, to provide a basis for improving reading performance. An oral reading miscue that interferes with the message or indicates an inability to attack an unknown word should be counted as a genuine error. Omitting *not* from a sentence changes the meaning of a message considerably and constitutes a serious error, especially if it is not corrected by the reader. Adding *and* to a sentence is unlikely to interfere with the message and can probably be ignored as an indicator of any serious reading problem.

Consider this situation: Juan is asked to read the sentence "A bird hopped across the grass." Instead, he reads: "A robin hopped across the green grass." Even though Juan's version is different from the written one, he evidently understand what he is reading. In fact, one might argue that Juan's version is more vivid and descriptive than the written one, thus suggesting extraordinary comprehension.

Contrast Juan's reading with Karl's, who says: "A bird hopped across the run." A tabulation of errors would show: Juan—2 errors; Karl—1 error. Juan's miscues "make sense." Karl's indicate something serious: He does not correct a miscue that is grammatically incorrect, the substitution involves a word with a different meaning, and the words look different.

The *Reading Miscue Inventory* or *RMI* (Goodman & Burke, 1972) gives extensive directions for analyzing miscues. The *RMI* requires that nine specific questions be asked about every miscue:

1. Is a dialect variation involved in the *miscue?*
2. Is a shift in intonation involved in the *miscue?*
3. How much does the *miscue* look like what was expected?
4. How much does the *miscue* sound like what was expected?
5. Is the grammatical function of the *miscue* the same as the grammatical function of the word in the text?
6. Is the *miscue* corrected?
7. Does the *miscue* occur in a structure that is grammatically acceptable?
8. Does the *miscue* occur in a structure that is semantically acceptable?
9. Does the *miscue* result in a change of meaning?

Goodman and Burke are interested in the nature of the child's responses in oral reading from a psycholinguistic perspective. Their view is based on the idea that all miscues are not of equal importance. In fact, some miscues may provide positive proof of a child's reading skill. For example, some substitutions may fit into the syntax of a sentence and not affect meaning (for example, Juan's substitution of robin for bird). Miscues of this type can indicate that the child is making heavy use of context and comprehending the message while reading. Additional evidence to support this view is obtained when other substitutions that alter the meaning of a sentence or fail to fit into the syntax of the sentence are corrected by the child.

Reading comprehension is assessed in two ways with the RMI procedure: first, the analysis of miscues as mentioned earlier (are miscues that alter meaning corrected by the child, for example?) and second, by means of a Retelling Score. The Retelling Score is based on the reader's recollections of what he or she has read immediately after finishing a story. Goodman and Burke indicate that both measures of comprehension are necessary to differentiate between readers who produce few miscues but gain little understanding and readers who miscue often but remember quite well what they've read.

The Retelling Score is based on an analysis of the material read, converted into outline form, with points assigned to main components. Story material, for example is analyzed as follows:

Character Analysis	Points
Recall	15
Development	15
Events	30
Plot	20
Theme	20

If five characters appear in the story, the child could receive three points for each one recalled, in this case. Information recalled about the characters' appearance, attitudes, behaviors, and so forth earns the reader points for understanding of character development. Similar analysis is made of the story in the other categories.

Following the child's initial response in retelling the story, questions are asked that stimulate expansion. If the child does not recall specific information, it is not supplied, and questions are kept general: "What was (name of character) like," for example? Detailed instructions for preparing a story outline and scoring retellings are provided in the RMI Manual (Goodman & Burke, 1972).

The classroom teacher can apply the general RMI principles to interpreting oral reading miscues without an extensive analysis. At times the thorough analysis of reading samples may be justified for a few individuals.

A special word is needed concerning the assessment of oral reading miscues of children with regional or subcultural dialects. Some teachers unwittingly record and score as reading errors pronunciations that "sound wrong" to them. For example, *that* pronounced *dat* is sometimes scored as a mispronunciation. In view of our earlier recommendation concerning what to regard as a genuine reading error, pronunciations learned in a particular region of the country or in a particular cultural group should not be regarded as reading errors.

The translation of graphic symbols into their oral counterparts depends largely on the reader's background of experience and resulting language patterns. For example, Kasdon (1968) reports that black subjects in a study of oral reading consistently read *was* for *were* and sometimes pronounced *with* as *wif*. Latin Americans frequently substituted *b* for *p*, as in *bet* for *pet*, and *v* for *b*, as in *vrilliant* for *brilliant*. There can be no doubt that these subjects were reading, if reading is defined as gaining meaning from the printed page. Regarding these "mispronunciations" as *reading errors* is indefensible.

Oral Reading Inventories

Teachers can make their own oral reading inventories by taking paragraphs from materials they use for instruction, arranging them in order of difficulty, and developing questions or standards for judging comprehension. Such inventories are called *informal reading inventories* (IRI) and have the advantage of being truly representative of the material children will read daily. Many publishers now provide such an IRI for use with their basal series.

There are also a number of commercially prepared oral reading inventories that are similar in design and purpose. These include the *Basic Reading Inventory, Classroom Reading Inventory,* and the *Standard Reading Inventory.* These inventories provide instructions for administration and some information on interpretation. Some also provide norms—a feature of questionable value. The fact that two or three forms are usually included in oral reading inventories is laudable. This permits retesting and makes them useful for assessment of a child's progress over a period of time.

Oral reading can be an excellent source of information. Its greatest value is that the teacher can watch for certain behaviors as the need arises. Furthermore, the goals of the instructional program can easily influence what is observed. Goals can be adjusted as oral reading diagnosis reveals the instructional needs of children. This is true because the teacher is so actively involved in this kind of assessment.

Oral Reading Assessment

1. Construct an informal reading inventory for the grade level of interest to you. Include paragraphs at least two levels above and below grade level. To check comprehension, either create questions to be answered or outline the key points to be covered when the reader retells what he or she can remember.
2. Administer your IRI (from Step 1) or a commercially prepared inventory. Differentiate between miscues that are important indicators of possible difficulty and miscues that can safely be ignored. If possible, examine the manual for the *Reading Miscue Inventory* (Goodman & Burke, 1972).
3. Compare the directions for scoring two or more commercial IRI's. Make a chart similar to the one on page 475 contrasting the errors to be noted.

Teacher Observation

Teacher observation provides another means for gathering information on children's needs. We regard teacher observation as the single most important element in an evaluation program. In a single day, the classroom teacher has countless opportunities to appraise the progress and needs of each learner. Teachers also have the opportunity to synthesize the diagnostic data gathered from all other sources and adjust their observations to fill in missing information. With the press of daily responsibilities, however, teacher observation often fails to provide the information desired (Cunningham, 1982).

This discrepancy between the potential and actual value of teacher observation can be overcome by three valuable techniques:

1. Systematic observation,
2. Anecdotal records,
3. Samples of products.

Systematic Observation

The variety of activities occurring during a reading lesson, as well as the number of children in a typical classroom, combine to form a complex set of interactions for the teacher to observe. It is essential that specific purposes for observation be outlined ahead of time. The teacher must decide on which child or children to focus attention and during which activities. These factors are determined by the need for information. For example, if test data, workbook performance, and daily work all point to specific instructional needs for a given child, the teacher may wish to confirm this information with his or her own observations. Through planning, systematic observations can be conducted. Haphazard observation on an incidental basis usually provides little useful information.

An example of systematic observation for a predetermined purpose may be helpful here. Suppose a teacher notices one of the students confusing the prefixes *pre* and *pro* in workbook assignment. By looking at an achievement test given in the fall, the teacher finds several vocabulary items answered incorrectly when *pre* is used, but several others of the same type are correct. The teacher also recalls a tendency on the part of this student occasionally to substitute the wrong prefix during oral reading. In view of this information, the teacher has a conference with the child to correct any misconceptions and thereafter pays special attention when the opportunity to observe this skill occurs. Evidence of continued confusion should lead to further instruction.

Anecdotal Records

Teacher observations can be further systematized by the use of rather simple anecdotal record keeping. Pertinent observations concerning an individual child, gathered in either a systematic or incidental manner, are entered in a notebook or noted on file cards. During the press of daily duties, a word or phrase can be noted on a slip of paper to aid in recall. Later, more explanation and detail can be written into a child's record. Patterns of behavior may emerge in such records, and careful documentation relieves the teacher of trying to recall all significant related incidents. Such records are often useful on a broader scale than simply for reading instruction. A sample anecdotal record follows:

<u>Ricky Owens</u>

Name

September 2—Ricky brought a book from home to share with the class. He read orally with excellent expression and phrasing. Title: *Rasmus and the Vagabond.*

September 12—Especially interested in basal reader story, "Hide Rack," story of a dog. *Note:* Check to see if he has read *Big Red* by James Kjelgaard.

October 14—Workbook poorly done. Careless errors. *Note:* Watch Ricky to see if this reading group is too slow for him.

October 18 Moved Ricky to top group. Seems very pleased and anxious to succeed. His best friend, George, is in this group. This may be troublesome.

November 7—Absent today. Missed introduction to Dewey decimal system. *Note:* Give Ricky individual help and a special work sheet to check his understanding.

November 21—Very emotional today. Disturbed his reading group during independent work. Check with principal to see if there are any known problems at home.

November 22—New brother born yesterday. Ricky is proud *and* more normal today.

December 4—Achievement test results indicate a deficiency in vocabulary. Use listening post and vocabulary-building record to begin corrective program.

Samples of Products

Samples of the child's work collected over a period of time can be especially valuable in evaluating a learner. Patterns of errors can be readily identified by this procedure, and progress can also be documented. Samples of work should be gathered in specific skill areas or spread across a broad range of skills, depending on the progress of an individual child. The simplest procedure for assembling a collection of products is to develop a folder for each child. Periodically a product from every member of the class can be filed; at other times a particularly revealing or timely product can be filed for individual children (*see* Fig. 14.1).

Information for individualizing instruction does not come from a single source, nor does it all arrive at one time. The instruments and techniques described in this section are used jointly and continuously to provide the information needed for properly individualizing instruction. As stated earlier, specific application of diagnostic procedures and techniques in specific skill areas will be made throughout the text.

The Cloze Procedure Is a Versatile Diagnostic Tool

A classroom teacher can gather useful and revealing information about a child's reading performance with the use of the *cloze procedure. Cloze* is a term derived from "closure," which refers to the human tendency

Martha   *Reading*   *March 18*

Frederick Douglas
fights for freedom
is about Frederick Douglas
born sometime in Febuary.
He was born as a slave in the
South.

coten feild

FIGURE 14.1 A Child's Daily Work. This sample of a child's daily work reveals a good deal about the child's comprehension of a story. Children's illustrations are useful sources of diagnostic data.

to fill in or complete pictures, sentences, or other stimuli that are incomplete. For example, you are inclined to complete the following sentence by inserting the missing word: "A flock of ducks flew overhead as the sun sank slowly in the _____ ." Past experience and your psychological processes cause you to add "west" or some other synonym in the open slot. Similarly, pictures, such as the ones that follow, are "filled-in" and perceived as wholes by the mind:

Diagnosing Needs and Assessing Progress   **481**

You are aware that parts are missing, to be sure, but you perceive the whole nevertheless.

This human tendency to bring closure has led to the use of the cloze procedure in identifying, measuring, and improving comprehension and in assessing language competence. By determining how effectively a child can supply words that have been deleted from a passage, you gain a measure of how much difficulty that child is having with the concepts and language it presents.

To illustrate, suppose you are interested in knowing which children in a class can be expected to profit from reading a book you have selected. You then follow these steps:

1. Take a passage from the selection of at least 275 words that is not dependent on previous information from the story or book. (The beginning of a section or chapter is usually appropriate.)
2. Begin with the second sentence, and delete every fifth word if you are working with an upper-grade children; every tenth word if you are working with lower-grade children.
3. Type up the entire passage, putting a blank in place of each deleted word. Be sure to make each blank the same length, and leave enough space for children to write in their answers.

Your cloze passage is now ready to be completed by the students. Give each child a copy of the passage. Ask all the children to write words that they think belong there in each of the blanks. Be sure to explain that you realize this is not easy, and it will be necessary for the child to guess occasionally. Encourage "educated guessing," based on what makes sense. Indicate that all blanks should be completed. Provide sufficient time for every child to finish the entire passage.

Next, compare the child's responses to the words that were deleted. Research with the cloze procedure suggests that you should rigidly adhere to the wording of the original passage in scoring the child's responses. The reason for being fairly strict about counting synonyms wrong is that the criteria developed for interpreting student performance are based on rigid scoring procedures. When you deviate by counting a synonym correct, you introduce a subjective variable that influences the results. Because you are usually after a general sense of the child's reading ability when you use this procedure and are not conducting a research investigation, your judgment concerning what to count as correct or incorrect *is appropriate.*

Students able to replace correctly 41 per cent or more of the words deleted will normally be able to read the book without undue difficulty. Those who get less than 41 per cent correct will probably find the book too hard to read. By studying the types of errors each child makes, you can gain further insight into their instructional needs. Many teachers obtain useful information by asking individuals to explain how they arrived at their answers. This can reveal much about the child's reading abilities.

Cloze Procedure

A series of cloze procedures can be developed—one from each level of a basal series, for example—to determine where each child should be placed for daily instruction. You can experiment with this assessment procedure to determine what scoring criteria and procedures are most appropriate for the instructional program in your classroom.

Rankin and Culhane (1969) established these criteria for interpreting the results of children's performances on cloze passages:

Independent level—The student correctly replaces 61 per cent or more of the deleted words.
Instructional level—The student correctly replaces 41 to 60 per cent of the deleted words.
Frustrational level—The student correctly replaces 40 per cent or less of the deleted words.

A sample cloze passage is now given. Using these criteria, you should be able to replace *eleven* words correctly:

An index is an alphabetical list of names, subjects, events, and so on, together with page numbers, and is usually placed at the end of a book. By consulting the index 1. _____ reader can locate exactly 2. _____ in a book the 3. _____ that he wants is 4. _____ . Because of its utility 5. _____ index is one of 6. _____ most frequently used features 7. _____ many reference volumes. The 8. _____ of an almanac, for 9. _____ , would be most unwieldly 10. _____ an index.

By the 11. _____ grades the increased use 12. _____ reading in the content 13. _____ will necessitate instruction on 14. _____ use of the index. 15. _____ must begin with the 16. _____ and move to the 17. _____ complex. At first, simply 18. _____ specific terms in the 19. _____ index and noting a 20. _____ page number is appropriate. 21. _____ , using cross-references, identifying 22. _____ that might provide information 23. _____ a topic, and employing 24. _____ indexes for the same 25. _____ can be undertaken. The 26. _____ exercise illustrates an activity 27. _____ using the index.

Words Deleted: 1. a, 2. where, 3. information, 4. located, 5. the, 6. the, 7. of, 8. use, 9. example, 10. without, 11. intermediate, 12. of, 13. areas, 14. the, 15. Instruction, 16. simple, 17. more, 18. locating, 19. alphabetical, 20, specific, 21. Later, 22. entries, 23. on, 24. multiple, 25. book, 26. following, 27. on.

Trial Teaching Yields Another Kind of Information

Trial teaching is a technique that can be helpful in gaining information about a child's needs and learning style. The label *trial teaching* is actually quite self-explanatory. The teacher identifies a skill or bit of information previous diagnosis has indicated the child needs to learn. A lesson is planned to achieve the desired goal and instruction is provided. By noting the child's responses, the teacher is able to see how prerequisite learning is applied and where confusion or misinformation creates a problem. The teacher can also note how the child goes about learning new information or skills. With insights gained from these observations, the teacher can adjust subsequent instruction to draw on the child's strengths.

Typically, trial teaching is most effective in a one-to-one setting. The reading clinician often employs this technique in working with a reading disabled child, for example. Insights can be gained from watching a child tackle a learning task that no test of recall or application of skills will reveal. The conference setting is an ideal one for trial teaching.

Let's look at an example. Teacher Rhoda Howsam has noticed that Jackie has difficulty in reading maps. At their next reading conference, Rhoda presents Jackie with information concerning how to interpret a road map. Symbols for a bridge, railroad, highway, and city are introduced. Jackie is asked to find an example of each on a map. Rhoda notices that Jackie confuses the symbols because she does not know how to interpret the map legend. Rhoda also discovers that unless the symbols are matched with pictures (symbol ⋈ with a picture of a bridge, for example), Jackie confuses them. As a result Rhoda learns that certain prerequisite information is not understood and that Jackie needs vivid visual stimuli to form the necessary perceptual images. Thereafter Rhoda plans instruction for Jackie that allows for these factors. Thus trial teaching has provided information that is immediately applied in the instructional program.

Summary

In order to individualize reading instruction, the classroom teacher must have information about each child's reading performance. Assessment can be undertaken with formal and informal measures to identify the child's instructional reading level and individual pattern of strengths and weaknesses. To be useful in planning daily classroom activities, assessment must relate to the teacher's instructional goals. Informal measures are usually more helpful in this respect that formal ones.

Diagnostic information can be gathered from everyday activities, such as workbook assignments, conferences, and oral reading performance. The cloze procedure and trial teaching can also yield valuable information regarding student progress and needs.

criterion-referenced test | informal measure
norm-referenced test | cloze procedure
instructional reading level | checklist
reading miscue | questionnaire
formal measure | anecdotal record

Discussion Questions

1. Why is individualization of reading instruction heavily dependent on thorough and continued diagnosis?

2. Mr. Humbert is preparing for a parent-teacher conference. He wants to show Mr. and Mrs. Walker what progress their son, Mark, has made over the course of the school year. How would you suggest he proceed? Why?

Recommended Readings

Dixon, Carol N. (1977, May). Language experience stories as a diagnostic tool. *Language Arts, LIV* (5), 501–505.

Dixon provides a simple evaluation checklist that can be used to determine students' language development and suggests instructional implications based on the scores.

Johnston, Peter H. (1984). Assessment in reading. In P. David Pearson et al. (Eds.), *Handbook of Reading Research*. New York: Longman.

Johnston reviews and summarizes investigations concerned with the assessment of reading and argues that the heavy reliance on product measures evident in the literature is largely inconsistent with the current emphasis on process in reading instruction and reading research.

Pikulski, John J., & Shanahan, Timothy. (Eds.). (1982). *Approaches to the informal evaluation of reading.* Newark, DE: International Reading Association.

This book summarizes alternative approaches that classroom teachers can take to formal, standardized tests of reading achievement on the premise that such approaches are especially helpful in planning and adjusting daily instruction.

Schreiner, Robert (Ed.). (1979). *Reading tests and teachers: A practical guide.* Newark, DE: International Reading Association.

Here is described testing as only one part of the evaluation process. The appropriate way to select tests, how to develop valid and reliable tests, and how to use test results in planning instruction are also discussed.

Wixson, Karen K., et al. (1984, January). An interview for assessing students' perceptions of classroom reading tasks. *The Reading Teacher, 37* (4), 346–352.

This article describes how a teacher-pupil interview can be conducted to gain insights into the strategy a student uses to understand while reading.

15

Adapting Reading Instruction for Exceptional Children

Some children learn school subjects quickly and easily, whereas others learn those same subjects slowly and laboriously. Both types are ill-equipped to learn at the same pace and in the same environment that is acceptable for the majority of students and, therefore, require special thought and attention from the classroom teacher. Public awareness and public law now require that *all* children be provided with educational opportunities that allow full development of their abilities. Teachers and schools must adapt instruction so that children formerly placed in special schools because of their handicaps can be integrated more fully into the regular classroom. They must also make provisions for children with special academic gifts so that these students can thrive in the subjects that match their talents. Children whose home language is not English must also receive special attention from classroom teachers.

Proficiency in reading, no matter how great or how limited the abilities of the individual child, stands at the center of academic learning. Classroom teachers, therefore, search daily for the means to lead all these children to a level of reading and thinking that will enable them to use their talents to grow as they can.

This chapter focuses on the following questions:

- *Who are "exceptional children"?*
- *What characteristics of these children need to be taken into account in planning reading instruction in the classroom?*
- *How can reading methods and materials be adapted for exceptional children?*

Who Are "Exceptional Children"?

Children who require extra attention and modified instructional programs in school have come to be identified as "exceptional children." Some of these children require more help than the average student because they have a physical handicap (such as impaired vision or hearing) that requires some adjustments in teaching procedures, and others need special attention because they are not able to learn in the same way or at the same rate as the average student. In addition to these children who have difficulty in learning, there are others who are able to perform at a higher level than most, either in terms of academic achievement or because of some particular talent or creative ability. Such gifted and talented students are also included within the term "exceptional children" (Blackhurst & Berdine, 1981, p. 9).

For the purposes of the present chapter, one other group of students will be included because they, too, require some modification of instructional procedures. These are the children whose ability to speak English is limited, often because they come from homes in which some language other than English is the dominant one. Such bilingual-bicultural children will need extra help until their ability to use English allows them to function in predominantly English-speaking classrooms.

Legislation Affecting Exceptional Children

Each of the groups of children just described has been affected by federal legislation that not only highlights their particular requirements but also provides funds and guidelines for instruction.

Legislation Affecting the Handicapped: P.L. 94-142

Public Law 94–142 (P.L. 94–142), the Education for All Handicapped Children Act, took effect in 1975 and guaranteed that all children would have available to them a free public education provided within the *least restrictive environment.* For those children with relatively slight learning problems or with manageable physical handicaps, this environment is often the regular classroom. When these children are placed with nonhandicapped students some provision will have to be made for their particular needs, but for the most part they will generally be expected to function as members of the class.

The term *mainstreaming,* although not mentioned in P.L. 94–142, is often used to refer to the practice of placing exceptional children into the regular classroom or into the mainstream of school life. Some handicapped students may need assistance from special educators as a supplement to regular classroom work, and for still more severely handicapped children it may be necessary to provide part of their instruction in special-education classes in addition to their work in the regular classroom. Regardless of the particular arrangement, the purpose is to find the "least restrictive environment" for each child as determined by his or her particular needs and abilities.

A significant feature of P.L. 94–142 is its requirement that an *Individualized Education Program* (IEP) be set up for each handicapped student. The IEP is a document prepared by the classroom teacher, special-education teachers (when they are to be involved), school administrators, the child's parents, and even the individual student whenever that is feasible. The IEP outlines the child's educational status (both strengths and weaknesses), presents a time schedule for instruction, and establishes criteria for evaluation. It thus becomes a blueprint to help the teacher provide meaningful instruction and to ensure that the child's educational needs are met. It also requires a diagnostic approach because assessing the student's strengths and weaknesses is one of the most important elements of effective teaching, especially where handicapped students are concerned. (For additional information on the structure of IEPs, see Gearheart & Weishahn, 1984, pp. 29–36; Lovitt, 1980; Radabaugh & Yukish, 1982, pp. 72–89; Tymitz, 1980.)

Legislation Affecting the Gifted and Talented: P.L. 95–561

In the past it was often assumed that gifted and talented children would succeed on their own without special assistance. However, in the early 1970s it was more fully recognized that gifted children were an educationally neglected group in American schools. In 1972, Congress established the Federal Office for the Gifted and Talented with the mandate to identify the nation's gifted children and to assist in developing their potential. Public Law 95–561 (P.L. 95–561), the Gifted and Talented Children's Education Act, was passed by Congress in 1978. It not only provides for the identification of gifted and talented children but also stipulates that funding shall be made available for programs to meet their needs.

Legislation Affecting the Bilingual-Bicultural: P.L. 93–380

With the passage of Public Law 93–380 (P.L. 93–380) in 1974, Congress established an Office of Bilingual Education within the Office of Education. This law "makes provisions for bilingual education in virtually every aspect of the educational process" (Baca, 1977, p. 17) and recognizes that students with a limited knowledge of English have special educational needs that must take into account the cultural heritage into which each child was born.

Affective Needs of Exceptional Children

The one element that is stressed continually throughout the literature on exceptional children is the importance of social acceptance and the development of a positive self-concept. Being singled out for special classes or appearing and behaving somewhat differently from their peers may make some children feel less worthy or less acceptable. Mainstreaming provides an excellent opportunity for many handicapped children to have the same educational experiences shared by most other children. Similar thought needs to be given to program development for the gifted and talented or bilingual-bicultural so that they, too, feel a part of the total social environment in schools.

A positive attitude toward reading is usually characterized by students' willingness to accept new information and make an effort to understand concepts, to respond to new material by completing reading assignments, and to believe that there is value in what they are doing. Teachers can help handicapped children develop such positive attitudes by providing activities that are simple enough to guarantee satisfactory completion and by showing each child how far he or she has progressed strictly in terms of individual accomplishment, not by comparison with superior readers in the class (Burns, Roe, & Ross, 1984, pp. 13–14).

The importance of the affective domain has been stressed in this book as well, especially with reference to language development (Chapter 3) and reading comprehension (Chapter 9). Because reading is so closely tied to social acceptance in school and therefore to self-esteem, it provides a particularly good way to involve handicapped children with others in the classroom. Through creative dramatics, peer-tutoring sessions, the sharing of written work, and the reading of favorite stories aloud, the child with special needs can feel a part of the classroom experience. Care should be taken to establish an atmosphere of cooperation in the classroom so that children all feel comfortable helping each other learn. It is often beneficial to undertake small group activities in which each member participates to help produce the group's final product, such as a report or book of short stories. Above all, it is vitally important for the teachers to let handicapped students know that they can learn and that the teacher strongly believes this.

Individualizing Reading Instruction

Chapters 12 and 13 of this text discussed ways of choosing and organizing instructional systems and materials in terms of the class as a whole. Although instructional objectives vary according to the needs of handicapped, gifted, or bilingual children, there are a number of teaching-learning principles that can be applied generally in all these groups.

Build on Strengths
Use those areas in which the child already has some competence to form the basis for further improvement. Continuing encouragement in areas of strength will help children to be more willing and confident in overcoming areas of weakness. For example, when a child explains a story, the teacher thanks that child for telling the class about something he or she knows, for helping the class grow.

Determine the Appropriate Pace and Duration of Instruction

Children with special needs may require an adjusted pace or duration for a lesson. Handicapped students who find it difficult to concentrate may need short, intense lessons. All too often this has resulted in too much fragmentation, insufficient time spent on learning, and little integration of prior knowledge to new learning. One way to compensate for this potential disparity is to keep up the pace of a lesson by changing the presentation technique or activity. For example, the reading of a short selection can lead to a short writing activity, which can lead to a role-playing exercise in which children act out and discuss words and ideas they learned from reading the selection. The original fifteen-minute reading thus becomes a forty-five-minute lesson integrating several aspects of learning.

The gifted and talented also need a different pace and duration for instruction. Often they choose to concentrate for long periods of time on something that holds their interest. Keeping up the pace for them may involve unit lessons continuing over several days or weeks that encourage their ability to concentrate, to solve problems, and to follow through to the completion of a project.

Use Effective Reinforcement

Most learners perform better if they see where they started and how far they have come. Therefore, children with special needs should have reinforcement that not only encourages success but also shows them their progress. Effective reinforcement varies according to the child and the instructional objectives. Progress may be adequately provided for the gifted and talented by verbal reinforcement or by the opportunity to produce something such as a book or drama. For the intellectually handicapped child, the display of progress may need to be more concrete. A goal that is not immediate, such as growth in reading comprehension, may seem too difficult to achieve. One way to reinforce progress for this child is to develop individual progress charts based on the child's interest or on stated objectives.

For example, if the child likes King Kong, design a chart showing the silhouette of the Empire State Building, with floors marked at regular intervals, and a King Kong figure that can be moved floor by floor to the top. Reward the child according to the progress being made on a particular objective. If the objective is comprehension, move the King Kong figure one floor higher *every* time the child performs well on a comprehension task. The child can see that the figure has moved up only one floor on the first day but several floors on the second day. Such charts appeal to all ages: The illustration may change, but the effect of actually *seeing* personal progress is beneficial for most learners.

Blend Group Work with Individual Work

Progress charts can serve as a vehicle for another valuable goal: blending group work with individual work. The significance of peer acceptance has been discussed in Chapter 13 ("Organizing for Instruction"). That acceptance reveals itself most effectively in group activities in which success is the result of the effort of several students working together, not simply of the work of an individual. The discussion of a story, for example, can be successful only when everyone participates actively. Turning stories into read-a-dramas can be successful only when reader-actors and their audience work together.

Group-participation activities can be charted in parallel with individual activities. To be successful, the children must move one King Kong up the individual objective chart and another King Kong up the group-participation chart. By inference, the child begins to appreciate that both are necessary; each benefits the other. With two charts, it is more likely that language and total reading will be kept in perspective rather than having isolated skills dominate the child's reading time. (For more information on how to individualize instruction, see Barbe & Abbott, 1975; Charles, 1980.)

The Role of Computers in Individualizing Instruction

The problems of adapting instructional procedures to meet the needs of exceptional students can be minimized to some extent by the use of computers to assist in both the management and the implementation of educational programs. Computer-managed instruction (CMI) can help with record keeping, with diagnostic tests adapted to suit the needs of particular students, and with all of the details related to evaluation of the effectiveness of instruction (Ragghianti & Miller, 1982). Furthermore, the computer can be of help in developing the IEP for each child (Hooper, 1981).

Recent advances have been made in the use of computers to help the handicapped by providing speech synthesis (enabling computers to "read" for blind or dyslexic students), speech recognition (allowing computers to "write" for physically handicapped students), and modified keyboards that can be used by those with problems of mobility (Bowe, 1984, p. 121). Although much of this technology lies within the realm of special education, it is helpful for the classroom teacher to know that such possibilities exist. It has also been found that slower-learning students, in particular, not only are capable of learning to use computers but also frequently "learn better with computers than with almost any other educational technology" because of the computer's patience and its capability for providing immediate feedback (Bowe, 1984, p. 122).

Kleiman and Humphrey (1984) report on "the experiences of teachers and students in two special education classes into which computers were successfully introduced" (p. 96). A total of twenty-nine children, ages seven to thirteen, participated in a project that involved the development and testing of software designed for spelling drill and practice. Some of these children had been mainstreamed and came to a special resource room only one hour per day whereas others received all their instruction in a special education classroom. The authors evaluated this experience in the light of commonly accepted views that hold that children with learning handicaps should *not* use computers because (1) the machines are too complex and students will become frustrated; (2) the children will break the computers; (3) students with poor social skills will only become more withdrawn and less communicative if they work with machines rather than people; and (4) teachers do not have time to learn how to use computers themselves, teach children how to use them, and make sure the machines are not damaged.

The outcome of this project completely refuted the negative arguments just presented. The children with learning difficulties quickly learned how to use the computer (often in only one practice session), were not intimidated, and accepted the idea that any mistake could be corrected simply by trying a second or a third time. The machines were not intentionally abused, and even students with problems of motor control did not have difficulty in adapting to the use of the keyboard. Students did not become more withdrawn but actually "opened up" as they discovered that they could master the computer, receive immediated feedback, and successfully deal with problems presented to them. Each child's self-esteem was enhanced by this positive experience.

Kleiman and Humphrey concluded that several positive arguments could be advanced in favor of using computers with children who are slow learners:

1. Computers are a great help in individualizing instruction, especially because they can be programmed to present lessons at different speeds and at varying levels of difficulty.
2. Children become *active* learners when using computers and develop better work habits as they interact with the machines.
3. The self-esteem of handicapped children increases as they develop better learning skills and come to realize that they *can* learn and succeed.
4. Parents, teachers, and other children change their attitudes as they begin to realize that handicapped learners can become more and more capable and self-confident (Kleiman & Humphrey, 1984, p. 101).

Reading programs suitable for slower learners will be discussed later in a section on reading materials and approaches. For now it is sufficient to point out that classroom microcomputers can help the handicapped child by providing individual tutorial or drill work in a situation that allows each child to proceed at a comfortable pace and to repeat work as needed. Although the quality of software designed specifically to meet the needs of exceptional children has been rated very low (Bowe, 1984, p. 128), it is possible to use currently available software, supplemented by any other appropriate materials, as one component in a program of individualized instruction for these students.

Reading for Children with Limiting Handicaps

Limiting handicaps are those that prevent a child's learning in the same way or at the same rate as other children do. Such handicaps may be physical (vision or hearing problems, orthopedic or neurological disorders) or mental (retardation, learning disability). Having a limiting handicap does not mean that a child cannot learn to read or read to learn; it simply means that extra effort must be brought to the task of determining the best instructional procedures.

The Education for all Handicapped Children Act discussed earlier (P.L. 94–142) has many implications for reading methods, materials, and instructional emphasis. These must be geared to the level and the strengths of the individual child. Because of previous educational experiences and the stigma of a "handicapped" label, the child should be given tasks, especially at first, that can easily be completed successfully. Both the instructional and interest levels of the child should be taken into account in providing reading instruction. Scores on standardized tests and other earlier evaluative information can be a help. However, in order to assess the child's individual strengths and weaknesses, teachers will have to develop informal tests on different aspects of reading (see Chapter 5). Discussions with the child's previous teachers can provide useful diagnostic information, and careful observation of the child is also most important. These data enable teachers to set both short- and long-term objectives.

Adapting Instructional Materials

In order to meet the selected objectives of the IEP, educators must find, adapt, or develop the methods and materials needed. Materials or assistance can be obtained from special-education personnel or resource centers. Existing materials can be adapted in a number of ways:

1. For children with short attention spans, two or three brief assignments can be provided instead of one long one.
2. Self-correcting materials at the child's reading level can be provided so that each student can work independently at the appropriate level.
3. A teacher or an aide can go over a reading lesson with the child before the whole class begins the assignment. This enables the child to be familiar with the material, to get reinforcement, and to keep up with the class.
4. Multilevel materials on the same topic can often be found; this allows each child to read about the same topic at his or her own level. (See information on basal readers and other approaches in Chapter 12.)
5. In some cases, special materials will have to be developed by the teacher, with the assistance of special-education teachers if necessary. Classroom volunteers might also help in this.

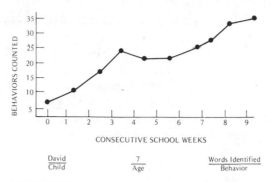

FIGURE 15.1   Example of a Precision Teaching Chart.

Keeping Records

In addition to setting objectives and adapting materials, it is most important for the teacher to keep appropriate records of the progress of the mainstreamed child. If the objectives are clearly and carefully laid out, this record keeping does not need to be a time-consuming task. Teacher-made tests or observations can be used to assess progress. Because such assessment is required by law, tests and observations have to be reported formally. One simple way to keep track of observations is through a method called *precision teaching.*

This procedure, originally developed by O. R. Lindsley in 1964, comprises five basic steps: *pinpoint, count, chart, aim,* and *evaluate.* As described by Lovitt (1977), *pinpoint* means to set specific objectives that can be observed, such as increasing the number of words the child knows. *Count* simply means to keep track of this number once a day or once a week. The count is then put on a *chart* such as the one given in Figure 15.1. Once the behavior has been identified and the starting point determined, the teacher establishes an *aim.* For example, as part of the IEP, the teacher might state that known words will increase from six to thirty over a two-month period. The chart is then kept for two months, and it is an easy task to *evaluate* whether or not the objective in the IEP has been reached.

Characteristics of Physical and Mental Handicaps

Classroom teachers will be called on to work with exceptional children who exhibit a wide range of problems and who must be taught using procedures that best suit their particular needs. The most prominent features of the various types of handicaps will be discussed here, followed by more detailed information on the way that these handicaps affect reading and on materials and approaches that can be used to help exceptional children learn.

494

Some of the most obvious handicaps that teachers may encounter among their students are those that are physical in origin. These may involve disorders that are more or less readily apparent (such as the inability to use limbs or to see or hear well); such problems do not usually *in themselves* mean that the child has any deficits in intellectual ability. (Of course, it is always possible that some children may have both physical and mental problems; this should not be overlooked when evaluating the needs of exceptional children.) Adapting to the needs of students with physical impairments can usually be done with relatively simple commonsense adjustments, as will be discussed later.

Children who do not "pay attention" are not necessarily misbehaving; it may well be that they simply cannot hear or see what is happening in the classroom. Any problems in attending to what is going on or in understanding written or verbal instructions should alert the teacher to possible difficulties in these areas, and an examination of hearing and vision should be suggested for any child who gives evidence of these problems.

Hearing-impaired students will usually exhibit symptoms that should be apparent to the teacher: frequent requests for repetition of spoken instructions, turning the head toward the speaker, frowning when trying to listen, and frequent earaches and spells of dizziness. Teachers can adapt instruction for the hard-of-hearing by seating the student near the front of the room, by always facing the class when given spoken instructions, by emphasizing silent reading with such children, and by relying on written instructions as much as possible.

Children with impaired vision will tend to squint or scowl when looking at the chalkboard, rub the eyes frequently, hold the book very close or far away, and make many errors when copying from the board. These students should be seated near the chalkboard, should be provided with adequate light, and may benefit from books and printed materials with large type. Teachers should utilize the child's senses of touch and hearing in developing concepts such as "smooth," "soft," "bumpy," and so on, and by having the child feel objects that match these terms. Recorded material can also be helpful in letting children hear stories and poems that may be too taxing for them to read for long periods of time. Frequent alternation between close work and other activities is important as well (Caton, 1981).

Physical handicaps *other* than those involving vision and hearing are of two basic types: (1) orthopedic and neurological impairments (cerebral palsy, muscular dystrophy, and multiple sclerosis, for example) and (2) other health impairments (diabetes, cancer, tuberculosis, cystic fibrosis, and so on). These do not create the problems associated with vision and hearing disorders and thus do not usually make the task of learning to read any more difficult than it is for nonhandicapped children. On the other hand, there are psychological problems associated with learning to cope with physical disability, and with incurable disease in particular. In general, the teacher should simply be on the lookout for signs of fatigue and frustration that may accompany these disabilities and should try to emphasize the positive aspects of each child's progress and accomplishments—in reading as well as in any other area of study.

Handicaps That Affect the Learning Process

Mental Retardation

Some children who learn more slowly than the average are classified as "mentally retarded." This term means that such children are below average in intellectual functioning and also experience problems in adaptive behavior. The emphasis is on *limitations in performance*—the child is unable to behave in ways normally considered appropriate for children of the same age. It is also important to point out that mental retardation is no longer considered an "incurable" condition, one that is a lifelong affliction comparable to cerebral palsy. "It is no longer thought of as a disease; instead, according to current understanding *a person may be considered retarded at one time in his life, but not at another"* (Hallahan & Kauffman, 1978, p. 64).

Hargis (1982) emphasizes the *performance* aspect of this label and points out that the British term *educationally subnormal* is more accurate because it does not imply a physiologically based cognitive defect. Most of the children labeled "mentally retarded" are, in fact, normal individuals who have a problem that can be expressed in educational terms. "Their level of maturity at any given chronological age and their rate of learning cause even more obvious discrepancies with curricular demands than those revealed by learning disabled children" (p. 7). If such children are forced to conform to a program of instruction that does not allow for their slower rate of learning, their "defective" performance causes them to appear to be "retarded" in comparison with more average students whereas they may need only a different instructional approach in order to be able to learn satisfactorily.

Children who are severely retarded—usually with IQs below 35—are not likely to benefit from the usual classroom situation and are usually not mainstreamed. Likewise, the moderately retarded or *trainable mentally retarded* (TMR)—those with IQs in the 35–50 range—are usually taught in self-contained classrooms. Mildly retarded children—the *educable mentally retarded* (EMR)—have IQs in the 50–80 range, and in the past they have been taught in self-contained classrooms. Today there is a trend toward including them within the regular classroom whenever possible, and many EMR children can deal successfully with schoolwork up to about the sixth-grade level or possibly higher in certain cases.

Intraindividual differences are common, and children with the same IQ may have vastly different educational needs. Many children score low on IQ tests for cultural and environmental reasons; one impetus for mainstreaming was the finding that a disproportionate number of black and Spanish-surnamed students were classified as EMR. Research has shown that IQ is *not* a constant, as was once supposed (Kagan et al., 1971). Instruction and changes in environment can alter

IQ scores significantly. Furthermore, IQ tests measure *only* the performance of the child at a given point on a given series of questions; such tests should not be viewed as an infallible guide to suggest how the same child might perform on another test at a later time. For all these reasons, educators have for some time moved away from the classification of children *solely* on the basis of an IQ score.

Learning Disabilities

During his youth, Thomas Edison was considered to be abnormal and mentally defective; he never did well or "fitted in" at school. Woodrow Wilson did not learn the alphabet until he was nine and could not read until he was eleven. Albert Einstein did not speak until age three, and until age seven he formulated even the shortest, simplest sentences silently with his lips before speaking aloud. Reading and writing remained difficult throughout his lifetime, and he always did poorly in foreign languages and arithmetic (Lerner, 1981, p. 5).

The situations described here all come under the general heading of "learning disabilities." This broad term has been used to describe children who seem to have no obvious mental or physical problem and yet do not learn as readily as other children of the same age do. The definition given as part of P.L. 94–142 indicates that a "specific learning disability" is a "disorder in one or more of the basic psychological processes involved in understanding or in using language spoken or written . . ." (Lerner, 1981, p. 7). Such disorders may be evident in an impaired ability to listen, think, speak, read, or write. Learning disabilities usually include those that affect perception and understanding but do *not* include specific physical problems such as impaired hearing or vision, epilepsy, cerebral palsy, and so on (Savage & Mooney, 1979, Ch. 2).

There are many types of learning disability, and the problem is particularly difficult to deal with because it is not always identifiable by physical characteristics. Some of the more commonly encountered indications of learning disability include perceptual-motor impairments (inability to copy letters, for example), general coordination problems (clumsiness), inability to focus attention for any length of time, and disorders of memory or thinking (recalling or understanding abstract concepts). It also happens that some children may have difficulty in one subject area and not in others (Gillespie-Silver, 1979, p. 24).

As with the mildly retarded, it is important for teachers to remember that children who have been labeled "learning-disabled" are not in fact incapable of *learning* but may simply require a different approach or more preparation than the majority of children who are considered "average." Once learning-disabled children have been reached with a teaching strategy that allows them to succeed, it is quite possible that some (or perhaps many) of them will be able to progress at a reasonable pace.

Because the learning-disabled child usually needs to improve reading ability before any other skills can be developed, it is important to adapt teaching methods to suit the needs of the individual student (even though content and sequence of presentation remain essentially the same as they are for other students). When they are working with learning-disabled students, it is most important for teachers to create a structured environment, to minimize and accept the students' mistakes (while showing them that *everyone,* even the teacher, makes mistakes sometimes), to help the student by supplying words that cause problems and by giving clear instructions, and to use a variety of teaching approaches and assessment techniques (Burns, Roe, & Ross, 1984, p. 472).

Communication Disorders (*Speech and Language*)

A study undertaken in 1969 by the National Institute of Health found that approximately 10 per cent of the population in the United States experienced some difficulty in communication (Culatta & Culatta, 1981, p. 109). "In fact, communication problems are probably the most pervasive of those discussed because they often affect all types of students" (Stephens, Blackhurst, & Magliocca, 1982, p. 35).

Although communication problems often involve both speech and general language functions, it must be stressed that the two are not synonymous even though we tend to think of speech as the most obvious and frequently used method of communication. *Language* is the total system of sounds and symbols used by mutual agreement to convey meaning and information, and it may be expressed in writing, in Braille, and by signs as well as by speech. Language has both a *receptive* and an *expressive* component: we must understand the meaning of words as conveyed to us from external sources (the receptive element), and we must also be able to convey our own messages to others (the expressive element). "Speech is the physical process of making the sounds and sound combinations of language. Language is much more complex than speech; speech production is one of its components" according to Culatta and Culatta (1981, p. 111).

Problems of communication, and especially of speech, are usually manifested in fairly obvious ways: We cannot understand what the speaker is trying to say, and we are distracted by unpleasant voice quality or physical mannerisms. Speech disorders are usually of three basic types: (1) articulation (omitting letters, especially initial and final consonants, or substituting sounds such as "pwetty thong" for "pretty song") (2) voice (awkward placement, lack of variation, poor quality) and (3) fluency (stuttering or speaking so fast that words are blurred in unintelligible) (Gearheart, 1980, p. 223). These problems do not in themselves affect the child's ability to learn to read, but they should be corrected by a therapist as soon as possible so that the child can read aloud and participate in normal classroom activities.

Language disorders present most serious and complex problems because they involve not only expressive skills (the ability to *use* language, especially speech) but also receptive skills (the ability to *understand* language). Basically, it may be said that a language problem exists when there is a noticeable gap between these two components, the expressive and the receptive. For example, a child may know the meaning of a number of words and may be able to point to the "door" or the "table" when these words are spoken, but if that child at age

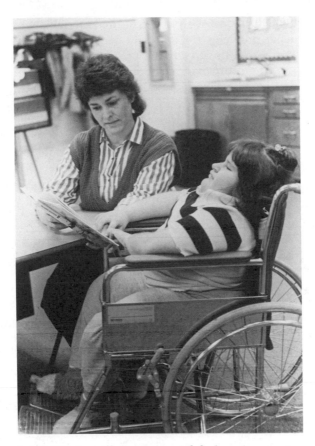

A child with a speech handicap will need special help when mainstreamed into regular classroom activities.

four or five cannot say, "This is a table," then a dysfunction in expressive language exists. On the other hand, if a child of five or six does not understand simple questions ("What is your name?") or statements ("Here is your book"), then there is clearly a receptive language problem.

Of course, it is impossible to say at exactly what moment children should be able to say or understand certain words and phrases, but there is clearly a problem if they lag noticeably behind their age-mates by the time they enter school. In some cases, difficulties that seem to be related to communication disorders do, in fact, have a physiological basis. Children cannot say words they do not *hear* clearly or understand words they cannot *see*. These factors should be checked whenever a child has difficulty in communicating.

In the absence of obvious causes, the problem may be one of *delayed language*. This inability to use language in a manner consistent with the child's age may related to the ability to understand or speak the language that the child hears in everyday life. Whatever the cause, "the person with delayed language *has not developed an understanding of how language works* in the normal time and/or manner" (Stephens, Blackhurst, & Magliocca, 1982, p. 36). This type of dysfunction is especially difficult to deal with in the normal school setting and obviously causes major problems for the child because everything involved in learning requires an understanding of language.

The complexity of communication disorders and the difficulty of dealing with them are underscored by the fact that some children may have good language skills (i.e., understand what they hear) but have major speech problems whereas others may have good speech and little understanding. "If a student has poor speech, teachers should not infer that the child also has poor language skills" according to Stephens, Blackhurst, and Magliocca (1982, p. 36). Especially in the case of children with cerebral palsy, it should not be assumed that their inability to speak means that they cannot hear, understand, and use language.

Characteristics of Reading Problems in Handicapped Children

Whatever the cause of their difficulty, most children who have problems in learning to read will exhibit one or more of the following characteristics. It is most important for the teacher to determine what specific problems a given child may have before any progress in reading instruction can be made.

Readiness Deficits

Exceptional children often enter school with problems in visual and auditory perception, limited development of language, and poor social and emotional skills. Because these elements provide the foundation for later development, reading readiness training programs have come to place more and more emphasis on the teaching of specific skills in highly organized and intensive periods of instruction. It is often necessary to extend this period of developing readiness skills and concepts until a firm foundation has been established.

Discrimination Problems

Handicapped children may have difficulty in seeing and hearing differences in various letters, sounds, and words. In particular, they may struggle to match various sizes and shapes and may not be able to see the difference between *b* and *d* or between *can* and *car*. Reversal of letters or words and problems in telling left from right are also typical examples of visual discrimination difficulties. Auditory discrimination problems are characterized by an inability to hear the difference between phonemic sounds or to determine whether or not words such as *bad* and *dad* sound the same. Such children may be confused by rhymes.

It is most important that teachers identify problems such as these and correct them by adapting instructional techniques. It should be obvious that letter discrimination, for example, is an important element in distinguishing one word from another and, therefore, in determining meaning. Multisensory learning methods are recommended for helping handicapped children with problems of word discrimination.

Word-Analysis Problems

Students who have problems in word analysis tend to make wild guesses about words while reading, to offer unreasonable word substitutions, and to read aloud in very slow, halting patterns. They do not use the wide variety of techniques needed to solve the problems presented by unknown words in the material they are reading. Use of context, use of phonetic analysis, and use of prefixes and suffixes are some of the techniques used by readers with a flexible approach to the solution of word problems. Handicapped children often rely on a single approach even when it is not appropriate. Teachers need to emphasize flexibility and to help students understand the variety of strategies that are available. (See Chapters 6 and 7 for details on word recognition.)

Attention and Memory Problems

Success in reading demands that the reader pay attention to the task and be able to store and then retrieve ideas and experiences generated during reading. Although attention and memory may be treated as two separate psychological phenomena, they are closely related in the act of reading. The ability to pay attention while reading gives intensity to the act of storing and retrieving information. Even short-term memory—retrieving information after only a few seconds or a minute—cannot function adequately when the individual cannot give sufficient attention to store it.

"Visual and auditory process problems usually are associated with memory disturbances," writes Wallace (1981, p. 460). Students who have not stored the letters and sounds of language in their brains will experience difficulty in retrieving written words that make use of those letters and sounds. Another example of attention and memory problems is the inability of a child to follow simple, clear directions. These problems are often approached first by eliminating as many external distractions as possible (Tarver & Hallahan, 1974) and then by conducting reading practice in a highly structured invironment. Working in a study carrel on very short-term reading tasks would be an example of instruction aimed at solving attention and memory problems. It is also helpful to involve all the major senses in learning tasks.

Comprehension Deficits

Understanding what has been read is a major problem for most handicapped students. Comprehension difficulties may involve recalling factual details just read ("It was raining. The wind was cold.") or making inferences ("Rattlesnake Pete was a bad man because . . ."). Most of the problems encountered with these readers involve such literal-comprehension deficits, and it follows that interpretive and critical skills are affected as well. Work in improving literal comprehension involves taking note of details, recalling events in proper sequence, and locating specific bits of information. Because of the difficulties such readers have with the mechanical process of reading, their comprehension naturally suffers.

Assessment of Reading Problems

A number of procedures can be followed in assessing the abilities and weaknesses of each child. A *list of priority skills* from a basal reader can be used to provide an overview of various skills associated with reading. By comparing the chart with the skills exhibited by the child, the teacher may be able to trace a weakness to certain skill deficiencies (Hammill & Bartel, 1982, pp. 41–51; Mandell & Gold, 1984, pp. 264–267).

In order to determine how to go about teaching the needed skills as indicated by the scope-and-sequence chart, teachers must obtain assessment information from a variety of sources. *Error analysis (miscue analysis)* can be particularly helpful in determining the types of errors the student makes and can pinpoint specific problems such as omitting or inserting letters or words. The teacher can have the child read words or short sentences and can then mark the type of error that occurs (Hammill & Bartel, 1982, pp. 53–59). Also see the discussion of oral reading miscue analysis in the preceding chapter of this text (pp. 474–478).

A *modified cloze procedure* can be used for both assessment and instruction (see pp. 480–483). Instead of omitting words according to a more-or-less arbitrary formula (every fifth word or every tenth word), the teacher could carefully prepare the passage so that only those words that can be readily inferred from context are omitted. Also, the teacher could write in two words above the blank and have the student choose the correct one.

Criterion-referenced tests can be used to identify problems and determine how to deal with them. Commercially made tests such as those described in the preceding chapter (pp. 463–465) can be used to determine the general problem, and teachers can make up other tests to focus on particular problems and to gain more specific data. For example, if a commercially made test indicates a problem with the CVC pattern, the teacher can then devise a test to determine the specific problem. The student may simply be confusing the letters *b* and *d,* for instance, or may be reading an *a* for an *o* or vice versa (Hargis, 1982, pp. 55–57).

All the material covered in the preceding chapter is relevant to the question of assessing the skills and needs of slower readers. In addition to the items discussed earlier, it will be helpful to review the information on oral reading inventories (pp. 472–478) and on teacher observation (pp. 478–480). More information on assessment by informal observation is given in Chapter 1 (pp. 18–19), Chapter 2 (pp. 34–37), and Chapter 5 (pp. 139–142). Finally, in addition to the informal procedures described so far, there are formal diagnostic tests and group reading tests that can be used to gain more information about the child's abilities and weaknesses (see pp. 465–468).

Reading Materials and Approaches

Much of the information on developmental reading approaches already given in this book can be adapted to the needs of exceptional students. The value and weakness of each type of approach will be discussed later, with reference to the broader discussion of each procedure as originally presented in Chapter 12 of this text. Handicapped learners may also need specialized approaches in order to overcome the problems discussed earlier. A number of remedial techniques will be considered in this discussion as well.

Developmental Reading Approaches

Gillespie-Silver (1979, p. 335) points out that the various teaching methods currently available must be combined or modified to meet the needs of mildly retarded or learning-disabled students. An elaborate analysis of traditional methods was made by Cohen and Plaskon (1978, pp. 969–970). They considered the relative advantages and disadvantages for the mentally handicapped child of the following approaches: Programmed Instruction, Alphabet, Phonics, Basal, Linguistic, and Language Experience. Another discussion of various developmental approaches and their applications in teaching handicapped learners is given by Wallace (1981, pp. 465–469).

Briefly, it can be said that *basal readers* are good for handicapped learners in that they provide a clear sequential structure and offer many suggestions in the teacher's manual, but this very structure often clouds the teacher's vision of how to adapt to individual needs or at least does not encourage deviation from the program. In order for teachers to use basal readers effectively, especially to serve the needs of the handicapped, it may be helpful to employ the concept of a directed-reading-thinking-activity (DRTA) advocated by Stauffer (1975). The DRTA procedure can be used to help students learn to think by "having readers set their purposes, then reading to find answers for their speculations and hypotheses, and finally judging their initial thoughts in light of the information gained through reading" (Hall, Ribovich, & Ramig, 1979, p. 100).

The *phonics method* may be particularly good for children who need constant reassurance of the orderliness of language. Its emphasis on word recognition encourages early independent reading and the child's natural interest in learning how to decode new words.

The *language-experience approach* is often quite effective in leading slower learners into reading, and it also allows adaptation to the needs of individuals or small groups (Hall, 1981). On the other hand, it requires a prolonged attention span, limits vocabulary to that of the student, and is difficult to manage because of the lack of structure. Many learning-disabled students may be having problems precisely because they have not been exposed to a variety of experiences; it follows that their ability to speak or write about themselves would be limited.

Programmed materials currently available in computer software can obviously be helpful because they allow students to work at their own pace without pressure. The very predictability of such programs, combined with the nonthreatening atmosphere permitted by individual work at the computer terminal, allows slower learners to develop at their own pace and to experience success in answering the questions posed by the program. In the case of children with severe problems such as autism, it has been found that working with the computer allows such children to take control of the situation (as opposed to being a "passive" receiver of instruction) and enables them to make progress that would have been thought impossible in any other situation (Goldenberg, Russell, & Carter, 1984, pp. 134–139).

One program that has been found effective in working with handicapped learners is *CARIS* (*Computer Animated Reading Instruction System*). With this program, children who have reached a developmental age of no more than 2.5 years have been able to learn to read and create simple sentences. The child is first presented with a list of nouns (*dog, boy, car,* and so on) from which one is chosen, and then a list of verbs is provided for the student's selection. When a noun-verb combination (such as "The dog jumps") has been chosen, the computer shows the action in animation. The system has been especially helpful in working with deaf children and those with other communication problems (Geoffrion & Geoffrion, 1983, p. 58).

The word-processing capability of the computer can be used to good advantage with both gifted and handicapped students. Stories generated through the language-experience approach can be entered quickly by the teacher or a student, and alterations can be made without rewriting an entire composition. Gifted students can use word processing as a part of their work on individual topics, and the computer is also helpful in allowing the gifted to work at an accelerated pace and to focus on problem-solving exercises rather than repetition of material already covered (Walkington & Babcock, 1984).

Although much of the emphasis in courseware has been on drill and practice, it is to be hoped that computer programs will soon focus on the tutorial capabilities of the machine and will permit greater student interaction and a broader range of possibilities for modification by teachers to suit the needs of individual students. Word processing and software designed to construct stories have already been used successfully by children with special needs. An extensive discussion of the possibilities of computers in developing language-arts skills for handicapped children is given by Goldenberg, Russell, and Carter (1984, Chapter 3). Also see the discussion of computers and reading in Chapter

12 of the present text; many of the ideas presented there can be adapted for handicapped learners as well.

Regardless of the approaches and techniques that may be considered best suited for each individual child, it is important to remember that such procedures alone will not guarantee results. Raim (1983) stresses the importance of interaction between teacher and student and points out that efforts to match teaching and learning styles may be secondary in importance to the influence of an involved teacher on the students. "If it is the interaction with an interested person which proves significant, then other aspects, such as method, need less scrutiny and perhaps less differentiation" (Raim, 1983, p. 810).

Specialized Approaches for Slower Readers

The following suggestions on reading instruction for learning-disabled children are offered by Richek, List, and Lerner (1983, pp. 144–147):

1. *Begin reading instruction at the level appropriate for the individual child.*
   Students should not waste time on material that is below their conceptual and readability levels, but must not be frustrated by being forced to attempt reading that is beyond them. The best progress is made when students are able to succeed consistently at the tasks set before them.

2. *Use time effectively.*
   Establish a firm routine for coming to class and getting down to work, call on specific students to get their attention, and observe students who are working independently to make sure that they are staying on task.

3. *Proceed logically from the simple to the complex.*
   As students grasp simple concepts, begin to introduce more difficult materials which demand greater effort and attention (paragraphs rather than sentences), increase the rate of teaching, and proceed from concrete to more abstract concepts.

4. *Capitalize on the student's strengths.*
   For example, if a student has a large base of sight words but does not have phonics skills, extend the sight-word vocabulary and introduce phonics only after the student is comfortable reading from a base of sight words.

5. *Teach, don't preach.*
   In order to learn, students must actively apply principles in words, sentences, and paragraphs. For example, instead of simply explaining that the suffix "-er" in words such as "painter," "teacher," and "writer" is used to denote "a person who does something," ask the students what these words mean and then have them discover what the definitions have in com-

mon (they all refer to someone who "does something") and then discover what the words have in common (each ends in "-er").

A number of reading-instruction methods have been developed specifically for disabled readers. These are discussed at length in Hammill and Bartel (1982, pp. 78–82), in Lerner (1981, pp. 303–310), and in Mandell and Gold (1984, pp. 275–280). A few of the more frequently used approaches will be summarized here.

Multisensory programs seek to stimulate several avenues of sensory input to stimulate learning. One of the best-known of such methods was developed by Grace Fernald in the 1920s and is called the Visual-Auditory-Kinesthetic-Tactile (VAKT) method (Fernald, 1943). This approach teaches the word as a whole and begins by having children ask about any word that interests them and that they do not know. The word is written in large letters on strips of paper about four by ten inches, and the child traces the outline of each letter with a firm two-finger contact while saying the word aloud. While tracing, the children see, say, and hear the letter or word as they feel the pattern of movement associated with it. Gradually, the tactile and kinesthetic modes are dropped, and the child is ultimately able to look at new words and decode them based on similarities to previously learned words.

Another multisensory approach is the Gillingham-Stillman method, originally developed for students who are dyslexic (Gillingham & Stillman, 1968). *Dyslexia* is a term that has been used to categorize a wide variety of problems, but, in fact, it simply means "an inability to read." It is a word that *describes* a condition; it is not the name of the *cause* for this condition. In one view the problem is essentially medical, caused by brain injury or stroke; but a great many dyslexics do not show any evidence of mental impairment. Another view holds that dyslexia is an educational problem and that dyslexics are simply those who have persistent difficulty in learning to read.

Whatever the cause or causes, this severe reading problem is characterized by symptoms such as "letter and word reversals, choppy oral reading patterns, transposition of letters in words, confusion of words with similar appearance, repetition of words or guesses during oral reading, and confusion of concepts such as *over* and *under*" (Mandell & Gold, 1984, p. 276). Such problems are often encountered in beginning readers, but in these special cases the problems are much more pronounced and persistent. The Gillingham-Stillman method focuses on the learning of individual letters and blends and uses a tracing technique to learn phoneme-grapheme correspondences. Single sounds are later combined into words, and the method emphasizes phonics and depends on a formal sequence of learning (Lerner, 1981, pp. 304–305).

Behavior-modification approaches require the setting of specified, measurable behavioral objectives and the introduction of environmental stimuli that are structured to bring about the desired change. One example of this approach is *DISTAR: An Instructional System* (Englemann

& Bruner, 1974), designed for very young children (preschool through grade three). "The program teaches children to decode various words through a series of highly structured and fast-paced drills which include symbol-action games, blending, and rhyming" (Wallace & Kauffman, 1978, p. 193). A teacher's manual and student books and work sheets are included. The program has been criticized in some instances for being rigidly structured, but many teachers have found the system to be effective with slower learners because of its well-organized and well-written material (Wallace, 1981, p. 471).

Behavioral principles are also applied in the *Peabody Rebus Reading Program.* It utilizes a *rebus*—a picture of a specific object or a symbol that suggests the sound of the word it represents—as the foundation for instruction, and it consists of three programmed workbooks and two reading books. The series is designed to prepare students for the beginning levels of a traditional reading program and allows them to progress at their own pace and provides immediate feedback. On completion of the program, the student "will have been exposed to 120 written vocabulary words and a significant number of comprehension and decoding skills commonly found in a basal reading program" (Mandell & Gold, 1984, p. 278).

In Chapters 6 and 7 of this text, we offered several suggestions for working on word recognition with both beginning and advanced readers. Exercises of the type presented there can be adapted to the needs of slower learners and can be supplemented by other collections of exercises such as those given by Deiner (1983).

A broad discussion of reading comprehension has been presented in Chapters 8 and 9 of this text. The principles included there should be reviewed with an eye to adapting them to the needs of the slower learner. In addition, there are detailed discussions of how to work on reading comprehension with slower learners in Hammill and Bartel (1982, pp. 62–66), in Lerner (1981, pp. 311–325), and in Wallace and Kauffman (1978, pp. 189–192).

All the suggestions offered so far could be used in any classroom of students learning to read. The difference with handicapped students is the manner in which the procedures are used. Of course, the older child is not going to be interested in the same concepts that concern

---

Teaching the Slow Reader

1. List ten techniques or strategies you would use with a first-grade EMR child who was not ready to begin to read. You can find some ideas in the chapters on language development and readiness. Try to devise at least two instructional strategies that could include other children as well.
2. Suggest ways you could adapt instruction for a fifth-grade classroom to include a child who was reading at the first-grade level. How would you adapt reading instruction as well as instruction in the content areas?

Mainstreaming

Activities mentioned throughout this book are suitable for handicapped children. For mainstreamed students, the following activities are especially appropriate:

1. Before a handicapped student enters the classroom, have him or her write or dictate an autobiographical sketch. Reproduce it and share it with the class. Discuss the disability if this seems appropriate. Such a discussion will help the other children be aware of the special needs of the mainstreamed child and will help that child be accepted by his or her peers.
2. Include the handicapped child in regular reading activities whenever possible. Design special reading projects that will team the handicapped child with other children.
3. Children who experience difficulty learning to read or spell by traditional methods may benefit from using a variety of senses—visual, tactile, auditory, kinesthetic—in working on letters, words, or sentences. Use tracing, listening, speaking, and even movement activities to help the child form the necessary cognitive associations.
4. For children who have attention or memory problems, give one simple direction at a time and write out the directions so that they can be referred to by students who forget. Let the child sit close to you so that you can help with focusing attention. Choose short reading selections so that the child can recall information easily.
5. Children who are slow in developing oral language should be given opportunities to talk and listen. Set aside part of each day as a sharing time when the handicapped child can talk with other children. This will provide a model of language usage for the child. Discuss pictures or the content of the reading selection with handicapped children before reading. This will give them some language cues to help them read.
6. For children with speech or phrasing problems, read along with the students so that they can hear the proper pronunciation and phrasing of a selection. Have the children keep track of their own progress by reading into a tape recorder at least once a week.
7. For all children, be sure the comprehension questions asked at the end of a selection are at the proper level. The child must be able to understand your questions as well as be able to read the selection.

a first-grader, so the teacher must adapt very basic and simple learning exercises to a wider range of interests. Older children, even though learning-disabled, will respond much better to things that interest them than they will to material obviously designed for use by much younger children.

Reading for the Gifted and Talented

Near the beginning of this chapter we gave a definition of gifted and talented children that stressed their high level of performance and their achievement or potential in intellectual and academic pursuits, creativity, leadership, and artistic endeavors (or any combination of these). Such children will require challenging educational opportunities if their abilities are to develop and their potential is to be realized.

Characteristics of the Gifted and Talented

The level of physical and emotional maturity of the gifted child is usually comparable to that of the average child. There are, however, a number of characteristics that can frequently be observed in gifted children, especially when they are placed in a stimulating environment. Several of these characteristics are listed by Ehrlich (1982, pp. 24–27), who indicates that gifted children are usually able to do the following:

> Use a large vocabulary including complex terms not usually encountered in younger children.
> Express clear thoughts in longer sentences than normally used by children of the same age.
> Remember details of past experiences and recall much of what has been read without the need for drill work.
> Learn quickly and efficiently without the need for elaborate explanation and repetition.
> Think clearly and logically, reason and generalize effectively, and recognize implied relationships.

It is important to realize that gifted children are not simply "average" children with a few extras. "For children above 145 IQ, their intellectual potential—the brain that drives them—is so fundamental to *everything* about them, that it cannot be separated from the personhood of the child," say Webb, Meckstroth, and Tolan (1982, p. 31). Such children must be helped to develop the social and self-development skills that will enable them to function in a world populated by a majority less intellectually gifted.

Although the regular classroom may be the least restrictive environment for many children with some types of physical and mental handicaps, this is usually *not* the case with gifted students. Such children may begin any given school year already having mastered the skills that their classmates will have to work on during the year. If the gifted student were forced to go through the same material presented to all the others, this would create an environment that would, in fact, be highly restrictive and not at all appropriate for his or her needs. For these reasons it is important to provide gifted students with special materials and instruction matching their abilities.

It has been generally assumed that gifted students usually become interested in reading at a very early age and often "teach themselves to read" before entering school (Price, 1976). The frequency with which this occurs may not be as great as one might expect, however. Cassidy and Vukelich (1980) found that less than 25 per cent of gifted children learn to read at an early age even if they possess readiness skills and are given special help. Furth (1970) suggests that they may need to perceive reading as functional before they will learn it. Regardless of when or how quickly gifted children actually do begin to read, their greater intelligence and intellectual curiosity enable them to grasp abstract concepts more readily, use their reading skills to obtain new information, understand relationships quickly and easily, and delve into areas of interest on their own. These same characteristics may also cause them to be easily bored and frustrated with routine school work, to rebel against rules and standardized procedures, and to dominate discussions with glib statements based on superficial knowledge.

Dealing with Individual Differences

In approaching reading or any other subject, teachers of gifted students must take into account the many intra- and interindividual differences found in such children (just as in handicapped children). There is no question that the gifted student must learn the basic skills needed to master reading, but the teacher should find out whether or not the child already has mastered a particular skill or can understand it after a brief explanation. On occasion, the gifted child will require a sequenced set of instructional activities just as any other child would to master a skill, but often a new idea can be grasped without the need for extensive repetition.

If the gifted child does not need the same sequence of study required by other students, then the type and level of material and instruction must be adapted to suit the requirements of such a child. In the past, there were two customary ways of adjusting the usual course of study to accomplish this: acceleration and enrichment. Acceleration may mean skipping grades, working with course content at a higher level or more rapid pace than is usual, enrolling in some college courses while still in high school, or in some cases becoming a first-year college student at the age of twelve. Most of these approaches do not directly affect the teacher who must work with gifted students in the classroom. Enrichment, on the other hand, is obviously a procedure that can be adapted by the classroom teacher.

It should not be assumed that "enrichment" simply means turning the child loose to follow his or her whim without guidance. It is possible for the child to read more material on a given topic than is normally required, to read about related subjects, and to expand on what is read by trips to museums, libraries, and the like. Particularly in the area of reading, it is likely that many gifted children will master the mechanics of the process fairly early and can then use this ability to develop more advanced skills in research, evaluation, and exploration on their own. In particular, the idea of independent research is one that ties in most closely with reading (especially comprehension) and that should be developed because of its importance in all areas of study throughout the child's entire lifetime.

Implications for Reading Instruction

Although reading programs for gifted children will vary to suit individual needs, Barbe and Renzulli (1975) point out several components that will be needed in every case:

1. *Early assessment of intellectual, perceptual, and reading abilities is vital.*

   Those gifted children who do begin to read at an early age may become disenchanted with a formal course of study in reading. A combination of intelligence and readiness tests, along with teacher observations and skill checklists, can be used to gain some idea of the child's level of competency. Repetition of material the child already knows can thus be avoided. For those who are not reading before beginning school, it is still likely that they will progress quickly and should not be expected to persist in drills already mastered.

2. *The reading program should be highly individualized.*

   The child should be allowed to work with the class when this is the best approach but should be provided with other work when it is needed to supplement or move beyond what the class is doing. If the child develops word-recognition skills quickly and easily, then it is not necessary to dwell on items such as phonics, generalizations, and rules of structural analysis, which are only devices to assist in word recognition. Gifted children can often "read" (decode) material that they do not fully understand. For example, the young child can first approach *Moby-Dick* simply as an adventure story without being concerned with the symbolism that could be grasped only by a more mature reader.

3. *The reading program should emphasize development of higher mental processes.*

   From the earliest grades, instruction should emphasize the value of reading as a way of getting information to form the basis of thinking and solving problems. Some skills to be developed include these:

Discovering clues from which to infer hidden meanings and probable outcomes.
Analyzing selections to detect author bias and subtle propaganda.
Locating materials on a given topic.
Organizing and synthesizing materials for purposes of reporting.
Evaluating materials in terms of worth and relevancy to purpose.

4. *The reading program should extend interest in reading.*

   Gifted children should not only master the mechanical skills of reading but should also establish permanent interest in reading as well. Children who are filled with intellectual curiosity should be provided with a variety of reading materials that will allow them to undertake in-depth study in those areas of greatest interest (Barbe & Renzulli, 1975, pp. 445–447).

In the earlier grades, when basic skills are the primary concern, the suggestions made earlier in this section are particularly relevant: Determine which skills the child has already mastered (and don't repeat them); present new skills in terms of their underlying principles rather than as a series of exercises (to see if the child can grasp them quickly); use the customary sequence of instruction only when it is needed. In the middle grades it is possible to permit more and more self-directed instruction, and it is also helpful to supplement work on specific skills by having the child undertake more long-range projects involving independent research and use of resources outside the school (see suggestions in Gold, 1965, pp. 210–211). The child is thus encouraged to extend and apply the classroom lessons into areas of personal interest.

Gallagher (1975) outlines a language-arts program for gifted students that stresses an active approach toward reading (pp. 179–181). In grades one to three, the objective of reading for gifted children should be the enjoyment of literature and the development of an awareness that stories can transport the reader back or ahead into other time periods. Even at this early stage, children can become involved in creating an ending different from the one in the actual story and can discuss what might have happened if characters had made different decisions. In grades four to six, children may begin to become more aware of other cultures and may come to appreciate language for its own sake. This can be accomplished through the study of folk fables and myths and through reading biographies. The child can be led to develop critical abilities and can apply skills in thinking and writing about what has been read and in organizing information gathered from reading.

Enrichment for the Gifted

1. Design enrichment activities for a gifted child using "space exploration" as a topic.
2. Design an appropriate study kit, or suggest several questions for long-range study that will motivate and challenge a gifted child.

Reading for Bilingual-Bicultural Children

As teachers are called on to work with more and more students whose first language is not English, it becomes necessary for them to consider the ways in which language instruction must be modified to meet the needs of these children. Federal regulations stipulate three factors that characterize an acceptable program of bilingual education:

> Instruction should be given in a child's native language to the extent that it will allow the child to achieve competence in English.
>
> Instruction should be given with attention to the cultural heritage of the child whose first language is not English.
>
> Instruction should be given in all subject-matter areas to the extent necessary to allow the child to progress effectively through the educational system.

Approaches to Working with Bilingual-Bicultural Children

Some guidelines for working with children of diverse ethnic backgrounds are suggested by the ASCD Multicultural Education Commission. These include learning about the students' culture and language to find out what is important to them, participating in community activities so that both parents and students will see that you care, valuing the students' contributions and listening to what they say, and discussing concerns that all children have, regardless of cultural background (Burns, Roe, & Ross, 1984, p. 487).

Teachers need to accept each bilingual-bicultural child without preconceptions and must value that child's native language because it is the language of home and family. "Language and self-concept are so closely intertwined that children can be made to feel foolish and worthless when their 'accent' or dialect is ridiculed by their teacher or peers" (Lapp & Flood, 1983, p. 429). The student must trust the teacher and feel confident before any attempt to teach a new language can be made.

The crucial importance of the child's cultural background can be seen in a report by Dixon (1976) of an evaluation of teaching procedures used in working with Mexican-American children. The individual identity of each of these children was defined primarily by his or her place within the total family unit and less by individual achievement. The effect of these cultural influences on teaching strategies is stressed:

1. Activities involving the entire group are more successful than those emphasizing individual improvement.
2. Activities requiring cooperation rather than competition may reflect the cognitive style of many Mexican-American children.
3. Activities involving interaction with the teacher and with other students are most profitable; paper-and-pencil work will be most effective if human interaction is also included.
4. The appearance of fellow students in roles of authority is natural and desirable in the classroom because Mexican-American children are accustomed to their older brothers and sisters assuming such roles at home (Dixon, 1976, p. 143).

These cultural characteristics suggest that peer teaching can be effective with Mexican-American children if the program is carefully designed so that such teaching is legitimately necessary. It has also been found that a group language-experience story has worked well with Mexican-American children, largely because it requires the group effort described earlier as each child tells his or her own story to the rest of the class. The student "author" may dictate a story entirely in Spanish, in a combination of Spanish and English, or entirely in English, depending on the state of development.

In addition to the advantage of allowing all children to share each other's stories, the language-experience approach allows each child to use the language skills and experiences he or she already has and avoids the problems that may be encountered in trying to read English aloud. This approach also helps children learn new words in context so that they can understand meaning more clearly, and it has the added advantage of presenting a limited number of words over and over again so that the child can eventually identify each word in isolation (Dixon, 1976, p. 144).

This discussion of the impact of cultural background and cognitive style on instructional approaches shows how significant these considerations can be. The teacher must be aware of these factors and make the effort to find out about the cultural and family environment of children with other backgrounds.

Implications for Reading Instruction

Approaches to reading instruction for bilingual students will vary depending on the background of each child. For example, the student who begins school speaking only Spanish will first need to be taught at least some of the rudiments of *speaking* English before any progress can be made in reading English. As a rule, such a child should begin to *read* in Spanish, moving to English at a later point. If the child can speak both Spanish and English, then reading instruction can begin in either language depending on preferences of the student and family. For the child who can already speak *and* read Spanish, it is necessary to begin with oral instruction in English before reading instruction begins (Lapp & Flood, 1983, p. 429).

Very young children whose first language is not English will usually begin to "pick up" words and short sentences in English as they play with other children. Not all children will progress very far without some instruction in English, however, and older children will definitely require a structured course of study if they are to learn English. Lapp and Flood (1983, pp. 437–441) provide a scope and sequence chart that can be used to determine how to go about teaching children who do need some direct instruction in English at the beginning level. They stress the need for teaching children how to form short declarative and interrogative sentences ("He is reading. Is he reading?"), use of the verb *to be* to show action in progress, and use of determiners (*the, a, an*). Other concerns at the earliest stages include use of basic verbs

Beyond the Fundamentals

other than *be,* formation of first-person singular, expression of time (verb tense), construction of negative statements (with *not*) and use of other qualifiers (*any, few, some, rarely,* and so on). Additional discussion of factors involved at the intermediate and more advanced levels is also included.

Vocabulary development for young children should focus on commonly used articles (eating and cooking utensils, foods, articles of clothing, furniture) and on other frequently encountered items and concepts (colors, days and months, telling time, numbers, and so on). Essentially the same approach can be used with non-English-speaking children as with any other younger students first learning to match names with objects; the difference here is that the children already have a background of knowledge in their first language and must be led to understand the new words within that context.

"For the learner who speaks no English, a very practical introduction to the language in a meaningful context is to begin with classroom instructions," suggest Rodrigues and White (1981, p. 8). The teacher or a tutor can list commonly used sentences ("Please pass in your papers"), and the tutor can teach the bilingual student the meaning of these statements using gestures and facial expressions. The tutor can hold up or point to objects (chalk, eraser, blackboard) and make simple declarative sentences ("This is an eraser") that are repeated by the learner. Later the tutor can formulate questions ("Is this a pencil or a piece of chalk?"), to which the learner can respond with more elaborate answers ("That is a piece of chalk. It is not a pencil.").

After the learner begins to use spoken English to some degree, it is possible to begin exercises in reading and writing. Reading assignments should relate to the immediate needs of the student. Because the most pressing need is to learn English, the teacher does not have to employ elaborate motivational strategies. The first reading activities can be developed by printing the words and sentences already learned in oral language. Students need to be able to understand instructions, and they want to feel that they are a part of the group. Therefore, "the choice of reading assignment can reinforce their feelings of accomplishment, making the teaching task that much easier" (Rodrigues & White, 1981, p. 6).

A detailed summary of teaching strategies for reading instruction of the bilingual child is given by Ching (1976, pp. 11–32). The author also discusses factors to consider in selecting reading approaches, including the following:

1. *Linking oral language and reading.*

   Present material in spoken form before it is presented in written form and use real-life situations (the language-experience approach). This approach has the advantage of building positive relationships between students and the teacher and of showing clearly the interrelation between thinking, saying, writing, and reading. Its limitations are that (a) vocabulary control is difficult, (b) content is limited to the experience of each child, and (c) unacceptable forms of speech are reinforced.

2. *Sequential development of reading skills.*

A basal reading approach can provide guidance in developing the basic reading skills, but any reading series must meet the following criteria: (a) content should be relevant to the culture of the child; (b) phonological and structural patterns must be within the child's speech repertoire; (c) vocabulary control should not be so rigid as to inhibit the child's interest in reading; (d) a variety of exercises should be provided to help in developing reading skills and extending reading experiences.

3. *Broadening reading experiences and stimulating recreational reading.*

It is most desirable that the bilingual child develop a positive attitude toward reading. Several approaches can be used to stimulate independent reading and broaden the child's reading experiences, including (a) listening centers that expose children to good books; (b) a film-viewing center with filmstrips relating to stories in children's literature; (c) an attractive library with good books on the child's reading level; (d) a regular storytelling time. Individualized reading is most effective in developing this positive attitude and in providing opportunities for interpersonal relationships between pupils and teachers (Ching, 1976, pp. 33–38).

Ching concludes by pointing out that "teaching reading to the bilingual child does not differ from teaching reading to the monolingual child, if the child is first helped to learn the phonemic and grammatical elements of English that differ from his first language before he is expected to learn to read English" (p. 38). Basically, the teacher must respect the cultural background of the child, become informed about the characteristics of the child's first language, and select the instructional approaches that best meet the needs of the individual bilingual child.

Summary

In this chapter we have tried to give you an overview of the major considerations involved in working with exceptional children in the regular classroom. There is an enormous amount of information on this topic, especially concerning handicapped children, and it will be necessary for you to augment our brief discussion with your own research.

All children who require special adaptations in their instruction will need particular attention paid to the affective aspects of learning and will require some thought and effort in order to provide extra materials and modifications in the pace at which they are expected to learn. As has been made clear throughout this chapter, most of the procedures that are effective with average children can also be used with slower learners and with gifted or bilingual children *if* you as the classroom teacher will take the time to determine exactly *what* the child needs in the way of additional material and instruction whether this takes the form of remedial work on the one hand or more challenging and rapidly paced work on the other. The most important factors to be kept in mind are that, when working with children who may be considered "exceptional" for any reason, you must determine what each child already knows (regardless of whether it is below or above the average for children of the same age), build on those strengths, and provide the materials and attention that will enable that child to develop as fully as possible.

Listings of High-Interest, Low-Vocabulary Books

Children who are having difficulty with reading, regardless of the reasons for that difficulty, can benefit by being provided with books that treat topics of interest to them but that use words they can readily understand. A list of thirty-one reading series that contain stories on interesting topics using a limited vocabulary is given in *Teaching Students with Special Problems* by Cecil D. Mercer and Ann R. Mercer (Columbus, Ohio: Charles E. Merrill, 1981, p. 296). Here are few of these:

Title	Publisher	Reading Grade Level	Interest Grade Level
Action Series	Scholastic Book Services	4–5	7–12
American Adventure Series	Harper & Row	3–6	4–8
Checkered Flag Series	Field Educational	2–4	6–12
Everyreader Series	McGraw-Hill	6–8	5–12
Interesting Reading Series	Follett	2–3	7–12
Reading for Concepts Series	McGraw-Hill	3–8	5–12
Space Science Fiction Series	Benefic Press	2–6	4–9

Other listings of similar material are given in the following:

Cushenbery, Donald C. (1977). *Reading improvement through diagnosis, remediation, and individualized instruction.* West Nyack, NY: Parker. (pp. 195–196).
Kochevar, Deloise E. (1975). *Individualized remedial reading techniques for the classroom teacher.* West Nyack, NY: Parker. (pp. 204–207).

Another source of material is *Good Reading for Poor Readers* (10th ed.) by George D. Spache (Champaign, IL: Garrard Publishing Co.,

1978; paperback edition 1974). This contains listings of trade books useful with poor readers, adapted and simplified materials, magazines and newspapers, series books, and many other resource materials. Also, an extensive listing of trade books that children like is given in *A Parent's Guide to Children's Reading* (5th ed.) by Nancy Larrick (Philadelphia: Westminster Press, 1982; paperback edition 1982, Bantam Books).

Finally, there is an annotated list of books *about* handicapped individuals—books written for children about other children, adults, and even animals—included in Gearheart and Weishahn, *The Exceptional Student in the Regular Classroom* (pp. 411–418) (St. Louis: C. V. Mosby, 1984). These books are grouped according to the type of handicap involved in the story, and there is an indication of the age range for which each is best suited.

Terms for Self-study

least restrictive environment
Individualized Education Program (IEP)
mainstreaming
educable mentally retarded (EMR)
learning disabilities
multisensory approaches
behavior-modification approaches
enrichment
language experience approach for bilingual children

Discussion Questions

1. What are the major types of handicapped children who may be included in the regular classroom? What characteristics of these types have implications for reading instruction?
2. What are some of the methods for adapting instruction or materials for teaching reading to the handicapped, to gifted students, and to the bilingual?
3. What steps might a teacher take if a child were unable to learn to read using traditional approaches and materials?
4. Why is it important to identify gifted children and to provide enrichment for them? What reading enrichment activities might be implemented?
5. What procedure should be followed when beginning to teach reading to a child who speaks only a foreign language? What approaches can be used if the child can speak at least some English?

Suggested Readings

In addition to the many books and articles cited in the text, the following books may be consulted for general information on working with exceptional children:

Epstein, Charlotte. (1984). *Special children in regular classrooms: Mainstreaming skills for teachers.* Reston, VA: Reston.

Gillespie, Patricia H., & Johnson, Lowell E. (1974). *Teaching reading to the mildly retarded child.* Columbus, OH: Charles E. Merrill.

Heward, William L., & Orlansky, Michael D. (1984). *Exceptional children* (2nd ed.). Columbus, OH: Charles E. Merrill.

Kirk, Samuel A., & Gallagher, James J. (1983). *Educating exceptional children* (4th ed.). Boston: Houghton Mifflin.

Information on teaching gifted children is available in the following:

Boothby, Paula R. (1980, March). Creative and critical reading for the gifted." *The Reading Teacher, 33*(6), 674–676.

Cassidy, Jack. (1981, October). Inquiry reading for the gifted. *The Reading Teacher, 35*(1), 17–21.

Feldhusen, John F., & Treffinger, Donald F. (1980) *Creative thinking and problem solving in gifted education.* Dubuque, IA: Kendall/Hunt.

Lake, Sara. (1981). *Gifted education: A special interest resource guide in education.* Phoenix, AZ: Oryx Press.

Laubenfels, Jean. (1977). *The gifted student: An annotated bibliography.* Westport, CT: Greenwood Press.

Moller, Barbara W. (1984, January). An instructional model for gifted advanced readers. *Journal of Reading, 27*(4), 324–327.

Books and articles providing information on bilingual education include these:

Allen, Virginia G. (1979, May). Books to lead the non-English speaking student into literacy. *The Reading Teacher, 32*(8), 940–946.

Escobedo, Theresa H. (Ed.). (1983). *Early childhood bilingual education: A Hispanic perspective.* New York: Teachers College Press.

Feeley, Joan T. (1983, March). Help for the reading teacher: Dealing with the limited English proficient (LEP) child in the elementary classroom. *The Reading Teacher, 36*(7), 650–655.

Omark, Donald R., & Erickson, Joan. (1983). *The bilingual exceptional child.* San Diego, CA: College-Hill Press.

Thomas, Carol H., & Thomas, James L. (1982). *Bilingual special education resources guide.* Phoenix, AZ: Oryx Press.

16

Current Issues in Reading

The student teaching seminar suddenly came alive when Darlene said, "My experience in the classroom is different from what I thought it was going to be. I thought I would be teaching what I learned in my methods courses. In a way I am, but it's also different from what I expected. For example, my supervising teacher sometimes uses instructional television to supplement reading. I wasn't prepared to teach with television. I'm not even sure how to develop a lesson based on a program."

Diane laughed and said that she had encountered something unexpected, too. She said that the parent-teacher organization in her school had purchased a microcomputer. "Now everyone is wondering how to use it. Several teachers asked me if I had any training at the university dealing with computers," she said. "I do know a little about computers, so I've become the 'expert' trying to help the other teachers and a few of the students in my class, too."

Roger said he had not realized how much testing went on in the classroom. "My students have to take state minimum competency tests in reading. I find myself wondering if I have covered the material they need to pass the test."

"Speaking of tests," Melanie added, "I learned from a friend that the state I want to teach in after graduation requires all teachers to take a minimum competency test to be certified. How do you study for a test like that? Can you take it over if you fail it the first time?"

These student teachers have identified several current issues that have a direct impact on reading instruction. Technology in the form of television and microcomputers and also competency testing of students and teachers are matters that you will encounter soon if they

520

aren't familiar to you already. This chapter will help you to deal with the questions that follow:

- *How can instructional television be used to enhance reading instruction?*
- *How do microcomputers fit into the reading program?*
- *What is included in a competency test for teachers?*
- *How does minimum competency testing of students influence what is emphasized in reading instruction?*

Reading, like other subjects in the school curriculum, does not exist in a vacuum. Just as reading instruction is influenced by the complex relationships between the learner's needs and the teacher's methods, it is also influenced by current trends or issues in the larger society. Although there is a variety of issues currently affecting schools, several we will examine here seem to have particular importance in the area of reading. We will first examine the impact of technology on reading instruction and then explore the topic of competency testing. Technology has the potential to alter how reading instruction is delivered, and competency testing has the potential to alter what is emphasized in instruction.

Technology and Reading Instruction

In his recent book, *High School,* Ernest Boyer, president of the Carnegie Foundation, made a special point of discussing the importance of bringing technology more fully into the schools of the United States (Boyer, 1983). Boyer argues that technology has the capacity to enhance the teacher's ability and broaden the horizons of the classroom.

As teachers we face the constant challenge of integrating technology into our classrooms in the most effective and efficient ways. One relatively recent product of technological advance, television, has become commonplace in the daily lives of our students and ourselves, but it is virtually unused in the classroom.

We see evidence daily of the important role television plays in the lives of the children we teach, and we know full well how difficult it is to compete with the television programs students watch. We understand that TV has enormous potential as a learning tool, but using that potential is evidently not as easy as it appears. A large part of the problem stems from the fact that print is still the dominant information source in our society today, and as a result our educational system is tied to print (Olson, 1977). Print technology is over three hundred years old and well entrenched in our lives and our schools. It is only natural that we rely so heavily on books and print as the major instructional tool.

However, the last fifty years have seen the development of telecommunications into an important information technology. Telecommunications, including the telephone, television, radio, and telegraph, are extremely rapid, thereby allowing people to gain more information and at a faster rate than they can from print. Furthermore, the technology is by no means static but is growing on a daily basis.

Instructional Television

Within the arena of telecommunications, we regard television as an instructional medium deserving special attention. Because it is a visual medium, TV's instructional use is quite different from that of print. Television, by its very nature, gains and holds attention. This can be seen readily by watching any child, including those who supposedly cannot concentrate beyond short periods of time, sit watching hours of television. Moreover, it is a powerful medium for modeling behavior. Everyone is exposed to new trends in manners, dress, behavior—good and bad—by watching television. From the standpoint of content, television has the capacity to present a wealth of information quickly. Evening news broadcasts illustrate this point. As many as twenty news items may be contained in a single thirty-minute news broadcast. It seems likely that students, as experienced watchers of television from infancy, expect the same fast pace in school.

Teachers are not often trained to use instructional television effectively, and, as a result, the potential of the medium goes largely untapped, in our view. Furthermore, as will be mentioned concerning computers later, many programs developed for instructional television do not take advantage of the medium as they might. Biggy (1975) suggests that the advantages of television can help "overwhelmed" teachers meet learner's individual needs. She believes that children are naturally fond of the medium and, therefore, attend to it. Television is compact in that it can present five or six different approaches to the same content in one program. It can also introduce and review content at several different levels, each in an entertaining way. Biggy points out, "For example, in a minute or two a concept can be presented at the level appropriate for teaching the entire age group. Then, in the next minute or so, the examples for reviewing and applying the concept can be alternately very easy, slightly more difficult, and extremely sophisticated to meet the needs of those children who are a cut or two above the common." (Biggy, 1975, p. 15). Furthermore, she suggests that television serves to free the teacher from presenting materials, thereby allowing the teacher to diagnose and prescribe for children's needs.

"Use of television as a major resource will provide time for the teacher to stand back and watch children react to instruction. Teachers can get immediate feedback and make the most of it in their planning. The opportunity to observe students at work and to make teacher-type decisions about how much more review and the like a child needs is really at the heart of the concept of the management role of the teacher," Biggy (1975, p. 16) writes.

What are the implications of a visual medium such as television for teaching reading? Instructional television is often thought of as more appropriate for supplementing subject areas such as social studies and science. However, certain programs like "Cover to Cover" are developed using televisions's motivation advantage to get students to read books. Almost any interesting instructional television program can become reading-oriented if the teacher develops a lesson based on it either to highlight reading skills or simply encourage children to read related books. A child who has watched a National Geographic special on lions may be led to read an article in the October issue of the magazine on the same topic, a nonfiction book about lions such as *Born Free,* or a novel in which lions play a prominent role such as *Nizambe.* If the television program has been viewed in class so that the teacher can provide planned introductory and follow-up activities, the impact of the viewing experience can be enhanced and even shaped in a desired direction. We have described how a teacher can use children's responses to shared experiences as productive jumping-off points for reading instruction elsewhere in the book (particularly in the chapter on creative reading). Some additional suggestions are offered in the next section.

Reading with Television

The following suggestions are especially appropriate for teaching reading with the aid of television:

1. Select any instructional television program that is highly motivational by virtue of its content. Using the five steps explained in Chapter 12 of this book, develop a language experience story. This activity is appropriate for a child of any age if the content of the shared program is interesting and meaningful to the group involved.

2. Select any instructional television program with different levels of content and about which there is a variety of print resources. Use television to pique curiousity about the topic. Let students use print resources to locate more information about the topic. Arrange for the sources found to be shared in a manner determined by the child.

3. Prior to showing an instructional television program, ask the children to listen for at least three new or interesting words. During the program have them write the words down along with any clues to meaning evident in the program. Follow up the program with a period during which the full meaning of the words is researched, using a variety of print resources. Have each child share his or her results. (This would make an excellent group activity as well.)

4. Have children predict what three, four, or five points a program will make about a topic prior to viewing a television program. Record the ideas generated. During viewing of the program, have the students take notes concerning their predictions. After the program, discuss the accuracy of their predictions. Identify other main points made in the program that were not predicted by the group. Relate recent stories or expository selections or both that the group has read for class to the topic of the program. Develop a bulletin board where newspaper and other printed items on the topic can be displayed.

5. After viewing an instructional television program, invite a speaker from the local community who has expertise on the

same or a related topic to visit your classroom. Ask the speaker to make a presentation, and then provide an opportunity for students to ask questions of personal interest. As a variation on this, simulate a news conference in which the students play the part of reporters who have the task of writing a news story based on the speaker's presentation. Students can be helped to prepare for the speaker's visit by reading relevant background material and developing questions for the speaker prior to the presentation.

6. If the necessary videotape equipment is available, help your students develop their own instructional program on a topic of general interest to be shown to the students in another classroom or school. Emphasize the importance of first developing accurate background on the topic and presenting a balanced report on all the key issues involved.

Computers and Reading Instruction

We are probably comfortable with print in a relative sense; it is familiar to us and hence does not pose much of a threat to our feelings of adequacy as teachers. Many of us are less comfortable with telecommunications when it comes to using them to teach in our classroom. But many of us are not at all comfortable with the implications of the latest form of information technology for our classroom—namely computers. The computer provides a new way to store, access, and use information. It is natural that its uses in a school setting are not fully understood, particularly in view of the rapid pace of change that characterizes the field. The introduction of inexpensive microchips that permit greater and greater miniaturization promises future development that staggers the imagination. (*Mindstorms* by Papert, 1980, and *The Micro Millennium* by Evans, 1983, are readable books that explore the potential developments of computers and the impact they will have on our lives.)

Some uses of computers that await only the general accessibility of machines in homes and places of business include electronic news and mail service, computerized shopping, electronic banking, and even medical diagnosis. Additional uses for computers in helping us manage our daily lives are reported nearly every week in the mass media. Predictions about the type of employment young people of today will find when they enter the job market in a few short years indicate that human services are being replaced by information services as the employment wave of the future. Boyer (1983) indicates that many of the jobs today's youth will hold do not even exist at the present time.

The advent of telecommunications technology may make it seem that the need to read and write will diminish in the near future. In many ways, we are moving into an oral and visual world. Marshall McLuhan predicted this shift away from reading and writing in the 1960s by suggesting that the "medium is the message." Those predictions now seem somewhat overdrawn in retrospect. Current predictions concerning the impending obsolescence of reading and writing skills may also be exaggerated. It seems likely that the computer will continue

Computers are having a marked impact on schools throughout the nation. Their potential for positively influencing reading instruction is just beginning to be realized.

to require literate users who can read a monitor screen and express their own thoughts in writing, perhaps even by developing their own computer programs. At least for now, the increased use of computers only underscores the importance of communication skills, including reading.

Many schools are feeling the impact of computers today because of the development of microcomputers, sometimes called personal computers. As microcomputers continue to become cheaper and more accessible generally, schools face the need to explore their potential in several arenas. Computers can serve administrative-management functions such as keeping student records and budget information in highly efficient ways. This capability has great potential for helping teacher and principal alike with the "bookkeeping side of education." More significantly, in our view, microcomputers have enormous potential for "revolutionizing" the instructional program in our schools.

Walker (1983) cautions that computers-in-education may simply be the latest "revolution" in education that goes the way of other revolutions such as career education and the new math if certain problems aren't recognized and addressed. Walker also sees the possibility of computers becoming just another part of the everyday classroom scene, being used much as chalkboards and textbooks are used, but not changing the fundamental nature of the teaching-learning environment. Whether we realize the tremendous potential computers have for schooling "depends on the instructional uses to which teachers and students" put them (Walker, 1983, p. 103).

On the positive side, microcomputers can contribute in a variety of ways to changing the complexion of classroom learning. Walker lists seven possible benefits: "(1) more active learning, (2) more varied sensory and conceptual modes, (3) less mental drudgery, (4) learning near the speed of thought, (5) learning better tailored to individuals, (6) more independent learning, and (7) better aids to abstraction" (Walker, 1983, p. 103). These potential benefits will not accrue if certain problems are not recognized and accommodated, however.

The problems according to Walker are these:

> (1) Microcomputers can supplement conventional education, but they cannot substitute for it. (2) Today's microcomputers are hard to use, and teachers prepared to use them are in short supply. (3) New products and systems are being created and marketed in such profusion, with such speed, and with so little standardization that systematic, long-term planning is nearly impossible. (4) Good programs are scarce because creating them for today's microcomputers is difficult, time-consuming, and expensive. (5) We are only beginning to understand how to use microcomputers in education; therefore, it is easy for a school or teacher to err, look foolish, or do harm. (6) Programs for teaching explicit, formal models can be created readily with known techniques, but it is much more difficult to use computers to teach subject matter that involves judgment, intuition, improvisation, and creativity. (7) Microcomputers will not solve (and may aggravate) several of the most serious current problems confronting education—notably equity, school finance, and divergent public expectations [Walker, 1983, p. 103].

To those problems we would add another difficulty that is closely related to point 7 in Walker's list (school finance). At a time when school budgets are being squeezed as never before, the need to make computers accessible to learners creates a genuine dilemma. Educators may never have the opportunity to give this latest revolution a fair trial for lack of enough computers in the classrooms. Even though the number of computers in classrooms is increasing at a rapid pace (from 131,000 in 1983 to 333,000 in 1984 according to a study by Ingersoll & Smith, 1984b), the average student in the United States has access to a computer on the average of only three minutes per day. Unless or until the problem of accessibility is solved, it makes little difference whether better software is written or teachers are trained to use computers because most students will never have a chance to become involved.

If we assume that the United States will find a way to make state-of-the-art computers accessible to students in the schools, several other issues come into focus. One we will mention only in passing because it carries us too far afield, but the second we will explore in greater depth. The issue we must largely ignore is, How much do all students need to know about the technical side of computers? Here we refer actually to knowing the intricacies of how computers are arranged internally, knowing how to write programs, and mastering various computer languages. Clearly, someone needs to learn the technical aspects of computers to advance the field, but how much does the average citizen need to know of the technicalities of computers? "No self-sufficient citizen who expects to live the bulk of his or her life in a computer-dominated world can be totally ignorant about how computers work," we hear our colleagues who are enthusiastic about computers say. Their argument is appealing, but how much technical knowledge is enough? How much does the average citizen of today know about the internal workings of a television set, a telephone, or a jet airplane? Very little, it seems to us, but we use these technological wonders nonetheless. Is the analogy apt? Are computers like telephones from a consumer standpoint—something we use but don't understand at a technical level? What constitutes computer literacy? The way we answer that last question as a society has significant implications for teachers and schools. To the extent that everyone needs to be conversant with technical details, the school curriculum will need to shift to cover these basics, and teachers will need to be prepared accordingly. These gains will be at the expense of topics and skills that must be dropped from the curriculum, which means the debate about curriculum content will touch nearly everyone. We offer no answer to the question, for it is enormously complex and goes far beyond the scope of this textbook, but it is a question that society must answer.

The second issue that flows from a solution to the problem of computer accessibility is the nature of the instructional uses to which computers will be put in the classroom. If and when terminals are available in sufficient numbers to make them a practical part of the instructional environment, how will they be used? There are at least four forms computer lessons now take. They are (1) drill and practice exercises, (2) games and simulations, (3) tutorials, and (4) problem-solving activities.

Drill and practice exercises are those in which a task is performed repetitively. Games involve competition according to a set of rules and may be against oneself, someone else, or the computer. Simulations involve the extraction of situations from the real world with conditions that change as input is made by the learner. Tutorials use the computer to interact with the learner by using a dialogue that is responsive to the errors made by the learner. Problem-solving activities place the learner in a situation that is solved through the process that the program is designed to teach. (Presently math and science programs make greater use of problem solving than do reading programs.)

Of the various types of programs just described, the drill and practice program is the easiest type to write and, therefore, the most common (Mason, Blanchard, & Daniel, 1983). A single correct answer is usually required, and the computer merely gives immediate feedback as to the correctness of the learner's response. The great potential of the computer for stimulating higher levels of thought is not reflected in drill and practice exercises. They do little more than convert workbooks into electronic form. Ingersoll and Smith (1984b) found that teachers desire features in computers for future use that suggest that repetitive functions such as drill and practice will continue to dominate the instructional uses of computers. This may reflect a simple lack of awareness on the part of teachers more than it does a conscious rejection

Even primary age children can use the computer as a learning device.

of tutorial, simulation, and problem-solving uses. We can't be sure. When the demand increases for software that features truly interactive learning, so will the availability of such programs, we predict. This assumes that teachers will become more sophisticated and more demanding in their evaluation of software. In that regard, we believe the principles and procedures outlined in Chapter 12 for evaluating instructional materials are relevant to software evaluation, though not without some further refinement. The fundamental rule stated in Chapter 12 is still the most appropriate place to start: Evaluate materials in terms of your own instructional objectives.

In evaluating computer software, the teacher must determine what is needed and search for materials that meet that need. The tendency is strong, especially in the case of instructional packages that include an audiovisual (technological) element, to be blinded by the flash, the bump, and the whirr. When this happens, the materials begin to control the curriculum rather than the other way around, as it should be.

Because there are special considerations in the evaluation of computer software, we offer special guidance here. Rosenstock, Dodl, and Burton (1984) suggest that users follow the steps listed next in evaluating computer software.

Suggested Evaluation Sequence
1. Inspect the packaging and descriptive material that accompanies the software (usually called the documentation).
2. Thoroughly read the documentation, noting in particular the requirements of the software (e.g., the amount of computer memory required, the type of disk-operating system required, the need for a printer or other peripherials or both, and so forth).

3. Load the software into the computer, and work through the program using the documentation.
4. Record your observations and comments on an evaluation form such as the one in Figure 16.1 by Rosenstock, Dodl, and Burton.
5. Work through the program on two other occasions, taking a different approach each time (i.e., deliberately make as many mistakes as possible one time and another time answer most

FIGURE 16.1   Educational-Administrative Software Evaluation.*

Program Name: _____
Author/Producer: _____
Distributor: _____
Address: _____
_____

Subject Area: _____
Description: _____
_____
_____
_____
_____

Price: _____

Instruction/Game/Administration
  (Check appropriate blanks.)

Instruction:

__ Inquiry and Dialogue
__ Drill and Practice
__ Simulation and Gaming
__ Problem Solving
__ Other_____

Administrative:

__ Student-oriented
__ Attendence
__ Grade storage
__ Class Schedules
__ Scheduler
__ General Information
__ Other_____

Games:

__ Graphics
__ Text
__ Adventure
__ Arcade
__ Other_____

__ Financial-Oriented
__ Ledger
__ Billing
__ Payroll
__ Inventory
__ Library Records
__ Other_____

Applicability in U.S. Schools: (Circle grades appropriate.)
Pre 1 2 3 4 5 6 7 8 9 10 11 12 College None

System Requirements: (Please check those appropriate.)

Computer:	__ IBM PC	__ IBM PC-XT	__ Apple][	__ Apple][e
	__ TRS80	__ VIC20	__ PET	__ Commodore__
	__ TI__	__ KAYPRO	__ ATARI__	Other_____
Language:	__ BASIC	__ Pascal	__ COBOL	__ FORTRAN
	__ Machine language (compiled)			__ Assembler
	__ PL/I	__ LISP	Other_____	

Memory: __ 16K __ 32K __ 48K __ 64K __ 128K __ 256K
                   __ >256K_____

External storage: __ Disk Drives How many?__ __ SS __ DS
                   __ Hard Disk ____ M __ Cassette __ none
                   other_____

FIGURE 16.1 *(Continued)*

Other Peripherals:

__ Color Monitor	__ Speech Synthesizer
__ Game Paddles	__ Printer_____
__ Z80 Card	__ Joystick
__ Clock	__ Graphics Tablet
__ Modem/Acoustic Coupler	__ Light Pen
__ Key Pad	__ Robot Arm

__ Other (Specify cards or peripherals.)

_____

_____

Maintenance Requirements:

Can backups of program disk be made? Yes/No

Are backups provided? Yes/No

Can backups of data be made? Yes/No

Does the program backup data? Yes/No

Are backup disk for data provided? Yes/No

Is it the user's responsibility to backup data? Yes/No

If so, how? _____

Does the user need to supply software? Yes/No

If so, what? _____

Manufacturer's Support:

Is manufacturer's support needed? Yes/No

Do they provide a phone number? Yes/No

If so, is it toll-free? Yes/No

Do they answer the phone? Yes/No

Estimate the amount of support or consultation needed.

__ Extremely Frequent   __ Frequent   __ Occasional
__ Seldom   __ Never   __ Always

Is customizing of the program needed? Yes/No

Is customizing of the program available? Yes/No

If so to either, at what cost? (specify briefly)

_____

External Documentation Adequacy:

Is documentation provided? Yes/No

Indicate level of computer knowledge needed to understand documentation.

None		Some		Literate		Conversant			Too much	
1	2	3	4	5	6	7	8	9	10	11

Rate the adequacy of the documentation in the following.

	Poor		Fair		Good		Excellent			
Setting Up	1	2	3	4	5	6	7	8	9	10	NA
Input of data	1	2	3	4	5	6	7	8	9	10	NA
Update data	1	2	3	4	5	6	7	8	9	10	NA
General Use	1	2	3	4	5	6	7	8	9	10	NA
Report Format	1	2	3	4	5	6	7	8	9	10	NA
Report Output	1	2	3	4	5	6	7	8	9	10	NA
Data Limits	1	2	3	4	5	6	7	8	9	10	NA
Program Limits	1	2	3	4	5	6	7	8	9	10	NA

Reports Generated:

Can the reports be customized? Yes/No

If so, by whom? Manufacturer/User

Are the reports complete for all needs? Yes/No

If not, why? _____

_____

FIGURE 16.1 *(Continued)*

Please rate the reports.

Poor			Fair		Good		Excellent		
1	2	3	4	5	6	7	8	9	10

Limitations:

Please state any limitations found in the program,

i.e., student population, teacher population, student preferences, number of classes, number of books, largest dollar figure handled.

Also state hardware/software limits (if any) and if the program and data are portable (to another computer).

_____

_____

_____

Communication Capability:

Does the program allow for communication with other computers?

Yes/No

If so, indicate the following:

Ease of up and down loading files:

difficult   moderate   easy

1 2 3 4 5 6 7 8 9 10

Ease of use:

difficult   moderate   easy

1 2 3 4 5 6 7 8 9 10

Please specify any limitations or requirements or both.

_____

_____

_____

Cleanliness of Program Code:

Are there any logical bugs in the program? Yes/No

If so, what are they and where:

_____

_____

_____

Are there any syntactical bugs in the program? Yes/No

If so, what are they and where:

_____

_____

_____

Please rate the smoothness of the program flow.

Rough Fair   Good Very smooth

1 2 3 4 5 6 7 8 9 10

Does the program's organization make sense? Yes/No

In General:

Please rate:

Ratings:	Poor		Fair			Good		Excellent		
Physical Characteristics	1	2	3	4	5	6	7	8	9	10
Usage Considerations	1	2	3	4	5	6	7	8	9	10
Presentation	1	2	3	4	5	6	7	8	9	10
Instructional Considerations	1	2	3	4	5	6	7	8	9	10
Administrative Considerations	1	2	3	4	5	6	7	8	9	10
Aesthetics	1	2	3	4	5	6	7	8	9	10
Practical Considerations	1	2	3	4	5	6	7	8	9	10
Price/Performance Rating	1	2	3	4	5	6	7	8	9	10
Overall Rating	1	2	3	4	5	6	7	8	9	10

FIGURE 16.1 *(Continued)*

Comments/Reactions:

_____

_____

_____

_____

_____

_____

_____

Reviewer: _____ Date: _____

* A Product of the Education Microcomputer Laboratory College of Education, Virginia Polytechnic Institute and State University.

questions correctly, but make errors occasionally to see how the program handles them).

6. Select three different children representing various achievement levels. Have each child work through the program and then give you his or her comments and reactions. Note the children's performance as they try the software, watching in particular their general level of success, their interest, and the appropriateness of the program for their instructional needs.

7. Make further entries on the evaluation form.

8. Ask another teacher to work through the program, and ask for evaluative feedback.

9. Leave the program for a week or so; then try it once again yourself.

10. Revise the entries made on the evaluation form, revise as appropriate, and share your recommendation with whomever is responsible for ordering instructional software.

Other evaluation criteria are listed in Mason, Blanchard, and Daniel (1983). In addition, many magazines designed for computer users carry regular reviews of new software that has entered the market. Examples include *Softalk, PC Magazine, Classroom Computer News, Creative Computing, Educational Technology,* and *Educational Computer.*

Competency Testing in Education

There is a very good chance that you are presently teaching in or will soon teach in a state that uses competency tests as part of the certification process. As of the 1983–1984 school year, only eight states did not require that candidates for teacher certification submit scores on the *National Teacher Examinations* (NTE) or similar competency test as part of the application process (Sandefur, 1984).

Teachers are not the only ones being tested. Students in over half the states are now required to pass competency tests in order to graduate from high school (Pipho, 1984). In many states, competency tests are also administered at various points in a student's school career to provide evidence that basic skills are being learned along the way.

Recent calls have been heard for testing all teachers on a regular basis, not just those who are seeking to gain initial certification (*Teacher Education Reports,* November 10, 1983). Authoritative voices such as the Southern Regional Education Board have recommended that school principals also be required to take paper-and-pencil competency tests. Some critics have suggested that those on college and university faculties who prepare teachers also be given competency tests (*Teacher Education Reports,* May 26, 1983).

In all these cases, the use of competency tests has not been proposed as a replacement for other means of evaluation that have been in place for decades such as requiring successful completion of certain courses on the way to a degree, diploma, or certification. Rather, these tests would be an additional requirement to ensure the competence of public school personnel.

What has given rise to the competency testing movement in education? As recently as 1977, only three states required teachers to take competency exams (Sandefur, 1983). Except for a few states, the use of competency tests for graduation from high school has occurred within the past ten years (Pipho, 1984). Opinions differ on what accounts for this increased emphasis on testing as a means of ensuring quality, of course, and one's own perspective tends to influence how the phenomenon is interpreted.

From our vantage point the main factor behind the increased interest in competency testing was a widespread concern among the citizenry in general that the quality of public education had eroded badly during the late sixties and early seventies. Though public education has been criticized periodically (see Ayres, 1909; Conant, 1959; Lynch, 1912; Lynd, 1950; Rickover, 1959, 1963; Smith, 1949), the most recent scrutiny occurred at a time when the print and electronic media had gained a new and awesome ability to focus public attention. Widespread publicity given to a fifteen-year decline of SAT scores seemed to arouse national concern (Venable, 1981; Wirtz et al., 1977). Several anecdotal stories about a teacher here or there who spelled poorly and evidenced poor language usage in notes sent home to parents received national attention (*Time,* June 16, 1980). Declining productivity of workers on the job, stagnation of the national economy, increased competition from foreign producers, the Iran hostage crisis, the oil embargo, increased pressure for a fully integrated society, and a host of other developments contributed to a general sense of doubt on the part of the public about the vitality and strength of nearly all its public institutions and agencies.

In response, governing bodies began to seek ways to deal with the perceived erosion of quality in American society. A fairly inexpensive way to solve the "problem of quality" in public schooling was to focus on the product—the learners. If high standards could be established for those who would graduate from the system, so the logic went, changes would be forced on those who had let the standards deteriorate. It was not a big step to conclude further that competent teachers would not have let the system decline so dramatically, and, therefore, quality assurances were also needed in this domain to get rid of incompetents. Why not keep incompetents out of the classroom through a rigorous testing program, critics reasoned?

Those who advocate the use of competency tests are not set on destroying the teaching profession. Their motives seem to be of a higher order: They want to be sure that certain standards are met. Advocates of competency testing believe that by meeting those standards the test taker will demonstrate he or she can perform at a particular level. One can hardly argue against the goal of ensuring that standards are met. What is debatable is whether a test being used in this fashion actually measures the skills and knowledge that are important and whether decisions that affect people's lives should be based solely or even primarily on a paper-and-pencil test.

Evidence that indicated schools are doing a rather admirable job under the circumstances was largely ignored by those who sought to legislate quality into education (Brandt, 1981; LaPointe, 1984). Neither was much attention paid to the social and economic conditions that affected schools. But it is beyond our scope and not central to our purpose here to explore in any depth either the nature or validity of the concerns that gave rise to the competency testing movement. A number of recent books by noted authorities (including Richard Brandt, former dean of education at the University of Virginia, 1981; Ernest Boyer, president of the Carnegie Foundation and former U. S. commissioner of education, 1983; John I. Goodlad, former dean of education at UCLA, 1984; Dianne Ravitch, adjunct professor at Columbia University, 1983; and Theodore R. Sizer, former dean of education at Harvard University and headmaster at Phillips Academy, 1984), have all written books that explore the complexities of public education and offer insights into the accuracy of charges that U. S. schools have recently deteriorated in quality.

Let us here devote our attention to preparing you and your students to perform well on the competency tests that now seem to have a firm foothold in public education.

The Nature of Competency Tests for Teachers

One battery of tests, the National Teacher Examinations (NTE), published by the Educational Testing Service (ETS) of Princeton, New Jersey, has gained a prominent role in the current movement to test teachers. We will concentrate our attention here on the NTE because of its widespread use throughout the United States. We should point out that not all school systems, agencies, and associations that require a competency test use the NTE, however. It is important that you explore the situation with respect to teacher testing in your own location to determine the type of test or tests you must take to be admitted to a professional school or to qualify for employment as a teacher or both. Many tests developed by local school systems such as Dallas, Texas, or individual states such as Arizona are similar to the NTE, so the description provided here will be helpful to some extent in those cases as well. Nevertheless, it is still important to know the exact nature of any competency test you will take so that you may prepare yourself accordingly.

The National Teacher Examinations

The NTE examinations are described by ETS as "standardized, secure examinations that provide objective measures of academic achievement for college students in teacher education programs, for college seniors completing teacher education programs, and for advanced candidates who have received additional training in specific fields" (*NTE Program Bulletin of Information, 1984*, p. 5). One battery of three tests, called the *Core Battery*, consists of (1) a *Communication Skills Test*, which measures listening, reading, and writing; (2) a *General Knowledge Test*, which covers literature and fine arts, mathematics, science, and social studies; and (3) a *Test of Professional Knowledge*, which "includes questions related to the social and cultural forces that influence curriculum and teaching as well as questions dealing with general principles of learning and instruction," (*NTE Program Bulletin of Information, 1984*, p. 5).

Depending on who has asked that you take the NTE and why, any or all of the *Core Battery Tests* may be required. The most common reason for requiring any of the *Core Battery Tests* is to assess how well a teaching candidate can perform certain basic tasks. Thus, performance on the *Communication Skills Test* provides evidence that a candidate can listen, read, and write at a particular level of proficiency. It is significant that ETS does not indicate a passing score on any of the NTE tests. In fact, ETS is careful to caution those who use the NTE *not* to make decisions about candidates solely on the basis of one or even all tests in the NTE battery. Nevertheless, the inability of anyone taking the test to perform certain basic communication tasks successfully can be useful information to have. Exactly how that information is used becomes a policy matter that often becomes infused with political considerations. Despite an absence of any compelling evidence indicating that competent teachers can be separated from incompetent teachers by using the NTE, the members of a school board, state legislature, or committee on admission to professional studies in a school, college or department of education, for example, may decide that those below a certain score on that particular test (or other test) should be excluded or rejected. As one who might be affected by such a decision, it behooves you to achieve a high and, therefore, passing score.

The Communication Skills Test
The *Communication Skills Test* is comprised of four half-hour sections, including a listening accuracy test presented on tape, a multiple choice reading and writing test, and an essay writing test. Following are sample questions that should help you understand how performance is tested.

Listening[1]

Direction: Choose the answer that is the best response to the question you hear.
Listen to the following example:
You will hear:

1. *How often do you go to the movies?*
   You will read:
   a. *The theater's close. We usually walk.*
   b. *No. We don't go all that much.*
   c. *Once every week or two.*
   d. *Because we both enjoy movies.*

Reading

Social and scientific revolutions must be sharply distinguished. Social revolutions are restricted to a particular time and place; they last for a while and then pass into history. Scientific revolutions, on the other hand, belong to all places and all times.

1. *The primary purpose of the statement is to*
   a. *argue that advances made in science cannot be undone or forgotten.*
   b. *identify several important aspects of scientific and social revolutions.*
   c. *discuss the social consequences of scientific revolutions.*
   d. *point out a fundamental difference between social revolutions and scientific revolutions.*
   e. *suggest that the importance of social revolutions is frequently overestimated.*

Writing Multiple-Choice

Directions: Indicate which of the underlined and lettered parts contains an error.

He spoke bluntly and angrily to we spectators. No error.
　　　　　a　　　　b　　c　　d　　　　e

The Test of General Knowledge

Many people who hold the opinion that teachers should be able to perform certain basic communication tasks at a minimum level of competency also believe that teachers should know certain concepts and facts. Consequently, those who support the use of the *Communications Skills Test* for screening teachers typically also support the use of the *Test of General Knowledge* for the same purpose. This two-hour test also consists of four half-hour sections that employ multiple-choice questions to assess understanding of literature and fine arts, mathematics, science, and social studies. We note that, like the *Communication Skills Test,* the knowledge tested in this test is not typically taught by an

---

[1] The sample questions provided here and in the pages that follow are all taken from the *Guide to the NTE Core Battery Tests: Communication Skills, General Knowledge, Professional Knowledge.* Princeton: ETS, 1984. Reprinted by permission of Educational Testing Service, the copyright owner. Permission to reprint the NTE test questions does not constitute endorsement by Educational Testing Service of this publication.

education faculty as much as it is by the arts and sciences faculty of a college or university. The *General Knowledge* section of the NTE Core Battery includes items such as the following:

Fine Art

Note: *In the test booklet, a photo of a bronze statue displayed at The Metropolitan Museum of Art is shown.*

1. This bronze statue derives much of its effect from the
   a. *lack of recognizable subject matter.*
   b. *open and inviting gesture.*
   c. *lines and folds of the garment.*
   d. *relaxed posture of the figure.*
   e. *pathetic facial expression.*

Mathematics

1. *If the sum of two numbers is 18, which CANNOT be true of the numbers?*
   a. *Their sum is 0.*
   b. *Their product is 0.*
   c. *One number is twice the other number.*
   d. *One number is eight times the other number.*
   e. *One number is greater than 18.*

Science

1. *The current in a wire can be increased by increasing the*
   a. *potential difference between the ends of the wire.*
   b. *resistance of the wire.*
   c. *temperature difference between the ends of the wire.*
   d. *length of the wire.*
   e. *layer of insulation around the wire.*

Social Studies

1. *During a recession in the United States, unemployment is likely to be highest among which of the following groups?*
   a. *public school teachers*
   b. *army officers*
   c. *office managers*
   d. *automobile assembly workers*
   e. *dairy farmers*

The Test of Professional Knowledge

Not all those who favor competency testing of teachers would see a need to use the third part of the *Core Battery*—the *Test of Professional Knowledge*. ETS provides this test as part of the *Core Battery* to measure the knowledge ordinarily taught by a college, school, or department of education. In the eyes of some, teaching itself has no knowledge base but instead is dependent almost entirely on knowing the subject matter to be taught. Thus, some believe a college graduate who majors in mathematics, for example, is sufficiently prepared to teach geometry to fifteen-year-olds despite having had no student teaching, child development, or professional education courses. Such people would not find much of value in the *Test of Professional Knowledge* but would probably favor using the other two parts of the *Core Battery*.

We personally attach some importance to teachers having knowledge about schools and schooling and also about teaching, learning, and curriculum. This textbook represents our beliefs about some information that teachers should master to be effective. Good teaching involves many abilities, attitudes, and traits that cannot be measured with any written test, of course, but all parts of the *Core Battery* are equally important in establishing the threshhold levels that teachers should meet.

The content of the *Test of Professional Knowledge* deals primarily with the context and process of teaching. Questions concerning the context of teaching focus "on the constitutional rights of students and the implications for classroom practice, the implications of state, federal, and judicial policies for school practices, forces outside the classroom that influence teachers and students, and the activities and functions of professional organizations and of teachers' rights and responsibilities" (*Guidelines for Proper Use of NTE Tests, 1983*, p. 4). Questions concerning the process of teaching focus on the appropriate techniques and means of instructional planning, implementation, and evaluation, as well as acceptable professional behavior.

Sample questions from the *Test of Professional Knowledge* are provided as follows:

1. *To satisfy the requirements of legislation regarding the education of handicapped persons, teachers of handicapped children are obliged to do which of the following?*
   a. *Make regular appointments with each child's parents to discuss the child's social adjustment.*
   b. *Count the number of times that objectives in each child's individualized education program (IEP) are included in lessons.*
   c. *Write an anecdotal record about the pattern of each lesson.*
   d. *Hold periodic conferences with the evaluation team to report student progress.*
   e. *Indicate the extent to which the instructional objectives in each child's individualized education program (IEP) have been reached.*

2. *Which of the following rules, designed to implement a school's discipline code, violates students' First Amendment rights?*
   a. *Students shall not forge or falsify notes or excuses.*
   b. *Students may not use tobacco in the school building or on school grounds.*
   c. *Students may not wear political buttons in school.*
   d. *Students may not leave school without a pass signed by a teacher or administrator.*
   e. *Students must identify themselves when requested to do so by school authorities.*

The Speciality Area Tests

If you are required to take the NTE at all, there is a very good chance you will be expected to take both the *Core Battery* and the *Speciality Area Test* for your teaching field. *Speciality Area* tests are available in

Beyond the Fundamentals

twenty-seven different fields, including early childhood education (ages three to eight), education in the elementary grades (grades one to eight), and most high school subjects such as mathematics, French, and industrial arts. In the field of reading, a *Speciality Area Test* is available at an entry level (i.e., *Introduction to the Teaching of Reading* for those who will teach reading) and an advanced level (i.e., *Reading Specialist,* primarily for those who will supervise and coordinate reading programs). Which, if any, of the speciality tests you would take to qualify for a teaching position depends on the requirements of the state and local school system where you hope to be employed. You should check with the appropriate officials for advice on which exams to take. (Remember that some states and school systems use exams other than the NTE). Because it is fairly expensive to take the NTE, you may not want to do so unless it is a specific condition of employment or certification in your locality. On the other hand, if you think you may move someday, you may want to take the NTE shortly after completing your academic work even if it is not required in your locality to avoid the potential decline in score that goes with forgetting the specifics learned in your college courses.

Each speciality exam is developed by ETS with the assistance of experts in the area being tested. The content of the exam is based on an analysis of the field and involves the identification of major topics the experts regard as basic. In the *Introduction to the Teaching of Reading Test,* for example, the eight areas examined are these:

1. Nature of the reading process, including interrelatedness of the processes of listening, speaking, reading and writing, and cultural factors that influence the desire and ability to read.
2. Reading skills and methods of teaching them, including word recognition and analysis, vocabulary and concept development, linguistic analysis, comprehension, flexibility in reading, study techniques, library and reference skills, and oral reading.
3. Utilization of diagnostic and prescriptive teaching to provide for individual differences, including tests, records, and skill profiles in planning instruction, organizing the classroom for learning, skillful questioning, student characteristics as related to reading, and differentiated reading assignments.
4. Theories of reading instruction, including those focusing on students' language, students' maturity and interest, the nature of English spelling patterns, the nature of basic sight words and syntax, and learning theory.
5. Reading instructional approaches, including changed orthography, analytic and synthetic phonics, linguistic approaches, systems such as programmed reading and individually prescribed instruction, language experience, basal reader, and individualized reading.
6. School organization for teaching reading, including nongraded and cross-graded plans, team teaching, open classrooms, tutoring, use of paraprofessionals, and the schoolwide approach.

7. Affective aspects of reading instruction, including stimulation of interest and teacher characteristics that affect reading instruction.
8. Teacher resources, including professional organizations, journals, texts, and other sources of knowledge [*NTE Programs: Core Battery and Speciality Area Tests, 1983,* pp. 89–90].

Questions asked on the *Introduction to the Teaching of Reading Test,* like all tests in the NTE battery, probe recall and identification of fact as well as understanding of concepts that require making associations, generalizations, and interpretations. Some questions involve the application of facts and concepts in solving problems.

Several sample questions from the reading test will help you gain a sense of what is required:

1. Of the following aids to the pronunciation of an unknown word, which would ordinarily be used by a reader after all others have failed?
   a. configuration clues
   b. context clues
   c. phonic analysis
   d. the dictionary
   e. structural analysis

2. In teaching a unit on words and their meanings, a classroom teacher probably would achieve the LEAST favorable results by
   a. making use of a wide variety of books that provoke controversial questions.
   b. encouraging the pupils to learn one word a day.
   c. having pupils discuss and write figures of speech.
   d. encouraging pupils to collect and categorize words in personal notebooks.
   e. providing lists of words that the pupils can memorize.

3. A bilingual program has just been started in a school in order to help students who are dominant in Spanish. Some indignant parents insist that their Spanish-speaking children learn to read in English immediately. The teacher can reassure the parents about the purpose of this program by telling them the program is designed to
   a. provide enrichment activities.
   b. promote an interest in cultural activities.
   c. teach basic skills in both Spanish and English.
   d. help the students learn in their native tongue.
   e. protect the Spanish-speaking students from the remarks of those who cannot understand them.

Registering to Take the NTE

The NTE is administered at dozens of sites scattered throughout the United States on several different occasions during the year. The *Core Battery* is typically administered on a Saturday in October and again in March at predesignated locations and the *Speciality Area Tests* on a Saturday in November and again in April. Special arrangements can be made in cases where religious convictions prevent a Saturday testing. ETS is also responsive to requests for special administrations of the tests from handicapped individuals and other individuals who cannot take the tests under the regular arrangements. Extra costs may be involved in special administrations of the NTE.

All individuals seeking to take the NTE must submit registration materials and a check or money order to ETS well in advance of the test day (more than thirty days). A comprehensive booklet designed for those wanting to take the NTE, titled *NTE Programs: 19XX–XX Bulletin of Information*, can be obtained by writing to ETS in Princeton, New Jersey (the full address is given later in this chapter) or by calling (609) 771-7670 during regular business hours.

Preparing to Take the NTE or Other Competency Test

In recent years a flourishing business has sprung up around the matter of helping people prepare for any number of standardized tests. The *Scholastic Aptitude Test* (SAT), for example, is one for which you may have seen study devices ranging from computer software to intensive workshops offered at a local community education center. Nearly any bookstore will offer books that promise to help you in doing well on the *Graduate Record Examination, Miller Analogies Test,* or other test used for screening or selecting candidates for any number of enterprises (e.g., certification, licensing, admission, and the like). Several such publications are available in connection with the NTE, as a matter of fact. We found the following titles at a local book store:

Fox, Daniel. (1983). *National Teacher Examinations* (NTE). New York: ARCO.
Rudman, Jack. (1984). *National Teacher Examinations—Common Examination: Admission Series: ATS-15.* New York: National Learning.

Experts on studying have found that the more one knows about a criterion task (a test, for example), the greater the effectiveness in studying and preparing for that task (Anderson & Armbruster, 1984; Armbruster & Anderson, 1981). It is helpful to know what content is covered by a test, for example, the number and types of questions, how long the test will last, whether external aids such as dictionaries or calculators can be used, and how the test will be scored (i.e., whether a correction for guessing is made).

To the extent that a book (like Fox, 1983, or Rudman, 1984) helps you understand the nature of the NTE, it can probably help you prepare more effectively. Actually, ETS provides several items free of charge and some at a minimal cost that are likely to help you improve your performance by clarifying a number of important matters concerning the nature of the tests. The *NTE Programs: 19XX–XX Bulletin of Information* mentioned earlier is one such aid. In addition to providing forms and information needed to register for taking the test, the *Bulletin* describes what to take with you to the testing session, what strategy to use in taking the tests, how the tests are scored, how your scores will be reported, and how and under what circumstances scores can be cancelled by the examinee or ETS.

When you register to take the NTE, a leaflet providing a brief content outline for the tests (much like the one provided for the reading test on p. 539 of this text) as well as sample questions for the NTE will be sent to you automatically by ETS with your ticket of admission to the testing session.

ETS also offers a *Guide to the NTE Core Battery Tests: Communication Skills, General Knowledge, Professional Knowledge* that includes three actual tests from earlier administrations, answer keys for the tests, and instructions for scoring the tests. The *Guide* also discusses the content of each test, provides explanations for correct answers, and gives strategy tips for taking the tests. The *Guide* is available for $7.95 per copy, including shipping and handling. Orders should be sent to:

NTE *Guide*
Educational Testing Service
CN 6058
Princeton, NJ 08541-6058

In addition to obtaining and studying the items described above, you might also read a text such as *Proven Strategies for Successful Test Taking* by Sherman and Wildman (1982) for general test-taking advice. These and other authorities make a number of excellent suggestions for taking tests. In the case of multiple-choice tests, a few of their tips include the following:

1. *Use good test-taking tactics.*
   a. *Quickly estimate at the outset about how much time you can afford to spend on each question.*
   b. *Move at a steady pace through the test. Come back to difficult questions that you cannot solve immediately.*
   c. *Respond to the questions according to directions.*
   d. *Find out in advance what the test will require of you.*
   e. *Aggressively attack the test with the idea that each question can be answered.*
2. *Know and take advantage of the characteristics of multiple-choice tests.*
   a. *If the correct answer is not immediately found, eliminate alternatives that are obviously absurd, silly, or incorrect.*
   b. *Compare each alternative to the stem and to other alternatives.*
   c. *Remember that when two alternatives are identical, then both must be incorrect.*
3. *Use logical reasoning to improve performance.*
   a. *Remember that if any two options are opposite, then at least one may be eliminated.*
   b. *Choose the alternative that is the most inclusive.*
4. *Use clues provided by flaws in the test.*
   a. *Correct answers are often ones that contain qualifiers such as these: in most cases, generally,* or *frequently.*

b. *Locate and eliminate alternatives that do not match the stem grammatically.*

c. *Certain words such as* **always** *or* **never** *often make an alternative too broad to be correct.*

d. *Longer alternatives are often correct because they elaborate or qualify an answer [Sherman and Wildman, 1982].*

Contrary to what many laypeople believe, it is not dishonest or unethical to enhance your own test performance (or that of your students) by learning to be a good test taker. Anything that enables people to reveal what they truly know about a topic that does not include practicing on the actual test to be used is simply good preparation. Scholars should scrimmage under actual game conditions just as athletes do before a big competition. This means learning as much as possible ahead of time about the tasks to be performed on a test and using every bit of knowledge you have about how to maximize your score. Everyone taking a test has the same opportunity—or should have— to maximize his or her own performance. One plausible explanation for the poor performance of some individuals on standardized tests such as the NTE is simply insufficient opportunity to learn good test-taking behaviors. We recommend that you give yourself the best possible chance to do well on the NTE or other competency test by preparing yourself properly.

If you are not satisfied with your score on the NTE or other teacher competency test, it is usually possible to retake them after a designated interval. The costs involved in doing so may make this approach unattractive, and you may not want to have a score on your record that is less than your best, but one way of gaining a better understanding of what is included in such a test is to take it for practice. Your efforts to prepare can be enhanced if you have had some previous experience with it. Many high school students are now adopting this strategy as a way of improving their SAT scores. ETS and other test publishers take the position that a score cannot be improved with this approach, but it is permissible.

Competency Testing of Students

Minimum competency testing (MCT) is a label that has come to have a fairly specific meaning in education. The following definition, which we judge to be widely accepted, was used in hearings held during the summer of 1980 by the National Institute of Education (NIE):

> Minimum competency testing refers to programs mandated by a state or local body which have the following characteristics: (1) All or almost all students of designated grades are required to take paper-and-pencil tests designed to measure basic academic skills, life or survival skills, or functional literacy; (2) a passing score or standard for acceptable levels of student performance has been established; and (3) test results may be used to certify students for grade promotion, graduation, or diploma award; to classify students for or to place students in remedial or other special services; to allocate compensatory

funds to districts; to certify schools or school districts; or to evaluate teachers (Thurston and House, 1981).

Not everyone agrees with this definition, particularly with the stipulation that the denial of high school graduation on the basis of a state-mandated test is an integral part of MCT. (For example, South Carolina did not use MCT tests that way in 1981, but many still regarded its program as a minimum competency testing program.) Most states having or considering an MCT program do deny high school graduation on the basis of test performance (Pipho, 1984). Impara, Andrew, McCluskey, and Weber reported in 1979 that thirty-five states were either planning or had instituted an MCT program (Impara et al., 1979). An update in 1984 revealed that of forty states responding to a survey, twenty used MCT for high school graduation, and three others left this option open to the local school system (Pipho, 1984). No state responding had dropped MCT as a graduation requirement.

Like competency testing of teachers, minimum competency testing appears to be a legislative or state education agency (or both) response to public concern for a perceived decline in the quality of education. Again, we will resist the temptation to explore here the validity of those concerns about quality and the efficacy of MCT as a response. These are important matters for your consideration, however, and we recommend that you study the writings of individuals such as Bracey (1983), Glass (1978), Madaus (1979), Pullin (1981), and Tittle (1982), who have examined the topic in depth. We will concern ourselves in this textbook with the consequences of MCT for your students and for your teaching.

The Nature of Competency Tests for Children

As we attempt to describe the nature of competency tests for children, we must first caution that not all competency tests are alike. Differences do exist in MCTs from locality to locality and from test to test. Even the subject areas tested are not always alike. At the same time, our area of primary interest in this textbook, reading, is nearly always one of those domains tested, and there is enough similarity across most reading competency tests to permit us to make some useful generalizations.

Competency Testing at the High School Level

Earlier we indicated that some states require students to pass a competency test in order to graduate from high school. We will spend a little time examining such tests even though this textbook is not written primarily for high school teachers because by doing so we can provide a sense of perspective on the nature of the tests the students you teach must pass eventually. You will find occasions when you might say or do something that will have a positive cumulative effect over time along with the efforts of other teachers. This is especially important in the domain of testing for high school graduation because many

Children need help in learning how to perform up to their ability on competency tests. Such preparation reduces test anxiety and increases the validity of the scores achieved.

of those MCTs focus on application situations that do not reflect what students have studied in English, science, math, history, and other courses.

With respect to reading, those interested in measuring minimum competencies typically focus on the uses of reading in everyday, even survival, situations. In Virginia, for example, the *Graduation Competency Test; Reading* is comprised of five parts as follows:

1. Following Safety Warnings (twenty-six items).
2. Completing Forms and Applications (thirteen items).
3. Using Reference Sources (thirteen items).
4. Determining Main Ideas (thirteen items).
5. Using Documents (thirteen items).

On the Virginia test, students read short passages from documents such as an employee manual or tourist guide in part 5, for example, and answer multiple-choice questions calling for literal interpretation. Other parts of the test require students to interpret the label on a medicine bottle or can of furniture polish, for example; decide what information belongs in a particular blank on an application form (such as a driver's license application); find numbers in a telephone directory; read a road map; and identify the main idea of a three- or four-para-graph expository selection. Students first take the *Virginia Graduation Competency Test* in grade ten and must earn a score that corresponds to 70 per cent on the original 1978 test to pass. The test may be taken up to five times—once each year in grades ten and eleven and three times in grade twelve. (Special provisions are made so that individuals who left school without a diploma can retake the test on one of four occasions when it is given each year.) Students must also pass a mathematics minimum competency test to graduate from a Virginia high school. Additionally, the local school division must certify that the student has demonstrated minimum competency in social studies and has been given career preparation or has been prepared for further education.

A few sample items from the Virginia test are presented here. You will notice that the items are not distinguishable from those found on many other tests of reading.

Toothache Pain Relief Cream

DIRECTIONS: Squeeze a small quantity of cream directly into cavity and on the gum surrounding the tooth.

CAUTION: This preparation is intended for limited use only. Use as a temporary measure until a dentist can be consulted. Do not use continuously. Do not use for other mouth ailments such as irritation or mouth soreness. Keep this and all drugs out of the reach of children.

1. *While on vacation, you develop a toothache. You use the toothache pain cream for two days until you get home to see your dentist. According to the warning above, you are acting:*
   a. *correctly*
   b. *incorrectly*

2. *You feel several sore spots on the roof of your mouth. You apply the toothache medication directly to the sores. According to the warning above, you are acting:*
   a. *correctly*
   b. *incorrectly*

If the test items on an MCT are not different from a typical criterion-referenced or norm-referenced test, you may be wondering, What is it about MCTs that make them notable? The answer lies in the way the test results are used. Impara (1979) indicates that test scores can be used for decisions about individuals and decisions about programs. Furthermore, insofar as individuals are concerned, decisions may be made about (1) placement (also called classification or screening), (2) selection (also called prediction, as, for example, predicting success in a particular job), and (3) diagnosis (i.e., identifying strengths and weaknesses). Without going into specifics that fit better in a book about educational measurement, it is important to recognize that different kinds of validity are important in each testing situation depending on the kind of decision to be made with the results. We need to pursue that thought for just a moment to describe one of the major problems facing the classroom teacher with respect to minimum competency tests.

Earlier we pointed out that MCTs often test skills that are not taught directly by any teacher in a typical high school program. Reading is a main part of the Virginia high school graduation test, yet the typical high school student in Virginia does not enroll in a reading course. Consequently, no teacher is directly responsible for teaching the skills being measured by that portion of the graduation test. It is often the English teacher who inherits the task of preparing students who may be having trouble with the reading section of the competency test. What occurs at this point is often frustrating to the teacher and disheartening to the student. The English curriculum must be abandoned to provide a repeat of instruction on basics that were probably taught in the elementary grades but not in the form required by the MCT. The teacher is seldom trained in providing the type of instruction needed, yet the student will not graduate if Shakespeare and grammar are taught and life or survival reading skills ignored. The problem is one of test validity—in this case, content validity (sometimes called instructional validity). What is being taught in the English program is not what the MCT measures.

The MCT typically does not have criterion or predictive validity, meaning that it has not been found appropriate for selecting those who will graduate by virtue of the fact that it correctly identifies those students who have met the criterion. In this case, the criterion would seem to be one of having the ability to become a contributing, self-supporting citizen. If you reflect for a moment on the difficulty of creating a paper-and-pencil test that is valid for predicting success in life, you can appreciate the complexity of the situation. Meanwhile, back in the classroom, the English teacher is faced with the dilemma of teaching what students need to know in order to pass the competency test or teaching what he or she thought high school English was supposed to include. Tests must be valid for the uses to which they are put, and that is often not possible when decisions made on political grounds are in conflict with sound educational practice.

Minimum Competency Testing at the Elementary School Level

At the elementary school level, MCTs often have a diagnostic-remedial function. That is, on the basis of a child's performance on an MCT, an instructional plan can be drawn and implemented. Not only are the tests somewhat different in scope and content (they often include more items than screening tests and focus on a particular skill, for example), but they are not a final hurdle that stands in the way of graduation. As a result, MCTs can be used for diagnosis and instructional planning—something that appears to be more positive than what happens with MCTs at the high school level.

Yet two factors that threaten the effectiveness of MCTs even at the elementary school level need to be considered. The first relates to what the MCT measures. Often MCTs break the reading act into myriad elements with performance on each element tested separately. Thus, knowledge of vocabulary is tested through matching synonyms in isolation rather than in gaining meaning from connected discourse, for example; word recognition ability is tested in a variety of ways ranging from dividing words into syllables to identifying words that rhyme; comprehension is typically measured via multiple-choice questions that call for recognition of details only. As a result, the reading process is treated in a mechanical and synthetic fashion that fails to reflect the way we believe it should be taught.

A second concern we have for MCT programs at the elementary school level is that the scope and sequence of the instructional program being used may not match the assumptions made by those who wrote the tests. A third-grade child who is making good progress in the Rainey River School District instructional program, for example, may do poorly on a state-mandated MCT because the skills and concepts being tested have not yet been introduced or fully developed in the program the child's teacher and school are following. Unless all the schools in a state adopt a standard curriculum with uniform objectives (a highly unlikely and perhaps unwise development), no single test of how well children in various school systems are progressing is possible. Thus, we can have the same mismatch between instruction provided and performance measured that exists in the high school graduation test.

In some states, MCTs are also being used at the elementary school level to determine who will earn promotion to the next grade. In such cases, the implicit assumption is being made by policymakers that success in the next grade is not possible (or at least probable) because performance on some presumably critical prerequisite skills measured by the MCT is inadequate. Typically, no evidence to support the validity of the tests for making that type of decision has been gathered, but the conventional wisdom of raising quality by holding up higher standards is invoked to justify the action.

Interestingly, the use of MCTs in making decisions about nonpromotion to a subsequent grade often work in one direction only. That is to say, a poor test score can keep a child from being promoted, but a good score cannot get him or her promoted. A child judged to be promotable on the basis of other sources of information (e.g., daily work, teacher judgment, scores on other tests) can still be denied promotion if the MCT is not "passed," but a child who passes the MCT is seldom promoted on the basis of that score if the other indicators of progress are not positive. Satisfactory performance on an MCT thus becomes a necessary but not sufficient condition for promotion. (The same practice usually holds sway in graduation decisions, too; passing all courses does not outweigh a nonpassing score on an MCT.) When this happens, the test has become the tail that wags the dog.

The good news is that most states do not use MCTs as the sole determinant of who will pass on to the next grade. As a professional, you will have the opportunity and responsibility, if you teach in one of those states, to exercise some judgment in deciding whether a child's poor performance on an MCT reflects (1) lack of opportunity to learn (as when the test does not match with your curriculum) or (2) inappropriate focus by the test on a nonessential skill (as when finding rhyming words to assess knowledge of phonics). Kept in proper perspective, MCTs can provide one additional piece of information that helps the classroom teacher gain a complete picture of each child's progress. In this case, the dog wags the tail.

Beyond the Fundamentals

Helping Students Do Their Best on an MCT

We indicated earlier that teachers have a responsibility for seeing that students perform as well on competency tests as their skill and knowledge permits. Many of the same steps involved in preparing yourself to take a teacher competency test are ones students can and should take as well. The classroom teacher is in a good position to help children prepare for an MCT ahead of time and to ensure that good test-taking strategies are used while taking the test.

We suggest that, if at all possible, you obtain a copy of a minimum competency test no longer in use and make it the basis of your instruction. Students need an opportunity to examine and then discuss an MCT as a group activity. Because most MCTs in the area of reading are of a multiple-choice nature, we suggest you introduce the suggestions made on page 540 in this book to your students. This would lead logically to some direct instruction on each of the points made by Sherman and Wildman (1982) such as calculating the amount of time that can be spent on each question in the test, for example. This scenario portrays what we have in mind.

Teacher: One thing we can do to improve our test-taking ability is to decide before starting the test about how much time we can spend on each question. That way we don't spend too much time on a few hard questions and miss the chance to answer other questions that are easier. One thing I've found helpful is to do a quick calculation that gives an average time that can be spent on each question. How many questions are there on the test you have in front of you?

Randy: Sixty-two.

Teacher: That's right. Let's round that off so we can do some fast arithmetic in our heads and call it sixty. How much time does the test allow to complete the test?

Alice: I think it's thirty minutes.

Teacher: Does that look correct, David?

David: Yes.

Teacher: How can we now figure the average amount of time to spend on each question? [pause] If we have thirty minutes to answer sixty questions, can we take a full minute for each question? Harry, how long would sixty questions take if we took one minute for each question?

Harry: I don't know. [pause] Sixty minutes, I guess.

Teacher: Right. So how much time can we spend on each question if we have only thirty minutes for the test? It won't be a full minute, will it?

Harry: Half a minute?

Teacher: Does that sound correct, class? Let's try that. In half a minute, or thirty seconds, we could answer one question, and in a full minute we could answer two questions. In thirty minutes we could answer how many questions?

Randy: Sixty!

Teacher: How did we calculate that? If we answered by dividing, which number is divided into which other number to get half a minute? Can we write that as a formula?

And the demonstration goes on, using other tests and other numbers to give a sense of how to calculate an appropriate pace for taking various tests.

If an old MCT is not available for the preceding and subsequent activities, many of the same suggestions can be conducted by using another test. The greatest benefit will accrue to the students if the test is similar in format and content to the test they will take. Differences can be anticipated; and necessary adjustments, made in the way the children are coached.

Next the wise teacher would probably simulate a test taking situation, we believe, while signaling thirty- or sixty-second intervals, thus encouraging students to develop a sense of pace. At the signal it would be time for students to move to the next question. The need for some flexibility in using this system must be explained, of course, so that a slavish adherence to the time allowance for each question does not develop. Students could be helped to see that the time interval is an approximation that needs to be adjusted if an item can be solved with a few more seconds of concentration. Conversely, if an item is an absolute mystery, even though the time signal has not been given, it is wise to guess at an answer and move along to the next item (unless a penalty for incorrect answers is to be assessed in scoring the tests).

In addition to those points Sherman and Wildman make (each of which should be demonstrated by the teacher using actual test items—preferably exactly like those the children will take on the MCT with respect to format, answer sheets, directions, and so forth), other skills and understandings the teacher can develop include the following: (1) read an entire item before selecting an alternative rather than selecting the first alternative that looks correct (especially when the best answer is being sought); (2) guess at an answer for a question that requires too much time to ponder (after quickly eliminating obviously wrong alternatives), but mark that item to go back to for further deliberation in the event time remains after all questions have been answered; (3) actually cross off alternatives on the test booklet once they have been eliminated as possibilities to focus attention and narrow down the choices to as few as possible (this is especially important if you come back to that question again toward the end of the testing session because it enables you to immediately concentrate on the alternatives not eliminated earlier).

You should be willing to share your own test-taking techniques along with an explanation as to why they seem to work for you as a way of helping children understand the value of monitoring one's own thinking. You can also encourage students to verbalize the strategies and processes that they employ with the intent of deciding whether they are productive or counterproductive. This activity will help raise test taking to a conscious level (in itself a healthy practice) and also cause students to realize that, like any other skill, good habits need to be practiced; and poor habits, extinguished.

Space will not permit us to develop an entire unit on test taking here, but we hope the preceding description and the list of suggestions we shared from Sherman and Wildman's book will give you a sense of direction.

Research evidence supporting the value of teaching test-wiseness (a label we believe is descriptive when it comes to test-taking behaviors that can be learned) is mixed. Weaver (1978) reported that some studies indicate training over time improves test scores, but some other studies have found that gains do not persist, nor do they always transfer to other situations. Many children learn test-wiseness on their own through experience, and this may explain the lack of clear-cut research support for the positive effects of training programs. We are not inclined to let the mixed research results dissuade us from recommending that children be helped to acquire and practice good test-taking techniques.

More detailed descriptions of how to teach test-wiseness may be found in the following ERIC documents reviewed by Weaver (1978):

Callenbach, Carl Anton. (1981). *The effects of instruction and practice in nonsubstantive test-taking techniques upon the standardized reading test scores of selected second grade students.* (Doctoral dissertation, Pennsylvania State University). 98 pp. ED 067 617. This is not available from EDRS; available from University Microfilms.

Crehan, Devin D., et al. 1977. *Developmental aspects of test-wiseness.* Paper presented at the annual meeting of the A.E.R.A., New York. 10 pp. ED 137 394.

Diamond, James, & Evans, William. (1972). *An investigation of the cognitive correlates of test-wiseness.* 5 pp. ED 065 508.

Ford, Valeria A. (1973). *Everything you wanted to know about test-wiseness.* 30 pp. ED 093 912.

Goolsby, Thomas M. Jr., & Wray, Grace A. (1969). *Practice test for pre-primary and beginning first grade.* Prepared for the Evaluation Division, Research and Development Center in Educational Simulation, University of Georgia. 8 pp. ED 054 219.

Jongsma, Eugene A., & Warshauer, Elaine. (1975). *The effects of instruction in test-taking skills upon student performance on standardized achievement tests.* Final Report. New Orleans: University of New Orleans, Department of Elementary and Secondary Education. 67 pp. ED 114 408.

Maryland State Department of Education. (1975). *Improving student attitudes and skills for taking tests.* Baltimore, State Department of Education. 245 pp. ED 128 352.

Millman, Jason, et al. (1965, Autumn). An analysis of test-wiseness. *Educational and Psychological Measurement, 25* 707–726.

Sabers, Darrell. (1975). *Test-taking skills.* Tucson, AR: Center for Educational Research and Development. 29 pp. ED 133 341.

Yearby, Mary Elizabeth. (1975). *The effect of instruction in test-taking skills on the standardized reading test scores of white and black children of high and low socioeconomic status.* (Doctoral dissertation, Indiana University). 280 pp. ED 117 677. This is not available from EDRS; available from University Microfilms.

One final point needs to be made. We believe the most important test-taking attribute of all is determination to perform well. In our experience, many children perform poorly on tests because they do not regard the task as an important one. Tests can be overemphasized, too, of course, but MCTs often play a bigger role in the lives of students than they realize. It seems appropriate at least to let students know how the results of a test they will take next week may be used. Threats or melodrama should be avoided, but a straightforward explanation should help students recognize the need to do their best.

Summary

This chapter has examined several issues that confront teachers and schools today. Included were technology in the form of television and computers and competency testing of teachers and students. Suggestions were made concerning ways of incorporating television into the classroom reading program. Computers were examined from the standpoint of their potential to enhance the instructional program, and guidelines were offered for evaluating computer software. The National Teacher Examinations were described in detail and suggestions provided for maximizing your performance. Minimum Competency Examinations (MCT) for pupils were also discussed with an emphasis on helping pupils prepare to perform well. Issues of test validity in MCT programs were explored.

Discussion Questions

1. What approaches other than competency testing of pupils and teachers might contribute to improved quality in public education?
2. What dangers are inherent in widespread adoption of computers into the reading curriculum? How can these dangers be minimized?

Recommended Readings

Becker, George J. (1973). *Television and the classroom reading program.* Newark, DE: International Reading Association.

Becker presents practical ways teachers can use the home television viewing habits of students to improve reading and language arts instruction.

Goodlad, John I. (1984). *A place called school: Prospects for the future.* New York: McGraw-Hill.

Goodlad reports the results of an extensive review of schooling in the United States, based on observations by the author and a staff of trained observers in schools throughout the country.

Mason, George E. The printout (a column appearing in each issue of *The Reading Teacher,* a publication of the International Reading Association).

Mason, George E., Blanchard, Jay S., & Daniel, Denny B. (1983). *Computer applications in reading.* Newark: IRA.

The authors discuss the rapidly changing environment of computers in reading, including specific program descriptions, readability and textbook analysis, services, uses in classroom, and research.

Ravitch, Diane. (1983). *The troubled crusade: American education, 1945–1980.* New York: Holmes Meier.

Here is an analysis of American schools from the post World War II era to the present from a historical, economic, sociological, and political perspective.

Appendixes

Appendix A Children's Book Clubs

The availability of books is an extremely important factor in whether children develop the habit of reading. When children themselves own books, they are easily accessible. The book clubs listed here can help the teacher place books within easy reach of every child.

American Heritage Junior Library, 336 West Center Street, Marion, OH 43302.

Arrow Book Club, Scholastic Book Services, 904 Sylvan Avenue, Englewood Cliffs, NJ 07632 (Ages 9–11).

Beginning Reader's Program 575 Lexington Avenue, New York, NY 10021.

The Bookplan, 921 Washington Avenue, Brooklyn, NY 11225 (Ages 8 months–11 years).

Catholic Children's Book Club, 260 Summit Avenue, St. Paul, MN (Ages 6–16). AP Dell Paperback Books, Educational Sales Department, 1 Dag Hammarskjold Plaza, 245 East 47th Street, New York, NY 10017.

Junior Literary Guild, 177 Park Avenue, New York, NY 10017 (Ages 5–16).

Lucky Book Club, Scholastic Book Services, 904 Sylvan Ave., Englewood Cliffs, NJ 07632 (Ages 7–9).

Parents' Magazine Book Club for Little Listeners and Beginning Readers, 52 Vanderbilt Avenue, New York, NY 10017 (Ages 3–8).

See Saw Book Club, Scholastic Book Services, 904 Sylvan Avenue, Englewood Cliffs, NJ 07632 (Ages 5–7).

Teen Age Book Club, Scholastic Book Services, 904 Sylvan Avenue, Englewood Cliffs, NJ 07632 (Ages 12–14).

Weekly Reader Children's Book Club, Education Center, 1250 Fairwood Avenue, Columbus, OH 43216 (Ages 4–10).

Young America Book Club, 1250 Fairwood Avenue, Columbus, OH 43216 (Ages 10–14).

Young Folks Book Club, 1376 Coney Island, Brooklyn, NY 11230.

Young People's Book Club, 226 North Cass Avenue, Westmont, IL 60559 (Ages 4–10).

Young Readers of America (Division of Book-of-the-Month Club), 345 Hudson Street, New York, NY 10014 (Ages 9–14).

Appendix B Magazines and Newspapers for Children

Boy's Life, P.O. Box 61030, Dallas, TX 75261.

Child Life, P.O. Box 567B, 1100 Waterway Blvd., Indianapolis, IN 46206.

Children's Digest, P.O. Box 567B, 1100 Waterway Blvd., Indianapolis, IN 46206.

Children's Playmate, P.O. Box 567B, 1100 Waterway Blvd., Indianapolis, IN 46206.

Cobblestone, 28 Main St., Peterborough, NH 03458.

Cricket, 1058 8th St., LaSalle, IL 61301.

Dynamite, 902 Sylvan Ave., Englewood Cliffs, NJ 07632.

Ebony Jr., 820 South Michigan Ave., Chicago, IL 60605.

Electric Company Magazine, One Lincoln Plaza, New York, NY 10023.

Highlights for Children, 2300 West Fifth Ave., Columbus, OH 43216.

Humpty Dumpty's Magazine, P.O. Box 567B, 1100 Waterway Blvd., Indianapolis, IN 46206.

Jack & Jill, P.O. Box 567B, 1100 Waterway Blvd., Indianapolis, IN 46206.

My Weekly Reader, 1250 Fairwood Ave., Columbus, OH 43216.

Ranger Rick's Nature Magazine, 16th St. N.W., Washington, DC 20036.

Scholastic News, 902 Sylvan Ave., Englewood Cliffs, NJ 07632.

Sesame Street, One Lincoln Plaza, New York, NY 10023.

Stone Soup, P.O. Box 83, Santa Cruz, CA 95063.

Wee Wisdom, Unity School of Christianity, Unity Village, MO 64065.

World, National Geographic, Dept. 00481, 17th & M Sts. N.W., Washington, DC 20036.

Young World, P.O. Box 567B, Indianapolis, IN 46206.

Appendix C Selection Aids for Children's Books

American Library Association. (1968). *Storytelling: Readings, bibliographies, and resource aids.* Chicago, IL, 60611: 50 East Huron Street.

The book includes versions of stories expressed in other art forms, such as poetry, dance, music, the cinema, and recordings.

Arbuthnot, Mary Hill, Mary Clark, Margaret, & Geneva Long, Harriet. (1966). *Children's books too good to miss.* Western Reserve University.

Here are descriptions of 265 books, many Newbery and Caldecott medal winners, grouped according to age group. A section with examples of distinguished children's illustrators is included.

Association for Childhood Education International. (1980). *A bibliography of books for children* (rev. ed.). Wheaton, MD: 11141 Georgia Ave., Suite 200.

An annotated bibliography of over 1,500 books for children of ages two to twelve, this work includes author and title index and a reference book section.

Brewton, John E. & Brewton, Sara W. (Comps.). (1954; 2d suppl., 1965). *Index to children's poetry*. Bronx, NY: The H. W. Wilson Company, 950 University Ave.

Here is a title, subject, author, and first-line index to poetry in collections for children and youth. Information about the poems is given in the title entries, with cross-references to 130 books of poetry. This listing gives author or authors, name of book, approximate price, a very brief summary, and the suggested grade level for the book.

Children's Catalog (a981). (14th ed.). Bronx, NY: The H. W. Wilson Company, 950 University Ave.

Designed to serve as a basic selection aid for elementary schools, the catalog is done in three parts: classified (subdivided by Dewey classification, fiction, easy books, and story collections) with full bibliographical data for each book plus an annotation and excerpts from a review or reviews; author, title, subject, and analytical indexes; directory of publishers and distributors.

Eastman, Mary H. (1926; 1st suppl. 1937). *Index to fairy tales, myths, and legends*. Westwood, MA: Faxon, 15 Southwest Park.

The book lists fairy tales, myths, legends, and stories in alphabetical order by title, with location or author. The author or book title is also listed in a second section with date of publication, publisher, and approximate price.

Gillespie, John T., & Gillespie, Christine. (1981). *Best books for children* (2d ed.). Ann Arbor, MI: R. R. Bowker Company, P.O. Box 1807.

This is an annual, annotated bibliography for kindergarten to grade twelve, arranged by grades and subjects.

————, & Lembo, Diana L. (1970). *Introducing books: A guide for the middle grades*. Ann Arbor, MI 48106. R. R. Bowker Company, P.O. Box 1807, 48106.

A book talk manual for the educator to use with ages eight through twelve, this volume suggests themes (and related book and nonbook follow-up) that reflect needs and concerns of the intermediate group's growing social and ethical awareness: family, friends, physical problems, values, adult roles, reading for fun. Eighty-eight books are concisely described and analyzed for use as book talks.

Hearne, Betsy. (1981). *Choosing books for children: A commonsense guide*. New York: Delacorte.

Here is a good guide for adults, with booklists and book selection from preschooler to young adult.

Huck, Charlotte S. (1979). *Children's literature in the elementary school* (3d rev. ed.). New York: Holt, Rinehart and Wilson.

Reviews current and historical books for children by subject matter and helps children, teachers, and librarians build a frame of reference for book selection. Gives guidelines for children's literature program in school and library and details audiovisual supplements. An author, publisher, and title index and subject index are included, as well as publishers' addresses, book selection aids, a pronunciation guide for children's book authors, and a listing of children's book awards.

Iarusso, Marilyn B. (Ed.). (1977). *Stories: A list of stories to tell and to read aloud* (7th ed.). New York: New York Public Library.

This book is divided into two main parts: list of stories to be told; stories and poems to read aloud. Another section includes a list of recordings by well-known storytellers or authors reading from their own works. Name and subject indexes are included.

Kimmel, Margaret Mary, & Segel, Elizabeth. (1983). *For reading out loud!: A guide to sharing books with children.* New York: Delacorte.

This book teaches adults how to read out aloud and what to read and includes cross-listings of books by subject, length, type, and setting.

Kingman, Lee (Ed.). (1968). *Illustrators of children's books, 1957–1966,* (Vol. 3). Boston: Horn Books.

This volume describes the history and development of the use of illustrations in children's books, includes illustrators from many countries, and describes various procedures used for printing illustrations. Also included is a bibliography of illustrators and authors.

_____ (Ed.) (1978). *Illustrators of children's books, 1967–1976,* (Vol. 4). Boston: Horn Books.

Here is a history of children's books illustrations. (See preceding reference.)

_____. (Ed.) (1965). *Newbery and Caldecott medal books, 1956–1965.* Boston: Horn Books.

_____, (Ed.) *Newbery and Caldecott medal books, 1966–1975.*

Here is an update of children's award-winning books (see Miller & Field reference later).

Lamme, Linda Leonard. (1980). *Raising readers: A guide to sharing literature with young children.* New York: Walker and Company.

The author annotates books according to age groups. In the selected book list for the beginning reader, activities for the book annotated are included.

Larrick, Nancy. (1983). *A parent's guide to children's readings* (rev 5th ed.). Garden City, NY 11530: Doubleday & Company.

Here is a handbook for parents, with an extensive annotated bibliography.

Mahoney, B. E., Latimer, Bouise P., & Folmsbree, Beulah. (Eds.). (1947). *Illustrators of children's books, 1744–1945* (Vol. 1). Boston: Horn Books.

Here is a history of children's books illustrations. (See Kingman reference earlier.)

Miller, Bertha M. (Ed.). (1958). *Illustrators of children's books, 1946–1956,* (Vol. 2). Boston: Horn Books.

Here is a history of children's books illustrations. (See Kingman reference earlier.)

_____ & Field, Elinor W. (Eds.). (1957). *Caldecott Medal books, 1938–1857.* Boston: Horn Books.

The book offers complete data on each medal-winning books and its illustrators from the beginning of the award to 1957. Includes the name of the author, a book note concerning the artist's technique, the artist's acceptance paper, and a biographical paper for each winner. Teachers will appreciate the value of distincive art examples that are available for use by and with children.

_____, and _____ (Eds.). (1955). *Newberry Medal books, 1922–1955.* Boston: Horn Books.

The volume presents brief comments about each year's Newbery Medal-winner, given for exceptional children's books, with a short excerpt from the book, a biographical note about the author or other qualified person, the author's paper of acceptance, and illustrations from some books.

Simmons, Beatrice. (1972). *Paperback books for children.* New York: Citation Press.

This annotated bibliography includes a topic and author index as well as grade level recommendations.

Spache, George. (1974). *Good reading for poor readers* (rev. ed.). Champaign, IL: Garrard Publishing Company.

Describes the "psychological interaction of a child and a story." Lists trade and library books, and also adopted and simplified material, textbooks, workbooks, games, magazines, newspapers, series books, and book club, with suggested grade levels.

Sutherland, Zena (Ed.). (1973). *The best in children's books.* Chicago: University of Chicago Press.

The book includes 1,400 reviews selected from "The Bulletin of the Center for Children's Books." Developmental and curricular values are discussed.

———, Monson, Dianne L., & Arbuthnot, May Hill. (1981). *Children and books* (6th ed.). Glenview, IL: Scott, Foresman and Company.

This volume reviews books for children by main characters and plots and suggests ways of using some of them for reading aloud and storytelling. It also discusses illustrations and illustrators of children's books and critera for judging illustrations and lists extensive reference materials at the end of each chapter.

Tway, Eileen (Ed.). (1981). *Reading ladders for human relations.* Urbana, IL: National Council of Teachers of English, 1111 Kenyon Rd.

Under topics related to feelings and human relations, this book provides an annotated bibliography that can be used to support any curriculum area where personal feelings and human interactions are subject for reading.

White, Mary Lou. (1981). *Adventuring with books.* Urbana, IL: National Council of Teachers of English, 1111 Kenyon Rd.

White includes suggestions for getting children involved with books and an annotated list of those books that emphasize adventure and excitement for children.

Winkel, Lois (Ed.). (1984). *Elementary school library collection* (14th ed.). Williamsport, PA: Bro-Dart Foundation, 500 Arch St.

This book lists and annotates basic print and nonprint materials in classifications of reference materials, nonfiction, fiction, easy books, periodicals, and professional tools for the teachers. It also contains an author, title, subject index with a graded listing, a classified listing of audiovisual materials, a list of large print materials, and a directory of publishers.

Appendix D   Sources of Information on Reading Instruction

Professional Associations

Individuals who are interested in belonging to a professional organization that offers information and activities related to the improvement of reading instruction will find the following professional associations helpful:

International Reading Association (IRA), 800 Barksdale Road, P.O. Box 8139, Newark, DE 19711. Is organized into local and state councils that hold regular meetings devoted to the improvement of reading instruction and offers an extensive list of publications available to members and nonmembers. Regional and national conferences are held annually. A world congress is sponsored every other summer.

National Council of Teachers of English (NCTE), 1111 Kenyon Road, Urbana, IL 61801. In organization and function, NCTE and IRA are quite similar. NCTE is divided into sections according to grade level (i.e., elementary, secondary, college) and has a broader focus than IRA, but it has a publications program, local and state councils, regional and national conferences, and so forth. NCTE is concerned with all communications skills including reading.

National Reading Conference (NRC), 1070 Sibley Tower, Rochester, NY 14604. The NRC is much smaller than IRA or NCTE and tends to have more of a research orientation. The organization publishes an annual yearbook and a journal (*Journal of Reading Behavior*) and sponsors one national meeting in early December each year. Membership is open to all but primarily includes college professors interested in reading instruction or research or both.

Agencies

Educational Products Information Exchange (EPIE) 475 Riverside Drive, New York, NY 10027. EPIE is an information center that periodically reviews, analyzes, and describes materials for reading instruction (as well as other curricular areas and audiovisual equipment). Trained reviewers at EPIE examine materials according to specific guidelines so they can inform consumers about available products. Evaluative judgments are left to the purchaser, but useful facts and figures basic to decision making are provided in publications available from EPIE.

ERIC Clearinghouse on Reading and Communication Skills (ERIC/RCS) NCTE, 1111 Kenyon Road, Urbana, IL 61801. ERIC/RCS is a federally sponsored clearinghouse for information on reading and reading-related matters, as well as other communication skills (e.g., writing, listening, speaking, and so on). Similar ERIC clearinghouses exist for other fields of education (Exceptional Learners, Teacher Education, and so on). The ERIC Clearinghouses select printed materials to be abstracted and indexed in several monthly publications (*Research in Education* and *Current Index to Journals in Education*). Copies of some materials are made available in microfiche and hard copy forms through ERIC Document Reproductive Service. Columns written by ERIC/RCS staff members appear regularly in several professional journals.

Center for the Study of Reading (CSR), 51 Gerty Drive, Champaign, IL 61820. The CSR is a research center funded by the National Institute of Education. The work of the Center is carried out at the University of Illinois and at Bolt, Beranek and Newman, Inc., in Cambridge, MA. Over forty senior researchers and a like number of research assistants representing a variety of disciplines conduct research intended to provide new knowledge about the reading process and reading instruction.

Periodicals in Reading

The Reading Teacher, published eight times per year by the International Reading Association, is an IRA membership journal for classroom teachers and reading specialists who work at the preschool and elementary school level. (See IRA for an address.)

The *Journal of Reading,* published eight times per year by the International Reading Association, is an IRA membership journal for those concerned with reading at the adolescent and adult levels in and out of formal school environments. (See NCTE for an address.)

The *Journal of Reading Behavior (JRB)* is published four times a year by The National Reading Conference, Inc. *JRB* is the membership journal for members of NRC and primarily publishes research reports of an experimental and descriptive nature. (See NRC for an address.)

Early Years is a magazine for professionals who are interested in the preschool, kindergarten, and early grades. Articles are practical in nature and provide teaching tips and activities that many find helpful. (Write to Early Years, 373 East Forty-third Street, New York, NY 10017.)

Instructor magazine is intended for elementary school teachers. Many contributors are themselves teachers who have ideas to share on topics ranging from bulletin boards to learning games. (Write to *Instructor* Magazine, 1000 River Road, Cincinnati, OH 23333).

References

Weintraub, Sam, Smith, Helen K., Plessaa, Gus P., Roser, Nancy L., Hill, Walter R., & Kibby, Michael W. (Eds.). (annually). *Annual summary of investigations relating to reading.* Newark, DE: International Reading Association.

The *Annual Summary* summarizes reports of reading research published between July 1 of one year and June 30 of the next. Reports are categorized into six major areas with further subcategorization in five areas. Entries are abstracted and include full bibliographic information. An author index is included.

Harris, Theodore L., & Hodges, Richard E. (Eds.). (1981). *A dictionary of reading and related terms.* Newark, DE: International Reading Association.

The *Dictionary* contains definitions for over 5,400 terms directly or indirectly related to the reading process and reading instruction. Entries follow the form of any standard dictionary, including a key to pronunciation, parts of speech designation, and multiple definitions for terms having several meanings. Some terms are presented in the context of a sentence to further illustrate correct use.

Mitzel, Harold E., Best, John Hardin, & Robinowitz, William. (Eds.). (1982). *Encyclopedia of educational research* (*EER*) (5th ed.). New York: The Free Press, a division of Macmillan.

Sponsored by the American Educational Research Association, the *EER* is a comprehensive compendium of educational research. Two hundred fifty-six essays in the nature of critical syntheses and interpretations of reported educational research authored by noted authorities on each topic are grouped into eighteen broad headings in this fifth edition. Earlier editions appeared in 1941, 1950, 1960, and 1969. Entries on "Reading." "Readability," and "Readiness" are particularly relevant to the subject matter of this textbook.

Buros, Oscar K. (1978). *Mental measurements yearbook* (*MMY*) (8th ed.). Highland Park, NJ: Gryphon Press, The *MMY* includes factual descriptive information on all known tests published in the English-speaking countries of the world as well as "candidly critical" reviews of those tests written especially for the *MMY* by carefully chosen professionals. Published reviews that have appeared elsewhere are also excerpted in the *MMY* for some tests. Entries on a particular test are followed by an extensive bibliography of references related to that test. Lastly, the *MMY* includes listings of books on measurement and excerpts from published reviews of those books. Tests reviewed in earlier editions of *MMY* are not necessarily reviewed again in the latest edition. Consequently, a special publication that collects reviews of all reviews of reading from earlier yearbooks appeared in 1968 under the title *Reading tests and reviews* (Vol. I) (Gryphon Press). An updated volume (Vol. II) was published in 1975 but obviously does not include reviews, appeared in the eighth edition of *MMY* (1978).

Beyond the Fundamentals

Anderson, Richard C., Spiro, Rand J., & Montague, William E. (1977). *Schooling and the acquisition of knowledge.* Hillsdale, NJ: Lawrence Earlbaum Associates.
A widely quoted collection of essays consisting of papers presented at a conference sponsored by the Navy Personnel Research and Development Center in San Diego, November 1975, this volume addresses the following questions: "How is knowledge organized?" "How does knowledge develop?" "How is knowledge retrieved and used?" "What instructional techniques promise to facilitate the acquisition of new knowledge?" (from the Preface, pp. ix–x). The notion of schema theory is a fundamental tenet of this text. Though theoretical in nature, the articles provide a basis for understanding the reading process as a complex interaction between reader and text.

Huey, Edmund. (1908). *The psychology and pedagogy of reading,* New York: Macmillan Publishing Co.
This classic text is remarkably compatible with contemporary thought insofar as the cognitive processes underlying reading are concerned. Many of Huey's early theoretical speculations have been verified by empirical research conducted since the publication of this book. More than a historical curiosity, it offers the serious student of reading a thorough, readable introduction to how the human mind processes textual information.

Gibson, Eleanor J., & Levin, Harry. (1975). *The psychology and pedagogy of reading.* Cambridge, MA: MIT Press.
The authors approach the reading act from a cognitive basis in this book. This volume would be especially useful to anyone interested in theory and research relative to the initial acquisition of reading and how the skilled reader extracts meaning from text.

Curry, Joan F., & Morris, William P. (1975). *Searching the professional literature in reading.* Newark, DE: International Reading Association.
This fifty-page booklet enables readers to identify sources of information in reading and describes how a topic can be pursued via a literature search. Suggestions are given on building a bibliography, note-taking, and keeping up-to-date on topics of current interest. Several helpful appendixes include "A Guide to Information Sources in Reading," a checklist for evaluating educational research, and a list of journals containing articles on reading.

Aukerman, Robert C. (1981). *The basal reader approach to reading.* New York: John Wiley & Sons.
Fifteen of the most widely used basal reading series are described in this book according to a consistent set of variables (i.e., physical components, instructional components, literacy components, graphic arts components, directed-learning components, individualized reading components, and management components). These descriptions follow the author's discussion of what makes a basal reader series and how one can be judged, and may also include a discussion on how to implement the use of a basal program.

Larrick, Nancy. (1983). *A parent's guide to children's reading* (5th rev. ed.). Garden City, NY: Doubleday & Co.
Written primarily for parents who are interested in helping young children develop an appreciation for, and love of, books and to help parents understand how reading instruction is typically provided in schools, Larrick's inexpensive paperback book is a valuable resource for teachers and administrators as well. Specific suggestions are made on a host of practical topics ranging from how to use television viewing as a starting point for reading to selecting books as gifts for children. This is a very readable book that demystifies many of the issues that confuse and alarm parents. The wise

teacher and school will have copies to lend to concerned parents as well as parents who simply want to be supportive.

Smith, Nila B. (1965). *American reading instruction*. Newark, DE: International Reading Association.

The history of reading instruction in the United States is traced in this thorough and detailed volume. Materials, teaching methods, and the social context of various eras are described in an interesting, often anecdotal fashion. Reprints of pages from the original blueback spellers of Webster and the McGuffey readers give the reader a visual sense of what young readers encountered in the "good old days" of American schooling. The ebb and flow of phonics and "look-say" emphases over the decades are also described. Greater perspective on the issues facing educators in the field of reading today is gained from being familiar with this book.

Appendix E Information on Computer Software for Reading Instruction

In order to keep abreast of developments in instructional software, you will need to consult the most recent issues of journals that include reviews and evaluations of this material. Some of these journals are now listed.

Classroom Computer Learning (Pitman Learning, Inc., 19 Davis Drive, Belmont, CA 94002. Nine issues per school year.) A column titled "Product News" gives information on new hardware, software, and services.

Computers, Reading and Language Arts (Modern Learning Publishers, Inc., 1308 East 38th St., Oakland, CA 94602. Published quarterly.) This journal contains not only software reviews but also EPIE and ERIC reports relating to the use of computers in language-arts instruction.

Educational Technology (Educational Technology Publications Inc., 140 Sylvan Ave., Englewood Cliffs, NJ 07632. Published monthly.) This journal contains evaluations of new software in "Educational Technology Product Reviews," brief descriptions of new software in "New Products and Services," and also includes ERIC reports on computers in education.

Media & Methods (American Society of Educators, 1511 Walnut St., Philadelphia, PA 19102. Nine issues per school year). A regular column is "Software Reviews and Previews."

The Reading Teacher (International Reading Association, 800 Barksdale Road, Newark, DE 19711. Nine issues per school year.) Software reviews given in "The Printout," a column by George E. Mason.

In addition to journals such as those just listed, you can find information on instructional software in the following:

Geoffrion, Leo D., & Geoffrion, Olga P. (1983). *Computers and reading instruction*. Reading, MA: Addison-Wesley. See especially pp. 170–172 (Public Domain Program Listings), pp. 172–208 (Commercial Software), and pp. 209–211 (Index to Commercial Reading Programs).

Mason, George E., Blanchard, Jay S., & Daniel, Danny B. (1983). *Computer applications in reading*, 2d ed. Newark, DE: International Reading Association. See especially pp. 140–147 (Instructional Software Publishers), pp. 150–152 (Current Software Directories), and pp. 156–163 (Software Evaluation).

A few directories devoted to educational software are listed here:

Educational Software Directory
   Sterling Swift Publishing Co.
   1600 Fortview Road
   Austin, TX 78704
   (Apple software only)
Educator's Handbook and Software Directory
   Vital Information, Inc.
   350 Union Station
   Kansas City, MO 64108
   (Apple software only)
Instructor Computer Directory for Schools
   Instructor Publications, Inc.
   757 Third Ave.
   New York, NY 10017

Directories that list all types of software include the following:

International Microcomputer Software Directory
   Imprint Software
   420 S. Howes St.
   Fort Collins, CO 80521
Skarbeck's Software Directory
   11990 Dorsett Road
   St. Louis, MO 63043

References

Alpha Time. (1970). Jericho, NY: New Dimensions in Education.

Altick, Richard. (1969). *Preface to critical reading.* New York: Holt, Rinehart & Winston.

Alvermann, Donna E., & Boothby, Paula R. (1982, December). Text differences: Children's perceptions at the transition stage in reading. *The Reading Teacher, 36*(3), 298–302.

Anderson, Richard C., Osborn, Jean, & Tierney, Robert J. (1984). *Learning to read in American schools: Basal readers and content texts.* Hillsdale, NJ: Lawrence Erlbaum.

Anderson, Richard C., & Pearson, P. David. (1984). A schema-theoretic view of basic processes in reading. In P. D. Pearson et al. (Eds.), *Handbook of reading research* (pp. 255–292). New York: Longman.

Anderson, Richard C., Spiro, Rand J., & Montague, William E. (Eds.). (1977). *Schooling and the acquisition of knowledge.* Hillsdale, NJ: Lawrence Erlbaum.

Anderson, Thomas H., & Armbruster, Bonnie B. (1984a). Studying. In P. D. Pearson et al. (Eds.), *Handbook of reading research* (pp. 657–680). New York: Longman.

Anderson, Thomas H., & Armbruster, Bonnie B. (1984b). Content area textbooks. In R. C. Anderson, J. Osborn, & R. J. Tierney (Eds.), *Learning to read in American schools: Basal readers and content texts* (pp. 193–224). Hillsdale, NJ: Lawrence Erlbaum.

Andrews, Theodore E. (Ed.). (1983, May 26). Florida considers merit plan. *Teacher Education Reports, 5*(8), 6–7.

Applebee, Arthur N. (1978). *The child's concept of story.* Chicago: University of Chicago Press.

Armbruster, Bonnie B., & Anderson, Thomas H. (1981, November). Research synthesis on study skills. *Educational Leadership, 39*(2), 154–156.

Ashton-Warner, Sylvia. (1963). *Teacher.* New York: Simon and Schuster.

Austin, Mary, & Morison, Coleman. (1963). *The first R: The Harvard report on reading in elementary schools.* New York: Macmillan.

Ayres, Leonard P. (1909). *Laggards in our schools.* New York: Charities Publication Committee.

Babbs, Patricia J., & Moe, Alden J. (1983, January). Metacognition: A key for independent learning from text. *The Reading Teacher, 36*(4), 422–426.

Baca, Edward J. (1977). Bilingual education in Public Law 93–380. In *Bilingual education resource guide* (pp. 10–25). Washington, DC: National Education Association of the United States.

Bailey, Mildred H. (1967, February). The utility of phonic generalizations in grades one through six. *The Reading Teacher, 20*(5), 413–418.

Baker, Linda, & Brown, Ann L. (1984). Metacognitive skills and reading. In P. D. Pearson et al. (Eds.), *Handbook of reading research* (pp. 353–394). New York: Longman.

Balow, Bruce. (1971, March). Perceptual-motor activities in the treatment of severe reading disabilities. *The Reading Teacher, 24*(6), 513–525.

Barbe, Walter B., & Abbott, Jerry L. (1975). *Personalized reading instruction: New techniques that increase reading skill and comprehension.* West Nyack, NY: Parker.

Barbe, Walter B., & Renzulli, Joseph S. (1975). *Psychology and education of the gifted* (2nd ed.). New York: Irvington.

Barrett, Thomas. (1972). Taxonomy of reading comprehension. *Reading 360 Monograph.* Lexington, MA: Ginn.

Bartlett, Frederic C. (1932). *Remembering.* London: Cambridge University Press.

Beaucamp, Wilbur L. (1925). A preliminary experimental study of techniques in the mastery of subject matter in elementary physical science. *Supplementary Education Monograph* No. 24 (pp. 47–87). Chicago: University of Chicago Press.

Becker, George J. (1973). *Television and the classroom reading program.* Newark, DE: International Reading Association.

Beebe, Mona J. (1980). The effect of different types of substitution miscues on reading. *Reading Research Quarterly, 15*(3), 324–336.

Berglund, Roberta L. (1983, February). A primer on uninterrupted sustained silent reading. *Reading Research Quarterly, 36*(6), 534–539.

Bernstein, S. (1973). The effects of children's question-asking behaviors on problem solution and comprehension of written material (Doctoral dissertation, Columbia University).

Bertrand, Carol W. (1976). The effect of letter deletion on word recognition (Master's thesis, Rutgers University).

Biggy, Virginia. (1975). A horrendous job. In *The essential skills television project: A working document* (pp. 14–17). Bloomington, IN: Agency for Instructional Technology.

Bisset, Donald J. (1969). The amount and effect of recreational reading in selected fifth grade classrooms (Doctoral dissertation, Syracuse University, Reading and Language Arts Center).

Blackhurst, A. Edward, & Berdine, William H. (Eds.). (1981). *An introduction to special education.* Boston: Little, Brown.

Blakely, W. Paul, & Shadle, Erma M. (1961). A study of two readiness-for-reading programs in kindergarten. *Elementary English, 38*(7), 502–505.

Bloomfield, Leonard, & Barnhart, Clarence L. (1961). *Let's read: A linguistic approach.* Detroit: Wayne State University Press.

Bond, Guy L., & Dykstra, Robert. (1967, Summer). The cooperative research program in first-grade reading instruction. *Reading Research Quarterly, 2*(4), 5–142.

Bond, Guy L., Tinker, Miles A., & Wasson, Barbara B. (1979). *Reading difficulties: Their diagnosis and correction.* Englewood Cliffs, NJ: Prentice-Hall.

Bowe, Frank. (1984, Mid-October). Micros and special education. *Popular Computing, 3* (13), 121–128.

Bowman, M. A. (1980). The effect of story structure questioning upon the comprehension and metacognitive awareness of sixth grade students (Doctoral dissertation, University of Maryland).

Boyer, Ernest L. (1983). *High school: A report on secondary education in America.* New York: Harper & Row.

Bracey, Gerald W. (1983, June). On the compelling need to go beyond minimum competency. *Phi Delta Kappan, 64* (10), 717–721.

Bradley, Beatrice E. (1956, February). An experimental study of the readiness approach to reading. *Elementary School Journal, 56,* 262–267.

Brady, Larry M. (1974). How stated purposes for reading affect reading comprehension scores of fifth grade students in a midwestern suburban school district (Doctoral dissertation, University of North Dakota).

Brandt, Richard M. (1981). *Public education under scrutiny.* Washington, DC: University Press of America.

Bransford, J. D., & Johnson, M. K. (1973). Considerations of some problems of comprehension. In W. G. Chase (Ed.), *Visual information processing.* New York: Academic Press.

Braun, Carl. (1969, Spring). Interest-loading and modality effects on textual response acquisition. *Reading Research Quarterly, 4* (3), 428–444.

Britton, James. (1970). *Language and learning.* New York: Penguin Books.

Brown, Ann L., Campione, J. C., & Day, J. (1981, February). Learning to learn: On training students to learn from texts. *Educational Researcher, 10,* 14–21.

Brown, Ann L., & Murphy, M. D. (1975). Reconstruction of arbitrary versus logical sequences by preschool children. *Journal of Experimental Child Psychology, 20,* 307–326.

Brown, James I. (1965). *Programmed vocabulary.* Chicago: Lyons & Carnahan.

Burger, I. Victor, Cohen, T. A., & Bisgaler, P. (1956). *Bringing children and books together.* New York: Library Club of America.

Burns, Paul C., Roe, Betty D., & Ross, Elinor P. (1984). *Teaching reading in today's elementary schools* (3rd ed.). Boston: Houghton Mifflin.

Buros, Oscar K. (1969). *Reading tests and reviews.* Highland Park, NJ: Gryphon Press.

Buros, Oscar K. (1975). *Reading tests and reviews II.* Highland Park, NJ: Gryphon Press.

Buros, Oscar K. (1978). *Seventh mental measurements yearbook.* Highland Park, NJ: Gryphon Press.

The case of 17 million children: Is our public school system proving an utter failure? (1912, August). *The Ladies Home Journal, 29.*

Cassidy, Jack, & Vukelich, Carol. (1980, February). Do the gifted read early? *The Reading Teacher, 33* (5), 578–582.

Caton, Hilda R. (1981). Visual impairments. In A. E. Blackhurst & W. H. Berdine (Eds.), *An introduction to special education* (pp. 206–252). Boston: Little, Brown.

Chall, Jeanne S. (1967; updated ed. 1983). *Learning to read: The great debate.* New York: McGraw-Hill.

Chall, Jeanne S. (1983). *Stages of reading development.* New York: McGraw-Hill.

Chall, Jeanne S. (1984). Readability and prose comprehension: Continuities and discontinuities. In J. Flood (Ed.), *Understanding reading comprehension.* Newark, DE: International Reading Association.

Chall, Jeanne S., & Feldman, Shirley. (1966, May). First grade reading: An analysis of the interactions of professed methods, teacher implementation, and class background. *The Reading Teacher, 19* (8), 569–575.

Charles, C. M. (1980). *Individualizing instruction.* St. Louis: C. V. Mosby.

Children's choices for 1983. (1983, October). *The Reading Teacher, 37*(1), 51–69.

Ching, Doris C. (1976). *Reading and the bilingual child.* Newark, DE: International Reading Association.

Chomsky, Carol. (1972, February). Stages in language development and reading exposure. *Harvard Educational Review, 42*(1), 1–33.

Chomsky, Carol. (1976). Approaching reading through invented spelling. In L. B. Resnick & P. A. Weaver (Eds.), *Theory and practice of early reading.* Hillsdale, NJ: Lawrence Erlbaum.

Clark, Charles H. (1982, January). Assessing free recall. *The Reading Teacher, 35*(4), 434–439.

Clay, Marie. (1972a). *Concepts about print.* London: Heinemann Educational Books.

Clay, Marie M. (1972b). *Reading: The patterning of complex behavior.* London: Heinemann Educational Books.

Clymer, Theodore. (1963, January). The utility of phonic generalizations in the primary grades. *The Reading Teacher, 16*(4), 252–258.

Cohen, Ruth. (1983, April). Self-generated questions as an aid to reading comprehension. *The Reading Teacher, 36*(8), 770–775.

Cohen, Sandra B., & Plaskon, Stephen P. (1978, November-December). Selecting a reading approach for the mainstreamed child. *Language Arts, 55*(8), 966–970.

Coleman, James. (1966). *Equality of educational opportunity.* U. S. Department of Health, Education and Welfare.

Combs, Warren E. (1977, October). Sentence-combining practice aids reading comprehension. *Journal of Reading, 21*(1), 18–24.

Conant, James B. (1959). *The American high school today.* New York: McGraw-Hill.

Cooper, David et al. (1972). *Decision making for the diagnostic teacher.* New York: Holt, Rinehart & Winston.

Cousert, Girly C. (1978). Six selected home reading environment factors and their relationship to reading achievement at third grade (Doctoral dissertation, Indiana University).

Covington, Martin V. (1967, February). Some experimental evidence on teaching for creative understanding. *The Reading Teacher, 20*(5), 390–396.

Cromer, W. (1970). The difference model: A new explanation for some reading difficulties. *Journal of Educational Psychology, 61,* 471–483.

Culatta, Richard, & Culatta, Barbara K. (1981). Communication disorders. In A. E. Blackhurst & W. H. Berdine (Eds.), *An introduction to special education* (pp. 108–148). Boston: Little, Brown.

Cullinan, Beatrice. (1974). Teaching literature to children, 1966–1972. In H. A. Robinson & A. T. Burrows (Eds.), *Teacher effectiveness in elementary language arts: A progress report.* Urbana, IL: National Conference on Research in English/ERIC-Clearinghouse on Reading & Communication Skills.

Cunningham, Patricia. (1982). Diagnosis by observation. In J. J. Pikulski & T. Shanahan (Eds.), *Approaches to the informal evaluation of reading* (pp. 12–22). Newark, DE: International Reading Association.

Dale, Edgar, & Chall, Jeanne S. (1948). A formula for predicting readability. *Educational Research Bulletin, 27,* 11–20, 37–54.

Dasch, Anne. (1983, January). Aligning basal reader instruction with cognitive state theory. *The Reading Teacher, 36*(4), 428–434.

Davis, Frederick B. (1972, Summer). Psychometric research on comprehension in reading. *Reading Research Quarterly, 7*(4), 628–678.

References

DeBoer, John. (1967). Teaching critical reading. In King, Wolf, & Ellinger (Eds.), *Critical Reading.* Philadelphia: Lippincott.

Deighton, Lee C. (1966). Flow of thought through an English sentence. *Vistas in Reading,* IRA Conference Proceedings, XI, Part I, 322–326.

Deiner, Penny Low. (1983). *Resources for teaching young children with special needs.* New York: Harcourt Brace Jovanovich.

DeStephano, Johanna S. (1978). *Language, the learner & the school.* New York: Wiley.

Dickerson, Dolores P. (1982, October). A study of the use of games to reinforce sight vocabulary. *The Reading Teacher, 36*(1), 46–49.

Distad, H. W. (1927, April). A study of the reading performance of pupils under different conditions on different types of materials. *Journal of Educational Research, 18,* 247–248.

Dixon, Carol. (1976, November). Teaching strategies for the Mexican American child. *The Reading Teacher, 30*(2), 141–144.

Don, Sue et al. (1973). *Individualizing reading instruction with learning stations and centers.* Evansville, IN: Riverside Learning Associates.

Downing, John. (1984, January). A source of cognitive confusion for beginning readers: Learning in a second language. *The Reading Teacher, 37*(4), 366–370.

Downing, John, & Oliver, Peter. (1973–74). The child's concept of a word. *Reading Research Quarterly, 9*(4), 568–582.

Dreyer, Hal B. (1973, May). Rx for pupil tutoring programs. *The Reading Teacher, 26*(8), 810–813.

Duell, Orpha K. (1978). Overt and covert use of objectives of different cognitive levels. *Contemporary Journal of Educational Psychology, 3,* 239–245.

Duffy, G., & McIntyre, L. (1980, June). A qualitative analysis of how various primary grade teachers employ the structured learning component of the direct instruction model when teaching reading. East Lansing, MI: Michigan State University Institute for Research on Teaching, Research Series No. 80.

Durkin, Dolores. (1961, January). Children who read before grade one. *The Reading Teacher, 14*(4), 163–166.

Durkin, Dolores. (1966). *Children who read early.* New York: Teachers College Press, Columbia University.

Durkin, Dolores. (1968). When should children begin to read? In *Innovation and change in reading instruction,* Chapter 2. Sixty-Seventh Yearbook of the National Society for the Study of Education, Part II. Chicago: University of Chicago Press.

Durkin, Dolores. (1972). *Teaching young children to read.* Boston: Allyn & Bacon.

Durkin, Dolores. (1974). A six year study of children who learned to read in school at the age of four. *Reading Research Quarterly, 10*(1), 9–61.

Durkin, Dolores. (1978–79). What classroom observations reveal about reading comprehension. *Reading Research Quarterly, 14*(4), 481–533.

Durkin, Dolores. (1984, April). Is there a match between what elementary teachers do and what basal reader manuals recommend? *The Reading Teacher, 37*(8), 734–744.

Durrell, Donald D. S. et al. (1958, February). Success in first grade reading. *Journal of Education, 140,* 1–8.

Dykstra, Robert. (1967). The use of reading readiness tests for prediction and diagnosis: A critique. In T. Barrett (Ed.), *The evaluation of children's reading achievement* (pp. 35–52). Newark, DE: International Reading Association.

Dykstra, Robert. (1968a, Fall). Classroom implications of the first grade reading studies. *College Reading Association, 9,* 53–59.

Dykstra, Robert. (1968b, Fall). Summary of the second phase of the cooperative research program in primary reading instruction. *Reading Research Quarterly, 4*, 49–70.

Earle, R. A. (1969). Use of the structured overview in mathematics classes. In H. L. Herber & P. L. Sanders (Eds.), *Research in teaching reading in the content areas: First year report.* Syracuse, NY: Syracuse University Reading and Language Arts Center.

Ehrlich, Virginia Z. (1982). *Gifted children: A guide for parents and teachers.* Englewood Cliffs, NJ: Prentice-Hall.

Ellis, DiAnn W., & Preston, Fannie W. (1984, April). Enhancing beginning reading using wordless picture books in a cross-age tutoring program. *The Reading Teacher, 37*(8), 692–699.

Elwell, C. E. et al. (1976). *Phonics is fun.* Cleveland, OH: Reardon, Baer.

Emans, Robert (1967, February). The usefulness of phonic generalizations above the primary grades. *The Reading Teacher, 20*(5), 419–425.

Englemann, Siegfried, & Bruner, E. C. (1974). *DISTAR: An instructional system.* Chicago: Science Research Associates.

Evans, Christopher. (1979). *The micro millenium.* New York: Washington Square Press.

Farr, Roger. (1969). *Reading: What can be measured?* Newark, DE: International Reading Association.

Farrell, Ellen. (1982, October). SSR as the core of a junior high reading program. *Journal of Reading, 26*(1), 48–51.

Feitelson, Dina. (1979). *Mother tongue or second language.* Newark, DE: International Reading Association.

Fernald, Grace. (1943). *Remedial techniques in basic school subjects.* New York: McGraw-Hill.

Fillmore, C. (1968). The case for case. In E. Bach & R. Harms (Eds.), *Universals in linguistic theory* (pp. 1–81). New York: Holt, Rinehart & Winston.

Fisher, K. D. (1973). An investigation to determine if selected exercises in sentence-combining can improve reading and writing (Doctoral dissertation, Indiana University).

Fisk, Lori, & Lindgren, Henry C. (1974). *Learning centers.* Glen Ridge, NJ: Exceptional Press.

Fitzgerald, Gisela G. (1980). Reliability of the Fry sampling procedure. *Reading Research Quarterly, 15*(4), 489–503.

Fitzgerald, Jill, & Spiegel, Dixie Lee. (1983). Enhancing children's reading comprehension through narrative structure. *Journal of Reading Behavior, 15*(2), 1–18.

Fitzgibbon, Thomas J. (1974). Reading tests and the disadvantaged. In William E. Blanton et al. (Eds.), *Measuring reading performance,* pp. 15–33. Newark, DE: International Reading Association.

Flesch, Rudolf T. (1948). A new readability yardstick. *Journal of Applied Psychology, 32,* 221–233.

Flood, James (Ed.). (1984a). *Understanding reading comprehension.* Newark, DE: International Reading Association.

Flood, James. (1984b). *Promoting reading comprehension.* Newark, DE: International Reading Association.

Forgan, H. W. (1978). *Forgan's phonics.* Santa Monica, CA: Goodyear.

Forman, Laurie Ann. (1977). Word attack emphasis in three basal reading systems during the 1930s, 1950s, and 1970s in first grade (Master's thesis, Rutgers University). *RIE,* January 1978.

Fox, Daniel. (1983). *National teacher examinations* (NTE). New York: ARCO.

Frase, L. T., & Schwartz, B. J. (1975, October). Effect of question production and answering on prose recall. *Journal of Educational Psychology, 67*(5), 628–635.

Frederiksen, C. H. (1972). Effects of task-induced cognitive operations on comprehension and memory processes. In J. Carroll & R. O. Freedle (Eds.), *Language comprehension and the acquisition of knowledge.* Washington, DC: W. H. Winston.

Frederiksen, C. H. (1975, July). Representing logical and semantic structure of knowledge acquired from discourse. *Cognitive Psychology, 7*(3), 371–458.

Frederiksen, C. H. (1977). Semantic processing units in understanding text. In R. O. Freedle (Ed.), *Discourse production and comprehension,* Vol. I. Norwood, NJ: Ablex.

Fries, Charles C. (1962). *Linguistics and reading.* New York: Holt, Rinehart & Winston.

Frith, Uta, & Vogel, Juliet M. (1980). *Some perceptual prerequisites for reading.* Newark, DE: International Reading Association.

Fry, Edward B. (1969, March). The readability graph validated at primary levels. *The Reading Teacher, 22*(6), 125–130.

Fulwiler, Gwen, & Groff, Patrick. (1980, Fall). The effectiveness of intensive phonics. *Reading Horizons, 21*(1), 50–54.

Furth, Hans. (1970). *Piaget for teachers.* Englewood Cliffs, NJ: Prentice-Hall.

Gallagher, James J. (1975). *Teaching the gifted child* (2nd ed.). Boston: Allyn & Bacon.

Ganschow, Leonore, Weber, Donald B., & Suelter, Susan K. (1984, April). To remediate reading-like behavior, teach a beginner to self-monitor. *The Reading Teacher, 37*(8), 718–721.

Gartner, Alan G., Kohler, Mary C., & Riessman, Frank R. (1971). *Children teach children.* New York: Harper & Row.

Gearheart, Bill R. (1980). *Special education for the '80s.* St. Louis: C. V. Mosby.

Gearheart, Bill R., & Weishahn, Mel W. (1984). *The exceptional student in the regular classroom* (3rd ed.). St. Louis: C. V. Mosby.

Geoffrion, Leo D., & Geoffrion, Olga P. (1983). *Computers and reading instruction.* Reading, MA.: Addison-Wesley.

Getman, G. N. et al. (1968). *Developing learning readiness.* Manchester, MO.: Webster.

Gibbons, H. D. (1971). Reading and sentence elements. *Elementary English Review, 18,* 42–46.

Gibson, E. J., & Levin, Harry. (1975). *The psychology of reading.* Cambridge, MA: MIT Press.

Gillespie-Silver, Patricia. (1979). *Teaching reading to children with special needs: An ecological approach.* Columbus, OH: Charles E. Merrill.

Gillingham, Anna, & Stillman, Bessie W. (1968). *Remedial teaching for children with specific disability in reading, spelling, and penmanship* (7th ed.). Cambridge, MA: Educators Publishing Service.

Glass, Gene V. (1978, Winter). Standards and criteria. *Journal of educational measurement, 15*(4), 237–261.

Gold, Milton J. (1965). *Education of the intellectually gifted.* Columbus, OH: Charles E. Merrill.

Goldenberg, E. Paul, Russell, Susan Jo, & Carter, Cynthia J. (1984). *Computers, education and special needs.* Reading, MA.: Addison-Wesley.

Goodlad, John I. (1984). *A place called school: Prospects for the future.* New York: McGraw-Hill.

Goodman, Kenneth S. (1963, March). A communicative theory of the reading curriculum. *Elementary English, 40*(3), 290–298.

Goodman, Kenneth S. (1969, Fall). Analysis of oral reading miscues: Applied psycholinguistics. *Reading Research Quarterly, 5*(1), 9–30.

Goodman, Kenneth S. (1970). Behind the eye: What happens in reading. In H. Singer & R. Ruddell (Eds.). *Theoretical models and processes of reading.* Newark, DE: International Reading Association.

Goodman, Kenneth S. (1976). Reading: A psycholinguistic guessing game. In H. Singer & R. Ruddell (Eds.), *Theoretical models and processes of reading* (2nd ed.). Newark, DE: International Reading Association.

Goodman, Kenneth S. et al. (1966). *Choosing materials to teach reading.* Detroit: Wayne State University Press.

Goodman, Kenneth S., & Niles, Olive S. (1970). *Reading: Process and program.* Urbana, IL: National Council of Teachers of English.

Goodman, Yetta M., & Burke, Carolyn L. (1972). *Reading miscue inventory.* New York: Macmillan.

Gordon, Christine J., & Braun, Carl. (1983, November). Using story schema as an aid to reading and writing. *The Reading Teacher, 37*(2), 116–121.

Goudey, Charles. (1970, February). Reading—directed or not? *Elementary School Journal, 70*(5), 245–247.

Greaney, Vincent, & Neuman, Susan B. (1983, November). Young people's views of the functions of reading: A cross-cultural perspective. *The Reading Teacher, 37*(2), 158–163.

Greenewald, M. Jane, & Pederson, Carolyn. (1983). Effects of sentence organization on the reading comprehension of poor readers. In J. A. Niles & L. A. Harris (Eds.), *Searches for meaning in reading/language instruction* (pp. 101–103). Rochester, NY: National Reading Conference.

Grimes, J. E. (1975). *The thread of discourse.* The Hague, Netherlands; Mouton.

Gunning, Robert. (1952). *The technique of clear writing.* New York: McGraw-Hill.

Guszak, Frank J. (1968, April). Questioning strategies of elementary teachers in relation to comprehension. Speech given at IRA Conference in Boston.

Gutek, Gerald L. (Ed.). (1983). *Standard education almanac, 1983–84* (16th edition). Chicago: Professional Publications.

Guthrie, John T. (Ed.). (1981). *Comprehension and teaching: Research reviews.* Newark, DE: International Reading Association.

Hall, MaryAnne. (1981). *Teaching reading as a language experience.* Columbus, OH: Charles E. Merrill.

Hall, MaryAnne, Ribovich, Jerilyn K., & Ramig, Christopher. (1979). *Reading and the elementary school child* (2nd ed.). New York: Van Nostrand.

Hall, Robert A. (1960). *Linguistics and your language.* New York: Doubleday Anchor Books.

Hallahan, Daniel P., & Kauffman, James M. (1978). *Exceptional children: Introduction to special education.* Englewood Cliffs, NJ: Prentice-Hall.

Halliday, M. A. K. (1977a). *Learning how to mean.* New York: Elsevier.

Halliday, M. A. K. (1977b). *Explorations in the functions of language.* New York: Elsevier North-Holland.

Hammill, Donald D., & Bartel, Nettie R. (1982). *Teaching children with learning and behavior problems* (3rd ed.). Boston: Allyn & Bacon.

Hanna, Paul R., Hodges, Richard E. & Hanna, Jean S. (1971). *Spelling: Structure and strategies.* Washington, DC: University Press of America (reprint, n.d.). Originally published: Boston: Houghton Mifflin, 1971.

Hargis, Charles H. (1982) *Teaching reading to handicapped children.* Denver: Love.

Harris, Albert J., & Jacobson, Milton D. (1982). *Basic reading vocabularies.* New York: Macmillan.

Harris, Larry A., & Niles, Jerome A. (1982, Spring). An analysis of published informal reading inventories. *Reading Horizons, 22*(3), 159–174.

References

Harste, Jerome C., Burke, Carolyn L., & Woodward, Virginia A. (1983). *The young child as writer-reader and informant: Final report.* Bloomington, IN: Indiana University, Language Education Department.

Hay, J., & Wingo, C. (1960). *Reading with phonics.* New York: Lippincott.

Heilman, Arthur W. (1981) *Phonics in proper perspective* (4th Ed.). Columbus, OH: Charles E. Merrill.

Hiebert, Elfreida. (1981). Developmental patterns and interrelationships of preschool children's print awareness. *Reading Research Quarterly, 16*(2), 236–260.

Hofler, Donald B. (1981, November). Word lines: An approach to vocabulary development. *The Reading Teacher, 35*(2), 216–217.

Holmes, Betty C. (1983). The effect of prior knowledge on the question answering of good and poor readers. *Journal of Reading Behavior, 15*(4), 1–18.

Hooper, George A. (1981, November/December). Computerize your IEPs. *Classroom Computer News, 2*(2), 34–37.

Hoskisson, Kenneth. (1974, March). Should parents teach their children to read? *Elementary English, 51*(3), 295–299.

Hoskisson, Kenneth. (1975, March). The many facets of assisted reading. *Elementary English, 52*(3), 312–315.

Huck, Charlotte S. (1976). *Children's literature in the elementary school* (3rd Ed.). New York: Holt, Rinehart & Winston.

Hughes, T. O. (1975). *Sentence-combining: A measure for increasing reading comprehension.* ERIC Clearinghouse on Reading [ED 112 421].

Hull, Marion A. (1981). *Phonics for the teacher of reading* (3rd Ed.). Columbus, OH: Charles E. Merrill.

Impara, James C. (1979). Technical issues associated with minimum competency testing. In J. C. Impara et al., *Minimum competency testing: State-of-the-art* (pp. 34–38). Washington, DC: National Association of State Boards of Education.

Impara, James C. et al. (1979). *Minimum competency testing: State-of-the-art.* Washington, DC: National Association of State Boards of Education.

Ingersoll, Gary M., & Smith, Carl B. (1984a). *1983 report on trends in the use of educational materials: Traditionals.* Dayton, OH: The Mazer Corp.

Ingersoll, Gary M., & Smith, Carl B. (1984b). *1983 report on trends in the use of educational materials: Microcomputers.* Dayton, OH: The Mazer Corp.

Jacques, Milton G. (Ed.). (1983, November). Arkansas adopts teacher literacy testing for recertification. *Teacher Education Reports, 5*(10), 7.

Jobe, Fred W. (1976). *Screening vision in school.* Newark, DE: International Reading Association.

Johns, Jerry L. (1982). The dimensions and uses of informal reading assessment. In J. J. Pikulski & T. Shanahan, *Approaches to the informal evaluation of reading* (pp. 1–11). Newark, DE: International Reading Association.

Jongsma, Eugene. (1980). *Cloze instruction research: A second look.* Newark, DE: International Reading Association.

Jorm, A. F. (1977, April). Children's reading processes revealed by pronunciation latencies and errors. *Journal of Educational Psychology, 69*(2), 166–171.

Kagan, Jerome et al. (1971). Personality and IQ change. In P. S. Sears (Ed.), *Intellectual development.* New York: Wiley.

Kasdon, Lawrence M. (1968, May). Oral versus silent-oral diagnosis. Paper presented at IRA Conference Proceedings in Boston.

Keedy, Marvin L., et al. (1970). *Exploring elementary mathematics,* V. New York: Holt, Rinehart & Winston.

Keller, Paul F. G. (1982, April). Maryland micro: A prototype readability formula for small computers. *The Reading teacher, 35*(7), 778–782.

Kephart, Newell C. (1971). *The slow learner in the classroom.* Columbus, OH: Charles E. Merrill.

Kintsch, Walter (1974). *The representative of meaning in memory.* Hillsdale, NJ: Lawrence Erlbaum.

Kintsch, Walter, & Miller, James R. (1984). Readability: A view from cognitive psychology. In J. Flood (Ed.), *Understanding reading comprehension* (pp. 220–232). Newark, DE: International Reading Association.

Kitagawa, Mary M. (1982, October). Improving discussions or how to get the students to ask the questions. *The Reading Teacher, 36*(1), 42–45.

Klare, George R. (1984). Readability. In P. D. Pearson et al. (Eds.), *Handbook of reading research* (pp. 681–744). New York: Longman.

Kleiman, Glenn M., & Humphrey, Mary M. (1984, October). Computers make special education more effective and fun. *Creative Computing, 10*(10), 96, 100–101.

Kounin, Jacob S. (1983, November). Classrooms: Individuals or behavior settings? In *Monographs in Teaching and Learning* (General Series, Number 1). Bloomington, IN: School of Education, Indiana University.

LaBerge, David, & Samuels, S. J. (1974, April). Toward a theory of automatic information processing in reading. *Cognitive Psychology, 6*(2), 293–323.

Laffey, James, & Shuy, Roger. (1973). *Language differences: Do they interfere?* Newark, DE: International Reading Association.

Lange, Bob. (1982, April). Readability formulas: Second looks, second thoughts. *The Reading teacher, 35*(7), 858–861.

Langer, Judith A., & Smith-Burke, M. Trika (Eds.). (1982). *Reader meets author/bridging the gap.* Newark, DE: International Reading Association.

LaPointe, Archie E. (1984, June). The good news about American education. *Phi Delta Kappan, 65*(10), 663–667.

Lapp, Diane, & Flood, James. (1983). *Teaching reading to every child.* New York: Macmillan.

Larrick, Nancy. (1980). The impact of television on children's reading. In C. M. McCullough (Ed.), *Inchworm, inchworm: Persistent problems in reading education* (pp. 65–74). Newark, DE: International Reading Association.

Larrick, Nancy. (1982). *A parent's guide to children's reading* (5th ed.). Philadelphia: The Westminster Press. Paperback edition 1982, Bantam Books.

Lass, Bonnie. (1982, October). Portrait of my son as an early reader. *The Reading Teacher, 36*(1), 20–28.

Layton, James R. (1980, December). A chart for computing the Dale-Chall readability formula above fourth grade level. *Journal of Reading, 24*(3), 239–255.

Lee, Doris M., & Van Allen, Roach. (1963). *Learning to read through experience.* New York: Appleton-Century-Crofts.

Legenza, Alice, & Elijah, David. (1979, July/August). The cloze procedure: Some new applications. *Journal of Educational Research, 72*(6), 351–355.

Lehr, Fran. (1983, November/December). Developing critical and creative reading and thinking skills. *Language Arts, 60*(8), 1031–1035.

Lehr, Fran. (1984, March). Peer teaching. *The Reading Teacher, 37*(7), 636–639.

Leibowicz, Joseph. (1983, November). Children's reading interests. *The Reading Teacher, 37*(2), 184–187.

Lerner, Janet W. (1981). *Learning disabilities: Theories, diagnosis, and strategies* (3rd ed.). Boston: Houghton Mifflin.

Lipson, Marjorie Youmans. (1984, April). Some unexpected issues in prior knowledge and comprehension. *The Reading Teacher, 37*(8), 760–764.

Loban, Walter. (1963). *The language of elementary school children.* Champaign, IL: National Council of Teachers of English Research Report No. 1.

Lorge, Irving. (1939). Predicting reading difficulty of selections for children. *Elementary English Review, 16,* 229–233.

Lovitt, Thomas. (1977, May). Precision teaching. *Early Years, 7*(9), 44–45, 64.

Lovitt, Thomas. (1980). *Writing & implementing an IEP: A step-by-step plan.* Belmont, CA.: Pitman Learning.

Lynch, Ella Frances. (1912, August). Is the public school a failure? It is: The most momentous failure in our American life today. *The Ladies Home Journal, 29,* 4.

Lynd, Albert. (1950). *Quackery in our schools.* Boston: Little, Brown.

McConnell, Campbell R. (1982, October). Readability formulas as applied to college economics textbooks. *Journal of Reading, 26*(1), 14–17.

McCracken, Robert A., & McCracken, Marlene J. (1972). *Reading is only the tiger's tail.* San Rafael, CA: Leswing.

McCullough, Constance M. (1957, September). Responses of elementary school children to common types of reading comprehension questions. *Journal of Educational Research, 51,* 65–70.

McCullough, Constance M. (1963). *McCullough word analysis tests.* Boston: Ginn.

McDonell, Gloria M. (1978). Effects of instruction in the use of an abstract structural schema as an aid to comprehension and recall of written discourse (Doctoral dissertation, Virginia Polytechnic Institute and State University).

McKenna, Michael C. (1983, March). Informal reading inventories: A review of the issues. *The Reading Teacher, 36*(7), 670–679.

McLaughlin, G. Harry. (1969, May). SMOG grading—a new readability formula. *Journal of Reading, 12*(8), 639–646.

McLuhan, Marshall. (1964). *Understanding media: The extensions of man.* New York: New American Library.

Madaus, George, & McDonagh, John. (1979). Minimum competency: Unexamined assumptions and unexplored negative outcomes. In R. Lennon (Ed.), *Impactive changes in measurement* (pp. 1–14). (*New Directions for Testing and Measurement,* No. 3) San Francisco: Jossey-Bass.

Mallon, Barbara, & Berglund, Roberta. (1984, May). The language experience approach to reading: Recurring questions and their answers. *The Reading Teacher, 37*(9), 867–871.

Mandell, Colleen, & Gold, Veronica. (1984). *Teaching handicapped students.* St. Paul, MN.: West.

Mandler, Jean M., & Johnson, Nancy S. (1977). Remembrance of things passed: Story structure and recall. *Cognitive Psychology, 9,* 111–151.

Manzo, Anthony V. (1975, January). Guided reading procedure. *Journal of Reading, 18*(4), 287–291.

Manzo, Anthony V. (1980, November). Three 'universal' strategies in content area reading and languaging. *Journal of Reading, 24*(2), 146–149.

Marshall, Nancy, (1983, March). Using story grammar to assess reading comprehension. *The Reading Teacher, 36*(7), 616–620.

Mason, George E., Blanchard, Jay S., & Daniel, Danny B. (1983). *Computer applications in reading* (2nd ed.). Newark, DE: International Reading Association.

Mason, Jana M. (1980). When do children begin to read: An exploration of four-year-old children's letter and word reading competencies. *Reading Research Quarterly, 15*(2), 203–227.

Mason, Jana M. (1984). Early reading from a developmental perspective. In P. D. Pearson et al. (Eds.), *Handbook of reading research* (pp. 505–544). New York: Longman.

Matsuyama, Utako K. (1983, March). Can story grammar speak Japanese? *The Reading Teacher, 36*(7), 666–669.

Meehan, Trinita. (1970). The effects of instruction based upon the questioning patterns of pre-service teachers (Doctoral dissertation, Indiana University).

Meyer, Bonnie J. F. (1975). *The organization of prose and its effect on memory.* Amsterdam: North-Holland.

Meyer, Bonnie J. F. (1984). Organizational aspects of text: Effects on reading comprehension. In J. Flood (Ed.), *Promoting reading comprehension* (pp. 113–138). Newark, DE: International Reading Association.

Meyer, Bonnie J. F., & Rice, G. Elizabeth, (1984). The structure of text. In P. D. Pearson et al. (Eds.), *Handbook of reading research* (pp. 319–352). New York: Longman.

Mier, Margaret. (1984, April). Comprehension monitoring in the elementary classroom. *The Reading Teacher, 37*(7), 770–774.

Mitzel, Harold (Ed.). (1982). *Encyclopedia of educational research.* New York: Free Press.

Monson, Dianne L., & McClenathan, Day Ann K. (Eds.). (1979). *Developing active readers: Ideas for parents, teachers, librarians.* Newark, DE: International Reading Association.

Moore, David W. (1983, November/December). A case for naturalistic assessment of reading comprehension. *Language Arts, 60*(8), 957–969.

Moore, David W., Readence, John E., & Rickelman, Robert J. (1982). *Prereading activities for content area reading and learning.* Newark, DE: International Reading Association.

Morse, J. M. (1975). Effect of reader-generated questions on learning from prose (Doctoral dissertation, Rutgers University.

Mosenthal, James H., & Tierney, Robert J. (1984). Cohesion: Problems with talking about text. *Reading Research Quarterly, 19*(2), 240–244.

Nardelli, Robert R. (1957, March). Some aspects of creative reading. *Journal of Educational Research, 50,* 495–508.

National assessment of educational progress: Reading and literature general information yearbook (1976). Washington, DC: U. S. Government Printing Office.

Neisser, Ulric. (1976). *Cognition and reality: Principles and implications of cognitive psychology.* San Francisco: W. H. Freeman.

Neuman, Susan B. (1981, January). Effect of teaching auditory perceptual skills on reading achievement in first grade. *The Reading Teacher, 34*(4), 422–426.

Nevi, Charles N. (1983, May). Cross-age tutoring: Why does it help the tutors? *The Reading Teacher, 36*(9), 892–898.

Newton, Beatryce T. (1980). Affective processes in critical reading. *Reading Improvement, 17*(1), 44–47.

Ollila, Lloyd O. (1977). *The kindergarten child and reading.* Newark, DE: International Reading Association.

Olson, David R. (1977). The language of instruction: The literate bias of schooling. In R. C. Anderson, R. J. Spiro, & W. E. Montague (Eds.), *Schooling and the acquisition of knowledge* (pp. 65–89). Hillsdale, NJ: Lawrence Erlbaum.

Olson, Mary W. (1984, February). A dash of story grammar and . . . Presto! A book report. *The Reading Teacher, 37*(6), 458–461.

Owens, A. M. (1977). The effects of question generation, question answering, and reading on prose learning (Doctoral dissertation, University of Oregon).

Papert, Seymour. (1980). *Mindstorms: Children, computers, and powerful ideas.* New York: Basic Books.

Patten, Simon N. (1911, March). An economic measure of school efficiency. *The Educational Review, 41,* 467–477.

Pearson, P. David. (1974–75). The effects of grammatical complexity on children's comprehension, recall, and conception of certain semantic relations. *Reading Research Quarterly, 10*(2), 155–192.

Pearson, P. David, Barr, Rebecca, Kamil, Michael L., & Mosenthal, Peter. (1984). *Handbook of reading research.* New York: Longman.

Pearson, P. David, & Johnson, Dale D. (1985). *Teaching reading comprehension.* New York: Holt, Rinehart & Winston.

Pederson, J. E. P. (1976). An investigation into the differences between student-constructed versus experimenter-constructed post-questions on the comprehension of expository prose (Doctoral dissertation, University of Minnesota).

Perfetti, Charles, & Lesgold, Alan. (1976). Coding and comprehension in skilled reading (Unpublished manuscript, University of Pittsburgh).

Pertz, Doris L., & Putnam, Lillian R. (1982, March). An examination of the relationships between nutrition and learning. *The Reading Teacher, 35*(6), 702–706.

Piaget, Jean. (1952). *The origins of intelligence in children,* trans. by Margaret Cook. New York: International Universities Press.

Piaget, Jean. (1963). *The child's conception of the world.* Paterson, NJ: Littlefield Adams.

Piche, Gene, & Slater, Wayne H. (1983). Predicting learning from text: A comparison of two procedures. *Journal of Reading Behavior, 15*(1), 43–57.

Pikulski, John J. (1984, March). Questions and answers. *The Reading Teacher, 37*(7), 687–688.

Pipho, Chris. (1984, January). State activity—minimum competency testing. Denver, CO: Education Commission of the States (mimeo.).

Platts, Sister Mary E., Marguerite, Rose, & Shumaker, Esther. (1960). *Spice.* Benton Harbor, MI: Educational Service.

Poulson, D., Kintsch, E., Kintsch, W., & Premack, D. (1979). Children's comprehension and memory for stories. *Journal of Experimental Child Psychology, 28,* 379–403.

Powell, Marvin, & Parsley, Kenneth M., Jr. (1961, February). The relationships between first grade readiness and second grade reading achievement. *Journal of Educational Research, 54,* 229–233.

Powell, William R. (1968). Reappraising the criteria for interpreting informal inventories. Paper presented at the thirteenth annual convention of the International Reading Association in Boston.

Price, Eunice H. (1976, October). How thirty-seven gifted children learned to read. *The Reading Teacher, 30*(1), 44–48.

Propp, V. (1958). *Morphology of the folk tale,* trans. by L. Scott. Bloomington, IN: Indiana University Research Center in Anthropology, Folklore, and Linguistics, Publication No. 10.

Pullin, Diana (1981, September). Minimum competency testing and the demand for accountability. *Phi Delta Kappan, 63*(1), 20–22.

Quandt, Ivan, & Selznick, Richard. (1984). *Self-concept and reading.* Newark, DE: International Reading Association.

Radabaugh, Martha T., & Yukish, Joseph F. (1982). *Curriculum and methods for the mildly handicapped.* Boston: Allyn & Bacon.

Ragghianti, Suzanne, & Miller, Rosemary. (1982, October). The microcomputer and special education management. *Exceptional Children, 49*(2), 131–135.

Raim, Joan. (1983, April). Influence of the teacher-pupil interaction on disabled readers. *The Reading Teacher, 36*(8), 810–813.

Rand, Muriel K. (1984, January). Story schema: Theory, research, and practice. *The Reading Teacher, 37*(4), 375–382.

Rankin, Earl F., & Culhane, Joseph W. (1969, December). Comparable cloze and multiple-choice comprehension test scores. *Journal of Reading, 13*(3), 193–198.

Rauch, Sidney J. (1969). *Handbook for the volunteer tutor.* Newark, DE: International Reading Association.

Ravitch, Diane. (1983). *The troubled crusade: American education, 1945–1980.* New York: Holmes Meier.

Raygor, Alton L. (1976). The Raygor readability estimate: A quick and easy way to determine difficulty. In P. D. Pearson (Ed.), *Reading: Theory, research and practice* (26th Yearbook of the NRC). Clemson, SC: National Reading Conference.

Reeke, Angela S., & Laffey, James L. (1984). *Pathways to imagination.* Glenview, IL Scott, Foresman.

Reimer, Becky L. (1983, January). Recipes for language experience stories. *The Reading Teacher, 36*(4), 396–401.

Resnick, Lauren B. (1970, October). Relations between perceptual and syntactic control in oral reading. *Journal of Educational Psychology, 61,* 382–385.

Richards, Jill. (1978). *Classroom language: What sort?* London: George Allen & Unwin.

Richek, Margaret Ann, List, Lynne K., & Lerner, Janet W. (1983). *Reading problems: Diagnosis and remediation.* Englewood Cliffs, NJ: Prentice-Hall.

Rickover, Hyman G. (1959). *Education and freedom.* New York: Dutton.

Rickover, Hyman G. (1963). *American education: A national failure.* New York: Dutton.

Robinson, Helen M. (1964). Developing critical readers. In R. G. Stauffer (Ed.), *Dimensions of critical reading* XI (pp. 1–11). Newark, DE: University of Delaware, Proceedings of the Annual Education and Reading Conferences.

Rodrigues, Raymond J., & White, Robert H. (1981). *Mainstreaming the non-English speaking student.* Urbana, IL: National Council of Teachers of English.

Roe, Anne. (1961). *The making of a scientist.* New York: Apollo Editions.

Rosenberg, Phillip E. (1968). Audiologic correlates. In A. Keeney & V. Keeney (Eds.), *"Dyslexia" diagnosis and treatment of reading disorders* (pp. 53–59). St. Louis: C. V. Mosby.

Rosenblatt, L. M. (1978). *The reader, the text, the poem: The transactional theory of the literary work.* Carbondale, IL: Southern Illinois University Press.

Rosenshine, Barak, & Furst, Norma. (1971). Research in teacher performance criteria. In B. O. Smith (Ed.), *Research in teacher education.* Englewood Cliffs, NJ: Prentice-Hall.

Rosenstock, Robert, Dodl, Norman, & Burton, John. (1984). *Educational microware assessment: Criteria and procedures for evaluating instructional software.* Blacksburg, VA: Education Microcomputer Laboratory, College of Education, Virginia Polytechnic Institute and State University.

Rosenthal, Robert, & Jacobson, Lenore. (1968). *Pygmalion in the classroom.* New York: Holt, Rinehart & Winston.

Rosso, Barbara R., & Emans, Robert. (1981, March). Children's use of phonic generalizations. *The Reading Teacher, 34*(6), 653–658.

Rudman, Jack. (1984). *National teacher examination—common examination: Admission Test Series:* ATS-15. New York: National Learning.

Rumelhart, David E. (1975). Notes on a schema for stories. In D. G. Bobrow & A. M. Collins (Eds.), *Representation and understanding.* New York: Academic Press.

Rumelhart, David E. (1977). Toward an interactive model of reading. In S. Dornic (Ed.), *Attention and performance VI.* London: Academic Press.

Rumelhart, David E. (1980). Schemata: The building blocks of cognition. In R. J. Spiro, B. C. Bruce, & W. F. Brewer (Eds.), *Theoretical issues in reading comprehension* (pp. 33–58). Hillsdale, NJ: Lawrence Erlbaum.

Rumelhart, David E., & Ortony, Andrew. (1977). The representation of knowledge in memory. In R. C. Anderson, R. J. Spiro, & W. E. Montague (Eds.), *Schooling and the acquisition of knowledge* (pp. 99–135). Hillsdale, NJ: Lawrence Erlbaum.

Russell, David H. (1956). *Children's thinking.* Boston: Ginn.

Russell, David H., & Karp, Etta. (1951). *Reading aids through the grades.* New York: Columbia University, Teachers College Press.

Sadow, Marilyn W. (1982, February). The use of story grammar in the design of questions. *The Reading Teacher, 35*(5), 518–522.

Samuels, S. Jay (1979, January). The method of repeated readings. *The Reading Teacher, 32*(4), 403–408.

Sandefur, J. T. (1984, March). State assessment trends. AACTE *Briefs, 5*(2), 17–19.

Sartain, Harry W. (Ed.). (1981). *Mobilizing family forces for worldwide reading success.* Newark, DE: International Reading Association.

Savage, John F., & Mooney, Jean F. (1979). *Teaching reading to children with special needs.* Boston: Allyn & Bacon.

Schach, Vita G. (1962, October). A quick phonics readiness check for retarded readers. *Elementary English, 39*(6), 584–586.

Schank, R. C., & Abelson, R. P. (1977). *Scripts, plans, goals and understanding.* Hillsdale, NJ: Lawrence Erlbaum.

Schaudt, Barbara A. (1983, May). Another look at sustained silent reading. *The Reading Teacher, 36*(9), 934–936.

Schell, Leo M. (Ed.). (1981). *Diagnostic and criterion-referenced reading tests: Review and evaluation.* Newark, DE: International Reading Association.

Schell, Leo M., & Hanna, Gerald S. (1981, December). Can informal reading inventories reveal strengths and weaknesses in comprehension subskills? *The Reading Teacher, 35*(3), 263–268.

Schmelzer, R. V. (1975). The effect of college student constructed questions on the comprehension of a passage of expository prose (Doctoral dissertation, University of Minnesota).

Schneider, Herman, & Schneider, Nina. (1968). *Science in our world.* Boston: D. C. Heath.

Schreiner, Robert. (Ed.). (1979). *Reading tests and teachers: A practical guide.* Newark, DE: International Reading Association.

Schuyler, Michael R. (1982, March). A readability formula program for use on microcomputers. *Journal of Reading, 25*(6), 560–591.

Sebesta, Sam L. (1968, April). Literature in the elementary school. Speech given at International Reading Association Conference Proceedings in Boston.

Sebesta, Sam L., Calder, James W., & Cleland, Lynne. (1982, November). A story grammar for the classroom. *The Reading Teacher, 36*(2), 180–184.

Sheldon, William D., & Carillo, Lawrence. (1952, January). Relation of parents, home and certain developmental characteristics of children's reading ability. *Elementary School Journal, 52*(3), 262–270.

Sherman, Thomas M., & Wildman, Terry M. (1982). *Proven strategies for successful test taking.* Columbus, OH: Charles E. Merrill.

Shores, J. Harlan (1960, November). Reading of science for two separate purposes as perceived by sixth grade students and able adult readers. *Elementary English, 37*(7), 461–468.

Shuy, Roger W. (1977a). *Linguistic theory: What it can say about reading.* Newark, DE: International Reading Association.

Beyond the Fundamentals

Shuy, Roger W. (1977b). Sociolinguistics. In R. W. Shuy (Ed.), *Linguistic theory: What it can say about reading* (pp. 80–94). Newark, DE: International Reading Association.

Silvaroli, Nicholas. (1964, June). Intellectual and emotional factors as predictors of children's success in first-grade reading. *Dissertation Abstracts, 24,* 5098.

Simons, Herbert D. (1971, Spring). Reading comprehension: The need for a new perspective. *Reading Research Quarterly, 6*(3), 338–363.

Singer, Dorothy G., Singer, Jerome L., & Zuckerman, Diana M. (1984). *Getting the most out of TV.* Glenview, IL: Good Year Books.

Sittig, Linda H. (1982, November). Involving parents and children in reading for fun. *The Reading Teacher, 36*(2), 166–168.

Sizer, Theodore R. (1984). *Horace's compromise: The dilemma of the American high school.* Boston: Houghton Mifflin.

Smith, Carl B. (1966, April). The double vowel and linguistic research. *The Reading Teacher, 19*(7), 512–514.

Smith, Carl B. (1967). *How to read and succeed.* New York: Simon & Schuster (Essandess Special Edition).

Smith, Carl B. (1978). *Teaching reading in secondary school content subjects: A bookthinking process.* New York: Holt, Rinehart and Winston.

Smith, Carl B., & Arnold, Virginia A. (1983). *Series r.* New York: Macmillan.

Smith, Carl B., & Fay, Leo C. (1973). *Getting People to Read.* New York: Delacorte Press.

Smith, Carl B., & Ingersoll, Gary M. (1984, January). Written vocabulary of elementary school pupils, ages 6–14. *Monograph in Language and Reading Studies* (Number 6). Bloomington, IN: School of Education, Indiana University.

Smith, Carl B., & Wardhaugh, Ronald. (1975). *Teacher's resource book—Series r.* New York: Macmillan.

Smith, Dora V. (1964). *Selected essays.* New York: Macmillan.

Smith, E. Brooks, Goodman, Kenneth S., & Meredith, Robert. (1976). *Language and thinking in the elementary school.* New York: Holt, Rinehart & Winston.

Smith, Frank. (1973). *Psycholinguistics and reading.* New York: Holt, Rinehart & Winston.

Smith, Frank. (1975, March). Role of prediction in reading. *Elementary English, 52,* 305–311.

Smith, Frank. (1977). Making sense of reading—and of reading instruction. *Harvard Educational Review, 47*(3), 386–395.

Smith, Frank. (1978). *Reading without nonsense.* New York: Teachers College Press.

Smith, Frank. (1982). *Understanding reading.* New York: Holt, Rinehart & Winston.

Smith, Marilyn, & Bean, Thomas W. (1983, December). Four strategies that develop children's story comprehension and writing. *The Reading Teacher, 37*(3), 295–301.

Smith, Mortimer (1949). *And madly teach.* Chicago: Henry Regnery.

Smith, Nancy J. (1984, March). A self-help checklist for parents on their role in reading readiness. *The Reading Teacher, 37*(7), 669–670.

Smith, Nila B. (1963). *Reading instruction for today's children.* Englewood Cliffs, NJ: Prentice-Hall.

Smith, Nila B. (1965). *American reading instruction.* Newark, DE: International Reading Association.

Spache, Evelyn B. (1976). *Reading activities for child involvement.* Boston: Allyn & Bacon.

Spache, George D. (1953). A new readability formula for primary-grade reading materials. *Elementary School Journal, 53,* 410–413.

Spache, George D. (1974). *Good books for poor readers.* Champaign, IL: Garrard.

Spache, George D. (1976). *Investigating the issues of reading disabilities.* Boston: Allyn & Bacon.

Spache, George D. (1981). *Diagnosing and correcting reading disabilities* (2nd ed.). Boston: Allyn & Bacon.

Spiegel, Dixie Lee (1980, December). Desirable teaching behaviors for effective instruction. *The Reading Teacher, 34* (3), 324–330.

Spiro, Rand J. (1977). Remembering information from text: The "state of schema" approach. In R. C. Anderson, R. J. Spiro, & W. E. Montague (Eds.), *Schooling and the acquisition of knowledge* (pp. 137–165). Hillsdale, NJ: Lawrence Erlbaum.

Spiro, Rand J., Bruce, Bertram C. & Brewer, William F. (Eds.). (1980). *Theoretical issues in reading comprehension.* Hillsdale, NJ: Lawrence Erlbaum.

Stauffer, Russell G. (1975). *Directing the reading thinking process.* New York: Harper & Row.

Stein, Nancy, & Glenn, C. G. (1979). An analysis of story comprehension in elementary-school children. In R. O. Freedle (Ed.), *New directions in discourse processing.* Norwood, NJ: Ablex.

Stephens, Lillian S. (1974). *The teacher's guide to open education.* New York: Holt, Rinehart & Winston.

Stephens, Thomas M., Blackhurst, A. Edward, & Magliocca, Larry A. (1982). *Teaching mainstreamed students.* New York: Wiley.

Stewart, Oran, & Green, Dan S. (1983, March). Test-taking skills for standardized tests of reading. *The Reading Teacher, 36* (7), 634–638.

Sticht, Thomas G., & Mikulecky, Larry. (1984). *Job-related basic skills: Cases and conclusions.* ERIC Clearinghouse on Adult, Career, and Vocational Education; Information Series No. 285. Columbus, OH: The National Center for Research in Vocational Education, The Ohio State University.

Strang, Ruth. (1968). *Reading diagnosis and remediation.* ERIC/CRIER (Reading Review Series). Newark, DE: International Reading Association.

Straw, Stanley B. (1978). An investigation of the effects of sentence-combining and sentence-reduction on measures of fluency, reading comprehension, and listening comprehension (Doctoral dissertation, University of Minnesota).

Straw, Stanley B., & Schreiner, Robert. (1982). The effect of sentence manipulation on subsequent measures of reading and listening comprehension. *Reading Research Quarterly, 17* (3), 339–352.

Strickland, Ruth. (1962, July). The language of elementary school children: Its relationship to the language of reading textbooks and the quality of reading of selected children. Bloomington, IN: Bulletin of the School of Education, Indiana University.

Sutherland, Zena B., Monson, Dianne L., & Arbuthnot, May Hill. (1981). *Children and books* (6th ed.) Glenview, IL: Scott, Foresman.

Tarver, Sara G., & Hallahan, Daniel P. (1974, November). Attention deficits in children with learning disabilities: A review. *Journal of Learning Disabilities, 7* (9), 560–569.

Thorndike, Robert L. (1974). Reading as reasoning. *Reading Research Quarterly, 9* (2), 135–147.

Thorndyke, P. W. (1977). Cognitive structures in comprehension and memory of narrative discourse. *Cognitive Psychology, 9,* 77–110.

Thurston, Paul, & House, Ernest R. (1981, October). The NIE adversary hearing on minimum competency testing. *Phi Delta Kappan, 63* (2), 87–89.

Tierney, Robert J., & Cunningham, James W. (1984). Research on teaching reading comprehension. In P. D. Pearson et al. (Eds.), *Handbook of reading research* (pp. 609–656). New York: Longman.

Tierney, Robert J., Mosenthal, James, & Kantor, Robert M. (1984). Classroom applications of text analysis: Toward improving text analysis. In J. Flood (Ed.), *Promoting reading comprehension* (pp. 139–160). Newark, DE: International Reading Association.

Tinker, Miles A., & McCullough, Constance. (1962). *Teaching elementary reading.* New York: Appleton-Century-Crofts.

Tittle, Carol K. (1982). Competency testing. In H. Mitzel (Ed.), *Encyclopedia of educational research,* Vol. I (pp. 333–352). New York: The Free Press.

Torrance, E. Paul (1969). Introduction. In *360 Reading Series.* Boston: Ginn.

Tovey, Duane R. (1980, January). Children's grasp of phonics terms vs. sound-symbol relationships. *The Reading Teacher, 33*(4), 431–437.

Trelease, James. (1982). *The read-aloud book.* New York: Penguin Books.

Tway, Eileen (Ed.). (1981). *Reading ladders for human relations.* Washington, DC: American Council of Education and National Council of Teachers of English.

Tymitz, Barbara L. (1980, September). Instructional aspects of the IEP: An analysis of teachers' skills and needs. *Educational Technology, 20*(9), 266–269.

Valmont, William J. (1983, November). Cloze deletion patterns: How deletions are made makes a big difference. *The Reading Teacher, 37*(2), 172–175.

Veatch, Jeannette et al. (1979). *Key words to reading: The language experience approach begins.* Columbus, OH: Charles E. Merrill.

Venable, T. C. (1981, February). Declining SAT scores: Some unpopular hypotheses. *Phi Delta Kappan, 62*(6), 443–445.

Vernon, M. D. (1958). *Backwardness in reading.* London: Cambridge University Press.

Voight, Ralph C. (1971). *Invitation to learning I: The learning center handbook.* Washington, DC: Acropolis.

Voight, Ralph C. (1974). *Invitation to learning II: Center teaching with instructional depth.* Washington, DC: Acropolis.

Vukelich, Carol. (1984, February). Parents' role in the reading process: A review of practical suggestions and ways to communicate with parents. *The Reading Teacher, 37*(6), 472–477.

Wagner, Guy, & Hosier, Max. (1970). *Reading games.* New York: Macmillan.

Walker, Decker F. (1983, October). Reflections on the educational potential and limitations of microcomputers. *Phi Delta Kappan, 65*(2), 103–107.

Walkington, Pat, & Babcock, Eloise. (1984, Summer). Educational computing and the gifted child: A how-to approach. *TEACHING Exceptional Children, 16*(4), 266–269.

Wallace, Gerald. (1981). Teaching reading. In J. M. Kauffman & D. P. Hallahan (Eds.), *Handbook of special education* (pp. 459–474). Englewood Cliffs, NJ: Prentice-Hall.

Wallace, Gerald, & Kauffman, James M. (1978). *Teaching children with learning problems* (2nd ed.). Columbus, OH: Charles E. Merrill.

Waller, Gary T. (1977). *Think first, read later! Piagetian prerequisites for reading.* Newark, DE: International Reading Association.

Ward, Evangeline. (1970, May). A child's first reading teacher: His parents. *The Reading Teacher, 23*(8), 756–760.

Wardhaugh, Ronald. (1975). Linguistics and reading. In C. B. Smith & R. Wardhaugh, *Teacher's Resource Book—Series r.* New York: Macmillan.

Wartenberg, Helen. (1969). The art of questioning (mimeograph). Ithaca, NY: Cornell University.

Waterhouse, Lynn H., Fischer, Karen M., & Bouchard, Ellen. (1980). *Language awareness and reading.* Newark, DE: International Reading Association.

Weaver, Gail C. (1978, October). Teaching children how to take standardized tests. *The Reading Teacher, 32*(1), 116–119.

Weaver, Phyllis A. (1979). Improving reading comprehension: Effects of sentence organization instruction. *Reading Research Quarterly, 15*(1), 129–146.

Webb, James T., Mekstroth, Elizabeth A., & Tolan, Stephanie S. (1982). *Guiding the gifted child: A practical course for parents and teachers.* Columbus, OH: Ohio Psychology. Psychology Publishing Co.

Weintraub, Samuel. (1969, April). Children's reading interests. *The Reading Teacher, 22*(7), 655, 657, 659.

Whaley, Jill F. (1981). Reader's expectations for story structures. *Reading Research Quarterly, 17*(1), 90–114.

Wheeler, George, & Sherman, Thomas F. (1983, April). Readability formulas revisited. *Science and Children, 20*(7), 38–40.

Wiesendanger, Katherine D., & Wollenberg, John P. (1978, May). Pre-questioning inhibits third graders reading comprehension. *The Reading Teacher, 31*(8), 892–895.

Wilson, Cathy R. (1983, January). Teaching reading comprehension by connecting the known to the new. *The Reading Teacher, 36*(4), 382–390.

Wirtz, Willard et al. (1977). *On further examination: Report of the advisory panel on the scholastic aptitude test score decline.* New York: College Entrance Examination Board.

Wolfram, Walt, & Fasold, Ralph W. (1974). *The study of social dialects in American English.* Englewood Cliffs, NJ: Prentice-Hall.

Woodcock, Richard W., Clark, C. R., & Davies, C. O. (1979). *Peabody rebus reading program.* Circle Pines, MN: American Guidance Service.

Yap, Kim Onn. (1979, Spring). Vocabulary; building blocks of comprehension? *Journal of Reading Behavior, 11,* 49–59.

Zirkelbach, Thelma. (1984, February). A personal view of early reading. *The Reading Teacher, 37*(5), 468–471.

Author Index

Neuman, Susan B., 91
Nevi, Charles N., 442
Newton, Beatryce T., 318
Niles, Jerome A., 475

Oliver, Peter, 130, 131
Olson, David R., 521
Olson, Mary W., 106
Ortony, Andrew, 231, 257
Osborn, Jean, 284
Owens, A. M., 280

Papert, Seymour, 524
Parsley, Kenneth M., 143
Pearson, P. David, 119, 245, 261, 341
Pederson, Carolyn, 245
Pederson, J. E. P., 280
Perfetti, Charles, 167
Pertz, Doris L., 126
Piaget, Jean, 28, 119, 257, 258
Piche, Gene, 286
Pikulski, John J., 88
Pipho, Chris, 533, 544
Plaskon, Stephen P., 503
Platts, Sister Mary E., 147, 447
Poulson, D., 266
Powell, Marvin, 143
Powell, William R., 461 n., 473
Premack, D., 266
Preston, Fannie W., 444
Price, Eunice H., 509
Propp, V., 266
Pullin, Diana, 544
Putnam, Lillian R., 126

Quandt, Ivan, 96

Radabaugh, Martha T., 488
Ragghianti, Suzanne, 491
Raim, Joan, 505
Ramig, Christopher, 503
Rand, Muriel K., 267
Rankin, Earl F., 201, 483
Rauch, Sidney J., 446
Ravitch, Diane, 534
Raygor, Alton L., 338, 340
Reeke, Angela S., 442
Reimer, Becky L., 71
Renzulli, Joseph S., 511–12
Resnick, Lauren B., 245
Ribovich, Jerilyn K., 503
Rice, G. Elizabeth, 265
Richek, Margaret Ann, 505
Rickover, Hyman G., 533
Riessman, Frank R., 444
Robinson, Helen M., 302
Rodger, Elizabeth B., 350
Rodrigues, Raymond J., 515
Roe, Anne, 95
Roe, Betty D., 489, 498, 513

Rosenberg, Phillip E., 123
Rosenblatt, L. M., 39
Rosenshine, Barak, 5, 19
Rosenstock, Robert, 528
Rosenthal, Robert, 90
Ross, Elinor P., 489, 498, 513
Rosso, Barbara R., 173
Rudin, Ellen, 350
Rudman, Jack, 541
Rumelhart, David E., 119, 153, 231, 257, 267
Russell, David H., 147, 302
Russell, Susan Jo, 504

Sadow, Marilyn W., 269
Salomon, Marilyn, 350
Samuels, S. Jay, 154 n., 391
Sandefur, J. T., 532, 533
Sartain, Harry W., 83
Savage, John F., 497
Schank, R. C., 283
Schaudt, Barbara A., 88
Schell, Leo M., 465
Schmeltzer, R. V., 280
Schneider, Herman, 334 n., 344 n.
Schneider, Nina, 334 n., 344 n.
Schreiner, Robert, 465
Schwartz, B. J., 280
Sebesta, Sam L., 90, 270
Selznick, Richard, 96
Shadle, Erma M., 143
Sherman, Thomas M., 542–43, 549–51
Shores, J. Harlan, 278
Shuy, Roger, 66
Silvaroli, Nicholas, 134
Simons, Herbert D., 259
Sittig, Linda H., 119, 130
Sizer, Theodore R., 534
Slater, Wayne H., 286
Smith, Carl B., 39 n., 160, 164, 170, 173, 178, 198, 209, 213, 214, 384, 392, 393, 412, 418, 444, 526, 527
Smith, Dora V., 94
Smith, E. Brooks, 69
Smith, Frank, 56, 61, 113, 119, 153, 168, 396
Smith, H. L., 335 n.
Smith, Marilyn, 270, 271
Smith, Mortimer, 533
Smith, Nancy J., 119
Smith, Nila Banton, 3, 196, 204, 387t., 388
Spache, Evelyn B., 147, 447
Spache, George D., 96, 121, 122, 338, 517–18
Spiegel, Dixie Lee, 37
Spiro, Rand J., 27, 48, 226, 227
Stauffer, Russell G., 503
Stein, Nancy, 267, 284
Stephens, Thomas M., 498, 499–500
Sticht, Thomas G., 9

Stillman, Bessie W., 506
Strang, Ruth, 235
Stratemeyer, C. G., 335 n.
Straw, Stanley B., 245
Strickland, Ruth, 392
Suelter, Susan K., 154
Sutherland, Zena, 100

Tarver, Sara G., 501
Terman, Lewis M., 126
Thorndike, Robert L., 184
Thorndyke, P. W., 267, 284
Thurston, Paul, 544
Tierney, Robert J., 267, 268, 284, 285, 286
Tinker, Miles A., 123, 196
Tittle, Carol K., 544
Tolan, Stephanie S., 508
Torrance, E. Paul, 319
Tovey, Duane R., 173
Trelease, James, 82
Tway, Eileen, 93
Tymitz, Barbara L., 488

Van Allen, Roach, 71
Veatch, Jeannette, 71
Venable, T. C., 533
Vernon, M. D., 126
Vogel, Juliet M., 122
Voight, Ralph C., 442
Vukelich, Carol, 83, 510

Wagner, Guy, 447
Walker, Decker F., 525–26
Walkington, Pat, 504
Wallace, Gerald, 501, 503, 507
Waller, Gary T., 119
Wardhaugh, Ronald, 169 n., 178, 202, 213
Wartenberg, Helen, 305
Wasson, Barbara B., 123
Weaver, Gail C., 551
Weaver, Phyllis A., 245
Webb, James T., 508
Weber, Donald B., 154
Weintraub, Samuel, 90
Weishahn, Mel W., 488, 518
Whaley, Jill F., 267
White, Robert H., 515
Wiesendanger, Katherine D., 279
Wildman, Terry M., 542–43, 549–51
Wingo, C., 175
Wirtz, Willard, 533
Wolfram, Walt, 67
Wollenberg, John P., 279
Woodward, Virginia A., 395

Yap, Kim Onn, 188
Yukish, Joseph F., 488

Subject Index

Affective domain, 21
  bilingual children, 513
  exceptional children, 488–89
  importance to reading comprehension, 274–78
Analytic approach to phonics, 159–60, 167–68
Analytic learning procedure, 163–64
Assessment
  affective factors, 274–78
  cloze procedure as diagnostic tool, 480–83
  content-area reading skills, 378–80
  criterion-referenced tests, 463–65
  critical reading, 316–17
  formal tests, 34, 459–60, 465–68
    evaluating, 465–68
    Mental Measurements Yearbook (Buros), 467
    Reading Tests and Reviews (Buros), 467–68
    standardized group tests, 465–68
  individualizing instruction, 461–62
  identifying reading level, 461–62
  identifying strengths and weaknesses, 462
  informal tests, 35–37, 460, 468–84
    checklists, 471
    conferences (teacher-student), 469–70

    cumulative record as diagnostic tool, 472
    interest inventory records, 471–72
    observation by the teacher, 478–80
    oral reading inventories, 472–78
    purposes, 460
    trial teaching, 484
    workbooks as diagnostic tools, 468–69
  instructional goals, 462–63
  interest in reading, 91–93
  norm-referenced tests, 464–65
  plan, 37
  reading comprehension, 292–94
    background experiences, 233–35
    language abilities, 245–48
    thinking abilities, 257–59
  reading difficulties in exceptional children, 502–03
  reading readiness, 137–42
  understanding of story structure, 272
  word recognition skills, 177–82
Association techniques for vocabulary development, 193–97
Attention problems in exceptional children, 501

Basal readers, 158–62, 384–95
  adapting for exceptional children, 503–505

  characteristics, 160–62
  content, 386–88
  computers and, 412, 418
  definition, 384–86
  developmental pattern, 385
  guidelines for selection, 390
  limitations, 392–93
  phonics, 158–59
  rationale, 390–92
  reading readiness, 385
  skills program, 386
  standards, 388–90
  vocabulary control, 384–85, 393–94
  word recognition, 160–62
Base words, 207–10
Behavior-modification approaches for slower readers, 506–507
Bilingual-bicultural children, 64–65, 488, 512–16
  affective domain, 513
  language experience approach, 514
  legislation affecting, 488, 513
  reading instruction, 512–16
Books, 81–83, 100–107
  evaluation by children, 103–105
  evaluation by teachers, 100–103
  importance for creating interest in reading, 81–83, 86, 100–107
  recommended for beginners, 82*t.*
  sharing, 105–106

586

Exceptional children (*Continued*)
assessing reading problems, 502–503
characteristics of physical and mental handicaps, 494–500
characteristics of reading problems, 500–502
children with limiting handicaps, 487–88, 493–508
computer-assisted instruction, 491–92, 504–505
definition, 487
gifted and talented, 508–12
Individualized Education Program (IEP), 488, 491
individualizing instruction, 489–92, 504–505
legislation, 487–88
mainstreaming, 487–88, 509
reading materials and approaches, 503–507
basal readers, 503
developmental approaches, 503–505
language experience approach, 503–504
phonics method, 503
programmed materials (CAI), 504–505
specialized (remedial) approaches, 505–507
Expressive language disorders, 498–500

Formal tests for diagnosis and assessment, 459–60, 465–68
Fry graph for estimating readability, 339–40

Gifted and talented children, 488, 508–12
characteristics, 508–10
inter- and intraindividual differences, 510–12
legislation, 488
reading instruction, 511–12
Gillingham-Stillman method, 506
"Go-go" reading (reading on the go), 376–78
Grouping for instruction, 423–36, 449–51
criteria, 424–27
individual differences, 424
individualizing instruction, 435
limitations and misuses, 434–36
managing activities, 449–51
plan for meeting with groups, 427–34
Guided reading lesson, 288, 294

Handicapped children, *see* Children with limiting handicaps

Harris-Smith outline of reading, 28–34
Hearing
deficiencies, 495
reading readiness, 121–26
High-interest, low-vocabulary books, 517–18

IEP, *see* Individualized Education Program
Independent learning activities, 437–51
contracts, 444–45
cross-age tutoring, 442–44
free-choice reading, 448–49
learning centers, 439–42
learning kits, 446–47
managing independent activities, 449–51
reading games, 447–48
reading selections as sources, 438–39
teacher aides as guides, 445–46
teacher planning, 437–38
Individualized Education Program (IEP), 488, 491, 493
Individualized reading instruction, *see* Personal interest approach
Individualizing instruction, 435, 437–51
differentiating assignments within groups, 435
exceptional children, 505
grouping by achievement, need, or interest, 424–27
independent work, 437–51
Inductive process, 159
Inflectional endings, 207–10
Informal tests for diagnosis and assessment, 460, 468–84
Instructional materials, 407–11
availability, 407–08
evaluation, 408–11
guidelines, 409–10
sources of information, 407–408
Instructional methods (systems), 384–406
basal readers, 384–95
language emphasis approach, 395–401
personal interest approach, 401–406
Intelligence Quotient, *see* IQ
Interaction as a motivating force, 25–27, 505
Interest in reading, 78–96
parents as significant influences, 79–83
schools as significant influences, 83–90
International Reading Association (IRA), 407–408

IQ (Intelligence Quotient)
exceptional children, 496–97
tests, 257–58
Isolated letter-sound approach, 168–69

Language
acquisition, 59–61
cues, 153–155
differences, 64–69
bilingualism, 64–65, 512–16
dialects, 65–69
meaning conveyed by, 57–59
Language arts integration (reading and writing), 13, 39–48, 75
Language development, 55–60
activities, 69–70
early stages, 54–55, 59–61
encouraging, 69–70
errors as important factors, 61–62
importance for reading, 55–57
language emphasis approach, 71–75
needs and interests of child, 62–63
prediction, 55–56, 58–59, 61–62
Language disorders, *see* Communication disorders
Language emphasis approach to reading instruction, 71–75, 395–401
exceptional children, 503–504
language experience stories, 398–401
limitations, 397–98
predictable stories, 396
rationale, 396–97
Language experience approach, *see* Language emphasis approach
Language experience stories, 398–401
Language skills, 153–55
Learning disabilities, 497–98
Legislation affecting exceptional children, 487–88, 493
Letter-sound approach, 168–69
Limiting handicaps, *see* Children with limiting handicaps
Listening table, 11
Literature program in the schools, 96–106; *see also* Books

Mainstreaming, 487–88, 509
Materials, *see* Instructional materials
Memory problems, 501
Mental retardation, 496–97
Methods, *see* Instructional methods (systems)
Miscue analysis (error analysis), 474–78, 502
Motivation for reading, 21, 25–27